LOCAL GOVERNMENT IN CANADA

EIGHTH EDITION

C. Richard Tindal
Susan Nobes Tindal
Kennedy Stewart
Patrick J. Smith

NELSON / EDUCATION

NELSON / EDUCATION

Local Government in Canada, Eighth Edition

by C. Richard Tindal, Susan Nobes Tindal, Kennedy Stewart, and Patrick J. Smith

Vice President, Editorial Higher Education:
Anne Williams

Acquisitions Editor:
Anne-Marie Taylor

Marketing Manager:
Ann Byford

Developmental Editor:
Jessica Freedman

Photo Researcher:
Sheila Hall

Permissions Coordinator:
Sheila Hall

Copy Editor:
Gail Marsden

Proofreader:
Liba Berry

Indexer:
Edwin Durbin

Senior Production Coordinator:
Ferial Suleman

Design Director:
Ken Phipps

Managing Designer:
Franca Amore

Cover Design:
Cathryn Mayer

Cover Image:
© Scott Barrow/Corbis

Printer:
RR Donnelley

COPYRIGHT © 2013, 2009 by Nelson Education Ltd.

Printed and bound in the United States
2 3 4 5 16 15 14 13

For more information contact Nelson Education Ltd., 1120 Birchmount Road, Toronto, Ontario, M1K 5G4. Or you can visit our Internet site at http://www.nelson.com

Statistics Canada information is used with the permission of Statistics Canada. Users are forbidden to copy this material and/or redisseminate the data, in an original or modified form, for commercial purposes, without the expressed permissions of Statistics Canada. Information on the availability of the wide range of data from Statistics Canada can be obtained from Statistics Canada's Regional Offices, its World Wide Web site at <http://www.statcan.gc.ca>, and its toll-free access number 1-800-263-1136.

ALL RIGHTS RESERVED. No part of this work covered by the copyright herein may be reproduced, transcribed, or used in any form or by any means—graphic, electronic, or mechanical, including photocopying, recording, taping, Web distribution, or information storage and retrieval systems—without the written permission of the publisher.

For permission to use material from this text or product, submit all requests online at www.cengage.com/permissions. Further questions about permissions can be emailed to permissionrequest@cengage.com

Every effort has been made to trace ownership of all copyrighted material and to secure permission from copyright holders. In the event of any question arising as to the use of any material, we will be pleased to make the necessary corrections in future printings.

Library and Archives Canada Cataloguing in Publication Data

Local government in Canada / C. Richard Tindal ... [et al.]. — 8th ed.

Includes bibliographical references and index.
ISBN 978-0-17-650396-3

1. Municipal government—Canada—Textbooks.
I. Tindal, C. R., 1943–

JS1709.T55 2012
320.80971   C2011-908698-0

ISBN-13: 978-0-17-650396-3
ISBN-10: 0-17-650396-X

About the Authors

Kennedy Stewart, Ph.D., lived in and around Wolfville, Nova Scotia, for much of his early life. He has a BA in History from Acadia University, an MA in Political Science from Simon Fraser University and in 2003 was awarded a Ph.D. in Government from the London School of Economics. He has held positions at a number of universities in Canada and the United Kingdom, including a term as Director of the Public Policy and Public Management Program at the top-ranked School of Politics and Sociology, Birkbeck College, University of London. Kennedy is a tenured associate professor in Simon Fraser University's School of Public Policy and writes and teaches about democracy, local government, and public participation. In 2011, Kennedy was elected Member of Parliament for Burnaby-Douglas, British Columbia, and currently serves as a member of Her Majesty's Loyal Opposition. Kennedy is married to Jeanette Ashe, who teaches in Douglas College's Department of Political Science.

Patrick J. Smith, Ph.D., is Professor of Urban Studies, and Political Science, as well as Director of the Institute of Governance Studies at Simon Fraser University in Vancouver where he has taught for the past 30 years. He has also taught at other universities (Victoria, Acadia, Dalhousie, and the Open University in the U.K.). He completed his Ph.D., in Government, at the London School of Economics. He has researched, advised, and written extensively about local, regional, and metropolitan politics and governing. His roots are in a small, rural (Simcoe County) Ontario community called Utopia, founded by his great-great-grandfather, and where a 175 year old farm is still a family operation. Patrick is married to Deborah Binnie Smith, Ph.D., who teaches ESL at Douglas College; and since May 2011 Patrick's Member of Parliament has been Kennedy Stewart, MP, Burnaby-Douglas.

C. Richard Tindal, Ph.D., has been teaching, researching, consulting, and writing about local government for more than 40 years. For much of that period, he was a Professor of Government at St. Lawrence College in Kingston, Ontario, and was Head of its Centre for Government Education and Training until taking early retirement in 1998. He also has been an occasional Visiting Professor in the School of Policy Studies at Queen's University, and has developed and taught courses via the Internet for Dalhousie University and the University of Alberta.

Susan Nobes Tindal, M.Ed., LL.B., worked in the field of law for 25 years and taught courses in law and municipal government for much of that time. She has served on the executive of a number of community organizations, particularly in the health field. In 2004 she retired from her position as legal counsel for a children's aid society in Eastern Ontario. Since the early 1970s, Susan and Richard have undertaken a wide variety of consulting projects with municipalities and other public bodies and have provided numerous workshops for councillors and staff.

Table of Contents

Preface ... xiii

Chapter 1 The Promise of Local Government ... 1
Introduction ... 1
What Is Local Government? ... 2
   Local Government ... 3
   Municipal Government ... 3
   Agencies, Boards, and Commissions ... 7
   Local Governance, Multilevel Government, & Multilevel Governance ... 8
   Aboriginal Governments ... 8
What Do Municipal Governments Do? ... 9
   Municipalities as Service Providers ... 9
   Municipalities as Democratic Governments ... 11
   Municipalities as Democratic Service Providers ... 14
The Changing Context ... 16
   The Demographic Context ... 16
   The Economic Context ... 18
   The Ideological Context ... 22
The Promise of Local Government ... 23

Chapter 2 The Legacy of the Past ... 27
Local Government Origins ... 27
   Aboriginal and Early Colonial Rule ... 27
   Ontario (Upper Canada) ... 31
   Quebec (Lower Canada) ... 36
   Nova Scotia ... 37
   Prince Edward Island ... 38
   New Brunswick ... 38
   Newfoundland ... 40
   Manitoba ... 41
   Saskatchewan ... 42
   Alberta ... 43
   British Columbia ... 43
   Northern Territories ... 44
Early 20th Century Growing Pains ... 46
   Housing ... 47
   Service Provision ... 47
   Transportation and Utilities ... 48
   Community Cohesion ... 48
   Corruption ... 49
The Reform Movements ... 50
   City Beautiful Movement ... 51
   City Healthy Movement ... 52

City Efficient Movement	53
The Reforms	54
Professional Planners and Planning	54
Changes to the Electoral Process	55
Boards of Control	56
City Managers and Executive Committees	57
Boards and Commissions	58
Concluding Comments	59
Chapter 3 Pressures of Growth and Change	63
Urban Growth in Canada	63
The Causes of Urbanization	66
Government Policies	66
Economic Influences	70
Growing Cities, Growing Benefits	72
Growing Cities, Growing Challenges	74
Solutions to Urban Challenges	80
Concluding Comments	84
Chapter 4 Local Government Restructuring	87
Introduction	87
British Columbia	88
Creation of Regional Districts	89
Assessing the Regional Districts	90
The Amalgamation Option	92
Alberta	93
Annexations and Amalgamations	93
Intermunicipal Agencies and Agreements	94
Saskatchewan	98
Manitoba	99
Restructuring in the Winnipeg Area	100
Metropolitan Winnipeg	101
Winnipeg Unicity	102
Assessing Unicity	103
Governing the Winnipeg Region	104
Ontario	106
Municipality of Metropolitan Toronto	106
Toronto Megacity	109
The Other Regional Governments	111
New Wave of Restructuring	112
Quebec	115
Early Amalgamation Efforts	115
Regional County Municipalities	116
Government of Major Urban Centres	117
New Upper Tier Governments	117
New Metropolitan Governing Bodies	118
Merger in the Major Centres	119

Demergers in the Major Centres	121
Recap: Multilevelled Municipal Restructuring	122
New Brunswick	125
Equal Opportunity Program	125
Governing Urban New Brunswick	126
Governing Rural New Brunswick	126
Reliance on Local Boards	128
Nova Scotia	129
Graham Commission: Too Much At Once?	129
Amalgamations in the 1990s	130
Cape Breton Regional Municipality (CBRM)	130
Halifax Regional Municipality (HRM)	131
Region of Queens	131
Amalgamations Assessed	132
Prince Edward Island	133
Newfoundland and Labrador	134
Municipal Amalgamations	135
The Regional Alternative	136
Resistant or Realistic?	136
Northern Territories	138
Concluding Comments	138
Chapter 5 Restructuring Limitations and Alternatives	141
Introduction	141
Recapping the Reforms	141
Comparing the Three Types of Reform	144
Intermunicipal Boards	145
Should We Shed a Tier?	146
The Case for a Two Tier System	147
The Case for a One Tier System	149
Reviewing the Rationale for the Reforms	150
Generating Savings	151
Focus on Savings Misplaced and Misleading	154
Controlling Sprawl	157
Ensuring Equity/Reducing Inequity	161
Policies That Address Equity	163
Eliminating Clash and Conflict	169
Less Government/Less Bureaucracy	171
A Different Perspective on Less Bureaucracy	173
To Compete in a Global World	174
Old and New Regionalism	178
Concluding Comments	180
Chapter 6 Intergovernmental Relations	185
Introduction	185
The Provincial-Local Relationship	186
Disentangling or Downloading?	189

The Rationale for Disentanglement	190
The New Brunswick Experience	192
The Quebec Experience	193
The Nova Scotia Experience	195
Ontario's Disentanglement Experience	197
Disentanglement Dissected	199
The Changing Legal Relationship	201
A More Positive Legislative Framework	206
Alberta	207
Manitoba	207
Nova Scotia	208
Newfoundland and Labrador	209
Saskatchewan	209
British Columbia	210
Ontario	212
Significance of the Legislative Reforms	214
Pursuing Individual City Charters	215
A More Positive Judicial Response	216
The Federal-Local Relationship	217
The Rise and Fall of MSUA	218
A New Deal with Municipalities?	221
Open Federalism and a Different Deal?	222
International Relations	223
Multilevel Relations	228
Making the Most of the Mushy Middle	232
Concluding Comments	236
Chapter 7 Local Government Finances	239
Introduction	239
Municipal Expenditures and Revenues	240
Municipal Finance and Fiscal Federalism	243
A Closer Look at Municipal Revenues	246
Transfer Payments	246
Rationale for Transfer Payments	247
The Transfer Record	249
The Territorial Difference	250
Federal Transfers	250
Revenue and Tax Sharing Agreements	252
Real Property Tax	254
Provincial Invasion of the Property Tax Field	258
Other Local Revenues	262
User Fees	262
The Case for User Fees	263
Development Charges	265
Fixing Municipal Finances	266
Far Away Fields Aren't Necessarily Greener	267
Increasing Revenues	270

New Municipal Revenue Sources ... 270
   New Taxing Powers for Canadian Cities ... 272
   Funding from the Provincial and Federal Levels ... 274
   Making Better Use of Existing Resources ... 277
     Confronting the Property Tax Mythology ... 277
     Being Sensitive to the Impact of Revenue Tools ... 278
Managing Expenditures ... 280
Concluding Comments ... 281

Chapter 8 Municipal Governing Structures ... 285
Introduction ... 285
The Machinery of Municipal Government ... 286
  The Municipal Council ... 287
    The Representative Role of Members of Council ... 288
      Ward Versus General Vote ... 289
      Trustee or Delegate? ... 291
  The Head of Council ... 292
  The Administration ... 295
  Changing Council-Staff Relations ... 297
    Reconciling Politics and Professionalism ... 298
    Clarifying Roles and Relationships ... 303
  Modifications to the Municipal Machinery ... 305
    The Standing Committee System ... 306
    Executive Committees ... 307
      Board of Control ... 308
      Other Forms of Executive Committee ... 308
    Coordinating Officers ... 310
      Chief Administrative Officer System ... 311
      The Council Manager System ... 311
      The Manager System in Canada ... 313
      The Commissioner System ... 314
      Canadian CAOs Today ... 316
    New Business Models of Government ... 318
  Effectiveness of the Modified Machinery ... 320
    Are Political Parties the Answer? ... 321
      The Case for Parties ... 321
      The Case Against Parties ... 323
Concluding Comments ... 324

Chapter 9 Municipal Governing Processes and Values ... 327
Introduction ... 327
The Importance of Values ... 328
  Community Values ... 328
  Organizational Values ... 331
  New Public Management Values ... 332
    NPM at the Local Level ... 333
      Partnerships and Joint Ventures ... 333

Measurement and Competition	336
Citizen as Consumer	341
Value Clashes	343
Meeting Your Waterloo	344
Ethics and Accountability	346
Show Me the Money	347
Crossing the Line	349
Moral Compass Missing	352
Governing as an Old Boys Club	353
Legislative Responses	354
Legislative Overkill in Ontario?	356
Going Beyond the Rules	358
When NPM Met MFP	359
Accountability for What to Whom?	361
Accountability in a Democracy	362
Concluding Comments	362

Chapter 10 Public Participation in Local Government — 365

The Importance of Citizen Participation	365
Local Government Elections	366
Voting in Local Elections	367
Local Council Composition	369
Political Parties and Local Elections	373
Party Activity in Montreal	373
Party Activity in Toronto	376
Party Activity in Winnipeg	380
Party Activity in Vancouver	382
Non-Electoral Participation in Local Government	385
Informative Participation Mechanisms	386
Consulting with the Public	391
Delegating to the Public	393
Concluding Comments	400

Chapter 11 Municipal Policy Making — 403

Introduction	403
Conflicting Perspectives on Policy Making	405
The Complexity of Policy Making	406
A Far From Tidy Process	406
Policy Definition: More Movement or Less?	408
Policy Linkages: Sprawl and All	410
Policy Linkages: Pursuing Healthy Communities	412
Influences on Municipal Policy Making	416
Socio-Economic Factors	416
Demographics	416
Economic Influences	417
Prevailing Ideology	419
Limits of the Neoliberal Market Model	420

Sources of Local Political Power 421
    Community Power Studies 421
    Public Choice Model 424
    Regime Theory 426
Legal and Jurisdictional Constraints 427
    Federal Neglect 428
    Provincial Paternalism 428
    Multilevel Governance 429
The Municipal Structure 430
    Municipal Policy Analysis Capacity 432
Illustrating Municipal Policy Making 433
Concluding Comments 436

Chapter 12 Future Prospects for Municipal Government 439
Introduction 439
Taking a New Look 439
What's Missing? 442
Reviving the Political Role 444
Improving the Service Delivery Role 448
    Escaping the Service Delivery Box 448
    Promoting Community Responsibility 450
    Using Resources Wisely 453
Striking a Balance 455
    A Vending Machine or a Barn Raising? 455
    The Representative or Administrative Role? 456
Concluding Comments 459

Select Bibliography 463

Index 487

Preface

Students and practitioners of local governing in Canada owe Susan and Dick Tindal a great debt. In the 1970s they took up the task of writing a comprehensive text on the subject. Crawford, Rowat, Higgins, and others had previously toiled in this field, but it was Richard and Susan Tindal who developed the franchise through seven (now eight) editions over more than thirty years. Each edition added value, and volume, to what we know – and what we should know – about local government. In the process we came to understand how much the authors themselves cared about the health of local government in Canada and local civic engagement.

As a text, *Local Government in Canada* has always been student focused. It demands that its readers have – or develop – an attitude about the state of Canadian local democracy. In doing so, the Tindals have contributed greatly to an important national dialogue.

When we were asked to help prepare an eighth edition of this classic, our keenness was tempered by a recognition that Susan and Dick had left very big shoes to try and fill. They turned this task over to us with generosity, a feature which has run through all of our conversations with them as they worked on each of the many earlier editions. And they continue to inform this work as it goes forward.

As with the Tindals, the community of urbanists and local government students across Canada (and some beyond) have continued to offer their thoughts, observations, and arguments to this discourse. These include the many colleagues who have participated in the Multilevel Governance project over recent years and more recent conversations with the likes of Peter Boswell (Memorial), Pierre Hamel (Montreal), Caroline Andrew (Ottawa), David Siegel (Brock), Chris Leo (Winnipeg), Joe Garcea (Saskatchewan), Jim Lightbody (Alberta), and Tom Hutton (UBC). Public servants in all provinces and territories of Canada have also taken the time to respond to queries for bits of local governing minutiae. Some of them are even our former students, or former students of colleagues who have also benefitted from studying from the Tindals' text. To each, our collective thanks for sharing their ideas.

We also wish to acknowledge the care, attention, and encouragement offered by the fine folks at Nelson Education, our publishers – including Anne-Marie Taylor, Acquisitions Editor for Higher Education; Jessica Freedman, Developmental Editor; Susan Calvert, Director, Content and Media Production; Vicki Gould, Manager, Rights and Permissions; Gail

Marsden, our Copy Editor; and Proofreader Liba Berry. They are all professional and fun to work with.

Beyond these, we have other debts of thanks and acknowledgement:

For Patrick Smith, I acknowledge my father's own example of community engagement, and that of his brothers, my uncles Clary and Eugene. Clary lived until November 2011 in the farm home where he was born almost 105 years ago. He knew about this new edition of *Local Government in Canada* and his commitment to community well being remained strong throughout his life. Eugene served for many years as Reeve of Essa Township in rural Ontario. Aunt Alice added the laughter to the mix. Eugene's grandson, Michael, now represents Ward One – including our 175 year old farm at Utopia, Ontario – on that same local council. The folks of Utopia epitomize community to me, and its keepers, like in so many of Canada's smaller communities, are treasures. I also acknowledge my mother, who came from a similar community (Minesing Station) seven miles away, and who always sought to ensure, by example, that civic engagement was an expectation of good citizenship; and Mr. Tuck, who pretended to "not have his glasses" so I would have to read him some of the *Toronto Star* news stories I delivered six days a week for five years. This developed into ongoing conversations which were filled with queries such as "what about that story last week?" I did not agree with Mr. Tuck's theory that you supported the outs until they were in and then immediately worked against them to make them outs again, but for a 9 to 13 year old, approaching Mr. Tuck's front porch, you had to be on your toes. Like any good teacher, he made you think, question, and form your own opinions.

For Kennedy Stewart, I am indebted to my wife and constant companion, Jeanette Ashe, who encouraged me to undertake this work and all things political. Her passion for politics flows from her parents, Tommy and Margie, who brought their Irish charm and sense of justice from inner city Belfast to Port Coquitlam, B.C. I am also indebted to my grandfathers Ed and Kennedy and grandmothers Mabel and Sybil who taught me at an early age what it meant to build community. Ed was the local gunsmith who erected swinging bridges and formed gun clubs to make life better for all living in his town. Kennedy was a local Anglican priest who visited homes to preside over births and deaths while providing the comfort of Latin verse in churches around Nova Scotia. Mabel and Sybil made sure there was always an extra potato in the pot just in case someone – even a stranger – was in need of a bit of nourishment. All these influences combine to inform my work about how to bring rural ideas of community to cities.

As teachers, we also owe a large debt to those who engaged us, and who continued the conversations – such as Peter Self and Keith Dowding (LSE/ANU), John Griffiths and George Jones (LSE), and to the many students who wander our way and who bring fresh questions about local governing. Our work would not be nearly as much fun without them all. Some of these students are also local government practitioners, from each of the ends of our country, and in between. Their perspectives enrich the dialogue that the Tindals have done so much to advance.

Saturna Island and Burnaby, British Columbia
November 11, 2011

Chapter 1
The Promise of Local Government

Local government plays an important role in the lives of Canadians. The thousands of municipalities dotted across our vast landscape have enormous potential to help Canadian communities address a wide range of challenges. For example, mayors and councils can help municipal residents find balance between increased participation in the globalized economy and protecting community values. Getting it right brings prosperity while maintaining local customs and traditions. Getting it wrong undermines the economy and threatens the local social fabric. Municipal officials also have the potential to help find a balance between supporting provincial and territorial government policies and ensuring these senior governments respect the will of local residents. Getting it right brings custom made services designed to fit local needs. Getting it wrong causes undue friction with senior governments or allows provincial and territorial officials to run roughshod over the local community. The key promise of the local government is this potential to achieve the correct balance on these and other important issues and, ultimately, make Canadian communities better places to live.

Introduction

Studying Canadian local government is often rich and fulfilling, but also a pursuit filled with paradoxes. For example, local political institutions are among the oldest in Canada, but frequent restructuring means many municipalities are also among our newest. Local government is said to be "closest to the people," but can hardly be said to be "local" when some cities and regions are now home to hundreds of thousands of residents. Local government allows communities to debate and resolve a wide range of issues, but many still argue "politics has no place in local government." Where local government often results in communities looking spectacular and feeling safe, municipal policies can sometimes produce adverse economic, environmental, and social consequences. The rest of this chapter explores these themes in more detail while at the same time providing crucial definitions and background context.

What Is Local Government?

While you might find definitions a bit boring, they are an important first step in understanding local government and related issues. This section defines and briefly explains local government, municipal government, and other institutions in which local decisions are made, as well as various other governance arrangements made at the local level. These definitions formally explain various institutions in Canada with latter parts of the book adding information about the wide array of individuals and groups involved in local decision making processes, including mayors, councillors, civil servants, businesses, nongovernmental organizations and, of course, residents. Explained throughout the rest of this section, Figure 1.1 diagrammatically illustrates these definitions.

Figure 1.1 Definitional Diagram

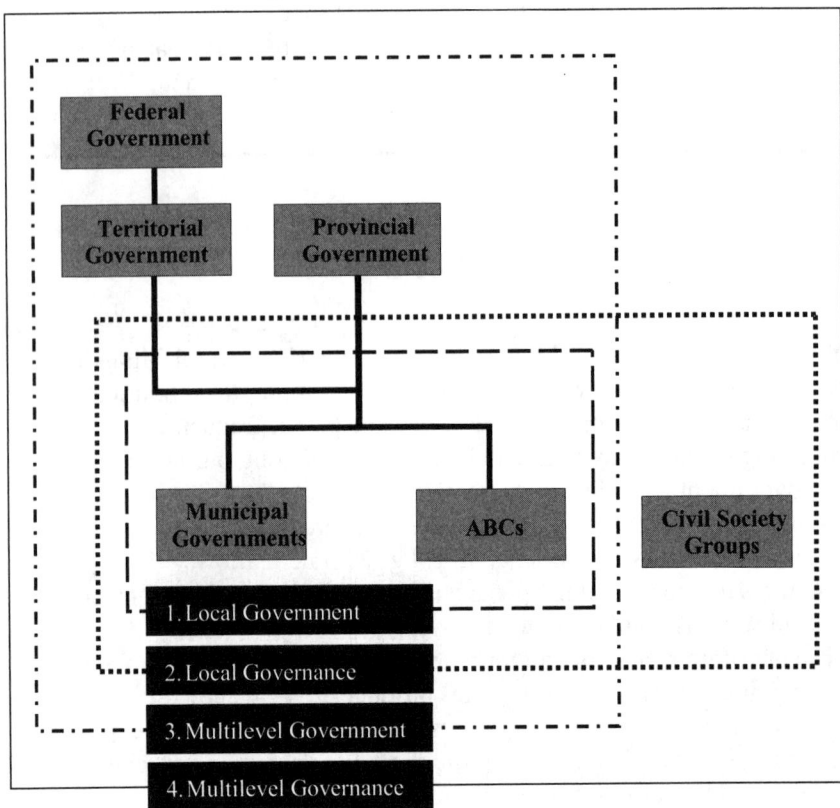

Local Government

"Local government" is a confusing term as it is used to describe (a) a particular *type* of government as well as (b) a *process* by which laws and policies are made within a specific geographic area. Regarding the first meaning, "local government" is a common synonym for "municipal government," used to describe an incorporated village, town, city, or other local entity with an elected council. For example, "municipal governments" and "local governments" are interchangeably used to describe the cities of Burnaby, Red Deer, Moose Jaw, Selkirk, Guelph, Laval, Fredericton, the Halifax Regional Authority, Summerside, Cornerbrook, Yellowknife, Dawson City, and Iqaluit.

As shown in Figure 1.1, "local government" can also pertain to the action of controlling or regulating people ("government") residing in a relatively compact ("local") geographic area.[1] Here the term describes a *process* of making local decisions that might involve a whole range of local officials and the institutions over which they preside. For example, some transportation decisions within a town or city are made by the mayor and council as they have authority over most local roads. However some municipal transportation decisions may also be made by a provincially appointed transit authority granted, for example, the power to decide bus routes. Together these two sets of decisions – those made by the council and those made by the provincially appointed transit authority – combine to provide "local government" in a municipality. To avoid confusion, this text uses the term "municipal government" to refer to villages, towns, or cities and "local government" to describe the process by which a number of official bodies make official decisions for a particular local area.

Municipal Government

"Municipal governments" sit at the core of Figure 1.1 and are the key focus of this text. From a formal perspective, a "municipal government" is a specific legal device created by provincial and territorial governments to allow residents of a specific geographic area the authority to provide services of common interest. Commonly known as a village, town, or city, a municipal government is a corporate entity – meaning it is empowered to enter into legally binding agreements with other

---

[1] Catherine Soanes and Angus Stevenson (eds.), *The Oxford Dictionary of English* (Rev. Ed.), Oxford University Press, 2005.

governments, businesses, organizations, unions, and individuals. A single municipal government is often referred to as a *municipality* with multiple municipal governments called *municipalities*. All municipalities are:

i) incorporated
ii) empowered to deal with a wide range of local issues
iii) defined by distinct geographic boundaries
iv) governed by elected councils
v) granted taxing power

One of the most important things to remember about municipal governments is although they are overseen by councils elected by local people, municipal governments exist at the whim of provincial and territorial governments. That is, provincial and territorial governments have unlimited authority to create municipal governments where they choose, merge, or amalgamate any two or more municipalities, or arbitrarily increase or reduce council authority. Provinces and territories even have the power to abolish municipal governments and instead directly deliver services and programs to local residents.

The provincial/municipal relationship was established in 1867 when the fathers of Confederation drafted Canada's constitution. The *British North America Act* (*BNA Act*), renamed the *Constitution Act* in 1982, lists Canada as having only two official levels of government: national and provincial. Sections 91 and 92 establish how various governmental powers and responsibilities are divided between the national and provincial governments, with Section 92(8) stating: "[i]n each Province the Legislature may exclusively make Laws in relation to Matters... including, "[m]unicipal Institutions in the Province." Where the Yukon and Northwest Territories and Nunavut do not enjoy the same constitutional status as Canadian provinces, the *Yukon Act*, *Northwest Territories Act*, and *Nunavut Act* grant northern territorial governments the authority to create, abolish, and restructure municipal governments as if the territories were provinces.

These constitutional and legislative arrangements are very important as they are the formal foundation upon which rests all other municipal government issues. First, municipal governments are not enshrined in the constitution as independent orders of government (that is, there is no section in the constitution listing powers exclusively held by municipal governments so they cannot be taken away by other levels of government). Provinces and territories have complete control over the existence and form of *their* municipal governments. Second, as the powers to make laws regarding municipal institutions are set out as exclusive to provinces, the national government cannot overturn or add to provincial laws regarding municipal governments.

Table 1.1 presents the 2006 Statistics Canada count of various types of municipal governments across Canada roughly listed from those types with the most population to those with the least. While cities and regional municipalities attract the most attention, we can see the vast majority of municipalities are still small and rural. The table also shows that Canada's 3813 municipal governments are not evenly distributed across the country. Quebec (1117) and Saskatchewan (804) lead the way with the most municipal governments, followed by Ontario (415), Alberta (349), and Newfoundland (283). While we might expect more populated provinces such as Ontario and Quebec to have more municipalities, the large number of municipal governments in Saskatchewan and Newfoundland suggest these latter provinces pursue a much more localized approach to providing municipal services.

Table 1.1 Canadian Municipal Governments – by Type (2006)

	City/Region	Reg Dist	Town/Tshp	Village	Mun/Canton	Cty/Dist	Hamlet Parish	Spec Reg	Rural Mun	Total
NL	3	-	279	-	-	-	-	1	-	283
PEI	2	-	7	-	100	-	-	-	-	109
NS	3	-	31	-	-	12	-	-	-	46
NB	8	-	26	69	-	-	152	-	1	256
Que	1	-	0	271	630	-	215	-	-	1117
Ont	50	-	299	11	55	-	-	-	-	415
Man	9	-	52	20	-	2	-	-	118	201
Sask	14	-	147	337	1	-	9	-	296	804
Alta	16	-	110	152	5	65	-	1	-	349
BC	48	27	15	42	1	50	-	-	-	183
Terr	3	-	7	5	0	0	35	0	0	50
Total	157	27	973	907	792	129	411	2	415	3813

Source: Adapted from Statistics Canada, 2006 Census of Population, http://www12.statcan.gc.ca/census-recensement/2006/ref/dict/tables/table-tableau-7-eng.cfm, accessed summer 2011. Similar categories are combined for presentation purposes. Please note that StatsCan categories may differ from those used by individual provinces.

In terms of population, many of our largest municipalities have grown larger than provinces and territories. For example, with just under 400 000 residents, Halifax Regional Municipality contains over 40% of the Nova Scotia population and covers over 10% of the provincial land area. As one long time municipal practitioner cautions, "…when the local order of government is expanded to a size where it approaches the size of a provincial government, it runs the risk of expanding its horizon to a point where it loses the proximity to citizens necessary to be an effective *local* government."[2] While some municipalities have grown to a size where they are perhaps in danger of losing the local status, the vast majority of Canadian municipalities have only a few thousand or even fewer residents. This enormous variety of municipal governmental arrangements makes it difficult to generalize about municipal government within a single province, let alone across Canada.

Box 1.1 Town of Wolfville shows you don't have to be big to lead

Where large cities and metropolitan regions usually dominate the headlines, the town of Wolfville, Nova Scotia has shown the world that small municipalities have big ideas. In 1997, Wolfville became the first municipality in Canada to ban smoking in vehicles in which a child is travelling as a passenger. In a first for the country, Wolfville Mayor Bob Stead and his council unanimously passed a by-law to issue first time offenders a warning with subsequent offences resulting in a $50 fine.

After Wolfville council passed the new by-law the Nova Scotia government quickly adopted a similar province-wide ban on smoking in vehicles with child passengers. Similar laws have now been adopted in six provinces across Canada and in cities around the world.

Despite having fewer than 4000 residents, Wolfville has become an international public health leader. Not content to rest, Wolfville town council also voted to become the first fair trade municipality in the country – committing to using fair trade coffees, teas, sugars, and other products in local restaurants and the local university.

These decisions made in Wolfville show municipalities do not have to have a large population to have a big impact. There are many other "Wolfvilles" across Canada – small municipalities providing efficient, effective, and innovative government for their communities and leaving their mark around the world. Their contribution and importance must not be overlooked in the current focus on big city government.

---

[2] André Carrel, *Citizens' Hall*, Toronto, Between the Lines, 2001, p. 92 (emphasis added).

Agencies, Boards, and Commissions

As shown in Figure 1.1, a variety of official local bodies also work with municipal governments to provide local government. These other bodies are often referred to as ABCs – agencies, boards, and commissions. Approximately 8000 of these bodies carry out their work across Canada, and include police commissions, regional health authorities, parks boards, and conservation authorities.[3] ABCs differ from formal municipal governments as they are for the most part appointed by provincial and territorial governments rather than elected by local people.[4]

Also considered ABCs, local school boards represent an important exception to the general rule as these elected bodies have a long history of working with education departments and agencies to deliver education within the local area. However, it is important to remember school boards do not qualify as municipal governments as they deal with a very narrow range of educational issues. In addition, most school boards are not granted direct taxation powers, but instead receive operating revenues from provincial, territorial, and municipal governments.

Agencies, boards, and commissions receive much less attention than municipalities in this text. While decisions made by these organizations can often greatly impact local government, ABCs are more a form of decentralized provincial and territorial administration than a vehicle through which local residents make decisions about the communities in which they live. In other words, ABCs provide an avenue for provincial and territorial governments to deliver top down policies, where municipal governments offer an opportunity for a more bottom up, organic policy generation. However ABCs are discussed sporadically throughout the text in order to highlight an often important role they play in local policy making process.

---

[3] Count estimate from Dale Richmond and David Siegel (eds.), *Agencies, Boards and Commissions in Canadian Local Government*, Toronto, Institute of Public Administration of Canada, Monograph No. 15, 1994, p. xv. For a discussion of developments in Western Canada, see Evan Jones and Susan McFarlane, *Regional Approaches to Services in the West: Health, Social Services and Education*, Canada West Foundation, February 2002.

[4] The Government of Canada also has a number of ABCs including, for example, appointed Port and Airport Authorities.

Local Governance, Multilevel Government, and Multilevel Governance

It is worth clarifying a few more terms before moving on. For example, some use the term "local governance" when talking about particular types of local decision making.[5] Numbered "2" in Figure 1.1, "local governance" moves beyond the idea of municipal governments and ABCs making local government decisions to describe particular local decision making scenarios involving municipal governments, ABCs, and civil society groups. The latter includes organizations such as registered charities, neighbourhood associations, faith based organizations, women's organizations, professional associations, trade unions, self-help groups, social movements, business associations, and advocacy groups. "Local government" describes collaborative arrangements only between officials in local institutions with formal powers derived from the constitution, while "local governance" defines scenarios where these local officials collaborate with civil society groups with less or even no formal authority.

Moving further along this path, arrangements between municipal and provincial government officials, municipal and federal government officials, or municipal and provincial and federal government officials are called "multilevel government" (numbered "3" in Figure 1.1). "Multilevel governance" (numbered as "4" in Figure 1.1) is a situation when municipal governments and one or both senior levels of governments and civil society groups form cooperative agreements to work on local issues.[6] Where some of these terms occasionally come up in this text, you are likely to encounter them the more you read about local government.

Aboriginal Governments

Another set of officials providing local government are those found in Canada's Aboriginal communities. Statistics Canada lists 2420 of these communities across Canada, described as Community Governments, Indian Reserves, Indian Government Districts, Indian Settlements, or as

---

[5] For example see Peter John, *Local Governance in Western Europe*, London, Sage, 2001.

[6] This term originated in Europe and first appeared in Liesbet Hooghe and Gary Marks, *Multi-level Governance and European Integration*, Lanham, MD, Rowman & Littlefield Publishers, 2001.

governments specific to particular First Nations such as Nisga'a or Cree Villages. These Aboriginal governments of Canada's First Nations, Indians, Inuit, and Métis are similar to municipal governments in that they are used by local people to make local decisions regarding local issues, but it is a mistake to describe any of these Aboriginal governments as municipal governments.

Aboriginal governments are not "creatures of the province" but rather a result of formal treaties between the specific Aboriginal group and the federal (and sometimes a provincial) government. Also, whether selected through customized election processes or hereditary leadership, Aboriginal governments are increasingly gaining authority over traditional and assigned lands and often have a much broader range of powers and responsibilities than municipal governments. It is perhaps better to think of Aboriginal governments as equivalent to mini-provinces – small groups of self-governing people with constitutional rights based on small parcels of land they have often lived on for centuries.

What Do Municipal Governments Do?

The last section described municipal governments as the key local government institutions. This section discusses the two main municipal government roles. On one hand, municipal governments are created by provinces and territories to deliver a wide range of necessary services, programs, facilities, and regulations to local residents. On the other hand, local residents expect elected municipal governments to express the will of the local community – even if what the community wants falls outside the authority of the municipal government to deliver or directly contradicts senior government policy. The growing scope of municipal government responsibility and pressures of living in a highly complex modern age often cause these two main roles to clash, but in combination they often offer the best local service provision approach.

Municipalities as Service Providers

Some people still think of municipal governments as similar to those shown below – slightly unsophisticated groups of elected male officials sitting around tables in quaint town halls making decisions about roads, sewers, parks, and other limited local matters. This image is seriously out of date, especially when it comes to the range of issues facing municipal councils in today's big cities.

Figure 1.2 Early Meeting of Vancouver's First City Council, 1886

Source: Vancouver Public Library, Special Collections, VPL #508.

Twenty-first century municipal governments have to deal with an enormous range of issues, actors, and organizations. This is true in our largest cities but, as the previous examples of anti-smoking and fair trade by-laws in Wolfville show, it is increasingly the case even in Canada's smallest towns. As described by Vander Ploeg, large Canadian cities:

> ... own telecommunications systems, fibre-optic networks, electrical transmission utilities, water and wastewater treatment plants, and airports. Big cities operate community welfare systems, public housing facilities, hospices, hostels, homeless shelters, and help run hot lunch and after school care programs, forensic laboratories, recreational facilities, concert halls, art galleries, and museums. Big cities also engage in the treatment of drug addiction and other medical and mental illnesses, as well as economic development, hazardous waste

remediation, environmental cleanups, and search and rescue. Big cities are also working on alternative fuel and energy technology as well as advanced transit systems, and are competing on the world stage to host the *Olympics,* the *Pan-American Games,* the *Commonwealth Games* and *World Expositions.* The list goes on.[7]

Despite the current myriad of duties performed by modern Canadian municipal governments, early documents show senior governments originally created municipal governments at the request of local property owners keen to protect their own interests. For example, when Halifax was formed in 1841 its charter limited the right to vote in local elections to about 800 people who could meet a property qualification and restricted candidacy requirements to a fraction of that number.[8] A study by Melvin Baker describes similar restrictions in St. John's where a number of measures ensured only merchants, lawyers, and shopkeepers made local decisions when the city was incorporated in 1888.[9] Similarly, Alan Artibise shows major Western Canadian municipal governments were dominated by a business elite, "partly because of a restricted franchise which effectively limited opposition."[10] While the franchise was gradually extended over the years, the influence of the propertied class and the business elites continues to prevail – a recurring theme in this text.

Municipalities as Democratic Governments

As valuable as it is to deliver all these services for provincial and territorial governments, many argue the core purpose of a municipal government is to provide a mechanism for local people to express, debate, and resolve local issues and concerns. To these local democrats, municipal governments perform a vital political role and provide local citizens opportunities to choose representatives who will make decisions reflecting, or at least addressing, community views and concerns. From

---

[7] From Casey Vander Ploeg, *Rationale for Renewal*, Canada West Foundation, September 2005, p. 27.

[8] Donald J. H. Higgins, *Local and Urban Politics in Canada*, Toronto, Gage, 1986, p. 39.

[9] M. Baker, "William Gilbert Gosling and the Establishment of Commission Government in St. John's, Newfoundland, 1914," *Urban History Review*, Vol. IX, No. 3, February 1981, pp. 37-39.

[10] Gilbert Stelter and Alan Artibise (eds.), *Shaping the Urban Landscape: Aspects of the Canadian City-Building Process*, Ottawa, Carleton University Press, 1982, p. 21. See also the Artibise article on pp. 116-147.

this perspective, the municipality is an extension of the community and depicts the community governing itself.[11]

The democratic role of municipalities has been emphasized by various 19th century scholars such as John Stuart Mill and Alexis de Tocqueville.[12] To Mill, municipal governments constitute a training ground where elected representatives learn how to govern before going on to serve at a more senior level of government and local citizens learn to exercise their democratic rights in the context of relatively simple to understand issues. Others view the democratic role of municipal governments in a much more fundamental light, agreeing with de Tocqueville's sentiments that "...municipal institutions constitute the strength of free nations....[a] nation may establish a free government, but without municipal institutions it cannot have the spirit of liberty."

No better expression of this latter sentiment can be found in Canada than in the famous Durham Report. Sent in the 1830s by the British Government to investigate a series of rebellions in what was then Upper and Lower Canada, Lord Durham was struck by the lack of municipal institutions in the colonies – especially in the rural areas still governed by unelected Courts of Quarter Sessions. He was concerned "the people receive no training in those habits of self-government which are indispensable to enable them rightly to exercise the power of choosing representatives in parliament."[13]

Indeed, the Canadian municipal expert K. G. Crawford views municipal governments as more than just training grounds, but as the level of government through which the democratic ideal was most likely to be fulfilled.[14] This is partly because local residents are more likely to understand the local issues more easily than the increasingly complex, technical matters predominating in senior governmental agendas. It is also due to the proximity of municipal institutions allowing local residents to more easily evaluate if their municipal officials act in the best interests of the community.

---

[11] For a more complete examination of this concept, see various writings by John Stewart including "A Future for Local Authorities as Community Government," in John Stewart and Gerry Stoker, *The Future of Local Government*, London, UK, Macmillan Education Ltd., 1989, and Michael Clarke and John Stewart, *The Choices for Local Government*, Harlow, Longman, 1991.

[12] See Alexis de Tocqueville's *Democracy in America* and John Stuart Mill's *Considerations on Representative Government* and *On Liberty*.

[13] Quoted in Engin Isin, *Cities Without Citizens*, Montreal, Black Rose Books, 1992, p. 132.

[14] See K. G. Crawford's *Canadian Municipal Government*.

Not everyone views the link between democracy and municipal government as positively as Mill, de Tocqueville, and Crawford. A contrasting vision is provided by Langrod who sees municipal government as "...but a technical arrangement within the mechanisms of the administrative system, a structural and functional detail...."[15] Langrod rejects the assumption municipal governments are vital to democracy and hints they can even undermine the democratic process:

> In some countries local [municipal] governments, with its structured anachronisms, the high degree of its internal functionalisation, the preponderance in practice of the permanent official over the elected and temporary councillor, its methods of work and its obstinate opposition to all modernization, can ... act as a brake on the process of democratisation.[16]

Opposition to the claim that municipal governments are somehow vehicles for democracy has a long history both in Canada and around the world. Over 100 years ago, many municipal politicians and administrators actively worked to insulate municipal governments from politics during what is often called the municipal reform movement. During this time reformers insisted local policy should be made according to objective and rational grounds and municipal administrators freed to provide municipal services without interference from elected representatives. In short, reformers believed municipal government should be run as if it were a business, instituting a number of structural changes designed to reduce the power of local politicians and elevate the role of appointed experts. The many agencies, boards, and commissions established during this era left the lingering notion municipal government decisions should never be based on political considerations.

Although efforts to separate municipal governments from political interference were often undertaken in the name of efficiency, some observers see these reforms as undemocratic or even antidemocratic. Pro democracy critics view reform era actions by property owners and businessmen as attempting to reduce the political influence of nonpropertied residents. That most reformers fighting to increase the power of middle class propertied businessmen were themselves middle class propertied businessmen reveals the bald self-interest of reformers.

---

[15] Georges Langrod, "Local Government and Democracy," in *Public Administration*, Vol. XXXI, Spring 1953, pp. 25-33. The frequently cited Langrod and Panter-Brick exchanges on the subject of local government and democracy are reprinted in Lionel D. Feldman (ed.), *Politics and Government of Urban Canada*, Toronto, Methuen, 1981, Section A.

[16] *Ibid.*, pp. 5-6.

According to Plunkett and Betts, the intention of those wishing to separate municipal decision making from politics:

> ... was not to try to halt the process of making decisions on public policy at the local level. Their intention, rather, was to exclude various groups from the process.... The reformers were interested in restoring the efficiency and effectiveness of municipal service delivery. At the same time, they were plainly concerned with restricting the influence of the cities' burgeoning population of working people upon the conduct of municipal affairs.[17]

The efforts of the early reformers to undermine the political role of municipal governments were misguided and harmful. Politics inevitably exists in every society because humans have wants and needs that must be satisfied from an insufficient pool of resources. As a result, competition and conflict arise, with the central purpose of any government being to resolve these disputes by deciding who gets what and how equitably scarce resources are distributed. Politics is an integral part of municipal government operations. Competition and conflict are equally prevalent at the local level as they are elsewhere. Divisions arise between different sets of interests: urban and rural, city and suburban, haves and have-nots, pro and anti development, men and women, and various ethnic groups, races, and religions. Since municipalities are democratically elected governments, not just vehicles for service provision, it is their role to mediate among the diverse interests, build consensus where possible, and to make and answer for choices. As Edward Banfield and James Q. Wilson state, "[p]olitics, like sex, cannot be abolished. It can sometimes be repressed by denying people the opportunity to practice it, but it cannot be done away with because it is in the nature of man to disagree and to contend."[18]

Municipalities as Democratic Service Providers

Where the administrative and political roles of a municipal government can sometimes conflict, the combination and interaction of these two essential functions make municipal governments an essential part of modern life. It is not just that municipalities are empowered by senior governments to provide a number of services that makes municipal

---

[17] T. J. Plunkett and G. M. Betts, *The Management of Canadian Urban Government*, Kingston, Queen's University, 1978, p. 27.

[18] Edward Banfield and James Q. Wilson, *City Politics*, New York, Random House, 1963, pp. 20-21.

government so important. Nor is it just because municipal governments represent the views of the local community. Municipal governments are vital to community well-being because they have the unique capacity to *provide services delivered in accordance with the needs and wishes of the local residents*. Neither the political nor administrative municipal roles are nearly as valuable if not interrelated so that one informs the other. Much of the potential benefit of a municipal government is lost if services are provided without regard to local needs or if local residents participate in a government lacking the capacity to deal with the issues of concern.

Of course there are also other reasons why municipal governments are so important to modern society. For one, history shows local service delivery cannot be merely left to the private sector. Just as governments cannot always provide goods as efficiently as the private sector, private firms do not always supply what is desired by a community, especially collective goods which are not usually profitable. This is a common theme in the development of local government in most modern industrialized countries. As Keith Dowding notes, the early history of local government,

> ... is the history of local communities petitioning central government for the right to raise taxes and regulate communities precisely because the market failed to provide all their wants....Markets may have some of the features of 'spontaneous order' but when the spontaneity of the market has failed to produce the goods, communities have sought the political powers to provide them for themselves.[19]

On the other hand, provincial governments do not on their own have the capacity to effectively deliver all local services. Where provincial governments might be able to build new roads or parks, it would be impossible for senior governments to effectively address more micro issues such as which potholes to fill or not fill, whether a park should allow pets or be dog free, or to decide if a homeowner should be allowed to plant a certain type of tree in his or her backyard. Municipal governments will always play a role in modern society as neither private firms nor provincial governments can deliver all local needs and wants, or at least not as effectively as more locally based governments.

Creating municipal governments also allows provincial and territorial governments to devolve authority and formally involve many decision makers in many different localities. Devolution allows locally

---

[19] Keith Dowding, "Public Choice and Local Governance" in Desmond King and Gerry Stoker (eds.) *Rethinking Local Democracy*, London, Macmillan, 1996, pp. 59-60.

generated knowledge to inform the process by which government policy is made for local areas. It also produces policy experimentation when different municipal governments employ different policy solutions to address similar types of problems. Experimentation at the local level allows policy makers to compare different policy responses and discover which best solves a local problem. Relying only upon centrally generated policy solutions limits prospects for innovation.

Finally, not only do provincial and territorial governments rely on municipal governments to deliver local services, but having a network of municipalities also broadens the opportunity to encourage greater public participation in government. Municipal governments are located within local communities and hence more immediately accessible than senior governments ever can be. Without municipal governments, senior governments would either be bombarded with more requests and demands than would be possible to adequately answer or accommodate, or the public would be virtually shut out of the policy making process due to the difficulties of accessing officials within a very centralized system.[20]

The Changing Context

To understand the nature and potential of municipal governments we need to appreciate the context in which they operate and how that context has changed over the years. Relevant factors include changing population patterns, the international economic framework, and the prevailing governing philosophy or ideology. The next section briefly discusses these three contextual variables, followed by concluding comments.

The Demographic Context

The upswing in the birth rate in the years immediately following World War Two is today reflected in uneven distribution of the Canadian population, as illustrated by the figure that follows.

---

[20] George W. Jones and John Stewart, *The Case for Local Government*, London, Allen & Unwin Inc., 1985.

Figure 1.3 Canadian Population Age Pyramid

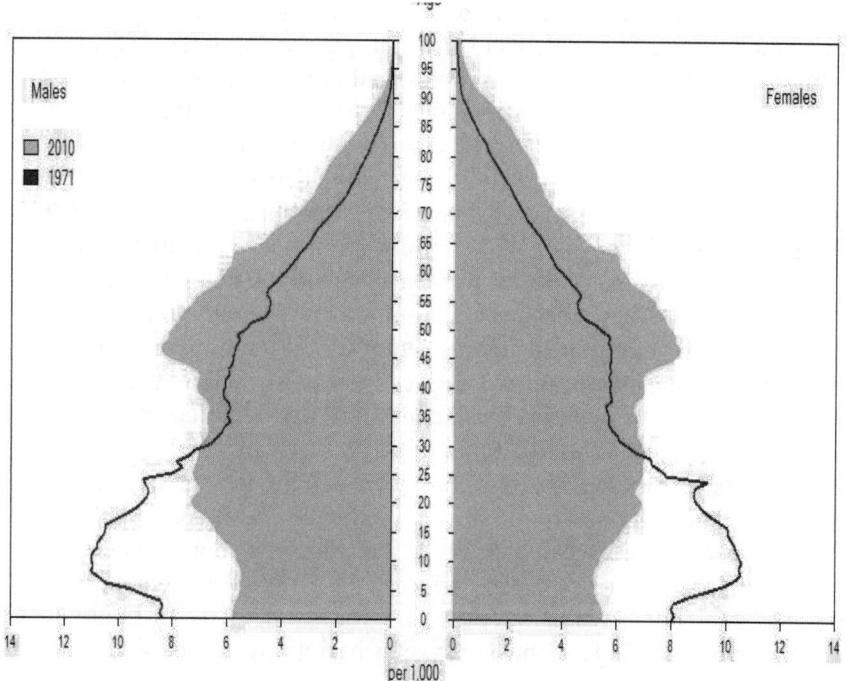

Source: Adapted from Statistics Canada publication *Report on the Demographic Situation in Canada*, Catalogue 91-209-XWE2011001, http://www.statcan.gc.ca/pub/91-209-x/2011001/article/11511/figures/fig-eng.htm; accessed November 2011.

As the population pyramid demonstrates, the effect of the "baby boomers" has many implications for all governments as this largest cohort of the population begins to near retirement age – especially as there are fewer younger people to pay taxes and provide essential services. Provincial and federal governments face rapidly increasing costs for health care and pensions. Local governments need to recognize and respond to the different preferences and servicing needs of seniors with respect to such matters as housing accommodation, public transit, and recreational facilities and programs.

With the birth rate in Canada now below what would sustain the current level of population, growth in this country is increasingly dependent upon immigration. The vast majority of immigrants settle in a few major urban areas, notably Toronto, Montreal, and Vancouver. They enrich the country with their diversity and they help to maintain a labour force that would otherwise soon face a shortage of workers. But immigrants often have settlement problems, can face discrimination, and place additional servicing demands on municipal governments. They also put to the test the inclusiveness of municipal policies and operations.

Canadian urbanization has long been driven by immigration. As discussed in Chapter 3, post-World War Two population growth in Canada's urban areas also greatly increased the demand for local services. As a result, some service provision was shifted upward to better resourced provincial or regional governments or intermunicipal boards when demands of local populations overwhelmed the delivery capacity of small municipalities. Services remaining locally based often were required to meet minimum standards set by provincial governments. Municipal financial shortfalls were eased by provincial grants, but these often came with attached provincial conditions and requirements. This period reduced the autonomy of municipalities as provincial governments became more involved in local affairs, leaving municipal governments with less ability to respond to the needs and preferences of local residents. Chapter 3 also discusses the concerns about how early patterns of urbanization adversely affected the political and democratic role of municipal government reduced by, for example, the difficulty in including people living amongst vast suburban sprawl.

The Economic Context

The influence of economic forces on government operations is certainly not new. Municipal responsiveness to the local community has always been constrained by an overriding preoccupation with satisfying business interests. The traditional municipal role of providing services to property owners has evolved into one of servicing land in support of the property development industry, an understandable preoccupation as the main source of municipal revenues has always been tax on real property. With the instantaneous transmission of information and capital and the lowering of trade barriers associated with the new globalized economy, municipalities feel even greater pressure to accommodate the interests of business or risk losing industry to other locales. These and other economic factors are discussed in more detail in Chapter 6. The rest of this section provides an initial overview of the general economic context in which contemporary municipalities operate – namely globalization and the changing nature of the international economy.

Stepping back for a moment to look at the global economy from a historical perspective, the horrors of World War Two prompted a change in the global economic system characterized by a new set of international arrangements and multilateral organizations established to ensure cooperation among trading partners.[21] Replacing the gold standard with fixed exchange rates to set the value of a currency provided stability in international economic transactions. An International Monetary Fund monitored exchange rate adjustments to prevent countries from unilaterally devaluing their currencies to gain a trade advantage on others and a new World Bank was set up providing funds for postwar reconstruction and aid and technical assistance to developing countries.[22]

These arrangements worked well for more than 25 years with most developed countries experiencing considerable economic growth. New and extensive social programs such as unemployment insurance ensured the resulting wealth was better distributed throughout most Western nations, with these programs viewed more as a stimulus to the purchasing power of citizens and a boost to economic growth than a government handout. Increased social spending reflected the economic ideas of John Maynard Keynes who proposed governments could adopt deliberate policies to minimize unemployment levels and support economic growth. Under Keynesian economics, economic growth *and* social justice were not only compatible but also mutually reinforcing.

As the 1970s unfolded, countries found themselves facing a combination of unanticipated economic problems including high and continued levels of unemployment and inflation. These problems were at least partly a result of the actions taken by a group of Oil Producing and Exporting Countries (OPEC) formed in 1973 to limit oil supplies and drive up prices. Keynesian economics fell out of favour as these combined economic problems continued to worsen. Once favoured social programs were now criticized for encouraging dependency among the less well-off and increasing taxation to a level seen as detrimental to business expansion.

---

[21] The description in this section is largely based on C. Richard Tindal, *A Citizen's Guide to Government*, 3rd Edition, Whitby, McGraw-Hill Ryerson Limited, 2005, pp. 316-331, which, in turn, draws from Ethan B. Kapstein, "A Global Third Way: Social Justice and the World Economy," *World Policy Journal*, Winter 1998/99, Vol. 15, pp. 23-35.

[22] When a country's currency is devalued, it is worth less in relation to the currency of its trading partners, making it cheaper for those countries to import goods from the country that has devalued. The reverse pattern is also true, of course, which is why the greatly strengthened Canadian dollar in 2011 was not universally a cause for rejoicing – since it made our goods more expensive for countries that would otherwise wish to import them.

While the OPEC oil crisis played out in the highly visible spectre of long lines at gas stations, abandoning fixed exchange rates proved an even more significant development. "Floating" exchange rates created entirely new financial markets with currencies becoming subject to speculation once values became determined by the impact of supply and demand. According to Linda McQuaig, daily trading in foreign exchange markets around the world grew from almost nothing to $150 billion by the mid-1980s, to $880 billion by 1992 and to $1.2 trillion by 1995. Most of this trading was not a reflection of the healthy flow of capital arising from nations trading and investing in each other but rather short term, speculative buying and selling of currencies to generate profits.[23] By the end of the 1990s, only about 2% of all global foreign exchange activity was connected to the export and import of real goods.[24]

Financial institutions understandably responded by diversifying their currency holdings to exploit the opportunities provided by floating exchange rates. Mobile capital was now free to roam the planet, giving it tremendous power over economic policy making and severely constraining the ability of national governments to pursue domestic policies. According to Howard Pawley, "[w]ith the click of a mouse, after entering a few numbers into the computer, bond markets and transnational corporations can change the course of any nation's development."[25] Canada experienced this harsh reality when Moody's Investor Services put the country's AAA credit rating under review a few weeks prior to the 1995 federal budget – the one in which Paul Martin famously stated that Canada's problem of steadily increasing annual deficits would be solved "come hell or high water." The message received by the government from Moody's was expenditures had to be cut, two-thirds of which were made up of social programs.[26] As one observer sees the situation:[27]

---

[23] Linda McQuaig, *The Cult of Impotence: Selling the Myth of Powerlessness in the Global Economy*, Toronto, Penguin Books Canada Ltd., 1998, pp. 153-158.

[24] Alex C. Michalos, "The Tobin Tax: A Good Idea Whose Time Has *Not* Passed," *Policy Options*, October 1999, p. 64.

[25] Howard Pawley, "Is Globalization Good for Canada?" *Toronto Star*, February 2, 1998.

[26] Andrew Johnson, "Strengthening Society III: Social Security," in Andrew Johnson and Andrew Stritch (eds.) *Canadian Public Policy: Globalization and Political Parties*, Toronto, Copp Clark Ltd., 1997, p. 180.

[27] Thomas L. Friedman, quoted in *ibid.*, p. 181.

> ...we live in a two superpower world. There is the U.S. and there is Moody's. The U.S. can destroy a country with bombs. Moody's can destroy a country by downgrading its bonds.

While capital now roams free, governments are increasingly constrained by international trade agreements and organizations established over the past couple of decades as the most visible manifestation of the new global economy. As discussed in Chapter 6, these include the Canada United States Free Trade Agreement (CUFTA or FTA) of 1988, the North American Free Trade Agreement (NAFTA) of 1994, and the World Trade Organization (WTO) created in 1995. The internationalization of economic activity is the key characteristic of this new era. Multinational corporations have become transnational corporations with no particular or permanent home base or domestic market. Modern technology allows companies to deploy resources spatially in whatever manner best serves the bottom line, resulting in most mass production and labour intensive work now being located in low wage regions of the world. The more mobility the international free trade regime provides these corporations, the more governments must balance pressure to accommodate transnational business interests with the risk of losing them to other jurisdictions.[28]

While there are considerable merits to freeing up world trade, there are also legitimate concerns about the specifics of the free trade agreements and the way they are enforced. It should be possible to structure free trade rules and regulations to provide a reasonable balance between the needs of business and the rights of individuals and their domestic governments. At the moment, this balance is lacking and the arrangements are skewered in favour of business interests. Much of the explanation for this imbalance can be found in the dominant ideology that has accompanied and rationalized the new economic order.

The 2008 global recession brought on by a collapse of banks in the United States and United Kingdom reveals the perils of an increasingly interconnected world and unregulated trade. Linked to reckless and unsustainable lending practices within the U.S. housing market, the recession resulted in a sharp drop in international trade and rising unemployment. That governments were forced to bail out or even assume ownership of some of the world's largest banks prompted some to call for a return to Keynesian economic policies and new international

---

[28] These developments are discussed, among others, in Murray Dobbin, *The Myth of the Good Corporate Citizen*, Toronto, Stoddart, 1998, and John Shields and B. Mitchell Evans, *Shrinking the State: Globalization and Public Administration "Reform,"* Halifax, Fernwood Publishing, 1998.

restrictions on international trade, although in 2010 the world's top economies scrapped plans for a universal global bank tax and other new financial trade regulations.

The Ideological Context

By the mid-1970s "neoliberalism" largely replaced Keynesianism as the dominant governance ideology. Neoliberalism offers a modern twist on classic liberal views most famously expressed in Adam Smith's *The Wealth of Nations* in which an "invisible hand" guides the interaction of supply and demand in a free marketplace and provides the greatest general benefit to individuals and the countries in which they live. Where classical liberalism rejects government regulation of domestic markets, neoliberalism moves further to include deregulation of the international sphere and extending market provision to cover new goods such as intellectual property rights.

The net economic and social benefits of a world organized on the basis of neoliberalism remains a matter of fierce debate, but there can be little doubt about the adverse impact of this ideology on the realm of government and the public domain. Various governments gave neo-liberalism practical expression by reducing social services, deregulating various industries, and privatizing public services, including those headed by UK Conservative Prime Minister Margaret Thatcher and American Republican President Ronald Reagan. These governments essentially hollowed out the state, with some suggesting private interests came to trump the public domain and related social priorities during the 1980s and 1990s.[29]

Canada was not long in following the example set by Thatcher and Reagan, dismantling the social safety net – either directly by curtailing programs or indirectly by undermining programs through expenditure cuts. The last decade of the 20th century saw the federal government shift responsibility by cutting transfer payments made to provincial governments. In turn, provincial governments shifted responsibility by cutting transfer payments made to municipal governments. Municipalities, as usual, often felt the worst effects of this "fend for yourself" federalism.

As discussed in Chapter 6, municipalities everywhere now face the combined impact of reduced provincial transfer payments and increased responsibilities arising from federal and provincial offloading. Yet because municipalities were not supposed to increase taxes, especially on

---

[29] David Marquand, *Decline of the Public, The Hollowing Out of Citizenship*, Cambridge, UK, Polity Press, 2004, p. 45.

business, they continually face pressures to reduce or abandon public services. As a result, many municipal governments have "reinvented" themselves and adopted core "new public management" practices to meet these local servicing and financing challenges resulting from senior government offloading.[30] As discussed in Chapter 9, most municipal governments have redefined their core business in line with neoliberal practices by developing business plans, setting measurable targets, and pursuing alternative service delivery strategies including joint ventures with other local government bodies, public private partnerships, and even outright privatization.

The Promise of Local Government

Those currently using new public management practices to reinvent 21st century municipal government echo early 20th century reform efforts to remove politics from the policy making process and force municipalities to cater increasingly to business interests. Modern municipalities often appear more focused on implementing senior government policies, preparing business plans, and pursuing economical service delivery options than on meeting the needs of the wider community. While it is important to maintain the local economy and assist provincial and territorial governments to implement policy, too narrow a focus on these objectives misses out on the main promise of local government: to capitalize on the unique capacity of municipalities to provide services in accordance with the needs and desires of the local community.

Too much top down or business oriented policy may cause local residents to express their preferences through alternative movements and venues, or become increasingly hostile toward local mayors and councils. Democracy has become so deeply ingrained that it is hard to imagine local residents allowing locally elected officials to favour the wishes of business and senior governments over those of the local community for too long. History shows unaddressed tensions often result in more community minded candidates standing during council elections or, if these efforts fail, protest or even violence.

---

[30] David Osborne and Ted Gaebler, *Reinventing Government*, New York, Penguin Books, 1993.

The only way to avoid these tensions and capitalize on the main promise of municipal government is to make local residents the heart of local government. Bringing residents in (or bringing them back in) will take considerable work, requiring a municipal council to first recognize its "obligation to engage citizens in democratic governance is far more important than its obligation to manage the services delegated to it by the provincial government."[31] It also entails, for example, recapturing the rebellious spirit of the Upper Canadian United Empire Loyalists who named new towns despite being ordered by British authorities to instead refer to their communities by an assigned number. However such local resistance will be difficult as most municipalities have fallen into a pattern of "comfortable subordination" after two centuries of colonial/provincial paternalism and federal indifference.[32]

Where globalization and senior government offloading present considerable challenges to municipal governments, these two conditions also offer new opportunities. Globalization makes for more mobile capital and increased competitiveness, but also elevates the role urban areas play in a service sector oriented economy. Reduced national and provincial government activities put pressure on local councils to deliver more services, but also provide municipal governments the chance to expand their scope of authority and put their own stamp on service delivery. These enhanced roles have been strengthened by provinces enacting legislation giving municipal governments greater operating freedom and flexibility and court decisions recognizing municipalities as local *governments* entitled to some latitude when taking action on behalf of their citizens.

One way municipal governments might realize these opportunities is to harness the power of the local community. As explained in Chapter 6, active participation and public support enhances municipal leverage when bargaining with senior governments or business interests but the extent to which residents get involved depends largely on the municipality and its practices. Global neoliberal forces do not require municipalities to be secretive about deliberations or resistant to the sharing of information with the public. Nor, as shown in Chapter 10, do these forces need to stop municipalities determined to actively engage the public in local decision making. Building strength from within the

---

[31] Carrel, *Citizens' Hall*, p. 108.

[32] This condition, and the preferred alternative, are explored in David Siegel and C. Richard Tindal, "Changing the Municipal Culture: From Comfortable Subordination to Assertive Maturity," *Municipal World*, March and April 2006.

community not only provides leverage but also reinforces the extent to which the municipality is viewed as a legitimate government.

Returning to the past is a very good place to start when trying to more fully understand where municipal governments find themselves today. Current municipal government structure, internal organization, machinery, and operating philosophy are more a reflection of historical evolution than is commonly appreciated. A surprising number of yesterday's issues and themes still affect contemporary municipal governments. The next few chapters explore the origins and evolution of municipal government in Canada as past legacies provide insight into what the future might hold for our villages, towns, cities, and metropolitan regions.

Chapter 2
The Legacy of the Past

When it comes to understanding the current state of local government in Canada, it is important to remember that we are largely prisoners of decisions made by our ancestors. It is also essential to keep in mind that there is really nothing new under the sun, with current happenings usually echoing past events. These lessons certainly apply to Canadian local government. Challenges faced by our predecessors are similar in nature to those we face today and, moreover, decisions made decades and even centuries ago continue to shape 21st century local government institutions and practices. This chapter traces local government development back to its turn of the 20th century origins in each Canadian province. It includes early attempts to deal with challenges such as rapid growth from an agrarian society. Understanding such roots can be crucial to decisions about future local governing choices.

Local Government Origins

This section provides an overview of the historical evolution of Canadian local government rules and practices. It begins with the very first governmental arrangements of our First Nations people then moves to discuss colonial and postcolonial local government developments on a province by province basis. Key historic figures are highlighted as well as crucial legislative choices – including those of a constitutional nature that greatly limit the flexibility of contemporary Canadian local government.

Aboriginal and Early Colonial Rule

The earliest local governments in what is now Canada were formed thousands of years ago by Aboriginal people. While the family was the basic organizational unit, Aboriginals often came together to form villages, with village leaders cooperating to make regional or even national policy decisions. For example, Iroquois communities governed themselves locally through tribal councils. Tribal council leaders from different villages gathered to make regional decisions through "councils of the nation." Once per year Iroquois leaders from different regions would gather to make national decisions at "grand councils"– sometimes known as a "confederacy."[1] While written records of these meetings are scant due to the oral traditions of Canada's first people, it is easy to imagine these early local and regional meetings concerning topics very similar to those faced by modern local governments.

While Vikings visited and briefly settled in what is now Newfoundland around AD 1000, European colonization of what is now Canada began when Jacques Cartier travelled up the St. Lawrence River and took possession of the territory in the name of the king of France in 1534. Cartier twice more returned with French settlers who stayed to form the first permanent European settlements in what was first called New France, then renamed Lower Canada, and is now known as the province of Quebec. Europeans' colonization changed many aspects of North America, including the process of local decision making.

Just as early Aboriginals dealt with local issues by forming villages and regional governments, so too did new waves of European immigrants. However, unlike Aboriginals, Europeans settling in North America were not free to run their own affairs, but rather were subject to the decisions made by European-based French or, later, British monarchs whose will was made known through governors whom these kings and queens appointed to run their overseas colonies. Scattered in small pockets over a vast area with very rudimentary forms of transportation and communication, North American settlers soon found local problems could not be effectively or directly addressed by centralized colonial governments. While some form of local administration was inevitable for quite practical reasons, the particular form of local government which evolved was strongly influenced by the settlers' political beliefs. Modern Canadian local government is a unique product of all these traditions.

European settlement continued under Samuel de Champlain who founded the City of Quebec in 1608 and went on to become the first governor of New France. Spreading out from Quebec City, the French founded Trois-Rivières in 1634, followed by Montreal (then called Ville-Marie) in 1642. Even with these colonization efforts, fewer than 500 French lived in New France in the mid-1600s, with the vast majority of the local population being Aboriginal.[2]

---

[1] http://www2.canadiana.ca/citm/themes/aboriginals/aboriginals2_e.html.

[2] Guy Frégault, *Canadian Society in the French Regime*, Ottawa, The Canadian Historical Association, 1981.

The first experiment with local self-government came in 1647 when the king of France permitted residents of the three French cities to elect local "syndics" to sit as members of the colonial council located in Quebec City. By definition, local self-government refers to local decision making processes where local residents can influence or control which issues are debated, what decisions are made, and who is empowered to make these decisions. In this early case, syndics had no decision making power, but merely presented electors' concerns to the appointed council and conveyed the council's decisions to the citizenry. Despite their meagre power, the office of syndic was discontinued in 1674 by a French government generally opposed to the concept of representative government, and local self-government disappeared from Canada for almost a century.

Although European colonization of North America began with the French, the British were also set on exploiting resources in foreign lands, and eventually amassed a vast global empire of colonies to accomplish this goal. Following a long series of wars, the British decisively defeated the French during the Battle of the Plains of Abraham in 1759 and, soon after, moved to take Quebec City and Montreal from the French in 1760. Under the terms of the 1763 *Treaty of Paris*, the British gained all French lands in what is now Canada, including approximately 65 000 French inhabitants. Largely in response to this overwhelming French presence in British North America, the British issued the Royal Proclamation of 1763 – creating the Province of Quebec and granting French residents religious freedom but barring Catholics from holding public office.[3]

In terms of local government, the British first vested all authority in the military then transferred these powers to appointed governors and councils. In 1764, the British established *Courts of Quarter Sessions*, an ancient English system for local administration overseen by justices of the peace. Courts of Quarter Sessions met in three districts around Montreal, Quebec City, and Trois Rivières to hear and decide relatively unimportant local matters. While an earlier proclamation promised the introduction of English law and the English system of land grants, little change was made to the traditional running of the affairs of Quebec. The 1774 *Quebec Act* officially restored French civil law for private matters but maintained English common law for public law – including criminal prosecution.

---

[3] Ralph Sarkonak, *A Brief Chronology of French Canada, 1534-1982*. Yale French Studies, 65, 1983, pp. 275-282.

The American Revolution of 1776 precipitated a flow of United Empire Loyalists to Nova Scotia and western Quebec. Loyalists rejected the demands of American revolutionaries and preferred the 13 colonies to remain under British rule. Between 1782 and 1783, more than 50 000 Loyalists fled the United States. About 10 000 arrived in the Saint John area of the Bay of Fundy, with another 25 000 landing in Nova Scotia and 20 000 moving to unsettled areas around Lake Ontario including present day Kingston, Toronto, and Niagara.[4]

Loyalist immigrants mainly hailed from the colonies of New York and New England. These areas had enjoyed significant input into local government decision making while under British control. Of note, these immigrants brought with them a long tradition of town hall meetings where citizens would make decisions about local issues with little interference from British governors. The town hall tradition saw *selectmen* (equivalent to modern day councillors) elected during annual town meetings by those residing within one-half mile of the meeting house. Selectmen (and they were all men) administered the affairs of the town between meetings. In theory, selectmen were to be approved by the governor, but in practice they operated very independently of the central authorities.

Loyalists retreating to Central Canada from the United States were unhappy living under French civil law, and were especially opposed to the French system of land grants under the seigneurial system and their limited local autonomy. There soon were numerous petitions from the Loyalists around Lake Ontario for some form of local courts and administration, English civil law, and separation from that area of Quebec east of Montreal. With much hesitation, but in response to the sheer numbers of immigrating loyalists, a 1787 ordinance divided western Quebec into four new districts with corresponding Courts of Quarter Sessions which assumed judicial, legislative, and administrative responsibilities including: maintaining the peace, regulating domestic animals, regulating licensed taverns, appointing minor officials, and overseeing highways.[5] As the only official agency dealing with local matters, British governors granted Courts of Quarter Sessions more and more powers to deal with new problems as they arose. The next sections explain further evolution of Canadian local government on a province by province basis.

---

[4] Figures from K. G. Crawford, *Canadian Municipal Government*, Toronto, University of Toronto Press, 1954, p. 21.

[5] *Ibid.*, p. 23.

Ontario (Upper Canada)

Continuing pressure from Loyalists for a separate province with English civil law and an English system of land tenure resulted in the *Constitutional Act, 1791*. New provisions under this act included: (1) dividing the province of Quebec into the provinces of Upper and Lower Canada; (2) providing each new province with a British Lieutenant Governor, appointed executive and legislative councils, and an elected legislative assembly; and, (3) enabling English law and land tenure in Upper Canada.

J. G. Simcoe, the first Lieutenant Governor of Upper Canada, strongly discouraged any form of local government. His stance reflected the prevailing view of the British government based in England fearful of the prospect of facing another American revolution and losing another important colony. Local governments were distrusted and considered breeding grounds for dissent and disloyalty.[6] To further discourage any strong attachment to a particular place, in 1783 British authorities directed that the first townships surveyed on the upper St. Lawrence be called "royal seigniories" rather than "townships," and that seigniories be numbered rather than named. However, even before the *Constitutional Act* of 1791 passed, Loyalists had already set up town meetings and designated their settlements as "townships." In an imaginative act of defiance, townships were named after King George and other members of the British Royal Family.

Loyalists still strongly believed they deserved local self-rule in Upper Canada as they constituted a good deal of the provincial population and felt they had proven their loyalty to the Crown by fleeing the rebellious American colonies. These sentiments were reflected in early legislation. The first bill of the first session of the legislative assembly of Upper Canada was "to authorize town meetings for the purpose of appointing divers parish officers," passing as the *Parish and Town Officers Act* in 1793. The Act permitted local voters to hold annual town meetings during which they appointed town clerks, assessors, tax collectors, road overseers, fence viewers, pound keepers, and town wardens who represented local inhabitants in the Quarter Sessions Courts of the district in which the township was located. Despite these various positions, the only actual legislative authority granted to local officials

---

[6] This point is made by Engin Isin, "The Origins of Canadian Municipal Government," in James Lightbody (ed.), *Canadian Metropolitics: Governing Our Cities*, Toronto, Copp Clark Ltd., 1995, pp. 60-61.

was to fix the height of fences and to regulate animals running at large.[7] A law dealing with assessment was also passed, allowing residents to raise money in order to pay for the costs of court and jail houses, officers' fees, and building roads.

The end of the War of 1812 in North America and the Napoleonic Wars in Europe brought a new wave of immigration. Between 1815 and 1850, approximately 800 000 British residents moved to British North America, with most settling in Upper Canada. This population growth magnified existing urban problems and increased the pressure for local self-government. In response to these pressures, the Upper-Canadian legislature created an elected police board in the Town of Brockville to take over local government functions previously exercised by the Courts of Quarter Sessions. The Brockville police board represents the first step toward establishing elected local government councils in Canada. These changes in Brockville proved popular. In 1834, legislation allowed York to become the self-governing City of Toronto, with eight more police towns and two additional cities created in Upper Canada by 1838.

It is important not to overstate the democratic significance of police boards as the vast majority of town residents were blocked from participating in the decision making process.[8] Eager to undermine local autonomy, British governors allowed only police board members to speak at local meetings and permitted only male royal subjects who owned homes to hold board positions or vote in elections. According to Isin, "[t]hese qualifications for board membership and voting demonstrate the calculated restrictions that were put upon participation in town politics."[9]

While the urban areas of Upper Canada were gaining more, although very limited, local self-government, the magistrates of the Quarter Sessions remained in almost total control in rural areas. Reform newspapers claimed many magistrates were unfit, intemperate, and prepared to use violence to silence those calling for local government reform. These same newspapers claimed that decisions as to which local works were to be carried out and how much tax revenue was to be raised often unfairly penalized or ignored those living in areas in which deciding magistrates had no personal interest.[10]

---

[7] In Ontario, town meetings were actually township meetings.

[8] Engin F. Isin, *Cities Without Citizens*, Montreal, Black Rose Books, 1992, pp. 112-114.

[9] *Ibid.*, p. 113.

[10] Fred Landon, *Western Ontario and the American Frontier*, Toronto, McClelland & Stewart Limited, 1967, p. 223.

Dissatisfaction with local government arrangements at least in part contributed to the 1837 rebellions in Upper and Lower Canada where local inhabitants clashed with British colonial governments. In response, the Earl of Durham was appointed to investigate the insurrection and the general state of government in all British North America provinces. Durham produced a comprehensive report containing important recommendations concerning local government. According to Durham, "...municipal institutions of local self-government ... are the foundations of Anglo-Saxon freedom and civilization."[11] Moreover, "[t]he latter want of municipal institutions giving the people any control over their local affairs, may indeed be considered as one of the main causes of the failure of representative government and of the bad administration of the country."[12] Durham's sweeping recommendations included reuniting Upper and Lower Canada into a single province with local matters to be overseen by separate municipal bodies.

In 1840, Lord Sydenham replaced Durham as Governor General. Sydenham largely agreed with Durham's assessment of the situation and the importance of reunifying Upper and Lower Canada and strengthening local self-government. Sydenham expressed his concerns in a letter to the British Colonial Secretary in which he writes:

> Since I have been in these Provinces I have become more and more satisfied that the capital cause of the misgovernment of them is to be found in the absence of Local Government, and the consequent exercise by the assembly of powers wholly inappropriate to its functions.[13]

While the British Government agreed to merge Upper and Lower Canada through clauses in the 1840 *Union Act,* it firmly rejected the idea of creating independent local governments in the colonies despite the strong recommendations of Durham and Sydenham. The importance of this omission cannot be overstated. Had the *Union Act* contained clauses providing for a system of local government, then such a separate and distinct provision for local government might well have been reproduced later in the *British North America (BNA) Act* of 1867. The *BNA Act* created only two levels of government for Canada – national and provincial – leaving matters of local government for the provinces to

---

[11] Gerald M. Craig (ed.), *Lord Durham's Report*, Toronto, McClelland & Stewart Limited, 1963, p. 60.

[12] *Ibid.*, p. 67.

[13] Landon, *Western Ontario*, p. 223.

decide. Had the *Union Act* of 1840 and the subsequent *BNA Act* contained distinct provisions for creating local government, Canada today would likely have three distinct orders of government – national, provincial, *and* local. Instead, as we shall see later, Canadian municipalities were and remain mere "creatures of the province" subject to the whims of provincial governments.

Undeterred by the actions of his superiors in England, Lord Sydenham pressed on with reforms in British North America. In 1841, Sydenham persuaded the legislature of the newly united colonies to establish elected district councils to take over the administrative authority formerly exercised by the Courts of Quarter Sessions in rural areas. While district council heads (wardens) were initially appointed by the Governor General, councils were eventually given the right to choose their own warden. Annual town meetings were held to elect various town officers as well as new district councillors. District councils were given responsibility for roads, municipal officers, taxing, justice, education, and welfare, and raising revenue by tolls or taxes on real or personal property. Despite this local discretion, the Governor General retained unlimited authority to disallow by-laws and dissolve councils.

Not only did the *District Councils Act* dramatically shift the approach to local administration in Canada, it preceded similar changes in England by almost 50 years.[14] While central authorities retained considerable power to offset local incompetence, district councillors proved capable and able to develop local economic activity through constructing and repairing roads and bridges and creating school districts. However, assessment problems and strict provincial control undermined council effectiveness. In terms of revenues available to district councils:

> These were paltry sums for the needs of large districts, and it is quite certain that the very light direct taxation on which Canadians long prided themselves was a rather important factor in the backward condition of the country for so many years.[15]

The next local government reformer of note in Upper Canada is Robert Baldwin, a Toronto lawyer first elected to the Assembly of Upper Canada in 1830. Baldwin twice formed a government with La Fontaine from Lower Canada, the second time from 1848 to 1851. He reformed

---

[14] Crawford, *Canadian Municipal Government*, p. 31.

[15] Adam Shortt and Arthur G. Doughty (gen. eds.), *Canada and its Provinces: A History of the Canadian People and Their Institutions*, Toronto, Glasgow, Brook and Company, 1914, Vol. XVIII, p. 437.

the judiciary of Upper Canada, created the University of Toronto, granted amnesty to the participants in the 1837 and 1838 rebellions, and, of particular importance for this text, created the legislative foundation on which Canada's modern local government structure rests.

In 1843, Baldwin significantly changed the structure of local government while serving as Attorney General in what was then Canada West (later Ontario) in the Province of Canada. However, his vision was not fully realized until the legislature and Governor General approved the *Municipal Corporations Act* of 1849 – often called the "Baldwin Act." The *Baldwin Act* combined all municipal legislation into one distinct Act and (as shown in Figure 2.1):

1) Designated counties, as the upper municipal government tier;
2) Established villages, towns, and cities as urban municipal units;
3) Excluded cities and most towns from county authority; and
4) Established townships as the primary rural municipal government unit.

Figure 2.1 Local Government Structure under the *Baldwin Act*

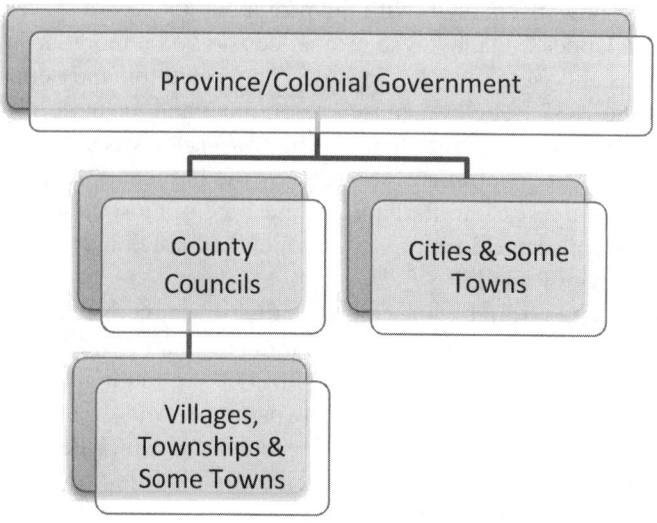

Quebec (Lower Canada)

Government by magistrates of the Quarter Session was also unpopular in Lower Canada, with local residents frequently demanding improved local administration. However, change did not come until 1832 when Quebec and Montreal were granted charters enabling citizens to elect mayors and aldermen – paralleling the introduction of the board of police and elected councils that same year in Brockville, Upper Canada. The Quebec incorporations were limited to a four year term, and were not renewed until after 1840 due to the political turmoil caused by the 1837 Rebellion.

Guided by Lord Sydenham, in 1840 a new series of laws enabled a system of local government in Lower Canada resembling the district councils later established in Upper Canada. These new laws divided Lower Canada into districts with local elected councils overseen by appointed wardens and outlined terms for electing clerks, assessors, tax collectors, surveyors, road inspectors, fence viewers, drain inspectors, and pound keepers. Large townships and parishes were constituted as corporate bodies and each permitted to elect two councillors to the district councils. Although the district councils were given the power of taxation, most power remained with the provincial Governor.

Unlike in Upper Canada, these ordinances proved unpopular in Lower Canada and were repealed in 1845. The execution and deportation of rebels of the 1837 Rebellion caused resentment and mistrust of Lord Sydenham and his motives for change. The *Union Act* was also unpopular and local government was seen by the French as another means of British oppression. Perhaps the measure of most concern to local residents concerned local taxation which had previously been unknown in Lower Canada.

A county system roughly based on the district councils was set up in 1847, but lasted only until the *Lower Canada Municipal and Road Act* of 1855. This Act established the foundation of Quebec municipal government by providing for parishes, townships, towns, and villages, while retaining the county as an upper tier municipal unit. The heads of the local councils sat on the county council and chose their own warden. Each level could appoint the officers it felt were necessary and could levy taxes. Cities continued to be created by special charters rather than being incorporated under the provisions of the general legislation. This system remained largely in effect until the beginning of the 20th century.

Nova Scotia

Municipal institutions in the Atlantic Provinces initially paralleled those of Ontario. In the early 1700s the area known as Acadia was ceded by France to Britain, renamed Nova Scotia and locally governed by Courts of Quarter Sessions. Waves of Loyalists migrated to the area during and after the American Revolution – although more from New York, New Jersey, Pennsylvania, and the South than New England. These Loyalists brought different traditions of local government, mostly based on the classed society of the American South in which the Courts of Quarter Sessions also discharged local government functions and the Governor appointed local officials. Anti-American feelings undermined New England Loyalists' attempts at promoting local self-rule in Atlantic Canada, at least partially explaining why local residents continued to tolerate Courts of Quarter Sessions.

Early local government in Nova Scotia was provided by Courts of Quarter Sessions established by the British authorities around 1750. A wave of immigration at the beginning of the 1760s brought settlers accustomed to the town meeting form of local government. However, colonial authorities were unwilling to consider such a democratic approach, especially after the American War of Independence. In addition, many Loyalists living in Nova Scotia worked to block local government reforms due to fears of revolution and concerns about increased taxation and the loss of patronage. Further, the compact nature of the province and availability of cheap water transportation rendered road construction, one of the major municipal functions, less important. The first municipal incorporation did not occur until 1841 when Halifax became a charter city.

Provincial authorities showed more willingness to allow local government after responsible government was introduced to the province of Canada in 1848. Legislation permitting county incorporation was enacted in 1855, followed by similar laws concerning townships in 1856. Ironically, many Nova Scotians did not exercise this newly granted right to local self-government. According to Higgins, early enthusiasm waned when it was discovered incorporation brought higher levels of taxation.[16] In response to this reluctance, the provincial government enacted the 1879 *County Incorporation Act* to shift local services provision costs to local residents:

---

[16] Donald J. H. Higgins, *Local and Urban Politics in Canada*, Toronto, Gage, 1986, pp. 39-40.

That Act was conceived in secrecy at the provincial level and it was the direct offspring of the financial difficulties of the provincial government. The then Attorney General, J.S.D. Thompson, who later became Prime Minister of Canada, frankly stated that the main object of the Act was "to compel Counties to tax themselves directly to keep up their roads and bridges."[17]

Under the *County Incorporation Act*, rural areas of the province were incorporated as counties or districts, single tier municipalities governed by a warden and an elected council. The *Towns Incorporation Act* of 1888 provided for urban areas, stipulating the geographic and population requirements to enable a town to apply for a charter of incorporation. Prior to the passage of this law, eight towns had been incorporated through individual charters.

Prince Edward Island

In 1769, Prince Edward Island separated from Nova Scotia. Two years prior, the island had been divided into counties, parishes, and townships for judicial and electoral purposes. However, these divisions were never used as municipal units. Indeed, the immediate need for municipal government or even decentralization was not apparent given the small geographic size and tiny population of Prince Edward Island.

The first municipality appeared in 1855 when Charlottetown was incorporated as a city. In 1870, new legislation enabled resident householders of a town or village to petition provincial authorities for the ability to elect three or more wardens empowered to appoint local officers and pass by-laws with regard to finance and police matters. Summerside was incorporated as a town in 1875, but only six more towns had been incorporated by the time the procedure fell into disuse in 1919.

New Brunswick

Fifteen years after Prince Edward Island separated from Nova Scotia, New Brunswick followed suit, with the break precipitated by an influx of United Empire Loyalists. The following year, 1785, Saint John was incorporated as a city, preceding by almost 50 years the creation of cities in the rest of Canada. Elsewhere in the colony, however, local

---

[17] A. William Cox, Q.C., in a 1989 paper, "Development of Municipal-Provincial Relations," quoted in *Task Force on Local Government*, Report to the Government of Nova Scotia, April 1992, Briefing Book, p. 13.

government was carried on by the Courts of Quarter Sessions and a grand jury. The local citizenry, according to Higgins, seems to have been largely indifferent to the idea of local self-government.[18] This attitude is at least partly due to the smaller number of Loyalists coming from New England. Whalen, however, rejects this viewpoint, contending that only about 7% of the Loyalists came from the Southern Colonies with their system of Quarter Sessions and that, in any event, even the Loyalists from New England made little demand for more democracy at the local level.[19] Nor did the province's French population, with its tradition of centralism, make such demands.

Much of the impetus for the incorporation of municipalities came from the central authorities concerned about "reducing the time consumed on endless debates and squabbles over parish and county issues in the legislature" and anxious to shift a growing expenditure burden.[20] An 1843 *New Brunswick Courier* editorial captures the extent to which local people opposed new municipal government legislation claiming new laws "…would have cut loose that many-headed monster, Direct Taxation and its Myrmidon, the Tax-Gatherer, into the happy home of every poor man throughout the land."[21] Although an act was eventually passed for the incorporation of counties in 1851, only six counties were established over the next three decades due to local reluctance.

The basic municipal system of New Brunswick was established with the passing of the 1877 *Counties Act* and the *Town Incorporation Act* of 1896. The *Municipalities Act* of 1877 mandated county incorporation, thus ensuring all residents were subject to by-laws passed by local councils. During this period a number of urban communities sought corporate status. Fredericton had received its charter in 1848, over 60 years after the first urban incorporation in Saint John. By 1896, nine towns had been established by separate charter and the province enacted laws allowing towns to elect mayors and aldermen. In 1920 the provincial government enacted laws allowing villages to incorporate.

---

[18] Higgins, *Local and Urban Politics in Canada*, p. 40.

[19] H. J. Whalen, *The Development of Local Government in New Brunswick*, Fredericton, 1963, Chapter 2.

[20] *Ibid.*, p. 20.

[21] Quoted in Whelan, *Local Government in New Brunswick*, pp. 20-21.

Newfoundland

The development of municipal institutions in Newfoundland was a slow and arduous process.[22] The early settlements were numerous, but geographically isolated from each other. They were also sparsely populated and, thus, financially unable to support any form of local government. Moreover, since Newfoundlanders only gained the right to own property in 1824, they jealously guarded against attempts to levy taxes.

Early settlers had little prior experience with local government. In addition, island residents were not influenced by the development of municipal government elsewhere in Canada due to Newfoundland's geographic isolation. Local residents in much of the province saw little need for municipal government since transportation needs were partly served by water and the central government provided local services such as roads.

After some unsuccessful attempts, the town of St. John's was created in 1888. As with other Atlantic provinces, pressure for incorporation came from colonial authorities attempting to offload the governmental costs to local residents. As Higgins explains, municipal status for St. John's was imposed partly to facilitate costly improvements to the sewerage and street systems and partly to be a mechanism whereby the privately owned and heavily in debt St. John's Water Company would become the financial responsibility of the City – a Water Company in which the Premier of Newfoundland and other prominent government supporters and business people were shareholders![23]

No other municipalities were formed in Newfoundland for 50 years. Acts authorizing incorporation were passed in 1933 and 1937, but without any local response. Desperate to form municipalities, the provincial government attempted to persuade local residents to incorporate by offering subsidies and taxation flexibility as a reward. By 1948, 20 municipalities had been incorporated by special charter, with only five imposing property tax on local citizens.[24]

---

[22] Higgins, *Local and Urban Politics in Canada*, pp. 33-34.

[23] *Ibid.*, pp. 34-35.

[24] Crawford, *Canadian Municipal Government*, p. 41.

Manitoba

The provinces of Manitoba, Saskatchewan, and Alberta were part of the original Hudson's Bay Company land grant and later of the Northwest Territories. The Company had complete judicial, legislative, and administrative authority over people living in lands under its control. In 1869, the newly created Dominion of Canada acquired the Company's rights in Rupert's Land and the Northwest Territories. However, substantial settlement did not occur in the new Prairie Provinces until the late 19th century. As in other parts of Canada, demands for local service and infrastructural investment increased pressure on these provinces to enact a local government system. Many of the related laws and arrangements enacted by prairie governments were modelled after those used in Ontario, but customized to meet local needs and conditions.

Manitoba became a province in 1870. The first provincial legislature provided for a system of local government by a grand jury and Courts of Sessions that were to administer a *County Assessment Act* and a *Parish Assessment Act*. Judges of the Sessions also chose local officers such as treasurers, assessors, highway surveyors, pound keepers, and constables from lists presented by the grand jury.

The first municipality was established in 1873, when Winnipeg was incorporated as a city. Incorporation, and the accompanying real property tax, was heavily resisted by the Hudson's Bay Company and four other large property owners, who together owned over half of the assessable property in Winnipeg.[25] In that same year, new legislation allowed local residents to establish municipalities provided a minimum number of local freeholders from within a district signed a petition requesting incorporation. However few such petitioning efforts were undertaken and only six areas were ever incorporated under this petitioning scheme.

The Manitoba government dropped the incorporation-through-petition scheme in 1883. Instead, the province introduced a municipal system for the whole province modelled on the two tier county system of Ontario. The province established 26 counties with councils composed of the heads of both rural and urban local (lower tier) municipal councils. The county council elected a warden from among its own members.

However, the county system proved ineffective. Local residents resented the two tier system and county councils proved unable to cope with the large and under-populated areas under their authority. The province replaced the county system after only three years, instead

---

[25] Higgins, *Local and Urban Politics in Canada*, pp. 50-51.

dividing unincorporated areas into smaller rural municipalities. In 1902, cities, towns, villages, and rural municipalities were recognized as the basic units of local government in Manitoba. Although Winnipeg is always treated differently than other Manitoba municipalities, this general local government system continues to endure.

Saskatchewan

Like Manitoba, Saskatchewan had been part of the lands granted to the Hudson's Bay Company. It was taken over by the Canadian government in 1870 and administered as a colony until gaining provincial status in 1905. The territorial council first provided for municipalities in 1883 by enacting a municipal ordinance patterned on Manitoba laws which, in turn, had been modelled on the Ontario *Municipal Act* of 1849. The ordinance provided for the creation of rural municipalities or towns depending on location, population size, and local demand.

While Regina received town status in 1883 and four rural municipalities were organized a year later, little incorporation occurred after 1884. By 1897, only one more town had been created and two rural municipalities had even dropped their municipal status. Despite these efforts, the vast land area and small, scattered population could not generate a sufficient financial base to support municipal government.

In an effort to overcome the problem of too much land and too few people, the provincial government passed an ordinance allowing "statute labour and fire districts" to be created in unorganized areas to oversee road provision and fire protection services. In 1897, the province expanded this program by enacting now elected "local improvement districts." Around the same time the province authorized the incorporation of cities, towns, and rural municipalities.

These changes were in part made to cope with the federal government's policy of encouraging Europeans and Eastern Canadians to settle in the West. These new residents brought with them their own ideas concerning municipal government, including a willingness to embrace incorporation. By the time Saskatchewan became a province in 1905, the new province could boast 4 cities, 43 towns, 97 villages, 2 rural municipalities, and 359 local improvement districts.[26]

---

[26] Horace L. Brittain, *Local Government in Canada*, Toronto, Ryerson Press, 1951, p. 179.

Alberta

The development of local governments in Alberta closely followed those in Saskatchewan. Like its eastern neighbour, Alberta was also part of the federally administered Northwest Territories from 1870 until 1905. The territorial council allowed municipal incorporation in 1883, with the town of Calgary becoming the first official local government in 1884. Further incorporation efforts were initially thwarted by large landowners who opposed taxes on their property, including the Canadian Pacific Railway.[27] Only two more urban municipalities were created over the next decade: Lethbridge in 1891 and Edmonton in 1892. However, residents living in the sparse and scattered rural areas did not petition for their own rural municipalities and, as in Saskatchewan, "statute labour and fire districts" and "local improvement districts" became the main local government arrangements used in Alberta.

Toward the end of the 19th century, a large influx of settlers began to stimulate the creation of local governments. The provincial population grew from 18 000 in 1881 to 170 000 in 1905. Local residents had already organized themselves into 2 cities, 15 towns, and 30 villages by the time Alberta became a province in 1905. By 1912, a new redesigned municipal system included cities, towns, and villages. Although large local improvement districts could be designated as rural municipalities upon reaching a specified population, few such changes occurred due to fears about tax increases.

British Columbia

Early European settlements in what is now British Columbia were scattered and isolated due to the mountainous terrain and the physical separation of Vancouver Island and the mainland. Like Alberta, Saskatchewan, and Manitoba, the area was also initially under the jurisdiction of the Hudson's Bay Company: Vancouver Island until 1849 and the mainland until 1858. In 1860, New Westminster, the capital of the mainland colony, became a municipality. Two years later, Victoria, the capital of the Vancouver Island colony, was incorporated as a town.

After gaining provincial status in 1871, British Columbia enacted the *Consolidated Municipal Act* providing for local petitions for municipal incorporation. However, only five municipalities were approved by 1874. Vancouver, originally known as Granville, was a small logging

---

[27] *Ibid.*, p. 54.

community with only about 300 residents at the time of its incorporation in 1886. A population boom began soon after the Canadian Pacific Railway chose Vancouver as the western terminus of the transcontinental railway in 1884.[28]

The *Municipal Clauses Act* of 1892 provided for a municipal government system similar to that in Ontario, but without a county level. Municipalities were either cities with mayors and councils or rural districts with reeves and councils, with 52 municipalities brought into being by the turn of the 20th century. The *Village Municipalities Act* of 1920 allowed small urban areas to incorporate, albeit with limited powers.

Northern Territories

The area of the Yukon and Northwest Territories was controlled by the Hudson's Bay Company until acquired by the federal government in 1870.[29] Its territory was reduced immediately when Manitoba was established as a separate province, further reduced in 1905 when Saskatchewan and Alberta became provinces, and reduced again in 1912 when the boundaries of Ontario, Quebec, and Manitoba were extended north to their present positions. The discovery of gold in the Klondike in 1896 sparked a rapid population increase, prompting the federal government to establish the Yukon as a separate territory in 1898. A third territory, Nunavut, was established in the eastern Arctic in April, 1999.

The context of municipal government in the far north greatly differs from conditions found in southern Canada. First, the three territories cover vast areas but contain very little population – much of it concentrated in the three capital cities. Second, the distances between municipalities are long and road connections limited. Third, municipal governments have very limited access to property tax as much of the land belongs to the federal and territorial governments. Finally, Aboriginal land claims have affected, and continue to affect, governmental development.[30]

---

[28] Higgins, *Local and Urban Politics in Canada*, pp. 57-58.

[29] The description in this section is partly based on *ibid.*, pp. 59-60.

[30] Katherine A. H. Graham, "Municipal Reform in the Northern Territories: Now for Something Different," in Joseph Garcea and Edward C. LeSage Jr. (eds.), *Municipal Reform in Canada*, Toronto, Oxford University Press, 2005, pp. 270-271.

Dawson City was incorporated as the first territorial municipality in 1901, but its charter was revoked and local service provision reverted to the territorial administration in 1904. Also in 1901, a provision was made for the establishment of unincorporated towns upon petition, but these units were not full municipal governments since residents could only elect one official and only assume a very limited range of services. One unincorporated town was created, but later disbanded when its population declined. The often temporary nature of northern settlements added to the problems caused by the very small, scattered population. Therefore, while both the Northwest Territories and the Yukon had municipal ordinances authorizing municipal governments, very few units were created. By 1964, only three municipalities had been incorporated: the towns of Yellowknife and Hay Bay and the village of Fort Smith.

Virtually all laws and government services within the Northern Territories stemmed from Ottawa. However, in 1967 the Territorial Council relocated from Ottawa to Yellowknife and new municipal structures were introduced to allow for more local decision making and to encourage greater public participation in government. Territorial governments also began to devolve authority to local governments and attempted to strengthen the political role of the municipalities. According to one study, "[In] the NWT the importance of the local level of government is of particular magnitude because of the cultural diversity and the vast distances between communities."[31]

While only a very small portion of the vast area of the Northern Territories is organized municipally, these organized portions of the territory contain three-quarters of the population with structures basically modelled upon those found in southern Canada. The territories also contain some 40 other municipal governments, mostly hamlets with limited power. There are also "charter communities" with customized local government arrangements allowing for procedural and administrative flexibility. This flexibility is especially important in communities accustomed to more traditional governmental practices, with the charter community approach blending Inuit and First Nations' traditions with the European-style approach to local governance.

---

[31] *Constitutional Development in the Northwest Territories, Report of the Special Representative* (Drury Report), Ottawa, 1980.

Early 20th Century Growing Pains

By the beginning of the 20th century, most provinces had established, or were in the process of establishing, local government. At the same time, Canada continued to experience seismic economic and population shifts. The country was industrializing, moving from farming, fishing, mining, and forestry to manufacturing and service provision with many of these jobs filled by the large number of immigrants pouring into Canadian cities. Between 1901 and 1911, Canada led the Western world in population growth, with the foreign born population increasing by over two million people during this period. Shown graphically in Figure 2.2, the effects of this growth cannot be understated. For example, by the end of the boom the population of Edmonton and Calgary was 40 times greater than at the beginning of the boom period – transforming what were small villages into cluttered cities.

Figure 2.2 Percentage of the Total Canadian Population Living in Urban Areas

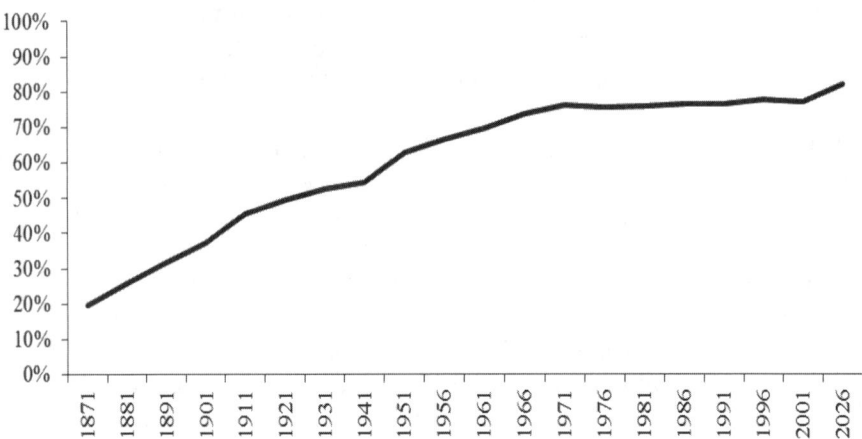

Source: Statistics Canada and World Bank data adapted by the authors.

This massive population increase and its urban nature brought a number of accompanying problems. These are related to housing, service provision, transportation and utilities, community cohesion, and corruption. Each is explained below in more detail.

Housing

Demand for new housing and accompanying property speculation drove up land values across Canada. One report shows a 900% increase in Victoria, British Columbia, properties over a mere six month period.[32] The increase in land values precipitated a change in downtown land use from a mix of small businesses and residential housing to office buildings. Changes in land use and higher real estate prices also pushed the working class out to the suburbs. Despite a building boom accompanied by large scale land assembly and suburban development, all major Canadian cities soon faced a serious housing shortage and the appearance of ghettos and slums.

Figure 2.3 Canadian Slum Housing, 1912

Source: City of Toronto Archives, Fonds 1244, Item 679. Reprinted with permission.

Service Provision

Another problem facing rapidly growing Canadian cities was just how to provide services to thousands of new residents. Immigrant workers were often housed in hastily built, low quality buildings, without sanitary conveniences. Families frequently shared accommodation and overcrowding

---

[32] J. B. Thornhill, *British Columbia in the Making*, London, UK, Constable and Company, 1913, pp. 126-127, quoted in Weaver, *Shaping the Canadian City*, p. 13.

became a strain on already overworked municipal water and sewer systems. A 1910 report shows many municipalities dumping untreated sewage into inland water systems then drawing drinking water from the same water systems into which they pumped waste. These factors produced serious health hazards that became only too apparent in the early 1900s with an alarming increase in the number of epidemics. During this period, one of every three deaths was caused by tuberculosis, and typhoid and flu epidemics caused more casualties than World War One.[33]

Transportation and Utilities

Overcrowded downtown districts plus an increased number of people commuting from the suburbs created the need for new modes of transportation or, at the very least, the construction of more roads and sidewalks. By 1913, most cities had electric streetcar systems (often privately owned monopolies) as well as electric power plants (often owned by the municipality). New and expanded municipal services meant higher municipal taxes. A 1907 report by Wickett states, "[t]he annual expenditure of Winnipeg clearly exceeds that of Manitoba; Montreal's that of the province of Quebec; and until the present year Toronto's that of the province of Ontario."[34]

Community Cohesion

Growing urban areas also faced community cohesion challenges. For example, Winnipeg, which had already shown an impressive increase in population from 1800 to 40 000 between 1874 and 1899, surged to 150 000 by 1913. The bulk of this increase came from immigration, and by 1911 no other Canadian city had as high a proportion of European born residents. The problems of assimilation that resulted led to what Allan Artibise calls a "Divided City."[35]

---

[33] The figures on pollution and health are from Alan H. Armstrong, "Thomas Adams and the Commission on Conservation," in L. A. Gertler (ed.), *Planning the Canadian Environment*, Montreal, Harvest House, 1968, pp. 20-22.

[34] Quoted in "Tomorrow's Metropolis: The Urban Reform Movement in Canada, 1880-1920," in Gilbert A. Stelter and Alan F. Artibise (eds.), *The Canadian City: Essays in Urban History*, Toronto, McClelland & Stewart, 1977, p. 376.

[35] *Ibid.*

Divisions also occurred along class lines. For example, working people organized labour unions to counterbalance the strength of business interests. With the end of the war, returning soldiers swelled the labour force, jobs were scarce, and many workers were dissatisfied with their wages and their hours. On May 13, 1919, the growing labour unrest exploded in a general strike in Winnipeg, paralyzing Canada's third largest city. Less intense sympathy strikes broke out in a dozen other cities, including Toronto, Vancouver, Edmonton, and Calgary. Gradually, civilian authorities reasserted their authority ending the strike by arresting its leaders more than a month after it began. As explained later, this polarization of business and labour contributes to ongoing clashes between these two interests for control of municipal councils in Canada's major cities.

Where formal political power, such as the right to vote and stand as candidates in local elections, had been long limited to propertied, middle-aged males, the local franchise was eventually expanded to those without property, women, and younger people during the first decades of the 20th century. Keating describes the concern of the business community and the professional middle class about the demands of an increasingly assertive working class, armed with the franchise.[36] The arrival of working class voters produced local political parties and in some provinces a civic socialist movement. The business community thought these new conditions might be curtailed by limiting the role of the poor and working class in local politics by stressing how political parties had no place in local politics which, they thought, should be non-partisan. As Keating points out, "attacks on politics or partisanship often mask objections to the use of political power to counteract inequalities in the social or economic spheres. Non-partisanship thus tends to be a conservative rallying cry."[37]

Corruption

Massive urbanization forced local councils to modernize and expand service provision, increase administrative capacity, and raise property taxes. Growing municipal coffers and increased local authority proved too tempting for many officials, leading to often deep and widespread corruption within city hall. Calls for structural reform first came from

---

[36] Michael Keating, *Comparative Urban Politics*, Aldershot, Edward Elgar, 1991, pp. 43-46.

[37] *Ibid.*, p. 43.

newspapers covering the corruption of the Tammany Society in New York City (and other American political machines) and subsequent American efforts at municipal reform. In fact, much as American immigrants had influenced the original development of Canadian municipal government, Americans also exerted a strong influence on Canadian reforms at the turn of the 20th century.

While municipal corruption had reached crisis proportions in the United States, the situation in Canada was somewhat less severe. However, Canadian municipal politicians were not immune to the opportunities presented by the sudden urban growth and get-rich-quick mentality. In Toronto, corporations bidding on contracts and franchises complained aldermen were "shaking them down" and precipitated an inquiry in which only a few were found guilty but the entire council was tarnished by association. Around the same time, the Toronto zoo keeper was found stocking his own kitchen with food meant for the animals. In Montreal, the Police Commission was discovered to be running a protection racket. In Regina, city councillors were being given unusually low property taxes and utility bills.[38] These revelations and others left the public disillusioned and prompted calls for action.

The Reform Movements

A new array of social groups formed in response to these emerging urban problems. The Women's Christian Temperance Union, YMCA, YWCA, Salvation Army, and White Cross Army focused on stamping out all evils associated with the wicked city, including crime, vice, and poverty. The Civic Art Guild of Toronto, City Improvement League of Montreal, Union of Canadian Municipalities, Good Roads Association, and the Civic Improvement League of Canada were founded to address servicing and financial pressures facing municipal governments. Urban scholars often classify these various groups as three different movements: the city beautiful movement; the city healthy movement; and the city efficient movement. While the city efficient movement began slightly later than city beautiful and city healthy, all three are important as they helped set the reform agenda.

---

[38] Examples from John C. Weaver, *Shaping the Canadian City: Essays in Urban Politics and Policy, 1890-1920*, Toronto, Institute of Public Administration of Canada, 1977, pp. 56-59.

City Beautiful Movement

The city beautiful movement is linked to a local pride of place as well as increased population growth and material success. This movement was largely led by city boosters who trumpeted the extent to which their city or town was better than many or all other cities or towns. Where some boosters sought to improve the city for its own sake, local councillors and businessmen often saw boosterism as simply another opportunity for generating new business activity.[39] Boosterism was difficult to oppose as those who disagreed were portrayed as lacking community spirit or good business sense. According to Artibise, in the eyes of city beautiful proponents "[g]ood citizenship and boosterism were synonymous."[40]

The city beautiful movement was embraced by many Canadian architects, engineers, and surveyors unhappy with the squalor and the ugly environment in rapidly developing Canadian communities. The objective of these civic leaders was to create a civic grandeur by, for example, developing extravagant city centres with monumental public buildings grouped around public squares connected by broad, tree-lined avenues. These expensive and grand designs provoked criticism, with opponents claiming the city beautiful movement encouraged indulgence and promoted "mere adornment" rather than addressing real housing and sanitation problems.[41]

In the forefront of the municipal reform movement were middle class merchants and businessmen. Many of these people had little sympathy for the democratic aspects of local government. They were mainly concerned with expanding local services in order to attract more growth (often on land they owned) which in turn would expand the local tax base to help pay for new services. To these boosters, mostly from the business community, local government was just a tool to serve personal and community prosperity, "...merely a device to be used for the benefit of the people who managed to gain political power or influence."[42]

---

[39] Alan J. Artibise, "In Pursuit of Growth: Municipal Boosterism and Urban Development in the Canadian Prairie West, 1871-1913," in Gilbert Stelter and Alan Artibise (eds.), *Shaping the Urban Landscape: Aspects of the Canadian City-Building Process*, Ottawa, Carleton University Press, 1982, p. 124.

[40] *Ibid.*, p. 125.

[41] Gerald Hodge and David L. A. Gordon, *Planning Canadian Communities*, 5th Edition, Toronto, Nelson, 2008, p. 75.

[42] Stelter and Artibise, *Shaping the Urban Landscape*, p. 128.

City Healthy Movement

The city healthy movement arose in response to deteriorating health conditions in urban areas. For example, Fort William tripled its population between 1896 and 1905 as the result of railroad expansion. In the winter of 1905-1906 a sewer that directly emptied into the city's water supply caused some 800 cases of typhoid.[43] Similar situations in other provinces prompted public health advocates to press for better public water supplies, proper sewer systems, and slum eradication.[44]

City healthy supporters became convinced of a connection between poor housing conditions and poor public health. Toronto's Medical Officer of Health described slums as "cancerous sores on the body politic, sources of bacteria spreading disease, crime, and discontent throughout the city."[45] Worried about their health and aware disease did not respect social standing, wealthy citizens pressed for measures to expand the powers of health and building inspectors and legislated housing standards. J. J. Kelso, an Ontario lobbyist for children's aid and urban renewal advocate, proposed "[r]ear houses and those built in the notorious alleys and lanes of the city should be pulled down. There should be a by-law that every dwelling must front on a forty or sixty foot street and that only one dwelling should be created to each 20 by 100 foot lot.[46] Despite often noble intentions, razing condemned houses often only served to worsen already severe housing shortages.

The early city healthy movement significantly affected municipal government development. Pressure for local government action resulted in the creation of municipal public works departments as well as parks, housing, and social services.[47] However, as 20th century medical advances shifted health policy priorities from prevention to treatment, local government spending priorities also shifted, from spending on preventive programming to massive expenditures on hospitals and

---

[43] Weaver, *Shaping the Canadian City*, p. 28.

[44] Hodge and Gordon, *Planning Canadian Communities*, p. 89.

[45] Paul Rutherford, "Tomorrow's Metropolis," in Paul Rutherford (ed.), *Saving the Canadian City: The First Phase, 1880-1920*. Toronto, University of Toronto Press, 1974, p. 375.

[46] *Labour Gazette*, July 1910, p. 128, quoted in Weaver, *Shaping the Canadian City*, p. 33.

[47] Trevor Hancock, "From Public Health to the Healthy City," in Edmund P. Fowler and David Siegel (eds.), *Urban Policy Issues: Canadian Perspectives*, 2nd Edition, Toronto, Oxford University Press, 2002, p. 257.

doctors. Only recently has the city health movement made a comeback, with local governments rediscovering the link between local preventative service provision and healthy local populations.

City Efficient Movement

City efficient proponents asserted that the business of running and planning urban areas should be seen less as a process where local people come together to discuss and make community decisions and more as a rational or even scientific exercise during which experts provide technical solutions to local challenges. According to one city efficient promoter, "if all the facts can be collected ... then a solution of any town planning problem becomes comparatively simple."[48] This perspective is consistent with, and reinforced by, the then newly emerging idea of "scientific management" where rational inquiry is used to find the "one best way" to run any organization. It also virtually eliminates any motivation to consult citizens or to engage in widespread political debate.

In addition to being local boosters, many local businessmen also supported the city efficient movement. They rejected the claim that population expansion could on its own cause urban problems, viewing growth as merely allowing nature to follow its own course. Instead, the business community blamed inefficient municipal governments and corrupt local politicians for local woes. They also claimed taking the politics out of municipal government would lead to more efficient and businesslike municipal administration. In one Hamilton election, the reform mayoral candidate ran on the slogan that "civic business is not politics."[49] Many newspapers supported this view as shown in this editorial comparing municipalities and joint stock companies:

> If we could only manage our business as private corporations manage theirs we certainly would not have such a queer lot of directors – aldermen as we call them – or make presidents – mayors as we call them – out of men who have never proven themselves as good businessmen.[50]

However, much of the city efficient reform fervour was also due to a certain amount of self-interest, with business owners using the idea of

---

[48] Gilbert Stelter and Alan Artibise, "Urban History Comes of Age: A Review of Current Research," *City Magazine*, Vol. 3, No. 1, September-October 1977, p. 31.

[49] Weaver, *Shaping the Canadian City*, p. 42.

[50] *Saturday Night*, 1899, quoted in Weaver, *Shaping the Canadian City*, p. 41.

city efficient to silence the voice of those outside the business community and "...scupper the rules of the game."[51] For example, many businessmen stood to gain financially through municipal actions and wanted as little interference as possible in these dealings. Winnipeg's Mayor Sharpe was a wealthy contractor who specialized in sidewalks. In Regina a reform candidate known as "the Merchant Prince" claimed he paid $3 out of every $100 of local taxes. Montreal business leaders, including the president of the Street Railway Company, privately financed a plebiscite on structural reforms. Zoning by-laws were used in many cities to remove substandard housing from upper and middle income neighbourhoods as wealthy residents believed slums "spoil the appearance of a neighbourhood" and lower property values.[52]

The Reforms

Turn of the 20th century growing pains and pressure for change by the various civic movements eventually resulted in significant local government reform. As discussed below, reforms included the rise of the planning profession, changes to the process by which local officials were elected, and the emergence of chief administrative officers, civic boards of control, and commissions. As we shall see in subsequent chapters, these reforms have had a lasting impact on local government in Canada.

Professional Planners and Planning

The urban problems and pressure for change influenced the rise of planning as a profession in Canada. For example, in 1909 the Canadian government formed the Commission for the Conservation of Natural Resources (CCNR) to monitor natural resource use in Canada. Despite what initially seemed a rural focus, the CCNR soon began to commit considerable time to problems in urbanizing areas.[53] As these conditions worsened, the CCNR increased its attention to these matters, appointing Thomas Adams as Advisor on Town Planning in 1914.

---

[51] *Ibid.*, p. 64.

[52] Weaver, *Shaping the Canadian City*, p. 407.

[53] Hodge and Gordon, *Planning Canadian Communities*, p. 86.

Born in Scotland and educated in law, Adams merged British ideas with North American practices to create a uniquely Canadian approach to urban planning. While in Britain, Adams had worked to implement the *British Town Planning and Housing Act* to improve urban conditions in the United Kingdom. The Act centred around the idea of the "Garden City" which sought to disperse urban populations and industry of a large city into a larger number of "new towns" or "satellite towns" so as to create more amenable living conditions. When he arrived in Canada, Adams had a reputation as "an eloquent author and speaker on the Garden City Movement, on agricultural land use and on town planning and housing as aspects of local government."[54]

While with the CCNR, Adams proceeded to draft local plans and model provincial town planning acts based on those developed in Britain. His work rapidly spread across Canada. By 1916, all provinces but British Columbia and Prince Edward Island had enacted planning statutes based on Adams' work. Adams' approach to planning also featured honorary planning boards, influenced by American prototypes. He also assisted many Canadian municipalities in the preliminary stages of local planning and promoted the creation of provincial departments of municipal affairs in Ontario and Quebec. This early foundation laid by Adams served as a base for modern planning departments in virtually every Canadian municipality.

Changes to the Electoral Process

Many early Canadian towns and cities followed the British council committee tradition to run their cities. Under this system, city councillors (sometimes called aldermen) were elected using a system where the municipality was divided into districts (also known as wards) with one councillor being elected to represent residents within this district using a first-past-the-post election formula. Once elected, district representatives selected one councillor to serve as mayor from among themselves. In addition to selecting a mayor, local councillors were also often charged with reallocating tax dollars or money for public works within the district from which they were elected. This system allowed district councillors a great deal of power in specific areas and, in some cases, resulted in corruption.

Reformers insisted corruption could be reduced by treating the municipality as one giant multimember "at large" district, where all

---

[54] Armstrong, *Thomas Adams and the Commission on Conservation*, p. 28.

council candidates would campaign across the whole city and local districts would be eliminated. One of the more convincing arguments for abolishing districts was that they fostered a parochial view of municipal issues rather than encouraging elected officials to take a more city wide view. It was thought that the at large system would eliminate perceived episodes of log-rolling – situations where district councillors say to one another "I'll give you what you want in your ward if you'll give me what I want in mine." In 1912, a *Financial Post* editorial stated that the ward system was one of the dominant evils of municipal life and that "all aldermen should hold their seats by the vote of all the electors and should represent all the city at all times."[55]

Montreal abolished the council committee system in 1857, instead installing a new system where citizens directly elected a mayor for their city – much like how Americans elect a president to oversee the affairs of the entire United States. Toronto switched to direct, at large mayoral elections in 1873, reducing the number of district councillors in 1891. In 1894, both Saint John and Fredericton abolished wards completely. In Toronto and Montreal an unsuccessful attempt was made to extend the right to vote to companies.

Boards of Control

Boards of control were also introduced to reduce the power of district councillors. Drawn from the U.S. experience, boards of control often took over from council important executive functions such as preparing budgets, appointing and dismissing department heads, and awarding contracts. The first Canadian board of control was instituted in Toronto in 1896 in response to a water and sewer crisis. Board members were initially chosen by the councillors from among themselves, but subsequently directly elected by citizens at large. Board decisions could only be overturned by a two-thirds vote of council, an often difficult feat since the board of control members were also voting members of council.

Boards of control proved popular in Ontario where this governing model became mandatory for municipalities of 100 000 population and over. It also spread to other provinces and was adopted by Winnipeg in 1906, Calgary in 1908, and Montreal in 1910. Decisions made by the Montreal board of control were subject to the approval of a majority of councillors. However, Western Canadian governments instead adopted systems in which appointed commissioners specializing in specific fields

---

[55] *Financial Post*, February 10, 1912, quoted in Weaver, *Shaping the Canadian City*, p. 67.

and without any formal decision making power would act as administrators and provide advice to councillors. Edmonton was the first city to implement this system in 1904, with Regina, Saskatoon, and Prince Albert all implementing similar measures by 1912.

City Managers and Executive Committees

Some Canadian municipalities adopted another American innovation known as the city manager. Especially popular in Quebec after 1920, city managers were appointed to coordinate and supervise all city departments and municipal affairs. The rationale behind the system assumed policy making should be the exclusive concern of a small elected council, and civic administration (policy implementation) the exclusive concern of the city manager. In other words, reformers thought it possible to divorce politics from policy, favouring this system as it appeared to make local government management more businesslike. In 1919, Guelph appointed a city manager and arranged the city administration in a way similar to that found in a joint stock company, with the aldermen as directors and the mayor as president. According to Guelph observers, "[t]he city manager through his different departments, plans the work, submits same to council for their approval. When approved, it is up to the city manager to carry it out in a business-like manner, without interference from the aldermen (councillors)."[56]

In some cities it was even suggested that elected councils be entirely abolished, with local affairs exclusively managed by appointed executives. For example, reformers in London, Ontario, proposed that council be replaced by an executive composed of representatives from a variety of special interest groups such as the Rotary club, various ratepayers associations, and the Board of Trade. Montreal reformers proposed to retain the mayor and council, but add a four member executive committee, with two members selected by council, one selected by the Board of Trade, and one by the Chambre de Commerce. While most of these proposals were not adopted, Montreal did have a council consisting of a mayor and 99 councillors in the 1940s, of whom 66 were elected and 33 were appointed by public associations.[57]

---

[56] Frank H. Underhill, "Commission Government in Cities (1911)," in Rutherford (ed.), *Saving the Canadian City*, p. 68.

[57] Paul Hickey, *Decision Making Processes in Ontario's Local Governments*, Toronto, Ministry of Treasury, Economics and Intergovernmental Affairs, 1973, p. 203.

Boards and Commissions

In a further effort to reduce council's control, reformers advocated various types of boards and commissions to oversee specific activities, thus removing them from the political arena. These boards were not a new phenomenon. Ontario used police boards in the 1840s. However, the practice greatly expanded between 1890 and 1920 as municipalities faced decisions in areas relating to sewers, pumping stations, streetcars, power systems, street and sidewalk paving, building codes, assessments, department budgets, tenders, debentures, and sinking funds.

Goldwin Smith, a member of a Toronto municipal reform group, sums up the general attitude in 1890 by stating that while city council is the proper setting for debates on principles, new challenges show that the "... city is simply a densely peopled district in need of a specially skilled administration."[58] Others argued special purpose bodies such as commissions would likely attract "the services of bright, able men who have not the time to serve in the council," as business people were more likely to serve in an appointed position than they were to engage in an election contest and, if successful, endure the tedious task of attending to constituents' requests.[59] These arguments succeeded. Toronto created parks, fire, hydro, and transportation commissions. Montreal created a parks commission while a water works commission was instituted in Vancouver. However, many became concerned over the amount of decentralization and fragmentation created by the proliferation of special purpose bodies. According to *Municipal World*:

> Decentralization has been carried too far. Town Planning Commissions, Suburban Road Commissions, Railway Commissions, Police Commissions, Boards of Education, Hospital Trusts, Utilities Commissions have usurped Council powers. The Council today is little more than a tax-levying body with little or no control.[60]

---

[58] Weaver, *Shaping the Canadian City*, p. 72.

[59] Mayor Bethune, Vancouver (1907), quoted in *ibid.*, p. 70.

[60] S. M. Baker, "Municipal Government Reform," *Municipal World*, Vol. 27, October 1917, p. 154, in Weaver, "Tomorrow's Metropolis Revisited," p. 411.

Concluding Comments

The early sections of this chapter outline the origins of local government in Canada. Beginning with the first Aboriginal governments and then those instituted by European colonists, these sections show how changing economic, political, and cultural conditions forced authorities to alter the rules and arrangements by which local decisions were made. They also reveal why Canadian local governments are so similar in nature despite being established in different provinces and during different eras, mostly due to the influence of provisions established in the 1849 *Baldwin Act*. This early legislation set a precedent where provincial and territorial governments still have local government systems with:

1. Distinct urban and rural municipal designations;
2. Very limited authority, most of which centred on servicing property; and,
3. Property tax as the main local government revenue source.

Today many Canadians demonstrate a romantic attachment to the cities and towns in which they live – often attributing these sentiments to their ancestors' long and bitter struggle to wrest local self-government from an unsympathetic and paternalistic British regime. This vision is often used to defend the status quo whenever change threatens historic municipal boundaries. Yet the true story of local government origins is considerably less stirring. With the possible exception of Upper Canada (Ontario), this chapter shows municipal government was less warmly received or even actively resisted elsewhere in Canada mainly due to fears about local property tax increases. In reality, most municipal governments were imposed on local populations by senior governments seeking to shift the growing burden of government expenditures to local populations and not because of strong local democratic values. Even in Ontario where pressure for local self-government was most pronounced, an important factor in the creation of municipal institutions was the inability of the Courts of Quarter Sessions to deal with growing urban problems.

As Canada moved into the 20th century, growth pressures spawned three distinct reform movements: city beautiful, city healthy, and city efficient. Each reform movement presented a different vision of tomorrow's city.[61] While many reformers undoubtedly were sincere in

---

[61] Rutherford, *Saving the Canadian City*, p. xvii.

their efforts, others had less noble motives behind their proposals. C. S. Clarke, an opinionated Torontonian, denounced crusaders who wanted to purify city life as "a small group of pious fanatics who bothered the respectable and terrorized the weak."[62] In only slightly more generous terms, Kaplan states that "the reform doctrine was self-congratulatory, contemptuous of outsiders, and thus highly vulnerable to charges of hypocrisy," especially since its main advocates were often prominent businessmen seeking to expand their personal wealth and influence.[63]

The expansion of the franchise and the emerging political power of the lower classes threatened the business community and pushed its leaders to call for reforms in the name of eliminating corruption and improving efficiency. The primary method of achieving reform was to remove powers from council control by decreasing the number and importance of ward politicians, increasing the power of a small executive through the board of control, strengthening the powers of the administration through the commissioner and city manager systems, and, finally, creating separate special purpose bodies to take over completely certain important functions which could not be entrusted to politicians. In this light, municipal government was regarded less as a level of government and more as a business. Consequently, the right to vote was viewed as less important than ensuring a well run municipal organization that would provide services efficiently. As Goldwin Smith said of the municipal franchise:[64]

> What is the power which we now exercise, and which is largely illusory so far as the mass of us are concerned, compared with our health, our convenience, and the rescue of our property from the tax-gatherers?

The net result of the reforms was a more complex, less accountable municipal government, more responsible to economy and efficiency than to voters. But as early as 1899, many recognized these reforms had not eliminated waste and corruption. There were also complaints about evasion of responsibility. For example, *Toronto Star* editors complained council and the board of control were merely playing "a game of shuttlecock and battledore."[65] In 1909, the Fort William–Port Arthur Utilities Commission admitted that service was poor. In 1913, Calgary's

---

[62] Rutherford, "Tomorrow's Metropolis," p. 371.

[63] Harold Kaplan, *Reform, Planning and City Politics: Montreal, Winnipeg, Toronto*, Toronto, University of Toronto Press, 1982, p. 173.

[64] Weaver, *Shaping the Canadian City*, pp. 45-46.

[65] *Ibid.*, p. 70.

commissioners purchased a $5000 car with special paint and a special siren horn for their use, perhaps not the most efficient use of public funds.[66] The problem, of course, was that even businessmen and experts were as prone to self-interest and corruption as those municipal officials they had previously chastised. In 1895, the *Telegram* observed that "the fault is not with the system but with the people"[67] – an insight that today's proponents of structural change might keep in mind.

There is a striking similarity between the problems and reforms of 100 years ago and those of today. Common to both periods are concerns over the adequacy of the municipal infrastructure, housing shortages and resistance to low income housing, rapid consumption of resources and environmental degradation, the promotion of preventive health programs, conflict of interest and corruption, and a feeling that structural changes make little difference if people and their practices remain unchanged.

The legacy of the reform era is evident in the continued existence of many of the structural reforms from the early 1900s and in the continued denial of the relevance of politics at the local level. Modern municipalities are told to embrace business principles and practices at the expense of engaging citizens. Many city officials brag about being open for business, often at the expense of more balanced policies and practices. These pressures are perhaps even greater today due to globalization and free trade. Economy and efficiency are once again the touchstones of a well run municipality, with the bottom line often replacing the broader public interest. If it is true that those who do not learn from history are condemned to repeat it, today's municipal leaders perhaps need to pay more attention to the lessons from their past.

---

[66] *Ibid.*, p. 72.

[67] *Ibid.*, pp. 72-73.

Chapter 3
Pressures of Growth and Change

The last chapter described how the foundations of Canada's local government system were laid 200 years ago for the small and scattered population of a primarily rural and agricultural society. It also showed that although we have come to be one of the most urbanized countries in an increasingly globalized world, our local government structure is very similar to that used by our ancestors. This chapter continues to explore the theme of growth, including how and why Canada's population has become more urbanized, some of the benefits of city life, and how Canadians might overcome the many challenges associated with urban growth.

Urban Growth in Canada

The proportion of Canada's population living in urban areas has grown from a mere 20% around the time of Confederation to now over 80%. These estimates are based on what Statistics Canada defines as an "urban area" or those places with 1000 or more residents and a population density of at least 400 people per square kilometre. The proportion of Canadians living in urban areas is similar in the United States, but is more than the proportions in other industrialized countries – except the United Kingdom where nearly 90% of the population lives in towns and cities.[1]

In 1871, the time of the first census, around 20% of Canadians lived in urban areas. However, this proportion increased to 80% at the beginning of the 21th century and is projected to climb even higher by 2026. This pattern was illustrated by the figure in Chapter 2 (page 46) that shows Canadian longitudinal growth patterns. No longer hewers of wood or drawers of water, most Canadians are now city dwellers. This trend toward urbanization is perhaps best illustrated by the changing nature of Canada's Aboriginal population: more than half of Canada's Aboriginal people now live in urban areas (most living in Canada's 10

---

[1] http://www12.statcan.ca/census-recensement/2006/as-sa/97-550/index-eng.cfm.

largest cities) as compared to fewer than 7% approximately a half century ago.²

Statistics Canada also tracks growth in Census Metropolitan Areas (CMAs) defined as regions having at least 100 000 residents and an urban core of at least 50 000. According to the 2006 census, Canada has 33 CMAs which now are home to more than two-thirds (68%) of the entire Canadian population. As shown in the table below, of the 21.5 million Canadians living in CMAs, 14.1 million lived in one of the six metropolitan areas with a population of more than 1 million: Toronto, Montreal, Vancouver, Ottawa–Gatineau, Calgary, and Edmonton.

Table 3.1 Six Largest Census Metropolitan Areas in Canada (2006)

Census Metropolitan Area	Province	Population
Toronto	Ontario	5,113,149
Montreal	Quebec	3,635,571
Vancouver	British Columbia	2,116,581
Ottawa–Gatineau	Ontario/Quebec	1,130,761
Calgary	Alberta	1,079,310
Edmonton	Alberta	1,034,945

Source: Statistics Canada "Portrait of the Canadian Population" at http://www12.statcan.ca/census-recensement/2006/as-sa/97-550/pdf/97-550-XIE2006001.pdf.

It is important not to confuse CMAs with municipalities as the two are not always the same thing. For example, in 2006 the population of the City of Toronto was 2 503 281 whereas the population of those living in the region designated as the Toronto CMA was just over 5.1 million.

Just as population growth is uneven across the country, so too is it unevenly distributed within major urban areas. Much of the growth over the past several decades has occurred beyond the central city cores, contributing to a pattern of urban sprawl. In terms of growth patterns, Bryant and Lemire report that during the 1980s, "almost 60 per cent of the net growth in Canada's CMAs and almost 50 per cent of Canada's net growth was located in the CMA's fringe areas beyond the urbanized core...."³ In addition, between 1996 and 2001, the combined population of the city centres of the four largest CMAs grew by only 0.9% per year, compared with a 2.3% growth per annum in the suburban and outlying

---

² Conference Board of Canada, *Mission Possible, Successful Canadian Cities*, The Canadian Project Final Report, Vol. III, 2007, p. 10.

³ Christopher Bryant and Daniel Lemire, *Population Distribution and the Management of Urban Growth in Six Selected Urban Regions in Canada*, Toronto, Intergovernmental Committee on Urban and Regional Research, 1993, p. 14.

areas.[4] Between 2001 and 2006, the growth rate of municipalities peripheral to Canada's 33 CMAs was 11.1% (double the national average of 5.4%), while the central cities grew by only 4.2%. In the Montreal CMA, for example, the City of Montreal and all but one municipality on the island of Montreal had growth rates below the province and the country, while 30 municipalities in the CMA grew by at least twice the national average. Similarly, population growth in five municipalities in the Hamilton to Oshawa corridor of the Greater Golden Horseshoe (GGH) was at least four times the national average. Other GGH municipalities grew even faster, such as Milton which had a staggering 71.4% increase in population between 2001 and 2006.[5]

While this chapter mainly focuses upon urban Canada, it is also important to note emerging trends in rural areas. Unlike urban Canada, Canada's rural population grew by a mere 1% between 2001 and 2006. Additional statistical analysis reveals two very different types of rural areas. Rural areas close to urban centres saw population increases of 4.7%, a rate very close to the overall national average. Fourteen of the twenty-five fastest growing rural communities are located less than 50 kilometres from Montreal, Toronto, or Vancouver, with another six located close to other large CMAs. However, in more remote rural areas the population declined slightly (0.1%). In many cases, the economies of these rural areas with declining populations rely on fishing, agriculture, forestry, mining, or other waning primary industries.

These statistics suggest that slow, no, or declining growth patterns is one of the main problems facing rural communities caused by changing economic patterns, remoteness, and lack of transportation or communication links. The movement of young people out of these areas in search of jobs also leaves rural areas with disproportionately older populations.[6] However, it would be a mistake to focus only on the constraints facing rural areas and overlook their importance to the country. Natural resource industries supported by rural communities make up over 13% of Canada's Gross National Product (GNP) and account for over 50% of the country's exports. Moreover, rural areas are the primary sources of the

---

[4] Toronto Dominion Bank, *A Choice Between Investing in Canada's Cities or Disinvesting in Canada's Future*, April 2002, p. 8.

[5] http://www12.statcan.ca/census-recensement/2006/as-sa/97-550/index-eng.cfm.

[6] David J. A. Douglas & Associates, "The Fiscal Balance and Rural Municipalities" in Federation of Canadian Municipalities, *Building Prosperity From the Ground Up: Restoring Municipal Fiscal Balance*, June 2006, Appendix 6.

natural capital (food, water, energy, and other resources) needed to sustain life in the urban part of Canada.[7]

Changing population patterns have created a divide between rural and urban Canadians. For example, where rural Canadians often feel neglected by governments preoccupied with urban issues, urban dwellers lament the overrepresentation of rural areas in provincial and federal legislatures. While those living in urban centres contend they generate far more wealth than is returned to their areas by provincial and federal governments, so, too, do those living in rural areas. In some cases these rural claims are justified. A 2007 report found the Ontario government earned $413 million from mining and water taxes and stumpage fees in 2006, while returning only $60 million for economic development and infrastructure through the Northern Ontario Heritage Fund. Even more strikingly, between 2001 and 2005 provincial revenues from the Ontario mining industry increased by 110% and federal revenues by 77%, while municipal property taxes from mining companies decreased by 4.5%.[8] How to find a balance between rural and urban demands is an increasingly difficult problem for federal and provincial politicians.

The Causes of Urbanization

While rural problems are important, the rest of this chapter continues to focus on urbanization as most Canadians now live in cities. "Urbanization" describes an increase in population as well as an increase in population density – or how the population is distributed across the country and within regions. This section focuses on the two main factors affecting population growth and distribution: government policies and economic conditions. Subsequent sections shed light on the benefits and challenges associated with urbanization.

Government Policies

Government has always had a major impact upon population growth and distribution within and across Canada. For example, every year the

---

[7] Federation of Canadian Municipalities, *Restoring Municipal Fiscal Balance*, p. 10.

[8] *Northern Lights, Strategic Investments in Ontario's Greatest Asset*, A Position Paper Presented to Ontario's Three Major Political Parties, April 18, 2007, pp. 9-10.

federal government decides how many immigrants to accept into the country, with immigration being one of the chief reasons for Canadian urbanization. Once in the country, new immigrants tend to settle in large urban areas such as Toronto, Montreal, and Vancouver. Immigrants are largely drawn to these areas by existing immigrant communities and are unlikely to relocate into slow growing rural areas "unless there is a significant change in the distribution of incentives, notably employment opportunities and cultural services."[9] If population growth remains a government priority, this reliance on immigration will likely continue unless the country's low fertility rate of about 1.5 children per woman increases to reach at least the replacement rate of 2.1 children.[10] Some suggest the current trend of immigrant clustering raises the possibility of "a permanent set of place-based winners and losers," as it creates one set of rapidly growing, socially diverse places with younger populations and another set of slow growing (or shrinking) socially homogeneous places with aging populations.[11]

While immigration partially explains why Canada has continued to urbanize, industrial policy sheds additional light on this issue. The impact of industrial policy on urbanization can be traced as far back as Sir John A. Macdonald's 1879 "National Policy," especially its use of high tariffs to protect new manufacturing industries in Central Canada, which led to the early (and continuing) concentration of manufacturing in a central corridor extending from Quebec City to Windsor. This development, in turn, contributed to the growth of a number of cities in this area, and to the dominance of the Montreal and Toronto areas as described by the Economic Council of Canada in its Fourth Annual Review:

> ... economic change in Canada has thus been marked by a relative shift in the focus of employment and output from on-site exploitation of the natural resource base to the processing of materials, to manufacturing and advanced fabrication, and to the provision of a rapidly widening range of modern private and public services. Inevitably this change has implied a shift in the location of economic activity away from the rural area and its small service centres towards the larger urban centre.[12]

---

[9] Enid Slack, Larry S. Bourne, and Meric Gertler, *Small, Rural, and Remote Communities: The Anatomy of Risk*, Panel on the Role of Government, August 2003, p. 5.

[10] Statistics Canada, *Portrait of the Canadian Population in 2006*, p. 7.

[11] Larry Bourne and Jim Simmons, "New Fault Lines? Recent Trends in the Canadian Urban System," *Canadian Journal of Urban Research, Supplement*, Summer 2003, p. 40.

[12] Economic Council of Canada, *Fourth Annual Review*, Ottawa, 1967, p. 181.

More recent patterns of urban development have been influenced by policies of the federal government, notably with respect to housing and urban renewal initiatives. With the 1935 *Dominion Housing Act*, and especially with the establishment of the Central (now Canada) Mortgage and Housing Corporation (CMHC) in 1946, federal financial assistance for single family dwellings reinforced low density sprawl. The actions of the CMHC also contributed to neighbourhood dislocations and attendant problems because of what has been described as a bulldozer approach to urban renewal. Urban growth became a prime instrument of public policy to stimulate and maintain high levels of economic activity.[13] After studying federal housing policy, Fallis finds that it is mainly influenced by federal macroeconomic policy and he observes: "the federal government has always used housing programs as instruments of fiscal policy."[14]

Leo describes how all three levels of government became involved in a massive postwar program of government support for suburban development, pursuing policies giving free rein and entrenching the private automobile over public transportation.[15] Such polices were consistent with the demands of the public driven, to a large extent, by families with young children in search of quiet suburban streets and backyards.[16] However, Leo suggests governments also responded to those who profited from suburban expansion including developers, Department of Finance and CMHC civil servants, and contributors to the Liberal Party of Canada.[17] These influences led to a uniquely Canadian response to urbanization, much different from, for example, the European response where suburban development was much less dominated by the automobile.

---

[13] Michael Goldrick, "The Anatomy of Urban Reform in Toronto," in Dimitrios Roussopoulos (ed.), *The City and Radical Social Change*, Montreal, Black Rose Books, 1982, p. 264.

[14] George Fallis, "The Federal Government and the Metropolitan Housing Problem," in F. Frisken (ed.), *The Changing Canadian Metropolis: A Public Policy Perspective*, Toronto, Canadian Urban Institute, 1994, Vol. 1, p. 376.

[15] Christopher Leo, "The State in the City: A Political-Economy Perspective on Growth and Decay," in James Lightbody (ed.), *Canadian Metropolitics*, Toronto, Copp Clark Ltd., 1995, p. 31.

[16] This point is made in David K. Foot, *Boom, Bust & Echo*, Toronto, Macfarlane Walter & Ross, 1996, Chapter 7, who also explains how the aging population has brought about a decline in public transit ridership and a growth in the suburbs and the reliance on cars.

[17] Leo, "The State in the City," p. 32.

James Lorimer contends "most of the development of Canadian cities in the three boom decades from the Forties to the Seventies was a direct consequence of the economic development strategy chosen by Ottawa for Canada."[18] In his view, this strategy had two principal components: the exploitation of natural resources for use mainly by the major metropolitan economies, and the expansion of a branch plant secondary manufacturing industry in Southern Ontario. Thus local government's primary role was to provide the physical services to support this style of growth and development. As a result, according to Lorimer, local government officials became servants of the very developers they were supposed to regulate.[19]

Bradford describes the period between 1940 and 1970 as one of "cities in the shadows of Keynesian space," referring to the economic policies of John Maynard Keynes then being pursued by government.[20] Central to those policies was spending as a stimulus to the economy, both through an expanding network of social programs and through the construction of housing to accommodate a rapidly growing population – fuelled by baby boomers and immigrants. Local governments were expected to do their part, in return for increased tax revenues and jobs.

Magnusson describes the federal government's efforts to support the housing market to ensure an expansion of the economy.[21] But, he also notes the provinces were just as concerned as the federal government about removing any possible checks on growth, which was one of their reasons for increasing conditional grants for improving public facilities in cities. He also suggests provincial legislation on planning and zoning was based on the assumption that urban development would be undertaken through private initiative, with municipalities playing a regulatory role, but one that facilitated private enterprise.[22]

Canada's contemporary settlement patterns can be seen as a product of the federal government's longstanding pro immigration policy.

---

[18] James Lorimer, "The post-developer era for Canada's cities begins," in *City Magazine Annual 1981*, Toronto, James Lorimer and Company, 1981, p. 7.

[19] See, for example, *The Real World of City Politics*, Toronto, James Lewis and Samuel, 1970; *A Citizen's Guide to City Politics*, Toronto, James Lewis and Samuel, 1972; *The Developers*, Toronto, James Lorimer, 1978; and *After the Developers* (with Carolyn MacGregor), Toronto, James Lorimer, 1981.

[20] Neil Bradford, *Why Cities Matter: Policy Research Perspectives for Canada*, CPRN Discussion Paper F\23, June 2002, Canadian Policy Research Networks, pp. 16-19.

[21] Warren Magnusson, "Introduction," in Warren Magnusson and Andrew Sancton (eds.), *City Politics in Canada*, Toronto, University of Toronto Press, p. 27.

[22] *Ibid.*

Settlement patterns are also affected by other government policies promoting housing, particularly single family housing, as an instrument of economic growth as well as massive investments in highway construction. However, the next section explains how the trend toward urbanization is also due to the transformation of Canada's economy from primary and secondary industry to service sector provision – from agricultural and manufacturing to retail sales, transportation, goods distribution, entertainment, insurance, banking, and health care.

Economic Influences

Where some suggest government policies created our highly urbanized country, others suggest private decision making has had a greater impact.[23] Perhaps the most powerful economic explanation for urbanization comes from what economists call "economies of scale." According to this theory, cities grow because it is cheaper to do business in a densely populated urban area than in a sparsely populated rural area. The growth of firms located in rural areas is restricted as these firms have only a small local market in which to sell their goods or services. This means they have to duplicate operations in other rural areas or transport goods or services over long distances to expand. However, firms located in urban areas have a much larger market in which to operate, allowing them to lower costs and increase production and profits. Firms located in urban areas also benefit from increased levels of public goods provisions such as urban infrastructure.[24] As firms locate to cities, so too do people looking for better jobs and a better life.

As firms and people rush to the cities, land becomes scarcer and more valuable – often driving land speculation. As property prices increase in the expanding inner city, developers buy cheap land just outside urban centres then market this land to those looking to capitalize on the city life but unable to afford expensive inner city property prices. As demand for suburban homes rises, so too do housing prices and developer profits. Escalating land costs then push the cost of housing beyond the reach of many would-be home owners, forcing them to move even further from the city core.

---

[23] See, for example, Boyce Richardson, *The Future of Canadian Cities*, Toronto, New Press, 1972, on which this section is based.

[24] Roger W. Caves, "Economics of Scale," from Roger Caves, *Encyclopedia of the City*, New York, Taylor and Frances, 2005, p. 208.

While some see these trends as beneficial, many do not.[25] For example, according to Castells, "it is impossible to understand both the urban sprawl which passes for development and the urban conflict it has produced unless one recognizes the determining power of the capitalist mode of production which governs these processes."[26] Rather than being haphazard and random, city growth is intimately linked with the changing needs of the economic system and "[t]he city is developed, redeveloped and moulded over time according to long term cycles in how profits are made and investment decisions taken."[27]

This view also addresses how governments aid the profit cycle. For example, Western nations emerging from the Depression of the 1930s needed to stimulate consumption to sustain the capitalist system. As such, these governments introduced a series of policies to facilitate urban growth. By shifting the focus of capital from production to consumption and by emphasizing urban development as a key vehicle to achieve it, these actions effectively changed the function of cities from that of workshops to "artifacts of consumption." Some argue the chief beneficiaries of these policies have been the property development industry, including financiers, real estate companies, construction companies, and property managers.[28]

Globalization has tightened the link between economics and urban life. Since information and capital now can be instantaneously transmitted around the world and trade rules changed to facilitate the international movement of goods and services, firms have even more freedom to reorganize to increase productivity.[29] Urban development is clearly affected by the economic transformation inherent in the forces of the global economy, making it very likely future employment opportunities will continue to be concentrated in Canada's major urban centres. Innovation, knowledge intensive production, and other forms of creative activity have become more concentrated geographically within large cities and city regions.[30]

---

[25] Dimitrios Roussopoulos, "Understanding the City and Radical Social Change," in Roussopoulos, *The City and Radical Social Change*, p. 61.

[26] M. Castells, as quoted in *ibid.*, p. 111.

[27] Goldrick, "The Anatomy of Urban Reform in Toronto," p. 263.

[28] *Ibid.*, pp. 264-265.

[29] Conference Board of Canada, *Mission Possible*, p. iv.

[30] Enid Slack, Larry S. Bourne, and Meric Gertler, *Vibrant Cities and City-Regions: Responding to Emerging Challenges*, a paper prepared for the (Ontario) Panel on the Role of Government, August 2003, p. 7.

Growing Cities, Growing Benefits

The previous sections show how government policies and economic forces have transformed Canada into a very urban country complete with an array of large metropolitan centres. This is not a uniquely Canadian phenomenon. Many industrialized countries are as densely populated as Canada and some have had giant cities centuries before Europeans set foot on North American soil. Ancient Rome might be considered the first true great city in the world, having a population of one million people as early as AD 100 – many centuries before Confederation. Throughout history, cities have been regarded as positively and negatively influencing humanity. This subsection briefly explores the economic and social benefits of living in cities with subsequent subsections exploring the downsides of living in densely populated areas. From the economic perspective, it is hard to imagine how Canada's modern economy could function without cities. Over the last century, Canada's economy has shifted from relying on jobs in primary industries to service sector employment. This change in our economic focus prompted urbanist Jack Layton to suggest cities are now critical to the Gross Domestic Product (GDP) of their respective provinces:

> ...cities are where most of Canada's GDP is created. Just the seven largest metropolitan areas generate 45 percent of the country's GDP. Regionally, the City of Winnipeg's gross domestic product accounts for two-thirds of Manitoba's economy; Calgary's and Edmonton's GDP is 64 percent of Alberta's; Vancouver's GDP is 53 percent of British Columbia's; Montreal's is just under half of Quebec's; and Toronto is responsible for 44 percent of Ontario's GDP.[31]

Where fishing, logging, farming, and trapping drove Canada's economy in the early stages of our development, cities are now Canada's economic engine. Jane Jacobs describes the new Canadian reality:[32]

> Without Vancouver, Calgary, Toronto, Montreal and Winnipeg ... Canada would be so poor it would qualify as a third world country. The ... taxes that businesses and residents in these five cities pay are what make federal and provincial programs and activities financially possible.

---

[31] Jack Layton. "A time to build Canada's cities," *Policy Options*, February 2004, pp. 33-38.

[32] Remarks at C5 meeting of big city mayors, May 25-26, 2001, from *Ideas That Matter*, Vol. 2, No. 1, p. 4, accessed May 1, 2003 from www.ideasthatmatter.com.

While the economic benefit of cities is readily apparent, cities can also be wonderful and vibrant places to live. The American historian Lewis Mumford goes further, stating cities are purposefully created "...to convert power into form, energy into culture, dead matter into the living symbols of art, biological reproduction into social creativity."[33] Urban historian Peter Hall describes cities as cultural crucibles and goes as far as to claim humanity only ever moves forward due to innovations created in urban areas.[34] For Hall, "[t]he Renaissance... was an urban phenomenon; so too was every great creative burst in human history."

The trend of cities as major engines of social development has continued into the 21st century. Urban areas now provide increasingly rich and diverse environments, cultural and creative activities, distinctive neighbourhoods, and high quality public services including education and health care. These qualities make cities great places to live and attractive places for talented people to work.[35] If a city can attract a talented workforce, these workers will, in turn, attract investment capital and the knowledge and innovative intensive forms of production to replace traditional economic activity.

Those cities that measure up well with respect to the three Ts – Technology, Talent, and Tolerance – are projected by Richard Florida to attract knowledge economy firms as the skilled workers needed for this type of industry wish to live in these types of locales. Florida contends "creative class" workers crave vibrant neighbourhoods, after-hours activity, ample recreational facilities, and an atmosphere that welcomes and nurtures creativity and diversity. Florida's research indicates cities filled with writers, designers, musicians, actors, painters, dancers, and other types of cultural workers attract high tech firms because they create conditions in which high tech workers like to live. On the other side, those cities lacking these types of people often fail to attract knowledge-based firms.[36]

---

[33] Lewis Mumford, *City in History: Its Origins, Its Transformation and Its Prospects*, New York, Harcourt Brace, 1961.

[34] Peter Hall, *Cities in Civilization: Culture, Technology and Urban Order*, London, Weidenfeld & Nicolson, 1998, p. 3.

[35] *Ibid.*, p. 14.

[36] Florida's books include *Technology and Tolerance: The Importance of Diversity to High-Technology Growth*, Washington, DC, The Brookings Institution, June 2001; *The Rise of the Creative Class*, New York, Basic Books, 2002; *The Flight of the Creative Class*, New York, HarperCollins, 2005; and *Who's Your City?*, Toronto, Random House, 2009.

Florida's writings have been enthusiastically embraced as well as criticized. Some question the extent to which coffee shops, trendy restaurants, and art galleries encourage economic growth. Others suggest the shift of many firms and jobs to the suburbs means that cities, even "cool" ones, are no longer magnets for talented workers. Harvard professor Edward Glaeser agrees skilled workers are the key to urban success, and their contribution includes creativity, but he disagrees with Florida's efforts to identify a distinct creative class or to link this class with other aspects of urban life.[37] Bradford contends Florida's focus on high end talent undermines contributions of the less advantaged and suggests that some of Florida's creative hot spots are also socially polarized.[38]

Growing Cities, Growing Challenges

While many of us have grown up in or been drawn to cities and are well aware of the associated social and economic benefits, living in densely populated cities also brings a great many challenges. Examining cities in the 1970s, Lithwick suggests challenges during the mid and late 20th century included poverty, housing costs, transportation congestion, environmental decay, and social unrest. However, he also stresses that properly understanding these challenges requires scholars to distinguish between problems *of* cities and problems *in* cities. In other words, solving urban problems requires identifying whether they happen to occur in cities or are inherent in the urban process. Applying this distinction shows many problems identified as the latter are really the former. For example, urban poverty in a depressed region reflects a weak regional economic base, not some particular urban phenomenon. Similarly, unemployment and inflation may be especially obvious within urban areas, but they are the result of national economic performance and the effectiveness of fiscal and monetary policies of governments.[39]

---

[37] Edward L. Glaeser, "Review of *The Rise of the Creative Class*," accessed February 12, 2007 from http://www.economics.harvard.edu/faculty/glaeser/files/Review_Florida.pdf.

[38] Neil Bradford, *Creative Cities Structured Policy Dialogue Backgrounder*, Ottawa, Canadian Policy Research Networks, August 2004, p. 4.

[39] N. H. Lithwick, *Urban Canada: Problems and Prospects*, Ottawa, Central Mortgage and Housing Corporation, December 1970, p. 14-19.

Lithwick also suggests transportation challenges, pollution, and poverty often persist as they are improperly diagnosed as problems rather than as symptoms of much larger, interdependent problems. He instead sees most urban challenges as flowing from the general urban trend of high land prices – where the growth of cities produces competing demands for scarce urban space, driving core property prices upward and households outward to the suburbs. Because of these interdependencies and misdiagnosis, efforts to deal with each problem in isolation have inevitably failed:

> Housing policy has added to the stock of urban accommodations, but has led to urban sprawl and fiscal squeeze for the municipalities. Transport policies have moved people faster initially, but have led to further sprawl, downtown congestion, pollution, and rapid core deterioration.[40]

Problems identified persist or have even worsened since the 1970s. High housing costs have led to homelessness levels not seen since the Great Depression. That Canada now has more food banks than McDonald's outlets indicates the pervasiveness of poverty.[41] Some inner city neighbourhoods suffer higher than average crime rates, driving those who are mobile into the suburbs and leaving those who remain with fewer resources to cope with their situation. In the words of one report:[42]

> A vicious cycle has been launched – where movement away from the urban core places downward pressure on residential and industrial densities and tax bases, forcing municipalities to hike downtown property taxes and other tax levies, which in turn prompts more urban flight. Making matters worse, stagnant or shrinking tax bases have made it difficult for downtown municipalities to address the very social problems that drove businesses and individuals to outlying areas in the first place.

These trends result in what scholars in the United States often deem "white flight," or the tendency of more affluent, white Americans to move to the suburbs and poorer, non-whites to live in decaying cities. Those left behind include the homeless, the mentally ill, transient unemployed youth, those on fixed incomes, the elderly, immigrants, and

---

[40] *Ibid.*, p. 15.

[41] C. Richard Tindal, *A Citizen's Guide to Government*, 3rd Edition, Whitby, McGraw-Hill Ryerson Limited, 2005, p. 284.

[42] Toronto Dominion Bank, *Investing or Disinvesting*, p. 8.

single mothers with children.[43] In Canada, this phenomenon has led to poverty rates in central cities being higher than rates in adjacent suburbs and to an increased geographic concentration of poor families.[44] According to studies completed by the Federation of Canadian Municipalities (FCM), quality of life is at risk and even deteriorating for a significant number of people living in urban areas. In addition, the FCM finds a growing income gap, cuts to social programs, and an increased strain on the urban environment is offsetting general improvements in rates of urban postsecondary education, employment growth, and home ownership.[45]

To a considerable extent, the growing urban income gap between rich and poor is an inevitable result of the impact of globalization. Highly skilled professionals do very well in today's knowledge based economy. However, "the local face of globalization has a darker side," reflected in manufacturing jobs moving from North American cities to countries where labour costs are lower.[46] In addition, immigrants have enjoyed less economic success in recent decades and are taking much longer to close the earnings gap between themselves and non-immigrant workers. As a result, "poverty in Canada's largest cities is heavily concentrated among the immigrant population."[47]

Beyond the income gap, another form of polarization exists in the increasing tendency for immigrants to settle within ethnic enclaves, technically measured as an urban area with 30% or more of the population from one visible minority. While there were only six such enclaves in Toronto, Montreal, and Vancouver in 1981, this number increased to 254 by 2001.[48] These neighbourhoods are often low income, reflecting the larger reality that visible minority families make up three-quarters of the country's poor. Opinions vary as to whether these

---

[43] Larry Bourne, "Urban Canada In Transition to the 21st Century: Trends, Issues and Visions," in Trudi Bunting and Pierre Filion (eds.), *Canadian Cities in Transition*, 2nd Edition, Toronto, Oxford University Press, 2000, p. 39.

[44] Kevin K. Lee, *Urban Poverty in Canada: A Statistical Profile*, Ottawa, Canadian Council on Social Development, 2000, p. xv.

[45] Federation of Canadian Municipalities, *Quality of Life in Canadian Communities*, Theme Report #3, *Growth, the Economy and the Urban Environment*, 2005, accessed June 7, 2007 from www.fcm.ca.

[46] John Lorinc, *The New City*, Toronto, Penguin Group, 2006, p. 59.

[47] Conference Board of Canada, *Mission Possible,* p. 10.

[48] Marina Jimenez, "Do ethnic enclaves impede integration?" *Globe and Mail*, February 8, 2007.

settlement patterns smooth the transition for immigrants or inhibit integration into Canadian society. However, fewer and fewer of us appear to be living in ethnically diverse neighbourhoods even if Canada is supposedly a multicultural society.[49]

Poor and polarized urban neighbourhoods undermine the development of *social capital* in these locales or, as described by Robert Putnam "the collective value of all 'social networks' and the inclinations that arise from these networks to do things for each other."[50] A Statistics Canada study on social engagement finds fewer Canadians now trust others to "do the right thing" such as return a lost wallet, especially those living in the country's largest urban centres. The study describes those living in large cities as having a weaker sense of belonging to their local community than those living in small towns.[51]

Cities also have a major environmental impact, the negative aspects of which may be intensifying in an increasingly global economy. According to one observer, "...cities are massive consumers of non-renewable resources and producers of solid wastes.... [a]s such, they confront major environmental challenges in air and waste pollution, waste management, destruction of agricultural lands, and disruption of ecosystems.[52] Historically, cities were much smaller and relied mainly on the raw materials available in their surrounding hinterlands. As they grew, they had to range further afield to obtain sufficient resources. Thanks to the global supply chain that now exists, cities can "scour the entire earth" to meet their resource needs.[53] Many doubt the current economic and urban model is sustainable given the rapidity with which it consumes resources and the extent of waste flows and pollution that result. One estimate suggests that in 20 years we will require on an annual basis the ecological equivalent of three or four earths.[54]

---

[49] Allan Gregg, as quoted in *ibid*.

[50] Putnam, Robert, *Bowling Alone: The Collapse and Revival of American Community*, New York, Simon and Schuster, 2000.

[51] Statistics Canada, *2003 General Social Survey on Social Engagement, cycle 17: an overview of findings*, Ottawa, July 2004, accessed August 12, 2007 from http://www.statcan.gc.ca/pub/89-598-x/89-598-x2003001-eng.pdf.

[52] Bradford, *Why Cities Matter*, p. 43.

[53] Roy Woodbridge, "Provisioning Cities – A New Urban Agenda," Montreal, Institute of Research on Public Policy, *Policy Options*, July-August 2005, p. 27.

[54] *Ibid.*, p. 29.

Of all the issues and problems associated with urbanization, urban sprawl is attracting increasing attention and controversy. Urban sprawl is usually associated with low density development, strip malls, and car dependency. The exact extent that Canadian cities have sprawled, as well as the very definition of sprawl, is contested. For example, the Canada West Foundation finds Western Canadian cities can be described as sprawling if sprawl is defined as "low density auto-dependent outward growth of an urban area." However our cities are not sprawling if sprawl is defined as "the unplanned, non-contiguous, *ultra-low* density development that characterizes many U.S. cities...."[55] In questioning the existence of sprawl, the Foundation notes Western Canadians have elaborate planning processes in place, that the outward growth is mainly contiguous and consists of connecting new neighbourhoods to existing urban infrastructure, and that new suburban neighbourhoods often have higher density than developments found in older suburban communities.[56]

Definitions aside, it is hard to contest the massive growth of Canada's suburbs and the challenges associated with this growth. For example, Fowler is very critical of North American growth patterns, suggesting we are increasingly living in cities "where we sleep en masse in huge residential complexes and work en masse in huge retail or industrial developments – and spend our lives travelling between them, from living room to kitchen, so to speak."[57] He also claims North Americans squander billions of dollars by living in built environments with "extravagant transportation system[s], life-threatening levels of pollution ... needlessly large infrastructure of utilities such as water mains and trunk sewers, and significantly more expensive housing and consumer goods."[58] Along these lines, a Greater Toronto Area task force estimates a more compact and efficient development pattern could save local taxpayers $1 billion per year.[59] In addition, time spent by individuals in long commutes along clogged artery roads and taken by

---

[55] Robert Roach and Karen Wilkie, *Project Update, Municipal Services and Environment Initiative*, August 2004, p. 1, accessed August 30, 2004 from www.cwf.ca.

[56] *Ibid.*, p. 2.

[57] Edmund P. Fowler, *Building Cities That Work*, Kingston, McGill-Queen's University Press, 1992, p. 31.

[58] *Ibid.*, p. 69.

[59] Report of the GTA Task Force, *Greater Toronto*, 1996, p. 111.

trucks to transport products from place to place result in economic waste and lost production.[60]

Urban sprawl also adversely affects the natural environment in a number of ways aside from increasing pollution due to traffic congestion. For one, sprawl often occurs in areas with good farmland located near our large cities. In the Greater Toronto Area, increasing levels of sprawl threaten the 42% of land classified as suitable for farming, including the vast majority of which is considered prime agricultural land.[61] In addition, low density suburban growth also threatens the natural renewal of water reservoirs as parking lots and roads cause precipitation to enter the storm sewer systems as runoff rather than filtering into underground aquifers, thus slowing reservoir replenishment.[62]

Different kinds of negative social impact and exclusion are experienced by those living beyond the central city. Those without vehicles (the young and the elderly) can feel isolated and trapped in the suburbs. Conversely, suburban commuters have little time, or opportunity, for interaction and participation in local community events. Lowi even suggests that the suburbs represent a failure of citizenship.[63]

> We have removed ourselves not only from the responsibilities of civic participation but also from the challenges of social relations by zoning poor families out of our neighbourhoods. The social and political skills of adults have declined; we have lost the ability, at a personal level, to say how we feel, to negotiate, to solve problems creatively – in short, to be publicly responsible individuals.

According to Jacobs, the physical diversity that has been disappearing from our cities made contact among neighbours more likely and encouraged people to care about what went on in their neighbourhood.[64] Fowler takes a similar position, arguing the physical characteristics of the postwar urban environment have an adverse impact on our social behaviour, including our political activities. What he terms "authentic politics" is, he contends, only possible in small scale, diverse spaces

---

[60] Liam Stone, with Roger Gibbins, *Tightening Our Beltways: Urban Sprawl in Western Canada*, Canada West Foundation, October 2002, pp. 3-4.

[61] Pamela Blais, *Inching Toward Sustainability: The Evolving Urban Structure of the GTA*, Report to the Neptis Foundation, March 2000, pp. 23-24.

[62] Stone and Gibbin, *Tightening Our Beltways*, p. 3.

[63] Theodore Lowi, *The End of Liberalism*, New York, W. W. Norton, 1979, p. 267.

[64] Jane Jacobs, *The Death and Life of Great American Cities*, New York, Random House, 1961.

where a variety of casual face to face interactions occur naturally, a development pattern disappearing as our cities have been rebuilt in the postwar period.[65]

Fowler and Layton find a direct relationship between traffic and neighbourhood vitality, suggesting an increased reliance on cars means streets are now used almost exclusively as thoroughfares rather than as public meeting places. In their view, the reduction in healthy street level contact contributes to the present distrust of government and the erosion of the public sector.[66] Doucet describes the series of urban villages that flourished in Ottawa 50 years ago along residential roads served by electric streetcar lines, and contrasts this with today's "traffic sewers" designed to move traffic across the city as quickly as possible.[67] Hume laments the "topography of globalization" that threatens Toronto with "not just an architecture of anonymity, but also a generic, lowest-common denominator approach to the built environment" one in which "marketplace logic leaves no room for a civic dimension."[68]

Solutions to Urban Challenges

Most accept that the challenges associated with urbanization need redress, with many modern reformers linking most environmental, social, and economic problems to increasing levels of urban sprawl. Over 50 years ago, Regional Growth Management (RGM) reformers began to call for measures such as limited growth, preserving communities and the environment, and limiting new infrastructural investment.[69] In the late 1980s, the New Urbanism movement pushed for compact development in which neighbourhoods would include housing, community facilities,

---

[65] Fowler, *Building Cities That Work*, p. 132.

[66] Edmund P. Fowler and Jack Layton, "Transportation Policy in Canadian Cities," in Edmund P. Fowler and David Siegel, *Urban Policy Issues*, 2nd Edition, Toronto, Oxford University Press, 2002, p. 125.

[67] Clive Doucet, *Urban Meltdown, Cities, Climate Change and Politics as Usual*, Gabriola Island, B.C., New Society Publishers, 2007, Ch. 6.

[68] Christopher Hume, "Topography of globalization threatens this city," *Toronto Star*, March 18, 2002.

[69] Oliver Gillam, *The Limitless City: A Primer on the Urban Sprawl Debate*, Washington, DC, Island Press, 2002, p. 155.

stores, and transit. In the 1990s, "Smart Growth" proponents began to call for less wasteful urban growth and development.[70]

Many of these anti-sprawl movements have been guided by the views and writings of Jane Jacobs. Jacobs turned conventional views of planning on their head with her 1961 book *The Death and Life of Great American Cities*. At a time when city planners were demolishing neighbourhoods and ramming giant highways through the middle of cities, Jacobs embraced crowded streets filled with mixed land uses. In her book she demonstrates density and diversity are essential to healthy city life as the mixture of workplaces, residences, and short city blocks ensure streets are filled with activity which provides constant observation and safety for residents. Turning words into actions, Jacobs led the (successful) effort to block the construction of Toronto's Spadina Expressway in 1968. Before her death in 2006, Jacobs lent her support to Canada's five largest cities in calling for more recognition and resources for cities from provincial and federal governments.

Figure 3.1 Jane Jacobs

Source: Frank Lennon/GetStock.com.

Other reforms heed international discussions about sustainable development, such as those promoted by the 1987 World (Bruntland) Commission on the Environment and Development Report to the United Nations. As summarized by Bradford, the Bruntland Commission argues

---

[70] Canadian Urban Institute, *Smart Growth in Canada*, Toronto, March 2001, p. 3.

it is possible to have economic development while protecting the environment:

> A sustainable city is dedicated to reducing its impact on the bio-region by shrinking the size of the ecological footprint. The strategies are by now well-known and involve government deploying a host of policy instruments and fiscal incentives to embed ecological factors into the decision making processes of citizens and governments. Familiar goals are substituting brownfield conversions for greenfield development, and higher density housing complexes for detached single family lots; ensuring local waste management and reuse rather than exporting it to distant landfill or incineration sites; limiting private automobiles; and protecting natural heritage sites or expanding green spaces.[71]

Despite the opposition to sprawl, many still defend existing settlement patterns and reject the alleged benefits of limiting growth. For these critics, sprawl is accepted as the longstanding practice of cities expanding outward and respects the desire of people wanting a home and more open space. Attempting to interfere with the operation of the marketplace by limiting suburban growth policies is rejected as ill advised, especially when these policies do not achieve their supposed benefits.

Defenders of sprawl suggest too much government interference with market forces in urban settings generates insufficient highway construction and worsens traffic congestion, which, in turn, increases air pollution. They also argue housing costs become excessive when growth is limited, making it difficult for young families and immigrants to enjoy home ownership.[72] Some assert mass transit will never substitute for automobile travel without population densities far beyond what people would find tolerable. In support of this notion, Cox points to the example of Portland, Oregon, the "poster child" of smart growth, where public resistance forced the authorities to abandon plans to increase density and, instead, to expand the urban growth boundary outward.[73]

Unfortunately, the debate about what to do in cities tends to focus on the extremes of growth limiting strategies versus sprawl as if they represent an either-or situation. Even if there are problems with limiting growth, continuing the pattern of urban sprawl hardly seems sustainable.

---

[71] Bradford, *Why Cities Matter*, p. 45.

[72] One of the most persistent critics of smart growth is Wendell Cox. His views are summarized in *Smart Growth, Threatening the Quality of Urban Life*, Winnipeg, Frontier Centre for Public Policy, February 2004 and form the basis for the points that follow.

[73] *Ibid.*, pp. 30-31.

Defenders of sprawl may be correct in asserting growth limitation policies may drive up housing costs and limit automobile travel, but it is hard to see how houses built in sprawling suburbs can be economically feasible when limited oil supplies inevitably drive gasoline prices to unaffordable levels.[74] It may be that congestion in cities causes more air pollution than arises from car travel on rural roads, but this allegation also ignores the benefits of getting people in urban areas to travel by public transit, bicycle, or by foot.

Opponents to limiting sprawl are also correct in pointing out the many impediments to implementing growth limiting policies. For example, green belt and growth centre initiatives for the Greater Golden Horseshoe were introduced by the Ontario government in 2005 with much fanfare, but a 2007 report found "a yawning gap between ... reality and planning goals."[75] Sprawl continues in the area, and almost certainly will for quite some time, given the amount of land zoned already for development. People still want to settle in the suburbs and have extra space. In addition, most municipalities encourage growth – whether compact or sprawled – because property taxes yield more revenues when assessment bases increase. Whatever the risks associated with attempting to limit sprawl, the much greater risk is entirely failing to address the problem.

Cities continue to change even as the debate about sprawl continues. Described by White as "turning the urban sock inside out," some inner cities are now attracting fewer immigrants and are becoming less violent and less stressful while their suburbs become increasingly heterogeneous, violent, and demanding.[76] For example, suburbs located outside Canada's three largest cities all have higher rates of poverty and immigration than their central cities.[77] A 2007 study of Toronto shows that the poor are increasingly concentrated in the city's periphery.[78] In addition, recent population growth in the York Region, a suburb just

---

[74] For more on this see Richard Gilbert and Anthony Perl, *Transport Revolutions: Moving people and freight without oil,* Gabriola Island, B.C., New Society Publishers, 2010.

[75] Pierre Filion, *The Urban Growth Centres Strategy in the Greater Golden Horseshoe,* Toronto, Neptis Foundation, May 2007, accessed from www.neptis.org July 12, 2007.

[76] Otis White, *Urban America in Transition,* posted August 19, 2006 at www.civic-strategies.com.

[77] Jill Mahoney, "Suburban myths demolished," *Globe and Mail,* July 31, 2006.

[78] Toronto Dominion Bank, *An Update to TD Economics' 2002 Report on the Greater Toronto Area (GTA) Economy,* July 2007, accessed from www.td.com/economics, August 25, 2007.

north of Toronto, now comes less from native born, second generation Canadians and more from new immigrants from Asia or the former Soviet Union. These changes greatly increased pressure on suburban social services and suggest we need to revise the traditional view of poor central cities struggling with poverty and crime surrounded by prosperous suburbs to which the middle class has fled.[79]

We might also need to re-examine the traditional view of population increases being more desirable than slow or limited growth. For example, comparing the rapidly growing and much-heralded Vancouver with the slower growing and less flamboyant Winnipeg, Leo and Anderson find moving from Winnipeg to Vancouver increases a person's income by 12%, but increases the cost of owning a home by 183%.[80] The authors also show that Winnipeg's economic growth usually outpaces its population growth and that the city's average unemployment rate was the same or lower than the rate in Vancouver between 1994 and 2003. Leo and Anderson suggest Winnipeg's diversified economic base of agriculture, manufacturing, government, and education, is not subject to booms, but relatively well insulated from busts.[81] This research shows municipalities need to recognize that both rapid growth and slow growth have advantages and drawbacks.

Concluding Comments

Canada's system of local government was born in the 19th century when pressures of growth and change forced senior governments to respond in ways appropriate for the country's mostly agricultural and rural economy. Local residents lived in a very large number of relatively small municipalities and worked in primary industry. The local government system provided by the 1849 *Baldwin Act* and other provincial legislation allowed municipalities to collect property taxes to provide a limited range of property services.

This chapter shows how Canada rapidly transformed into an urbanizing, industrialized society during the early stages of the 20th

---

[79] James Rusk, "Suburban fences hide new poverty," *Globe and Mail*, March 13, 2006.

[80] Christopher Leo and Kathryn Anderson, "Being Realistic About Urban Growth," *Journal of Urban Affairs*, Vol. 28, No. 2, 2006, p. 178.

[81] *Ibid.*, p. 179.

century, and then into the highly urbanized, knowledge-based economy we know today. As these changes unfolded, population growth and overspill outstripped municipal boundaries. With this sprawl came increasing concerns about a growing concentration of poverty in inner city neighbourhoods, low density development, the loss of farmland and a variety of environmental concerns, and a weakened sense of community and citizenship.

However, as shown in subsequent chapters, while Canada has morphed into one of the most urbanized countries in the world, our municipal structures have largely stayed stuck in the 1800s. This institutional paralysis has created three distinct problems. First, the ability for local officials to respond to local problems has been undermined as many traditional local government responsibilities such as health, education, and welfare have been uploaded to senior governments. Second, senior governments have offloaded many program delivery responsibilities to local governments, lessening the ability for policies to be custom made to fit local needs. Finally, senior governments continue to cut back on the money directly provided to local governments while at the same time failing to provide new revenue raising powers. This has resulted in a widening gap between increasing expenditures and available revenue sources. This growing fiscal squeeze is a key problem for all municipalities and undermines their ability to ready local communities for 21st century challenges.

Chapter 4
Local Government Restructuring

Amalgamations that created enlarged cities in places such as Winnipeg, Montreal, Quebec City, Toronto, and Ottawa have attracted most of the attention on local government reform in Canada. But the failure to reform municipal government – or even to *establish* municipal government – in the rural areas of many provinces has been one of the greatest shortcomings in such reform initiatives in recent decades.

Introduction

As the previous chapter made clear, the pressures of growth and change brought many challenges, especially in relation to rapid urbanization, extensive sprawl, and global competition. This chapter examines one particular response to these challenges, that of municipal reform and restructuring. Other relevant responses also occurred – such as new municipal legislation, initiatives to disentangle and realign provincial and local responsibilities, and limited changes affecting municipal revenue sources – and they are discussed in Chapters 6 and 7. Many other responses could have been introduced, as will be evident from discussions in Chapter 5. But it was particularly through municipal amalgamation and restructuring that most provinces attempted to address perceived local problems and, as will become clear, dealing with just this one type of response makes for a full chapter all by itself.

The description of the extensive reforms must inevitably be quite brief,[1] and any major analysis of these reforms and their strengths and shortcomings is reserved for the following chapter. That chapter will also offer some examples of the many other responses that could have been introduced – responses that arguably would have been more effective than restructuring in addressing the areas of concern.

---

[1] More detail on local government reforms can be found in Chapter 4 of the previous two editions (2009 and 2004) of this book and Chapters 5 and 6 of the 5th (2000) edition.

The reforms have included the amalgamations of municipalities (and school boards, although they are not included in this examination), the creation (and subsequent merger) of two tier metropolitan and regional government systems, and the creation of intermunicipal joint servicing bodies. These reforms extend back over a period of more than 50 years and they have altered the municipal system in virtually every province, although to markedly varying degrees. A strict chronological outline of developments would involve jumping back and forth among provinces, and even returning to the same municipality more than once in those instances where there have been repeated reforms. Instead, developments will be described by province and since the examination of the historical foundations of local government in Chapter 2 essentially travelled east to west as did the settlement of the country, we will reverse direction in this chapter and travel west to east.

British Columbia

Reform in British Columbia has been very pragmatic and directed mainly at problems related to the absence of a municipal structure over much of the province. In 1966 only 2870 out of 266 000 square miles in British Columbia were within organized municipalities.[2] The remainder of the province, containing one-sixth of its population, received some services (mainly policing and roads) directly from the provincial government. It also received services from improvement districts, most of which provided at least water and fire protection. The organized municipalities also faced problems, with small, financially weak areas finding it difficult to provide services and some municipalities suffering from sprawl and poor land use. The locally recognized need for a joint approach to the provision of services in the Greater Vancouver area had already prompted the establishment of a number of regional special purpose agencies for such matters as drainage, water, health, planning, and parks.[3]

---

[2] The figures are from D. W. Barnes, "The System of Regional Districts in British Columbia," in Advisory Commission on Intergovernmental Relations, *A Look to the North: Canadian Regional Experience*, Washington, DC, 1974, p. 110.

[3] On this early history see Patrick Smith, "Regional Governance in British Columbia," *Planning and Administration,* Autumn 1986, pp. 7-20, and H. Peter Oberlander and Patrick Smith, "Governing Metropolitan Vancouver," in Donald Rothblatt and Andrew Sancton, (eds.), *Metropolitan Governance: American/Canadian Intergovernmental Perspectives*, Berkeley, University of California Press, 1993, pp. 329-374.

Creation of Regional Districts

The British Columbia government's response was to provide for the creation of regional districts that could administer functions over wide areas, including unincorporated territory. In marked contrast to the imposition of reforms that will be evident in the experiences of a number of other provinces, the government used a strategy of "gentle imposition" to create structures capable of becoming significant regional governments, especially in the Vancouver and Victoria urban areas.[4] It did so by not assigning any functions to these new districts initially.[5]

There are now 27 regional districts, covering all of British Columbia except for the Stikine Region in the far north-west corner, which is administered by the province. They vary greatly in area and population, from the 2.4 million in Greater/Metro Vancouver to about 1500 in the Central Coast (and just over 600 in the Stikine). Their key features include the following:

> ➤ Each district is governed by a board of directors made up of councillors appointed by and from the councils of incorporated municipalities within its boundaries and representatives elected from the population of the unorganized electoral areas. Differences in the numbers represented by the board members are reflected in a weighted voting system that applies for budgetary matters and when decisions are being made about the provision of services to particular areas within a district. Only representatives from the affected areas vote in these latter instances.

> ➤ The province has mandated very few functions for the regional districts. They act on behalf of municipalities in dealings with the Municipal Finance Authority, from whom all municipalities (except Vancouver) must obtain their long term borrowing. They are responsible for preparing comprehensive plans for managing solid waste and for emergency planning. They also finance the local share of the capital costs of new hospitals.

---

[4] Paul Tennant and David Zirnhelt, "Metropolitan Government in Vancouver: the strategy of gentle imposition," *Canadian Public Administration*, Spring 1973, pp. 124-138.

[5] Robert L. Bish, "Evolutionary Alternatives for Metropolitan Areas: The Capital Region of British Columbia," *Canadian Journal of Regional Science*, Special Issue, Spring 2000, p. 75.

- The 1995 *Growth Strategies Act* authorizes the districts to undertake regional planning on a voluntary basis. Ten of them have developed/adopted regional growth strategies.[6]
- The districts also provide a wide range of other services, some across the region, and others to the rural (unincorporated) areas, where the regional district serves as the local government, and still others to two or more member municipalities.
- The regional districts do not levy taxes. They send to each municipality a separate requisition for each service, which includes the appropriate share of the administrative costs – and the municipality must pay.[7] In the case of services provided to unincorporated areas, the requisition goes to the province, which in turn collects property taxes from inhabitants of those areas. In 2011, British Columbia added a small Towns of Tomorrow grant/fund of over $17 million for rural/small town infrastructure.

Assessing the Regional Districts

While the Greater Vancouver Regional District (GVRD) has received most of the attention, the districts have arguably played a more important role in the less populated areas of the province, by providing a flexible structure for addressing servicing needs in unorganized areas and across municipal boundaries. Existing municipalities continue under the district structure, thereby contributing to a sense of community, allowing for diversity within the regional area, and helping to ensure accessibility and responsiveness in the municipal system.[8] At the same time, the services provided by the regional districts promote the common interests of area municipalities, and the fact that these regional services have been assigned by the area municipalities means that they are determining their common interests rather than having this definition imposed from above.

However, there are longstanding and growing concerns about the governing structure of the regional districts, especially the indirect

---

[6] Information accessed June 13, 2011 from the Ministry of Community, Sport and Cultural Development website at www.cscd.gov.bc.ca/lgd/planning/growth_strategies.htm, and information provided by Ministry staff, June 28, 2011.

[7] Allan O'Brien, *Municipal Consolidation in Canada and its Alternatives*, Toronto, ICURR Press, May 1993, p. 53.

[8] This point and the subsequent ones in this paragraph are based on Lionel D. Feldman Consulting Ltd. and the Institute of Local Government, Queen's University, *Evaluation of Alternative Structures and a Proposal for Local Governance in the Edmonton Region*, January 1980, especially pp. 37-42.

election of a portion of board members. A Regional District Review Committee set up in 1977 found insufficient efforts by the districts to explain their responsibilities and encourage public involvement and public concerns that the districts were inaccessible and secretive.[9] Smith has expressed concern about the extra responsibilities being given to the regional districts, such as the shift of public transit from the province to the Greater Vancouver area, effective April 1, 1999, with the creation of what has become known as Translink – though here, the province has since moved to regain greater control over the regional transportation entity.[10] He and Stewart conclude[11] that a municipal accountability crisis is looming, in part because of the way that the regional boards are chosen, and they call for direct election of a Greater Vancouver authority to replace the GVRD. There is little indication that such change is pending.

Artibise also believes that reform of the GVRD is necessary. He argues that its mandate is too limited, since it is delegated to the district by member municipalities and "changes with the fortunes of the regional interest at the local ballot box."[12] Because all of the board members are part time regional politicians, no one speaks out forcefully and consistently for the region and, as a result, the staff of the GVRD have too much influence. Artibise also points to what he terms a complex and confusing system of weighted voting. On the other hand, Bish concludes that the present governing arrangements are beneficial in that they do not engender competition and rivalry between elected councillors at the local and regional levels. This problem was very much in evidence in Ontario when it introduced directly elected upper tier councils within a number of its regional government systems. He also points out that only a small percentage of services are provided across the whole area of a district. As

---

[9] Regional District Review Committee, *Report of the Committee*, Victoria, Ministry of Municipal Affairs and Housing, 1978.

[10] For a brief discussion on accountability concerns re these more recent Translink changes, see P. Smith, "British Columbia Changes Metro Vancouver's Transportation Governance: A Re-Examination of Peter Self's Dilemma Thesis: Efficiency vs. Accountability?" in *Local Matters*, vol. 2, Auckland, NZ, Institute of Public Policy, Local Government Centre, April 2008, pp. 2-5.

[11] Patrick J. Smith and Kennedy Stewart, *Making Accountability Work in British Columbia*, Report for the Ministry of Municipal Affairs and Housing, June 1998.

[12] Alan F. J. Artibise, *Regional Governance Without Regional Government*, background report prepared for the Regional Municipality of Ottawa-Carleton, April 1998, p. 23.

a result, it is not inappropriate to have a structure that gives priority to local citizens' interests rather than some concept of a regional interest.[13]

The regional district model, now more than 45 years old, is the most enduring of the forms of restructuring introduced in Canada. If it is to continue its successful run, it must find a way to address the demands for a more accountable governing structure – at least in the major metropolitan settings – without introducing the conflicts that typically arise when upper tier councils are directly elected. That may explain some of British Columbia's reticence to so act – though accountability concerns also have promoted broader amalgamation ideas as well.[14]

The Amalgamation Option

Before leaving British Columbia, it should be noted that some municipal restructuring has resulted from local initiatives. Some 35 municipalities were the subject of a substantial municipal restructuring between 1985 and 2000, including the amalgamation of the districts of Abbotsford and Matsqui to form the City of Abbotsford in 1995.[15] The tradition that amalgamations are not provincially imposed but must have the agreement of the municipalities to be merged has been codified in legislation passed in 2003 (the *Community Charter*, discussed in Chapter 6). In February 2008, the province did intervene in a Vancouver Island regional district (Comox-Strathcona). It had some history of component parts not getting along. Despite being relatively small – just over 100 000 in population – the province stepped in and split the RD into two new Regional Districts: Comox Valley Regional District (approximately 60 000 population with three municipalities and three electoral areas) and Strathcona Regional District (an amalgam of five municipalities and four electoral areas, population 42 000).[16]

---

[13] Robert L. Bish, *Accommodating Multiple Boundaries for Local Services: British Columbia's Local Governance System*, paper presented at Indiana University, Bloomington, October 21, 2002, p. 16.

[14] On this, see, for example, Kennedy Stewart, "Inaction Costs: Understanding Metropolitan Governmental System Reform Dynamics in Toronto," *Canadian Political Science Review*, vol.2, #1, Spring 2008, pp. 16-34.

[15] For an analysis of this amalgamation and four others, see Igor Vojnovic, *Municipal Consolidation in the 1990s: An Analysis of Five Canadian Municipalities*, Toronto, ICURR Press, 1997.

[16] From a Ministry of Community, Sport and Cultural Development, BC, Local Government Department communication with authors, June 30, 2011.

Alberta

The Alberta government has taken an approach similar to that of British Columbia, leaving restructuring largely to the decision of the municipalities. The rapid population increase that accompanied the development of the petroleum industry in the postwar period led to a number of changes in municipal boundaries in the Calgary and Edmonton areas. These are discussed first. The province began to encourage the notion of amalgamation more actively in the mid-1990s, but the choice was still left to the local level, and few changes resulted. Local needs have been addressed mainly by joint servicing arrangements and intermunicipal collaboration. Municipal governments were given broader and more flexible governing powers through pioneering Alberta municipal legislation discussed in Chapter 6.

Annexations and Amalgamations

A Royal Commission recommended in 1956 that the boundaries of Edmonton and Calgary be enlarged to encompass their full metropolitan areas,[17] but no action was taken on this proposal. Instead, there were frequent annexations of adjacent territory, usually at the initiative of landowners and developers wishing an extension on services. But when the Alberta government (between 1974 and 1976) unilaterally imposed restricted development areas around both cities as future utilities and transportation corridors, these were viewed with alarm as barriers to future city expansion. Edmonton responded with a March 1979 application for a massive annexation, including the City of St. Albert and the entire County of Strathcona. After complex and expensive hearings that lasted almost a year, the outcome was a compromise solution in which Edmonton got some land from Strathcona for expansion, but not St. Albert and its considerable assessment.

Attempting to reform municipal structures this way presents a number of problems besides the extensive cost involved. It is at best a piecemeal, fragmented approach that does not consider the overall needs of the entire urban area, but instead focuses on particular territories affected by proposed annexations, and in an invariably confrontational atmosphere. Moreover, the relentless pace of urban sprawl makes

---

[17] *Report of the Royal Commission on the Metropolitan Development of Calgary and Edmonton* (McNally Commission), Edmonton, Queen's Printer, 1956.

frequent annexations necessary in an attempt to keep up. "For the past 20 years Edmonton has been involved in never-ending annexation and amalgamation battles with its surrounding municipalities."[18] In spite of its efforts, Edmonton finds itself ringed by four cities and four urbanizing rural municipalities, whereas Calgary's aggressive annexation efforts have extended its boundaries to encompass over 90% of its regional population.[19] That pattern is confirmed by the 2006 census data, which shows that the City of Calgary contains 91.5% of the population of the Calgary census metropolitan area, whereas Edmonton contains only 70.6% of the population of its CMA.[20]

Amalgamation as an option for other municipalities in Alberta gained attention in the mid-1990s, when the province launched an initiative that encouraged municipalities to assess their viability.[21] Those not measuring up well could, with provincial assistance, dissolve or amalgamate with other municipalities. The municipal response was "underwhelming," with a couple of amalgamations in the 1990s (involving the Town of Cold Lake and the City of Drumheller) and with three villages reverting to hamlet status between 2000 and 2002. A small number of others – such as the Town, and County, of Two Hills and the Villages of Derwent, Myrnam, and Willingdon – were considered more recently (in 2008).[22]

Intermunicipal Agencies and Agreements

Reliance on joint service agreements and agencies has long been a prominent feature of Alberta local government. The services most commonly subject to these joint arrangements are fire protection, ambulance service, recreation facilities, garbage disposal, libraries,

---

[18] Susan McFarlane, *Building Better Cities: Regional Cooperation in Western Canada*, Canada West Foundation, October 2001, p. 13.

[19] James Lightbody, *The Comparative Costs of Governing Alberta's Metropolitan Areas*, Edmonton, Western Centre for Economic Research, Information Bulletin Number 48, January 1998, p. 4.

[20] Statistics Canada website, *Portrait of the Canadian Population in 2006: Findings*, accessed June 1, 2007 at www.statcan.ca/english/census06/analysis/popdwell/index.cfm.

[21] The description of this initiative is based on Edward C. LeSage Jr., "Municipal Reform in Alberta," in Joseph Garcea and Edward LeSage (eds.), *Municipal Reforms in Canada*, Toronto, Oxford University Press, 2005, p. 73.

[22] See Alberta Municipal Affairs, *Two Hills Regional Partnership: Governance Review-Final Report* at www.townoftwohills.com/updates/gov, (accessed June 7, 2011).

family and community support services, airports, roads, and disaster services.[23] Examples of intermunicipal agencies include the following:

- Regional planning commissions were established to prepare regional plans to which the plans of all member municipalities were expected to conform.[24] Beginning with the Edmonton area in 1950, 10 of these commissions were created, covering 70% of the area of the province. Governed by elected representatives from the councils of the member municipalities, they were abolished in 1994, supposedly as an economy measure.
- Regional services commissions, first authorized in 1981 to provide limited (utility) services to more than one municipality, were given expanded responsibilities in 1994 – including airports, emergency response, and intermunicipal planning administration, and to serve as more general vehicles for municipal cooperation. In response, the number of these commissions has jumped from 32 in 2001 to 52 in 2004. By mid-2011, this had grown to 66.[25] These are "made up of two or more municipalities to provide any utility or service they are authorized to provide." They are "an alternative corporate structure for municipalities to provide joint services." They have "natural person powers." As one form of governance to provide regional services historically (in Alberta) they have been "used by municipalities to provide utility, planning, emergency and assessment services on a regional basis."[26]
- Alberta established 17 regional health authorities (RHAs) in 1994, responsible for hospitals, continuing care, community health services, and public health programs. The 17 health regions were amalgamated into 7, effective April 2003, with mental health services being integrated into their operations.
- There were also 18 regional Child and Family Services Authorities established in 1994. Of all Western provinces, Alberta has gone the farthest in devolving decision making to

---

[23] O'Brien, *Municipal Consolidation*, p. 60.

[24] *Ibid.*

[25] LeSage, *Municipal Reform in Alberta*, p. 74. Also information from Municipal Services Branch, Local Government Services, Alberta Municipal Affairs, June 15 and June 21, 2011 and from www.municipalaffairs.alberta.ca/mc_municipal_profiles.cfm, accessed June 18, 2011.

[26] From information provided by Municipal Services Branch, Local Government Services, Alberta Municipal Affairs, June 15 and June 21, 2011.

regional authorities, raising questions about the possible overlap of responsibilities between local governments and these regional authorities and about the extent to which these authorities are becoming political actors in their own right.[27]

In addition, there have been a number of initiatives over the years designed to provide some form of broader, regional jurisdiction for larger urban areas. The Alberta Capital Region Forum was created in March 1995, comprising 14 municipalities and relying on voluntary funding, mostly from Edmonton. One analysis found that during its short life the Forum was unsuccessful either in land use planning or in developing any coherent regional economic strategy.[28] It was replaced at the beginning of 1999 by the Alberta Capital Regional Alliance (ACRA), comprising the City of Edmonton and 19 surrounding communities. It was governed by a board mainly comprising the mayors and reeves of member municipalities (now 23 in number). A February 2002 report from the Alberta Capital Regional Governance Review set up by the Minister of Municipal Affairs recommended various ways of improving cooperation, but the province rejected the Review's call for a new regional body to which all area municipalities would have to belong. In 2006, Edmonton voted to leave ACRA, citing its unanimity requirements as too large an obstacle to regional decision making. ACRA was disbanded but when regional tensions continued, the province stepped in, threatening intervention unless the now 25 municipalities and counties could agree on more coherent regional planning. The premier also created a new regional board. In March 2009, a regional plan was approved in a 19 to 6 vote.[29] Lightbody has suggested that this "regional plan" agreement was primarily to allow local governments to access provincial infrastructure dollars.

Opinions vary on how much the Alliance accomplished through the voluntary cooperation of its member municipalities. The fact that Edmonton contains 70% of the population of the region makes the other municipalities suspicious of most efforts to collaborate, while a frustrated Edmonton has increasingly pushed for a revenue sharing plan and more action on regional issues. Lightbody is quite unimpressed with the

---

[27] Evan Jones and Susan McFarlane, *Regional Approaches to Services in the West: Health, Social Services and Education*, Canada West Foundation, February 2002, p. 10.

[28] *Ibid.*, p. 14.

[29] See, for example, CBC News, Edmonton, "Capital Region Mayors Approve Growth Plan," March 19, 2009. An additional nine "summer villages" are also covered by such decisions but are not formally members of the CRB.

Alliance, noting that it provides no services, has neither dues nor fees, has had minimal policy activity, and depends on the unilateral actions of individual members to implement decisions, should it make any.[30] LeSage, on the other hand, finds that the Alliance completed a regional transportation master plan, a regional emergency response plan (with federal and provincial financial support), and a regional GIS (geographic information system).[31] In the end, it took provincial intervention, creating a new regional board to get majority support in the region for growth planning – an outcome agreed upon in 2009, though Lightbody remains skeptical about its actual capacity to plan regionally versus to provide a platform for municipalities to get provincial funds for basic services such as roads and transit. Having a "regional plan" was a prerequisite for such provincial spending in the region.[32]

There is also a Calgary Regional Partnership (CRP) representing 18 municipalities, including Calgary, and promoting improved service delivery through intermunicipal initiatives. While generally modelled on the Alberta Capital Regional Alliance, the Calgary organization sought to define voting decision rules to promote collective action, rather than relying on the consensus approach which caused the Edmonton Alliance to fail.[33] There are similar regional partnerships in other areas of the province, including Red Deer (where the focus is mainly on economic development). The CRP also agreed on a new *Calgary Metropolitan Plan* (in June 2009) with a 15 to 3 vote and emphasis on three key goals: regional transit, regional water and waste water servicing, and regional GIS/Economic Development.[34] In 2010, the Calgary Region Economic Partnership – an operational branch of the CRP – produced a 10 Year Regional Economic Development Strategy which is in the early stages of implementation.

---

[30] James Lightbody, *City Politics, Canada*, Peterborough, Broadview Press, 2006, p. 443.

[31] LeSage, *Municipal Reform in Alberta*, p. 74.

[32] We are grateful to Dr. Lightbody, University of Alberta, for sharing his assessment on the most recent Edmonton area plan (June 2011).

[33] LeSage, *Municipal Reform in Alberta*, p. 75.

[34] See www.calgaryregion.ca/crp/projects/projects/calgary-metropolitan-plan.aspx, (accessed April 1, 2011). On international aspects of this see Patrick Smith and Kennedy Stewart, *Global Calgary: A Globalist Strategy for the City of Calgary*, Ottawa, Canadian Policy Research Network, April 2006, 35 pp.

Saskatchewan

Most municipal restructuring has been limited in Saskatchewan, mainly taking the form of small scale annexations. According to O'Brien, as urban places grew, they were usually able to annex land required for urban development, partly because rural municipalities didn't favour suburban fringe development within their boundaries. Writing in 1993,[35] he notes that there had been 315 annexation and incorporation initiatives in Saskatchewan since 1979, of which 280 were approved, and that 12 of these were annexations to Regina and Saskatoon. As a result, these two single tier cities cover, respectively, (according to census data from 2006) 92% and 87% of their census metropolitan areas.[36] Intermunicipal agreements have also been common in Saskatchewan, especially for fire protection and road maintenance, and single purpose intermunicipal agencies are used for economic development, planning, and water.

The provincial government introduced legislation in 1996 to provide for service district boards modelled on British Columbia's regional districts and the regional service commissions in Alberta. No action was taken in the face of strong local opposition. However, there is extensive regionalization in the province, including health boards, regional tourism boards, and regional agriculture and development boards.[37]

The provincial government established a *Task Force on Municipal Legislative Renewal* in 1998, and its interim report contemplated a dramatic reduction in the number of municipalities from 1000 to about 125. The local response was very negative, highlighted by referendums held in 145 rural municipalities in which 98% of participants opposed forced amalgamations.[38] No action was taken on the recommendations, but the Municipal–Provincial Roundtable and Northern Municipal Roundtable were formed in 2000, and their deliberations identified a number of financial and legislative impediments to voluntary municipal restructuring in Saskatchewan, which were removed in legislation passed in 2001.[39] Garcea, who had a front row seat as Chair of the Task Force, wryly observes that the new legislation for voluntary amalgamation

---

[35] O'Brien, *Municipal Consolidation*, p. 58.

[36] Statistics Canada, *Portrait of the Canadian Population in 2006*.

[37] McFarlane, *Building Better Cities*, pp. 12-13.

[38] Saskatchewan Association of Rural Municipalities, *News Release*, May 2, 2000.

[39] McFarlane, *Building Better Cities*, p. 12.

"ended up serving a symbolic rather than a practical function."[40] The *Cities Act* (2002) allowed natural person powers and "areas of jurisdiction" for cities voting to be so covered by the new Act. It provided for no new taxation powers.

Saskatchewan continues to function with a large number of very small municipalities. The northern half of the province faces particularly pressing problems.[41] It contains approximately 60 communities, some under municipal governments and some under First Nations governments. There is a need for improved municipal infrastructure and community services but northern municipalities lack the financial resources and professional staff to respond effectively. They are covered by a separate Act, the *Northern Municipalities Act*. As of January 2006, Saskatchewan added the *Municipalities Act*, covering smaller urban and rural municipalities. While allowing for traditional differences between urban and rural settings, the Act is also "wherever practical and possible" to apply equally to both urban and rural municipal authorities.

The most recent innovation in Saskatchewan is around funding: the province has initiated a municipal revenue sharing formula designed to transfer to municipalities the equivalent of 1% of the province's sales tax. In 2011, the first year it was fully implemented, this represented a transfer of $216.8 million, up 70% from 2007.[42] Meanwhile, the provincial government has taken control over setting a uniform property tax mill rate across the province.[43]

Manitoba

A 1964 Royal Commission report proposed comprehensive reform that would divide Manitoba into 11 administrative regions, each governed by

---

[40] Joseph Garcea, "Saskatchewan's Municipal Reform Agenda," in Garcea and LeSage (eds.), *Municipal Reform in Canada*, p. 87.

[41] Task Force on Municipal Legislative Renewal, *Municipal Governance for Saskatchewan in the 21st Century*, Summary of Final Report, August 2000, p. 64.

[42] See Ministry of Municipal Affairs, News Release, June 3, 2011, "Province's Revenue Sharing Approach Gains National Interest."
http://www.gov.sk.ca/news?newsId=d22a9a19-da04-4115-9d2c-6262de7b5b1b.

[43] We are grateful to Dr. Joe Garcea, University of Saskatchewan, for sharing his assessment of recent changes and the new funding formula (June 2011).

councillors from municipalities within the region, and would amalgamate the existing 106 municipalities in Manitoba to form 40 or 50 units.[44] Faced with strong opposition, the province moved instead to formalize a system of single purpose districts for providing services on an intermunicipal basis.[45] Examples included planning districts, conservation districts, regional development corporations, community round tables, weed control districts, and veterinary services districts.

The municipal structure outside of Winnipeg was reviewed again in the early 1990s, through a process of public consultations conducted by a panel established by the Minister of Rural Development. A major issue identified was the need for better coordination in service delivery, given that there were nearly 300 special purpose bodies along with over 200 municipalities beyond the boundaries of Winnipeg – most of them very small and financially weak.[46] However, with the power base of the ruling Conservative party largely in rural Manitoba, the province had every reason to "tread lightly."[47] Accordingly, the panel's report avoided any suggestion that amalgamations would be mandated, leaving the desired coordination of services to be achieved through local initiative. As in many such settings, local "self-reform" was often not forthcoming under such arrangements.

Restructuring in the Winnipeg Area

Municipal reform activities in Manitoba have focused on Winnipeg, which, as the provincial capital and the centre for over half of the population and two-thirds of the economic activity, understandably dominates the local government scene. Population growth after the Second World War brought the usual urban problems. Expenditures soared, notably in education, while revenues were distributed unevenly and there were wide variations in property assessment. There was inadequate sewage disposal for the area and water rationing became common. A number of intermunicipal special purpose bodies operated in

---

[44] *Report, Manitoba Royal Commission on Local Government Organization and Finance* (Michener Report), Winnipeg, Queen's Printer, 1964.

[45] This section is based on O'Brien, *Municipal Consolidation*, p. 31.

[46] Province of Manitoba, *Final Report: Meeting the Challenges of Local Government*, 1995, pp. vi-vii.

[47] Christopher Leo and Mark Piel, "Municipal Reform in Manitoba," in Garcea and LeSage (eds.), *Municipal Reforms in Canada*, p. 109.

the Greater Winnipeg area and, while they enjoyed some success, their existence was seen as evidence of the need for area wide government.

A Greater Winnipeg Investigating Commission report in 1959 called for the establishment of a two tier system of metropolitan government. Apparently the Commission was strongly influenced by the Metropolitan Toronto system and had frequently consulted with its chair, Fred Gardiner.[48] However, the reform introduced by the province in 1960 was more modest than the Commission's recommendations and differed from Toronto in significant respects.

Metropolitan Winnipeg

The two tier system established in 1960 had 10 municipalities within the jurisdiction of the new Winnipeg metropolitan government and 9 more partly within and partly in the outlying "additional zone" over which Metro Winnipeg had planning authority. The metro government was given full authority over all planning, zoning, and issuing of permits as well as such operating functions as assessment, civil defence, flood protection, sewage disposal, and water (excluding local distribution). Many responsibilities that had previously been exercised by separate special purpose bodies were vested directly in the metro council.

To encourage an area wide perspective, the 10 members of the metro council were directly elected from pie shaped districts that included both central and suburban areas and they could not also hold local office. Most metro councillors were successful in taking a broader view, with more specific, parochial demands being directed at lower tier councils. But they were rather aggressive in their initiatives and insufficiently sensitive to the concerns of local councils. Adding to the problems was the extent of opposition to the new system. While some negative reaction had been expected, "[W]hat occurred instead was a virtual municipal insurrection, an assault on metro far exceeding anyone's expectations. During its ten year history, but especially in 1961–65, metro lived under a state of siege."[49] Attacks on the system subsided somewhat after 1965 when the premier reaffirmed his support for it. The election of an NDP government in 1969, however, led to a whole new approach to the governing of the Winnipeg area.

---

[48] T. Axworthy, "Winnipeg Unicity," in Advisory Commission on Intergovernmental Relations, *A Look to the North*, p. 90.

[49] Harold Kaplan, *Reform, Planning and City Politics: Montreal, Winnipeg, Toronto*, Toronto, University of Toronto Press, 1982, p. 554.

Winnipeg Unicity

As its name implies, Unicity replaced the two tier metro system with one enlarged city government. But much more than amalgamation of municipalities was involved, and the administrative centralization for efficiency in service delivery was to be offset by various provisions for political decentralization. In sharp contrast to most other reform initiatives, Unicity was not created with the objective of reducing governments or cutting costs; it was intended to increase the capacity of municipal government to control and shape urban development and to promote greater social and economic equality.[50]

The representative role of local government and the importance of citizen participation was a central feature of the new system, reflected in:

- The provision for an unusually large council of 50 members (plus the mayor), each elected from a separate ward.
- The establishment of 13 community committees, each covering a number of wards and consisting of the councillors from these wards. These committees were intended to maintain two way communications between Unicity and its residents and to have responsibility for preparing budgets for services with a local orientation (and variation).
- The election of resident advisory groups (RAGs) to advise and assist each community committee.

These arrangements were intended "to weaken the alliance between public officials and land-based business by promoting the formation of alternative governing coalitions."[51]

A second significant feature of the new system was the attempt to build in the elements of the parliamentary governing model, particularly in terms of a separate executive responsible for providing leadership and answering to the elected council. A key provision of this model, proposed in the White Paper but deleted from the legislation, was the stipulation that the mayor be chosen by and from the members of council. Through this process, mayors could provide leadership on council because of majority support. It was envisaged that executive committee members would be chosen the same way and, with the mayor as chair, this body would be akin to the cabinet in the parliamentary

---

[50] Andrew Sancton, "Why Unicity Matters: An Outsider's View," in Nancy Klos (ed.), *The State of Unicity – 25 Years Later*, Winnipeg, Institute of Urban Studies, 1998, p. 4.

[51] Paul G. Thomas, "Diagnosing the Health of Civic Democracy: 25 Years of Citizen Involvement with City Hall," in Klos, *The State of Unicity*, p. 47.

system. An important element of this system, of course, was the existence of organized political parties. Some form of party activity had been evident in Winnipeg since 1919, but it was hoped that a more formalized party system would evolve to complement the new structure.

Assessing Unicity

Unfortunately, the actual performance of Unicity has been rather disappointing – perhaps inevitably so, given the innovative and ambitious objectives that had been set for the system. A number of reviews and reforms, briefly summarized below, failed to overcome its shortcomings.

> - A Committee of Review appointed in 1975 laid much of the blame for Unicity's performance on the fact that the mayor was directly elected rather than chosen from council (as originally intended), thereby removing the focus of leadership and accountability central to the parliamentary model. This lack of political leadership was especially significant given the large size of the council and the potentially fragmented outlook inherent in election by ward. As a result, considerable attention was directed to the securing of public services for particular wards – often taking the form of a city/suburbs division, rather than the establishment of overall policies for the Winnipeg area. After reviewing the new system, Plunkett and Brownstone concluded that "city policy making has not been altered drastically, and that it has only been improved slightly from what it seems likely to have been if the former structure had remained unchanged."[52]
> - In June 1977 the Manitoba government adopted a number of amendments to the Unicity structure but, ironically, these changes did little to resolve the weaknesses identified and, in some cases, intensified them – notably with respect to the position of mayor. The council was reduced from 50 members to 29 and the number of community committees (12 since 1974) was reduced to 6 and their vague and limited powers were further reduced. They dealt only with libraries, parks and recreation, and some planning functions,[53] a reflection of the growing trend toward centralization in program design and service delivery. With greatly increased areas and populations of

---

[52] T. J. Plunkett and M. Brownstone, *Metropolitan Winnipeg: Politics and Reform of Local Government*, Berkeley, CA, University of California Press, 1983, p. 173.

[53] Feldman Consulting Ltd., *Evaluation of Alternative Structures*, p. 67.

about 100 000, the community committees and RAGs lost the close contact and familiarity with local issues which had been their main (and just about only) strength. Overall, the changes made in 1977 "essentially kept a weak-mayor political system, but strengthened the professional administration through centralizing power in their hands at the expense of the Community Committees and the Standing Committees."[54]

➤ A Conservative government replaced the NDP and legislated (in 1992) a reduction in the Unicity council from 29 to 15 members. This change was supposed to reduce parochialism and encourage the council to take a broader, city wide approach to planning. It was also expected to streamline and speed up the decision making process. But Gerecke and Reid argue that this change also meant that there were now only three members from the inner city, leaving the old City of Winnipeg as "nothing more than three wards on the rump of a suburban council."[55] Other changes in the 1992 legislation saw the community committees further reduced in number from six to five, and the RAGs abolished outright. The bold experiment in citizen participation launched in 1972 was all but gone 20 years later!

Governing the Winnipeg Region

Much urban development has been taking place beyond the Unicity boundaries in recent decades. Between 1971 and 1991, Unicity's population increased a modest 15.2%, while the population in the surrounding municipalities increased by 69.4%.[56] Between 1991 and 1996, the city's population growth was 0.3%, while municipalities bordering Winnipeg grew at a rate of more than 10% and even more than 20% in some instances.[57] Even so, the 2006 census found that the City of Winnipeg still contained 91% of the population of the Winnipeg CMA.

---

[54] Greg Selinger, "Urban Governance for the Twenty-First Century: What the Unicity Experience Tells Us," in Klos, *The State of Unicity*, p. 90.

[55] Kent Gerecke and Barton Reid, "The Failure of Urban Government: The Case of Winnipeg," in Henri Lustiger-Thaler (ed.), *Political Arrangements: Power and the City*, Montreal, Black Rose Books, 1992, p. 127.

[56] Institute of Urban Studies, University of Winnipeg, *Prairie Urban Report*, Issue No. 1, Vol. 1, May 1996.

[57] Richard Lennon and Christopher Leo, *Stopping the Sprawl: How Winnipeg Could Benefit from Metropolitan Growth Strategies for a Slow-Growth Region*, Canadian Centre for Policy Alternatives, January 2001, p. 9.

Efforts to address regional issues have not had much success. In 1989 the Manitoba government established what became known as the Capital Region Committee, comprising three provincial ministers and the heads of council for Winnipeg and 15 surrounding municipalities. Since each municipality was given one member on the committee, this meant that Winnipeg had the same representation as the other 15 municipalities that averaged 5000 in population. Moreover, most fringe municipalities had an incentive to build their tax revenues through low density urban development. Not surprisingly, the committee made little progress in tackling urban sprawl.[58]

Ten years later, a Capital Region Review Panel that had been set up to provide an avenue for better understanding between Winnipeg and its neighbours reported that some form of regional association was needed to address the growth and development occurring beyond the boundaries of Unicity.[59] A further review, by a Regional Planning Advisory Committee, recommended in 2003 that there be more regulation of metropolitan growth and intermunicipal sharing of services and tax revenues.[60] One assessment of the situation contrasts the revolutionary initiative that created Unicity with the approach of recent years, which has been "cautious almost to the point of invisibility."[61]

Table 4.1 Restructuring Highlights – Western Provinces	
British Columbia	Regional districts that allow flexibility and diversity and preserve a sense of community but raise concerns about accountability.
Alberta	Annexations, especially for the cities of Calgary and Edmonton. Regional boards to promote intermunicipal cooperation across the Calgary and Edmonton metropolitan areas. Various regional bodies re planning, hard services, social services.
Saskatchewan	Many small scale annexations, but major reforms rebuffed and still very large number of (mostly small) municipalities. Intermunicipal bodies for economic development, water, planning.
Manitoba	Two tier Metropolitan Winnipeg system in 1960s. Winnipeg Unicity provided both administrative centralization and political decentralization, including emphasis on citizen participation and an attempt to create a parliamentary governing model.

---

[58] Leo and Piel, *Municipal Reform in Manitoba*, p. 119.

[59] *Final Report of the Capital Region Review Panel* (Scarth Report), Winnipeg, Department of Intergovernmental Affairs, 1999.

[60] Regional Planning Advisory Committee, *A Partnership for the Future: Putting the Pieces Together in the Manitoba Capital Region* (Thomas Report), Winnipeg, Department of Intergovernmental Affairs, 2003.

[61] Leo and Piel, *Municipal Reform in Manitoba*, pp. 118-119. In the summer of 2011, Dr. Chris Leo kindly shared recent reflections on local governing in Winnipeg and Manitoba.

Ontario

The experiences in Ontario provide a marked contrast to those of Western Canada. Municipal restructuring began almost 60 years ago with the establishment of the Municipality of Metropolitan Toronto, continued with the creation of a series of two tier regional government systems in the 1960s and early 1970s, and then resumed with a vengeance over the recent past during which the number of municipalities was almost cut in half. Not only has the restructuring been much more widespread, but also it has been largely imposed or induced by the provincial government.

Municipality of Metropolitan Toronto

With the postwar "population explosion," the rapid growth of a number of municipalities surrounding the City of Toronto produced serious servicing difficulties including:

- Expanding the water supply and sewage treatment facilities (when only 6 of the 13 municipalities involved had direct access to Lake Ontario);
- Providing arterial roads for the increasing traffic volume;
- Integrating public transportation and the highway network;
- Building many new schools;
- Meeting increased welfare demands within the City of Toronto;
- Growing traffic congestion from the extent of commuting; and
- The difficulty and cost of borrowing, especially for the outlying municipalities that then had limited industrial assessment.

In response to these problems, a federated form of government embracing the City of Toronto and the 12 surrounding municipalities was introduced, effective January 1, 1953. As the lower tier or level in a two tier structure, these 13 municipalities retained their existing boundaries and a wide range of responsibilities. An upper tier unit, the Municipality of Metropolitan Toronto, was established with responsibility for such major functions as debenture borrowing, water supply and trunk mains, sewage treatment works and trunk sewers, and designated roads. There were also some responsibilities shared between the two tiers. With an indirectly elected metropolitan council (that is, composed of individuals elected initially to designated positions on the lower tier councils), the new structure was similar to Ontario's century old county system. The major differences were the inclusion of the city in the metropolitan system and the much stronger powers given to the upper tier council.

In its early years, Metropolitan Toronto was substantially successful in combating the servicing problems facing the member municipalities, particularly as regards sewers, water supply, education, and general financial stability. This success helped ease initial opposition from many localities on the provincially imposed metro system.[62] To a considerable extent, these early successes have been attributed to the forceful, skilled leadership of the first chair of the metro council, Fred Gardiner, who held this position from 1953 to 1961. But Colton notes that there were concerns even before Gardiner retired.[63] There was a massive expansion of housing, but mainly in the form of high rise apartment construction that was accompanied by an increasing concentration of power in the development industry. Toronto enjoyed a boom in downtown development but fears mounted about an excessive growth mentality and disruption of established neighbourhoods – as reflected in the activism of citizens and citizen groups in the 1960s. This activism was also reflected in a growing anti-expressway sentiment culminating in the "Stop Spadina" (expressway) movement.

Quite apart from these changing public attitudes, Kaplan emphasizes the significance of the indirect election of metro councillors, noting that they stood, succeeded, or failed largely on the basis of their records in their lower tier council, only referring to the metro level when it was politically expedient to blame it for not delivering enough for the local municipality in question.[64] With Gardiner astutely avoiding issues that would threaten local municipalities, councillors were largely indifferent to everything else and prepared to accept his leadership. But the limitations of this passive support became all too apparent when council turned to the more complex issues of the 1960s, especially under the less forceful chairs who succeeded Gardiner. Noting that metro's main successes were between 1953 and 1957, Kaplan contends that "in retrospect, the early burst of activity was the aberration and the subsequent prolonged retreat a more accurate expression of the system's character."[65]

---

[62] Kennedy Stewart, "Why Insulate New Institutions? Evaluating Pre- and Post-Change Support for Metropolitan Reform in Greater London and Toronto," in Eran Razin and Patrick Smith (eds.), *Metropolitan Governing: Canadian Cases, Comparative Lessons*, Jerusalem, Magnes Press, Hebrew University of Jerusalem, 2006, pp. 187-213.

[63] Timothy Colton, *Big Daddy*, Toronto, University of Toronto Press, 1980, pp. 177-178.

[64] Kaplan, *Reform, Planning and City Politics*, pp. 685-690.

[65] *Ibid.*, p. 694.

A Royal Commission review of Metro Toronto's first decade endorsed the new two tier system.[66] The main change was the merger of the original 13 municipalities at the lower tier into 6, effective January 1967. In addition, the metro council was increased to 32 members, with 20 of these coming from the 5 newly merged suburban municipalities in recognition of their much greater population growth over the decade. A few responsibilities, notably waste disposal and social assistance, were transferred from the lower tier to the upper, continuing a trend that had been evident throughout the 1950s. But as Kaplan observed, there was little in these reforms to revive Metro Toronto.[67] The suburban municipalities now enjoyed a majority position, but had no regional aspirations on which to use their power. They had received the necessary expansion of their basic services during the first decade. Now it was the City of Toronto that needed the upper tier more – to help finance the renewal of aging facilities. But Kaplan concludes that with a complacent suburban majority, the metro council was even less inclined to blaze new trails.

Major changes in the election of the metro council were introduced for the 1988 municipal elections. While the mayors of the 6 lower tier municipalities continued to serve as members, the remaining 28 were directly elected, and did not hold seats on the lower tier councils. The metro chair was henceforth to be chosen by council only from among the directly elected members. These changes appeared to reflect a belated concern by the Ontario government for the representative role of municipal government and its accountability and responsiveness.

By this time, the area of urban development that Metro Toronto had been established to embrace and to stimulate had long since expanded beyond its boundaries. Just as the population growth of the City of Toronto failed to keep pace with that of the suburban local municipalities within metro, so too did metro itself fall behind the rapid pace of growth of areas adjacent to it. It found itself "hemmed in" on all sides by four regional governments (discussed below) and by Lake Ontario. Until 1971 Metro Toronto had absorbed the bulk of the new population growth in this area – now known as the Greater Toronto Area (GTA) – but since

---

[66] *Report of the Royal Commission on Metropolitan Toronto* (H. Carl Goldenberg, Commissioner), Toronto, Queen's Printer, 1965. See also Anne Golden and Enid Slack, "Urban Governance reform in Toronto: A Preliminary Assessment of Changes Made in the Late 1990s," in Razin and Smith (eds.), *Metropolitan Governing,* pp. 29-74.

[67] Kaplan, *Reform, Planning and City Politics,* p. 697.

then its growth has dropped off sharply. In fact, metro's share of the population of the GTA had fallen from 77% in 1961 to 54% by 1991.[68]

Gradually, the view developed that a new governing body was needed for the GTA. A major impetus for this approach came from the 1996 "Golden Report," which proposed replacing metro and the four surrounding regional governments with a single, streamlined Greater Toronto Council and giving lower tier municipalities added powers and responsibilities to deliver a wider range of services.[69] This proposal was endorsed later that year by the *Who Does What* panel on provincial and local services headed by David Crombie. Thus, the stage seemed set for the abolition of the regional governments in the GTA including Metro Toronto.

Toronto Megacity

Given these developments, most were caught off guard by the province's announcement in late 1996 that all six lower tier municipalities and the metro level would be combined to form a new City of Toronto of some 2.4 million people, thereby creating a municipality more populous than five of Canada's provinces. If Manitoba, as discussed above, had been influenced by Metro Toronto in setting up its Metro Winnipeg structure in 1960, this time it appeared that Ontario drew inspiration from Winnipeg's Unicity in creating Toronto's Megacity (although the latter name did not endure, and even the term Unicity is passing out of usage).

The main rationale for this unexpected initiative seemed to be the savings supposedly generated by amalgamation. In addition, however, it may be that the Conservative government hoped and expected that submerging the old City of Toronto into a larger municipality where its elected representatives were outnumbered by members from the suburbs would rein in what the province saw as the free spending ways of the old city. In that regard, the motivation for amalgamation was mainly ideological – the imposition of the values of the ruling Conservatives upon the more left leaning council of the old City of Toronto.[70]

---

[68] Frances Frisken, "Planning and Servicing the Greater Toronto Area," in Rothblatt and Sancton (eds.), *Metropolitan Governance*, p. 157.

[69] Report of the GTA Task Force, *Greater Toronto* (Anne Golden, Chair), January 1996.

[70] For analysis of possible explanations of the Megacity decision, see Neil Thomlinson, "When Right is Wrong: Municipal Governance and Downloading in Toronto," in Mike Burke, Colin Mooers, and John Shields, *Restructuring and Resistance: Canadian Public Policy in an Age of Global Capitalism*, Halifax, Fernwood Publishing, 2000, pp. 226-260.

There was strong opposition to the creation of the Megacity, with a large majority voting against it in referenda held in all six of the lower tier municipalities. But the province pushed ahead and effective January 1, 1998, the area previously under a two tier metropolitan government system became one municipality, governed by a council of 57 members elected by ward (subsequently reduced to 44), plus the mayor elected at large. Perhaps the most striking thing about this reform – apart from the fact that there was no previous rationale for it, either in restructuring studies or in the Conservative party's past positions – is that it created a municipality with boundaries both too large and too small. Its massive size, at least in the Canadian context, presents major challenges for representation and local democracy. Yet its creation did nothing to address the need for an overall governing body for the GTA.

To respond to this latter need, the province established a Greater Toronto Services Board in January 1999. It had only one specific power, the control of GO Transit (the provincially established commuter train system that operated across the bottom of the GTA) and was governed by a board with members from every municipality in the GTA. The hope was that the Board might gradually improve coordination in growth and development, but many member municipalities opposed any expansion of its role. When the province resumed responsibility for GO Transit, the Board lost its main raison d'être, and was abolished at the end of 2001.

A Greater Toronto Transportation Authority (now known as Metrolinx) was created in 2006 to plan, finance, coordinate, and develop an integrated transportation network for an even larger area around Toronto known as the Greater Golden Horseshoe. On the surface, this agency is very similar to the Greater Toronto Services Board that preceded it, but whether its fate will be similar remains to be seen. What is clear is that after successive rounds of restructuring of Toronto area municipalities, we are no closer to a municipal structure that corresponds to the ever growing regional metropolitan area.

That has produced some of its own dynamics. In October 2010, Toronto Mayor Rob Ford led a rightist coalition to victory, defeating 39 other candidates for the new Megacity Toronto mayor.[71] Early in 2011, Mayor Ford posed the idea of an uploading of Toronto's Transit Commission responsibilities to the province – by transferring the TTC to the province's regional transportation agency, Metrolinx.[72] The imminent

---

[71] See www.toronto.ca/elections/results/results_2010.htm, (accessed April 1, 2011).

[72] See Adam Radwanski, "For both Ford and McGuinty, an Ontario-run TTC has its perks," *Globe and Mail,* January 25, 2011, and "Ford tried to upload costly TTC to Metrolinx," *National Post*, January 26, 2011.

provincial election (of October 2011) might have stimulated some provincial commitment but none was forthcoming. Nor does it seem likely now, given that the Liberals were reelected, albeit with reduced numbers.

The Other Regional Governments

The ongoing developments in the Toronto area are by no means the only municipal restructuring activities that occurred in Ontario. The original Metro Toronto was really the first of the regional governments and within a decade it had been transplanted to a dozen other areas. While Metro Toronto was seen as an ad hoc response to specific servicing problems, the broader regional government program developed, at least officially, from an overall government policy. That policy recognized the need to provide not only efficient delivery of services but also adequate access and effective representation of local views and concerns. It called for regional governments based on such criteria as community of interest, an adequate financial base, and sufficient size to generate economies of scale. The policy also proposed varied structural options including both two tier and one tier government and the direct or indirect election of the upper tier councillors in the former instance.[73]

Eleven regional governments were created between 1969 and 1974.[74] If we add the prototype, Metro Toronto, and the Restructured County of Oxford (described below), we had 13 regional governments in Ontario, containing two-thirds of its population. While the reform policy was potentially quite broad and imaginative, in practice the reforms introduced were all two tier systems closely resembling Metro Toronto. As such, they can best be described as a modification of the traditional county system in Ontario featuring:

- ➢ Regional boundaries that followed the boundaries of one or more counties with minor exceptions.
- ➢ Indirectly elected regional councils, but with increasing provision for direct election over the years.
- ➢ Costs for regional services apportioned to lower tier municipalities according to their share of total assessment.

---

[73] The Honourable John Robarts and the Honourable W. Darcy McKeough, *Design for Development Phase Two*, statements to the Legislature of Ontario, November 28 and December 2, 1968.

[74] These were Ottawa-Carleton, Niagara, York, Waterloo, Sudbury, Peel, Halton, Hamilton-Wentworth, Durham, Haldimand-Norfolk, and Muskoka.

- More powers than traditional county governments, including welfare, roads, water supply, sewage disposal, planning, and capital borrowing.
- Lower tier municipalities formed by the merger of existing municipalities and including any cities or separated towns.

As the unpopularity and political cost of the regional reforms became increasingly apparent, the government announced that it was winding up the program, which, it claimed, had served its purpose. In its place, a County Restructuring Program was announced early in 1974, but very little action was taken on the local studies carried out under this program. Ironically, the one restructured county in Ontario, Oxford County, was created prior to this program being announced. County government reform resurfaced at the end of the 1980s, with several provincial reports calling for restructuring based on the amalgamation of lower tier units and the expansion of county powers. As with the program 15 years earlier, virtually no action was taken on the studies carried out.

New Wave of Restructuring

By the 1990s, attention was shifting away from structural changes to process improvements. The Ontario government was increasingly focused on matters of function (disentanglement) and finance (deficit reduction). No new regional governments had been established for more than 20 years, and it began to look as if major municipal restructuring activities were a thing of the past. But then June 1995 brought the election of the Conservatives, led by Mike Harris – and the municipal world was in for a shock.

Within a few months of taking office, the Conservatives introduced provisions (in the *Savings and Restructuring Act*) that they claimed were intended to make it easier for municipalities to implement annexations and amalgamations. These provisions laid out a two pronged approach to reform, designed in a way that put enormous pressure on municipalities to act. Reform could be achieved by reaching local agreement – if the change was supported by a majority of the affected municipalities containing a majority of the population and, where applicable, a majority of the members of the upper tier council as well. If no local agreement could be reached, however, and if even only one municipality requested, the minister could appoint a commission with total authority to determine the new structure for the municipal area defined by the minister.

Two dramatic events added significantly to the pressure for change. When the province forced through the amalgamations in Toronto, most small municipalities understandably wondered what chance they had to resist if the wishes of such a large population area were ignored. Events in Kent County were even more threatening. A commission was appointed that led to the amalgamation of all municipalities within the county, the county government, and the separate City of Chatham – against the wishes of 22 of the 23 municipalities affected! The message for municipalities in the rest of the province was that there was no telling what might happen if a commission was appointed. Better to make changes yourself, however unpalatable, than to have more drastic changes imposed upon you.

The high pressure campaign pursued by the province was quite effective in achieving the substantial pace of restructuring it desired. Following the reelection of the Conservative government, the pace of municipal restructuring increased even more – this time with particular focus on a number of the regional government areas that had not been covered by the *Savings and Restructuring Act*. The province appointed Special Advisors who were given 60 days to consult and prepare final reports for restructuring in Ottawa-Carleton, Hamilton-Wentworth, Sudbury, and Haldimand-Norfolk. In all but the last instance, the reports led to the establishment of one amalgamated city replacing both existing upper and lower tier units. A modified version of this approach was introduced in Haldimand-Norfolk, with one amalgamated city covering Haldimand and a second one covering Norfolk. A number of other amalgamations were also introduced prior to the November 2000 municipal elections, one of the most dramatic being the creation of the City of Kawartha Lakes through the amalgamation of all municipalities within the former Victoria County, following the recommendations of a provincially appointed Special Advisor.

In early 2001, the province let it be known that it would proceed with amalgamations in the future only on the basis of strong local support. Queen's Park sources were quoted as saying that major savings expected from amalgamation had failed to materialize, that implementation costs had been a drain on the provincial budget, and that the political costs of forced amalgamation were too high.[75] By this time, however, the number of municipalities was down to 446 (it is now 444),[76] almost 100 fewer than the 539 that existed in Ontario at Confederation.

---

[75] See James Rusk, "Province plans to stop forcing cities to merge," *Globe and Mail*, February 2001.

[76] Ministry of Municipal Affairs and Housing, Province of Ontario, *List of Ontario Municipalities,* at www.mah.gov.on.ca/page1591.aspx (accessed May 24, 2011).

No clear explanation has ever been offered for the aggressive program of municipal amalgamations pursued by the Conservatives in the second half of the 1990s. Siegel and Hollick suggest that the province felt that municipalities would be better able to handle the additional services being downloaded to them (as a result of the *Who Does What* exercise, discussed in Chapter 6) and the reduction in provincial transfer payments, if they were amalgamated.[77]

The Ontario government never provided policy guidelines for municipal restructuring, along the lines of the *Design for Development* policy that applied to the earlier regional government reforms. It did offer restructuring principles, but rather than explaining how a new system should be designed, these principles focused on what the outcome of restructuring should be – in the form of less government, fewer municipal politicians, lower taxes, less bureaucracy, and more efficient service delivery. The emphasis of these principles made it sound as though "one consolidation is as good as another."[78] However, they placed amalgamation "within the government's neoconservative agenda as reflected in the *Common Sense Revolution*."[79] This ideological explanation is reflected in other Harris legislation like the *Fewer Politicians Act* (1996).[80] In addition, the pursuit of lower taxes and greater efficiency, though seldom mentioned explicitly, "fits in well with concerns about globalization and the need to make Ontario more competitive in the international environment."[81]

Since the October 2003 election of Liberal Premier Dalton McGuinty, there has been a somewhat different focus – with Greenbelt legislation effective since February 2005. This enables creation of a

---

[77] Thomas R. Hollick and David Siegel, *Evolution, Revolution, Amalgamation: Restructuring in Three Ontario Municipalities*, London, University of Western Ontario, Local Government Case Studies No. 10, 2001, p. 29.

[78] *Ibid.*, p. 97.

[79] Ajay Sharma, *The Paradox of Amalgamation: An Analysis of Municipal Restructuring Practices in Ontario*, paper presented to the Canadian Political Science Association, Annual Conference, Saskatoon, May 30-June 1, 2007, p. 15.

[80] See Thomas Maidwell, "Does Size Matter? Has the Reduction in Its Size Lessened the Legislative Assembly of Ontario's Ability to Hold the Executive to Account?" Canadian Political Science Association paper, May 2011, for an analysis of the effects of such efforts.

[81] David Siegel, "Municipal Reform in Ontario," in Garcea and LeSage, *Municipal Reform in Canada*, p. 129. Dr. David Siegel, Brock University, and Dr. Caroline Andrew, University of Ottawa, both offered collegial insights on Ontario cases. See also C. Andrew, "Evaluating Municipal Reform in Ottawa-Gatineau: Building for a More Metropolitan Future," in Razin and Smith (eds.), *Metropolitan Governing*, pp. 75-120.

greenbelt plan to protect 1.8 million acres of countryside, preserve farmland, limit development across the Greater Golden Horseshoe of Ontario, and allow area municipalities to add to the protected areas.[82] For smaller, rural municipalities, Ontario also added a *Municipal–Rural Infrastructure Fund Agreement* (2004-2011).[83] Given the reelection of the McGuinty government in October 2011, this shift away from major municipal restructuring initiatives is likely to continue.

Quebec

Municipal restructuring efforts in Quebec have proceeded on several fronts, some more successfully than others. There have been repeated efforts to promote municipal amalgamations, culminating in much activity in the past decade. A network of upper tier municipalities has been introduced across the province in place of the old county governments. In addition, two tier systems have been established, merged, and then re-created (after a fashion) in some of the largest urban areas. Merged municipalities have demerged again. Overall, the restructuring story in Quebec is one of great variety and complexity.

Early Amalgamation Efforts

The 1960 election of the Liberals led by Jean Lesage, and the launching of the "Quiet Revolution," ushered in a series of reforms aimed at modernizing Quebec and its institutions. At that time, over 90% of Quebec's 1600 municipalities had less than 5000 population and nearly 50% had less than 1000 population.[84] Successive governments attempted to promote amalgamations in various ways. A 1965 *Voluntary Amalgamation Act* allowed two or more municipalities to amalgamate following a council's resolution to that effect. Not surprisingly, this approach wasn't greeted enthusiastically, and the number of

---

[82] On the *Greenbelt Act* (2005) see www.mah.gov.on.ca/Page195.aspx.

[83] See *Agreement,* November 2004 (and as amended, November 2006) at http://comrif.ca/eic/site/comrif-fimrco.nsf/eng/h_00001.html (accessed April 30, 2011).

[84] Jean Godin, "Local Government Reform in the Province of Quebec," in Advisory Committee on Intergovernmental Relations, *A Look to the North: Canadian Regional Experience*, Washington, DC, 1974, p. 50.

municipalities was reduced by less than 100 between 1965 and 1971. Legislation in 1971 gave the Minister of Municipal Affairs more power to force amalgamations, but this power was little used because of local opposition and because (as will be discussed) the province was by then preoccupied with metropolitan reforms. The number of municipalities was only reduced by 84 between 1971 and 1975.[85] The next couple decades saw only a limited number of voluntary amalgamations (and a few forced ones).

Regional County Municipalities

Another restructuring initiative was the 1979 *Land Use Planning and Development Act*, which established a network of 95 new upper tier units called regional county municipalities (RCMs). These new units replaced all the former 72 county municipalities, which had consisted entirely of rural units and exercised very limited responsibilities. They originally covered the province but a number of them have been disbanded in those urban areas in which enlarged cities have been created, as discussed below. Each RCM had to adopt a regional land use plan, and was also to take over the functions of the old counties, at least for the mainly rural areas in which counties had been operating.[86]

Each RCM is governed by a council composed only of the head of council (or representative) of each member municipality. In Sancton's view, the message was clear: "a new source of elected political authority was *not* being established." The RCMs were to represent existing municipalities acting together – nothing more. They are less genuine political institutions than flexible mechanisms for handling assigned responsibilities, rather like the regional districts of British Columbia.[87] Tomalty offers a similar assessment,[88] finding that the RCMs failed to become a political forum of action independent from local municipalities. Their ineffectiveness as regional planning agencies he attributes in part to the fact that they do not have responsibility for providing infrastructure, such as roads and sewage treatment, and thus have little

---

[85] O'Brien, *Municipal Consolidation*, p. 39.

[86] Louise Quesnel, "Political Control over Planning in Quebec," *International Journal of Urban and Regional Research* 14, 1990, pp. 25-48.

[87] Andrew Sancton, *Local Government Reorganization in Canada since 1975*, Toronto, ICURR Press, April 1991, pp. 16 and 23.

[88] Ray Tomalty, *The Compact Metropolis: Growth Management and Intensification in Vancouver, Toronto and Montreal*, Toronto, ICURR Press, 1997, p. 159.

leverage with local municipalities. He also cites the indirectly elected governing councils and elaborate voting arrangements as constraints.

Concerns about the adequacy of the representation arrangements have increased as the expenditures of the RCMs have grown, a pattern noted earlier with respect to the regional districts in British Columbia. Costs are shared by municipalities in proportion to their share of the area's taxable assessment. Cities with a healthy assessment base are, not surprisingly, critical of the fact that their voting strength on council is not nearly as large as their expenditure burden. In response, the province amended the legislation in 1987 to provide new options for voting arrangements within the RCMs.

Government of Major Urban Centres

As the main cities in Quebec grew and spilled over their boundaries, the by now familiar challenges arose. Annexations were used early and often in response to problems of urban sprawl in the Montreal area. The need for a vehicle to address intermunicipal problems in the area led to the establishment of the Montreal Metropolitan Corporation in 1959. It was authorized to exercise a number of important functions including sewers, water distribution, arterial roads, planning, mass transit, major parks, and all other services considered as intermunicipal by agreement among the municipalities or by decision of the Corporation. Its jurisdiction extended over the City of Montreal and 14 island municipalities and its governing body comprised 14 representatives from the city, 14 from the suburbs, and a chair appointed by the province. In large part because of vigorous opposition from Montreal's Mayor Jean Drapeau, the Corporation was never a major force in spite of its impressive terms of reference.

New Upper Tier Governments

In June 1969, the Union Nationale government announced plans for a new governing structure for the Montreal area (and for Quebec City and Hull as well). The Montreal Urban Community (MUC) came into existence on January 1, 1970. The new structure had a governing council made up of the mayor and councillors of the City of Montreal and one delegate from each of the other 29 municipalities under its jurisdiction. The city was also given 7 of the 12 seats on the powerful executive committee and provided the first chair in the person of Lucien Saulnier, who had been Mayor Jean Drapeau's chief lieutenant.

The MUC's initial priority was the unification of all police forces on the island[89] and it then moved on to such activities as subways and sewers. But its effectiveness was hampered by the city-suburb split and by the fact that while Montreal had a majority of the votes on council, a motion could only pass if supported by at least half of the suburban delegates present. The original legislation contemplated that internal boundary adjustments would be made, but any such changes would involve some merging of French speaking and English speaking populations – a task no politician wanted to tackle. As a result, the MUC's role became a passive one of accepting provincial money and implementing provincial decisions, especially after the Parti Québécois came to power in 1976.[90]

An urban community (upper tier municipality) was also created for Quebec City and the Regional Community of Outaouais was established for Hull and environs. A primary motivation for the latter municipality was apparently the perceived need to provide a counterweight to the adjoining Regional Municipality of Ottawa-Carleton in Ontario, and to represent the area's interests to the National Capital Commission. The fact that the Outaouais Urban Community contained major portions of rural as well as urban territory resulted in an uneasy partnership that placed strains on the organization. Following a ministerial statement and a study (the Giles Report) in 1990, two new structures were put into place effective January 1, 1991 – a new regional county municipality covering the rural areas and a modified Outaouais Urban Community confined to the urban areas of Gatineau, Hull, Aylmer, Buckingham, and Masson. The latter five have since merged into a single municipality.

New Metropolitan Governing Bodies

Changing population patterns presented growing challenges and problems for the urban community governments, especially the one in the Montreal area. Rapid growth in the outer suburbs beyond the MUC made its boundaries increasingly irrelevant.[91] While the MUC had contained 71% of the population of the Montreal census metropolitan area in 1971, that proportion was down to 57% by 1991. Yet expansion

---

[89] In fact, it was a Montreal police strike that accelerated the formation of the Montreal Urban Community, which became a vehicle through which suburbs were drawn into the financing of this service on a regionalized basis.

[90] The assessment in this paragraph is based on Andrew Sancton, "Montreal's Metropolitan Government," Hanover, *Quebec Studies*, No. 6, 1988.

[91] Sancton, *Canada's City Regions*, p. 84.

of the MUC boundaries seemed unlikely, since the adjacent areas were governed by regional county municipalities – leaving Montreal hemmed in much the way Toronto had been with regional governments around it.

The 1990s saw a series of reports and recommendations for new structures in the Montreal area. Of particular note was a provincially appointed task force (chaired by Claude Pichette) that recommended in December 1993 that a Montreal Metropolitan Region be established covering the entire census metropolitan area and its more than 100 municipalities. In 2001, two new metropolitan communities were created, covering roughly the census metropolitan areas of Montreal and Quebec City. Only a planning coordinating commission was established in the Gatineau-Hull area, given that this metropolitan area was much less complex structurally, with just one large city and one regional county municipality.[92]

The Montreal Metropolitan Community (MMC) is a planning, coordinating, and funding body serving 82 municipalities and a population of 3.6 million.[93] It is governed by a 28 member council with representatives from member municipalities or groups of municipalities. The MMC is to develop a shared vision for the area and to harmonize government policies and programs within the area. There is little indication that it has made much impact so far. In that regard, it is noteworthy that Hamel doesn't even treat the MMC as a structural reform but instead as a functional one in his examination of municipal initiatives in Quebec.[94]

Merger in the Major Centres

By the 1990s, the province was taking an increasingly tough stand on amalgamations, partly out of a desire to create larger municipal institutions to which responsibilities could be downloaded. Indeed, the 1990 provincial budget downloaded $400 million in responsibilities, mostly in the area of public transit and police services, along with local roads in rural areas. The Parti Québécois took power in 1994 and introduced an amalgamation program bolstered by financial incentives

---

[92] Andrew Sancton, "Why Municipal Amalgamations? Halifax, Toronto, Montreal," in Robert Young and Christian Leuprecht (eds.), *Canada: State of the Federation 2004: Municipal-Federal-Provincial Relations in Canada*, Montreal and Kingston, McGill-Queen's University Press, 2006, Chapter 5.

[93] Information from the CMM website at www.cmm.qc.ca, accessed June 24, 2007.

[94] Pierre Hamel, "Municipal Reform in Quebec," in Garcea and LeSage, *Municipal Reform in Canada*, pp. 151 and 153-154.

and penalties. Its greater success is evident from Hamel's observation that only Ontario amalgamated more municipalities than Quebec in the 1990s. Close to 200 more were eliminated in 2001 and 2002 (including in major urban areas such as Montreal and Quebec City, as discussed below), but that still left Quebec with over 1100 municipalities.[95]

In March 2000, the Minister of Municipal Affairs issued a reorganization plan for Quebec local government particularly focused on comprehensive mergers in the three urban community or regional government systems in Montreal, Quebec, and Hull-Gatineau that by then contained 70% of the province's population. Local opposition was widespread and referenda in the suburban areas brought voter turnout of between 10% and 35%, and a 90% rejection of amalgamation.[96] Undeterred, the province merged all of the municipalities within the Montreal, Quebec City, and Hull-Gatineau areas (including the upper tier urban communities governing these areas) to form three enlarged single tier cities as of January 2002.[97] Amalgamations were also introduced to create enlarged cities for Lévis, Longueuil, Trois-Rivières, Sherbrooke, Saguenay, Shawinigan, and Saint-Jérôme.

Community or borough councils (conseils d'arrondisement) were established in several of the newly merged cities, including Montreal and Quebec City. In Montreal, 27 boroughs were initially created, with boundaries closely following those of the urban neighbourhoods of the old Montreal and the old suburban municipalities. There are 40 borough councillors elected to serve only at the borough level, with the rest being elected from within each borough to serve on its council and also to sit on the Montreal city council. The boroughs don't have any taxing power, but they play a significant role, essentially running local services and also making final decisions on local zoning matters (without any appeal to Montreal council or any provincial tribunal). Their status is enhanced by the fact that the chair of each of the 19 borough councils that currently exist is a directly elected mayor who also sits on Montreal city council.

---

[95] *Ibid.*, p. 159.

[96] Louise Quesnel, "Municipal Reorganization in Quebec," *Canadian Journal of Regional Science*, Special Issue, Spring 2000, pp. 125-127.

[97] This reform was strikingly similar to the mass merger that had taken place in the Toronto area in 1998 (and was cited by proponents of the Quebec initiative) and also the mergers that took place within several of Ontario's former regional government areas.

Demergers in the Major Centres

Not surprisingly, there was a great deal of local resistance to these widespread amalgamations, much of it found among the suburban municipalities that became part of the new City of Montreal. In addition to the common suburban perspective that their well run administrations would be submerged into a less efficient and more costly city operation, the Montreal mergers, of course, were also sensitive because of the issue of language. In one of those "It seemed like a good idea at the time" moments, Jean Charest promised, while leader of the opposition party in Quebec, that he would provide a way for municipalities to demerge if they were unhappy with being amalgamated into large cities. Charest became Premier in 2003 and, to his credit, carried out his promise. While the process he outlined seemed designed to make demerger unattractive and difficult to obtain, at least he provided an option – unlike his Liberal counterparts in Ontario, who opposed forced mergers when in opposition but then shied away from accommodating any local demerger initiatives that flared up in that province.[98]

The key demerger provisions were:[99]

➢ A referendum had to be requested by 10% of the electors in the territory of a former municipality and approved by a majority of votes representing 35% of total eligible voters.
➢ Any municipality that demerged would have to participate in an urban agglomeration council comprising all the municipalities formerly part of the amalgamated municipality and retaining most of the powers previously vested in the amalgamated city.

Even with these provisions, 89 former municipalities gained enough signatures to hold referendums and demerger was approved in 2004 in 31 former municipalities, including 15 of the 28 that had been brought together to create the new City of Montreal.[100] Where such demergers have been approved, agglomeration councils (ACs) have now been established, effective January 2006, comprising representatives from the demerged municipalities and the city from which they have extracted themselves.

---

[98] The experiences of the two provinces are compared in Andrew Sancton, *Municipal Mergers and Demergers in Quebec and Ontario*, paper prepared for the Colloque sur les réalisations du gouvernement Charest, Université Laval, December 9-10, 2005.

[99] Andrew Sancton, "The Governance of Metropolitan Areas in Canada," *Public Administration and Development*, 25, 2005, p. 324.

[100] Hamel, *Municipal Reform in Quebec*, p. 155.

The Montreal agglomeration council, for example, is headed by the mayor of Montreal and had 15 representatives from the Montreal council and 15 from demerged municipalities, although changes were provided in Bill 22, passed in June 2008. Since then, the governance structure has allowed for adjustments to take account of a number of suburban concerns: Bill 22 created an Agglomeration Secretariat, quota share financing (with just one local tax bill from each person's own municipal hall), return of arterial road jurisdiction to individual municipalities, an audit committee, and a working group to continue consideration of how much suburbs should pay for downtown Montreal developments.[101]

Representatives of the city, because of its population, hold the vast majority of the voting power on council, and Montreal initially provided the services delivered by the agglomeration council. The AC Secretariat now takes on much of this work, which addresses one suburban concern. The agglomeration council is essentially a vehicle to ensure demerged municipalities continue to pay their share of the services being provided across the metropolitan area. As a result, demerged municipalities in Montreal (and in other areas such as Longueuil) have expressed growing frustration with their lack of power within these councils. Bill 22 went some way to rectify these suburban concerns.

After considerable restructuring reform over recent years, Hamel has suggested that as no institutional change can be perfect, the task in Montreal, and Quebec more generally, is "just make it work." Having time to adjust to the range of changes brought forward – and trying to make them work – might offer the most productive local and provincial response.[102]

Recap: Multileveled Municipal Restructuring

As will by now be evident, the new millennium ushered in a dizzying series of changes in municipal structure in major urban areas of Quebec, leaving residents in some areas governed by three or even four – in the case of Montreal – levels of administration. Prior to these changes, there had been two tiers of municipal government in the Montreal, Quebec City, and Hull areas – local municipalities and the upper tier, "urban communities" established by the province in 1970, as discussed above. How did we get from two levels to three or four? Let's review.

---

[101] See, for example, David Johnson, "How the agglomeration council will work: Suburbs will get some of the things they were asking for," *The Gazettte,* June 13, 2008.

[102] With thanks to Dr. Pierre Hamel, University of Montreal, Lac Brome reflections, June 27, 2011.

Chapter 4 • *Local Government Restructuring* 123

> ➢ In response to population overspill beyond the boundaries of the urban community governments, new governing bodies were established in 2001 covering the entire census metropolitan areas of Montreal, Quebec City, and Gatineau-Hull.
> ➢ Almost at the same time, the province introduced a massive merger in which all the municipalities within the Montreal, Quebec City, and Gatineau-Hull areas (including their upper tier, urban communities) were amalgamated to create three enlarged cities, as of January 2002. So even as larger governing bodies were being created, covering the entire census metropolitan area, the existing two tier system was being merged into enlarged, single cities. In effect, we had added a tier and taken away a tier. By this point, you are probably shedding a tear as well, but bear with us.
> ➢ In recognition of the large size of the newly merged cities, community or borough councils were established in several of them, including Montreal and Quebec City. This brings us to three levels of administration – the large metropolitan communities, the newly merged, large cities, and the borough councils within some of these cities, intended to replicate the local municipalities lost through amalgamation.
> ➢ The final component arises from the demerger process set up by the Liberals when they gained power in 2003. It led to yet another level in the form of an agglomeration council, made up of representatives from demerged municipalities and the city from which they departed.

Putting all of this together, residents of Montreal are under four levels of administration, as depicted in the accompanying chart. Residents of municipalities that demerged from Montreal find themselves under three levels and that arrangement would also apply to the residents of the two municipalities that demerged from Quebec City and are now governed by their own demerged municipality, the Quebec City agglomeration council, and the metropolitan community governing the Quebec City CMA. The agglomeration council, city council,

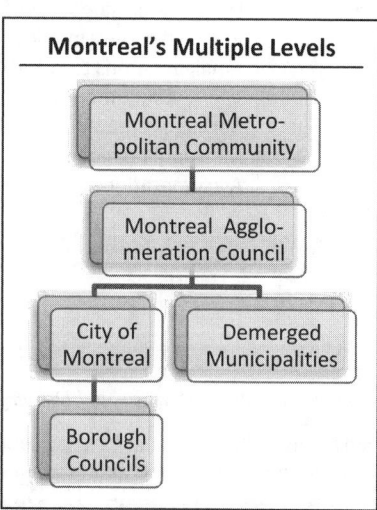

Montreal's Multiple Levels

Montreal Metropolitan Community

Montreal Agglomeration Council

City of Montreal

Demerged Municipalities

Borough Councils

and borough councils are all part of the same corporate entity (the City of Montreal).

If, as often alleged, two tier municipal systems cause confusion and weaken accountability, residents in some parts of the province of Quebec face quite a challenge. Much of the complexity arises from the demerger process that has recently unfolded. The former municipalities that successfully demerged have regained the authority to tax their property owners to pay for local services. However, apart from that aspect – and perhaps that is enough – it is not evident that the position of the municipalities that demerged from Montreal is much different than if they had remained as boroughs within the city government.[103] Hamel has added that Montreal's changes "raise(s) more questions than it answers....The Government of Quebec has chosen an extremely conservative path. It has opted for an institutional reform that hardly modifies the prerogatives and powers of the existing actors." .... Major changes *might* result, but "everything will depend on the willingness of the CMM authorities to become involved in a true political debate concerning metropolitan issues and to invite civil society actors to participate in this debate."[104]

Table 4.2 Restructuring Highlights – Central Canada	
Ontario	Metro Toronto system subsequently merged into City of Toronto. Network of two tier regional governments, several of which were subsequently merged into large single cities. Widespread amalgamations across Ontario, reducing the total number of municipalities from 815 to 444.
Quebec	Limited amalgamation of small municipalities. Regional county municipalities replaced former counties. Amalgamations to create large cities in Montreal, Quebec City, Hull, and several other urban areas. Boroughs created within several of these new cities. Metropolitan communities for Montreal and Quebec City areas. Agglomeration councils over cities with demerged municipalities.

---

[103] Sancton, *Municipal Mergers and Demergers*, p. 21.

[104] Pierre Hamel, "Institutional Changes and Metropolitan Governance: Can De-Amalgamation Be Amalgamation? The Case of Montreal," in Razin and Smith (eds.), *Metropolitan Governing*, pp. 114-115. Dr. Pierre Hamel also offered more recent comments on Quebec and Montreal (June 2011).

New Brunswick

New Brunswick was in the forefront of municipal reform early on, but seems determined never to be caught in that position again. There was a push in the 1990s to restructure municipal government in urban areas, with limited results, but it is in rural New Brunswick where deficiencies in the municipal structure are most problematic.

Equal Opportunity Program

Comprehensive local government reform initiatives were undertaken in New Brunswick in the 1960s as a result of the report of the *Royal Commission on Finance and Municipal Taxation* (chaired by Edward Byrne). The emphasis on fiscal matters in the title reflected the difficulties facing local governments in the province at the time. Service standards varied widely (especially in education), there were marked inequities in municipal taxes and high tax arrears, municipalities were finding it difficult to finance their servicing needs, and three of the single tier rural counties were virtually bankrupt. To provide all citizens with minimum standards of service regardless of the financial resources of their local municipalities, the report proposed that the province take over full responsibility for a number of services to people to ensure uniformity, leaving municipalities responsible for more localized services to property. It also recommended that the province take over the provision of local services in the rural areas of the province.

The New Brunswick government responded with an Equal Opportunity Program in 1967 under which the main recommendations of the Commission were implemented. The province took over responsibility for the administration of justice, welfare, and public health, and financial responsibility for the provision of education. Property assessment and collection of property taxes became provincial responsibilities. The 15 single tier counties that had governed the rural areas of New Brunswick were abolished, and the province took over the provision of services to these areas through new local service districts (discussed in more detail below) established for the purpose. Some 90 villages were established, in partial compensation for the loss of the county governments.

The reforms substantially improved the quality of such services as education, justice, and welfare – but at the price of the municipal level losing all or partial responsibility for these functions to the province. But the reforms did not deal with the need for boundary changes in urban areas and the fact that municipalities had been eliminated in rural areas added to the problems caused by growing population overspill.

Governing Urban New Brunswick

A December 1992 government report[105] acknowledged that the equal opportunity reforms had not addressed the problems of urban centres and proposed that they be studied with a view to possible restructuring. The results of these studies are very briefly summarized below.

- A Moncton report of April 1994 ruled out amalgamation of Moncton, Dieppe, and Riverview, primarily out of sensitivity to the predominantly French population of Dieppe. Instead, a joint services board was created. This Commission of the Three Communities operated for three and one-half years but was hampered by municipal turf wars and resistance to service sharing and by conflicting directives from provincial departments.[106]
- The City of Miramichi became the fourth largest municipality in the province in 1995 with the merger of all 11 communities in the Miramichi area (only 5 of which were municipalities).
- Effective January 1, 1998, the eight suburban municipalities in the Saint John area were consolidated into three, with the Saint John boundaries remaining the same. In addition, a Regional Facilities Commission was established to integrate the financing of major facilities in Saint John that benefited the region.
- Three municipalities and a portion of a local service district were amalgamated with the City of Edmundston in 1998.

These urban restructuring initiatives ended with the June 1999 election that brought Bernard Lord and the Conservatives to power (1999-2006).

Governing Rural New Brunswick

While the reforms in urban areas were limited, they far exceed the changes in rural areas. As already mentioned, the abolition of county governments left the rural areas of New Brunswick without municipal

---

[105] Ministry of Municipalities, Culture and Housing, *Strengthening Municipal Government in New Brunswick's Urban Centres*, December 1992.

[106] Daniel Bourgeois, "Municipal Reform in New Brunswick," in Garcea and LeSage, *Municipal Reform in Canada*, pp. 246-247.

Chapter 4 • *Local Government Restructuring* 127

governments. About 100 local services districts were established initially, to provide local services to unincorporated areas according to local preference, and there are now 269 such LSDs.[107] For more than 30 years, there have been unsuccessful initiatives to restore some form of municipal government to rural New Brunswick.

> A 1976 report[108] identified a number of problems, including the lack of elected councils to represent the people, inequities in the financing of services, and difficulties implementing services such as community planning. But no action was taken on the proposal that the LSDs be replaced by 11 rural municipalities.
> A 1993 report also found numerous problems, including conflicting land uses, sprawl, and unmanaged development just outside major centres. It called for rationalization of local service districts into rural communities with elected councils.[109] One pilot community was created in 1995, but no others followed.
> A June 2001 report[110] outlined several options for municipal structures in the rural areas, including models similar to British Columbia's regional districts and Quebec's regional county municipalities. Consultations found little public support for these proposals, largely because residents in unincorporated areas feared that incorporation would bring increased taxation. As a result, no municipal structure was introduced for rural areas. Instead various locally initiated changes were encouraged, with respect to such matters as the boundaries of local services districts and joint provision of services by regional bodies.[111]
> A very modest provincial initiative was introduced in 2005, with the passage of *An Act Respecting Rural Communities*, which was designed to allow local service districts, on their own or in combination, to become incorporated rural municipalities with elected councils. Given the voluntary nature of the provisions,

---

[107] Government of New Brunswick, *Local Government Resource Manual*, Section 1, p. 4, accessed June 14, 2011 at www.gnb.ca/0370/index-e.asp.

[108] *Report of the Task Force on Nonincorporated Areas in New Brunswick*, Fredericton, Queen's Printer, 1976.

[109] Government of New Brunswick, *The Commission on Land Use and the Rural Environment: Summary Report*, April 1993.

[110] *Report of the Minister's Round Table on Local Governance*, June 2001.

[111] Final Report of the Select Committee on Local Government and Regional Collaboration, *Executive Summary*.

however, there has been very little local response to date.[112] This was perhaps mostly due to the 2006 defeat of the Bernard Lord Conservatives, the subsequent defeat – after one term – of the Shawn Graham Liberals in 2010, and the first term settling in of David Alward's Conservatives (since October 2010).

The population growth in the rural areas now exceeds the rate of growth within municipalities, especially in the areas adjacent to the eight cities in New Brunswick. While the problems already identified also continue to grow, political realities make provincial intervention unlikely. Municipal incorporation would bring tax increases since residents in these rural areas are presently being subsidized by more than $20 million a year – the amount by which the fixed provincial levy on owner occupied residential properties in unincorporated areas falls short of the cost of the services provided to these areas by the province. But since the 40% of the population living in unincorporated areas controls 60% of the seats in the legislature, the province hesitates to increase the levy, or to impose municipal governments on the rural areas.[113]

Reliance on Local Boards

A distinctive feature of local government in New Brunswick has been the creation of single purpose boards to deliver services that transcend political boundaries. There are currently 12 district planning commissions, 12 solid waste commissions, and 15 community economic development agencies. There are also commissions dealing with such matters as wastewater, airports, police, and libraries. Joint service bodies are particularly prevalent in urban areas, where they handle services such as public transit, pest control, and emergency planning.[114] Bourgeois reports that many of the boards are single purpose bodies operating within their silos and not adequately coordinating services that are related (though, collectively, these agencies have sometimes made presentations to the respective Ministers).[115] These boards are insufficiently accountable to the public.[116]

---

[112] Geoffrey R. Martin, "Municipal Reform in New Brunswick: Minor Tinkering in Light of Major Problems," *Journal of Canadian Studies*, Winter 2007, p. 93.

[113] Bourgeois, *Municipal Reform in New Brunswick*, p. 249.

[114] Government of New Brunswick, *Local Government Resource Manual*, Section 1, p. 4.

[115] The authors acknowledge the assistance of staff at the New Brunswick Local Government Department, (June 17 and June 20, 2011).

[116] Bourgeois, *Municipal Reform in New Brunswick*, p. 245.

Nova Scotia

Local government reform initiatives in Nova Scotia came in two main waves, almost 20 years apart. A comprehensive report in the early 1970s led to some changes over the ensuing decade. The 1990s brought restructuring in a few urban areas, but there have not been any changes since.

Graham Commission: Too Much At Once?

The Royal Commission on Education, Public Services, and Provincial–Municipal Relations in the Province of Nova Scotia (chaired by Professor John F. Graham) lived up to its lengthy title by releasing a massive report in June 1974. Like the Byrne Commission in New Brunswick a decade earlier, the Graham Commission report concluded that the province should be responsible for such general services as education, health, social services, housing, and the administration of justice, and that it should provide such support services to municipalities as capital borrowing, assessment, tax collection, water and sewer user billing and collection, and the administration of municipal pension funds. The Graham Commission also recommended that the existing rural municipalities, towns, and cities be replaced by 11 one tier counties covering the province.

While the major restructuring recommended by the Commission was not pursued, a number of boundary changes did take place through more localized annexations and amalgamations. These included major expansions to Dartmouth and Halifax and the creation of the Town of Bedford – all involving lands taken from Halifax County. The increasingly intertwined relationships between these four municipalities led to the establishment of the Metropolitan Authority of Halifax,[117] which was originally set up to operate a regional jail and gradually took on the operation of a regional transit system and a sanitary landfill operation. But this body was hampered by internal wrangling over the financing of its work and different views of its priorities,[118] and was ineffective in pursuing regional planning and in dealing with such challenges as the environmental cleanup of Halifax harbour.

---

[117] Andrew Sancton, *Local Government Reorganization*, p. 35.

[118] Katherine A. Graham, Susan D. Phillips, and Allan M. Maslove, *Urban Governance in Canada*, Toronto, Harcourt Brace & Company, 1998, p. 83.

Amalgamations in the 1990s

The impetus for further restructuring (in the Halifax area and elsewhere) came as a result of a 1992 report of a task force established by the Minister of Municipal Affairs. As in New Brunswick and elsewhere, the fact that rural development was outpacing growth in the established urban centres was a cause for concern. In addition to recommendations for a significant realignment of functions between the provinces and municipalities – rather similar to the proposals arising from the disentanglement process unfolding in Ontario during this same period – the report also called for a major restructuring of municipal governments in the five most urbanized counties in the province (including Halifax County) that together contained 67% of the Nova Scotia population. It stated that one tier amalgamated municipalities would be the preferred restructuring model.[119] The following year saw reports from municipal reform commissioners for Cape Breton County and Halifax County.

Cape Breton Regional Municipality (CBRM)

Previous reports had recommended amalgamations for the Cape Breton area and there was growing criticism of the complex network of special purpose bodies in the area. The Cape Breton Commissioner called for amalgamation of all eight municipalities including the county and the new municipality commenced operations on August 1, 1995. The limited resistance to this change probably reflected the widespread recognition of the financial difficulties facing a number of the municipalities, and public hope and expectation that savings would result from restructuring. The Commissioner had estimated annual savings of $13.8 million, of which $7.3 million was to come from the realignment of provincial and municipal services that had been introduced across Nova Scotia. Instead, the service swap resulted in an additional cost of $5 million a year, contributing to the $15 million shortfall that the new municipality faced in its initial (1995-1996) operating budget. The 2010-2011 operating budget was set at $128.1 million – in balance.[120]

---

[119] Report to the Government of Nova Scotia, *Task Force on Local Government*, April 1992, p. 33.

[120] This included a "jump" in gas tax revenues to $3.9m from $2.5m the year before. See www.cbrm.ns.ca/images/stories/financial%20stmts/Budget%20summary%202010-11.pdf (accessed May 31, 2011).

Halifax Regional Municipality (HRM)

In contrast with Cape Breton, there was considerable opposition to the amalgamation of the City of Halifax, the City of Dartmouth, the Town of Bedford, and the surrounding County of Halifax, which took effect on April 1, 1996. The new municipality is huge, covering almost 6000 square kilometres or almost 10 times the area of Metropolitan Toronto (now the amalgamated City of Toronto). It contains 40% of the population of Nova Scotia, only a small proportion of it located in its substantial rural area and dozens of small towns and fishing villages. The HRM council has a mayor and 23 members, elected from wards. Councillors also sit on one of six community councils that make decisions about local land use issues.[121]

The reasons offered for the creation of the HRM include:[122]

> The possibility of savings (estimated at $10 million) appealed to a provincial government then facing its own fiscal challenges. [These anticipated savings failed to materialize.][123]
> The province wanted to eliminate what was seen as excessive and harmful economic competition between the business and industrial parks of the municipalities, highlighted by the battle between Halifax and Dartmouth over the location of a Price Club big box store.
> Since Halifax County was facing an adverse financial impact from the provincial–local service swap then underway, and the other three municipalities were looking at a financial gain, the amalgamation produced a more equitable, and politically acceptable, impact.

Region of Queens

A third amalgamation during this period, which merged the County of Queens and the Town of Liverpool to form the Region of Queens municipality, was locally initiated. It was intended to improve services, achieve some economies of scale, and recognize the community of

---

[121] Sancton, *Governance of Metropolitan Areas*, p. 320.

[122] Dale Poel, "Municipal Reform in Nova Scotia," in Garcea and LeSage, *Municipal Reform in Canada*, p. 177.

[123] See, for example, Terri Evans, *Mega Cities. Mega Savings: Efficiency Debates in the Halifax Regional Municipality and the Capital Regional District in Victoria*, M.A. Thesis, Department of Political Science, Simon Fraser University, Vancouver, 2000. See pp. 88-89 re the lack of such savings.

interest between the areas brought together. It has apparently been a successful amalgamation in terms of improved financial capacity, financial management, and the provision of services.[124] Other counties, such as Kings, have also had some history of regional thinking. In 1979, Kings County (which forms part of Nova Scotia's agriculturally productive Annapolis Valley) was able to agree on the province's first county wide plan. It did so at a time when neighbouring Halifax failed to come to such an agreement.[125]

Amalgamations Assessed

It is difficult to assess the impact of these three amalgamations because of the many other changes that were occurring at the same time. For example, Industrial Cape Breton's losses of fishing, coal mining, and a steel industry have worsened the Island's economy, irrespective of the municipal structure in place, while there has been extensive growth in the Halifax area because of offshore oil and natural gas developments, not the new municipal structure.[126] Far from saving money, the Halifax Regional Municipality saw amalgamation costs of some $40 million in the early years, increased taxes and user charges, and low levels of satisfaction with post-amalgamation services.[127] The vast and diverse area that has been merged has not melded and a 2004 survey found that 61% of respondents were completely or mostly supportive of the division of the HRM into two separate municipalities, one urban and one rural. However, experience elsewhere (notably Ontario) suggests that public dissatisfaction eases over time.[128] In addition, there is no doubt that Halifax has a stronger political voice and that all of the new municipalities have a stronger capacity for policy analysis and management.[129]

Not surprisingly, the amalgamation that was not imposed from above (Queens) appears to be the most successful and well regarded. Its method

---

[124] Poel, *Municipal Reform in Nova Scotia*, p. 178.

[125] On this, see Patrick Smith, "Planning and Open Government: Recent Policy Options and Applications in Canada," *Planning and Administration*, Vol.11, No.2, Autumn 1984, pp. 54-62.

[126] Poel, *Municipal Reform in Nova Scotia*, p. 180.

[127] Brian Crowley (Atlantic Institute for Market Studies), *Municipal amalgamations in Atlantic Canada and beyond: Why amalgamate?*, presentation to the Annual Meeting of the B.C Municipal Finance Authority, March 29, 2001.

[128] For example, see Kennedy Stewart, "Why Insulate New Institutions?," in Razin and Smith (eds.), *Metropolitan Governing*, pp. 187-213.

[129] Poel, *Municipal Reform in Nova Scotia*, p. 180.

of creation also seems to be the model for the future. The revised *Municipal Government Act* of 1999 requires a plebiscite in which a majority of those voting must support creation of a regional municipality. With the New Democrats taking over in 2009 – after 10 years of Hamm/ Macdonald Conservatives – Darrell Dexter's administration early in its first term found itself having to take over the administration of the small Annapolis Valley town of Bridgewater (population, 970) when the mayor and council all resigned over concerns about financial irregularities. The province had to advance funds against future grants but this cash crunch in a small town might force local amalgamations and could put such matters higher on the provincial agenda.[130]

Prince Edward Island

With some 30% of the population in unincorporated areas and most municipalities small and financially weak, the PEI government has actually provided many of the municipal services except in a few of the largest urban centres.[131] In what is now a familiar scenario, most rural residents seem quite content with these arrangements, which spare them the property taxes that would come with municipal incorporation and a more fully developed local service role.

The impetus for reform and restructuring came from a 1990 report of the *Royal Commission on the Land*. It found that land management required an improved municipal structure and was very critical of the limited capacity, resources, and initiatives of the small municipalities found in rural PEI. The report also described the familiar problem of municipal boundaries not keeping up with population overspill and gave particular attention to the Charlottetown area where nine suburbs and the city struggled to achieve a coordinated approach voluntarily.[132] As it happened, the ensuing public debate centred on possible amalgamations

---

[130] See Oliver Moore, "Bye-bye, Bridgetown? Hello Bridgevillage? Staggering financial problems, now under police investigation, spark fears that N.S. town could disappear as independent entity" – after existing for 114 years. *The Globe and Mail,* June 4, 2011, p. A7.

[131] John Crossley, "Municipal Reform in Prince Edward Island," in Garcea and LeSage, pp. 229-230.

[132] O'Brien, *Municipal Consolidation*, pp. 27-30. The Commission's findings are also discussed in Crossley, *Municipal Reform in PEI*, pp. 221-222.

in the Charlottetown and Summerside areas, the Land Commission's recommendations on rural municipal reform were ignored, and this issue has yet to be addressed. It remains arguably the most pressing municipal issue facing the province.[133]

A June 1993 *White Paper on Municipal Reform* called for restructuring in both the Charlottetown and Summerside areas, which it found overgoverned. A Commissioner was appointed and his December 1993 report[134] called for the complete merger of the five municipalities in the Summerside area (along with some unincorporated territory) and for mergers that created three enlarged municipalities in the Charlottetown area, including an expanded City of Charlottetown. These changes were legislated in 1994 and the new cities began operations the following year. It had been anticipated that further restructuring might be undertaken, especially to "complete" the mergers in the Charlottetown area, but there has been no further action on this front.

In June 2005, the *Municipal Legislative Reform Report* was released by the Municipalities Act Review Committee (set up under the Minister of Community and Cultural Affairs in July 2003). Its report called for greater accountability and increased local authority.[135] It also recommended "more efficient" municipalities (by enlarging/ amalgamating smaller ones) and the consolidation of all municipally related provincial statutes into one *Municipalities Act*.[136]

In 2011, there were still 74 municipalities in PEI, for a provincial population of 143 401[137] – an average of 1 for every 1938 islanders.

Newfoundland and Labrador

Within a few years of joining Confederation in 1949, Newfoundland experienced rapid growth and the number of municipalities had risen to almost 300 by the early 1970s when the province set up a royal

---

[133] Crossley, *Municipal Reform in PEI*, p. 228.

[134] Prince Edward Island, *Report of the Commission on Municipal Reform (Charlottetown and Summerside Areas)*, December 1993.

[135] Municipalities Act Review Committee, *Municipal Legislative Reform Report*, Province of PEI, June 2005, p.15.

[136] *Ibid.*, pp. 93-94.

[137] www.princeedwardisland.com/original/pt-pop-oroj.pdf, (accessed May 14, 2011).

commission chaired by H. G. Whalen. Its 1974 report called for the gradual creation of as many as 20 regional governments with upper tier units similar to, but stronger than, British Columbia's regional districts. It also recommended tightening up incorporation procedures, the introduction of the property tax because of the poor financial conditions in most municipalities, and a new system of provincial grants. The latter proposals were gradually incorporated in revisions to the *Municipalities Act*.

Municipal Amalgamations

Shortly after the election of the Liberal government headed by Clyde Wells in 1989, the province launched an ambitious program of municipal consolidations. But for a variety of reasons, including strong local opposition, many of the proposed amalgamations were not pursued. By the time the consolidation program was put on hold in 1992, to allow for a review of the process and its accomplishments, 33 former communities had been reduced to 13.[138]

The main changes occurred in the Northeast Avalon area, which included the City of St. John's and about 20 smaller surrounding municipalities largely dependent on St. John's for employment and retail services.[139] A St. John's Metropolitan Area Board had operated in this area since 1963, gradually assuming a larger role with respect to such matters as planning, supplying services to outlying areas, and operating a regional water supply system.[140] With restructuring effective January 1992, St. John's absorbed two municipalities and most of the area previously under the Metropolitan Area Board, which was abolished at the same time. It also gained regional responsibilities for public transit, solid waste management, water supply, fire protection, and secondary processing of sewage. In effect, St. John's became a regional service provider with respect to these responsibilities, a role that it did not welcome.[141] While it would prefer to annex or merge with the surrounding areas to which it is providing services, the provincial

---

[138] Peter Boswell, "Municipal Renewal in Newfoundland and Labrador," in Garcea and LeSage, *Municipal Reform in Canada*, p. 199.

[139] Peter Boswell, "Regional Government for St. John's?" *Urban Focus*, Institute of Local Government, Queen's University, January-February 1979.

[140] This summary is based on O'Brien, *Municipal Consolidation*, p. 24.

[141] Andrew Sancton, Rebecca James, and Rick Ramsay, *Amalgamation vs. Inter-Municipal Cooperation: Financing Local and Infrastructure Services*, Toronto, ICURR Press, 2000, p. 42.

position is that no municipalities will be amalgamated against their will.[142]

The Regional Alternative

Continuing provincial concern about the number of municipalities directed attention to the possibility of a regional focus for service delivery. It was reflected in several developments, including:

- The division of the province into 20 economic zones to facilitate economic development and the establishment, in 1995, of regional economic development boards for each zone.
- The fall 1996 release of a consultation document, *Reforming Municipal Government in Newfoundland and Labrador*, which stated that municipalities could be expected to play a greater role in economic development in their respective regions, and which suggested that the boundaries of the new economic zones might be used to delineate new regional groupings of municipalities.
- The appointment of a task force the following spring which recommended in September 1997 establishing a regional county services board in each of the 20 economic zones, to be governed by a board of directors comprising both elected and appointed members representing unincorporated areas and municipalities, respectively. These boards would be given few initial powers, but could take on additional functions with local agreement.[143] The proposed boards were quite similar to British Columbia's regional districts, but they have not been established. Those opposed cited by now familiar arguments about fear of taxation in rural areas that had been receiving municipal services courtesy of the province and concern that any new regional structure would give the province an opportunity to download services and costs.[144]

Resistant or Realistic?

There have been few changes with respect to municipal consolidation or regionalization, in spite of a number of reports and recommendations. At

---

[142] Boswell, *Municipal Renewal in Newfoundland and Labrador*, pp. 200-201.

[143] Newfoundland and Labrador, Department of Municipal and Provincial Affairs, *Final Report, Task Force on Municipal Regionalization*, 1997, p. 9.

[144] Boswell, *Municipal Renewal in Newfoundland*, p. 202.

first glance, it appears that local resistance to change and lack of political will at the provincial level have left Newfoundland and Labrador saddled with far too many municipalities. But Boswell makes an interesting alternative case. He suggests that the need for widespread municipal reform is not as great in Newfoundland as in other parts of Canada and that many of the province's nearly 300 municipalities are very small and often operate quite efficiently with minimum staff and expense. He points out that some voluntary sharing of resources is occurring and more formal joint arrangements are being considered. In Boswell's view, it is possible that the existing structure of many small municipalities is the most cost effective way of delivering services while providing democratic representation.[145]

Conservative Premier Danny Williams (2003-2010) was succeeded by Kathy Dunderdale who led the Conservatives to another victory in December 2010. Before he departed, Williams undertook municipal consultations on (i) municipal reform, (ii) regional government, and (iii) seven regional governance models. That consultation continued into the term of his successor in 2011, with any new outcomes pending.[146]

Table 4.3 Restructuring Highlights – Atlantic Provinces	
New Brunswick	Mergers in a few urban areas, notably Miramichi and Saint John. Limited success in resolving the loss of municipal government in rural areas following the Byrne Commission. Some 300 boards to deliver services, often on behalf of municipalities and unincorporated areas.
Nova Scotia	Imposed amalgamations in Halifax and Cape Breton and voluntary amalgamation in Queens.
PEI	Charlottetown and Summerside enlarged by amalgamation. Limited, weak municipal structure in rural areas a concern.
Newfoundland	Amalgamation program produced few results, mostly in the St. John's area.

---

[145] *Ibid.*, pp. 207-208.

[146] See *Regional Government Initiative*, Municipalities Newfoundland and Labrador, at www.municipalitiesnl.com/?Content=CCRC/The_Regional_Government_Initiative, (accessed, June 4, 2011.) We are also grateful for suggestions from Dr. Peter Boswell, Memorial University of Newfoundland, on this topic.

Northern Territories

There is no restructuring story to tell with respect to municipalities in the Northern Territories. Indeed, when restructuring was underway 50 years ago, in places like Ontario and Manitoba, there were but three incorporated municipalities in the North. There are still fewer than 50, almost all of them without a property tax base. While the Northwest Territories government announced that most local communities would assume full responsibility for property taxation in the 2007-2008 fiscal year as part of a shift toward greater local control,[147] to date only the six municipalities incorporated under the *Cities, Towns and Villages Act* are operating as municipal taxing authorities.[148] The gradual development of Northern municipalities was outlined in Chapter 2. Given the great distances between most municipalities in the North, the usual restructuring through annexation and amalgamation simply does not enter the picture. Other than Whitehorse (2006 population, 20 461) and Yellowknife (2006 population, 18 700) all other municipalities in the three territories are under 7000. Thus, municipal reform in the Northern Territories has focused mainly on changes in municipal legislation[149] – as discussed briefly in Chapter 6.

Concluding Comments

The following chapter offers an assessment of our local government restructuring experiences, and of other options not pursued. For now, we offer a few observations to summarize and conclude this lengthy chapter.

> ➢ Approaches to restructuring have varied markedly, from the forceful, top down imposition most evident in Ontario, through the sporadically strong provincial position exhibited in Quebec

---

[147] Northwest Territories, Ministry of Municipal and Community Affairs, *The New Deal for NWT Community Governments*, Fall 2006, accessed at www.maca.gov.net/resources, October 1, 2007.

[148] See www.maca.gov.nt.ca/resources/Differences_in_Comm_Govt_Structure.pdf.

[149] See Katherine A. H. Graham, "Municipal Reform in the Northern Territories," in Garcea and LeSage (eds.), *Municipal Reform in Canada*, Chapter 12.

and, to a lesser extent, the Maritime provinces, to the much more laissez-faire posture of most other provincial administrations. A return to municipal restructuring does not appear to be on the provincial agendas at the moment and the issue did not figure prominently in the slew of provincial elections that were held in the fall of 2011 – all of which returned the governing parties.[150]

➢ Strong local opposition has stymied efforts at restructuring in provinces such as Saskatchewan and Newfoundland and has reduced its scope in others such as Quebec and New Brunswick. This has been particularly evident, for example, with the failure of rural reforms in provinces such as New Brunswick and Manitoba because the governing parties at the time had their power base in the rural areas.

➢ While reforms in some provinces acted as a model for action in others, the apparently similar initiatives often did not have the same motivation or objectives. For example, it was an NDP government that created Unicity, with the expectation that it would equalize service standards across the urban area. A similar amalgamated city was introduced in the Toronto area in 1998, but by a very conservative regime led by Mike Harris and for the declared purpose of reducing costs. The merger that created the enlarged City of Montreal in 2002 may have been partly inspired by Toronto's merger in 1998, but the Quebec government's motivation was to strengthen the central city by bringing in the suburbs and their assessment, whereas the Ontario government's motivation in merging the Toronto municipalities was to use the more conservative suburbs to restrain what the province perceived as a left leaning, free spending council in the old city.

➢ Intermunicipal boards have been widely used to pursue regional planning and joint service delivery, especially where municipal restructuring has been resisted.

➢ Not surprisingly, given the large populations involved, restructuring efforts in urban areas have received most of the attention, and have frequently been justified as a response to the competitive pressures in this age of globalization.

➢ However, there are also problems with the municipal structure in the rural areas of many provinces, especially in relation to the

---

[150] These were the Liberals in PEI on October 3, the NDP in Manitoba on October 4, the Liberals in Ontario on October 6, the Conservatives in Newfoundland and Labrador on October 11, and the Saskatchewan Party in Saskatchewan on November 7. There were also elections in the Yukon and Northwest Territories in the fall of 2011 but, as noted above, municipal restructuring is a non-issue in these areas.

extensive population living in unorganized territory and reluctant to accept any municipal incorporation and the taxation that would accompany it. As a result, there may be little in the way of planning and land use controls, leaving more vulnerable the natural capital (including food, water, and other resources) on which the population – including the urban population – ultimately depends for its survival.
- The regional districts of British Columbia have been one of the most enduring reform initiatives and also one of the most effective at addressing the combined needs of urban, rural, and unincorporated areas. Even where questions emerge in BC's largest urban centres, this is still the case.
- Urban restructuring in Ontario, Quebec, and Manitoba (with respect to the Winnipeg area) has gone through a two stage amalgamation process that first saw the creation of merged two tier systems and then the collapsing of those systems into single enlarged cities.
- Even these enlarged cities, however, cannot keep up with the relentless pace of population overspill, creating continuing demands for regional or metropolitan institutions that can take action on a wider scale. The multilevelled government structure in the Montreal area includes one such institution but there is no counterpart for the Toronto/Golden Horseshoe area.

Chapter 5
Restructuring Limitations and Alternatives

Municipal restructuring efforts in Canada have been limited in a number of respects – in the reforms actually carried out; in the emphasis on amalgamation (especially in the 1990s); in the alternative approaches to reform that have received too little attention; in the broader, external changes that should occur and often haven't; and in the internal changes and innovations that have been relatively neglected because of the preoccupation with boundary changes.

Introduction

To keep its length manageable, Chapter 4 concentrated on describing, without much analysis, the reforms to municipal structures in Canada over the past almost 60 years. The primary objective of this chapter is to evaluate that restructuring experience, including the validity of the underlying rationale for the reforms and the effectiveness and potential of the resulting structures. In the process, we will also identify a number of alternatives to restructuring, many of which received limited attention.

It is beyond dispute that local governments in Canada have faced growing challenges over the past half century plus, many of them related to the pressures of growth and change described in Chapter 3. That chapter documented what appears to be a permanent, polarized pattern of growth in Canada. Major urban areas must contend with increasing global competition and with the economic, environmental, and social costs associated with sprawl. Much of the rest of the country struggles with slow growth or no growth and governing in rural areas is hampered by a weak economic base, limited assessment (and tax revenues), and an underdeveloped system of municipal government in several provinces.

Recapping the Reforms

The restructuring response to these challenges can be grouped, somewhat arbitrarily, into three main categories as described and illustrated below.

1. The establishment of intermunicipal boards to provide a forum for addressing issues that cross municipal boundaries and/or for providing particular services (such as planning, economic development, water and sewer systems, and transit).

Table 5.1 Intermunicipal Boards	
Metropolitan Authority of Halifax	Originated in 1962 as Halifax-Dartmouth Metropolitan Authority, and over the years gained responsibility for operating a regional jail, regional transit, and a regional landfill site. Abolished when the Halifax Regional Municipality was established in 1996.
St. John's Metropolitan Area Board	Established in 1963, for planning, then provided a number of urban services. Abolished in 1992, with the newly enlarged municipality of St. John's becoming a regional service provider in its place.
Commission of Three Communities (Moncton, Dieppe, Riverview)	Set up in 1996 as an alternative to amalgamation, and charged with regionalizing common services including fire, police, water treatment, cultural facilities, industrial parks, economic development, urban planning, public transportation, solid waste, and emergency measures. Disbanded in 2000, although close to 10 other agencies oversee provision of services in the Greater Moncton area.
Montreal Metropolitan Community (MMC)	Set up in 2001 with representatives from all municipalities in the Montreal CMA. Duties include metro planning and economic development, social housing, and planning for urban transit and solid waste disposal.
Greater Toronto Services Board (GTSB)	Established in 1999 with representation from all municipalities in the Greater Toronto Area, but with responsibility only for the GO Transit commuter train system. Dissolved at the end of 2001, but a somewhat similar Greater Toronto Transportation Authority (now Metrolinx) was set up in 2006.
Manitoba Capital Region Committee	Set up in 1989 with heads of council for Winnipeg and 12 (now 15) surrounding municipalities, and focused on developing a strategy for sustainable development, but there has been little progress over the years.
Alberta Capital Region Forum	Created in 1995 with representatives from 14 municipalities, including Edmonton. Limited success and replaced in 1999 by the Alberta Capital Regional Alliance comprising Edmonton and 19 surrounding communities. Some progress, including at least an outline of a growth management plan.

2. The establishment of regional or metropolitan two tier municipal systems, with the upper tier unit responsible for addressing the

cross boundary issues and lower tier municipalities (enlarged through merger or not) providing the more localized services.

Table 5.2 Two Tier Systems	
Ontario	Metropolitan Toronto, 1953-1997. Eleven regional government systems set up during 1969-1974.
Manitoba	Metropolitan Winnipeg, 1960-1971.
British Columbia	Regional Districts, 1965.
Quebec	Urban communities: Montreal, Quebec City, and Hull, 1970-2001. Regional county municipalities, 1979.

3. The amalgamation of two or more (often many more) municipalities to create one unified jurisdiction.

Table 5.3 Amalgamated Single Tier Municipalities	
St. John's, Newfoundland	St. John's combined with two municipalities and most of the area formerly under the Metropolitan Board, January 1992.
Summerside, PEI	Five municipalities merged in 1995.
Charlottetown	The city, a town, and five communities merged in 1995.
Cape Breton, NS	Eight municipalities merged, effective August 1995.
Halifax	Four municipalities, including Halifax county, April 1996.
Miramichi, NB	Merger of 11 communities (five municipalities), effective 1995.
Edmundston	Merged with 3 municipalities and portion of rural district.
Montreal, Quebec	Merger of 28 municipalities, including an upper tier urban community, to form enlarged City of Montreal, effective 2002.
Quebec City	Merger of 13 municipalities, including an upper tier urban community, effective 2002.
Gatineau-Hull	Merger of 5 municipalities, including an upper tier urban community, effective 2002.
Longueuil	Merger of 8 municipalities, effective 2002.
Lévis	Merger of 10 municipalities, effective 2002. (Trois-Rivières, Sherbrooke, Saguenay, Shawinigan, and Saint Jérôme also enlarged through merger in 2002) (32 municipalities demerged in 2006, 15 from Montreal)
Toronto, Ontario	Merger of 7 municipalities, including upper tier metro government, effective January 1998.
Chatham-Kent	Merger of 23 municipalities, including upper tier county government and separated city, effective January 1998.
Kawartha Lakes	Merger of 17 municipalities, including county, January 2001.
Ottawa	Merger of 12 municipalities, including regional government, January 2001.
Hamilton	Merger of 7 municipalities, including region, January 2001.
Sudbury	Merger of 8 municipalities, including region, January 2001.
Haldimand-Norfolk	Merger of 7 municipalities, including region, to form two municipalities, January 2001.
Winnipeg, Manitoba	Merger of 13 municipalities, including upper tier metro government, January 1972.

Comparing the Three Types of Reform

It is possible, as illustrated below, to place the three types of response on a spectrum from least intrusive to most in terms of how much they affect existing municipal structures.

Figure 5.1 Gradations of Restructuring

| Intermunicipal Boards | Two Tier Systems | Amalgamation |

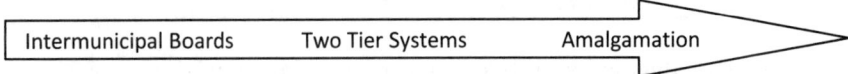

When intermunicipal boards are established, all municipalities usually continue to exist. When metropolitan and regional government systems are established, lower tier municipalities continue to exist, although usually with some amalgamations. With the third option, full amalgamation, all previously existing municipalities are subsumed within a single enlarged municipality.

Deciding where a particular structure fits along this spectrum, however, is not always straightforward. While we have classified the Montreal Metropolitan Community, for example, as an intermunicipal board, should it be recognized instead as a two tier system? Not according to Hamel and Rousseau, who contend that it has few powers or resources and is not fully a regional government.[1] At this point, it is still too soon to tell how the MMC will evolve and whether it will become a significant level of government. The same argument was made about regional districts in British Columbia in their first years of operation after 1965. Few dispute they are part of two tiered governments now.[2] What about the regional county municipalities, also found in Quebec? Have they been effective enough to warrant their inclusion in the list of two tier systems? While they are broadly similar in structure to British

---

[1] Pierre Hamel and Jean Rousseau, "Revisiting Municipal Reforms in Quebec and the New Responsibilities of Local Actors in a Globalising World," in Robert Young and Christian Leuprecht (eds.), *Canada: The State of the Federation 2004: Municipal-Federal-Provincial Relations in Canada*, Montreal & Kingston, McGill-Queen's University Press, 2006, p. 150.

[2] Patrick Smith and H. Peter Oberlander, "Restructuring Metropolitan Governance: Greater Vancouver–British Columbia Reforms," in Donald Rothblatt and Andrew Sancton (eds.), *Metropolitan Governance Revisited: American/Canadian Intergovernmental Perspectives,* Berkeley, University of California Press, 1998, pp. 371-373. Then B.C. Municipal Affairs Minister Dan Campbell insisted that regional districts were "not conceived of as a fourth level of government, but as a functional rather than a political amalgamation." (*Ibid.*, p.376.)

Columbia's regional districts (which we have now recognized as upper tier governments), they have not yet been as successful. It is because of these sorts of considerations that our threefold groupings and examples must inevitably reflect subjective judgment.

The spectrum illustrated above might also appear to depict a somewhat natural or inevitable progression with respect to the reform and restucturing of municipal government, an interpretation encouraged by those who prefer the amalgamation option. From their perspective, intermunicipal boards have major limitations, especially relating to the coordination of services and to public accountability, and two tier systems involve duplicated services that add to costs and cloud accountability. A closer examination suggests that the progression depicted in Figure 5.1 is neither inevitable nor necessarily preferable.

Intermunicipal Boards

The examples in Table 5.1 disprove the notion that these boards are inevitably a temporary arrangement on the way to more complete municipal restructuring. Yes, some intermunicipal boards (such as those in the Halifax and St. John's areas) were abolished when municipalities were amalgamated. But in many other areas, joint boards have continued or have been established *after* amalgamations occurred. This is true, for example, in the Montreal and Toronto areas, where a variety of inter-municipal bodies have been created in an attempt to find a means of addressing the wider issues of their urban areas.

As to whether intermunicipal boards and the joint servicing arrangements that they represent are less desirable than municipal restructuring, opinions vary. There are obvious economies of scale when municipalities join together in providing a number of specific services, especially those of a capital intensive nature such as water supply, sewage treatment, and public transit. Intermunicipal agreements, whether or not under the aegis of a joint board, are also a very flexible way for municipalities to combine in whatever numbers and configurations are most appropriate (and efficient) for the provision of particular services. As a result, these arrangements continue to be prominent even where amalgamation has taken place. One study found, for example, that in the Ontario regions of York and Durham, "even within two-tier systems designed specifically to provide an upper-tier government for the provision of services that transcend any particular lower-tier municipality (municipalities that are themselves the result of significant amalgamations when the reorganized systems were created), there is still a dense network of inter-municipal agreements covering everything from animal control to public transit."[3]

On the other hand, it is argued while intermunicipal boards may be effective in providing their own particular service, each board operates in isolation. Planning and coordination of service provision is a major challenge when a number of these boards operate in one urban area. There are also criticisms that the boards stifle public participation and erode accountability. The servicing role "reigns paramount," and boards resist public efforts to become more involved as inappropriate "political" intervention into matters of a technical nature.[4] When servicing decisions are dispersed among various intermunicipal boards, it becomes difficult for citizens to understand the structure and to enforce accountability. Accountability challenges are substantial concerns across many jurisdictions, as discussed elsewhere in this volume.

Should We Shed a Tier?

While intermunicipal boards don't necessarily evolve into restructured municipalities, it appears that two tier systems evolve into amalgamated single tier municipalities. Most restructured two tier systems were created 40 to 50 years ago, and even the most recent such systems (Quebec's urban communities and regional county municipalities) were set up in the 1970s. Moreover, many of these two tier systems have been abolished in the past few years through amalgamations that created large single tier municipalities. Gone are Quebec's urban communities[5] and almost half of Ontario's regional governments; long gone (since 1972) is Winnipeg's metropolitan system. The most enduring two tier system (now close to 50 years in existence) is that of British Columbia's regional districts, their longevity no doubt partly attributable to the modest scale and flexible nature of their operations. Indeed, a few might perhaps still place the regional districts in the first category above – as an intermunicipal board rather than as an upper tier government. Their hybrid nature is part of what makes the regional districts distinctive. Where the fraying occurs in this argument in B.C. is in the major Metro

---

[3] Andrew Sancton, Rebecca James, and Rick Ramsay, *Amalgamation vs. Intermunicipal Cooperation: Financing Local and Infrastructure Services*, Toronto, ICURR Press, 2000, p. 73.

[4] James Lightbody, *City Politics, Canada*, Peterborough, Broadview Press, 2006, p. 451.

[5] The two tier model has been continued in the form of the new Montreal Metropolitan Community and the similar body established for the Quebec City area – depending, as already noted, on how these bodies evolve.

Vancouver region. Here the push is beyond two tiers to a more amalgamated form. For much of the rest of the province, the existing regional district system continues to function fairly efficiently as part of a two tier system, and it continues to have many boosters in the Vancouver region as well.

The Case for a Two Tier System

Notwithstanding the trend in Canada, Stephens and Wikstrom claim that the establishment through amalgamation of one municipality covering an entire metropolitan area (popular among scholars during the first half of the 20th century) has virtually no support in the scholarly community today. Instead, "most present-day scholars of urban affairs predisposed toward metropolitan government reform endorse a federative, two tier type of metropolitan governmental structure."[6] Some would add that metropolitan *governance* models have become more common as a more flexible variant in governing city regions across much of North America. According to Rosentraub and al-Habil "the expansion of governance is growing but it needs to be flexible or 'elastic' in nature, not formal in structure."[7] Hall's assessment of developments in the USA concurs that "formal metropolitan government structures are not the trend line."[8] In Canada they are more common.[9]

A report recommending a two tier system of government for the Hamilton area at the end of the 1960s offered this justification.[10]

> The Commission believes that the two tier system for the area offers the best opportunity of reconciling the two main aspects of municipal government – efficiency and access. The larger administrative unit would provide a greater chance for efficiency, but the sheer size, number of people and volume of business would mean that the elected council of the metropolitan community would have difficulty

---

[6] G. Ross Stephens and Nelson Wikstrom, *Metropolitan Government and Governance*, Oxford, Oxford University Press, 2000, p. 29.

[7] Mark Rosentraub and Wasim al-Habil, "Why Metropolitan Governance is Growing, As Is the Need for Elastic Governments," in Don Phares (ed.), *Governing Metropolitan Regions in the 21st Century*, Armonk, NY, M. E. Sharpe, 2009, pp. 39-53.

[8] John S. Hall, "Who Will Govern American Metropolitan Regions, and How?" in Phares (ed.), *Governing Metropolitan Regions*, pp. 221-236.

[9] On this see, for example, A. Sancton, "A Review of Canadian Metropolitan Regions," in Phares (ed.), *Governing Metropolitan Regions*, pp. 39-53.

[10] The Hamilton-Burlington-Wentworth Local Government Review, *Report and Recommendations*, November 1969, p. 72.

in hearing all persons wishing to express aspects of local concern. There are many functions that are not of overall concern but are of extreme local importance. These functions may be more readily dealt with by the lower tier council who will have the knowledge of local conditions.

The report went on to explain that a two tier system of municipal government allows different decisions to be made and different levels of service to be provided in various areas of the region to best meet the desires and needs of its inhabitants.

Sharpe makes a similar point when noting that some find an inherent logic in the two tier model of municipal government "since it can help resolve the eternal conflict within local government between the values of participation, access and local identity on the one hand and functional optimality and production efficiency on the other."[11] He also states that the unitary type is not an option that works for the very largest cities, simply because of scale.[12]

Kitchen offers several benefits from the existence of both lower tier and upper tier municipalities.[13] The first is that the larger geographic area of the region can better address and control spillovers (positive or negative externalities) that might arise if some services were provided by lower tier municipalities. As an example of a negative externality, he cites the problem that could arise if solid waste disposal were a lower tier responsibility and if a solid waste disposal site were opened by one municipality near the boundary of an adjacent municipality, generating negative impacts on the residents of that neighbouring municipality.

Another benefit of a regional level is ensuring consistent standards in the provision of certain services. If, for example, social welfare assistance were administered at the lower tier, and if support differed among lower tier municipalities, there would be an incentive for recipients to relocate to those municipalities offering the highest level of support. Until changes introduced in the late 1990s, this pattern was evident in those areas of Ontario without a county welfare system where cities, with their wider range of services and programs, carried a disproportionate share of the welfare burden.

---

[11] L. J. Sharpe, *The Government of World Cities: The Future of the Metropolitan Model*, Chicester, John Wiley & Sons, 1995, p. 18.

[12] *Ibid.*

[13] Harry Kitchen, "Does Amalgamation Really Produce Cost Savings?," paper presented to Municipal Amalgamation Conference, Halifax, April 25, 1995.

A further benefit of the two tier system, according to Kitchen, is that where spillovers are not prevalent and uniform standards are not required, local preferences can be reflected in the quantity and quality of services provided by lower tier municipalities. In addition, the existence of a number of separate municipalities looking after these services generates a competitive atmosphere that provides a stimulus for improved service delivery.

Bird and Slack[14] also find merit in the two tier system, partly as a way of getting around the fact that each urban service will likely achieve the lowest per unit cost at a different scale of production.

> ...the optimum form of government will likely turn out to be a two tier or multi-tier structure where some services are provided by the upper tier – either a province or a regional government – and some by the lower tier or tiers. Indeed, since most government activities consist of a cluster of functions, what appears to be unnecessary overlap of government functions may sometimes represent a rational solution to the spillover problem. In Europe, this is termed the "subsidiarity principle" – placing specific responsibility at the level where it can most efficiently be provided.

The Case for a One Tier System

In spite of this impressive list of potential benefits, two tier systems have come under increasing attack in Canada and, as noted, many of them were eliminated in the extensive restructuring of the 1990s. Typical of the criticisms of the two tier model were these comments of the commissioner who recommended the amalgamation that created the Halifax Regional Municipality:[15]

> A two tier structure is more expensive: there are more elected officials, more administrators, and more facilities. It is more confusing to the taxpayer, since there are always questions about which of the two tiers is responsible for what. As a result, it is less responsive.

The relationship between the upper and lower tier is often problematic in two tier systems. Depending on the area and population covered by the system, there are often complaints about domination by the former city or suburbs. Where the upper tier councillors are chosen

---

[14] Richard M. Bird and N. Enid Slack, *Urban Public Finance in Canada*, 2nd Edition, Toronto, John Wiley & Sons, 1993, p. 35.

[15] Nova Scotia, *Interim Report of the Municipal Reform Commissioner, Halifax Metropolitan Area*, July 8, 1993, p. 39.

by indirect or double direct election – in that they hold their positions by virtue of being selected by lower tier councils or by being elected to councils at both levels – the concern is that they are too focused on the interests of the local municipalities from whence they come.

However, when upper tier councillors are directly elected, as was the case with Metropolitan Winnipeg in the 1960s and Metropolitan Toronto (for the most part) and Regional Ottawa-Carleton in the 1990s, the result is to sharpen the clash between upper and lower tier.[16] Lower tier municipalities complain that they lack representation on the upper tier council. For upper tier councillors, direct election gives them a sense of greater legitimacy and a better opportunity to direct their attention to region wide issues, but it also tends to make them less sensitive to local views and concerns. The result is usually growing conflict and confrontation, which becomes one of the justifications for the provincial governments to eliminate the two tier systems in these areas.

In contrast to these alleged defects of two tiers, proponents of a one tier system claim that it is simpler, avoids duplication, is more efficient and therefore saves money, and provides clearer lines of accountability.

Bearing in mind the arguments outlined thus far, let us turn to the reasons that have most often been given for municipal restructuring in Canada and how well they measure up under closer examination.

Reviewing the Rationale for the Reforms

Among the reasons advanced, to a greater or lesser extent in Canada, to justify municipal restructuring are the following:

1. To generate savings
2. To address the problem of sprawl
3. To ensure equity (or at least less inequity)
4. To eliminate intermunicipal clashes and turf wars
5. To reduce bureaucracy and have less government
6. To compete more effectively in a global world

---

[16] Andrew Sancton has discussed this problem: see "The Municipal Role in the Governance of Cities," in Trudi Bunting and Pierre Filion, *Canadian Cities in Transition*, 2nd Edition, Toronto, Oxford University Press, 2000, pp. 437-438, and "Signs of Life? The Transformation of Two-Tier Metropolitan Government," in Caroline Andrew, Katherine A. Graham, and Susan D. Phillips (eds.), *Urban Affairs: Back on the Policy Agenda*, Montreal and Kingston, McGill-Queen's University Press, 2002, pp. 180-181 and 187.

A closer examination of these justifications indicates that some of them appear to have much more validity than others. Ironically, it is the least valid reasons that have often been advanced most forcefully by a number of provincial governments.

Generating Savings

Especially over the past two decades, proponents of municipal amalgamation or consolidation have emphasized the need to overcome fragmentation, reduce duplication, and generate savings. Every news release from Ontario's Ministry of Municipal Affairs in the second half of the 1990s announcing an amalgamation repeated the standard statement: "Municipalities across Ontario are eliminating waste and duplication and providing better service at lower cost, through local restructuring." The municipal mergers introduced in Nova Scotia, New Brunswick, and Quebec over the past two decades were also preceded by predictions of savings. Opponents of amalgamation responded, among other objections, by disputing the savings predictions. The efforts of newly amalgamated municipalities, not surprisingly, have been largely devoted to the pursuit of the promised savings – with, at best, mixed results – and evaluations of the success of the new structures have also focused primarily on how well they have held the line on expenditures and taxes.

It is felt that this issue has unduly monopolized attention, to the neglect of other considerations that are at least as important in judging the merits of amalgamation versus fragmentation. However, it is examined first because it has loomed so large in discussions.

Those who anticipate savings from amalgamation seem to proceed from three main assumptions.

i) That economies of scale will result from providing services over larger areas;
ii) That reducing duplication means substantial staff reductions that will account for the bulk of the anticipated savings; and
iii) That the existing range and level of services will continue largely unchanged within the new municipality.

Economies of scale arise where the per unit cost of delivering a service falls as the quantity of the service provided increases. However, each municipal service is likely to achieve these economies at a different scale of production. The optimum size of government may be different for fire services than for roads or police. For example, studies by Kitchen have shown that the lowest cost per gallon of water supplied existed in municipalities in the range of 25 000 to 35 000, whereas the least expensive delivery systems for solid waste collection were found in municipalities under 5000, with per capita costs then rising until the population reached about 325 000 residents.[17] According to Bish, most research indicates that "approximately 80 percent of local government activities do not possess economies of scale beyond relatively small municipalities with populations of 10 000 to 20 000."[18]

If one wants to achieve economies of scale, amalgamation is a problematic choice, because while the larger municipality that results may be more efficient for delivering some municipal services, it will be less efficient for delivering others. As already noted, a better option – if savings is the objective – is for municipalities to join in a variety of combinations for different services, or even for different aspects of the same service. For example, there are many activities within the policing function, each with a different optimum scale of operation. A detailed study of production arrangements for policing in Standard Metropolitan Areas in the United States found that police patrols are best handled by very small detachments, while dispatching systems, detention facilities, crime labs, and training facilities are best handled over successively larger areas.[19] From this perspective, the best arrangement isn't a single amalgamated municipality *or* a two tier system; it is a large number of separate municipalities. Such a structure not only allows for flexible service production, as needed, but also provides a competitive atmosphere because of the multiple service producers. However, there are problems with this public choice rationale for multiple service providers via a more "elastic governance" model, to which we will turn later in this chapter.

The second assumption, that savings would arise from a substantial reduction in staffing, has also proven to be elusive. Staff layoffs or buyouts result in increased costs in the early going because of the severance packages that must be paid. Before long, municipalities often find that they have downsized too much and lost too much experience and expertise – leading to increased costs as the staff complement is expanded again. Savings that have been sustained have usually arisen from the introduction of more efficient work processes, but it is arguable

---

[17] Kitchen, "Does Amalgamation Really Produce Cost Savings?"

[18] Robert L. Bish, *Local Government Amalgamations: Discredited Nineteenth-Century Ideals Alive in the Twenty-First*, Commentary No. 150, C. D. Howe Institute, March 2001, p. 14.

[19] Discussed in *ibid.*, pp. 13-14.

that such improvements could have been made (and were in numerous municipalities) without amalgamation.

Savings on staffing costs are hard to achieve because there are strong upward pressures on these costs after amalgamation. There is pressure to standardize services by moving to the highest level previously prevailing, by levelling up, not levelling down. There is pressure to standardize salaries and wages, by levelling up to the highest remuneration that previously existed. Additional staff may be needed because of a loss of volunteer activity associated with the previous, smaller municipalities. The new municipality may also face demands for additional levels of supervisory personnel, more support staff, or new specialized positions.

Box 5.1 Why Do Predictable Results Surprise Anyone?

When the two tier system of municipal government in Hamilton-Wentworth was merged to create a large, single tier City of Hamilton, effective January 2001, new union contracts resulted in wages that moved up to the highest level found in any of the six former municipalities that were merged. Inexplicably, the chair of the amalgamation transition team indicated that this wage inflation had not been anticipated.[20] That any savings would be expected from this particular merger is especially puzzling, given that the administrative structures of the upper tier government and the City of Hamilton – accounting for 91% of the total expenditures of all municipalities in the system – had already been combined in 1998.[21] With less than 10% of expenditures left to merge, there was clearly no justification for the Hamilton merger on the grounds of savings.

Partly because of upward pressures on costs, the substantial savings predicted by amalgamation proponents have not usually materialized. Sancton makes this point on the basis of examples drawn from Britain, the United States, and Canada. He notes that numerous studies in the United States have shown that larger municipalities spend more money per capita on most services than do smaller ones, and that the federal government's Advisory Commission on Intergovernmental Relations had reversed its position by 1987 and no longer advocated municipal consolidation.[22] According to Cox,[23] an analysis of U.S. census data indicates that larger municipal units generally have higher expenditures

---

[20] Marvin Ryder, as quoted in Jeffrey Cohan, "MetroVisions: 5 suburbs melted in Ontario's 'Steeltown'," *Pittsburgh Post-Gazette*, September 21, 2004.

[21] David O'Brien, *Report of the Special Advisor, Local Government Reform for Hamilton Wentworth*, Toronto, Ministry of Municipal Affairs and Housing, 1999, pp. 27-28.

[22] Andrew Sancton, "Reducing costs by consolidating municipalities: New Brunswick, Nova Scotia and Ontario," *Canadian Public Administration*, Fall 1996, p. 272.

[23] Wendell Cox, *Reassessing Local Government Amalgamation*, Backgrounder, February 2003, Frontier Centre for Public Policy, accessed June 10, 2007 from www.fcpp.org.

and that consolidated governments are more costly than governments typified by multiple government units. It is a view reiterated by Norris, Phares, and Zimmerman.[24] A study of the determinants of municipal expenditure in Ontario also found that within a regional government structure, the larger the municipality, the higher the per capita expenditures.[25]

On the other hand, Lowery and Lyons found little support for the contention that a fragmented municipal structure reduces delivery costs.[26] Lightbody claims just the opposite, on the basis of an analysis of expenditure patterns in Alberta's two largest cities in the mid-1990s. He found that "the governmentally polycentric CMA region of Edmonton had higher costs in providing a practically identical package of urban services than the more unitary government of the Calgary CMA."[27]

An analysis of the experience of three amalgamations in Ontario found neither the savings predicted by the province nor the significant cost increases feared by opponents of amalgamation.[28] It also found, however, that total expenditures in one of the three (Kingston) were kept in line by reducing capital expenditures – which it labelled a questionable strategy for a municipality already coping with infrastructure problems. Since factors such as the size of the municipalities being amalgamated had a bearing on resulting costs and possible savings, the analysis concluded that one should not generalize about the final impact of amalgamations. That has not stopped such arguments being used, most often by amalgamation proponents.

Focus on Savings Misplaced and Misleading

Vojnovic's preliminary analysis of the effects of five amalgamations of Canadian municipalities[29] demonstrates the futility of trying to establish

---

[24] See Donald Norris, Don Phares, and Tonya Zimmerman, "Metropolitan Government in the United States? Not Now ... Not Likely," in Phares (ed.), *Governing Metropolitan Regions*, pp. 11-38.

[25] J. Kushner, I. Masse, T. Peters, and L. Soroka, "The determinants of municipal expenditures in Ontario," *Canadian Tax Journal* (1996), Vol. 44, No. 2.

[26] David Lowery and William Lyons, "The Impact of Jurisdictional Boundaries: An Individual-Level Test of the Tiebout Model," *Journal of Politics*, February 1989.

[27] Lightbody, *City Politics, Canada*, p. 436.

[28] Joseph Kushner and David Siegel, "Do Municipal Amalgamations Result in More Efficient Service Delivery?" *Municipal World*, January 2006, pp. 21-24.

[29] Igor Vojnovic, *Municipal Consolidations in the 1990s: An Analysis of Five Canadian Municipalities*, Toronto, ICURR Press, 1997.

a precise link between amalgamation and costs, and also debunks the third assumption listed above – that services and service levels continue unchanged after amalgamation. In some instances where costs decreased, it was because provincial grants were provided to smooth and sweeten the transition process. In other instances, costs went up significantly, but at least partly because of provincial downloading, increased service standards, or other factors not directly related to the act of amalgamation. Poel's assessment of restructuring in Nova Scotia leads to the same conclusion. He points out that the amalgamation in Cape Breton can't be blamed for the area's economic problems related to the loss of fishing, coal mining, and a steel industry any more than Halifax's amalgamation can be given credit for economic growth derived from offshore gas and oil developments.[30] Whatever the costs of a merger, moreover, we have no way of knowing what the costs would have been had it not occurred.

Followers of public choice theory argue that fragmented municipal structures generate savings because such structures most closely approximate the marketplace, allowing individuals to make choices about services and taxes. Bish, for example, has made this point with regard to the Victoria/Capital Region in British Columbia.[31] But many residents are not mobile and can't easily shift locations even if they have information that suggests more attractive alternatives. The poor and disadvantaged are especially lacking in mobility, and a fragmented municipal structure can give rise to policies that reinforce this reality.

Urban sprawl traditionally included the movement of middle class families to suburbs where they could pursue their objective of having single family homes on large lots, free of the congestion and crime associated with the inner city. By practising "exclusionary zoning,"[32] suburban municipalities attempt to keep out the poor and (often) racial minorities. The more these groups become concentrated in the central city, the more the suburbs attempt to dissociate themselves from the city and its social problems, which they usually try to blame on inefficient and spendthrift city administrations. As a result, municipal fragmentation

---

[30] Dale Poel, "Municipal Reform in Nova Scotia," in Joseph Garcea and Edward LeSage (eds.), *Municipal Reforms in Canada*, Toronto, Oxford University Press, 2005, p. 180.

[31] Robert Bish, "Local Government Service provision in the Capital Region," Local Government Institute, University of Victoria, LGI Report #5, April 1999.

[32] David Rusk, *Inside Game Outside Game*, Washington, DC, Brookings Institution Press, 1999, p. 8.

(especially in suburban America) "is largely a mechanism for preserving racial and social segregation and protecting private property values."[33]

Lightbody finds a somewhat similar situation in Canada, arguing that suburban communities such as Westmount, Quebec and St. Albert, Alberta have lived a variation of the *Field of Dreams* movie slogan. Their motto has been "if you don't build it, they can't come," as reflected in restrictions on the construction of multifamily residential buildings and low rent apartments, insufficient transit services to support shift workers, and limited social services and supports.[34] The issue is really one of equity, a rationale for restructuring examined separately below.

Keating points out that just because smaller jurisdictions have lower costs doesn't mean that they are more efficient. "It might equally reflect the tendency for the American middle classes to retreat into small, homogeneous communities which do not face the high costs of areas with more social stress or central place functions, and to provide more services privately."[35] Nor should it be surprising that amalgamated municipalities have increased costs in those instances when the real reason for their creation (notwithstanding the government rhetoric outlining the rationale) was to increase expenditures and to equalize standards across the enlarged area. This was certainly the objective with the creation of Winnipeg Unicity and it was also the outcome with some of the amalgamations in Ontario such as Chatham-Kent.

By emphasizing the savings that were to result from municipal amalgamations, provincial governments created a situation in which opponents of amalgamations could claim that the reforms had failed when the savings did not materialize. But a fragmented municipal structure gives rise to a number of considerations other than the cost of services and failure to take these into account leaves incomplete any assessment of the effect of reforms to that structure. This misplaced focus has been expressed as follows:[36]

> Instead of highlighting the political advantages of metropolitan integration in terms of information, equity in service provision, and democratic control, supporters of consolidation all too often make

---

[33] Michael Keating, "Size, Efficiency and Democracy: Consolidation, Fragmentation, and Public Choice," in David Judge, Gerry Stoker, and Harold Wolman, *Theories of Urban Politics*, London, Sage Publications, 1995, p. 122.

[34] Lightbody, *City Politics, Canada*, p. 391.

[35] Keating, *Size, Efficiency and Democracy*, p. 125.

[36] W. E. Lyons, D. Lowery, and R. H. deHoog, *The Politics of Dissatisfaction: Citizens, Services and Urban Institutions*, Armonk, NY, M. E. Sharpe, 1992, p. 192.

insupportable claims about economies of scale that shift the terms of the debate to the wrong issues.

Controlling Sprawl

By its nature, urban sprawl spills over the boundaries of a central city to adjacent suburban municipalities and beyond. Amalgamation is touted as a way of bringing the entire urban area under a single municipality that would then be in a position to address sprawl and its problems. While such a response is more likely under a unified jurisdiction, one should not assume that an amalgamated municipality would necessarily tackle the sprawl issue effectively. The same forces contributing to sprawl over the decades (including public preference for single family homes on large lots) would still be at play within the enlarged municipality.

Moreover, amalgamation as the solution for sprawl presupposes that the resulting enlarged municipality extends over the entire area of the sprawl. This is manifestly not the case in Canada's two largest cities, in spite of their recent controversial amalgamations. According to 2006 census information, the City of Toronto contains only 49% of the population of the Toronto census metropolitan area and Montreal contains only 45% of the population of its CMA.[37] Given the population and settlement patterns in Canada (discussed in Chapter 3) amalgamating municipalities as a means of controlling sprawl would most usually mean having to restructure on a continuing basis, constantly expanding boundaries outward in an attempt to catch up with the ongoing population overspill. Any such attempt is almost certain to create municipalities that are too large in relation to their other important roles, as would clearly be the case if Toronto or Montreal were expanded to embrace their CMAs. Some city region amalgamations have come closer to capturing the urban boundary solution, even into the near future. Ottawa, for example, arranged for future metro growth in its 2001 amalgamation.[38]

---

[37] Statistics Canada, *Portrait of the Canadian Population in 2006, 2006 Census*, accessed from http://www12.statcan.ca/english/census06/analysis/popdwell/index.cfm, June 1, 2007, pp. 22 and 27.

[38] Caroline Andrew, "Evaluating Municipal Reform in Ottawa-Gatineau: Building for a More Metropolitan Future," in Eran Razin and Patrick Smith, *Metropolitan Governing: Canadian Cases, Comparative Lessons,* Jerusalem, Hebrew University of Jerusalem, Magnes Press, 2006, pp. 75-94.

> **Box 5.2 You Can't Get There From Here**
>
> Amalgamating municipalities as a response to sprawl is likely to require frequent expansion of boundaries outward. It also is likely to result in municipalities that become too large for dealing effectively with local matters and yet remain too small to encompass the population overspill.

Rather than expanding local governments until they cease to be local, it can be argued that provincial governments should provide more leadership with respect to sprawl, since they obviously have the broader jurisdiction needed and the authority and resources to be effective. Indeed, in the largest urban agglomerations in Canada, it seems evident that only the provincial level is in a position to provide the overall planning and control necessary to manage growth effectively. Some provinces have come to recognize this, notably British Columbia and, more recently, Ontario.

British Columbia provided a positive example of provincial leadership in regional planning and development with its 1995 *Growth Strategies Act*. It established a framework for coordinated, long term planning in high growth areas of the province through the development of regional growth strategies, which have been completed by 10 regional districts.[39] The legislation required municipalities to plan regionally, authorized the province to intervene where they failed to act cooperatively, and provided for dispute resolution as a last resort.

An early and impressive outcome was the *Livable Region Strategic Plan* of the Greater Vancouver Regional District, the first such initiative, which enabled municipalities across the Lower Mainland to take actions to control sprawl, limit car use, and protect environmentally sensitive lands. This has since been updated as the Sustainable Region Initiative and in June 2011, a "Sustainability Congress" met to build a shared roadmap for the "next" future of the region.[40] For those contending that amalgamation is needed to control sprawl, this initiative was taken even though the City of Vancouver contains only 27% of the population of the Vancouver CMA. According to Smith, this example demonstrates that provincial governments can contribute to urban solutions and that regional governance is a viable alternative to regional government.[41]

---

[39] See "Status of Regional Growth Strategies in BC," accessed June 15, 2011 at http://www.cscd.gov.bc.ca/lgd/planning/growth_strategies.htm.

[40] See http://www.metrovancouver.org/region/congress/Pages/default.aspx, (accessed June 24, 2011).

[41] Patrick Smith, "Restructuring Municipal Governance: Vancouver and B.C. Reforms," *Policy Options*, September 1996, pp. 7-8.

Regional growth strategies continue to be a priority in British Columbia, with the current legislation (the *Local Government Act*) outlining minimum content requirements but leaving regional districts with considerable flexibility on the development of the strategy. Once a regional growth strategy is in place, member municipalities must amend their community (local) plans accordingly. As mentioned, there are currently 10 regional districts (within the three higher growth areas of the province) with completed regional growth strategies.[42]

The Toronto area provides another good example, in this case one in which provincial leadership has been sporadic and often ineffective, until very recently. Efforts to limit further growth in already built up areas coupled with policies and incentives to attract and stimulate growth in less developed areas were the basis of Ontario's regional development initiatives of the 1960s and its *Toronto Centred Region Plan* of the early 1970s. The logic underlying this provincial involvement was the recognition that "the province was not dealing with a metropolis and a set of lesser centres that could be allowed to develop autonomously, but with a highly integrated urban complex which spread right across the southern portion of the province."[43]

These provincial initiatives ran their course without having much impact on the unfolding development patterns and the provincial role had declined by the 1990s even as the need for growth management in the Greater Toronto Area had increased. Stein has argued that the lack of provincial investment in roads, sewers, and water mains in the right places demonstrated a "failure of nerve" that contributed to the worsening urban sprawl.[44] He is even more critical of the Ontario government following the election of the Conservatives in 1995, claiming that they took the province out of planning (by allowing regions to amend official plans on their own), cut financial support for cities, and downloaded provincial costs on them.[45]

In a generally positive analysis of the Toronto area at the beginning of the 21st century, Savitch and Kantor also raise concerns about developments on the planning front. They describe what had been a "cooperative confluence of power," a "triple alliance" involving the

---

[42] For details, see the Ministry of Community, Sport and Cultural Development website at www.cscd.gov.bc.ca.

[43] Warren Magnusson, "Metropolitan Reform in the Capitalist City," *Canadian Journal of Political Science*, September 1981, p. 565.

[44] David Lewis Stein, "The Region at 25," *Toronto Star*, January 1, 1999.

[45] *Ibid.*

province, Metropolitan Toronto, and its six lower tier municipalities, that successfully oversaw planning and development in the area up until the late 1990s.[46] But they note that the province then began to undercut provincial planning, softened restrictions, and allowed localities more discretion on development – with the predictable result that "development has begun to slip past smaller suburbs into a formless sprawl...."[47]

This sprawl posed an increasing threat to the Oak Ridges Moraine, a unique area that stretches for 160 kilometres east from the Niagara Escarpment across the top of the Greater Toronto Area and into neighbouring Durham Region, acts as a rain barrel feeding 65 rivers and streams that flow into Lake Ontario, and also directly provides water to over 250 000 people. The Conservative government did respond with a six month freeze on development in the moraine, followed by legislation in December 2001 that provided the province with regulatory power over the types of development that could occur there. Not all environmentalists were especially happy with the new legislation or the fact that any protection for the moraine was covered by regulation and could be amended or removed the same way.

This initiative has since been overtaken by a much more interventionist approach on the part of the Liberal government that gained power in 2003. Key provisions include:

- Legislation that provides for a green belt area and plan that will contain urban sprawl in the Greater Golden Horseshoe and protect the Niagara Escarpment and the Oak Ridges Moraine and a broader greenbelt area.
- A 2005 *Places to Grow Act* that will implement the province's plan to concentrate growth within the Golden Horseshoe in 26 key urban areas.[48]
- A revised Provincial Policy Statement (PPS) – with which all local planning activity must be consistent – that supports intensification of land use, more compact, high density development, and more transit friendly land use.

By 2011, some aspects of the *Greenbelt Act* (2004) and the *Green Energy Act* (2009) had caused some local upsets. Under the latter, wind

---

[46] H. V. Savitch and Paul Kantor, *Cities in the International Marketplace*, Princeton, Princeton University Press, 2002, pp. 176-180.

[47] *Ibid.*, pp. 279-281.

[48] *A Growth Plan for the Greater Golden Horseshoe*, 2006. For the latest developments, go to https://www.placestogrow.ca/index.php?lang=eng.

turbines can be built without local control, for example,[49] but in general the local-provincial angst in late 1990s Ontario subsided.

It remains to be seen whether these provincial initiatives will have a significant effect on the sprawl problems within the area surrounding Toronto. While there has been generally strong praise for these initiatives from proponents of smart growth, one analysis by such an organization expresses a number of concerns. These include exceptions allowed, weak intensification and density targets that seem to affirm "business as usual," further highway projects that continue automobile dependent sprawl, and weak protection for natural areas and prime farmland outside of the green belt area.[50] These examples illustrate the difficulty of arresting sprawl and we also acknowledge (as discussed in Chapter 3) that not everyone agrees with the wisdom of attempting to control sprawl. It is not our intention to reopen that debate. Rather, we are suggesting that *if* sprawl is to be tackled, amalgamations are less likely to be effective than appropriate provincial intervention.

Ensuring Equity/Reducing Inequity

For reasons already discussed, a fragmented municipal structure can give rise to serious concerns about equality and equity. In fact, such a structure tends to perpetuate, and even accentuate, inequalities in income, economic opportunity, and quality of life. Not only do those in the suburbs avoid the social costs of the inner city as much as they can, but also – in a cruel irony – inner city residents are called upon to subsidize those in the suburbs, to the extent that they pay through their taxes to finance the very expensive extension of road, water and sewer lines, and other major infrastructure investments that facilitate the suburban development. After studying 165 metropolitan areas in the United States, Rusk found[51] that those that had created metropolitan governments by annexation or consolidation were less segregated by race and class, economically healthier, and more equitable for their residents.

The problems outlined above have been more pronounced in the United States than Canada, which may help to explain why the issue of

---

[49] We are grateful to Dr. David Siegel, Brock University, and Dr. Caroline Andrew, University of Ottawa, for pointing out some of these developments.

[50] Mark S. Winfield, *Analysis of the Government of Ontario's Greater Golden Horseshoe Growth Plan*, Pembina Institute, July 4, 2006, accessed March 12, 2007 from www.pembina.org.

[51] David Rusk, *Cities Without Suburbs*, Washington, DC, Woodrow Wilson Centre Press, 1993.

equity has scarcely been mentioned in the Canadian context, at least until recently. It is instructive to examine briefly the solutions that have been advocated by observers of the American scene, and then to compare the situation here in Canada. Apart from Rusk, cited above, most of the others writing about this subject have largely ignored the issue of boundaries and have encouraged various mechanisms that would enable municipalities in a metropolitan area to cooperate with each other.[52]

Myron Orfield has done more than observe the urban scene in the United States; he has meticulously documented the spread of urban poverty from inner city to inner suburb and the rise of affluent outer ring suburbs. By so doing, he managed to split the normal suburban alliance against the city and forged a new one between the declining central city and older, threatened blue collar suburbs – leading to a number of intermunicipal collaborations in the Minneapolis–Saint Paul area.[53]

Orfield calls for seven reforms to address the problems facing America's urban areas.[54] The first three – fair housing, property tax sharing, and reinvestment in infrastructure – are needed to deconcentrate poverty, provide fiscal equity, and support the physical rebuilding needed to bring back the middle class and restore the private economy. He also calls for broader land use planning, an expansion of transit, and a combination of welfare reform and job creation centred on local public works projects, all designed to provide growth that is balanced socio-economically, accessible by transit, economical with government resources, and sensitive to the environment. Finally, he suggests that the previous six reforms can be most effectively administered and sustained by an elected metropolitan coordinating structure.

Two things about Orfield's list come immediately to mind. The first is that structural reform, which has received so much attention in Canada in the 1990s, is but one of seven reforms that he advocates. The second is that the other six proposals on his list all relate to policies and programs that can be introduced without any municipal restructuring, especially since many of these policies are best provided by higher levels of government. Ironically, Canada already had most of these policies in place to some degree, but has been abandoning them somewhat at the same time that provinces have been pushing restructuring.

---

[52] Andrew Sancton, *Merger Mania*, Montreal and Kingston, McGill-Queen's University Press, 2000, pp. 80-81.

[53] Myron Orfield, *Metropolitics: A Regional Agenda for Community and Stability*, Washington, DC, Brookings Institution Press, 1997, is his personal account of the battle he waged to bring about regional collaboration.

[54] *Ibid.*, pp. 11-12, on which the following discussion is based.

Policies That Address Equity

Equity issues can be addressed in a number of ways besides restructuring. In fact, while the existence of a number of separate municipalities within one urban area can give rise to problems of coordination in the provision of services and of equitable sharing of costs, restructuring doesn't necessarily help to alleviate problems caused by spillovers or externalities. This is particularly the case where urban and rural municipalities with widely varying service standards are brought together. Vojnovic points out that if differences in levels and standards of service among the merging municipalities are not recognized in the design of the tax structure, externalities may actually be exacerbated, with some unknowingly paying for services from which they get no benefits.[55]

One way to address inequities, and to counter excessive municipal competition for growth at the same time, is to introduce a tax sharing scheme under which some portion of the yield from new growth brought to an area is shared among municipalities in return for joint marketing and promotion efforts and, sometimes, joint investment in infrastructure.

Box 5.3 Sharing the Wealth in Minneapolis–St. Paul

One of the best known and longest operating tax sharing plans is the one found in Minneapolis–St. Paul. It was introduced in 1971, overcame fierce opposition from wealthy municipalities that would have to share, and was finally enacted as the *Fiscal Disparities Act* in 1975. The rules, which apply to the close to 200 municipalities in the seven county Minneapolis–St Paul area, as well as to school districts and other taxing authorities, are quite simple. Each jurisdiction contributes 40% of the growth in its commercial-industrial tax base (since the base year of 1971) to a regional pool. The funds in the pool are then redistributed based on whether a community has higher or lower fiscal capacity than the regional average. The plan has been successful in reducing inequities significantly while also reducing, but certainly not eliminating, municipal competition for industry and growth.[56]

Provinces can provide unconditional grants to bolster the revenues of municipalities with a weak assessment base (in much the same way as the federal government has long provided equalization payments to have-not provinces). A majority of the provinces have had such programs over the years, but not on a scale that would suggest that equalization was a

---

[55] Igor Vojnovic, "Municipal Consolidation, Regional Planning and Fiscal Accountability: The Recent Experiences in Two Maritime Provinces," *Canadian Journal of Regional Science*, Special Edition, Spring 2000, pp. 49–72.

[56] Orfield, *Metropolitics*, examines the tax sharing plan, and another assessment is provided in Citizens League, *Minnesota Journal*, April 2007, accessed June 28, 2007 at www.citizensleague.org.

major priority.[57] Provinces can also promote a more equitable distribution of public housing throughout an urban area to offset the fact that lower priced housing is associated with higher levels of demand for publicly funded social services and education. The Ontario Housing Corporation was established in 1964 to access federal funding for public housing and had considerable success in dispersing public housing across the Metro Toronto area.[58] However, the federal government abandoned the public housing field in the 1990s (only recently to return on a smaller scale) and the Ontario government turned what is now usually termed "social" housing over to the private sector (with little response) when the Conservatives assumed power in 1995. Subsequently, the province downloaded responsibility for social housing to municipalities in what must be considered a backward step with respect to equity concerns. In other provinces, such as British Columbia, B.C. Housing has sought to carve out a role in "saving" SROs (single room occupancy hotels) in Vancouver's poorer Downtown Eastside (DTES) as part of its support for local emphasis on dealing with central city homelessness. Between 2006 and 2011 the province of British Columbia acquired 26 SRO hotels (with 1500 rooms) in Vancouver, New Westminster, and Victoria.[59]

Ontario's withdrawal from such shared cost programming was part of a fairly widespread cutback evident in most provincial jurisdictions as they struggled to combat deficit and debt problems that had been made worse by cuts in the transfer payments that they received from the federal government. Any such reduction in provincial support, however, leaves municipalities more vulnerable to inequities and social problems. There were two studies in the Greater Toronto Area, one on homelessness in Toronto at the end of the 1990s and the other at the beginning of this decade. The first concluded that Toronto risked suffering the "inner city" poverty of American cities without concerted multilevel policy responses.[60] The second found similar features such as:

---

[57] The discussion in this section is largely based on Frances Frisken, "Jurisdictional and Political Constraints on Progressive Local Initiative," in Timothy L. Thomas (ed.), *The Politics of the City*, Toronto, ITP Nelson, 1997, pp. 163-166.

[58] Frances Frisken, L. S. Bourne, Gunter Gad, and Robert A. Murdie, "Governance and Social Sustainability," in Mario Polese and Richard Stren (eds.), *Social Sustainability of Cities: Diversity and the Management of Change*, Toronto, University of Toronto Press, 2000, p. 85.

[59] See, for example, Press Release, B.C. Housing, "Single Room Occupancy Hotels," at www.bchousing.org/initiatives/Renovating/SRO (accessed June 26, 2011).

[60] See Report of the GTA Task Force, *Greater Toronto*, 1996 and Mayor's Homelessness Action Task Force Report, Toronto, 1999 (www.toronto.ca/pdf/homeless_action.pdf).

- a deepening city suburban split;
- an increasing polarization of income and social status;
- a relative decline of parts of the older mature suburbs;
- the continued geographical concentration of low income and socially disadvantaged households; and
- the intense separation of social groups with nontraditional social and cultural backgrounds.[61]

A study of the Montreal area noted that social programs from the provincial and federal level had helped to ensure its social sustainability and questioned whether this sustainability would be undermined by the cutbacks in social programs since the mid-1990s.[62] The record of new provincial spending on such social programs into the early 21st century is, at best, spotty.

Transit is another example in which provincial government grants have played a positive role, only to be cut back as part of the retrenchment of the 1990s/early 2000s. Ontario's actions were again quite dramatic, with the province withdrawing from all funding for municipal transit systems and transferring to the municipal level the cost of an intermunicipal train service across the Greater Toronto Area known as GO Transit. Saner heads prevailed eventually, and the province took back responsibility for GO Transit and also introduced grant payments covering 33% of transit operations (well down from the 75% that it used to subsidize). The province also established, in 2006, a Greater Toronto Transportation Authority (now Metrolinx) that was supposed to plan, finance, coordinate, and develop an integrated transportation network within the Greater Golden Horseshoe. It has been successful in obtaining (in June 2010) $9.5 billion in provincial funding for an ambitious public transit plan covering five major transit projects over the next decade.[63]

As Chapter 7 describes, provinces such as British Columbia, Alberta, and Ontario provide support for public transit by sharing a portion of their fuel taxes with their major cities. But Chapter 7 also documents the very limited federal financial support for public transit, as compared with the situation in the United States. In addition to inadequate financial support from the senior levels, part of the problem in Metro Vancouver is related to how the metropolitan municipalities will pay their share of

---

[61] Larry Bourne, *People and Times: A Portrait of the Evolving Social Character of the Greater Toronto Region*, Toronto, Neptis Foundation, 2000.

[62] Anne-Marie Séguin and Annick Germain, "The Social Sustainability of Montreal," in Polese and Stren, *Social Sustainability of Cities*, pp. 52-53.

[63] Details can be found at the Metrolinx website at www.metrolinx.com.

such programs. Translink, the now provincially appointed metro transportation authority, has been hundreds of millions of dollars short on its share of the long-planned Evergreen Line – from Burnaby, Vancouver's next door neighbour, to northeast regional municipalities Port Moody and Coquitlam. A combined $1 billion is available from the federal and provincial governments but the Mayors' Council, Translink's governing body, had resisted calls for its $400 million share of the ll kilometre line to be paid from local property taxes.[64] In October 2011, however, agreement was reached on a two cent per litre gas tax increase plus two years of increased property taxes (of approximately $24 per unit each year) to fund the Evergreen rapid transit line, new bus services, and road improvements. With this decision, senior government funding will flow and completion of the next phase of rapid transit to the northeast corner of the Vancouver region is expected by 2017.[65]

Another approach that provinces can pursue is to take over or fully fund particular local services as a way of ensuring uniformity of service delivery. New Brunswick's Equal Opportunity Program is the most dramatic example of this approach, under which that province assumed full responsibility for the administration of justice, welfare, public health, and educational finance. Paradoxically, the Ontario government moved in the opposite direction, shifting downward functions that, by their nature, increase inequities and inconsistencies. As a result of a local services realignment introduced in 1996, Ontario took over a substantial portion of education costs but gave its municipalities increased or total responsibility for such services as social assistance, public health, social housing, land ambulances, and public transit.

It should be noted that the social programs downloaded in Ontario were assigned to single tier and upper tier municipalities, including the network of regional (and one metropolitan) governments covering the urban areas of the province. As a result, the various amalgamations that collapsed these two tier regional systems into enlarged single cities did nothing to advance the cause of equity. The same areas that financed the provision of social programs through the Metropolitan Toronto upper tier government, for example, now finance the provision of these programs by the enlarged City of Toronto. Without these upper tier governments in

---

[64] On this see, for example, Kelly Sinoski and Jonathan Fowlie, "Evergreen Line Faces Another Year's Delay and Uncertain Future: It could be cancelled outright because of a funding dispute between the province and Metro Vancouver mayors," *The Vancouver Sun*, June 1, 2011.

[65] Kelly Sinoski, "Evergreen Line construction to begin next summer: transportation minister," *Vancouver Sun*, October 27, 2011.

most American urban areas, the equity issue is certainly valid. It is misleading, however, to import it to justify amalgamations that simply replace a two tier system with a single municipality covering the same territory. That two tier system had been successful "in ensuring a relatively high degree of intermunicipal equity in the quality of local services, through the pooling of tax revenues."[66]

There are also several examples of cost sharing across an urban area as a way of addressing equity considerations – whatever municipal structure is in place. To illustrate:

> ➤ After transferring responsibility for a number of social programs to the municipal level in the late 1990s, the Ontario government acknowledged the externalities associated with local delivery of such services by mandating a scheme under which social assistance and social housing costs were equalized across all municipalities in the Greater Toronto Area. The spring 2007 Ontario budget announced the phasing out (by 2013) of this cost sharing scheme, which had always been opposed by the other municipalities. In 2011, in another good example of being careful what you wish for, however, these municipalities may soon prefer that the regional cost sharing scheme had been continued. Now that the "urban sock is turning inside out," as discussed in Chapter 3, it is the surrounding municipalities, not the City of Toronto, that are likely to face growing social costs in the coming years.
> ➤ Across Ontario more generally, after the 1998 Local Services Realignment process undertaken by the Harris Conservative government, shared cost arrangements were changed for social housing, employment and financial assistance, child care, long term care, paramedic and public health services, and the Municipal Property Assessment Corporation. The municipal share of funding increased for all these provincially mandated services – not a positive development in terms of equity considerations. The City of Ottawa calculated in 2011 that the local property tax share for such growth raised taxes by $670.[67] Ontario is the only province in which the property tax funds major social service

---

[66] New Local Government Network, City Regions Commission, *Seeing the Light? Next Steps for City Regions*, December 2005, p. 15, accessed May 14, 2007 from www.nlgn.org.uk.

[67] See, for example, City of Ottawa, "Provincially Mandated and Cost Shared Programs." http://ottawa.ca/city_hall/financial/lrfp3/financial_profile/part_a/prov_mandated_en.html (accessed July 1, 2011).

costs (over $3.5 billion). Gradually, however, this unfair burden has been addressed. The province increased its share of public health costs from 50% to 75% between 2004/5 and 2007/8. As a result of the fall 2008 report of the Provincial-Municipal Fiscal and Service Delivery Review, the province is uploading various social program costs over a 10 year period, saving Ontario municipalities $1.5 billion by 2018.[68]

> A regional transit coordinating agency was established in 1989 to bring together representatives of the Montreal Urban Community transit system, the south shore system, and the system of the City of Laval. By setting up such an agency, the province combined financial responsibility for subway operating deficits and for previous municipal long term transit debt among all municipalities served by the three systems.[69] December 1995 legislation created the Metropolitan Transportation Agency, which serves a population of 3.2 million in 64 municipalities and 13 regional counties with its 21 transit authorities.[70] By 2010, the Société de Transport de Montreal (STM) had a ridership of 382.2 million, an increase of 5.4%.[71]

> Translink (the Greater Vancouver Transportation Authority – renamed the South Coast British Columbia Transportation Authority) was set up in 1998 to plan and finance a regional transportation system that supports the regional growth strategy of this area.[72] Translink was initially governed by a board of directors comprising mostly local representatives appointed by and from the Greater Vancouver Regional District. (There is now a mayor's council composed of the heads of the municipalities in Metro Vancouver and they appoint a board of directors of individuals chosen for their skill and expertise.) Translink is authorized to raise revenues through various means including taxes, levies, toll charges, and user fees. Using these sources has

---

[68] See *Provincial-Municipal Fiscal and Service Delivery Review Report*, Province of Ontario, AMO/City of Toronto, at www.mah.gov.on.ca/page6002.aspx, accessed March 17, 2011.

[69] Andrew Sancton, "Metropolitan Government in Montreal," in Sharpe, *The Government of World Cities*, pp. 138-139.

[70] Information from the agency's website www.amt.qc.ca/english/welcome.asp, accessed June 28, 2007.

[71] See STM, *On The Move: 2009 Activity Report*, Montreal, 2010.

[72] Information on this agency is available at www.translink.bc.ca.

proven to be exceedingly difficult politically, however. Translink also receives three cents per litre of the fuel taxes collected by the province. In 2011, 92% of Translink's total budget of $229.2 million came from residential and business property tax. Fuel tax revenues were the next largest share[73] and, as noted above, it was decided in late 2011 to add two cents per litre to the regional fuel tax to help fund the Evergreen Line.

Box 5.4 Equity Solutions Lie Elsewhere
To sum up, if improving equity is a major objective, it can be achieved through a wide range of policies and programs that are best provided by senior levels of government. The fact that a number of these programs have been provided in Canada presumably helps to explain why equity issues have not been as pronounced here as in the United States. But government restraint over the past decade has undermined some of these programs, with the result that equity may become more of a concern despite all the restructuring there has been.

Eliminating Clash and Conflict

Proponents of amalgamation often point to intermunicipal disagreements and turf wars as reasons why boundary changes are needed. It is widely held, for example, that the merger creating the Halifax Regional Municipality was precipitated by excessive competition between the business parks of the separate municipalities.[74] We are told that municipalities are too parochial, that they won't cooperate sufficiently. They won't pursue the joint ventures that might bring about savings. Their wrangling makes it difficult for joint boards to function. Combining these fractious municipalities into one governing unit resolves these problems. It facilitates urban planning and economic development. But does amalgamation eliminate wrangling and, more to the point, should it?

Presumably not all of the different points of view expressed by municipalities prior to their amalgamation are shortsighted or selfish. To some extent, they reflect underlying values and concerns within their local populations. These differences don't magically disappear just because there is an amalgamation. In fact, when amalgamations bring together quite diverse areas – such as when urban and rural areas are

---

[73] See Translink, "Translink releases 2011 Property Tax rates," April 8, 2011, Press Release and Translink, *2011 Budget.*

[74] Dale Poel, *Municipal Reform in Nova Scotia*, p. 177.

combined in Ontario's Chatham-Kent or Ottawa or in Nova Scotia's Halifax – it may be that the differences will be heightened or exacerbated. The rural–urban conflict has been quite evident in amalgamated municipalities in Ontario such as Hamilton and Ottawa. Former provincial Conservative leader John Tory, whose party imposed these amalgamations, acknowledged the problem in discussions with the City of Hamilton.[75] Ottawa responded to rural unrest by holding a Rural Summit and introducing a number of changes designed to address rural concerns.[76] According to one study, Ottawa has been struggling with the differing cultures of the former municipalities that were merged – reflected in a more politicized and inclusive decision making process in the old city, policy processes driven by professional staff in most of the suburbs, and more informal, personalized operations in the rural areas.[77] Caroline Andrew has suggested that in Ottawa, the rural-urban divide which was evident immediately postamalgamation has been ameliorated by the Rural Summit and increased provincial interest in such issues.[78]

If an amalgamation process is "softened" by introducing a ward system of election based on the former municipal boundaries, this electoral system tends to perpetuate and reinforce the differing views and values that have been thrown together. The same is true if community councils or committees are established with boundaries that encompass the municipalities that have been amalgamated.[79] These bodies will attempt to ensure that the particular interests and concerns of their area are not overlooked by the new, enlarged municipality – and fulfilling this role is presumably why they were established in the first place. Even without a ward system or community councils, the diverse views found within an enlarged municipality will continue to demand attention – as they should in a democratic system. It must be appreciated, then, that amalgamation doesn't eliminate differences and clashes; it brings them inside a single council chamber.

---

[75] Kevin Werner, "Amalgamation not working in Hamilton: Tory," *Flamborough Review*, June 9, 2006.

[76] Details at http://ottawa.ca/residents/rural_connections/rural_summit_02/index_en.html, accessed June 15, 2006.

[77] Laura A. Reese and Davia S. Cox, "Local culture and governmental change: The endurance of culture in the face of structural change," *Canadian Public Administration*, Summer 2007, p. 256.

[78] Communication with authors, June 25, 2011.

[79] As discussed in Chapter 9, such bodies were established in such amalgamated cities as Winnipeg, Toronto, Montreal, and Halifax, although in this last instance boundaries were deliberately not based on the old municipal boundaries.

> **Box 5.5 All For One and One For All?**
>
> Consider the council of the new City of Montreal, elected in November 2001. Former Mayor Pierre Bourque had fought hard for the amalgamation that created the new city and suburban voters responded by defeating Bourque and electing Gerald Tremblay and a majority of his Montreal Island Citizens Union Party. Proponents of amalgamation had claimed that it would end decades of conflict and bickering between the suburbs and the city. Instead, this split simply carried over into the new council, with the suburban representatives holding the upper hand, hardly an arrangement conducive to a harmonious term of office.

It is also important to recognize that amalgamation is likely to alter the balance of power on the local scene. For example, by merging middle class suburbs with inner city areas, amalgamation may push local politics to the right.[80] It is likely that this kind of consideration was on the mind of the Conservative government in Ontario when it imposed the merger that created the new City of Toronto. The expectation was that representatives elected to city council from the more conservative suburban areas would be able to curb the more free spending inclinations (at least from the province's perspective) of councillors from the old city. This observation is also made by Savitch and Kantor, who note that the province also believed that once social programs were downloaded to the city, councillors would have an added incentive to be more frugal.[81]

Less Government/Less Bureaucracy

This argument for amalgamation reflects the view that people are overgoverned and desire less government, less "red tape," and fewer politicians. It is consistent with the antigovernment bias that is central to the right wing revolution that swept across North America in the past several decades. The reduced role of government and government regulations is also very consistent with the demands of the business community and the perceived requirements of the new global economy.

Nowhere has this rationale been more in evidence than in the restructuring initiatives pursued by the Conservative government in Ontario in the second half of the 1990s. They premised restructuring on the notions that local politicians and staff are "the problem," that there are too many of them, that they are wasteful in their practices, that their

---

[80] Keating, "Size, Efficiency and Democracy," p. 122.

[81] Savitch and Kantor, *Cities in the International Marketplace*, p. 182.

operations are inefficient, that they tax too readily, and that they spend irresponsibly.[82]

The answer, according to the Ontario Conservatives, was to provide less government. Every amalgamation in Ontario prompted a press release from the Ministry of Municipal Affairs that tracked how many fewer municipalities and municipal politicians there were as a result. By the time the restructuring initiative was abandoned in early 2001, the number of councillors had been reduced by almost 2000, representing a 40% reduction in local representation. This reduction was presented by the province as a self-evident gain to society, but why is it so desirable to have fewer elected local politicians in a democracy? What are the implications of enlarging municipalities to the point where serving on council ceases to be a part time activity available to all, and becomes the preserve of the full time professional politician? One consequence of this change is that council salaries go up to handle increased workloads, often cancelling out virtually all of the savings that were supposed to result from reducing the number of politicians – not that councillors' salaries are in any way a significant factor in overall municipal costs. Across Canada, most municipal councillors serve as part time politicians, even when supervising multimillion dollar budgets and significant numbers of professional staff.[83]

The provincially promoted amalgamations did not really produce less government, of course; instead, they produced bigger government and, as discussed below, more bureaucratic government as well. One explanation for this obviously incorrect provincial message may be that what the Conservatives really meant (and wanted) was not less government in terms of size, but a reduction in the prominence and role of local governments. Less government for them might be equated with the enhanced role for the private sector reflected in the enthusiastic provincial promotion of alternative service delivery options including public private partnerships and outright privatization. Students of local government elsewhere in Canada would not be surprised by this approach.

---

[82] T. J. Downey and R. J. Williams, "Provincial agendas, local responses: the 'common sense' restructuring of Ontario's municipal governments," *Canadian Public Administration*, Summer 1998, p. 234.

[83] For a comparative analysis of this across eight major Canadian cities see Patrick Smith and Kennedy Stewart, "Immature Policy Analysis: Building Capacity in Eight Major Canadian Cities," in Laurent Dobuzinskis, Michael Howlett, and David Laycock (eds.), *Policy Analysis in Canada: The State of the Art*, Toronto, University of Toronto Press (Institute of Public Administration of Canada Series in Public Management and Governance), 2007, Ch.11, pp. 265-288.

Another concern about the supposed virtues of less government is the very large populations that are now represented by relatively small councils. When restructuring proponents cite with approval the reduction in the number of local politicians that has been achieved, they are really talking about a reduction in local representation. Each councillor now represents a much larger number of people, usually over a much larger area. The link between citizens and their *local* government is weakened as a result – and concerns about local accountability grow.[84]

A Different Perspective on Less Bureaucracy

In addition to the doubts about less government, it is equally hard to understand the claim that amalgamation brings less bureaucracy. To the contrary, the result is larger municipalities that have more complex organizations, more layers of management, and more opportunities for red tape. Moreover, equating less bureaucracy with reduced duplication and reduced barriers and red tape for business is a very narrow way of looking at this subject. Research on the features of what are termed post-bureaucratic organizations[85] describe them as people centred, change oriented, results oriented, decentralized, revenue driven, and competitive. The presence or absence of these features has virtually nothing to do with amalgamation.

It is sometimes suggested that creating a new municipality through amalgamation provides the opportunity to introduce such features. But the upheaval caused by amalgamation, and the lengthy process involved in bringing about its implementation, can divert the time and energy of new municipalities and keep them from pursuing these innovations. This was the Montreal experience,[86] as it was in Toronto. At least two-thirds of the very substantial savings predicted for Toronto (about $150 million to $250 million annually) was not related to amalgamation but was to arise from "efficiency enhancements." These savings did not materialize in the first few years, according to the Director of Toronto's Amalgamation Office, who claimed that achieving such savings was not a

---

[84] *Ibid.*

[85] See, for example, Kenneth Kernaghan, Brian Marson, and Sandford Borins, *The New Public Organization*, Toronto, Institute of Public Administration of Canada, 2000.

[86] Pierre Hamel has suggested that after perhaps "too much" reform, Quebec municipalities like Montreal should be left alone to "just make it work" instead of undergoing more restructuring to respond to earlier reform changes. Personal communication with authors, June 27, 2011.

reasonable expectation "in the short run." [87] Poel reports similar experiences in Halifax, where the theme in the first three years was not savings but "don't drop the ball." He emphasizes that a great deal of time and energy is needed to get a new organization up and running effectively.[88] Hamel would agree.

To Compete in a Global World

Amalgamation is advocated to reduce harmful intermunicipal competition and "beggar-thy-neighbour" policies designed to attract industry, and also to create an enlarged municipality more capable of holding its own in the increasingly competitive global marketplace. It may be recalled that reducing intermunicipal competition for business was cited in the amalgamation that created Halifax, and the amalgamations in Montreal, Toronto, and Ottawa were also promoted as creating bigger cities that could handle themselves better on the world stage.

The argument that amalgamation is required because of globalization is very much open to dispute. It appears to be derived from the fact that globalization has made cities and city regions increasingly important – and on that point there is no argument. "City-regions have come to be recognized as key nodes of the global economy; as places where capital, workers, institutions and infrastructure (soft and hard) come together to provide the foundations for successful economic activity."[89] While national boundaries (and their governments) may have become less important in the new global economy with its various international trade agreements and organizations, major urban centres have come to the

---

[87] As quoted in Laura Eggerston, "Becoming One: Lessons Learned From Amalgamation," *Forum*, Ottawa, Federation of Canadian Municipalities, Nov/ Dec 2000, p. 18.

[88] D. Poel and M. Dann, "The development of political leadership in the context of change," unpublished paper.

[89] Meric S. Gertler, "City-Regions in the Global Economy: Choices Facing Toronto," *Policy Options*, September 1996, p. 12. See also Patrick Smith (with T.H. Cohn), "North American Cities In An Interdependent World: Vancouver and Seattle as International Cities," in Earl Fry, Lee Radebaugh, and Panayotis Soldatos (eds.), *The New International Cities: The Global Activities of North American Municipal Governments*, Provo, UT, Brigham Young University, 1989, pp. 73-116; Patrick Smith, "Globalist vs. Globalized Cities: Redefining Urban Responses to Globalization," in T. H. Cohn, S. McBride, and J. Wiseman (eds.), *Power in the Global Era: Globalization and its Discontents*, London, Macmillan, 2000; and Patrick Smith and Kennedy Stewart, *Global Calgary: A Globalist Strategy for the City of* Calgary, Ottawa, Canadian Policy Research Network, April 2006.

forefront because their very concentration of population and economic activity enhance efficiency and innovation.[90]

But does it follow that this increased economic importance of cities and city regions requires amalgamations that create municipalities large enough to embrace them? To the extent that broader, regional strategies and actions are needed, are there alternative mechanisms for achieving them? It is instructive to recall the findings of Richard Florida (discussed in Chapter 3) that in today's knowledge based economy businesses are attracted to areas that have a talent pool, which, in turn, means that places that can attract talented people will enjoy economic success. Vibrant neighbourhoods, ample recreational facilities, an atmosphere that welcomes and nurtures diversity and creativity, a good public education system – all of these contribute to the rich quality of life that is the key to success. Building healthy and vibrant communities is less about formal government structures and more about building relationships. Thomas describes the required emphasis on governance rather than government:[91]

> It involves sharing power, the creation of formal and informal networks of interaction, more open and responsive flows of information and intelligence in all directions, decision-making on multiple levels and across multiple sectors and dynamic changes. This more complicated and kaleidoscopic approach to agenda setting recognizes that governments do not have a monopoly on the knowledge, skills and capacity to achieve economic and social improvement.

The argument that amalgamation is needed to contend with global competition falters in the face of the fact that many of the most dynamic and competitive regions in North America (such as the Boston and Dallas areas and Seattle–King County) are among the most fragmented. To illustrate:

> ➢ Pittsburgh has enjoyed an economic renaissance with more than 120 separate elected municipal governments in the central city and Allegheny County.[92] It has a limited tax sharing plan

---

[90] Peter Dreir, John Mollenkopf, and Todd Swanstrom, *Place Matters: Metropolitics for the Twenty-First Century*, Lawrence, University Press of Kansas, 2001, p. 25. See also Allen J. Scott, John Agnew, Edward W. Soja, and Michael Storper, *Global City-Regions*, in Allen J. Scott (ed.), *Global City-Regions*, Oxford, Oxford University Press, 2002.

[91] Paul Thomas, *Globalization, Competitive Regionalism and Municipal Tax Sharing*, July 2002, accessed June 15, 2007 from www.gov.mb.ca/ia/capreg.

[92] Sancton, *Merger Mania*, pp. 77-78. See also Sancton, "Globalization Does Not Require Amalgamation," *Policy Options*, Montreal, Institute for Research on Public Policy, November 1999, pp. 54-58.

operated by the Allegheny Regional Asset District established in 1993. It receives one half of the proceeds from the 1% Allegheny County Sales and Use Tax (the other half is paid directly to the municipal governments) and uses this money to support libraries, parks and recreation, and cultural, sports, and civic facilities and programs.[93] There is also an Allegheny Conference on Community Development, a private sector leadership body with over 300 regional investors, that works in collaboration with public and private partners to promote economic growth in Pittsburgh and the 10 counties of southwestern Pennsylvania.[94]

➤ It wasn't a unified municipal structure that spearheaded the economic success of Silicon Valley, California; rather it was a private sector initiative that brought together key stakeholders (including municipalities) in the San Jose region to develop a vision and discuss ways of attracting and maintaining computer-associated manufacturing. Collaboration and networking have been the distinguishing features of governance in this area, highlighted by such initiatives as Joint Venture: Silicon Valley, a public private partnership that addressed key regional issues such as education and brought together a group of business, government, and community leaders to develop a vision for 2010. This project, in turn, led to the Silicon Valley Civic Network, which is promoting public discussion of the 2010 vision and goals.[95]

➤ Critics of the City of Toronto often praise the achievements of Chicago and advance it as a model to emulate.[96] The irony is that the Chicago metropolitan area has 270 local governments and over 1000 other governing bodies and special districts.[97]

➤ Regional coordination in the Denver area has evolved from an intercounty planning association that became in 1968 the Denver Regional Council of Governments (DRCOG), a nonprofit, voluntary membership association that now comprises 52 municipal and county governments. It is the region's recognized

---

[93] From the District's website www.radworkshere.org, accessed June 28, 2007.

[94] Its website, accessed June 28, 2007, is www.pittsburghregion.org.

[95] Douglas Henton, "Lessons from Silicon Valley: Governance in a Global City-Region," in Scott, *Global City-Regions*, pp. 396-397.

[96] *Globe and Mail* columnist Margaret Wente rhapsodized about Chicago in a May 29, 2007 piece entitled "What's wrong with Toronto? Nothing a good mayor couldn't fix."

[97] New Local Government Network, *Next Steps for City Regions*, p. 14.

metropolitan planning agency, overseeing transportation and water funding and planning, even though it cannot impose taxes, issue bonds, or legislate. DRCOG adopted a growth management plan in 1997 which has to date been accepted by municipalities representing almost 90% of the region's population.[98]

➢ In Seattle, the city region has developed an international governance model both formal and informal. Under auspices like the Trade Development Alliance – an amalgam of the cities of Seattle, Everett, and Tacoma and the port of Seattle and the greater Seattle Chamber of Commerce – international 7-10 day "study tours" are organized annually to competitor cities around the world. Seattle also has 21 "sister cities," one of the highest numbers of municipal international connections in the United States.[99]

If the municipalities within an urban area are amalgamated, the unified structure will doubtless make it easier to promote and market that area. But amalgamation is not a prerequisite to economic growth, as the preceding examples illustrate. Even if there is an amalgamation, much will still depend on the degree of collaboration that can be achieved between the enlarged municipality, the local business community, and the wide variety of agencies and organizations that collectively contribute to the well-being of the area. Ultimately, as discussed further in the next section, broader collaboration is arguably more important than the particular municipal structure that is in place. The Seattle example demonstrates this point clearly.[100]

---

[98] Kathleen McCormick, *Regional Thinking*, Urban Land Institute, September 2006, accessed June 14, 2007 at www.uli.org.

[99] The authors are grateful to Dr. Keith Orton, Director, International Relations, Office of Intergovernmental Relations, City of Seattle, February 2011.

[100] See also Patrick Smith (with T. H. Cohn), "Developing Global Cities In The Pacific Northwest: The Cases of Vancouver and Seattle," in Peter K. Kresl and Gary Gappert (eds.), *North American Cities and the Global Economy: Challenges and Opportunities*, Thousand Oaks, CA, Sage, 1995; *Urban Affairs Annual Review* 44, Chapter 11, pp. 251-285; and "Transborder Cascadia: Opportunities and Obstacles," *Journal of Borderlands Studies*, Vol.19, No.1, Spring 2004, pp. 99-121.

Old and New Regionalism

The varied options that are available to address regional issues can be grouped into two categories of old and new regionalism. Traditional or old regionalism is preoccupied with the need for boundary changes and with structural reforms through amalgamation and the establishment of one or two tier municipal systems. Over the past couple of decades, however, other ways of addressing these issues have come to the fore and have become known as the new regionalism. One of the best known expressions of this new approach is found in the writings of Myron Orfield cited earlier in this chapter. Another is Neal Peirce's *CitiStates*, which chronicles both the challenges facing major centres in the United States and the varied ways in which these are being tackled through the combined efforts of many players, of which municipal governments are but one, and not always the leading one.[101]

Key features of the new regionalism are summarized below.[102]

Box 5.6 Features of the New Regionalism

- Focusing on governance, not government, by establishing a vision and goals and setting policies to achieve them.
- Focusing on process instead of structure, through such means as strategic planning, resolving conflict, and building consensus.
- Accepting that boundaries are open and elastic and building cross-sectoral governing coalitions that vary with the issues being addressed.
- Emphasizing collaboration and voluntary agreement rather than hierarchy and top down power.
- Building trust as a binding element in relations among regional interests.
- Moving away from a focus on power and how it is allocated among levels of government, and shifting to an emphasis on empowering neighbourhoods and communities and drawing them into regional decision making.

It is fair to say that the old regionalism has prevailed in local government reform and restructuring in Canada, including the wave of reform in the 1990s that saw amalgamations imposed in Ontario and Quebec and, to a lesser extent, in Nova Scotia and New Brunswick. However, elements of the new regionalism are also evident in Canada, and are reflected in

---

[101] Neal R. Peirce, *CitiStates: How Urban America Can Prosper in a Competitive World*, Washington, DC, Seven Locks Press, 1993.

[102] Allan Wallis, "The New Regionalism: Inventing Governance Structures for the Early Twenty-First Century," paper presented to the Elected Officials Symposium at the University of Alberta, June 21, 2000.

earlier examples of urban and metropolitan agencies made up of public and private representation and devoted to promoting cooperative action on cross boundary issues.

Consistent with the new regionalism is the work of the Toronto City Summit Alliance, which describes itself as a multisector coalition working to meet the Toronto region's challenges. Its Steering Committee includes company presidents, university chancellors, mayors and CAOs, three former provincial premiers, and various other luminaries. The Alliance released a 2003 action plan with recommendations for all levels of government as well as business, labour, voluntary organizations, and citizens. It remains active and hosted a 2007 Summit to review progress on various fronts and to set out new priorities.[103] In February 2011, the Civic Action Alliance brought together over 700 "leaders" of the GTA (including three former Ontario premiers) to a summit meeting. It has emphasized diversity and sustainability of the city region and reflects this new regionalism.[104] In the absence of formal governing structures covering the broader Toronto area, the Alliance has emerged as a potential vehicle for providing some leadership at this level, just as a semiformal structure does in the Seattle city region.[105] The fact that the Toronto Alliance operates within an area that has gone through municipal restructuring is a reminder that old and new regionalism can exist side by side and, indeed, the combined approaches may offer the most effective way to address the challenges we face.

Whatever formal municipal structure may exist in an area, and however it may be reformed, there is also a need for alliances between the public and private sector and broader community interests. The number, nature, and geographic focus of these alliances may vary over time, depending on the issue being addressed. The new regionalism defines its area on the basis of the policy issue that needs attention rather than the municipal boundaries that exist. The result has been described as a *virtual* region, rather than one institutionalized and fixed in space.[106]

---

[103] For details see the Alliance website at www.torontoalliance.ca.

[104] See www.civicaction.ca/greater-toronto-summit-2011, accessed June 30, 2011.

[105] See Patrick Smith, "Branding Cascadia: Who Gets To Decide? Considering Cascadia's Conflicting Conceptualizations – The Case for a Global City Region Definition," *Canadian Political Science Review*, Vol. 2, No. 2, Summer 2008, and Andrew Sancton, "The Governance of Metropolitan Areas in Canada," *Public Administration and Development*, Vol. 25, 2005, p. 325.

[106] Tassilo Herrschel and Peter Newman, *Scale, "Virtual Regions" and Structures in City Regional Governance – a North American – and European Perspective*, paper prepared for the City Futures Conference, Chicago, 2004.

But such regions can only become real and visible to the public through specific projects on the ground – and, for that, traditional administrative entities with their powers and funding are still needed. Thus, old and new regionalism must be combined for effective action at that level.[107]

Concluding Comments

We began this chapter with three structural responses to the challenges facing municipal governments, ranging from intermunicipal boards through two tier systems to municipal amalgamations. Our examination of experiences with these three responses does not support the notion that they represent a natural and desirable progression, with the shift from two tier systems to amalgamated single municipalities as the ultimate objective – notwithstanding the attention given to amalgamation in the municipal reforms of the recent past.

If amalgamation is the answer, what was the question? If saving money is the primary objective, there are many other responses that are at least as likely to be successful. In any event, getting bogged down in a debate over whether amalgamation saves money is pointless. There are too many variables to be able to isolate the impact of amalgamation alone. There is no way to predict the changes that will arise and affect the operations of amalgamated municipalities – just as there is no way to know how events would have unfolded if municipalities had not been amalgamated. Statistics can be assembled to demonstrate almost any point of view that one wants to promote, but ultimately this debate simply diverts attention from more important issues.

One of those is certainly the concern about equity, but this problem is most effectively addressed by provincial and federal government programs and financial supports – the same programs and supports that have been eroded by more than a decade of deficit and debt reduction initiatives on the part of these governments. These continue in the second decade of the 21st century. As one example, the 2011 plans of the British Columbia government to repeal its *Drainage, Ditch and Dike Act* left regional districts such as Metro Vancouver "balking" at assuming the

---

[107] Tassilo Herrschel, *Urban Governance, the "Virtual Region" and Policy Making: Moving Towards "Integrated" City-Regionalism?*, paper presented at the Urban Affairs Association annual conference, Seattle, April 25-28, 2007.

"assets, rights, claims, obligations and liabilities" for areas potentially affected by BC's abandonment of its former obligations.[108]

As for problems associated with urban sprawl, it is arguable that these also may require more action on the part of the provincial level – at least in the largest urban agglomerations in Canada. These areas are so large that they cannot be brought within the boundaries of a "local" government. This is still the case in spite of the mergers of the past decade that created the enlarged cities of Toronto and Montreal. These new municipalities have the same outer boundaries as the two tier systems of Metro Toronto and the Montreal Urban Community that were eliminated through merger. Neither city has jurisdiction over its wider urban area. Even in Metro Vancouver which does cover a good percentage of the CMA, sprawl and density issues continue. In 2011, GVRD Chair and Delta Mayor Lois Jackson mused about Delta "quitting" Translink due to inadequate services despite Delta's pattern of sprawl and aversion to extensive diversification.[109]

Since the Quebec government was willing to impose amalgamation in Montreal, Hamel and Rousseau wonder why it then settled for a much weaker body (the Montreal Metropolitan Community) for planning and coordination over the wider metropolitan area.[110] The same question is applicable, even more so, to the Ontario government, which created the new City of Toronto in the face of strong opposition, but has shown no such willingness to create structures that can address the broader problems of the Greater Toronto Area. The very fact that areas such as these are so vital to the economies of their provinces, and of Canada, makes one wonder why it should be left to the local level alone, however restructured, to address the problems caused by sprawl – and as Hamel has noted, to the time consuming tasks of adjusting to the new politics of postamalgamation life.

If the issue is the fragmented structure within urban areas, is this inevitably a problem, and one that requires amalgamation to resolve? Commenting on the much more fragmented structure found in the United States, Stephens and Wikstrom contend that although it may be assailed as "chaotic, confusing, crazy-quilt, or simply incomprehensible to the average citizen," it is "seemingly viable and far from broken." That is Hamel's point regarding contemporary Montreal and other reformed city

---

[108] See, for example, Kelly Sinoski, "Metro balks at assuming diking job," *Vancouver Sun,* June 11, 2011, p. A12.

[109] See CBC News, "Delta ponders leaving Translink," February 3, 2011.

[110] Hamel and Rousseau, "Revisiting Municipal Reforms in Quebec," p. 14.

regions in Quebec. Stephens and Wikstrom go on to argue that "the bewildering structural array of general-purpose and special-purpose government bodies splashed across the usual metropolis are largely responding to and meeting the varied service needs of the citizenry," although they acknowledge that the less fortunate may, to some extent, fall outside "this deft generalization."[111]

Policy makers in Canada have been too narrowly focused on mergers as the response to urban and metropolitan issues. We agree with the assessment that "structures by themselves are seldom, if ever, either the basic cause, or the probable solution, of the problems they are designed to fix" but that "institutional reform is the most visible and readily identifiable step that a government can take to effect change."[112]

There are many other mechanisms that can be used to address issues that cross municipal boundaries. In Walker's whimsically titled *Snow White and the 17 Dwarfs*, Snow White is metropolitan American and the 17 dwarfs are 17 approaches to regional service delivery – ranging from informal cooperation and local service agreements through special purpose bodies and councils of government all the way to two tier restructuring and amalgamation.[113] Some of these other approaches have been used in Canada, as evidenced by examples in this and the preceding chapter, but not nearly as much as in other jurisdictions. Why is this?

Box 5.7 Questions To Consider

Do other jurisdictions have to resort to alternative approaches because they lack the authority (as a result, for example, of the home rule provisions in many U.S. states) to impose amalgamations as several Canadian provinces have done? Or is it the case that provincial governments have not bothered to explore and utilize thoroughly the many alternatives potentially available because they have the power to force amalgamations, thereby creating a highly visible response?

Are municipalities too parochial to cooperate voluntarily, requiring forced collaboration through amalgamation? Or do they resist because cooperative ventures and joint agreements have often been used against municipalities in the past as proof that they are interdependent and should amalgamate?

---

[111] Stephens and Wikstrom, *Metropolitan Government*, p. 169.

[112] Mary Louise McAllister, *Governing Ourselves? The Politics of Canadian Communities*, Vancouver, UBC Press, 2004, pp. 116-117.

[113] David B. Walker, "Snow White and the 17 Dwarfs: From Metro Cooperation to Governance," *National Civic Review*, January-February 1987, pp. 14-28.

> Could it be that the longstanding and relatively successful example of the British Columbia regional districts works as well as it does precisely because municipalities know that they do not face the threat of forced amalgamation?[114]
>
> As discussed in Chapter 6, do municipalities have the capacity to act as what might be termed '"eager beavers" initiating action on local and regional issues on their own?

The debate will continue, as will periodic reform initiatives. But it would be helpful if provincial policy makers who have zeroed in on amalgamation as an all-purpose solution to municipal problems demonstrated a greater appreciation of both the nature and causes of these problems and the varied ways in which they can be addressed – and if municipalities sought to use some of their inherent capacity to act locally and regionally to show the way. Vancouver's initiatives on a supervised injection site and introduction of a harm reduction strategy discussed in Chapter 6 and elsewhere suggest possibilities here.

---

[114] This point is made by Andrew Sancton, "Canadian Cities and the New Regionalism," *Journal of Urban Affairs*, 2001, Vol. 23, No. 5, p. 553. See also Patrick Smith (with H. Peter Oberlander), "Greater Vancouver: l'exception canadienne metropolitaine," in Razin and Smith (eds.), *Metropolitan Governing: Canadian Cases, Comparative Lessons*, pp. 153-188, and "Even Greater Vancouver: Metropolitan Morphing in Canada's Third Largest City Region," in Phares, (ed.), *Governing Metropolitan Regions*, Chapter 13.

Chapter 6
Intergovernmental Relations

Traditional views of local governments are no longer sufficient. Local governments must get beyond the limiting mindset that they are but constitutional orphans who must constantly plead for better treatment from the provincial (and federal) government. They need to recognize their growing importance, seek out alliances within the public and private sectors, and pursue a collaborative approach to the issues and challenges that they face. They might find becoming "eager beavers" produces new, more locally oriented, results.

Introduction

It's a brave new intergovernmental world for municipal governments today. As indicated by the discussion of new regionalism in the previous chapter, municipalities are now increasingly involved in complex multilevel and multisector relations with other levels of government, business groups, and organizations from civil society.

The relationship between municipalities and provincial governments commands attention because the provinces determine the structures, functions, and finances – even the very existence – of municipal governments within their jurisdiction. Federal-local relations have assumed increased importance, however, especially as they affect cities and in response to the impact of globalization. It is not just that 80% of Canadians now live in cities as compared to over 80% of the country's 3 463 000 population being rural/agricultural in 1867. Now, nearly half of the population resides in three urban agglomerations. It is also that the social, economic, and environmental challenges that we face are found particularly in our cities. It is in urban areas that "many of the major questions and challenges of our civilization are being raised."[1] It is also, as Jane Jacobs argued over a quarter century ago, that the large cities and

---

[1] Mario Polèse, "Learning from Each Other: Policy Choices and the Social Sustainability of Cities," in Mario Polèse and Richard Stren (eds.), *The Social Sustainability of Cities*, Toronto, University of Toronto Press, 2000, p. 9.

city regions are viewed as the key to Canada's competitiveness in the new global economy.[2] Many of the problems *in* our cities are not problems *of* our cities (as Lithwick noted over 40 years ago),[3] and it is inappropriate and unreasonable to expect them to be resolved by city governments acting alone. Recognition of this reality has been slow and sporadic – not least by senior level governments.

There is growing appreciation that municipalities are also involved in international relationships of considerable significance, as a result of globalization and free trade agreements and associated organizations. Given the multiplicity of relationships critical to municipal operations, effective inter-governmental relations are likely to be characterized by increasingly complex, often changing, combinations of players. In an effort to simplify presentation of this subject, we begin by examining municipal relations with the various levels – provincial, federal, and international. To use terms that will become clear as we proceed, our examination starts with the traditional view of federalism as structure rather than as process.

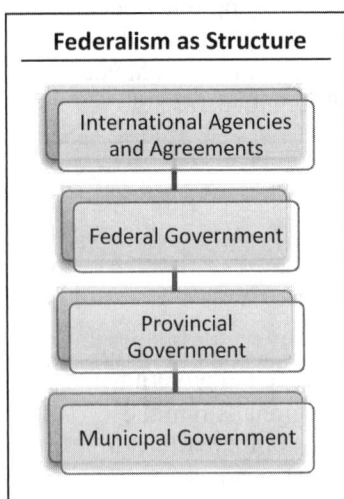

The Provincial-Local Relationship

The evolution of provincial-local relations in Canada has involved, for the most part, a pattern of increasing provincial supervision, influence, and control. Departments of municipal affairs were established by the beginning of the 20th century in a number of provinces "to give leadership and guidance in municipal development and to provide for the continuous study of the problems of municipalities." The Depression of the 1930s and attendant municipal defaulting on financial obligations led in several provinces to the establishment (or strengthening) of municipal

---

[2] Jane Jacobs, *Cities and the Wealth of Nations: Principles of Economic Life*, New York, Random House, 1983.

[3] N. H. Lithwick, *Urban Canada: Problems and Prospects*, Ottawa, Central Mortgage and Housing Corporation, December 1970, p. 14.

departments and municipal boards exercising a variety of supervisory powers in relation to local government.[4]

The period following the Second World War brought a further increase in provincial supervision and control, largely because of growing service demands on local government arising from the extensive urbanization of the time. As the revenues from the real property tax became less and less adequate to finance growing municipal expenditures, the provinces increased their financial assistance, mostly in the form of conditional grants. By attaching conditions, provinces were attempting to ensure that certain services were provided to at least a minimum standard regardless of the varying local financial capacities. But as municipalities participated in more of these shared-cost programs, their local expenditures increasingly reflected provincial priorities.

In some instances, intervention was even more direct, with the province assuming all or partial responsibility for functions traditionally exercised by the local level on the grounds, often quite valid, that the function had outgrown local boundaries and now had much wider implications. Especially during the first half of the 20th century, this pattern of functions shifting upward occurred with respect to such matters as roads, assessment, public health, education, administration of justice, and social services. A related development in some provinces saw the establishment or enlargement of intermunicipal special purpose bodies that were ostensibly part of the local government structure and yet came under increasing provincial control. Here again there was a valid concern on the part of the province about minimum standards in such areas as health and education, but the end result was a further weakening of municipalities in relation to the province. As one analyst saw it:[5]

> The succession of efforts to enlarge local administrative structures in education, public health, welfare, and toward regional municipalities has simply reduced the number of units confronting the provincial administrator at any one time.... The taxpayer's dollar has been the fulcrum of power for the bureaucrat to use in organizing things, ostensibly for the citizen's benefit but inevitably for the bureaucrat's benefit as well.

---

[4] K. G. Crawford, *Canadian Municipal Government*, Toronto, University of Toronto Press, 1954, p. 345. Chapter 17 of this text provides a good description of the historical evolution of provincial-local relations.

[5] Vernon Lang, *The Social State Emerges in Ontario*, Toronto, Ontario Economic Council, 1974, p. 61.

By the 1960s, local governments had been subjected to three decades of developments that undermined their independence and brought them increasingly into the orbit of the senior levels of government. The sun at the centre of most such municipal orbiting was the province.

> **Box 6.1 Three Decisive Decades**
>
> 1. As a result of the Depression of the 1930s, municipalities experienced increased provincial surveillance over their financial activities and they lost their historical place in the social services field to the provincial and federal governments.
> 2. During the 1940s, massive centralization occurred because of the war effort. As part of the tax-rental and then tax-sharing agreements brought on by the wartime emergency, municipal governments were squeezed out of such fields as income tax and sales tax, and confined to their historical dependence upon the real property tax as their main source of revenues.
> 3. By the 1950s, the greatly increased demands of the postwar period resulted in further provincial and federal encroachment on local operations.

Even where municipalities retained some jurisdiction over traditional functions, they found themselves increasingly entangled with the senior levels of government. To a considerable extent this intertwining of activities is inevitable, and reflects the interdependence of the programs and policies of all three levels of government. As O'Brien pointed out,[6] the various functions are interrelated in ways that would require intergovernmental activity even if they were all parcelled out in separate pieces to one level only – which they aren't and can't be (and arguably shouldn't be, as discussed later in this chapter).

Swainson has noted that in such intertwined settings *both* levels of government have the capacity to frustrate the other but neither is likely to benefit from such results.[7] A Smith and Stewart corollary to this *frustration thesis* is that when push does come to shove in such matters, constitutional standing trumps further frustration for the province. In support of this corollary position, we offer examples such as the Ontario government's response to Toronto area efforts to resist imposition of a

---

[6] Allan O'Brien, "A Look at the Provincial-Municipal Relationship," in Donald C. MacDonald (ed.), *Government and Politics of Ontario*, Toronto, Van Nostrand Reinhold, 1980, p. 167.

[7] See Neil Swainson, "The Provincial Municipal Relationship," in J. T. Morley, Norman Ruff, Neil Swainson, Jeremy Wilson, and Walter Young, *The Reins of Power: Governing British Columbia*, Vancouver, Douglas & McIntyre, 1983, Ch.8, pp. 237-269.

unified megacity and reminders like British Columbia's *Significant Projects Streamlining Act* (2003).[8]

That said, the line between health and welfare, or other intermingled policy dilemmas, is not always easy to find. Welfare and social housing are part of one policy. Housing density depends on transit or the automobile. The latter affects the environment and depends on energy policy. Add the need for planning and financing and there is no escaping the fact that governance in our society requires a lot of communication among governments at various levels.

Disentangling or Downloading?

Notwithstanding the inevitability of overlap, there have been a number of provincial initiatives to reallocate and disentangle responsibilities. While the New Brunswick changes go back 45 years, the 1990s saw major initiatives in Ontario and Quebec partly in response to increased fiscal restraint facing the provinces as a result of cuts in federal transfers to them. Reducing duplication and overlap in provincial and municipal service delivery was seen as a way of cutting mostly provincial costs. It was also felt that the entanglement obscured lines of responsibility and reduced political accountability, thereby removing or weakening the pressure on governments to strive for more efficient service delivery.[9]

The approaches taken in the various provinces, the underlying objectives, and the results achieved have all varied widely, as will be seen from the brief descriptions that follow. It will also be apparent that a number of the more recent initiatives were more concerned with downloading than disentangling and some resulted in arrangements that are at least as entangled as before. Examining the provincial experiences is useful background for the later discussion of the disentangled federalism continuing to be pursued by the majority Harper government in the second decade of the 21st century.

---

[8] Discussed in Patrick Smith and Kennedy Stewart, "Local Government Reform in British Columbia, 1991-2005: One Oar in the Water," in Joseph Garcea and Edward LeSage (eds.), *Municipal Reform in Canada: Reconfiguration, Re-Empowerment and Rebalancing*, Toronto, Oxford University Press, 2005, pp. 25-56.

[9] Igor Vojnovic, "The fiscal distribution of the provincial-municipal service exchange in Nova Scotia," *Canadian Public Administration*, Winter 1999, pp. 512-513.

The Rationale for Disentanglement

To the extent that a rationale for service reallocation was spelled out, the prevailing view was that local governments should be refocused on their historic role of providing services to property (funded, appropriately, by a property tax)[10] and that services to people should be the responsibility of the provincial level. The latter services, such as education, it was argued, provide benefits well beyond the boundaries of one municipality and should be financed from broader revenue sources (available to the province). Social services involve income redistribution tied to broad provincial (even national) standards and objectives, should not be open to local variation and, as a result, were also held to be inappropriate for local administration.

These distinctions were used, at least in part, in several studies related to disentanglement, including the Byrne Commission in New Brunswick (1963), Manitoba's 1964 Michener Commission, the Graham Commission in Nova Scotia (1974), and Ontario's *Who Does What* panel (1996). For example, the Graham Commission contended that municipal responsibilities should be divided into two groups: "... local services, which are of primarily local benefit or which might best be provided by municipal government, and general services, which are of more general benefit to the province or which the province might best provide."[11]

Cameron[12] is critical of the approach posed by Graham, which suggested that municipal responsibilities don't extend beyond the provision of services, however defined and disentangled, and therefore ignores the representative and political role of municipal government. Second, he finds the allocation of responsibilities arbitrary and likely to result in a municipal system that is responsible only "for that which is unimportant or inexpensive." Sancton and others working on multilevel interpretations are critical of disentanglement's underlying rationale that municipalities should concentrate on those responsibilities that are inherently local, an approach which he suggests inevitably means a narrower range of municipal functions. In Sancton's words:[13]

---

[10] Although, as noted in Chapter 2, the fear of a property tax to pay for local services fostered resistance to the establishment of municipal institutions in several provinces.

[11] *Royal Commission on Education, Public Services, and Provincial-Municipal Relations, Report*, Halifax, Queen's Printer, 1974, Vol. II, p. 3: 22.

[12] David Cameron, "Provincial Responsibilities for Municipal Government," *Canadian Public Administration*, Summer 1980, pp. 222-235.

[13] Andrew Sancton, "Provincial-Municipal Disentanglement in Ontario: A Dissent," *Municipal World*, July 1992, p. 23.

To base municipal government's existence on a mission to concern itself with inherently local issues is to insure its quick death. Does anyone really believe that there are *any* issues which are still inherently local?

If, as argued elsewhere in this text, municipalities are to act as a political mechanism through which a local community can express its collective objectives, then it is essential that municipalities be involved in as many activities as possible that are of interest and concern to the local community. This means expanding, not reducing, their sphere of influence. It means becoming (or staying) involved in functional areas in which the municipalities cannot expect to be autonomous. As Sancton wryly observes: "If municipal politicians are not interested in *all* government policies that affect their community, they can hardly complain if many in the community are not interested in municipal government."[14]

Even viewed only from the narrow perspective of services and their delivery, it can be argued that disentanglement efforts are misguided and are as likely to reduce efficiency as to increase it. In this regard, it is instructive to recall the discussion in Chapter 5 about the production of local government services.[15] It cited research that demonstrated how within any one function (such as policing) different activities possessed different characteristics and, as a result, economies of scale were best achieved by allocating these activities over varied areas of jurisdiction – some small and some large. British Columbia's "Missing Women Commission of Inquiry," chaired by former Attorney General Wally Oppal, offers insight into this with respect to local/regional policing.[16]

While the discussion in Chapters 4 and 5 related to the benefits of flexible governing arrangements, there is also a lesson here with respect to disentanglement. When a responsibility is shared by more than one level of government – and even by adjacent jurisdictions – it should not automatically be assumed that this arrangement represents wasteful duplication. Yes, it may, but it might also represent a logical and beneficial division of responsibility that is much more likely to generate

---

[14] *Ibid.*, p. 24. This reality is also recognized in Patrick Smith and Kennedy Stewart, "Beavers and Cats Revisited: Creatures and Tenants or Municipal Charters and Home Rule? Has the Local-Intergovernmental Game Shifted to the Mushy Middle? Canadian-American Comparisons/Vancouver and British Columbia Lessons," *Korean Local Government Review*, Vol. 6, No.1, 2004, pp. 123-156.

[15] Sancton, *Provincial-Municipal Disentanglement in Ontario*, p. 139.

[16] See www.missingwomeninquiry.ca, accessed July 2, 2011.

economies of scale and operating efficiency than would arise from consolidating total responsibility for the function in question at one level only. Some of this discussion in Canada has been informed by the European Union's deliberations about subsidiarity: the organizing notion of placing particular responsibilities where they can most efficiently and competently be conducted.[17] In the European Union, this might be at the supranational level, nationally, with internal states or regions, and/or locally.[18] More often, in the Canadian case, (as discussed below in this chapter) cost cutting was the rationale for the *Who Does What* discussions, even when efficiencies were the stated goals.

The New Brunswick Experience

The earliest reallocation of services, and one of the most substantial, began with the Byrne Commission of 1963 (discussed in Chapter 4) and led to the 1967 Program for Equal Opportunity. On the basis of the Commission's identification of services appropriate for the provincial and local levels, the New Brunswick government took over responsibility for the administration of justice, welfare, and public health, and financial responsibility for the provision of education. Property assessment and property tax collection also became provincial responsibilities. The primary objective of achieving greater equity in services was achieved, but the extent of the provincial takeover of local responsibilities, and the fact that the province replaced municipalities in providing services in rural New Brunswick, caused many to worry that the improvement had been achieved at the price of municipal government. The local, especially rural, backlash which followed meant that local accountability was countermanded by efficiency concerns.[19]

---

[17] See Dion Curry, *Multi-Level Governance Frameworks in Canada and the United Kingdom, or How I Learned to Stop Worrying and Love the Concept,* Ph.D Thesis, University of Sheffield, 2001; and "Relations Revisited: A Nuanced Approach to Types of Multi-Level Governance" in *CEU Political Science Journal,* Vol. 1, No. 5, 2007, pp. 79-93.

[18] See *Subsidiarity,* European Parliament Fact Sheets, accessed April 7, 2011 at http://www.europarl.europa.eu/parliament/expert/displayFtu.do?language=en&id=73&ftuId=FTU_1.2.2.html.

[19] The Canadian Institute for Research on Regional Development, *The Robichaud Era, 1960-1970:* Colloquium Proceedings, Moncton, NB, 2001; Georges Cyr, "The 1967 Municipal Reform in New Brunswick," in *ibid.*, pp. 135-159. See also Norman Ruff, *Administrative Reform and Development: A Study of Administrative Adaptation to Provincial Development Goals and the Reorganization of Provincial Government and Municipal Government, 1963-1967,"* Ph.D Thesis, McGill University, 1973.

The political costs associated with the changes were high for the New Brunswick Premier, even as many realized the benefits of fairer taxes. In New Brunswick, older fissures (Anglo-French, rich-poor, North-South divisions) re-emerged. While the playing field in terms of local taxation was considerably levelled, the repercussions continued into subsequent administrations. The Frank McKenna administration (1987-97) moved to create new "rural communities" to address some of this lingering discontent and to introduce a new local grants system. This initiative was halted by the subsequent Bernard Lord government (1999-2006).

The lack of local democracy in rural areas arising from the Byrne Report and Robichaud reforms of the 1960s[20] received further attention during ongoing discussions of a revised *Municipalities Act* over the past decade. This issue was reflected in the creation of the Commission on the Future of Local Governance (September 2007- December 2008, chaired by Jean-Guy Finn), under Shaun Graham's one term Liberal government (2006-2010).[21] This sense of unfinished local democratic business (the Finn Report recommendations were shelved) has continued with Premier David Alward (elected in 2010). His government's plans for second decade 21st century local governing reforms include a new round of public consultations and plans to revise and decentralize the operations of the 105 municipalities and 266 Local Service Districts in the province.[22]

The Quebec Experience

Beginning in 1980, the Quebec government realigned provincial and local finances and responsibilities. The province took over a significant portion of the education costs that had been financed from property taxes, while reducing provincial transfer payments a proportionate

---

[20] Under the Robichaud reforms, fully 30% of New Brunswick's population was left with no local government. For subsequent reform ideas, see Geoffrey Martin, "Municipal Reform in New Brunswick: Minor Tinkering with Major Problems," *Journal of Canadian Studies,* Vol. 41, No. 1, Winter 2007, pp. 75-99.

[21] Commissioner Jean-Guy Finn recommended cutting the number of municipalities from 105 to 53, adding to their efficiency, improving local governance, ensuring a more coherent and effective system, and allowing more local voice to unincorporated areas of the province. See Province of New Brunswick, *Building Stronger Local Governments and Regions: An Action Plan for the Future of Local Governance in New Brunswick,* Fredericton, NB, December 18, 2008.

[22] Information provided by the Local Government Department, Province of New Brunswick, June 17 and June 21, 2011.

amount.[23] While the financial changes offset each other, the fact that almost all of their revenues now came from their own sources left Quebec municipalities with a greater degree of fiscal autonomy than that enjoyed by municipalities in other provinces.

Two further changes were introduced at the beginning of the 1990s, prompted by the provincial government's concern about its growing expenditure burden and its perception that the revenue raising potential of the property tax had not yet been fully tapped.[24] In 1990, the province transferred to Quebec school boards the expense of maintaining school facilities while authorizing the boards to levy a property tax (to be collected by municipalities) covering up to 10% of their expenditures.[25] The result was to reduce the share of provincial financing of school board operations to about 88%.[26] The following year the Quebec government introduced changes that shifted to municipalities greater responsibility and financing obligations for public transit, roads, and policing. Both of these changes were seen, at least in part, as an attempt by the province to shift back to the property tax the burden for financing some of the expenditures that had been assumed by the 1980 reforms – a move strongly opposed by the Quebec Union of Municipalities.[27]

There were two servicing shifts during the first decade of the 21st century in Quebec. Municipalities with populations of 50 000 and over were required to provide more complete police services or, by June 2002, to contract with the Quebec Provincial Police force for these services. In addition, the regional county municipalities and the enlarged cities created through mergers in the Montreal and Quebec City areas were required to take on some responsibility for social housing.[28] Ongoing discussions about the effectiveness of the Montreal metropolitan agglomeration, the Communauté metropolitaine de Montreal (CCM), and the capacity of the merged island of Montreal suggest that recent

---

[23] F. Vaillancourt, "Financing Local Governments in Quebec: New Arrangements for the 1990s," *Canadian Tax Journal*, 1992, Vol. 40, No. 5, pp. 1123-1139.

[24] This view is frankly expressed by Claude Ryan, Minister of Municipal Affairs, in *The Sharing of Responsibilities Between the Government and Municipalities: Some Needed Adjustments*, December 14, 1990.

[25] *Ibid.*

[26] Vaillancourt, "Financing Local Governments in Quebec," p. 1137.

[27] Katherine A. Graham, Susan D. Phillips, and Allan M. Maslove, *Urban Governance in Canada*, Toronto, Harcourt, Brace & Company, Canada, 1998, p. 72.

[28] Pierre Hamel, "Municipal Reform in Quebec," in Garcea and LeSage (eds.), *Municipal Reform in Canada*, p. 159.

metropolitan reform efforts have failed to produce policy and structural agreement in Quebec's largest city-region.[29]

The Nova Scotia Experience

The disentanglement process in Nova Scotia arose out of a provincial initiative originally focused on reducing the number of municipalities. The *Task Force on Local Government*, which reported in April 1992, cited the position of the Union of Nova Scotia Municipalities that:[30]

> Property services should be supported by property taxes and delivered by municipal government. People services are the responsibility of the provincial government and should be financed by general provincial revenues. Both orders of government should continue efforts to reallocate the delivery and financing of services recognizing this basic principle.

Apart from reflecting the mantra of the 1974 Graham Commission, the report also reflected the position of the municipal association in calling for any reallocation of services to be revenue neutral, meaning that neither the provincial nor the local level would be better or worse off financially as a result of the changes.

The Graham Liberal government elected in 1993 adopted the principle of service exchange proposed in the 1992 task force report. Consistent with the services to property versus services to people distinction noted above, the exchange was based on municipalities being relieved of responsibility for social welfare services and contributions to the cost of correctional services while assuming greater responsibility (especially rural municipalities) for roads and bridges and policing. As these changes were being implemented, however, the province became increasingly preoccupied with deficit reduction. As a result, it capped the amount available for equalization payments to financially weak municipalities, causing particular hardship to a number of coastal towns formerly dependent on the ground fishery.[31]

---

[29] See, for example, Henri Aubin, "Trent Bent on Municipal Reform: Former Westmount mayor eyes a political comeback," The *Gazette*, Montreal, August 25, 2009. The authors also are grateful for a 2011 assessment by Dr. Pierre Hamel, Université de Montreal.

[30] Report to the Government of Nova Scotia, *Task Force on Local Government*, April 1992, p. 11.

[31] Kell Antoft and Jack Novack, *Grassroots Democracy: Local Government in the Maritimes*, Halifax, Dalhousie University, 1998, p. 12.

More generally, an analysis by Vojnovic finds that while the service swap in Nova Scotia was intended, in part, to assist financially distressed municipalities, it resulted in an increased financial burden for some of the fiscally weakest municipalities. In his view:[32]

> The overwhelming emphasis on maintaining a revenue-neutral exchange between the province and the municipalities, and ensuring a government structure where one level of government provides a single public service or governance function, redirected the attention of the province and the municipalities away from the basic distributional aspects of the reform.

Poel points out that the services swap was not as straightforward as originally intended.[33] The municipal and provincial levels continued to exercise a degree of shared responsibility – a policy phenomenon apparent across virtually all local governing settings – with respect (in Nova Scotia's case) to bridges, some social services, and correctional services. In addition, the development of provincial solid waste resource regions across the province involved a combination of provincial policies and performance targets and municipal responsibility for operations – providing another example of the difficulty of distinguishing between general and local services.

A further realignment was introduced in 1998, with an agreement to phase out municipal contributions to social service costs over a five year period (which concluded on schedule in 2003, under the John Hamm Conservative government). This uploading of social service costs into a unified provincial program "eliminated the variations in social service benefits found in municipal social assistance."[34] Nova Scotia's first time (and first term) New Democratic Party government (Darrell Dexter, Premier since 2009) does not appear to have new local governing changes high on its agenda. The 2011 Provincial Budget contained $560 million in capital expenditures on roads/bridges/schools construction (from an over $9 billion total) but no hint of any municipal structural reform.[35]

---

[32] Vojnovic, "The Service Exchange in Nova Scotia," p. 516.

[33] This discussion is based on Dale H. Poel, "Municipal Reform in Nova Scotia," in Garcea and LeSage (eds.), *Municipal Reform in Canada*, pp. 182-185.

[34] *Ibid.*, p. 183.

[35] See Province of Nova Scotia, *Budget, 2011*, Halifax, 2011.

Ontario's Disentanglement Experience

Disentanglement first arose in Ontario in the form of a 1990 report that proposed following the example of most other provinces by shifting the costs of social assistance to the provincial government. While agreeing in principle, the province balked at the approximately $800 million in extra costs that would result from such a shift. Instead, a follow up study was undertaken, this time of the entire division of responsibilities between the provincial and local levels. The resulting Hopcroft Report[36] formed the basis for discussions between the then newly elected Bob Rae NDP government (1990-1995) and the Association of Municipalities of Ontario (AMO) – discussions that took place under the guiding principle of fiscal neutrality, the same revenue neutral objective specified in Nova Scotia's disentanglement exercise. A tentative agreement was reached, centred on provincial assumption of social assistance in exchange for greater municipal responsibility for roads (again rather like the Nova Scotia experience). But the deal fell through when the province introduced major cuts in local transfer payments in response to its growing deficit and debt problems.

Disentanglement returned, albeit with some important changes in approach and emphasis, following the election of the Mike Harris Conservative governments (1995-2003) in June 1995. A *Who Does What* panel, chaired by former Toronto mayor and MP David Crombie, was appointed on May 30, 1996, to begin a complete overhaul of who does what in the delivery and funding of many government services. The panel's recommendations culminated in a summary report in December 1996, which largely followed the services to property versus services to people distinction cited earlier. It called for increased municipal responsibility with respect to roads, transit, ferries, airports, water and sewer systems, and policing, and increased provincial responsibility for social services and education.

The Ontario government's response, in January 1997, was a services swap that ignored the recommendations of *Who Does What* in several key respects. In particular, the province proposed to download to municipalities increased responsibility for a number of social programs, including public housing, public health, homes for special care, long term care, and general welfare assistance. In return, the province would assume all of the education costs previously borne by residential property taxpayers. The nature and speed of the government's response suggested

---

[36] *Report of the Advisory Committee to the Minister of Municipal Affairs on the Provincial-Municipal Relationship* (universally referred to as the Hopcroft Report after the committee chair, Grant Hopcroft), Toronto, January 1991.

that it had been pursuing its own internal, and more ideological, agenda, while using the *Who Does What* panel almost as a front or a diversion. That agenda, it seemed, was to gain full control of education decision making in Ontario.[37] Subsequent events (discussed below) support this interpretation.

In the face of widespread criticism and evidence that the proposed service swap was not fiscally neutral, the province accepted a number of modifications that arose from joint discussions with the Association of Municipalities of Ontario. As a result, residential taxpayers continued to pay half of the education costs that they had been financing (estimated at about $2.5 billion) and as a result of this provincial "savings," the Ontario government continued to finance such services as long term care and homes for special care. Even so, the end result of what has now become known as the local services realignment or LSR is that the province shifted downward responsibilities and/or costs for such social programs as public (social) housing, public health, land ambulances, and social assistance, as well as public transit, water and sewer systems, and policing (in rural areas).

While the province continued to insist that these new "improved" arrangements were definitely fiscally neutral, few believed the claim this time either. In fact, subsequent years have witnessed a series of financial adjustments or concessions from the province that effectively acknowledge the lack of fiscal neutrality in the LSR arrangements. For example, effective 2007 the provincial share of the cost of public health programs was increased from 50% to 75%, representing the uploading of some $125 million a year in costs. During late 2006, 2007, and 2008, the province, the Association of Municipalities of Ontario, and the City of Toronto conducted a joint review to improve the delivery and funding of municipal services, and its autumn 2008 report gave particular attention to the services downloaded under the LSR. In its consensus report, *Provincial Municipal Fiscal and Service Delivery Review: Facing the Future Together*,[38] there was agreement on an uploading of funding for $1.5 billion per year in services (by 2018) that were previously, under the LSR, paid for by municipal governments. Through joint working tables on infrastructure, service delivery, accountability, fiscal architecture, and

---

[37] This view, with which we concur, is offered by, among others, Katherine A. Graham and Susan D. Phillips, "Who Does What in Ontario: The Process of Provincial-Municipal Disentanglement," *Canadian Public Administration*, Summer 1998, pp. 186-187.

[38] Report, *Provincial-Municipal Fiscal and Service Delivery Review: Facing the Future Together*, Toronto, Province of Ontario/AMO/City of Toronto, Autumn 2008. Message from the Political Table.

economic competitiveness, Ontario will see a series of phased changes regarding housing and homelessness, cooperation on social service delivery, a greater share of the provincial gasoline tax (for local transit), new funding arrangements for roads and bridges, court security cost sharing, reworking of the Ontario Municipal Partnership Fund, etc.[39]

Disentanglement Dissected

Opinions vary as to whether attempts to disentangle provincial and local responsibilities are desirable, and we have our doubts on that score. But even if one agrees with the objective, it is clear that the disentanglement experiences in several provinces were seriously flawed. The intentions may have been good initially, but by the 1990s provincial financial concerns (aggravated, in part, by federal downloading of costs to their level) began to override considerations of what functions would best be handled at the provincial or local level. This was evident in Ontario (particularly), Quebec, and – to a lesser extent – Nova Scotia. Subsidiarity principles were sacrificed to senior government fiscal exigencies. Adding to the disentanglement process the guiding principle of fiscal neutrality may have been politically necessary, but it meant that mathematics – how to achieve a neutral result – trumped what distribution of functions was most logical. The result in Ontario, in the memorable phrasing of Siegel, is that "the ugly face of expediency impinged on the elegance of the task force's recommendations."[40]

The functional distortions that resulted from the financial concerns are particularly evident in the Ontario experience. The province's underlying objective was to take over responsibility for education, to rein in what it regarded as excessive spending by school boards. There is logic in having education financed by the province, but it is based on the need to ensure adequate spending and high and consistent educational standards at a time when educated workers are the key resource in the knowledge based economy. The case for provincial responsibility for education extends equally to other social programs such as social assistance and social housing. But taking over all of these social programs, however consistent and logical, would have increased provincial costs and that was unacceptable – especially to a provincial

---

[39] *Ibid*, pp. 2-4 and with thanks to Dr. David Siegel, Brock University, for recent impressions.

[40] David Siegel, "Recent Changes in Provincial-Municipal Relations in Ontario," in Robert Young and Christian Leuprecht (eds.), *Canada: The State of the Federation, 2004: Municipal-Federal-Provincial Relations in Canada*, Montreal & Kingston, McGill-Queen's University Press, 2006, p. 185.

governing party committed to cuts in expenditures and taxes. So the Ontario exercise was reduced to "basic arithmetic," with the province downloading other responsibilities until it had shifted enough costs to offset the uploading of education (more than enough, according to the municipal level). This explains why social housing, which had not even been part of earlier discussions, got tossed into the mix.[41]

Surprisingly, however, it could be argued that the Ontario government got it right, even if for the wrong reasons. Those taking this position would remind us of the caution that municipalities need to remain involved in as wide a range of services and programs as possible to demonstrate their relevance to their citizens. The fact is that not all municipalities were opposed to the downloading of social services in Ontario. Regional governments and a number of the large cities recognized the importance of social programs as a way of "connecting to diverse communities and promoting quality of life" and they also recognized that the quality of life in urban areas is "the key instrument of economic development in a global economy."[42] As a result, they have shown a willingness to exercise greater responsibility for social programs, *if* commensurate financial resources are provided – a condition that they would argue has not yet been met. This is not a situation pertaining only to Ontario municipalities, as British Columbia's "harm reduction/drug treatment" initiatives of Vancouver attest.

Ultimately, it may be that efforts at disentanglement are not only flawed in ways described above, but pointless or inappropriate. Consider the outcome of the Ontario exercise. Because the province downloaded responsibilities of wider than local significance, it has been obliged to introduce or expand the standards that must be maintained with respect to many of these services – such as public health, social housing, and water and sewage services. Ironically, the result is that provincial and local entanglement has been increased, not decreased.

That re-entanglement, and the apparent duplication and overlap that it represents, may – oddly enough – be the most effective way to address the needs of citizens. For example, "acknowledging the legitimate local interest in human-service delivery, while retaining responsibility for income redistribution at the provincial level, would contribute to recognition of the diversity of circumstances and needs across communities and affirm a vital role for local governments in the social domain."[43]

---

[41] Graham and Phillips, *Who Does What in Ontario*, p. 187.

[42] *Ibid.*, pp. 194 and 205.

[43] *Ibid.*, p. 205.

In addition, as argued elsewhere in this volume, having different aspects of a responsibility handled by more than one level of government, rather than being wasteful duplication, may be the best way to achieve economies of scale. Some of these same considerations cast doubts about the wisdom of the essentially disentanglement stance recently exhibited by the federal government, as examined later in this chapter.

Box 6.2 Disentanglement Dilemmas
Did the Ontario government get it right, even if for the wrong reasons? Were disentanglement efforts not only flawed but also inappropriate and pointless? Is re-entanglement – with its potential for overlap and duplication – the most effective arrangement?

The Changing Legal Relationship

Unlike provincial and federal governments, local governments were not given any guaranteed right to exist under Canada's constitution, but were simply identified (in Sec. 92.8, *British North America Act*, 1867) as one of the responsibilities that provinces could exercise. In response, as discussed in Chapter 2, provincial governments passed legislation that provided for the kinds of municipalities that could be incorporated, their governing structures, functions, and financial resources. These statutes were traditionally prescriptive in nature, detailing what municipalities could do – and often how they could do it – in what was commonly described as a "laundry list" approach. The courts usually took the position that if a provincial legislature had specified some items, then anything not specified was not intended. As a result, if municipalities could not find express legal authority for an action, they could not undertake it – or would face the risk of a court challenge (usually successful) if they proceeded in the absence of such express authority.

In their mid-1980s comparison of local/senior jurisdictional relations in Canada and the United States, Victor Jones and Patrick Smith described local governments as being either "beavers" or "cats."[44] They suggested that within the long held view of Canadian local governments as "creatures of the province" and American municipalities as either

---

[44] Victor Jones, "Beavers and Cats: Federal-Local Relations in the United States and Canada," in H. Peter Oberlander and Hilda Symonds (eds.), *Meech Lake from Centre to Periphery*," Vancouver, Centre for Human Settlements, University of British Columbia, 1986, pp. 88-115, and Patrick J. Smith, "Local-Federal Government Relations: Canadian Perspectives, American Comparisons," in Oberlander and Symonds (eds.), *Meech Lake*, pp. 127-136.

"tenants at will" or "home rule" activists, Canadian *beavers* were seen as formally weak creatures prone to danger avoidance and fleeing from interjurisdictional conflict. "Home-rule/charter city" *cats,* more common in the United States, were described as relatively autonomous units enjoying considerably more policy making discretion.[45]

Using this Jones and Smith metaphor to more effectively classify local governmental ability to affect policy formulation, Smith and Stewart suggested that beavers and cats – and hence all local governments – might be portrayed as sitting along a no discretion versus absolute formal authority continuum, with the two animal families further described as "strong" or "weak" depending on the potency of their formal powers. Most local governments, in both countries, would fall at neither extreme but along a "mushy middle."[46]

Figure 6.1 The Mushy Middle Continuum

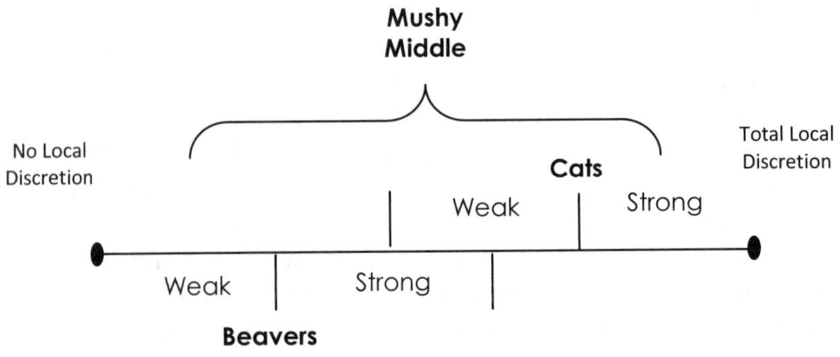

```
                        Mushy
                        Middle
                     ╱─────────╲
 No Local         ╱              ╲        Total Local
 Discretion      ╱       Cats     ╲       Discretion
                │   Weak │ Strong  │
●───────────────┼────────┼─────────┼──────────────●
      Weak      │ Strong │
                Beavers
```

As demonstrated in a number of settings, such as in the City of Vancouver, aggressive, "eager beaver" councils and mayors can overcome formal limits to their authority to "get it done even when they are not in charge."[47] The city's push of senior governments to allow the creation of North America's first officially sanctioned Supervised Injection Site (SIS) for local heroin users, and its utilization of the 2010 Winter Olympics to leverage additional senior resources for social housing both reflect "eager beaver" tendencies.

---

[45] Jones, *Beavers and Cats*, p. 90.

[46] For more on this theme see Patrick Smith and Kennedy Stewart, "Local Whole-of-Government Policymaking in Vancouver: Beavers, Cats and the Mushy Middle Thesis," in Young and Leuprecht (eds.), *Canada: The State of the Federation 2004*, pp. 251-272.

[47] R. Fisher and A. Shar, *Getting It Done: How to Lead When You're Not in Charge*, New York, Harper, 1998.

Such actions support the argument, as described by Jones and Smith, that local governments can be either beavers – those with a strictly delimited range of authority – or cats – those with freedom to expand into policy areas without the express permission of upper tier jurisdictions. This runs contrary to the view that in Canada municipal governments are limited creatures of the provinces versus institutions with extensive discretion for taking action.

In the United States, local governments tend to place themselves along both ends – and the middle – of the discretionary action spectrum. Some U.S. states made conscious efforts to create cats by giving local authorities "greater leeway to undertake a variety of actions of their own without first having to obtain expressed state permission."[48] This idea first found formal expression in 1875: Missouri amended its state constitution to allow what became known as "home rule."[49] Other states, especially in western U.S. states, followed to varying degrees. Yet despite a more than 110 year old home rule movement, America is still more a land of beavers than cats.

That is more consistent with a Dillon's Rule interpretation of U.S. local governing, more akin to traditional Canadian definitions. "Dillon's Rule was set down by Iowa Supreme Court Judge John F. Dillon in the 1860s; Dillon equated municipalities with business corporations, both of them limited to the powers expressly granted through their incorporation.[50] Like Canadian municipalities being "creatures of the province (under Sec. 92.8), Dillon described local governments as "tenants at will" of the states.[51]

---

[48] Bernard H. Ross and Myron A. Levine, "Home Rule and Home Charters," in *Urban Politics: Power in Metropolitan America*, 6th Edition, Itasca, IL, F. E. Peacock, 2001, p. 94.

[49] See Dale Krane and Robert Blair, *The Practice of Home Rule*, Report for the Nebraska Commission on Local Government Innovation and Restructuring, Omaha, January 29, 1999. In a 1985 case, the majority on the Missouri Supreme Court found *for* Dillon's Rule; the minority dissent argued that Article VI, Sec. 19 (a) repealed Dillon's Rule. See State ex rel. St. Louis Housing Authority v. Gaertner, 695 S.W. 2d 460. MO, 1985.

[50] See Victor Jones, "Beavers and Cats: Federal-Local Relations in the United States and Canada," in H. Peter Oberlander and Hilda Symonds (eds.), *Meech Lake: From Centre to Periphery – The Impact of the 1987 Constitutional Accord on Canadian Settlements: a Speculation*, Vancouver: Centre for Human Settlements: University of British Columbia, 1988, pp. 80-126.

[51] On Dillon, see Patrick Smith "Local-Federal Government Relations: Canadian Perspectives, American Comparisons – A View Through a Kaleidoscope," in Oberlander and Symonds (eds.), *Meech Lake*, pp.127-140.

> **Box 6.3 Dillon's Rule** [52]
>
> A municipal corporation possesses and can exercise the following powers and no others; first, those granted in express words; second, those necessarily implied or necessarily incident to the power expressly granted; third, those absolutely essential to the declared objects and purposes of the corporation – not simply convenient but indispensable; and fourth, any fair doubt as to the existence of a power is resolved by the courts against the corporation.

Some U.S. cats do exist, but there is much disagreement on the significance of the range of powers afforded to local governments depending on their size and home state. Thus, there is little agreement as to which local governments fit into which category on the spectrum. For example, one study found 19 home rule states, 26 states with legislative home rule where local governments exercise any powers granted to them or not prohibited by either the U.S. or state constitution, and just 5 strict Dillon's Rule states.[53] In contrast, a 2003 Brookings Institution paper identified 40 Dillon's Rule states.[54] Clearly, there are disagreements, not about the spectrum, but about where to put U.S. municipalities along its length.

While the contrasting approaches associated with these two rules provide a useful spectrum along which to measure efforts to reform municipal legislation in Canada, the contrast between them should not be exaggerated. The reality, as depicted in the figure below, is that between these two extremes lies a "mushy middle" in which the scope for municipal action is greater than Dillon's Rule would suggest and less than home rule would imply.[55] We will return to this point toward the end of this chapter where we assess some actions of eager beavers versus lazy cats.

---

[52] John F. Dillon, from an 1868 decision in *Merriam vs. Moody's Executors*, as quoted in Harold Wolman and Michael Goldsmith, *Urban Politics and Policy: A Comparative Approach*, Cambridge, Blackwell Publishers, 1992, p. 72.

[53] T. D. Mead, "Federalism and State Law: Legal Factors Constraining and Facilitating Local Initiatives," in J. J. Gargan (ed.), *Handbook of Local Government Administration*, New York, Marcel Dekker, 1997, Ch. 3.

[54] Jesse Richardson, Meghan Zimmerman Gough, and Robert Fuentes, "Is Home Rule the Answer? Clarifying the Influence of Dillon's Rule on Growth Management," Washington, DC, The Brookings Institution, January 2003.

[55] Patrick J. Smith and Kennedy Stewart, "Local Whole-of-Government Policy-making in Vancouver: Beavers, Cats, and the Mushy Middle Thesis," in Young and Leuprecht (eds.), *Canada: The State of the Federation, 2004*, Chapter 11.

Figure 6.2 The Scope for Municipal Action

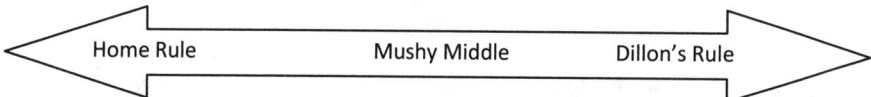

Municipal governments and their associations, notably the Federation of Canadian Municipalities (FCM), long lobbied for some constitutional recognition that might provide them with at least a degree of protection from arbitrary provincial actions, the flip side of lack of discretionary authority. These requests always fell on deaf ears. Municipal governments were ignored in both the Meech Lake and Charlottetown constitutional accords and they were also left out of the 1982 *Constitution Act* that repatriated the constitution. Given the widespread feeling that the country has wasted too many years in divisive and ultimately futile attempts to bring about constitutional change, few now seem interested in pushing constitutional recognition for municipalities. In any event, a number of observers have argued that it would be more realistic and appropriate to protect municipal interests by way of provincial constitutions. In Cameron's words:

> Municipalities have no place in a federal constitution, at least not beyond the present references which consign them to provincial jurisdiction. Any further reference could only serve to remove decisions about the provincial-municipal division of power to extra-provincial constitutional processes. Any direct participation by municipalities in the federal-provincial constitutional process could only occur at the price of their becoming special interest groups.[56]

Since the beginning of the 1990s, municipal associations in a number of provinces have pushed for some form of provincial charter that would recognize the existence of a separate level of municipal government. The Union of British Columbia Municipalities (UBCM) called for a charter or bill of rights in 1991, followed by similar demands from the Union of Nova Scotia Municipalities (UNSM) in 1993 and the Association of Municipalities of Ontario (AMO) in 1994. This lobbying seemed to have an impact, since most provinces over the past two decades have enacted new legislation that reflects – to varying degrees – the changes being sought.

---

[56] Cameron, "Provincial Responsibilities for Municipal Government," pp. 222-235.

A More Positive Legislative Framework

The first breakthrough came with Alberta's *Municipal Government Act* of 1994 and the most recent initiative is found in Ontario in 2006, with major amendments to the *Municipal Act* and a new *City of Toronto Act*. In the intervening years, positive legislative changes were also enacted in several other provinces, notably Manitoba, Nova Scotia, Newfoundland, Saskatchewan, and British Columbia. That sequence is obviously not geographic but reflects the order in which the changes were introduced and will be followed in the summaries below. These changes usually incorporated some combination of the following key features:

i) the provision of natural person powers;
ii) authorization to act within broad spheres of jurisdiction;
iii) a commitment to advance consultation;
iv) a requirement for municipal approval before certain actions (notably amalgamation) could proceed; and
v) a commitment to provide resources commensurate with the municipal responsibilities being allocated.

While the last three points are self-explanatory, the significance of the first two features is explained in the following table.

Box 6.4 Key Concepts in New Municipal Legislation	
Natural person powers	Vesting municipalities with natural person powers gives them a general authority to do those things that a person can do – such as hiring and dismissing staff, contracting for services, purchasing land or buildings, or selling or otherwise disposing of assets. These are things that municipalities have always done, but they had to find express authority in statutes before taking any such actions. While granting natural person powers gives municipalities greater flexibility, no additional powers are conveyed with this designation. Rather, the natural person powers are used as a tool for implementing the responsibilities otherwise assigned to municipalities.
Spheres of Jurisdiction	Spheres of jurisdiction (or spheres of authority) authorize municipal action on the basis of broad and general categories such as waste management, transportation systems, public utilities, economic development services, and culture, parks, and recreation. They provide an alternative to allocating powers to municipalities by itemizing specifically what they can do – as in the previously cited laundry list approach. The problem with such a list is that anything not mentioned, even inadvertently, is likely to be ruled beyond municipal jurisdiction on the grounds that if the provincial government had intended such a matter to be assigned, it would have been specified.

> Assigning broad spheres of jurisdiction is supposed to give municipalities greater flexibility and discretion. However, the scope of these spheres is constrained by limits that may be provided elsewhere in legislation, and there are also subjects not covered by the spheres and addressed separately and in a more prescriptive fashion.

Alberta

Alberta's *Municipal Government Act* was the first to give municipalities natural person powers and spheres of jurisdiction. But many municipal powers still require provincial approvals and nothing in the Act requires the province to consult with municipalities. A number of provisions in the legislation are designed to increase public participation, including citizen power to petition a public meeting and to force votes on new by-laws or on the amendment or repeal of existing by-laws and also more openness requirements relating to public meetings. Overall, the new Act represents "an effort to shift the burden of democratic oversight and control from the provincial government to the local citizenry."[57]

After agitating for greater authority and operating flexibility, Alberta municipalities apparently haven't made that much use of the new legislative framework. One explanation suggested has been a hesitancy to take new initiatives lest court challenges result.[58] One of the few legal challenges to the new legislation did initially give rise to some cause for concern but was ultimately resolved satisfactorily. This Calgary taxi-licensing by-law case is discussed in a later section.

Manitoba

Manitoba passed a *Municipal Government Act* in October 1996, but it limits municipal discretion to a narrower range of permissive powers than the Alberta legislation and it does not give them natural person powers. It does, however, grant corporate powers to municipalities and one analysis suggests that this may be as effective an approach to expanding municipal powers.[59] It also points out that the new Act has eliminated many of the detailed instructions that used to severely constrain municipal operations. It further observes that new provisions

---

[57] LeSage, "Municipal Reform in Alberta," in Garcea and LeSage, *Municipal Reform in Canada*, p. 58.

[58] *Ibid.*, p. 77.

[59] Christopher Leo and Mark Piel, "Municipal Reform in Manitoba," in Garcea and LeSage, *Municipal Reform in Canada*, p. 111.

encouraging contracting for services are intended to create a more competitive atmosphere in which market pressures will bring about greater collaboration and integration in service delivery (without the need for the municipal restructuring for which there has been strong public opposition in the province) and expresses some reservations about the implications of relying on this type of market model.[60]

The 1996 legislation does not apply to the City of Winnipeg, which has had its own charter since its formation in 1972. That charter was amended in 1998, but mainly in connection with internal restructuring relating to the council and senior administration. However, a new *City of Winnipeg Charter Act* was enacted in 2002 (effective January 2003), partly to incorporate or keep up with the changes that had appeared in the 1996 general municipal legislation. The new Act combines large numbers of previously detailed and scattered powers into 14 broad spheres of authority, and also gives Winnipeg natural person powers.[61] However, the analysis previously cited finds that natural person powers are limited to a brief reference at the beginning of the Act, which otherwise deals with the more traditional corporate powers, and it suggests that over time the concept of natural person powers may contain "more politics and public relations than legal substance."[62]

Nova Scotia

Nova Scotia amended its *Municipal Government Act* in December 1998. The new legislation does not give municipalities natural person powers or broad spheres of jurisdiction, continuing instead the traditional approach of giving municipalities a list of specific powers. But it does provide somewhat more autonomy by reducing the number of provincial approvals relating to financing and by-laws. In addition, the Act provides that the province must give municipalities (through the Union of Nova Scotia Municipalities) 12 months' notice of any initiatives that may affect municipal finance and the Minister must consult with the Union before amending the *Municipal Government Act*.[63]

According to Poel, municipalities and their association would have been more impressed with these provisions if the province hadn't added

---

[60] *Ibid.*, pp. 111-112.

[61] *City of Winnipeg Charter Act* (Bill 39), S.M. 2002, c. 39.

[62] Leo and Piel, *Municipal Reform in Manitoba*, p. 120.

[63] Department of Housing and Municipal Affairs, "Municipal Legislation Gets Makeover," October 27, 1998.

$1 million to municipal expenditures by making a change without consultation and without the 12 month notice, a change that adhered to the letter of the law (but not the spirit) by being made through legislation other than the *Municipal Government Act*.[64] This is but one of many examples demonstrating the overriding authority possessed by provincial governments no matter how they may amend their municipal legislation.

Newfoundland and Labrador

The Government of Newfoundland and Labrador enacted a new *Municipalities Act* in May 1999 that removed many restrictive provisions, expanded the authority of municipalities, and authorized a greater degree of local decision making. It also provided greater municipal autonomy with respect to taxation and financial management and new authority to pursue economic development through partnership agreements. Indicative of how paternalistic the provincial regime had been, until this 1999 legislation all municipalities were required to have their budgets approved by the Ministry.[65] In what has become a familiar pattern, "the greater autonomy, flexibility and powers are combined with increased requirements for accountability, transparency and public participation."[66]

Saskatchewan

Saskatchewan passed a new *Cities Act* in July 2002, in response to prolonged pressure from cities for their own separate legislation to provide them with greater authority and operating freedom. Modelled on similar legislation in other provinces (notably Alberta and Ontario), the *Cities Act* included provisions for natural person powers and areas (spheres) of jurisdiction.[67] The Act also includes some new public accountability provisions that balance the increased autonomy and flexibility for cities with requirements to involve and inform the public of decisions.

---

[64] Poel, *Municipal Reform in Nova Scotia*, p. 189.

[65] All these points are from Peter Boswell, "Municipal Renewal in Newfoundland and Labrador," in Garcea and LeSage, *Municipal Reform in Canada*, pp. 212-213.

[66] Donald Lidstone, "A Comparison of New and Proposed Municipal Acts of the Provinces: Revenues, Financial Powers and Resources," prepared for the 2001 annual conference of the Federation of Canadian Municipalities, May 27, 2001.

[67] Garcea, "Saskatchewan's Municipal Reform Agenda," in Garcea and LeSage, *Municipal Reform in Canada*, p. 98.

British Columbia

There have been several positive legislative changes in this province, dating back to the Clark NDP Government (1996-2001). The first of these legislative shifts was begun in 1996 with then Municipal Affairs Minister Mike Farnworth, a former Greater Vancouver city councillor, who initiated a review of British Columbia's *Municipal Act*. What most impressed the new Minister was how often his approval was required for what he termed "normal" municipal actions. Thus began work on a new *Local Government Act*. When finally passed in 2001, this replacement of British Columbia's *Municipal Act* reduced the length of the legislation considerably. The new *Local Government Act* also provided more opportunities for local initiatives.

This was followed by a Community Charter (Bill 14), which passed in April 2003 under the new Gordon Campbell Liberal Government (2001-2011) and came into effect January 2004. Its key features included:[68]

- recognition of municipalities as an "order of government" within their jurisdiction;
- requirement of provincial consultation prior to changes in the Act or to provincial grants to municipalities;
- provision for consultation agreements between the provincial government and the Union of British Columbia Municipalities on matters of mutual interest;
- provision of a dispute resolution process, including binding arbitration where all parties to a dispute choose this method;
- provision that municipal amalgamations cannot proceed unless approved by a vote in the affected jurisdictions;
- provision of natural person powers;
- provision of power to provide any service that the council considers necessary or desirable;
- provision of autonomous or concurrent authority (with the province) to regulate, prohibit, or impose requirements in relation to 13 broad spheres of authority in which municipalities typically operate; and
- new accountability requirements including an annual municipal report and a public meeting to present this report.

---

[68] For further details, see Ministry of Community, Sport and Cultural Development, www.cscd.gov.bc.ca/lgd/gov_structure/community_charter/index.htm.

When the community charter appeared, it was characterized as the most empowering local government statute in Canada. Lidstone's 2003 report card on municipal legislation ranked the British Columbia legislation near the top, along with the *Winnipeg Charter*, well ahead of the other legislation that had been enacted across Canada over the preceding decade.[69] The 2006 Toronto legislation would also be found near the top of this list as well.

Smith and Stewart, however, have a number of reservations about the community charter legislation, including its supposed empowerment of municipalities. They note, for example, that the legislation continues the province's authority to impose limits on municipal property tax increases in particular circumstances, and continues the commitment to "work toward the harmonization of provincial and municipal enactments, policies, and programs,"[70] and they wonder how this latter provision will work in those instances where a municipality wishes to pursue a unique approach.[71] They also cite several examples of provincial intervention where municipal actions or planned actions were deemed inappropriate, and suggest that these instances serve as a reminder that "constitutional authority does matter when significant policy differences arise between local and provincial players."[72]

In a by now familiar refrain, the province indicated that its municipal reforms included shifting responsibility for monitoring local councils from provincial ministries to local citizens. But Smith and Stewart are particularly critical of the legislation's failure to address municipal accountability, which, in their view, requires such responses as electoral financing reform and the removal of such barriers to electoral participation as at large elections in large municipalities including Vancouver.[73] There is early evidence that the call for annual reports and public meetings has not been an adequate means of strengthening local accountability. Carrel is very concerned about measures in the charter legislation that would structure local government on the corporate model

---

[69] Donald Lidstone, "Municipal Acts of the Provinces and Territories: A Report Card," prepared for the June 1, 2003 "Future Role of Municipal Government" Forum held during the annual conference of the Federation of Canadian Municipalities.

[70] Bill 14, *The Community Charter*, "Principles of the Provincial-Municipal Relationship," Part 1, Sec 2.

[71] Patrick Smith and Kennedy Stewart, "Local Government Reform in British Columbia," in Garcea and LeSage, *Municipal Reform in Canada*, p. 43.

[72] *Ibid.*

[73] *Ibid.*, pp. 40-41.

and dismisses the new annual report requirement as a very inadequate tool for accountability.[74]

Perhaps most tellingly, in 2003 (the same year as the Community Charter) British Columbia also passed a *Significant Projects Streamlining Act* – a clear reminder to any local authority that provincial priorities, such as Olympic-related construction, would not be thwarted by contrary municipal actions. When such actions did occasionally occur, as when West Vancouver sought alternative construction of part of the Whistler Sea to Sky Highway, the B.C. government had the judiciary quickly quash such local efforts. The new Christy Clark Liberal administration (since 2011) shows few early signs that municipal interests matter, despite concerns identified by a Local Government Elections Task Force report around issues such as the lack of limits on local election contributions and spending in British Columbia.[75]

Ontario

Ontario passed a new *Municipal Act* in December 2001, which, with minor exceptions, took effect on January 1, 2003. It authorized municipalities to exercise natural person powers and governmental powers within 10 general spheres of jurisdiction. It also retained, however, many prescriptive sections, especially dealing with financial matters. In a response reminiscent of the Alberta experience noted above, Ontario municipalities were slow to respond to the greater discretion inherent in the spheres of authority.[76] The legislation combined the increased powers given to municipalities with greater accountability and reporting requirements, a pattern evident in several other provincial initiatives. It also endorsed the principle of ongoing consultation with municipalities in relation to matters of mutual interest, and the province and the Association of Municipalities of Ontario signed a memorandum of understanding (in December 2001) setting out these consultation arrangements. These were utilized in the previously cited *Provincial Municipal Fiscal and Service Delivery Review: Facing the Future*

---

[74] André Carrel, "The Community Charter: Strengthening or Weakening the Citizen Voice at City Hall?" Langara College Continuing Studies, May 10, 2002.

[75] The *Local Government Elections Task Force* was a joint Government of BC/Union of BC Municipalities exercise, co-chaired by the Minister responsible. It reported in 2010, to allow time for legislative changes before the November 2011 municipal elections. No such changes occurred, partly due to truncated legislative sittings and leadership change for both Government and Opposition.

[76] David Siegel and C. Richard Tindal, "Changing the Municipal Culture: From Comfortable Subordination to Assertive Maturity – Part I," *Municipal World*, March 2006, p. 38.

Together (an Autumn 2008 report from the Province, AMO and the City of Toronto).

Two other major legislative changes occurred in Ontario in 2006. The first was a new *City of Toronto Act*, the provincial response to Toronto's campaign for a city charter that would recognize its special status amongst the municipalities of Ontario (and Canada). The new Act gave Toronto some limited additional revenue raising powers in relation to such matters as motor vehicle ownership, land transfer, sale of alcohol and tobacco, entertainment, parking lots, billboards, and roads (tolls).[77]

In lieu of spheres of jurisdiction, Toronto was given a new blanket power to provide any service or thing considered necessary or desirable for the public. This new power suggested an even broader, more flexible scope for municipal action (than the spheres of jurisdiction). Potentially offsetting these gains, however, was another provision that authorized the province, by regulation, to suspend *any* city by-law for 18 months. The increased discretion in the Toronto legislation was also offset by an elaborate new accountability regime mandated in the Act, including the appointment of an Integrity Commissioner, a Lobbyist Registrar, and an Auditor General. This new regime is examined further in Chapter 9.

The second legislative change in 2006 saw major amendments to the *Municipal Act* that mostly took effect in January 2007. The new Toronto legislation was reflected in these amendments, but with important differences. All municipalities were given the new blanket power to provide any service or thing considered necessary or desirable for the public, again potentially offset by the new provincial power to suspend any municipal by-law for 18 months. But in addition, all municipalities continue to have authority to take action within broad spheres of jurisdiction (in fact, an expanded version of these spheres). It was decided that the spheres were needed to deal with the division of responsibilities between upper and lower tier municipalities, which is not an issue in the single tier City of Toronto.

The result is that all other municipalities in Ontario arguably have as much or more scope for action than Toronto, since they have both the new blanket power *and* the (broadened) spheres of jurisdiction. They don't, however, have the same capacity for action, since they have not been given any of the additional revenue raising powers provided to Toronto. Neither have they been required to install the accountability regime mandated for Toronto, but they are authorized to appoint all the same oversight agencies on an optional basis. What has happened in the

---

[77] Details are at www.toronto.ca/finance/revenue_tools.htm, accessed August 15, 2007. Toronto's troubled initial experience with the new taxes is discussed in Chapter 7.

interim is that rather few Ontario municipalities have taken up the offer of self-accountability. A very few municipalities have created Integrity Commissioners, essentially by hiring a local lawyer to so act on a case by case basis. This has kept local governmental costs at a minimum as little is referred to these commissioners. And despite some calls (for example, by the Niagara Chamber of Commerce) for a municipal auditor general, there has been even less take-up of this accountability option, given that costs can run into the hundreds of thousands of dollars and must be borne by local taxpayers.[78] Local bureaucrats are ambivalent about the extra oversight and local councillors are disinclined to add to the local property tax burden to take on this responsibility.

Significance of the Legislative Reforms

The key features of the reforms, not found in all provinces, are the provisions for natural person powers, more general municipal authority within broad spheres of jurisdiction, and a commitment to advance consultation with municipalities. These changes are most welcome, although in several instances (notably British Columbia, Saskatchewan, and Ontario) they are accompanied by new requirements presented as enhancing the accountability of municipal governments. It is also clear that the new legislation is being used in some provinces to further ideological leanings of the provincial governing parties. As noted above, Leo and Piel describe the promotion of partnerships and the market model in Manitoba, and this theme is also reflected in the legislation in British Columbia and Ontario. A business or corporate emphasis is also evident in provisions for accountability in both the British Columbia and Ontario legislation, with efficiency and effectiveness measures and annual reports and meetings advocated.

While the new legislative initiatives are generally positive and a welcome step in the right direction, they don't protect municipalities from adverse actions being taken by their provincial governments. This is evident from the Smith and Stewart analysis of British Columbia and the unilateral action of the Nova Scotia government – both described above. It is also the case that Alberta and Ontario introduced their new municipal legislation during times when they were also curtailing, or had curtailed, their provincial grant support. Yet another example from Ontario is the way that the provision of a new blanket power for municipalities to take action is accompanied (offset) by a new provincial regulatory power to suspend any municipal by-law for 18 months.

---

[78] With thanks to Dr. David Siegel, Brock University, for pointing this out (July 6, 2011).

Pursuing Individual City Charters

Paralleling the demand for more permissive provincial legislation for local governments in general has been a growing demand that Canada's largest cities receive individual charters that would set out responsibilities appropriate to their size, resources, and importance. Having specific charters is not a new idea, of course, as indicated below.

	Box 6.5 Charter Cities in Canada
Saint John	Incorporated by royal charter in 1785. City has natural person powers. The Charter is exclusive of generally applicable municipal legislation unless there is a conflict with provincial statutes.
Vancouver	Charter dates from 1886 and is the exclusive authority except for a few provisions from generally applicable municipal legislation.
Montreal	Original charter dates from 1890s. New "city contract" entered into between province and new City of Montreal in June 2002 in support of the city charter.
Winnipeg	Charter dates from the amalgamation that created the city in 1972. Major revisions effective 2003 to provide greater autonomy, in line with changes in the Manitoba *Municipal Act* of 1996.

Conspicuous by their absence from this list of charter cities are Calgary, Edmonton, and Toronto (especially). Toronto made a concerted effort to join this list, arguing that it was quite distinct from most other municipalities in Canada and needed special governing arrangements best provided by having its own charter.[79] In a parallel development, the Big City Mayors Caucus of the Federation of Canadian Municipalities adopted a model framework for a city charter on May 30, 2002.[80] Much of the agitation for city charters revolved around the challenges now facing them in a global economy and their need for special powers that could not be provided in general municipal legislation. The symbolic value and status of a separate charter is obviously significant, but from a legal perspective, a charter provides no greater autonomy for a city than could be provided in a generous municipal Act, since both are provincial statutes subject to amendment or repeal.[81] In fact, Toronto did succeed in obtaining a generous statute of its own, as described above. But the city

---

[79] For a series of articles relating to this issue, see Mary W. Rowe, *Toronto: Considering Self-Government*, Owen Sound, The Ginger Press, Inc., 2000.

[80] Available from the Federation website at www.fcm.ca, accessed May 2, 2003.

[81] Mariana Valverde and Ron Levi, *Still the Creatures of Provinces? Canadian Cities' Quest for Governmental Status*, report submitted to the Law Reform Commission of Canada, February 2005, p. 42.

has been reluctant to use the new revenue raising powers that they gained and has recently scrapped one of them (the personal vehicle registration fee). What impact this action will have on future municipal calls for more sources of revenue beyond the property tax remains to be seen.[82]

Selecting large cities for special attention could be seen as relegating all other municipalities to second class status, a concern that will become evident when we turn shortly to federal relations with the local level. On the other hand, such differentiation could be beneficial for the small and rural units that make up the vast majority of Canada's municipalities. They often feel that policies are enacted to address concerns of the larger centres, without sufficient regard to how appropriate such policies may be for them and their much different conditions. If the needs of the largest cities can be handled through separate charters or statutes for them, then it may be possible to develop general municipal legislation that is more suitable for the smaller and more rural municipalities to which it will apply. If we can countenance asymmetrical federalism at the federal and provincial levels, it would not seem unreasonable for us to consider comparable arrangements between provinces and their widely varied municipal governments. Agreeing that one size does not fit all, one analysis suggests reversing the approach traditionally taken.[83]

> This reversal involves switching from a policy that starts with the idea that big cities are the same as smaller municipalities and creating exceptions for the big cities, to one that views all municipalities as big cities and makes exceptions for smaller municipalities. In this way, the Big City Agenda pulls along other municipalities with it.

A More Positive Judicial Response

The potential of the various initiatives to improve municipal legislation is also somewhat dependent on the interpretations that will be given by the courts in the cases that will inevitably arise. There are grounds for optimism, notwithstanding the shaky beginning with respect to Alberta's groundbreaking 1994 legislation. The City of Calgary had passed a by-law limiting the number of taxi licences and while this action was upheld initially, the Alberta Court of Appeal quashed the by-law. Seeming blissfully unaware of the move away from "laundry list" legislation, the Court of Appeal found that while the old legislation had conferred a specific power to limit the number of taxi licences, this power was not

---

[82] David Siegel, July 6, 2011.

[83] Kari Roberts and Roger Gibbins, *Apples and Oranges? Urban Size and the Municipal-Provincial Relationship*, Canada West Foundation, October 2005.

found in Alberta's *Municipal Government Act* of 1994. The Supreme Court of Canada, however, unanimously upheld the Calgary by-law, noting that a number of provinces had passed legislation providing more general powers to municipalities and that "this shift in legislative drafting reflects the true nature of modern municipalities which require greater flexibility in fulfilling their statutory responsibilities."[84] There have been several other significant Supreme Court decisions over the past decade that recognize the need for municipalities to have some flexibility in taking necessary actions on behalf of their citizens.

A frequently cited example is the Supreme Court of Canada ruling in the Hudson (Quebec) pesticide case.[85] The court upheld a municipal by-law prohibiting the use of pesticides (with specified exceptions), a by-law enacted under an omnibus provision in the municipal legislation that authorized by-laws to secure peace, order, good government, health, and general welfare in the community. Such provisions had rarely been relied upon successfully in the past as an independent source of authority for municipal actions. But the court held that a broad approach to the interpretation of this omnibus provision was needed to give municipalities flexibility "to deal with unforeseen or changing circumstances, and to address emerging or changing issues" within their communities.

Ultimately, the potential of the various legislative initiatives will depend on how actively municipalities exert themselves within the broader framework of operation that they now enjoy. The municipal response is likely to be careful and cautious, as noted above in relation to experiences in Alberta and Ontario. Municipalities that have been treated like children for a century and longer will take some time to feel comfortable with their new operating freedom, though some local "eager beavers" will lead the way.

The Federal-Local Relationship

While municipalities don't have any formal link with the federal government under the constitution, federal programs and policies have

---

[84] *United Taxi Drivers' Fellowship of Southern Alberta v. Calgary (City) (2004)*, 46 M.P.L.R. (3d) 1, (S.C.C.) [United Taxi], para 6.

[85] 114957 *Canada Ltée (Spraytech, Société d'arrosage) v. Hudson (Town)* (2001), 19, M.P.L.R. (3d) 1 (S.C.C.) [Spraytech].

long had a major impact on local government operations. As described in Chapter 3, there is no better example than the way federal financial assistance for housing contributed to low density sprawl and associated municipal servicing problems. Transport ministry decisions concerning rail services have had a critical impact on the economic vitality of communities, as have various industrial incentives and other programs offered by the federal government. Immigration policy is another federal responsibility that affects municipalities, dramatically so in the case of Canada's largest urban centres. But as Frisken notes, "federal immigration policy makes little attempt to ease the strains imposed on cities or city neighbourhoods by large influxes of new immigrants...."[86]

These examples should suffice to demonstrate that a kind of federal-local relationship existed long before it was given any formal recognition during the 1970s. Indeed, one study found that by the late 1960s, "more than 117 distinct programs administered by 27 departments in Ottawa influenced metropolitan development plans."[87] But in almost every case, the federal programs were introduced without regard to their impact on the local level. Municipalities had no opportunity for advance consultation and little hope of obtaining adjustments after the fact. In many cases, the federal initiatives were not even coordinated with each other.

The Rise and Fall of MSUA

By the end of the 1960s, however, two major factors combined to produce strong pressure for a closer and more formalized federal-local relationship. First, there was a growing municipal interest in the possibility of increased federal funds being made available to deal with major service demands, especially in urban areas. Second, there was a growing federal appreciation that, because of the large number of Canadians living in urban areas, the ability of municipal governments to meet their needs was of more than local, or even provincial, interest.

A federal task force on Housing and Urban Development was appointed in mid-1968 and its report recommended a greatly expanded

---

[86] Frances Frisken, "Introduction," in Frances Frisken (ed.), *The Changing Canadian Metropolis*, Vol. 1, Toronto, Canadian Urban Institute, 1994, p. 19.

[87] Elliot J. Feldman and Jerome Milch, "Coordination or Control? The Life and Death of the Ministry of Urban Affairs," in Lionel D. Feldman (ed.), *Politics and Government of Urban Canada*, Toronto, Methuen, 1981, p. 250. See also H. Peter Oberlander and Arthur Fallick (eds.), *The Ministry of State for Urban Affairs: A Courageous Experiment in Public Administration,* Vancouver, Centre for Human Settlements, UBC, 1987.

federal role. The government responded by establishing a Ministry of State for Urban Affairs (MSUA). As recommended, the new Ministry was not a traditional operating department but was to focus on developing policy and coordinating the projects of other departments. Also emphasized was the need to increase coordination among all three levels of government in dealing with the challenges of urbanization. If this sounds familiar, it is because the same need is being emphasized more than 40 years later, only now it is to deal with the challenges of globalization.

The new Ministry began with ambitious objectives considering "the absence of any authority with which to control the legislative or spending proposals of other agencies."[88] One analysis observed that "it was created as a new David without a sling; the new Ministry of State could fulfill its mission only with mutual trust and goodwill."[89] These commodities turned out to be in short supply and few of the approaches attempted by the Ministry had much success.

Two national trilevel conferences were held, in 1972 and 1973, and the fact that the municipal level was represented in its own right was something of a breakthrough. But the first conference, in Toronto, made little progress because of the uncompromising attitude of the provinces, led by Ontario. At the second conference, in Edmonton, agreement was reached to undertake a study of public finance with particular reference to the adequacy of municipal revenues. This study eventually confirmed that the local level was being shortchanged in the distribution of revenues in the Canadian federal system,[90] but by the time it appeared a third trilevel conference had been postponed – forever as it turned out. The Canadian Federation of Mayors and Municipalities (CFMM) – predecessor of today's Federation of Canadian Municipalities (FCM) – published its own conclusion about the municipal status with respect to trilevel finances in 1976. The pessimistic assessment was entitled *Puppets on a Shoestring*.[91]

By the spring of 1979, the MSUA was gone, ostensibly a victim of the politics of austerity. "Total savings would be less than $4 million (perhaps closer to $500 000), but the public would be impressed by a government prepared to abolish a whole ministry in the name of fiscal

---

[88] Cameron in *ibid.*, p. 245.

[89] Feldman and Milch, "Coordination or Control?," p. 254.

[90] *Tri-Level Task Force on Public Finance, Report*, 3 Vols., 1976.

[91] *Puppets on a Shoestring,* Ottawa, CFMM, April 28, 1976.

responsibility."[92] Lacking the clout that comes with specific program delivery, regarded with suspicion by federal bodies protecting their turf, disliked by provinces protecting their (municipal) turf, and hassled with constitutional wrangling over federal intrusion into areas of provincial jurisdiction, MSUA never really had a chance. Even Peter Oberlander, its first Secretary (Deputy Minister), called the effort – in the words of the *Yes Minister* television series advisor Sir Humphrey – "courageous."

The death of MSUA did not in any way signify the end of trilevel relations in Canada (just as such relations did not start with its birth). In fact, the federal influence may have been greater during the 1980s, as evidenced by large development projects in almost all of Canada's major metropolitan areas. Some of these projects (such as Harbourfront in Toronto and the Rideau Centre in Ottawa) were the result of election promises, while others reflected the regional influence of a member of the cabinet – such as the Winnipeg Core Area Initiative promoted by Lloyd Axworthy.[93] Whatever their impetus, these projects demonstrated the continuing significance of the federal presence in urban Canada. Oberlander would add that they also reflected a real "on the ground" legacy of MSUA efforts. He also argued that urban waterfront developments such as Granville Island in Vancouver should be included in the Ministry successes.[94]

The disappearance of the MSUA also did nothing to stem the repeated calls for a trilevel approach to infrastructure financing. The election of the Liberals in 1993 led to a *Canada Infrastructure Works* program under which the federal level provided $2 billion over a two year period, matched by similar amounts from the provinces and municipalities. But by the beginning of the new century there were a series of reports and analyses documenting the plight of Canadian cities and the need for greater federal (and provincial) involvement. What made these reports noteworthy is that many of them came not just from "the usual suspects" (municipal associations) but from the business and banking community as well. There appeared to be a growing consensus that the time for greater action had come.

---

[92] *Trilevel Task Force on Public Finance*, p. 260.

[93] Caroline Andrew, "Federal Urban Activity: Intergovernmental Relations in an Age of Restraint," in Frisken, *The Changing Canadian Metropolis*, p. 430.

[94] Oberlander's views herein have been expressed to the authors and are also reflected in Oberlander and Fallick (eds.), *The Ministry of State for Urban Affairs: A Courageous Experiment in Public Administration*.

Box 6.6 Cities to the Forefront
In March 2001 the Federation of Canadian Municipalities released its second report on the quality of life in urban Canada, which found that poverty and income inequality had continued to expand in large urban communities since the first study in 1999.[95]
A May 2001 research paper from the Federation found that European and American governments were investing powers and financial resources in their cities at a much greater rate than was happening in Canada.[96]
May 2001 saw a historic meeting of the mayors of Vancouver, Calgary, Winnipeg, Toronto, and Montreal, a group that became known as the C5. Discussions emphasized that far more revenues flow out of Canada's largest cities (in the form of taxes collected by the senior levels of government) than flow back into them.
The Toronto Board of Trade picked up on this theme in its June 2002 report *Strong City: Strong Nation*, in which it contended that in 2000 there was a net outflow of $9 billion from Toronto to the provincial and federal governments – the bulk of it ($7.6 billion) going to the federal level.
An April 2002 report from the TD Bank concluded that Canada's cities were at a disadvantage because of lack of access to revenue streams other than the property tax.[97]

A New Deal with Municipalities?

In an interesting parallel with the past, the federal response was once again the appointment of a task force – this time a Prime Minister's Task Force on Urban Issues, chaired by former Toronto councillor Judy Sgro. Once again, the recommendations focused on increased federal financial support (for affordable housing, transit/transportation, and infrastructure) and for the appointment of a federal minister to develop an urban strategy for Canada.[98]

The initial federal response was encouraging from the municipal perspective and was symbolized by the appointment of John Godfrey as Minister of State for Infrastructure and Communities – a variation of the Minister of State for Urban Affairs of three decades earlier. Acknowledging federal withdrawal from urban policy implicit in the abolition of

---

[95] Federation of Canadian Municipalities, *Quality of Life in Canadian Communities, 2001 Report*, Ottawa, March 27, 2001. This report is available at the Federation's website at www.fcm.ca, accessed December 12, 2002.

[96] Federation of Canadian Municipalities, *Early Warning: Will Canadian Cities Compete?*, Ottawa, May 2001, accessed December 12, 2002 at www.fcm.ca.

[97] TD Economics Special Report, *A Choice Between Investing in Canada's Cities or Disinvesting in Canada's Future*, April 22, 2002.

[98] Final Report, Prime Minister's Caucus Task Force on Urban Issues, *Canada's Urban Strategy: A Blueprint for Action*, November 2002.

the MSUA, Godfrey remarked that since 1979, federal urban policy had become "a bit like Sleeping Beauty's castle where vines are creeping up and nobody has been there for a long time."[99]

The 2004 federal budget, the first under Prime Minister Paul Martin, accelerated federal infrastructure support, provided GST relief for municipalities, and provided a share of federal gasoline taxes. There was much talk of the "New Deal" underway for Canada's cities. A cities secretariat was established in the Privy Council Office and an External Advisory Committee on Cities and Communities (EACCC) was set up, under the chairmanship of Mike Harcourt, former mayor of Vancouver. In a major shift in focus, however, the gas tax transfer that was originally intended to support public transit in cities was changed to a per capita transfer to all municipalities and the New Deal was broadened to cover communities, not just cities (much less just big cities).

Open Federalism and a Different Deal?

While the New Deal arguably lost its focus during Martin's short-lived government, the federal government of that period did make an attempt to develop policies that would address municipal needs. It also emphasized the need for collaboration between all levels of government (and the private sector). Since the election of the Conservatives under Stephen Harper in 2006, there has been a very significant shift in the federal position. The new approach, which has been given the disarming name of open federalism, is particularly directed at the federal-provincial relationship. It includes a commitment to respect the constitutional division of powers, to resist federal forays into provincial jurisdiction, and to redress the fiscal imbalance from which the provinces claim to suffer. Consistent with this approach, Prime Minister Harper has also made it clear that:[100]

- ➢ The federal government was excessively involved in provincial and local matters.
- ➢ New program spending will be concentrated in jurisdictional areas that are clearly federal.

---

[99] The Honourable John Godfrey, notes for an address to the C. D. Howe Institute, Toronto, May 6, 2005. This renewed federal interest was also reflected in Caroline Andrew, Katherine Graham, and Susan Phillips (eds.), *Urban Affairs: Back on the Policy Agenda*, Montreal and Kingston, McGill-Queen's University Press, 2002.

[100] Prime Minster Stephen Harper, address to the 2006 Annual Conference of the Federation of Canadian Municipalities, Montreal, June 2, 2006.

> Once the provincial fiscal imbalance is corrected, he does not anticipate large federal surpluses in the future.
> The provinces will have the financial capacity to fulfill their obligations (including any municipal fiscal imbalance).

For Harper, any New Deal will be with the provinces, not the municipal level. Indeed, the 2007 federal budget promised $39 billion over the next seven years to restore fiscal balance between the federal government and the provinces. From a strict constitutional perspective, it is logical – and tidy – to have the federal government improve the financial position of the provinces which then, in turn, improve the financial position of municipalities. However, the federal government's determination, accelerated by Harper's parliamentary majority after May 2011, to disentangle itself from its involvement in provincial and municipal matters goes against the increasingly widespread view (discussed below) that increased multilevel collaboration is the answer.

International Relations

In addition to relations with the provincial and federal levels, municipalities are also affected, directly and indirectly, by the globalization of the economy and the international organizations and agreements related to that process. What is less clear is whether the overall impact of these developments on municipalities will be positive or negative.

The negative or pessimistic view is that globalization has increased the power of private capital and that municipal governments have no choice but to implement the prevailing neoliberal, free market agenda.[101] Municipalities now have reduced bargaining power in dealing with developers and Leo comments that "mobile companies often call the tune in their dealings with local governments, and, in the process, they can cancel development plans, zoning rules, building code regulations, and even the taxes that are levied to support the city's services."[102]

---

[101] For example, see Gary Teeple, *Globalization and the Decline of Social Reform*, Toronto, Garamond Press, 1995.

[102] Christopher Leo, "Planning Aspirations and Political Realities," in Edmund P. Fowler and David Siegel (eds.), *Urban Policy Issues*, Toronto, Oxford University Press, 2002, p. 223.

There is also growing evidence of the extent to which municipalities (as well as provincial and federal governments) are constrained by such factors as the North American Free Trade Agreement (NAFTA) and the World Trade Organization (WTO). For example, NAFTA created extensive rights for foreign firms to sue governments under a very broadly defined category of expropriation. In 2001 a British Columbia Supreme Court Justice reviewed the decision of a NAFTA Tribunal that had ruled that American toxic waste firm Metalclad had to be compensated for a number of actions taken by the federal, state, and local governments in Mexico. Lidstone's observation that "Metalclad is a wake-up call for municipalities throughout North America,"[103] is understandable in light of a B.C. Justice's finding that:

> In addition to the more conventional notion of expropriation involving a taking of property, the Tribunal held that expropriation under the NAFTA includes covert or incidental interference with the use of property that has the effect of depriving the owner, in whole or in significant part, of the use or reasonably-to-be-expected economic benefit of the property. This definition is sufficiently broad to include a legitimate rezoning of property by a municipality or other zoning authority.[104]

A study of the impact of NAFTA on the United States and Mexico also sounds the alarm concerning the extent to which this agreement is constraining subnational and local government authority. Designed to advance privatization of public services, the effect of NAFTA is to "undermine the very ability of local governments to use markets for public goods by defining traditional state and local government mechanisms as 'non-tariff barriers to trade'."[105] Stephen McBride has called this effect "quiet constitutionalism."[106]

---

[103] Lidstone, *A Comparison of New and Proposed Municipal Acts*, p. 11.

[104] Supreme Court of British Columbia, "Reasons for Judgment of the Honourable Mr. Justice Tysoe, *United States of Mexico v. Metalclad Corporation*, May 2, 2001, as quoted in Ellen Gould, *International Trade and Investment Agreements: A Primer for Local Governments*, Union of British Columbia Municipalities, June 2001.

[105] Mildred Warner and Jennifer Gerbasi, "Rescaling and reforming the state under NAFTA: implications for subnational authority," *International Journal of Urban and Regional Research*, 2004, Issue 4, p. 858.

[106] Stephen McBride, "Quiet Constitutionalism in Canada: The International Political Economy of Domestic Institutional Change," *Canadian Journal of Political Science*, Vol. 36, No. 2, June 2003, pp. 251-273.

Lidstone also points out that the General Agreement on Trade in Services (GATS) expressly applies to services provided by or on behalf of municipalities, and requires the federal government to ensure that local authorities fulfill the obligations and commitments made by the federal government. From the way services are defined under the GATS, Lidstone concludes that public private partnerships, contracting out, design build arrangements, and privatization would be subject to the GATS provisions.[107] In this regard, the Greater Vancouver Regional District dropped plans to construct a water filtration plant under a $400 million public private partnership (P3) plan because it could not receive satisfactory assurances about the possible risk of losing control of this plant in the future from trade challenges under the NAFTA and GATS provisions.[108]

Another analysis also sounded a caution, pointing out that the GATS adversely affects the ability of municipal governments to supply and to regulate basic services such as water and sewage services, waste management, transportation services, public transit, road building, land use planning, and library services.[109] In 2011, debates over control of local water supply that animated an initial joint P3 initiative between Abbotsford and Mission, British Columbia were based on similar concerns.[110] And in BC's Powell River, a P3 sewage treatment proposal has been sold by proponents as not a P3 but a "service agreement."[111] Each such "Water Watch" issue was a factor in British Columbia's November 2011 municipal elections, contributing to the defeat of the mayors of Abbotsford and Mission.

Globalization has had quite an impact on the local level in an indirect way through the pressure that it has placed on senior levels of government to scale back and downsize their operations in support of the more competitive atmosphere demanded by the international marketplace. One

---

[107] Lidstone, *A Comparison of New and Proposed Municipal Acts*, p. 11.

[108] See *GRVD Decides Against Design-Build-Operate Arrangements for Constructing Drinking Water Filtration Facilities*, GVRD Press Release, June 29, 2001 and Murray Dobbin, "Municipalities Take on Ottawa's Trade Agenda," *National Post*, September 17, 2001.

[109] Michelle Swenarchuk, *From Global to Local: GATS Impacts on Canadian Municipalities*, Ottawa, Canadian Centre for Policy Alternatives, May 2002, p. v.

[110] See, "Mission, Abbotsford Debate Private Water Investment," CBC News, Vancouver, April 12, 2011.

[111] See http://prwaterwatch.wordpress.com/2011/04/ for a discussion of concerns about this project.

of the primary ways that they have made this adjustment is by shifting responsibilities and costs downward, where they have ultimately landed in the laps of local governments.

Local governments are also affected by the fact that globalization and international trade rules and regulations now make it almost impossible for senior governments to pursue the kinds of regional policies that used to be provided in support of have-not areas; such policies are deemed to be unfair trade practices under NAFTA or by the World Trade Organization.[112] The result is that local economies face increasingly stiff competition – from virtually anywhere in the world – and must respond without at least some of the provincial and federal government supports that used to exist.

Globalization has had a positive impact in making cities and city regions increasingly important as key players in the world economy. But does it follow that the municipalities within these urban areas have also become more important? Courchene seems to have no doubts about the positive future for cities. As he sees it, "the issue is not so much *whether* they will be able to extricate themselves from their current 'constitution-less' status as wards of their respective provinces, but rather *how* they will increase their autonomy and forge more formal linkages with both levels of government."[113] [emphasis in the original]

But Sancton questions the presumption that because cities are growing in importance, municipalities must as well.[114] He argues that cities are not governed by municipalities – at least not exclusively – since municipal governments always share functional responsibility for urban areas with other levels of government. Moreover, usually these other governments are responsible for functions that are most important to the city – such as money and banking, immigration, commercial law, unemployment insurance, and social assistance. He concludes, therefore, that municipalities will always be only a part of a multilevel system of government for cities and their importance may not grow as cities become more important – though the Canadian inclinations toward

---

[112] Christopher Leo, with Susan Mulligan, "City Politics: Globalization and Community Democracy," in Joan Grace and Byron Sheldrick (eds.), *Canadian Politics*, Toronto, Pearson Prentice Hall, 2006, p. 153.

[113] Thomas Courchene, *A State of Minds*, Montreal, Institute of Research on Public Policy, 2001, p. 277.

[114] Andrew Sancton, *The Limits of Boundaries: Can City-Regions Be Self-Governing?*, paper presented to the Urban Affairs Association Annual Conference, Montreal, April 22, 2006.

amalgamated municipal structures in many major centres do speak to recognized responses to globalization forces.[115]

The next section takes a closer look at these multilevel systems and how municipalities may fare within them. The case below provides an effective transition to that next section since the border issue in the City of Windsor illustrates both the intergovernmental and international influences on municipal government and the need for multilevel collaboration in addressing an issue that has a major place based component.

> **Box 6.7 Building Bridges in Windsor**[116]
>
> There is no better example of the intergovernmental complexities within which municipalities operate and the many players that are involved in resolving issues than the story of the border crossing between Windsor and Detroit. Globalization and free trade greatly increased the flow of traffic through the Windsor tunnel and across the Ambassador Bridge. In fact, this privately owned bridge carries the largest volume of truck traffic in North America. Windsor has become not just a key connection on the NAFTA superhighway but also increasingly the centre of an integrated trade axis that extends beyond North America. As traffic volumes increased, however, so did the need to upgrade or expand border crossings to accommodate this growth. This need suddenly became extremely pressing when the terrorist attacks of September 11, 2001 prompted the United States government to introduce border security measures that created a major backlog at the border and an adverse economic impact.
>
> Resolving the border crossing issue is an important agenda item for senior governments in both Canada and the United States. But it is also an extremely important item for the City of Windsor, where municipal streets carry the 12 000 trucks daily that cross the Ambassador Bridge, as well as the traffic to the Detroit-Windsor car tunnel. Windsor's primary objective has been to ensure that any new crossing and its access routes have the least impact possible and result in reduced truck traffic on city streets. Not content to be consulted on the issue as one of the many local stakeholders, city council even developed and advanced its own border solution at one stage.

---

[115] On this see, for example, Smith and Stewart, *Global Calgary: A Globalist Strategy for the City of Calgary* Ottawa, *Canadian Policy Research Network*, April 2006, and Smith, "Branding Cascadia: Who Gets To Decide? Considering Cascadia's Conflicting Conceptualizations – The Case for a Global City Region Definition," *Canadian Political Science Review*, Vol. 2, No. 2, Summer 2008, pp. 57-83.

[116] This description draws in part from information provided by John Skorobohacz, CAO, City of Windsor, and is mainly based on C. Richard Tindal, *The World of the Assessor*, Institute of Municipal Assessors, Summer 2007, Lesson 7, pp. 13-14 and John B. Sutcliffe, *Municipal Influences in a Multi-national Setting? The Windsor-Detroit Border Crossing*, paper presented to the Canadian Political Science Association Annual Conference, Toronto, June 2006.

> Agreement on a new bridge has now been reached by all three levels of government in Canada but the approval of the Michigan legislature is still required for the project to proceed. A committee of the Michigan Senate voted against recommending the project in late October 2011, allegedly as a result of the influence of the owner of the Ambassador Bridge who has fought the plans for a new bridge at every step[117] (and who claims an intention to build a second private bridge instead). But there are also other private interests involved, including the major industries that rely on the border for trade and they have increasingly lined up in support of the government's bridge project.
>
> Whatever the result, there are clearly many linkages underlying the new Windsor-Detroit link. The free trade regime promoted by international agencies and agreements made Windsor a key component of the global supply chain. The terrorist attack on 9/11 prompted responses that accelerated the backlog at the Windsor border. The U.S. and Canadian governments, as well as provincial and state governments, are all involved in addressing this backlog, as are various private interests. Since Windsor is so vitally affected by factors and forces beyond its control and beyond its municipal boundaries, the city's active participation in the resolution of this matter seems entirely appropriate.

Multilevel Relations

This term does not refer to the passionate couple who lived in a triplex, although that is a concept much easier to imagine than what is to follow. Instead, the title of this section refers to the reality of municipal government relationships today.

To understand these relationships, we need to begin by viewing federalism less as a structure – as outlined in the preceding pages – and more as a process. Instead of a constitutional hierarchy, focused on delineating the separate responsibilities of levels and orders of government, a combined and collaborative approach is the most effective way of addressing many of today's issues. This is not a new concept and, indeed, the federal system has shown a fair bit of flexibility over the years, notably through use of the so called federal spending power to enable the federal government to provide funds and establish standards in matters otherwise under provincial jurisdiction. In addition, creativity has been shown in developing policies that take account of the regional differences in Canada by allowing for variations in the application of

---

[117] Chris Vander Doelen, "Bridge struggle drags on," *The Windsor Star*, November 5, 2011.

these policies within the provinces.[118] This same combination of flexibility and cooperative arrangement needs to be extended to embrace the local level as well.

As Stein points out, "[f]ederal and provincial governments bump up against each other all the time on policies that directly affect cities."[119] Immigration, for example, is a federal and provincial responsibility that is manifested at the local level and its successful implementation, therefore, requires collaboration among all three levels of government. For difficult, complex problems, "the resources, expertise and jurisdictional authority of all levels of government need to be deployed in a coordinated way" in what Stein terms networked federalism.[120]

The final report of the External Advisory Committee on Cities and Communities described as follows the appropriate roles and responsibilities for an integrated approach to policy making:[121]

> To shape better cities and strong communities, federal capacities are needed to make connections, provincial and territorial powers are needed for strategic integration and municipal abilities are needed to engage citizens and deliver change locally. Cooperative relationships are essential ... working with [municipalities] and civil society in new governance partnerships tailored to city-regions and neighbourhoods.

Bradford argues that the pivotal role of cities in determining the quality of national life demands close collaboration among all levels of government. In his view, it is not just a matter of helping municipalities handle their responsibilities but of ensuring that federal and provincial policy interventions benefit from the insights provided by the local level.[122] To achieve effective area based policy, Bradford calls for what he terms joined up governance, in which various levels of government work with and through local partnerships including community based

---

[118] The federalism as process theme has been explored by Thomas J. Courchene, notably in *Celebrating Flexibility: An Interpretive Essay on the Evolution of Canadian Federalism*, Montreal, C. D. Howe Institute, 1995.

[119] Janice Gross Stein, "Canada by Mondrian: Networked Federalism in an Era of Globalization," in *Canada by Picasso: The Faces of Federalism*, Conference Board of Canada, 2006, p. 34.

[120] *Ibid.*, p. 37.

[121] External Advisory Committee on Cities and Communities, *From Restless Communities to Resilient Places: Building a Stronger Future for All Canadians*, 2006, p. ix.

[122] Neil Bradford, *Why Cities Matter: Policy Research Perspectives for Canada*, Discussion Paper F\23, Ottawa, Canadian Policy Research Networks, June 2002.

organizations and municipal councils.[123] Australians refer to this as whole of government policy making.[124] This term denotes "public agencies working across portfolio boundaries to achieve a shared goal and an integrated government response to particular issues. Approaches can be formal or informal. They can focus on policy development, program management or service delivery."[125]

Leo also endorses the importance and benefits of multilevel collaboration. While cities have become more important in a global economy, he makes a persuasive case against the charter city movement (described above) as the appropriate response. He notes provincial unwillingness to share power along with resistance from those who have doubts about the competence and democratic tendencies of municipal councils.[126] Leo also points out that municipalities given greater autonomy in today's very competitive environment might fail more often than succeed and that a case can be made for greater federal involvement in setting standards and financing programs. But he explains that the alternatives of greater municipal autonomy or a stronger central government represent a false choice, one premised on the traditional, hierarchical view of intergovern-mental relations – the federalism as structure approach outlined above. As he sees it, the question is: "How can we have policies that are truly national and yet fully take into account the very significant differences among regions and communities?"[127] The answer is a collaborative intergovernmental process that Leo terms deep federalism, one he finds evidence of since the late 1970s. His examples include:[128]

> ➤ The federal Neighbourhood Improvement Program (NIP), which took into account local features and differences by requiring a

---

[123] Neil Bradford, *Whither the Federal Urban Agenda?*, Research Report F\65, Ottawa, Canadian Policy Research Networks, February 2007, p. 5.

[124] See, for example, Tiffany Morrison and Marcus Lane, "What 'Whole of Government' Means for Environmental Policy and Management: An Analysis of the Connecting Government Initiative," *Australasian Journal of Environmental Management*, Vol. 12, No. 1, March 2005, pp. 47-54.

[125] Australian Public Service Commission, *Connecting Government: Whole of Government Responses to Australia's Priority Challenges*, April 2004 at www.apsc.gov.au/mac/connectinggovernment1.htm, accessed October 15, 2011.

[126] Christopher Leo, "Deep Federalism: Respecting Community Difference in National Policy," *Canadian Journal of Political Science*, September 2006, p. 485.

[127] *Ibid.*

[128] *Ibid.*, p. 489.

public participation process before urban renewal plans were developed for any targeted neighbourhood;
- ➢ Winnipeg's Core Area Initiative, a trilevel agreement for the social, economic, and physical renewal of the inner city; and
- ➢ The Vancouver Agreement among partners from all three levels of government to focus on economic development, the health of residents, and public safety in Vancouver's Downtown Eastside.

Unless local distinctions and differences are taken into account, federal policies that are effective in some parts of the country are inevitably ineffective or inappropriate in other areas. A classic example was the National Homeless Initiative launched by the federal government in the late 1990s.[129] It was a response to publicity about the increasing numbers of people living – and in some cases dying – on the streets of our large cities. Not surprisingly, the focus of this initiative was on homeless shelters and services to homeless people. There was no provision for spending on housing and yet in many cities, such as Winnipeg, a major problem was not street people but what were termed the relatively homeless – that is, people who were paying more than they could afford for housing and/or living in very inadequate accommodation. The Winnipeg Housing and Homeless Initiative is an attempt to respond to local needs and conditions. Under this initiative, all three levels of government provided funding for strategies developed by community groups active in such matters as housing renovation, relief of homelessness, and community development.[130]

To recap federalism as process – also known as networked federalism, deep federalism, joined up governance, whole of government and multilevel governance (among others) – the basic points are as follows:

- ➢ In today's global economy, national borders are less significant and national governments are constrained, whereas cities and city regions have elevated importance as the key drivers of a country's economic competitiveness.
- ➢ As a consequence, effective action is now increasingly needed on a regional scale.
- ➢ The response is found in new configurations that go beyond the constitutional division of powers and bring all levels of government together, along with community groups and other players as needed. (This is often referred to as rescaling, as in creating new scales of operation – to give you another term to assimilate.)

---

[129] The description of this initiative is based on Leo, *Deep Federalism*, pp. 500-502.

[130] Leo, with Mulligan, *City Politics: Globalization and Community Democracy*, p. 158.

> The result can be initiatives that combine the legal and financial backing of the provincial and federal levels and the insights and local knowledge of municipalities and community groups – into policy or program applications appropriately tailored to the local needs and circumstances.

Like Canada, the European Union has identified that not all change can come from constitutional reform. In Europe, the new Open Method of Coordination has replaced seeking legislative solutions.[131] As logical as these collaborative approaches sound, their achievement in practice is a continuing challenge, as is evident from recent research into multilevel governance experiences in eight countries (not including Canada). It found that the role of non-government bodies is not as prominent as expected and the interaction between governments very much reflects the formal hierarchy, with city governments being policytakers and not policymakers with respect to national programs that affect their jurisdictions.[132] Instead of top down forms of governing, bottom up has much to offer, as will be evident from the examples in the next section.

Making the Most of the Mushy Middle

There seems little doubt that municipalities will increasingly be part of multilevel governance arrangements. How well these arrangements work will depend, in part, on how effective municipalities are in asserting themselves and ensuring that local knowledge and circumstances are given proper consideration in the development and application of federal and provincial policies and programs.

In this regard, it was noted earlier that Smith and Stewart have identified a mushy middle that may characterize more accurately where municipalities operate – or at least where they have the potential to operate – than the supposedly precise locations defined by Sec. 92.8 (creatures of the province/Dillon's Rule) status and significant local discretion/home rule. In support of their contention, they provide two examples of what they termed "eager beavers vs.

---

[131] See http://ec.europa.eu/invest-in-research/coordination/coordination01_en.htm.

[132] Harvey Lazar and Christian Leuprecht (eds.), *Spheres of Governance*, Montreal and Kingston, McGill-Queen's University Press, 2007, p. 2.

lazy cats"[133] to show the capacity of local governments to act effectively in dealings with other levels of government by working more actively on policy matters further along the discretionary end of the mushy middle spectrum.

Figure 6.3 Revised Mushy Middle Continuum

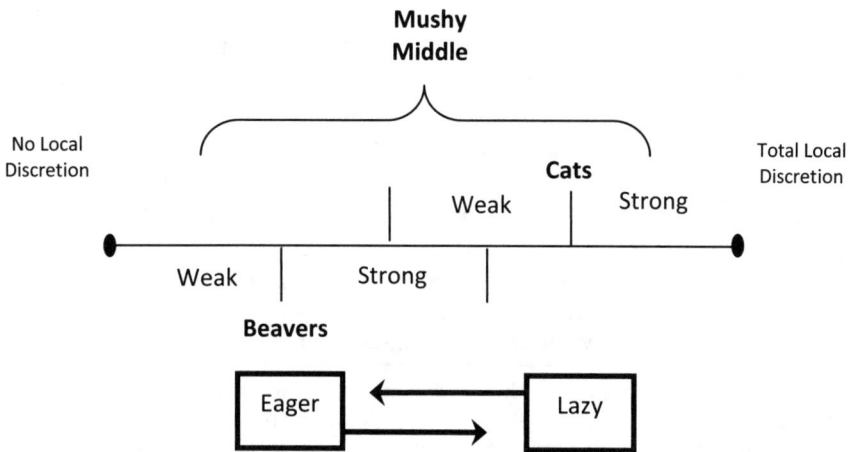

One of the cases describes how Vancouver led the way in intergovernmental discussions in pursuit of a new approach to drug treatment emphasizing harm reduction through the operation of safe injection sites. Key to this success was strong leadership initially from two mayors, Phillip Owen – whose support for the drug initiative cost him the backing of his local party, the rightist Non-Partisan Association (NPA) – and Larry Campbell of the left leaning Committee of Progressive Electors (COPE). Owen and Campbell's initiative was supported by their successors – Mayors Sam Sullivan (of the NPA) and Gregor Robertson (of the centre left Vision Vancouver). Part of pushing this agenda has been a case to the Supreme Court of Canada over federal versus provincial jurisdiction given the ambivalence/ hostility of the Harper Conservative government to a supervised injection site (SIS) for heroin users in Vancouver. Three different local political parties, right, left, and centre left have all supported this one of a kind in North America harm reduction imperative. As part of the Vancouver Agreement, the city kept all levels of government in a true multilevel solution to a significant local social concern.

---

[133] Smith and Stewart, *Beavers, Cats, and the Mushy Middle Thesis*, in Young and Leuprecht (eds.), *Canada: The State of the Federation, 2004*, pp. 258-263.

Vancouver's decision to hold a referendum on Canada's bid to hold the 2010 Winter Olympics in that city is the basis for the second case study. It reveals how the city used bargaining leverage that it enjoyed temporarily (while there was uncertainty about how much the newly elected leftist mayor and council might oppose the Olympic bid) to gain some concessions from both the province and the federal government with respect to a Vancouver social housing initiative. Even the holding of a *municipal* referendum after the federal and provincial governments had committed to the 2010 Winter Games was designed to deal the city some better cards in the multilevel discussions on social housing. The result was that the province stepped up its support.

Another positive example is that of Toronto's response to the challenges of being the country's largest recipient of immigrants. Its experience illustrates the benefits of collaborative action and provides an encouraging perspective of the influence that the local level can exert.[134]

Box 6.8 Meeting the Immigration Challenge

The potential of cooperative approaches is demonstrated by the way Toronto has become a national leader in the development of multicultural policy and programs. The story begins with the city facing severe financial pressures because of actions taken by the provincial and federal levels. The federal government promoted high levels of immigration without sufficient regard to, or financial support for, those municipalities in receipt of this immigrant population. The province downloaded responsibilities and costs as part of a local services realignment and then indirectly downloaded responsibility for immigrant settlement and multiculturalism policy by substantially withdrawing from these fields. The province also forced amalgamation on the municipalities in the Toronto area in 1998 but that mobilized the local population, including the immigrant population.

Engaged citizens and groups, including the Citizens for Local Democracy (C4LD), turned their attention to gaining increased autonomy for the new City of Toronto. There were calls for Toronto to become a province and demands for a city charter. The city formed strategic alliances through means such as participation in the C5 (mayors of big cities) and the Toronto City Summit Alliance (a coalition of leaders from more than 50 organizations representing business, labour, and the not-for-profit sector) that was first discussed in Chapter 5.

One of the priorities of the Toronto City Summit Alliance was to become a centre of excellence in the integration of immigrants. In furtherance of this objective, the Alliance set up the Toronto Region Immigrant Employment Council (TRIEC) to help immigrants with access to jobs. TRIEC is supported by a secretariat initially funded solely by a private foundation but now backed by federal funding as well. Consistent with the

---

[134] The description of this initiative that follows is summarized from Kristin Good, *Urban Regime-Building as a Strategy of Intergovernmental Reform: The Case of Toronto's Role in Immigrant Settlement*, paper presented to the Canadian Political Science Association Annual Conference, Saskatoon, May 30-June 1, 2007.

> concept of multilevel governance, TRIEC's members include community organizations, employers, labour unions, occupational regulatory bodies, educational institutions, and representatives of all three levels of government. This successful initiative is a very good example of how Canadian municipalities can build urban regimes by pooling public and private resources to create the capacity to develop and implement local policy agendas.

If more municipalities are to take the initiative by moving toward the mushy middle or fine tuning the local application of senior government programs, they need to stop seeing their roles and potential only through the perspective of the constitutional lens. That cities need to become much more assertive is a theme which has been advanced by several others as well. Jane Jacobs delivered this message at the first meeting of the C5 (the big five cities of Vancouver, Calgary, Winnipeg, Toronto, and Montreal) and her words merit repeating at some length.[135]

> I think you have an ingrained mindset of dependency and that this is going to be the hardest thing for you to overcome....You must somehow gather your self-esteem not to be apologetic about yourselves. Certainly the country needs to be educated about how important the cities are. But if the cities themselves don't believe it or are apologetic about it, or are afraid to bring it up, even aggressively, the education of the country and the understanding of what really is necessary and what ails us, is never going to come about.

Andrew advances a similar argument after expressing a number of concerns about the approach that federal and provincial governments have been taking to the needs of the cities.[136] Her view is that the future of local governments depends more on their actions than on some constitutional breakthrough. In her words: "City governments will not become more effective actors through provincial or federal recognition or power-sharing arrangements; rather, they can become more effective through their creation of more inclusive urban governance regimes."[137] Her concluding observation, reminiscent of the above noted advice of Jane Jacobs, is: "We should not ignore our cities, but this will happen only when they demonstrate to us and to the other levels of government that we cannot ignore them."[138] The Vancouver "eager beaver" examples above illustrate this more assertive posture.

---

[135] Quoted in *Ideas That Matter*, p. 20.

[136] Caroline Andrew, "The shame of (ignoring) the cities," *Journal of Canadian Studies*, Winter 2001, pp. 100-110.

[137] *Ibid.*, p. 109.

[138] *Ibid.*, p. 110.

Concluding Comments

The examination of intergovernmental relations in this chapter began with the traditional hierarchical approach, tracing municipal relations upward – to the province, the federal level, and even the international sphere. While these relationships are essential to an understanding of municipal operations and their scope and constraints, they certainly do not tell the whole story. Viewing municipalities through only the constitutional lens presents a limited and, in some respects, distorted picture as we have attempted to demonstrate throughout this chapter.

The chapter also makes clear the growing prominence of multilevel governance arrangements – that is, federal, provincial, and municipal governments and private, non-profit, and community organizations collaborating through processes that combine broad general policies with special local needs and conditions. The benefits of these arrangements cast doubt on the wisdom of the open federalism espoused by Prime Minister Harper, with its emphasis on withdrawing the federal government from entanglements with the provincial and local levels. The same misguided preoccupation with administrative tidiness was also noted with respect to disentanglement initiatives in several provinces.

Finally, this chapter has an important message for Canada's municipalities. It is time for the constitutional orphans to realize that they have grown up and need to get on with their lives. Municipalities now have a strengthened legislative foundation (in a majority of provinces) and favourable interpretations of their scope for action from the Supreme Court of Canada. Quite apart from their improved legal position, they have the ability to exercise more control over their destinies if they will but exert themselves forcefully and take full advantage of every opportunity – however fleeting – in which they have potential bargaining leverage.

There are encouraging signs of this more assertive stance. The mayor of Vancouver used a city-initiated Olympics referendum to gain concessions from the provincial and federal levels. Vancouver took the lead in reshaping federal health policy to address harm reduction for drug users, just as Toronto worked with organizations such as the Toronto City Summit Alliance to develop effective multicultural policies and programs. Mississauga used the threat of delays and refusal to provide municipal services to exert influence over the federal government in the early 1990s as the latter pursued privatization initiatives in connection with an expansion of Pearson Airport and to force the developer chosen to build a new terminal to pay development charges.[139] Not all such local efforts will be successful, but changing the channel can have some effect.

Bird is correct in observing that the image of municipal governments when approaching the provincial or federal level "is characterized more by the outstretched hand than the upraised municipal fist."[140] But that subservient posture is changing, as evidenced by the examples above. The outstretched hand may still be an apt image if, instead of being held out in search of money, it is being offered as an invitation to potential allies to collaborate in multilevel governance.

As for the money – and sooner or later it's always about the money – that is the focus of the next chapter.

---

[139] Tom Urbaniak, "Rhetoric and Restraint: Municipal-Federal Relations in Canada's Largest Edge City," in Young and Leuprecht, *Canada: The State of the Federation, 2004*, pp. 275-279.

[140] Richard Bird (ed.), *Who Decides? Government in the New Millennium*, Montreal, C. D. Howe Institute, August 2004, p. 14.

Chapter 7
Local Government Finances

To the extent that municipalities suffer from a fiscal imbalance, the problem is partly of their own making, just as the solution also lies partly within their grasp. The provincial and federal governments are far from blameless, but calling constantly for them to open their coffers is not the most productive use of municipal time and energy. Ideas of multilevel governing (MLG) support notions of the need for "whole of government" solutions to many of the policy dilemmas confronting Canada's larger municipalities. [1]

Introduction

It would surprise almost no one to open the morning paper and read: "A report on Canadian public finance, released today, foreshadows the decline and fall of municipal government as we know it in Canada within five years." According to this report, if present trends continue "autonomous municipal government will not survive without huge increases in property taxes or unacceptable cutbacks in services city residents now demand, or both." This is certainly a viewpoint widely expressed today, but the report being quoted is actually more than 35 years old.[2] Municipalities are obviously still very much with us, and to some extent they have become victims of "crying wolf" when it comes to their financial situation. But the concerns about the financial problems they face have remained and intensified. How real are these financial concerns, what is behind them, and how can they be resolved or eased?

---

[1] On MLG and "whole of government" solutions to urban policy challenges see, for example, P. Smith and K. Stewart, "Local Whole-of-Government Policymaking in Vancouver: Beavers, Cats and the Mushy Middle Thesis," in Robert Young and Christian Leuprecht (eds.), *Canada: The State of the Federation 2004: Municipal-Federal-Provincial Relations in Canada,* Montreal and Kingston, McGill-Queen's University Press, 2006, pp. 251-272.

[2] Canadian Federation of Mayors and Municipalities, *Puppets on a Shoestring*, Ottawa, April 28, 1976. Both quotes are from p. 1.

Attempting to answer these questions is the central purpose of this chapter. Clear municipal challenges exist, but senior governments ignore these matters at their own peril. Jane Jacobs has reminded all involved in Canadian governing that *not* dealing with local government exigencies puts real policy solutions in jeopardy.

Municipal Expenditures and Revenues

In a nutshell, the financial problem facing municipalities is that their expenditures are growing more rapidly than their revenues and they don't have complete control over either. Municipalities were established originally to provide a limited number of services to property in a predominantly rural and agricultural society and to fund these services from a tax on property. In contrast, consider their responsibilities today.[3]

> Municipal roles have evolved to include services oriented to people and income redistribution such as immigration and settlement services, affordable housing and homelessness, urban Aboriginals, and child care services. Cities have also seen an expansion in their responsibilities to include economic development, emergency preparedness, public security, cultural and recreational facilities, environmental protection and cleanup, alternative fuel and energy technologies, higher standards in clean water and air.

Many of the increased expenditures are related to the urbanization described in Chapter 3 and the accompanying sprawl with its expensive servicing requirements. Such growth requires investment in infrastructure (such as roads and bridges, water supply and sewage treatment facilities, solid waste disposal facilities, schools, libraries, and arenas and other recreational facilities) and, in addition, much existing infrastructure has deteriorated and now needs replacing – at a cost of many billions of dollars. Competitive pressures in a global economy increase the need for investment in infrastructure, not just in traditional hard services but also in the cultural, recreational, and other amenities that enhance the quality of life that attracts and retains knowledge workers.

---

[3] Big City Mayors' Caucus, *Our Cities, Our Future*, Ottawa, Federation of Canadian Municipalities, June 2006, p. 10.

While the emphasis on urban infrastructure is understandable, the fact is that rural areas also have major infrastructure needs.[4] The lack of broadband access to the Internet is a significant impediment for economic development in many rural areas. To improve the quality of life in rural communities requires social and cultural infrastructure such as libraries, parks, and community centres. The lack of infrastructure to support health service delivery also makes it more difficult to attract businesses and individuals to rural communities, an issue particularly felt in northern Canada.

Surprisingly, there isn't any precise or definitive measure of the infrastructure backlog or gap in Canada and studies variously estimate its magnitude as ranging from $60 billion to $125 billion.[5] Differences relate to such factors as the scope of the infrastructure being measured and whether the study includes both maintenance/replacement and new investment. It is also the fact that many of the studies obtain their data from people who may have a vested interest in overstating the size of the deficit and that these studies usually assume no policy changes in the future such as new user fees that could result in reduced demand.

We do know that there has been a dramatic increase in the portion of infrastructure owned by the municipal level. From 1961 through 2002, the municipal portion increased from 30.9% to 52.4%, while the federal portion declined from 23.0% to 6.8%.[6] It is also evident that the infrastructure is aging and is not being sufficiently maintained, largely as a result of

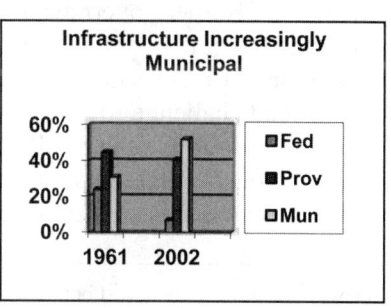

municipalities reluctant to undertake the necessary long term borrowing and anxious to hold the line on taxes. Whether it is Montreal freeways collapsing or municipal water systems malfunctioning, the infrastructure deficit remains. At the end of the first decade of the 21st century, the Federation of Canadian Municipalities stated the problem clearly:

---

[4] The discussion that follows is based on Federation of Canadian Municipalities, *Building Prosperity From the Ground Up: Restoring Municipal Fiscal Balance*, June 2006, p. 8.

[5] Enid Slack and Richard M. Bird, *Cities in Canadian Federalism*, Toronto, University of Toronto, May 2006, p. 11.

[6] Federation of Canadian Municipalities, *Submission to Transport, Infrastructure and Communities Canada*, September 8, 2006, p. 5.

> With growing responsibilities and limited revenues, municipalities are often forced to choose between providing necessary services ... and making necessary investments in the maintenance and construction of their public infrastructure.... Municipalities are required by law to balance their budgets each year, so the funding shortfall is inevitably pushed off the balance sheet onto our streets in the form of reduced maintenance and delayed replacement of aging infrastructure.... Canadians see the consequences of the deficit all around them: potholes, rusting bridges, water treatment and public transit systems that cannot keep up with demand, poor air quality and lack of affordable housing.[7]

All too often, the approach to infrastructure has been one of "design, build, and forget."[8] Even after the federal economic stimulus package of 2009-2011 to deal with the global recession that continued into the second decade of the 21st century, this pattern continued. In 2007, the infrastructure deficit was pegged at $123 billion.[9] The *Economic Action Plan* of the federal Conservative government put several billions of dollars into "Building Infrastructure to Create Jobs," much of it matched by provincial and municipal funds.[10] Despite continuing buffeting of the economy, the Harper government has so far reiterated its commitment to balance the federal budget by 2014-2015, leaving municipalities where they were in 2007-2008 in terms of ongoing infrastructure funding.[11]

An added challenge for municipalities is that a considerable portion of their expenditures is the result of services offloaded by the provincial and federal levels without commensurate financial resources. These expenditures are usually referred to as unfunded mandates.[12] Examples

---

[7] This was the view in 2008, just before the federal government's economic stimulus package of 2009-2010, set up to combat the global recession. See FCM Backgrounder: *The Municipal Infrastructure Deficit,* at www.fcm.ca/CMFiles/infrastructure1PFA-7676, (accessed August 20, 2011).

[8] McGill University Civil Engineering Professor Saeed Mirza, quoted in Steven Chase, "Cities struggling to keep up infrastructure," *Globe and Mail*, October 9, 2006.

[9] Mizra, *The Coming Collapse of Canada's Municipal Infrastructure,* FCM, 2007.

[10] On Canada's Economic Action Plan see *What Has Been Done* at http://www.actionplan.gc.ca/eng/feature.asp?featureId=4 (accessed August 19, 2011).

[11] As noted by Jim Flaherty to the Commons Finance Committee. See "Canada well-positioned to face global economic challenges, Flaherty tells Finance Committee," Finance Ministry Press Release, August 9, 2011 at www.fin.gc.ca/n11/11-069-eng.asp.

[12] These unfunded mandates are discussed in Enid Slack, "Fiscal Imbalance: The Case for Cities," in Federation of Canadian Municipalities, *Restoring Municipal Fiscal Balance*, Appendix 3, p. 76, and in Thomas J. Courchene, *CitiStates and the State of Cities*, Montreal, Institute for Research on Public Policy, June 2005, p. 12.

include immigration and social housing, social programs (particularly in Ontario), and water quality standards.

While their responsibilities and costs have grown in response to greatly changed conditions, municipalities continue to rely on the historic real property tax as their main source of revenue. The only other major local revenue source they have is user charges. While there are other possible sources – as discussed later in this chapter – municipalities don't have any authority to exercise them unless authorized by their provincial government, as a result of their subordinate constitutional position. To close the gap between these local revenues and their requirements, municipalities depend upon financial assistance from the provincial (especially) and federal levels of government. While there has been recognition of the importance of senior level financial assistance more recently, its erosion over the last two decades of the 20th century was a major contributor to the increasing financial stress experienced by municipalities. As we will see, that erosion is evidence of the extent to which municipal financial issues are affected by the changing nature of fiscal federalism. For local governments, this is not a new situation.

Municipal Finance and Fiscal Federalism

The story of municipal finance is entangled with that of provincial and federal finances. In fact, there are some intriguing – if somewhat superficial – parallels between municipal-provincial financial relations and provincial-federal financial relations. Just as municipalities contend that their responsibilities have increased greatly in importance and cost, well beyond the revenue sources available to them, so too have provinces complained about an unfair distribution of responsibilities and revenues vis-à-vis the federal government. The *British North America Act* of 1867 (now part of the *Constitution Act* of 1982) gave the federal government all of the important government responsibilities of the day and unlimited taxing powers to finance them. Provinces were given only direct taxation powers, which were expected to be more than adequate to fund the local and more minor matters given to them – not unlike the expectation that the real property tax would be more than adequate to handle the limited services to property being provided by municipal governments in the early years.

As the 20th century advanced, it became clear that the supposedly minor matters given to the provinces (especially education, social assistance, and health care) were becoming very important and expensive government powers. In response, the federal government provided a number of grants or transfer payments to the provinces, just as the provinces were extending similar financial support to municipalities wrestling with their increased costs. By the mid-1980s, however, the federal government was becoming increasingly concerned about its growing annual budget deficits and overall public debt and it began to introduce cuts in the transfer payments to the provinces. For example:[13]

> ➤ The early 1990s saw a freeze on payments to the provinces under a block grant known as Established Program Financing (EPF) and a cap on the growth of payments to Ontario and British Columbia under the Canada Assistance Plan.
> ➤ These two payment plans were consolidated into a Canada Health and Social Transfer (CHST) effective the 1996-1997 fiscal year and then reduced by $6 billion the next two years.

By the end of the decade, the federal government's financial position had improved significantly, in large part because of low interest rates that dramatically reduced the cost of borrowing charges on the national debt. It committed more than $5 billion to the provinces over a three year period as part of the 1999 Social Union Framework Agreement. An additional $2 billion for health care was promised in a January 2003 Health Accord, at which time the Canada Health and Social Transfer was split into two separate payments (for health and for social programs). A further $41 billion was committed in the "deal for the decade" health agreement reached in September 2004. This is up for federal-provincial negotiation in 2013 – and with the federal commitment to balance its budget in 2014-2015 new federal dollars will be limited. In addition, as will be discussed below, the federal government responded to its improved financial position in the early 21st century by introducing several initiatives (such as the GST exemption and the sharing of federal gas taxes) that directly involved them with municipalities and with other matters under provincial jurisdiction. This left the provinces, saddled with rapidly growing health costs, as the squeezed middle of the division of powers hourglass.[14]

---

[13] The summary that follows is based on C. Richard Tindal, *A Citizen's Guide to Government*, 3rd Edition, Whitby, McGraw-Hill Ryerson Limited, 2005, pp. 249-251.

[14] Courchene, *Citistates and the State of Cities*, pp. 14-15.

What is of particular interest for our purposes is the way in which the changes in federal-provincial financial relations were reflected in provincial-local financial relations. The cuts in federal transfers to provinces "were almost perfectly matched by cuts in provincial transfers to local governments," but the increase in federal government transfers since the late 1990s "has not been matched by increases in provincial transfers to local governments – the most significant departure from the pattern in more than 40 years."[15]

It is clear that provinces were able to insulate themselves from the adverse impact of reduced federal transfers by passing this financial burden to the local level, but municipalities – at the bottom of the fiscal food chain – had nowhere to pass the buck. The adverse impact on the municipal level is evident in the table below which shows the average annual rate of expenditures and revenues per capita between 1988/89 and 2004/05 for all three levels of government.[16]

Table 7.1 Average Annual Rate of Expenditures and Revenues per Capita			
	Municipal	Provincial	Federal
Expenditures	+0.9%	+0.6%	-0.9%
Revenues	+0.7%	+0.8%	+0.6%
Net Position	-0.2%	+0.2%	+1.5%

These figures and the story behind them reveal just how superficial were the earlier comparisons of municipal-provincial and provincial-federal fiscal relations. Yes, both the provincial and local levels have experienced financial pressures because their expenditures increased far more than anticipated. The local level received financial assistance from the provinces and the provincial level received financial assistance from the federal level, and they continue to seek such assistance. But there are also very significant differences affecting the municipal situation. In spite of all their protests, the provinces do have access to a wide range of tax sources from which they could generate all of the revenues that they need.

In fact, their financial woes have less to do with the cuts in federal transfers in the 1990s than with the self imposed cuts in provincial

---

[15] Hugh Mackenzie, *The Art of the Impossible: Fiscal Federalism and Fiscal Balance in Canada*, Canadian Centre for Policy Alternatives, July 2006, p. 31.

[16] Based on Harry Kitchen and Enid Slack, "Trends in Public Finance in Canada," in Federation of Canadian Municipalities, *Restoring Municipal Fiscal Balance*, Appendix 2. See also Slack's presentation on Infrastructure Planning and Financing to the European Union Workshop on Metropolitan Regions in Federal Systems, June 20, 2011, available at the Institute of Municipal Finance and Governance, University of Toronto, at www.utoronto.ca/mcis/imfg/resources.htm#pub.

income and corporate taxes that were introduced in a number of provinces beginning with Ontario in 1996 (shortly after the election of a Conservative government led by Mike Harris). Alberta, British Columbia, and a number of other provinces followed over the next few years and it is estimated that these tax cuts removed, as of 2005, over $30 billion in annual provincial fiscal capacity.[17] Municipalities, of course, do not have the many taxing powers available to the provinces. They have but one tax, on real property, and while it could presumably be increased (at least on residential properties, which have long been undertaxed relative to business properties), the increased revenues resulting would be far from sufficient for municipal needs.

A Closer Look at Municipal Revenues

A closer look at the main sources of revenue for Canadian municipalities, and how they have been changing and evolving, will provide further insight into the nature and magnitude of the financial problems facing municipalities and helpful background for considering possible solutions to these financial problems.

Transfer Payments

An important source of municipal revenues is in the form of transfer payments from the provincial (especially) and federal levels of government. These payments can take several forms, as follows:

- Conditional grants, which, as their name suggests, require that certain conditions be met – usually that the money be spent on a specified purpose and, often, that municipalities provide the matching funds (as in, for example, providing 25% of the funds to complete a 75% grant).
- Unconditional grants, which are funds provided without strings attached and available to be spent as the municipality sees fit.
- Payments in lieu of taxes (often referred to as PILs or PILOTs), which are essentially unconditional grants paid to municipalities with respect to provincial or federal properties that are exempt from taxation. Since these payments are being made to

---

[17] Mackenzie, *The Art of the Impossible*, p. 39.

compensate for taxes that can't be collected, it can be argued that they should not be treated as a transfer payment but included instead in the discussion of property taxes.
➢ Revenue sharing or tax sharing agreements, which (as described below) can provide more stable and ongoing revenue sources. These agreements usually provide for unconditional transfers but conditions may be attached in some instances.

Rationale for Transfer Payments

Transfers from the provincial level are offered for a variety of economic and political reasons.[18] One of the strongest economic arguments is that of externalities – the fact that a service provided by one municipality generates benefits (or costs) that spill over into other jurisdictions. Conditional grants can be used to cover the value of that spillover. Without such grants, inequities are likely to arise in the provision of, and costing for, services, with some municipalities enjoying a "free ride" at the expense of others. Grants also can be provided to close a fiscal gap and ensure that municipalities have sufficient funds to cover their expenditures. These usually take the form of an unconditional per capita or per household grant. Unconditional grants are also provided for equalization purposes – to shore up the financial base of municipalities in remote areas, or in areas with low levels of assessment and tax capacity, for example, or to ensure the provision of comparable services at comparable taxes by supplementing municipalities with a weak assessment base. In much the same way, the federal government has long provided equalization payments to ensure that all provinces are financially able to maintain minimum standards in the provision of services.

The rationale for some grants is much more political than economic in nature. Conditional grants may be provided simply to induce municipalities to provide a service that the province regards as a priority. Such grants are even provided sometimes as a way of making local governments (and their citizens) aware of the benefit of a new service, on the assumption that it will then be possible to withdraw the grant and have the service continued at local expense. Of course, it is precisely this instability with respect to transfers that municipalities find so troubling.

---

[18] This discussion is based on Harry Kitchen, *Municipal Revenue and Expenditure Issues in Canada*, Canadian Tax Paper No. 107, Toronto, Canadian Tax Foundation, 2002, pp. 159-163. See also his "A State of Disrepair: How To Fix The Financing of Municipal Infrastructure in Canada," C. D. Howe Commentary, Toronto, December, 2006 at www.cdhowe.org/pdf/commentary_241.pdf (accessed August 13, 2011).

There are also federal transfers to the local level, in spite of the provincial responsibility for this level of government. While these transfers are quite small, one can make a case for federal grants to local governments (and especially to cities).[19] One rationale is that federal grants are appropriate, indeed desirable, when it is federal policies or actions that give rise to municipal expenditures. The best example is federal immigration policy, under which the vast majority of immigrants settle in Canada's largest cities, giving rise to additional municipal expenditures that the federal government does not cover. Another example is international commitments made by the federal government, such as the Kyoto protocol on the environment, that require expenditures by local governments to implement.

Federal grants also can be justified with respect to matters of national interest, such as the problems of homelessness and lack of affordable housing. These problems are played out in the streets of our cities, but they are arguably a matter of national concern justifying much more federal financial assistance than has been forthcoming to date. Since these problems have largely arisen because of neglect by the federal and provincial levels, the prospect of substantial transfer payments from them to address these problems seems unlikely. City based studies have all concluded that the only solution to such issues is multilevel engagement, however.[20]

Another rationale derives from the recognition that the infrastructure and services provided by cities confer benefits beyond the municipal boundaries. This is the externalities or spillover argument again, although infrastructure benefits are fairly local and most spillovers are likely to stay within a regional context. In addition, it is increasingly appreciated that cities generate the bulk of the economic activity and growth in Canada – a notion popularized by Jane Jacobs, in her 1976 publication of *Cities and the Wealth of Nations*. As a result, the health of the cities is a matter of national interest, one justifying federal transfers. This is essentially the argument advanced at the beginning of the 1970s as one of the main reasons for the introduction of a Ministry of State for

---

[19] This discussion is based on *ibid.*, pp. 183-184 and Enid Slack, *Intergovernmental Fiscal Relations and Canadian Municipalities: Current Situation and Prospects*, Report to the Federation of Canadian Municipalities, May 8, 2002, p. 11, accessed July 12, 2007 at www.fcm.ca/english/documents/slack.html.

[20] See, for example, "Breaking the Cycle of Homelessness: The Mayor's Homelessness Action Task Force, Interim Report, City of Toronto, July 1998. See also "Homeless Action Plan," City of Vancouver and Federation of Canadian Municipalities, 2005 and "Maintaining the Momentum – Recommendations for a National Action Plan on Housing and Homelessness," Ottawa, January 2008.

Urban Affairs and it was echoed in the November 2002 report of the Task Force on Urban Issues and its call for a federal Ministry and new federal funding for affordable housing, transit/transportation, and sustainable infrastructure. As discussed elsewhere, the federal MSUA was a short-lived experiment in public administration, floundering on a sea of provincial protests over federal intrusions into areas of provincial jurisdiction.[21] It was shut down in 1979. Its successor, the Ministry of State for Infrastructure and Communities, was established in 2004, under the Paul Martin Liberals; it was subsumed under the Minister of Transportation after the Stephen Harper Conservatives won minority governing status in 2006 and continued as such in the second decade of this century.[22]

The Transfer Record

As municipal expenditures increased in the 20th century and the inadequacy of the real property tax became more pronounced, provinces began to introduce a variety of grants to local governments, mostly conditional in nature. For example, the 1901 *Highway Improvement Act* in Ontario introduced the roads grant, the first conditional grant apart from education. The number and variety of these grants proliferated, especially following World War Two, reaching over 100 in Ontario by the 1980s.

The 1990s saw a dramatic change, with provincial and (very limited) federal transfers declining from 45.7% of municipal government revenues in 1990, to 25.4% in 1994, to only 17.9% in 2000.[23] In some cases, the provinces attempted to soften the blow by making the reduced grants less conditional. Alberta and Ontario typified this approach. Alberta terminated its Municipal Assistance Grant and replaced it with a new Unconditional Grants Program. Funds from four

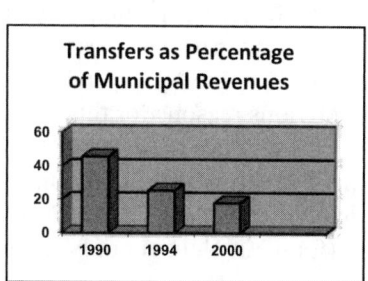

---

[21] On this see, H. Peter Oberlander and Arthur Fallick (eds.), *The Ministry of State for Urban Affairs: A Courageous Experiment in Public Administration,* Vancouver, Centre for Human Settlements, University of British Columbia, 1987, and Zac Spicer, "Was There Learning in the System: Making Sense of the Ministry of State for Urban Affairs and the Ministry of State for Infrastructure and Communities," paper for the Canadian Political Science Association, Montreal, June 2010.

[22] See *Transport, Infrastructure and Communities Portfolio,* accessed August 20, 2011 at www.infc.gc.ca/department/ticp-eng.html.

[23] Statistics Canada information as compiled in Kitchen, *Municipal Issues,* p. 16.

other conditional grants programs (relating to urban parks, public transit, policing, and family and community support services) were then transferred into the new unconditional program. But the budget for the unconditional program was then steadily reduced, from $169 million in 1994-1995 to $126 million the next year and to only $88 million in 1996-1997.[24] In strikingly similar fashion, the Conservative government in Ontario announced following its election in 1995 that three existing grant programs (the unconditional grant, roads grant, and northern roads assistance) were being converted into a single block grant – the Municipal Support Grant. This new grant was then reduced from what would have been a $1.4 billion transfer to $887 million in 1996 and $666 million in 1997, before disappearing as a separate grant in 1998.

The downward trend in transfers is also evident from the fact that between 1988 and 2004, the annual per capita decline in provincial/territorial transfers to municipalities was 3.7% and these transfers as a percentage of municipal revenue declined by 1.4% annually.[25]

The Territorial Difference

A major exception to this pattern is found in the territories. Just as the territorial governments are heavily dependent on federal transfer payments (75% of revenues in the NWT, 83% in the Yukon, and 91% in Nunavut) so too are municipal governments in the north heavily dependent on territorial transfers (42% of municipal revenues in the Yukon, 48% in the NWT, and 59% in Nunavut).[26] There are several fairly obvious reasons for this situation – including the higher cost of delivering services in the north because of the harsh climate, scattered population, and isolated communities; the limited taxing powers of municipalities in the north; and the scarcity of privately owned properties to tax (found in Nunavut only in the territorial capital of Iqaluit).[27]

Federal Transfers

Federal transfers to the local level over recent decades did show a modest but steady improvement. Highlights include:

---

[24] Figures from Alberta Municipal Affairs, *News Release*, February 24, 1994.

[25] Federation of Canadian Municipalities, *The Municipal Fiscal Imbalance By the Numbers*, 2006. See also, *FCM 2009: Pre-Budget Submission to the Standing Committee on Finance*, House of Commons, October 5, 2009.

[26] Federation of Canadian Municipalities, *Restoring Municipal Fiscal Balance*, p. 24.

[27] *Ibid.*, p. 29.

> A *Canada Infrastructure Works* program introduced in 1993 provided $2 billion in funding for approved projects, matched by the same amount of funding from provinces and municipalities, and directed toward upgrading the quality of infrastructure in local communities.
> A federal *Grants in Lieu of Taxes Act*, passed in 2000, provided for the first time for interest charges on late federal payments and for an improved dispute resolution process – both helping to improve the flow of federal payments in lieu to municipalities.
> Two "green" municipal investment funds with a combined value of $250 million were established in June 2000.[28] Administered by the Federation of Canadian Municipalities, these funds provide support to projects that help to improve the environmental efficiency and cost effectiveness of municipal infrastructure.
> The 2003 budget committed $100 million a year over 10 years for infrastructure, a disappointing response to the Sgro Report of the previous autumn, which had recognized the need for much greater federal financial assistance for Canada's cities.[29]
> The 2004 budget accelerated the infrastructure support by compressing it over a five year period. It also promised to increase to 100% the GST rebate to municipalities, providing $7 billion the following 10 years.
> The 2005 budget pledged to transfer five cents a litre of federal gasoline taxes annually over five years, generating a total of $5 billion for municipalities. Presented initially as a key component of the government's "New Deal for Cities," the gas transfer has been distributed through agreements with the provinces and territories on a per capita basis as part of a broadened (watered down?) focus on cities and communities.
> The Conservative government elected in January 2006 continued the GST rebates and the gas tax transfer, and, in the February 2007 budget, this gas transfer was extended another four years (from 2010/11 to 2013/14), which amounts to another $8 billion.
> The 2007 budget also announced a new $8.8 billion Building Canada Fund, but it is mainly a packaging up of several existing programs. Prime Minister Harper has made it clear (as discussed in the previous chapter) that the federal government will be

---

[28] The 2005 federal budget more than doubled these green funds by providing an additional $300 million.

[29] Prime Minister's Task Force on Urban Issues (Judy Sgro, Chair), *Canada's Urban Strategy: A Blueprint for Action*, November 2002.

refocused on matters within its constitutional jurisdiction (which does not include municipalities), will correct the fiscal imbalance experienced by the provinces, and will expect the provinces to address municipal financial needs in the future. To that end, the 2007 budget promised $39 billion to the provinces over the next seven years. As long as the Conservatives remain in power – as they did in 2008 and again with a majority in 2011 – any significant federal funding for municipalities seems unlikely; although a federal New Deal with provinces could presumably lead to increased provincial funding for municipalities.

- In spring 2011, the federal government indicated it could not guarantee hundreds of millions of federal dollars for affordable housing.[30]
- The surprise December 2011 announcement that the 6% annual increase in federal transfers for health care will be extended to 2017 leaves little room for new federal money for municipalities.

While this incomplete summary of federal transfers may still look fairly impressive, it is important to keep it in perspective. McMillan points out that the federal government contributed only 0.4% of municipal revenues in 2001 and he estimates that even after the Martin New Deal initiatives, including the full GST rebate, the federal contribution is only about 2%.[31] About 40% of current federal investments in municipalities are scheduled to expire by 2014 and the annual gas tax is shrinking since it is not indexed to inflation.[32]

Revenue and Tax Sharing Agreements

In their search for a more stable and continuing source of financial support, municipalities have often sought long term revenue sharing or tax sharing agreements. Ontario was the first to enter into such an arrangement – with its 1973 "Edmonton Commitment"[33] to increase its transfers to local governments at the rate of growth of total provincial

---

[30] See, for example, CTV News: "No Guarantee Funding for Affordable Housing will be Renewed" Canadian Press, March 15, 2011.

[31] Melville L. McMillan, "Municipal Relations with the Federal and Provincial Governments: A Fiscal Perspective," in Young and Leuprecht (eds.), *Canada: The State of the Federation 2004*, p. 73.

[32] Federation of Canadian Municipalities, *Keep Moving Forward*, Pre-Budget Submission, Fall 2011.

[33] So named because it was made by the Ontario government during the second (and last) tri-level conference (in Edmonton) sponsored by the Ministry of State for Urban Affairs.

revenues – but it was also one of the first to abandon revenue sharing, in 1977. In the second half of the 1970s, provinces such as Manitoba, Saskatchewan, and British Columbia introduced plans that guaranteed their municipalities specified levels of transfer payment, but these last two did not endure (at least in their original form).

Manitoba continues to have a Provincial Municipal Revenue Sharing program, known as the Building Manitoba Fund, under which the province shares with municipalities 4.15% of provincial income taxes (personal and corporate), two cents per litre of provincial gasoline tax revenues, and one cent per litre of provincial diesel fuel tax. Revisions to the program in 2011 now provide funds equivalent to the existing sources *or* 1% of the provincial sales tax, whichever is greater.[34] There is also limited revenue sharing in several other provinces, including:[35]

- ➢ The British Columbia government remits 11 cents per litre of provincial fuel tax revenues to the Greater Vancouver Regional District, which applies this money to the capital and operating costs of transit services and major roads within its jurisdiction. As noted in Chapter 5, the Mayors' Council of Translink agreed in October 2011 to an additional 2 cent per litre hike in metro fuel rates (and two years of limited property tax increases) to fund completion of its oft delayed Evergreen rapid transit line – to serve the North East sector of the metropolis.
- ➢ In a similar arrangement, Calgary and Edmonton receive from the Alberta government for transportation infrastructure an amount equal to five cents per litre of taxable gasoline and diesel fuel delivered to service stations in those cities.
- ➢ A new revenue sharing formula in Saskatchewan, described in Chapter 4, transfers the equivalent of 1% of the province's sales taxes to municipalities, amounting to $216.8 million in 2011.
- ➢ The Ontario government shares with municipalities two cents per litre of provincial gasoline taxes in support of public transit.
- ➢ Montreal's Metropolitan Transportation Agency receives 1.5 cents per litre from provincial fuel taxes collected on motor fuel sold in the Greater Montreal area.

These examples indicate that joint arrangements with individual municipalities are more prevalent than general provincial-municipal revenue sharing agreements. Whatever the arrangement, however,

---

[34] See http://web5.gov.mb.ca/mfas/grants_payments_fund.aspx.

[35] This summary is mainly based on Slack and Bird, *Cities in Canadian Federalism*, pp. 23-24.

municipalities still remain vulnerable to changing provincial priorities. For example, Ontario's ill fated Edmonton Commitment of the 1970s, tying transfers to the rate of growth of provincial revenues, was unilaterally altered by the province when it created a sizeable revenue stream that helped municipalities to increase expenditures to an extent deemed undesirable by the province. Twenty-five years later, Alberta reduced the gas transfer payment to Calgary and Edmonton to 4.2 cents per litre in October 2001 and then to 1.2 cents per litre in its budget of March 2002, only to restore it to 5 cents per litre shortly after – in response to strenuous local opposition. By 2010 Alberta had transferred $477 million in a Gas Tax Fund and $131.4 million under its Public Transit Fund, from Alberta's share of the federal gas tax for the province's municipalities.[36]

The prevailing view is that, despite such infusions, municipalities do not have access to the variety of tax sources and transfer payments available to municipalities in the United States and elsewhere, leaving them overly dependent on the property tax in attempting to meet their growing expenditure needs.

Real Property Tax

From the outset it was envisaged that the new municipal institutions being established in Canada would be financed by a tax on real property, defined essentially as land and buildings on land. In Upper Canada, for example, the first *Assessment Act* was passed in 1793, to provide a basis for the collection of property taxes to finance the expenditures of the townships that were then being established across the colony. Since the very limited services then being provided by municipalities (such as roads and fire protection) were services to property, it made sense to pay for them out of a tax on property – especially since property was the main form of wealth in those days. As Chapter 2 pointed out, so closely was the property tax associated with municipal government that the development of the municipal system was delayed in several provinces by public antipathy toward the introduction of this tax.

The enduring and pervasive nature of the property tax has certainly done nothing to alter the negative feelings toward it that were recorded from the days of the earliest settlers. Indeed, in the words of Bird and Slack: "No tax in Canada has been more vilified than the property tax."

---

[36] See KPMG Report, *Alberta Transportation Gas Tax Fund and Public Transit Fund Outcomes Report,* Province of Alberta, December 2009.

It has been called inherently regressive, inelastic, and an inadequate generator of municipal revenues. It has been labelled "unfair" because it is unrelated to ability to pay, "unrealistic" because it is unrelated to benefits, and "unsuitable" because it supports services unrelated to property.[37]

> **Box 7.1 In Praise of the Property Tax**
>
> Notwithstanding its negative image, there is much to be said for the property tax. It is easily administered within the relatively small areas encompassed by most municipalities. It is also easily enforced, since the tax base – property – cannot be concealed and can be sold by the municipality if taxes are not paid. In addition, there is at least some link between taxes paid and benefits received, which is one measure of a valid tax. The property tax is stable, meaning that revenues don't increase dramatically when there is economic growth, but neither do property values and revenues plummet when there is economic decline. Bird and Slack observe that "the residential property tax on the whole appears to be about as fair and efficient a tax as can be administered at the local level," and that its defects are largely correctable, in part through more frequent reassessment of property values.[38]

Indeed, a number of the problems attributed to the property tax have really been problems relating to assessment. Properties were traditionally underassessed, often markedly so. It was not unusual in Ontario to refer, as recently as the 1970s, to a "typical" house assessed at $10 000. There was no consistency in the degree of underassessment of properties either, resulting in widespread inequities when the tax rate was applied to the assessments. Business properties have usually been unfairly assessed (and taxed) in relation to residential properties. Ontario introduced current or market value assessment in 1998 but, along with the accompanying property tax reform, the new system has been complex, controversial, and frequently amended. Over the years, provincial governments have become increasingly involved in the assessment process, in an attempt to achieve consistency. Assessment is a local responsibility only in Alberta and Quebec and in the cities of St. John's, Winnipeg, and a number of urban municipalities in Saskatchewan.[39]

Provincial governments have also introduced a variety of payments to ease the tax burden on those with lower income levels, in an effort to offset the regressive nature of the property tax. Such programs are found

---

[37] Richard M. Bird and N. Enid Slack, *Urban Public Finance in Canada*, 2nd Edition, John Wiley & Sons, 1993, p. 100.

[38] *Ibid.*, p. 101.

[39] Karin Treff and Deborah Ort, *Finances of the Nation 2009*, Toronto, Canadian Tax Foundation, 2010, p. 6:10.

in virtually every province today, and range from grants to exemptions to tax credits to deferrals. In most provinces, as well, municipalities are given discretion to reduce property taxes for those in need of relief. These various forms of tax relief are provided almost exclusively with respect to residential and farm properties.[40]

Tax relief programs are in part a response to the visibility of the property tax. It is not deducted at source, in the quietly efficient manner of an income tax, but is collected directly from citizens in a few large, lump sum payments,[41] on the basis of tax rates set in highly publicized municipal council meetings. In one respect, this visibility is desirable in that it enhances municipal accountability. On the other hand, the highly visible nature of the tax makes councillors very reluctant to increase it, even when failure to do so can postpone necessary expenditures that only become greater over time. This pattern is very evident in the growing infrastructure backlog faced by most municipalities today.

Councillors are understandably attracted by opportunities to increase the assessment base in their municipality, and thus be able to generate more revenues without increasing taxes. This can lead to an acceptance of growth and development that is not always best for the municipality, a shortsighted approach sometimes referred to as "dollar planning." Ironically, it can also lead to financial problems rather than a financial windfall, since growth sometimes overloads existing services and infrastructure and triggers new expenditures that can more than offset the revenues gained from the enlarged assessment base.

While critiques of the property tax often focus on its inadequacy in meeting municipal revenue needs, economists are more concerned about the inefficiency of the property tax as it currently operates.[42] As a benefits tax, the property tax would be efficient as long as it is used to fund services that benefit the local community. As long as those who benefit from local public services are paying for them, the property tax can be considered fair and municipalities are clearly accountable to the

---

[40] Kitchen, *Municipal Issues*, p. 73.

[41] Municipalities, however, are increasing the number of installment payments, and some even offer a monthly payment plan. In addition, those paying mortgages often have their property taxes included.

[42] See Kitchen, *Municipal Issues*, Chapter 5; Kitchen, *Municipal Finance in a New Fiscal Environment*, Commentary No. 147, C. D. Howe Institute, November 2000, pp. 7-12; Bird and Slack, *Urban Public Finance*, Chapter 5; and Paul A. R. Hobson, "Efficiency, Equity and Accountability Issues in Local Taxation," in Paul A. R. Hobson and France St-Hilaire (eds.), *Urban Governance and Finance*, Montreal, Institute of Research on Public Policy, 1997, pp. 113-132.

local taxpayers for the cost of the services provided.[43] But a number of factors distort these relationships.

> As already noted, underassessing properties to varying degrees creates inequities and unfairness, although this problem has been at least partly addressed by provincial assumption of the assessment function in most jurisdictions.
> When a constant tax rate is applied to these varying assessments, it results in differences in the effective property tax rate within and across properties within a community. Since this differential tax treatment of properties does not reflect differences in the cost of providing municipal services to them, it creates a number of distortions and inefficiencies.[44]

Further distortions arise from the fact that every province has authorized the imposition of higher taxes on commercial and industrial properties, even though studies have shown that it is residential properties that receive proportionately more benefits from local government services.[45] The result is what businesses call an unfair burden of taxes on businesses, one that can make them less competitive at a time when they are exposed to much greater international competition as a result of globalization.

In some jurisdictions, this has led to significant debates as municipalities seek to alter this traditional imbalance by shifting more of the property tax to homeowners. In Vancouver, for example, since 2004, groups such as the business-led Fair Tax Coalition have pushed to even the property tax for business and homeowners. Others, including the leftist COPE-led city council of 2001-2004, rejected a shift from the more than 3% to 1% difference for businesses.[46] In a repeat effort with a new right-wing NPA city council (2005-2008) business concerns over two key issues – tax share and volatility – caused a city Property Tax Policy Review Commission to be created. Its Final Report of September 2007 was based on six principles:[47]

---

[43] Kitchen, *Municipal Issues*, p. 102.

[44] Kitchen, *New Fiscal Environment*, p. 9.

[45] *Ibid.*, pp. 9-10.

[46] See Matthew Burrows, "Cadman Flags Property Tax," *The Georgia Straight,* October 19, 2006.

[47] See City of Vancouver, *Property Tax Policy Review Commission: Final Report,* September 2007 (http://vancouver.ca/taxcommission/final_report.htm), p. 2.

- Fairness, based on benefits received
- Fairness, based on ability to pay
- Neutrality
- Accountability
- Stability and predictability
- Simplicity and ease of administration

The Vancouver Commission recommended that despite a lessening of the business to residential property tax share over the previous decade it should be reduced again to 48% from a 2006 average of 55% – by a phased reduction of 1% each year; that it should then be pegged at that level for five years; and that a "phase in" mechanism replace the city's three year averaging regarding real estate volatility.[48] It also concluded that residential properties consumed three quarters of all municipal services provided. In May 2011, the new left-centre Vision-led city council shifted the tax burden to add 3.82% to residential properties while reducing the burden for non-residential owners by 0.18% – a $23.8 million shift away from business and on to residential owners, based on the Tax Review Commission recommendations.[49] This response to the equity issue has not gone unnoticed in other jurisdictions across Canada.

More generally, the way the property tax is used contributes to the urban sprawl that has become such a concern in Canada and elsewhere. Since it costs much more to provide services to scattered, low density development, an efficient property tax would reflect these higher costs and, in turn, serve to discourage further sprawl. Instead, property taxes are often higher in the urban core, providing an incentive for movement to the suburbs and thus further sprawl.[50] In the words of Slack: "Higher property taxes provide an incentive for less dense projects and lower densities mean that the city is likely to expand in a way that is socially inefficient.[51]

Provincial Invasion of the Property Tax Field

The ability of municipalities to finance an increasing portion of their expenditures from their own revenue sources is threatened by the fact

---

[48] *Ibid.*, p. 6.

[49] See City of Vancouver, *City News: Your Property Taxes and the Budget*, May 2011.

[50] Kitchen, *Municipal Issues*, p. 113.

[51] Enid Slack, *Municipal Finance and the Pattern of Urban Growth*, Commentary No. 160, C. D. Howe Institute, February 2002, p. 8.

that the real property tax is less and less their own to use as they wish. Since the beginnings of municipal government in Canada, this tax has been portrayed as the mainstay of municipal finances. Yet municipalities have been gradually losing control over the use of the property tax.

Much of the provincial incursion has occurred with respect to education financing. At one time, education costs were mainly funded from the property tax. Gradually, provincial financial assistance grew, along with increasing provincial control and supervision of educational matters. Provincial governments also amalgamated school boards, in a move paralleling and often exceeding in scope the amalgamation of municipalities described in earlier chapters. Prompted by the desire to reduce costs and to improve access and equity, provinces began – as early as the 1930s in Alberta – to consolidate school boards and school areas.[52] This process continued and intensified in the 1990s.

While there are many issues that could be raised with respect to the educational reforms, of particular concern in this context is the extent to which provincial governments have invaded the property tax field to fund at least a portion of the educational costs – an incursion found in British Columbia, Alberta, Manitoba, Ontario, New Brunswick, and Prince Edward Island.[53] Currently, only Manitoba and Saskatchewan retain traditional property tax supported school boards.[54] McMillan points out that the school property tax made sense when a local contribution to schooling was required and the only sufficient local tax base was property, but that it is not well related to school benefits or ability to pay. He suggests that eliminating provincial property taxes for education (at least on residential properties) would free up some tax room that might then be available to meet other municipal expenditure needs.[55]

This provincial incursion has not been confined to the field of education. Beginning with New Brunswick's Equal Opportunity Program in the mid-1960s, provinces have been appropriating a portion of the property tax field and directing it to the financing of specified provincial services. As a result, the provincial role in the property tax field is much

---

[52] For a summary of consolidations up to the mid-1990s, see Robert Carney and Frank Peters, "Governing Education: The Myth of Local Control," in James Lightbody (ed.), *Canadian Metropolitics: Governing Our Cities*, Toronto, Copp Clark Ltd., pp. 248-251.

[53] Andrew Sancton, "The Municipal Role in the Governance of Cities," in Trudi Bunting and Pierre Filion (eds.), *Canadian Cities in Transition*, 2nd Edition, Toronto, Oxford University Press, 2000, p. 431. See also Treff and Ort, *Finances of the Nation 2009*, Chapter 9, for a summary of public school financing, by province and territory.

[54] Kitchen, *Municipal Issues*, p. 28.

[55] McMillan, "Municipal Relations with Federal and Provincial Governments," p. 63.

larger than the role of state governments in the United States. "Not only is the tax now basically provincial in New Brunswick, Prince Edward Island, and, for education, in British Columbia, but the local tax rates are at least partly determined by provincial grant levels...."[56] In Prince Edward Island and New Brunswick the province acts as the collection agency for both its own property tax levies and those of municipalities.

The disentanglement exercises of the 1990s added to this pattern of encroachment. For example, when Nova Scotia took on administrative responsibility for a number of people services in the 1995-1996 program of service exchange, it still required municipalities to include a provincial education levy in their tax bills and to contribute to the social and correctional services programs that became provincial responsibilities.[57] As a result, a substantial portion of the municipal tax base is devoted to supporting provincial programs. Similarly, under Ontario's local services realignment, the province assumed responsibility for half the education costs previously paid by residential property taxpayers. As noted above, the province also took over responsibility for setting the residential property tax rate to finance the other half of those costs, and for setting the property tax rate paid by business properties.

More recently, the Ontario government has shown a willingness to encroach on municipal decision making with respect to property taxes. While the property tax reforms introduced toward the end of the 1990s were supposed to give municipalities greater discretion to set tax policy, the province was not satisfied with the extent to which municipalities employed their tax tools to reduce the tax burden on business properties. As a result, the province imposed a cap on tax increases on business properties – at first for a three year period and then, under the *Continuing Protection of Property Taxpayers Act 2000*, on an ongoing basis. The gravity of this provincial action was well expressed by the executive director of the province's largest municipal staff association in commenting on the initial three year capping.[58]

> Make no mistake, this is a devastating decision for municipal government in Ontario. For decades, municipal associations have been lobbying for access to more revenue sources to supplement property taxes and reflect the scope of municipal responsibilities. This decision

---

[56] Bird and Slack, *Urban Public Finance*, p. 92.

[57] Kell Antoft and Jack Novack, *GrassRoots Democracy: Local Government in the Maritimes*, Halifax, Dalhousie University, 1998, p. 95.

[58] Ken Cousineau, "Editorial," *Municipal Monitor*, December/January 1998/1999, Association of Municipal Managers, Clerks and Treasurers of Ontario.

places the Provincial Government firmly in control of property taxes in Ontario.

On the Pacific edge of the country, in 2011, British Columbia's Liberal Premier Christy Clark called for the introduction of a Municipal Auditor General (MAG). Business saw the creation of this provincial auditor of municipalities as "an important part of ... creating equity in the property tax system."[59] British Columbia's major newspaper agreed.[60] In contrast, the Union of B.C. Municipalities called for caution, questioning what problem the new MAG was intended to fix. Its *Context Paper* called for more municipal consultation and more policy development on the issue – a clearly more ambivalent view of this perceived province intrusion into municipal governing.[61]

In September 2011, around the annual convention of the Union of B.C. Municipalities, the UBCM expressed "serious concerns" about this provincial initiative, not least the tight timetable for municipal consultations. A special session at its end of September 2011 Annual Convention was devoted to the issue. UBCM President Barbara Steele stated the local government case simply: "We don't know what the problem is that they are trying to solve with a municipal auditor general."[62] Only Nova Scotia and Quebec, and more recently the City of Toronto, have local government auditors-general (although the position is authorized – not mandated – for other municipalities in several provinces). For the UBCM, they "remained in the dark" and continued to express concern about the speed of implementation – the Minister stating that a B.C. Municipal Auditor General would be hired in spring 2012.[63] Some local ambivalence, no doubt, arose from the Minister's comment that while the province would initially fund the MAG position, if it proved successful, "local governments could be expected to assume the costs."[64]

---

[59] See *B.C. Chamber of Commerce News*, "Christy Clark calls for Municipal Tax Review," News Release, January 18, 2011. The Chamber called B.C.'s property tax system unfair to business.

[60] *The Vancouver Sun*, "Editorial: Auditor-general for municipalities will help cities cut costs," August 16, 2011.

[61] See Union of B.C. Municipalities, *Municipal Auditor General Context Paper,* July 2011.

[62] See Jeff Lee, "Municipalities cool to auditor-general," *The Vancouver Sun*, August 26, 2011, A3.

[63] See, for example, www.ubcm.ca/EN/meta/news/municipal-auditor-general.html.

[64] Cited in Jeff Lee, *Municipalities cool to auditor-general.*

While the property tax is not as bad as its critics often claim, neither is it as good as it could be. In particular, inequities in tax burden (as between multiresidential and single family properties and between business and residential properties) still need to be addressed more effectively and tax levels should be more closely aligned with the cost of delivering services. These and other suggestions will be examined more fully in a later section on possible ways of fixing municipal finances.

Other Local Revenues

In addition to the property tax, some provinces have authorized limited use of amusement taxes, land transfer taxes, and hotel taxes. Local government revenues also include "grants in lieu of taxes, sales of goods and services, rentals, concessions and franchises, licences and permits, remittances from own enterprises, interest, interest and penalties on taxes, fines and other miscellaneous local revenues."[65] Historically very limited, these other local revenues have increasingly been called upon in recent years as the main alternative for municipalities facing falling transfer payments and public resistance to property tax increases.

User Fees

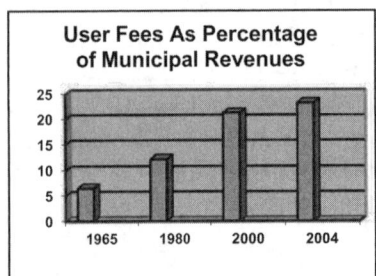

User charges or fees, in particular, have become more prominent, almost doubling from 6.5% of municipal government revenues in 1965 to 12.2% in 1980, almost doubling again, to 21.3% by 2000, and rising to 23.4% by 2004.[66] As we will see, user fees have been both promoted as a panacea for municipal revenue needs and criticized for their failure to bring a more efficient allocation of resources.

In simplest terms, a user fee is a charge levied upon an individual for the use of a specific public service. User fees work best when the service involved is a private good (a private sector type service) that benefits the individuals who use it and that can be kept from those who don't pay for it. Examples would be water, sanitary sewers, solid waste management, and airports – all of which can be fully or substantially funded by user

---

[65] Bird and Slack, *Urban Public Finance*, p. 63.

[66] Kitchen, *Municipal Issues*, p. 16, Table 2-2, and Kitchen and Slack, *Trends in Public Finance in Canada*, p. 4.

fees. In contrast, police and fire services are more in the nature of pure public goods, readily available to the whole community and not easily divisible into separate lots for purchase. Such public goods are more appropriately funded from the property tax.

A variety of revenue earning enterprises at the local level employ user fees to finance at least a part of their operations. Examples include recreational and cultural facilities such as arenas, libraries, pools, golf courses, and community centres, and public utilities providing such services as water supply, sanitary sewage collection and disposal, electricity, public transportation, airports, public housing, and municipal parking. Many of these services and facilities are administered by local boards and commissions – such as arena boards and public utility commissions – and rely heavily on user fees as they are increasingly called upon to bring their operations closer to break even.

The Case for User Fees

Economists point out that user fees promote efficiency in the consumption of goods and services – if the price equals the marginal cost of providing the service.[67] In practice, however, the user fee either bears no relation to the cost of providing the service or, at best, is based on average cost, which is easier to calculate.[68] As a result, such user fees often result in unplanned consequences and do nothing to promote conservation of resources. For example, Kitchen cites the still common practice of charging a flat rate for water, regardless of the quantity consumed. Far from encouraging conservation, this effectively provides a subsidy for wealthier individuals with larger lawns and gardens to water. He goes on to offer the following observations and suggestions:[69]

> ➢ The underpricing of water and sewage results in investments in water and sewage treatment facilities that are larger than would exist under a more efficient pricing policy.
> ➢ While user charges are employed for many parks and recreational facilities, they cover only a small portion of

---

[67] See, for example, Bird and Slack, *Urban Public Finance*, and Kitchen, *New Fiscal Environment*.

[68] The efficiency measures now being provided by many municipalities across Canada are based on average costing, in that the total volume of the service (tonnes of garbage, for example) is divided by the total cost of the service to arrive at a unit price (per tonne). Marginal cost pricing, by contrast, would establish a user fee per unit of output equal to the extra cost of providing the last unit (last tonne of garbage collected).

[69] These points are based on Kitchen, *New Fiscal Environment*, pp. 14-18.

operating costs. In addition, the lack of a peak load pricing policy, which would even out demand over days and weeks, has resulted in an overinvestment in recreational facilities.

- A user charge that covered the full costs of solid waste collection and disposal would prompt a more efficient use of local resources and provide an incentive for individuals to reduce the amount of garbage that they generate. Realistically, however, a somewhat lower fee is prudent to avoid negative spillover in the form of individuals avoiding the fee by dumping their garbage in rural areas or along roadways.
- While public transit fees (fares) cover only 50% to 75% of operating costs, higher transit fees would only be efficient and fair if automobile users paid a charge that reflected their social cost – which they certainly do not. One study suggests user fees in the area of non-public transportation by making use of new technologies to collect tolls. It argues that charging the full cost of travel for highways and roads in the downtown core of large cities like Toronto would benefit both society and the municipal bottom line.[70] This is no longer a radical idea, given the success of the congestion tax in London, England, for example, or Barcelona, Singapore, or Stockholm and the similar tax more recently advocated for New York City.[71]
- Having fire services funded from general municipal revenues does not take into account the variables that fire insurance companies consider when setting their rates. If there is no differentiation in the price of fire services, there is no incentive for owners of risky properties to take steps to minimize their need for fire protection (through such actions as using fire resistant building materials and installing sprinkler systems).

While there is considerable logic in the arguments advanced by Kitchen and other economists, expanding user fees in this manner is not without problems. Shifting the financing of municipal services from the property tax to user fees is likely to appeal to middle and upper income citizens. They would have no difficulty in paying such fees, and would presumably welcome the arrangement by which they only pay if they use the service. This option may lead them to obtain some services from the

---

[70] Toronto Dominion Bank, *The Greater Toronto Area (GTA): Canada's Primary Economic Locomotive In Need of Repairs*, May 22, 2002, p. 26.

[71] See for example, Kenneth Small and Erik Verhoef, *The Economics of Urban Transportation,* New York, Routledge, 2007.

private sector instead, with recreational facilities being one example where such alternatives exist in the form of private fitness facilities. But the more they use private alternatives, the more they are likely to resent paying property taxes to underwrite the cost of municipal services (such as recreational facilities) that they don't use. Yet lower income families certainly cannot afford to finance these facilities solely through user fees. Indeed, such fees may make municipal services less accessible for them.

While Kitchen acknowledges that lower user fees for services like recreation permit individuals to use facilities comparable to those they cannot afford in the private sector, he contends that "this type of subsidization is neither efficient nor fair because municipalities ought not to be concerned with major questions of income redistribution."[72] That may be true, but there seems little reason to expect provincial governments to accept increased responsibility for income distribution policies and programs at a time when they have downloaded some programs of this type (notably social services and social housing in Ontario) to the local level. Unless municipalities are prepared to introduce some form of income relief policies at their level, any substantial increase in user fees, at least for some services, is likely to have an adverse impact on lower income individuals and families.

Development Charges

Another local revenue source of note is that of development charges, also known as development cost charges, development cost levies, off site levies, and assessment levies. These charges are levied by local governments in British Columbia, Alberta, Saskatchewan, Ontario, and the Yukon and Northwest Territories to cover the growth related capital costs associated with new development (in some cases redevelopment).[73] Traditionally, such charges have been used to finance the building of water supply systems, sewage treatment plants, trunk mains and roads, but rather more services are covered in provinces such as Ontario.

In areas experiencing growth, development charges are obviously an important source of revenue and a way of ensuring that servicing costs relating to new development are paid for by the developer (and, ultimately, by the occupants of the new buildings) rather than by all property taxpayers. But these charges are, or can be, more than an alternative source of revenue; they can be a useful tool in encouraging

---

[72] Kitchen, *New Fiscal Environment*, p. 16.

[73] Slack, *Municipal Finance*, p. 14. In Ontario, school boards can also levy such charges, but only for land acquisition.

efficient use of land and infrastructure. To do so, however, the charges have to be structured to reflect the true cost of providing public services.[74] These costs are usually higher for low density neighbourhoods and for developments located farther away from existing services. Accordingly, development charges should be higher for developing land on the outer edges of a community, which would discourage urban sprawl. Uniform development charges across a municipality, as is often found, subsidizes inefficient uses of land and contributes to urban sprawl.

Unfortunately, development charges are not usually employed to reinforce planning goals. One analysis finds that development charges in Ontario "are geared almost exclusively to their revenue-raising role and are disconnected from planning goals."[75] It suggests that this usage reflects the underlying political reality that local politicians are more concerned with reducing the impact of growth on their taxpayers than on maximizing benefits for society as a whole. It further suggests that while provincial politicians are in a better position to reconcile the revenue and planning issues involved, they are also primarily interested in how much revenue development charges can generate – to help municipalities fund the provincial responsibilities and costs being downloaded to them.

Fixing Municipal Finances

On the surface, the solution seems obvious. Municipalities need more money. It is conventional wisdom that Canadian local governments do not enjoy the financial capacity and support experienced by their counterparts in other jurisdictions – a discrepancy of growing concern now that Canadian cities are increasingly in competition with cities in these other jurisdictions in today's global economy. While 93% of local tax revenues in Canada come from the property tax, income and sales taxes provide a large portion of local tax revenues in many other countries – as illustrated by the examples in the table below from 2002.[76]

---

[74] This discussion is based on *ibid.*, pp. 16-17.

[75] Ray Tomalty and Andrejs Skaburskis, "Development Charges and City Planning Objectives: The Ontario Disconnect," *Canadian Journal of Urban Research*, Vol. 12, Issue 1, Summer 2003, p. 158.

[76] Drawn from Slack, *Fiscal Imbalance*, p. 75.

Table 7.2 Tax Source as a Percentage of Local Tax Revenues				
	Income	Sales	Property	Other
Sweden	100			
Denmark	93.1	0.1	6.8	0.0
Switzerland	83.2	0.3	16.6	0.0
Germany	75.8	6.4	17.7	0.3
Japan	44.6	21.3	33.0	1.0
Spain	25.2	49.3	24.3	1.1
Italy	21.6	23.0	13.6	41.8
United States	5.2	22.2	72.6	0.0
Netherlands	0.0	43.4	56.6	0.0

International comparisons also reveal that municipalities in Europe and the United States were receiving financial support from their state and national governments at a much higher level than Canadian municipalities. One example cited was the Liveable Communities for the 21st Century initiative in the United States, which established a wide range of programs that included substantial financial support for transportation, the environment, and housing. By contrast, financial support for infrastructure investment in Canada was criticized as quite limited.[77] Even with a sizable portion of the 2009-2011 Economic Action Plan's federal fiscal stimulus being directed to municipal "shovel-ready" infrastructure projects, this was essentially a one time program rather than anything resembling ongoing federal involvement in reworking municipal finance.

Far Away Fields Aren't Necessarily Greener

While the financial situation for municipalities in other jurisdictions appears superior in some respects, a closer look at American experience suggests a more qualified assessment. The supposedly bright financial picture for American cities (as compared to Canadian) has dimmed considerably in recent years, as a result of unforeseen developments, changed federal priorities, and reduced state revenues.[78] Homeland security understandably became a top priority in the aftermath of the September 11th 2001 terrorist attacks, but only a fraction of municipal

---

[77] See, for example, Federation of Canadian Municipalities, *Early Warning: Will Canadian Cities Compete?*, Ottawa, May 2001.

[78] These changed circumstances are described in several reports from The Brookings Institution including an article by Bruce Katz, "American Cities: Federal Neglect Imperils Their Rise," *Baltimore Sun*, January 9, 2003, on which the following discussion is partly based.

spending on new security measures has been covered by promised federal transfers (essentially an example of the unfunded mandate problem discussed earlier in this chapter). American states faced a collective deficit of $60 billion or more, largely because of weak tax collections and American cities continue to bear the brunt of the cuts that will be required to address this fiscal crisis. The cities experienced a fiscal recession from 2001 to 2004 and face growing expenditures for infrastructure, public safety, and employee health care and pensions, for which their tax revenues have not kept pace.[79] The global economic collapse of 2008-11, much of it triggered by the sub-prime mortgage and banking meltdown in U.S. cities, left many state governments close to their own bankruptcy.

Even the much more varied local revenue sources available to American municipalities are not without their problems. At least 46 of 50 states have some kind of tax and expenditure limits (TELs) on their local governments.[80] The best known, and most severe, of these TELs is Proposition 13, in California, which dates from 1978. Not surprisingly, one effect of the TELs has been to reduce local government reliance on the property tax and to increase reliance on state aid and on other local revenue sources such as income taxes, business taxes, and sales taxes. But state aid has been cut substantially by state governments facing fiscal challenges. Yet many municipalities are unable to close the gap with tax increases because of the tax limits under which they must operate.

The strict limits on the property tax are also problematic in that they remove the discretion for municipal councils to vary tax rates as part of the process of balancing costs and benefits in local budgeting processes. This discretion is needed for flexibility and for accountability to local taxpayers, who pay much closer attention when local councils set tax rates than when services are funded by "other people's money."[81] The alternative is an increasingly centralized financial regime, as has already happened to education financing in the United States and in Canadian provinces such as Alberta and Ontario.

---

[79] Bruce Katz, *Local and Metropolitan Governance: Lessons from the U.S.*, The Brookings Institution, April 3, 2006, p. 40.

[80] According to a 1995 study of the Advisory Commission on Intergovernmental Relations, *Tax and Expenditure Limits on Local Governments*, as quoted in Robert L. Bish, "Local Government Finance Issues in the United States," LGI, University of Victoria, Working Paper 5, June 2002. See also Leah Brooks and Justin Phillips, "Municipally Imposed Tax and Expenditure Limits," *Land Lines*, Lincoln Institute of Land Policy, April 2009.

[81] Bish, *Local Government Finance Issues*, p. 13.

The fact that American municipalities have access to other local tax sources is also a mixed blessing. While these sources provided a healthy yield during the prolonged expansion in the economy during the 1990s, revenues from sales and income taxes fall sharply during a decline in the economy and this has caused some serious financial problems in cities dependent upon these sources.[82] The rapid increase in shopping via the Internet is also raising concerns about future sales tax yields.

The growing dependence on sales tax, especially where use of the property tax is restricted because of imposed limits like Proposition 13, is encouraging some strange behaviour with respect to local planning and development. Municipal governments dependent on sales taxes have been actively wooing big box stores and even car lots. At a time when cities are urged to enhance the local quality of life as a way of attracting knowledge workers, they may find it difficult to choose a research institute, mixed use development, or arts centre, if they can land instead a Wal-Mart or a car lot.[83] It would appear that it is not only the property tax that can lure municipalities into "dollar planning." That such thinking is counterproductive has engaged futurists such as Richard Florida. For Florida, future "world cities" will emphasize diversity, public service, quality of life, creativity, and innovation. His Creativity Index ranks cities across the globe.[84]

One analysis of the financial status of Canadian and American municipalities concludes that cities on each side of the border face a series of trade-offs. In its words:[85]

> Is it better for a city to be overly reliant on property taxes, but at the same time free from restrictions on the tax rate, the revenue generated, and the use of revenues? Or is it more desirable to have access to a small local general sales tax and more selective sales taxes that provide better revenue-generating capacity during good times, but where the tax rates are capped, revenues are earmarked, and any slowdown in the economy threatens the tax base?

---

[82] *Ibid.*, p. 5.

[83] This discussion is based on Otis White, *Give Us Your Car Lots*, Urban Notebook, posted August 11, 2006 at www.governing.com.

[84] See Richard Florida, *The Rise of the Creative Class: And How It Is Transforming Work, Leisure and Everyday Life,* New York, Basic Books, 2002, and *The Great Reset: How New Ways of Working and Living Drive Post Crash Posterity,* New York Harper Collins, 2010.

[85] Canada West Foundation, *Big City Revenues: A Canada-U.S. Comparison of Municipal Tax Tools and Revenue Levers*, September 2002, p. 31.

Increasing Revenues

Fixing municipal finances by generating more revenues means either new revenue sources for municipalities or increased transfers from the provincial and federal levels.

New Municipal Revenue Sources

Over the years, a variety of tax sources have been suggested by and for Canadian municipalities, including the poll (or head) tax, income tax, sales tax, and fuel tax. Some of these taxes, of course, were once used by municipalities in this country. For example, they used to have access to the income tax field and were levying these taxes (along with provincial governments) long before the federal level entered the field – as a "temporary" measure – in 1917. "By the end of the 1930s, some form of municipal income tax was accepted in every province in Canada."[86] But when the provinces entered into wartime tax rental agreements with the federal government in 1941, they surrendered their right and the right of their municipalities to levy income taxes – and no municipality has been authorized to levy an income tax since.

A similar pattern unfolded with respect to the poll tax, which used to be authorized for municipalities in every province. It was used primarily by municipalities in Atlantic Canada and then gradually abandoned, beginning in the 1950s, although it is still authorized in Newfoundland and Labrador. Experience with a municipal sales tax was much more limited, being confined to municipalities in the province of Quebec, between 1935 (when it was introduced by Montreal) and 1964.[87]

Of all the potential alternatives, Kitchen believes that a municipal fuel tax would make considerable economic and political sense, especially in large urbanized areas that are suffering from severe traffic congestion. He also states that a general municipal sales tax and, more specifically, a hotel and motel occupancy tax could be justified, on a basic level, as a benefits-based approach to municipal taxation.[88] Kitchen points out that giving municipalities additional tax sources would permit a broader distribution of the tax burden among those who benefit from municipal services, whether they are residents, commuters or visitors,

---

[86] Kitchen, *Municipal Issues*, p. 224.

[87] *Ibid.*, p. 226.

[88] Kitchen, *New Fiscal Environment*, p. 21.

and would make the municipal tax structure more flexible and adaptable to local conditions.[89]

A key issue is the basis on which municipalities would be given access to tax fields already occupied by the provincial and federal governments. Giving municipalities authority to set their own tax rates provides the greatest discretion and the greatest local accountability. But any significant variation in the level of sales tax or fuel tax, for example, from one municipality to the next is likely to prompt consumers to cross municipal boundaries in search of a better deal – a pattern experienced between Metro Vancouver (with regional gas taxes for Translink) and neighbouring Fraser Valley (without these taxes) or nearby Washington State. The fact is that the small size of most municipalities makes it too easy to avoid some of the alternative tax sources under consideration.

In McMillan's view, motorists are likely to travel across borders to avoid locally set gas taxes. For a locally determined tax relating to vehicles, he suggests a municipal vehicle registration charge, which could be collected as part of the provincial registration system to minimize administration and compliance costs. Since vehicle registration is linked to residence, such a tax could not be easily avoided. McMillan also offers tolls on road use as another possibility, particularly for controlling congestion in urban areas – as with the toll that has been introduced in central London, England,[90] and in cities such as Barcelona, Stockholm, and Singapore.

In some respects, the simplest approach is to have municipalities piggyback on to existing federal or provincial tax programs and receive a predetermined share of the yield collected by them. This approach also provides an opportunity to avoid an increase in the overall tax burden that could otherwise result from municipalities gaining access to these fields. As discussed above, the federal government is currently transferring to municipalities five cents per litre of gasoline taxes. It has also been asked to give municipalities the equivalent of one cent of the GST. But giving municipalities a previously agreed upon portion of the tax yield of the provincial or federal level is essentially providing them with an unconditional grant, not an additional taxing power to be used at their discretion. Other drawbacks with this arrangement, according to McMillan, are municipal vulnerability to potential arbitrary changes by the "sharing" government and a weak tax-benefit linkage.[91] Canada's

---

[89] Kitchen, *Municipal Issues*, p. 337.

[90] McMillan, *Municipal Relations with Federal and Provincial Governments*, pp. 69-70.

[91] *Ibid.*, p. 68.

"permanent" federal gas tax sharing with municipalities came about with the 2008 Federal Budget. In 2011, this represented over $2 billion for Canada's municipalities in transfers.[92]

Another option might be a municipal personal income tax, especially for large, metropolitan municipalities.[93] These governments are increasingly being called upon to respond to region wide issues such as poverty, crime, land use planning, and transportation and to provide social services. An income tax, which is more closely related to ability to pay than a property tax, is a more appropriate revenue source in these circumstances. Moreover, an income tax can be applied more effectively in large geographic areas where there is less likelihood of taxpayers moving beyond municipal boundaries to avoid such taxes. One relatively recent analysis suggested an earned income tax on residents, applied to employment and self-employed earnings of municipal residents and collected by the province through the regular income tax system. It estimated that a 1% earned income municipal tax would generate over $6 billion across all provinces.[94]

New Taxing Powers for Canadian Cities

The calls for new taxing powers for municipalities have been answered, to a limited degree, as a result of recent changes affecting the cities of Toronto and Montreal. The *City of Toronto Act* that took effect January 1, 2007 provided the city with the authority to introduce new taxes relating to such matters as alcohol, motor vehicle ownership, land transfer, tobacco, amusement, parking, billboards, and road pricing/ congestion. Montreal gained some taxing powers that were "inspired by the *City of Toronto Act*," with the passage of amendments to Bill 22 in 2008.[95] This legislation introduced a number of changes to reduce the conflict between Montreal and suburban municipalities arising from the operations of the agglomeration council (described in Chapter 4). Montreal was given the power to set the rate it charges for the "welcome

---

[92] See, for example, CBC News' "Quebec arena could get federal gas tax funds," February 11, 2011.

[93] Richard M. Bird and Enid Slack, *Fiscal Aspects of Metropolitan Governance*, University of Toronto, January 2004, p. 33.

[94] Jack M. Mintz and Tom Roberts, *Running on Empty: A Proposal to Improve City Finances*, Toronto, C. D. Howe Institute, February 2006, p. 25.

[95] See *Montreal Gazette*, "City of Montreal Strikes Deal with Suburbs, Province," June 12, 2008.

tax" on property sales over $500,000 – an obvious variation on the land transfer taxing power given to the City of Toronto.

The Alberta government in 2007 received recommendations from its Minister's Council on Municipal Sustainability that municipalities be allowed to impose new levies such as an amusement tax, property transfer tax, tourism tax, vehicle registration tax, and expanded development levies for directly related local services.[96] In July 2007, Alberta accepted most of the recommendations of the Council, adding revenue sources to local financing.[97]

New taxing powers will only generate revenues, however, if they are actually used. While self-evident, it seems necessary to add this qualifier in light of Toronto's early experiences with its new taxing powers.

Box 7.2 Taxing Times in Toronto

Facing a projected $575 million deficit for 2008, council received in July 2007 a report from staff, backed by then Mayor David Miller, recommending that it use its new taxing powers to introduce a land transfer tax of up to 2% on the sale of a house and a $60 fee to register ownership of a motor vehicle. Together, these new taxes would generate $350 million a year in additional revenue. There was considerable opposition to the proposed new taxes, in part from bodies such as the Toronto Board of Trade, which contends that the city could do more to reduce its expenditures. While the opposition was predictable, council's action was not. By a 23-22 vote, council refused to approve the new taxes. Instead, it deferred a decision until after the October 2007 provincial elections in Ontario, on the grounds that it wanted to see what additional money would be available from the newly elected provincial government. There wasn't any new provincial money when the tax proposals returned to council on October 22, but some changes in the land transfer tax and the appointment of a blue ribbon panel to review city spending resulted in a 26-19 vote of approval. By then, however, the damage was done. Toronto had failed in its first major test as a newly empowered municipality. It proved unable to get beyond its traditional knee jerk response of crying poor and holding out its hand for provincial largesse. One wonders why the city campaigned so long and hard for new tax powers if it does not have the political fortitude to use them.

In contrast, consider the actions of Mississauga in November 2007.[98] Already facing a proposed property tax increase of 3.9% for 2008, city council agreed to impose a 5% surcharge on property taxes. Revenues from this surcharge, which could remain in place for 20 years, will be

---

[96] Minister's Council on Municipal Sustainability, *Report to the Minister of Municipal Affairs*, March 5, 2007, p. 3.

[97] See Province of Alberta, "Province responds to report of the Minister's Council on Municipal Sustainability," *Press Release,* July 16, 2007.

[98] Royson James, "A new tax, yet Hazel smells of roses," *Toronto Star*, November 8, 2007.

allocated to infrastructure. This new tax was approved by a nine to two vote on council, after minimal debate and no apparent public opposition. It was coupled with a vigorous attack by Mayor Hazel McCallion on federal failure to provide adequate financial support for cities.

One can argue that Mississauga is hardly in a position to cry poor, since it has healthy reserves and no long term debt. But its financial position may be a strong point, one not lost on the mayor, who dared the provincial and federal governments to suggest that Mississauga was not well managed – a criticism often levied against Toronto. One can also argue that Toronto has faced much greater service demands without the benefit of the rapid growth enjoyed by Mississauga. But the issue here is not the respective merits of the demands for assistance from these two cities. What we are considering is the way in which they responded to their financial difficulties. Toronto initially threw itself on the mercy of the province by refusing to use the new taxing powers it had long sought, thereby calling into question the frequent assertion that the financial problems of Canadian cities would be resolved if only they were given more taxing powers like their American counterparts. Mississauga increased its taxes *first*, gaining credibility for its attack on the federal level. To those who argue that the differences between Mississauga's and Toronto's responses reflect little more than posturing and spin, one must remember that perception is reality, and nowhere more than in politics.

Toronto's experiences have hardly improved with the 2010 election of Rob Ford, labelled by Richard Florida as "the most anti-urban mayor to preside over a large global city."[99] One of Ford's first acts was to cancel the vehicle registration tax and he has insisted that he will also cancel the other new taxing power used by Toronto – the land transfer tax. However, these counterproductive steps did not keep Ford, as with mayors before him, from appealing to the province for financial help in closing the city's budget deficit.

Funding from the Provincial and Federal Levels

Provincial (and federal) financial assistance remains the other main source of revenue for municipalities – and the one that many seem to prefer. Probably the strongest case for transfer payments is with respect to the social programs that are found at the local level, especially in Ontario. It is almost universally accepted that income redistribution programs are not an appropriate responsibility for local government, and

---

[99] See Richard Florida, "The London Riots: A Virus of Globalization That Canada Could Catch Too," *The Globe and Mail,* August 20, 2011, p. F3.

especially not for funding from the property tax on which municipalities heavily rely. The best solution to this problem would be to transfer such responsibilities to the provincial and/or federal levels, where they arguably belong. Unless and until that happens, however, there is a strong case for increased transfer payments in support of such programs.

The other area in which there is widespread support for increased transfers is with respect to municipal infrastructure. While the overwhelming majority of transfer payments have come from the provincial level, there is an emerging consensus that the backlog in infrastructure investment facing our cities can only be addressed through action by the federal government and that, in any event, the importance of cities to the economic health of Canada more than justifies such a federal involvement. As noted above, a Federal Task Force on Urban Issues cited affordable housing, transit/transportation, and sustainable infrastructure as the three pillars of a new urban strategy and called for investment in these areas to reduce pressures on municipalities for large capital expenditures.[100] The subsequent improvements in federal financial support, including the short term economic stimulus package at the end of 2010 with a significant emphasis on local infrastructure, were summarized earlier in this chapter.

Kitchen is not persuaded that infrastructure funding requires more transfer payments from the federal and provincial levels. In fact, he flatly rejects the much heralded federal transfer of five cents of gasoline taxes as essentially an unconditional grant that lacks accountability and transparency.[101] Kitchen argues that municipal infrastructure, as much as possible, should be financed by the residents who benefit from it because this provides the best guide as to how much to invest in what.[102] An excellent candidate for this method of financing is water and sewers, charged on the basis of litres of water used. In addition to properly set user fees, infrastructure financed from long term borrowing is desirable from the point of view of fairness, efficiency, and accountability.[103] Yet instead of more long term borrowing over the past couple of decades many municipalities have turned to pay as you go financing for capital projects. Mintz and Roberts also contend that transfer payments undermine accountability and can contribute to an escalation in costs

---

[100] Final Report, *A Blueprint for Action*, p. 10.

[101] Kitchen, *Financing City Services*, p. 27.

[102] Harry Kitchen, *A State of Disrepair: How to Fix the Financing of Municipal Infrastructure in Canada*, Toronto, C. D. Howe Institute, December 2006.

[103] *Ibid.*, p. 7.

when municipal politicians don't have to raise taxes (and answer for them) to obtain the funds they need.[104]

One of the biggest problems with reliance upon provincial and federal transfers is that they leave the municipal level totally dependent upon the whims of the party in power and vulnerable to changes in governing party and ideology. For example, municipalities in Ontario experienced transfer cuts and downloaded costs with the election of the Harris government in the mid-1990s, and federal funding improvements during the brief regime of Paul Martin have less support now with the agenda of the Harper Conservative government. "Senior governments are fickle friends when it comes to providing grants."[105]

A simpler, more effective, and entirely appropriate way of addressing municipal financial needs would be to have the provincial and federal levels directly provide funding for the programs that are more properly their responsibility. A prime example, already cited, is Ontario, where "a return to provincial responsibility for funding all social service, social housing, and land ambulance expenditures, in keeping with the practice in the rest of Canada, would not only assist the municipal sector but also make sound economic sense – all income-distributional services should be the responsibility of the two senior levels of government."[106] Another example is the number of provinces that tax real property to finance schooling costs that they have assumed. Such costs should be financed, more appropriately, out of the varied revenue sources available to the provinces, thereby freeing up a significant portion of the property tax for more legitimate municipal use.

A strong case can be made that the federal level has a responsibility to assume more of the costs relating to immigration, the rapidly increasing population of urban Aboriginals, and affordable housing. Vander Ploeg argues that if the property tax is to continue as the main source of municipal revenues, "then cities should not have to engage in activities that redistribute income, whether they be affordable housing, homeless shelters, or programs for the disadvantaged." In his view, "a comprehensive disentanglement exercise focused tightly on core civic competencies would leave redistributional programs to senior governments."[107]

---

[104] Mintz and Roberts, *Running on Empty*, p. 2.

[105] McMillan, *Municipal Relations with Federal and Provincial Governments*, p. 68.

[106] Kitchen, *Municipal Issues*, p. 336.

[107] Casey Vander Ploeg, "Same old Fiscal Song out of Tune with the Times," *Calgary Herald*, April 29, 2002.

Making Better Use of Existing Resources

There is much that municipalities can do to address their financial problems. They need to start by ensuring that they are making the best, and wisest, use of the revenue sources that they already have.

Confronting the Property Tax Mythology

"The property tax has reached its upper limits." "People will not tolerate any further increase in the property tax." Statements like this have been repeated so often that they have become accepted wisdom, seldom challenged. Yet the reality is that the property tax has become less burdensome, not more burdensome, over the past few decades. Consider these examples:

> Municipal property taxes as a percentage of gross domestic provincial product declined by 1.5% (from 3.8% to 2.3%) in Canada between 1971/72 and 2001/02, and declined in all provinces except Newfoundland and New Brunswick.[108]

> An examination of selected Canadian and American cities found that while the property tax burden is higher in the Canadian cities, the overall tax burden at the local level was higher in the American cities.[109]

> The portion of personal disposable income allocated to property taxes in Edmonton declined from 2.46% in 1989 to 2.21% in 2004.[110]

> The property tax in Toronto, the city experiencing its annual fiscal crisis of inadequate revenues, is much lower than that of other cities in the GTA, as is evident from the accompanying table that shows 2007 property taxes on a house valued at $400 000.[111]

Oshawa	$5797
Mississauga	$2954
Markham	$3033
Oakville	$2973
Richmond Hill	$3039
Pickering	$4367
Vaughan	$3022
Toronto	$2355

---

[108] Kitchen, *Financing Canadian Cities*, pp. 8-9.

[109] Enid Slack, *Are Ontario Cities at a Competitive Disadvantage Compared to U.S. Cities?*, report for the Institute for Competitiveness and Prosperity, June 2003, p. 33.

[110] City of Edmonton, *New Fiscal Deal*, accessed July 10, 2007 from www.edmonton/ca.

[111] Jennifer Lewington, "Seeking Public Input, TTC Puts Off Service Cuts," *Globe and Mail*, July 21, 2007.

It is well documented that business properties bear a higher portion of property taxes, especially when the bulk of municipal services (approximately 75%) go to residential properties. Quite apart from considerations of equity, this imbalance could create a less competitive business environment.[112] But municipalities have considerable scope to increase residential property taxes, and in most provinces they also have various tools that can be used to provide tax relief where such increases create an intolerable burden for individual homeowners. While many have lacked the political fortitude to introduce such tax increases and the leadership and vision needed to justify the increases to a cynical and tax averse public, (as noted above) there are signs that local business lobbies have made this a priority and have made headway in promoting city action on this issue in municipalities such as Vancouver and elsewhere.

Being Sensitive to the Impact of Revenue Tools

The financial tools available to municipalities not only raise revenues, they can also affect the behaviour of local residents and ratepayers. "Where people choose to live (in the city core, existing suburbs or green-field suburbs), where businesses choose to locate (close to transit or far away) and where municipalities choose to invest in infrastructure are all influenced by fiscal incentives."[113] This is evident from discussions earlier in this chapter, including the following examples:

> ➤ The fact that business properties are more heavily taxed relative to residential, downtown properties relative to suburban, and rental housing relative to owner occupied housing, drives business and people out of the downtown core, contributes to urban sprawl and its associated costs, and discourages the construction of rental units and contributes to the problem of homelessness.[114] Instead, differences in tax burden – to the extent that municipalities have this discretion – should reflect differences in the production, environmental, and social costs of providing municipal services to different properties or property types.[115]

---

[112] Kitchen, *Financing City Services*, p. 14.

[113] Enid Slack, *The Impact of Municipal Finance and Governance on Urban Sprawl*, paper presented to the International Symposium on Urban Impacts: Global Lessons for the Great Lakes Basin, Chicago, September 25-26, 2006, p. 3.

[114] Toronto Dominion Bank, *Primary Economic Locomotive*, p. 2.

[115] Kitchen, *Financing City Services*, p. 13.

> User fees could be the basis for funding more municipal services and could reflect the marginal cost of providing these services. Properly set user fees help to ration services to those willing to pay for them, promote conservation, and militate against overinvesting in services and infrastructure.
> Development charges that vary according to the cost of providing services to the land in question would encourage higher density development within the core and discourage sprawl development in outlying areas.

A good, if ultimately unsuccessful, example of the use of municipal revenues to alter behaviour positively was the New Deal advocated by Winnipeg in 2003.[116]

Box 7.3 Winnipeg's New Deal
Winnipeg entered the 21st century with a population stagnating because of sprawl into outlying areas and a growing shortfall in the revenues needed to operate. Instead of the usual search for new revenues wherever they could be found without regard for the impact, Mayor Glen Murray and city council embraced an innovative plan of tax shifting, designed not only to generate additional revenues but also to promote more environmentally friendly behaviour. In simplest terms, the original plan called for property taxes and bus fares to be reduced over time by 50%, while there would be new taxes on things like garbage, gasoline, alcohol, natural gas, electricity, and 911 calls, and a 1% increase in sales tax. The overall result would be an annual increase in city revenues of $120 million. More importantly, the new tax structure would give people a choice. They could avoid taxes by changing their behaviour – putting out less garbage, reducing energy use, using public transit, or driving a more fuel efficient car, for example.

Winnipeg's New Deal had much to recommend it, but it was a radical concept that depended upon public support and provincial cooperation. Neither was sufficiently forthcoming. The public opposed new taxes and expressed concern that proposed property tax reductions would not be sustained. The province refused to give the city a 1% sales tax or a portion of the gasoline tax. City council regrouped with a simplified New Deal that did not include many of the consumption taxes that had been proposed, but also called for only a 4% decrease in property taxes. It too failed to gain necessary provincial support and the New Deal ended with Glen Murray's departure to run for the Liberals in the 2004 federal election.

---

[116] See http://winnipeg.ca/cao/media/news/nr_2004/nr_20040406.stm (accessed July 25, 2007).

There is much to admire, however, in the initiative shown by Winnipeg. Courchene notes approvingly that Winnipeg's specific tax or user fee proposals – as well as raising revenues – were one or more of "accountable, pro-environment, transparent, and efficient," and he expresses surprise that more cities have not taken similar action.[117] Developing an imaginative new approach to resolving its financial needs rather than simply seeking a provincial or federal handout provides a marked contrast to the behaviour too often exhibited by municipalities. It deserved a better fate than it received. Most importantly, the Winnipeg effort showed a kind of "eager beaver" behaviour available to municipalities and which so few attempt. Not all lead to full success, but challenging existing and overly traditional thinking may offer more opportunities for local problem solving than yearning for greater municipal recognition in a new Canadian constitution.

Managing Expenditures

While revenues, or lack thereof, have understandably attracted attention and energy, municipalities also need to make every effort to ensure that their expenditures are appropriate and represent best value.[118] This means more long term planning and priority setting by councils, so that the scarce resources of the municipality can be directed toward the achievement of a limited number of major goals and objectives rather than being used to perpetuate past spending patterns without any discernible priorities. It may call for municipalities to refocus and to get back to their "core programs," just as many private companies are pulling back from overly ambitious expansion plans and rediscovering the value of "sticking to the knitting."[119] It may mean having to eliminate some programs, or find someone else to deliver them, and reducing the level of service in others. Taking the trouble to survey local citizens may identify areas that are not regarded by the public as high priorities and where some curtailment is acceptable.

---

[117] Courchene, *Citistates and the State of Cities*, p. 17.

[118] Much of the opposition to Toronto's use of new taxing powers (discussed above) appeared to stem from doubts that the city had done all it could to control expenditures. Some of those doubts may explain the "End the Gravy Train" campaign that saw Rob Ford become Toronto's mayor in 2010.

[119] The phrase used by Tom Peters and Robert H. Waterman Jr., *In Search of Excellence*, New York, Warner Books, 1982, p. 15 and pp. 292-305, to describe companies that stuck with the businesses they knew and avoided venturing into different areas of operation.

Ensuring best value for expenditures does not mean holding the line on taxes (although that may be one result). Too many municipalities react to financial pressures by cutting expenditures (often "across the board") until they achieve a zero increase in taxes. But this approach leads to cuts that are ill considered, usually made in haste, and often without an appreciation of the long term impact on municipal operations. That impact is often felt in reduced quality of service.

In contrast, a growing number of municipalities have taken a different approach that harnesses the creative energy and ideas of all employees in seeking new and more efficient ways of delivering programs. Much of the focus is on streamlining procedures and removing "red tape" to improve service to local citizens. Such changes can also reduce costs and improve productivity, with the result that municipalities can reduce expenditures (and hold the line on taxes) while maintaining, or even increasing, the level of service. This outcome is particularly likely if programs are in place for measuring, reinforcing, and rewarding gains in productivity – programs that approximate the bonus pay or pay for performance long found in the private sector.

These latter suggestions obviously relate to the way municipalities are governed and to the central relationship between councillors and staff, matters that are the focus of the next chapter.[120]

Concluding Comments

A central issue in this chapter has been the extent of the fiscal imbalance facing Canada's municipalities. Delineating the scope of any such imbalance is not an easy task. Indeed, on one level, it can be argued that there is not, by definition, any imbalance, since municipalities must balance their budgets every year – and they have continued to do so. Those not persuaded about a fiscal imbalance can also point to the fact that the much maligned property tax, as a proportion of income or of the provincial domestic product, has not significantly increased over the years and that user fees could be employed more effectively to increase

---

[120] Here, see also Kennedy Stewart and Patrick Smith, "Immature Policy Analysis in Eight Canadian Cities" in Laurent Dobuzinskis, Michael Howlett, and David Laycock (eds.), *Policy Analysis in Canada: The State of the Art,* Toronto University of Toronto Press – Institute of Public Administration of Canada Series in Public Management and Governance, 2007, Ch.11, pp. 265-288.

revenues and, more importantly, to dampen demand and ease the strains on municipal infrastructure. Beyond this, other forms of local revenue raising can be more fully explored.

But it must be recognized that beneath the annual balanced budgets lies a growing imbalance in the form of unfunded municipal liability for infrastructure maintenance. Postponing investment in infrastructure has been an easy – but foolish – way for councils to avoid or minimize tax increases. But the crunch is coming, in two ways. Municipal infrastructure is showing its age and its neglect and servicing breakdowns will become more common unless action is taken. Second, since January 2009, municipalities have had to adhere to new accounting and financial reporting requirements from the Public Sector Accounting Board with respect to the infrastructure and all capital assets.[121] Under this new reporting model, the annual cost of owning and using a capital asset (essentially the depreciation costs, which have long been recorded in private sector operations) must be recorded. Municipalities now need to maintain a complete inventory of all capital assets, to have an asset or infrastructure management plan, and an accompanying financial plan that demonstrates that sufficient funds are being set aside to cover depreciation and to update and replace infrastructure as needed. These changes are most welcome, and they will bring to the forefront the overextended financial position of many municipalities that have been balancing their budgets off the back of their neglected infrastructure.

While the fiscal imbalance issue is almost always raised in reference to Canada's cities, and their need to be competitive in the global economy, it is likely that the financial position of rural, and especially northern, municipalities is at least as problematic. Their assessment base is not only small and usually weak, but it is often dependent on one industry and very vulnerable to changing economic circumstances. Economies of scale aren't available in small municipalities. Those that are isolated find it much more difficult to enter into joint service delivery and other partnership ventures. Limited staff and expertise are a shortcoming, as are sometimes traditional attitudes and ways of doing things.

The fact that there is some fiscal imbalance, about to become more evident, however, doesn't automatically mean that municipal governments need a major influx of revenues, particularly in the form of provincial and federal grants and their rigidity, uncertainty, and erosion

---

[121] On the PSAB, see www.psab-ccsp.ca/index.aspx (accessed August 4, 2011). See also the ASOB (Accounting Standards Oversight Board) which helps to set public sector accounting standards.

of accountability. It would be much better if those levels would own up to their rightful responsibilities and relieve municipalities of inappropriate costs for such areas as immigration, urban Aboriginals, affordable housing and homelessness, and (in Ontario) various social programs. Beyond that, some limited new tax sources have merit, especially growth taxes that would help to offset and to complement the less elastic, but more stable, property tax. It is also desirable that provinces provide municipalities with as much flexibility as possible to use whatever tax and revenue raising powers they have. A classic example of what is *not* desirable is the way property taxation in Ontario is subjected to continuing intervention by the province, manifested most obviously in the ongoing limits or caps placed on the municipal utilization of taxes on business properties.

It must be said, though, that at least part of the financial imbalance troubling municipalities is self-imposed.[122] The preceding chapter concluded with the image of the outstretched municipal hand, seeking financial assistance. This image was dramatically reinforced in July 2007 by Toronto's initial refusal to use new revenue raising powers it had long sought, and again in 2011 when a new mayor (Rob Ford) abolished one of the new revenue sources that had been introduced and then asked for provincial money to address the city's budget shortfall. This image is also evident in the inability of Metro Vancouver's transportation authority (Translink) to operationalize similar "new sources" in support of public transit improvements, in favour of holding out for provincial and (in the case of Vancouver's Translink) federal money.

Municipalities have legitimate grievances, and they should continue to seek redress. Indeed, a recent update of a 2002 report on the GTA economy documents the loss of 100 000 manufacturing jobs and a decline in the standard of living,[123] lending support to Toronto's case for financial help. But the bargaining position of municipalities in any approach to the provincial or federal level will be much greater if they first make full, effective, and imaginative use of the powers that they have. On that basis, there is definitely a municipal deficit – one of self-definition.[124]

---

[122] For a recent examination of this issue, see C. Richard Tindal and David Siegel, "Municipal Time Bombs Need a Municipal Bomb Squad," *Municipal World*, October 2011, pp. 23-25.

[123] *An Update To TD Economics' 2002 Report on the Greater Toronto Area Economy*, July 2007, accessed August 12, 2007 from www.td.com/economics.

[124] Higgins, Frisken, and Smith/Stewart have each offered reflection on this self-perception aspect of the municipal deficit.

Chapter 8
Municipal Governing Structures

Many of the various governing models used over the years, and the philosophies underlying them, have focused on efficiency and coordination in the delivery of services to the relative neglect of the political, representative, and accountability aspects that are (or should be) equally a concern of municipal government. Peter Self has called this efficiency-accountability dilemma *the* question in all of public administration.[1]

Introduction

An examination of how municipalities are governed logically starts with their internal governing machinery, and particularly the way councils and staff are organized and interrelate. A number of different governing structures have been found in Canada's municipalities over the years, each with particular strengths or shortcomings. Institutional structure is important "because it is the vehicle through which the basic purposes and values a society wishes to pursue through local government are carried out. It is thus presumed that institutions matter – that political and policy outcomes will differ as institutional structure differs."[2]

A number of variations on the basic municipal structure have been introduced over the years. These institutional reforms have usually been a response to changes in the prevailing values and roles associated with municipal government and, in turn, the new structures arising from the reforms have their own impacts on the local level and the distribution of power within it. As will become evident, much of that impact tended to affect adversely the representative, political, and accountability aspects of municipal government.

---

[1] Peter Self, *Administrative Theories and Politics,* London, Allen and Unwin, 1977, pp. 277-279.

[2] Harold Wolman, "Local Government Institutions and Democratic Governance," in David Judge, Gerry Stoker, and Harold Wolman, *Theories of Urban Politics*, London, Sage Publications, 1995, p. 135.

But in recent years the focus has shifted from municipal institutions to new governing arrangements that increasingly extend to organizations and operations outside the municipal structure. This broader focus reflects the growing appreciation of the distinction between government and *governance*, a distinction briefly introduced in Chapter 1 and referred to several times since.[3] Government refers to the formal institutions of the state, election arrangements, and decision making processes. Governance is a broader term that refers to the relationships between the formal institutions of government and civil society. Governance is more flexible (and less well defined) and can embrace a wide variety of relationships. Local government, therefore, refers to democratically elected municipal councils and their departments of municipal staff. In contrast, local governance encompasses these governing structures as well as other public, private, and voluntary bodies that are harnessed to address community needs.

Some view the concept of local governance as little more than a device for shifting responsibilities from local governments to the private and voluntary sectors – a means of offloading expenditures or providing an opening for private companies to pick up business. A more positive view is that local governance is not a replacement for local government but an additional mechanism for achieving broader cooperation and coordination at the local level. More insights into the nature of local governance will be provided in the next two chapters.

The Machinery of Municipal Government

Before venturing into the larger and less distinct world of local governance, let's begin with the machinery of local government. More specifically, we will examine the machinery of *municipal* government – not including the structures that may be found amongst the wide variety of agencies, boards, and commissions that form part of local government.

---

[3] The discussion of terms that follows is an amalgam of definitions and comparisons provided by Robin Hambleton, Hank V. Savitch, and Murray Stewart (eds.), *Globalism and Local Democracy*, London, Palgrave Publishers Ltd., 2002, pp. 150-151; H. V. Savitch and Paul Kantor, *Cities in the International Marketplace*, Princeton, Princeton University Press, 2002, pp. 329-330; and Mario Polese and Richard Stren (eds.), *The Social Sustainability of Cities*, Toronto, University of Toronto Press, 2000, pp. 17-20.

On the surface, this approach sounds quite straightforward, and the basic structure of municipal government is certainly simpler than that found at the provincial and federal levels, with their separate executive and legislative branches. There aren't separate branches of government at the municipal level; responsibilities are concentrated in the elected council and are carried out by appointed staff who are mostly organized into a number of functionally specialized departments.

The Municipal Council

The powers assigned to a municipality are exercised on behalf of its residents and ratepayers by a council elected by them. Provincial legislation usually includes provisions for the form of council and such details as the number of councillors and whether election is by general vote or by ward (a distinction discussed below). However, the new municipal legislation passed in most provinces over the past decade (and discussed in Chapter 6) often gives municipalities somewhat more discretion with respect to such matters. Municipal councils consist of a head (known as warden or chair in counties and other upper tier governments, as mayor in cities and towns, and as reeve, chair, or overseer in villages and townships) and a widely varying number of councillors. While the total membership varies greatly, there has been a tendency to have small councils of from 5 to 15 members, largely on the grounds that a small group is less unwieldy and more efficient in making decisions.

Members of council are expected to represent the local community and act on its behalf – although that role is not nearly as simple or straightforward as it sounds, as discussed below. They also exercise a policy making role through which they determine services and service levels, approve budgets, enact rules and regulations, and generally shape the local community and the quality of life within it. A third general role of councillors is managerial (for want of a better term) and it involves providing an oversight of municipal operations to ensure that policies are implemented as intended, funds are expended as authorized, and programs are delivered efficiently and effectively. This local politician-civic staff relationship is sometimes a bit more nuanced, with suggestions that permanent professional staff can at times have more policy sway than is generally understood.[4]

---

[4] See, for example, Patrick Smith and Kennedy Stewart, "Immature Policy Analysis: Building Capacity in Eight Major Canadian Cities," in *Policy Analysis In Canada: The State of the Art*, in Laurent Dobuzinskis, Michael Howlett and David Laycock (eds.), Toronto, University of Toronto Press, 2007, Ch.11, pp. 265-288.

Figure 8.1 Kingston City Council Meeting December 2006

Source: Ian MacAlpine, *Kingston Whig-Standard*. Reprinted with permission.

The Representative Role of Members of Council

The roles of councillors in making policy and overseeing implementation of policy by municipal staff receive a good deal of emphasis and will be explored in a subsequent section on council-staff relations. But it is a consistent theme of this text that the representative role of municipal government is most important and it is the elected members of council who fulfil this role, well or poorly. The longstanding bias in favour of small councils makes it more likely that they will not represent adequately the diversity of the population. Relatively small councils are even found in many of Canada's largest municipalities. Edmonton, for example, has had 12 councillors (plus a mayor) since the beginning of the 20th century, even as it grew from a small town to a city of over 700 000 people. Winnipeg has had twice as many members of the provincial legislature as it has councillors – even though the latter are representatives of the level of government supposedly closest to the people.[5] To cite one more example, the city of Mississauga has a council

---

[5] These two examples are from Jonathon Barker and Christopher Leo, "Introduction," in André Carrel, *Citizens' Hall: Making Local Democracy Work*, Toronto, Between the Lines, 2001, p. 3.

of 10 (plus mayor) for a population of 700 000. It is in Ontario that the provincial government, at least under the Conservative regime of Mike Harris in the 1990s, has been particularly keen to reduce the size of municipal councils in the name of efficiency, without any apparent regard for the representative role that these councils are supposed to play.[6]

Ward Versus General Vote

Quite apart from the size of the council, the representative role of councillors is affected by the method of their election. While directly elected heads of council are chosen by a general vote of the entire municipality, members of council may be elected on the basis of a ward system or neighbourhood constituency. In the latter case, the municipality is divided into several geographic areas with a number of members (usually an equal number) to be chosen from each of these areas. Candidates don't run over the whole municipality but only in "their" ward, and voters are limited to choosing from among the candidates in their particular ward. Whether election is by ward or general vote may be dictated by provincial statute; it may be at the discretion of the council; or it may be decided by council subject to the approval of the municipal electors.

Both methods of election have their proponents and their alleged advantages and disadvantages. Supporters of the ward system argue that under this approach the voters are much more likely to be familiar with the limited range of candidates from whom they must choose and the candidates will be more aware of the particular needs and interests of their constituents. It is also contended that ward elections ensure that all areas of the municipality will be represented on council, that they mean less expensive campaign costs, and that they bring a higher voting turnout, an assertion that appears to have some validity.

On the other hand, those supporting election by general vote claim that ward elections tend to perpetuate and even accentuate differences and divisions in the municipality. It is argued that a ward council is very parochial in outlook, with councillors worrying about their individual bailiwicks wherein they must seek reelection rather than being concerned about the good of the whole municipality. It is also contended that some representatives get elected on a ward basis who would not have been

---

[6] A survey of three amalgamated municipalities in Ontario found that a sizeable minority of residents felt that their access had been diminished, although this view was not shared by councillors or by community leaders. See Joseph Kushner and David Siegel, "Do municipal amalgamations reduce political representation and accessibility?," *Municipal World*, May 2004, pp. 7-9.

chosen if they were running over the entire municipality. Election by general vote is therefore felt to result in stronger, better qualified candidates since they must have support throughout the municipality. Proponents of a general vote also assert that it results in a council more capable of taking a broad view of the overall needs of the municipality.

There are rebuttals and counter arguments for most of these points. Ward elections do not ensure representation on council for every area of the municipality since candidates do not have to live in the ward in which they run – although "outside" candidates rarely succeed unless they have some sort of attachment to the ward. To the allegation that representatives get elected from wards who would not be chosen in at large elections, this result (if it happens) is precisely why ward elections are needed – to ensure a broader cross section of elected representatives, including those who may lack the profile and deep pockets to succeed in an at large campaign. To take one more example, where is the proof that elections at large result in better quality candidates, and how is this quality measured? Is it on the basis of education, income, and social class, or is a high quality candidate one who serves with dedication and integrity regardless of socioeconomic background? Stewart has suggested that given different levels of participation across more well-to-do versus poorer areas of a city like Vancouver, at large systems – as found by U.S. courts – also may discriminate in class or ethnic terms.[7]

Whatever the respective merits of these two methods of election, it might be assumed that beyond a certain population size (which is difficult to specify precisely) election by ward becomes almost inevitable to ensure that the citizens will have some prospect of knowing the candidates and that the candidates will not be faced with the financial and time demands of canvassing an excessively large population. While this relationship between the population of a municipality and the method of election generally holds true, there are exceptions, with the most notable one being the system of elections at large in the city of Vancouver, and indeed in *all* British Columbia municipalities. Vancouver voters have on more than one occasion given their support to the system of ward elections abandoned in 1936, but never with the 60% approval required by the province to bring about the change.

As was very evident during the turn of the century reform era of 100 years ago (discussed in Chapter 2), the issue of ward elections versus elections at large revolves around the distribution of power within city government. Ward elections make it more likely that the diversity of

---

[7] See Kennedy Stewart, "Measuring Local Democracy: The Case of Vancouver," *Canadian Journal of Urban Research*, 6:2, 1997, pp. 160-183.

interests within a municipality will have a voice on council. Indeed, it was precisely for this reason that the middle class business people who were central to the reform movement of a century ago pushed for the abolition of wards. In Western Canada, for example, wards were viewed with disfavour because they provided a means through which the growing labour movement and the large numbers of impoverished Europeans settling in major cities could gain a voice.[8] It remains true today that efforts to abolish ward systems of election, and to reduce the size of councils, have the effect of diminishing local representation. As has been the case with reforms to federal and provincial voting systems, real reform may take judicial prodding in municipal settings too where these issues predominate.

Trustee or Delegate?

Another major consideration affecting the representative role of councillors is whether they view their role as a trustee or a delegate. Those who view the councillor as a trustee believe that successful candidates should exercise their own judgment as to the best course of action with respect to the various issues that arise, while recognizing that the public will pass judgment on their performance at the next municipal election. The classic expression of the elected representative as trustee was provided by Edmund Burke, the 18th century British statesman and politician, who agreed that constituents' wishes and opinions ought to have great weight but stated that a representative "owes you not his industry only, but his judgment; and he betrays, instead of serving you, if he sacrifices it to your opinion."[9]

While eloquently expressed, Burke's views might not be warmly received at a time when there are calls for greater accountability on the part of those elected and even for more avenues for direct democracy, through which the public can substitute its judgment for that of the elected representative. The alternative to the councillor as trustee is the view that the councillor is chosen as a delegate, to govern in accordance with the wishes of the electorate and to act as a mirror faithfully reflecting their views. It is unclear how the councillor is to identify the views that are to be reflected so faithfully, how a diversity of viewpoints

---

[8] Jack Masson with Edward C. LeSage Jr., *Alberta's Local Governments: Politics and Democracy*, Edmonton, University of Alberta Press, 1994, p. 274.

[9] *The Works of the Right Honourable Edmund Burke: A New Edition*, Vol. III, London, 1826, p. 18.

is to be handled, or how to avoid being overly influenced on issues by a vocal minority.[10]

The Head of Council

No discussion of municipal council would be complete without an examination of the position of head of council. This position has become important over the years in spite of its lack of formal powers. While heads of council in Canada are not limited to the largely ceremonial role of their British counterparts, neither are they comparable to the American "strong mayor" who, in many states, has extensive authority with respect to preparation of current and capital budgets, planning, hiring, and firing.

Consider Ontario's new *Municipal Act*, which took effect on January 1, 2003. It provides that the role of the head of council is to act as chief executive officer, preside over council meetings, provide leadership to the council, represent the municipality at official functions, and carry out the duties of the head under this or any other Act. Not only are these duties quite vague and general, but also the new Act actually omits three provisions that used to be found in the legislation.[11] For reasons that were never explained, the province ignored the opportunity to strengthen the position at the time of the new *Municipal Act*. Nor was this oversight addressed in any significant way in major amendments to the *Municipal Act* (in Bill 130) at the end of December 2006. The amendments defined the role of the head of council as chief executive officer but again in vague terms such as uphold, promote, participate in, and foster.

The legislation goes a little farther in some provinces. For example, Manitoba, British Columbia, and Quebec provide a limited form of veto by authorizing the head of council to return any matter to the council for reconsideration. The latter two provinces and Saskatchewan empower the head of council to suspend any officer or employee, subject to confirmation by council. Changes to the *City of Winnipeg Act* in 1998 provide for the mayor to chair the Executive Policy Committee (EPC), to

---

[10] For a discussion of these conflicting perspectives, and the way they also manifest themselves when councillors also sit on other bodies such as upper tier governments and separate boards, see George Cuff, David Siegel, and C. Richard Tindal, "Representation Riddle: Conflicting demands on the local councillor," *Municipal World*, December 2004, pp. 9-12 and 35. See also, Frances Morell, *From the Electors of Bristol, The Record of a Year's Correspondence Between Constituents and their Members of Parliament,* London, Rountree Trust, 1977.

[11] These provisions were: to be vigilant and active in causing the laws of the municipality to be executed and obeyed, to oversee the conduct of all subordinate officers, and to communicate to council from time to time such measures as may improve the municipality.

appoint its members (four of whom are simultaneously appointed as chairs of the city's standing committees), and to suspend the chief administrative officer for up to three days – by which time the EPC must reinstate the CAO, extend the suspension for 30 days, or recommend to council dismissal of the person. With these changes, Winnipeg's mayor "became arguably the most powerful municipal executive in Canada."[12]

The position of mayor in the City of Toronto has been strengthened in a similar fashion, as a result of changes that occurred in conjunction with the new *City of Toronto Act* that took effect in 2007. It was widely held that if the city was going to be given more powers it also had to acquire a more effective governing model. So strongly did the province hold this view that the legislation included a provision authorizing it, by regulation, to require the city to appoint an executive committee and to require the mayor to exercise various appointment powers. To avoid the risk of such highhanded action by the province, city council moved to introduce similar changes *before* the legislation was passed.

The main specific power given to the mayor (echoing Winnipeg's reform of 1998) was the right to appoint the chairs of the standing committees and the deputy mayor, who make up 8 of the 12 members of the executive committee, along with the mayor who is chair. But even if all 13 members support a particular issue, they still represent a distinct minority in a council of 45 members. This political reality was all too evident in the mayor's embarrassing setback in July 2007 when his proposal to introduce two new taxes, backed by his executive committee, was defeated 23-22 in council (with the help of one defection from the executive committee). It may be that only political parties can provide the cohesion necessary for sustained direction on a council of this size. The merits of local political parties are examined later in this chapter, but Canadians usually respond quite negatively to attempts to introduce them into the municipal scene, reflecting a long established notion of non-partisanship in matters local.

In spite of their lack of formal power, Canadian mayors have high local political visibility, in large part because of the tendency for local media in a community to contact the mayor for short summaries of municipal business or comments on current controversies.[13] Their

---

[12] Christopher Leo and Mark Piel, "Municipal Reform in Manitoba," in Joseph Garcea and Edward C. LeSage Jr. (eds.), *Municipal Reform in Canada*, Toronto, Oxford University Press, 2005, p. 117.

[13] Andrew Sancton, "Mayors As Political Leaders," in Maureen Mancuso, Richard Price, and Ronald Wagenberg (eds.), *Leaders and Leadership in Canada*, Toronto, Oxford University Press, 1994, pp. 179-180.

ceremonial and symbolic functions are also important and can be the basis for popularity and reelection, and – if used effectively – for building links between the diverse elements of a local community. The mayor does not have any real authority over staffing and the administrative structure, but can exercise considerable influence by providing a link between senior managers and council. "With easier access to senior officials than other council members enjoy, and the ability to interpret council's wishes when they have not been clearly stated, the mayor can exert considerable influence within the municipal bureaucratic apparatus."[14]

Given these limits on their formal power, heads of council in Canada must rely heavily on their personality and persuasive skills in attempting to provide leadership. Except in those limited instances where organized political parties exist, a council is made up of a group of individuals with potentially different interests and concerns and no sense of cohesion or collective will. As a result, the challenge facing a mayor has been likened to "herding cats" in an article discussing the task facing Bob Chiarelli when he was elected in November 2000 as the first mayor of the new city of Ottawa. The new council was described as divided by geography, political beliefs, urban-rural concerns, ethnicity, and specific interests. A number of factions were in evidence: "left wing versus right wing, downtown councillors, rural councillors, the east-end group, the west-end group, the French lobby, the youth wing, and the old Nepean lobby.[15] Expecting any head of council to build a consensus and provide effective direction in circumstances such as these is quite a tall order.

Yet the record shows that mayors, even when facing opposition from council members, can accomplish a good deal "if they are competent, shrewd, and, most important, popular with the electorate."[16] A number of colourful and long serving mayors certainly "put their stamp" on their cities, with names like Elsie Wayne of Saint John, Stephen Juba of Winnipeg, and Jean Drapeau of Montreal coming readily to mind. Colourful mayors are still plentiful if we can judge by the results of a 2004 contest for craziest mayor run by Rick Mercer's Monday Report on CBC TV.[17] The winner was Saskatoon's mayor, Don Atchison, who

---

[14] *Ibid.*, p. 180.

[15] Ken Gray, "Mayor's job like herding cats," *Ottawa Citizen*, January 17, 2001.

[16] Allan Levine (ed.), *Your Worship: The Lives of Eight of Canada's Most Unforgettable Mayors*, Toronto, James Lorimer and Company, 1989, p. 2.

[17] The description that follows is based on Saskatoon (CP), *Saskatoon's mayor dubbed 'craziest,'* February 3, 2004.

began his term by proclaiming that anyone who wanted to see him at city hall had to come in business attire. Reminded that he had campaigned on a platform of being "the people's mayor," he soon rescinded the dress code. Surprisingly, he won over such likely prospects as St. John's irascible Andy Wells and Houston, B.C.'s mayor, Sharon Smith, who posed nude except for her chain of office, in pictures that somehow found their way into the public domain.

For longevity, accomplishments, and colour, it is hard to imagine a better example than Hazel McCallion of Mississauga whose political skill in responding to financial pressures was profiled in Chapter 7. Her career demonstrates how personality and temperament can forge an indelible public image.[18]

Box 8.1 Hurricane Hazel[19]
In November 2010, Hazel McCallion was reelected, at age 89, to what she has called her last four year term as mayor. She has been mayor of Mississauga since 1978 and has presided over a period of rapid growth during which the city has remained debt free. Her public image was established early in her career by her response to an incident in November 1979, when a chemical laden CPR train went off the tracks at a Mississauga crossing, forcing the evacuation of a large portion of the city. Early on in the weeklong drama, McCallion injured a leg, but she remained on the scene throughout, hobbling around on a cane. The perception of her as tough and graceful under pressure was fixed forever, and she remains a formidable figure to this day, legendary for her seven day work week and apparently boundless energy. When she was back at work only a couple of days after being hit by a pickup truck in February 2003, this incident only served to reinforce her image of invincibility. She is a member of the Order of Canada and placed second (out of 65 mayors shortlisted) in a 2005 World Mayor Project.

The Administration

In addition to council, the municipal governing machinery includes the appointed staff, responsible for administering the programs and policies of council and assisting council in making decisions by providing expert advice. There is, of course, a tremendous variation in the number and organization of staff, depending on the population of the municipality

---

[18] See Tom Urbaniak, *Her Worship: Hazel McCallion and the Development of Mississauga*, Toronto, University of Toronto Press, 2009.

[19] The following description is largely based on Jim Coyle, "Hazel's world reigns supreme," *Toronto Star*, October 11, 2000; John Barber, "Hurricane Hazel going strong at 80," *Globe and Mail*, February 12, 2001; Jim Coyle, "Mayor Hazel 1, pickup truck 0," *Toronto Star*, February 18, 2003; and D'Arcy Jenish, "Hurricane Hazel: going and going and going," *Forum*, Federation of Canadian Municipalities, November/December 2005.

and range of functions. At one extreme, increasingly rare, is the staff of one, perhaps part time at that. This person may act as clerk, treasurer, tax collector, by-law enforcement officer, building inspector, and dog catcher while performing a variety of other duties – and all without any formal job description whatsoever.

Box 8.2 Carrel the Crusader[20]

André Carrel wasn't the dog catcher, but he couldn't find one anywhere, so he was stuck with the responsibility for doing something when a pack of stray dogs became a serious problem during his first municipal job in Fort Simpson in the Northwest Territories. He got that job, as secretary-manager, in 1970, because the other applicant for the position couldn't type and he could. He could also fire a gun and that is how he addressed the dog problem after some small children were attacked. Carrel's next position was as city manager of Dawson City where he learned that a municipal manager who hoped to survive in a hostile political environment "needed to be one-quarter lawyer, one-quarter accountant, one-quarter engineer, and three-quarters son-of-a-bitch." He left Dawson City in 1981 to become the first full time executive director of the Association of Yukon Communities, headquartered in Whitehorse. From there he moved to the senior staff position in Rossland, British Columbia, where he played a key role in that municipality's innovations in direct municipal democracy, discussed in Chapter 9. While municipal staff are known to wax eloquent about the latest budgeting or managerial technique, Carrel is unusual in that his passion is the importance of municipal democracy and of the central role that must be played by local citizens, as outlined in his already cited book, *Citizens' Hall, Making Local Democracy Work*.

At the other extreme is the staff of thousands, grouped into twenty-odd functionally specialized departments, with job descriptions and operating manuals and an elaborate hierarchy. In this latter instance, the municipality obviously has much greater staff resources and expertise available. Bigger is not always better, however, and it is often difficult to draw these resources together into a coordinated operation.

Traditionally, there has been a requirement for municipalities to appoint certain statutory officers, but new legislative requirements in several provinces have removed or reduced this requirement, ostensibly to provide municipalities with flexibility to develop staffing arrangements that best meet their needs. For example, 1998 amendments (Bill 31) in B.C. eliminated the required titles of municipal clerk, regional district secretary, and treasurer, but gave formal recognition to the position of chief administrative officer. Ontario's *Municipal Act 2001* still requires the appointment of a treasurer and clerk, but neither now

---

[20] Based on information provided in Carrel, *Citizens' Hall, Making Local Democracy Work*, especially Chapter 2.

needs to be an employee of the municipality – a change that facilitates the currently popular philosophy of contracting out municipal services.

A brief look at the roles of staff indicates that they are closely related to the roles of councillors cited earlier.[21] The most obvious role is to administer the policies and programs of the municipality. Those staff directly involved in the provision of services are the ones with whom the local public most often have contact. As a result, such staff also have a public relations role because most citizens form their opinion of their municipal government on the basis of the chance encounters that they have with municipal staff. In the course of this public contact, staff often find themselves acting as brokers or arbiters of conflicting local interests, seeking to find common ground. Senior staffs have two very important roles – advising council on policy matters and managing and supervising the staff within their departments or sections.

These general roles in no way convey the magnitude and variety of responsibilities of a municipal official. When one of us was teaching an Internet course a few years ago, one student email did a much better job of illuminating the work involved, and it is reproduced below.

Box 8.3 All In a (Half) Day's Work

Today, as Town Manager, I wrote a letter to our local seniors group to renew a lease agreement (which I also re-wrote), got a flu shot, reviewed our Municipal Emergency Plan with our local Disaster Services rep, agreed to co-facilitate a Disaster Training exercise with a neighbouring community, set up a public meeting to establish a local Community Health Council, confirmed attendance at a weekend strategic planning session with the local Health Region, reviewed the minutes of last night's council meeting and delegated some assignments, telephoned our contractor about the delay in material shipment of a Public Works building expansion, set up a meeting with an engineer to complete a site review of a municipal commercial development, met with the mayor and a local community group president about an outstanding issue, met with our police Sgt about his need for additional hours to clear a backlog of tickets on the computer system, completed changes to a Traffic Control by-law as a result of last night's council meeting, and explained to my Public Works foreman why he might not be getting a new grader next year ... and I did all this before lunch.

Changing Council-Staff Relations

The council-staff relationship, and the operation of municipal government in general, is complicated by the difficulty of striking a balance between the concerns and emphasis of the politicians and the

---

[21] This discussion is partly based on C. R. Tindal, *Municipal Administration Program*, Unit Two, Association of Municipal Managers, Clerks, and Treasurers of Ontario, 2010.

professionals. In theory, the latter serve at the behest of the former, lending their expertise to the development and implementation of policy decisions made by the politicians. Rather than political and professional perspectives blending in the service of the local community, however, they have often appeared to operate at cross purposes. Increasingly, the claims of professionalism, and the associated emphasis on improvements in efficiency, have come even more strongly to the forefront – to the relative neglect of political considerations and the associated emphasis on serving the public interest and local democracy. A brief review will illustrate how this pattern evolved over time.

Reconciling Politics and Professionalism

The notion of professionalism in the local public service arose in both North America and Britain as a result of concerns about whether local governments could handle the increased responsibilities that they were acquiring as a result of industrialization and urbanization. As early as the mid-19th century, British reformers worried about corruption and nepotism in local government and criticized the fact that "new public works projects and new regulatory powers created conditions conducive to corruption and the capture of municipal officers by local interests."[22] In response, they encouraged the development of a professional corps of staff who would be immune to inappropriate local pressures.

The push for professionalism in North America arose during the reform movement of 100 years ago. Like the earlier British reforms, the impetus was a reaction against corruption and inefficiency in local government operations. As discussed in Chapter 2, reformers sought to replace patronage appointments and the spoils system with a municipal public service appointed for their technical qualifications. The belief that sound administration could solve municipal problems was reinforced by a scientific management movement that also developed in the early 20th century and promoted the benefits of general management principles.

Because much of the professionalization developed in response to the expansion of local responsibilities, it was specialized in nature and was focused on separate technical disciplines such as public health, social work, planning, and education. But the specialized knowledge that was a key feature of each of these professions also made their members insular, protective of their turf, and resistant to coordination, with the

---

[22] Martin Laffin and Ken Young, *Professionalism in Local Government*, Harlow, Longman, 1990, p. 13.

result that local governments were "in essence loose confederations of semi-autonomous empires."[23]

Central authorities in Britain and North America supported and encouraged professionalism in local government as a way of achieving minimum standards and consistency in the provision of services. They saw professionalism as a countervailing force to localism. It advanced the standardization favoured by central governments at the expense of local autonomy and diversity.[24] The impact on British local government following the Second World War is described by John Stewart in the following terms:[25]

> The politics of consensus was based on acceptance of the universalism of expertise and knowledge. Councillors of all parties had confidence in the services and in the advice given by officers on their development. Officers put their faith in established professional practice. Universal solutions based on expert knowledge were pursued for what were seen as common problems for all local authorities. There was little apparent need for local government or local choice.

The experience in Canada was similar, with the desire to maintain minimum standards in the provision of services leading not only to an emphasis on professionalism and consistency, but also to an increase in provincial supervision and control. Specialists at the local and provincial levels often felt allied in a common cause in furtherance of their particular discipline. Both the fragmentation of local administration and the strong links between local and provincial professionals were reinforced over the years by provincial grants that ensured expenditures on specified functions and by the isolation of functions into separate special purpose bodies – such as school boards, planning boards, and health boards.

Inherent in the professionalism of municipal staff was the sense of a commitment to certain public service ideals, including the protection of the public interest. This concept has been associated with the historic office of British Town Clerk for well over a century.[26] How it is interpreted today varies widely, but some senior staff believe that they

---

[23] T. Smith, *Town and Country Hall*, London, Acton Society Trust, 1966, p. 29.

[24] Laffin and Young, *Professionalism in Local Government*, p. 17.

[25] John Stewart, *The New Management of Local Government*, London, Allen & Unwin, 1986, p. 10. See also J. A. G. Griffith, *Central Departments and Local Authorities*, London, Royal Institute of Public Administration, 1966.

[26] T. E. Headrick, *The Town Clerk in English Local Government*, London, George Allen & Unwin, 1962.

have an obligation to argue against councillor views that they feel are misguided. Some staff have experienced "a sense of belonging to a public service which was both larger and more continuous than their immediate service with their current council suggested."[27] Taken to an extreme, the commitment to professionalism can be viewed as a kind of countervailing force that exists to limit or moderate political power in the interest of local democracy. From this perspective, "professional officers have a duty to moderate and constrain any abrupt policy changes thrown up by local politicians."[28] Mind you, staff who take this position to an extreme may find that "their immediate service with their current council" doesn't last as long as they had expected or desired.

Given their background and expertise, municipal staff may understandably feel that they have the best grasp of matters requiring policy action by council. It may seem to them that some of the policy ideas being championed by individual councillors are little more than an attempt to placate or please some specialized segment of the local populace. If they hold these views strongly enough, senior staff may resist the policy overtures of councillors and use a variety of tactics to thwart those that they find unworthy.[29] If that doesn't work, staff still have a great deal of influence because of their role in researching and recommending a specific course of action. Anthony Downs, in *Inside Bureaucracy,* describes this bureaucratic resistance to innovative policy change.[30]

> ...the amount and kind of information, the method of presentation, the manner in which alternatives are identified and appraised, and the making of, or abstention from, recommendations – all provide opportunities for the bureaucracies to impress their own discretion and preferences....The object is constant; to guide the official's decision into the channels that the bureaucrats regard as wise and prudent.[31]

In fairness to staff, the policy direction provided by council is often far from clear. There may be a variety of different and even contradictory policy signals provided by individual councillors, since the absence of a governing group within the council (with the exception of municipalities

---

[27] Laffin and Young, *Professionalism in Local Government*, p. 75.

[28] *Ibid.*, p. 77.

[29] Masson and LeSage, *Alberta's Local Governments*, p. 222.

[30] A. Downs, *Inside Bureaucracy*, Boston, Little, Brown, 1967.

[31] Wallace S. Sayre and Herbert Kaufman, *Governing New York City*, New York, W. W. Norton, 1965, pp. 420-421.

in Quebec and a very limited number in British Columbia) makes it difficult to develop a coordinated position. Sometimes the only way for councillors to achieve such a position is to compromise until the policy direction has become vague enough to avoid offending anyone. Even when members are not divided, they may still find it difficult to identify precisely what they want from staff. With respect to matters such as land use planning and economic development, staff may be told: "This is the sort of direction we want to move in. We would like you to negotiate with the relevant groups and do the best you can to move us in that direction."[32] When council essentially abdicates its policy making responsibility in this manner, staff are placed in an ambiguous and difficult position.[33] In addition, there are situations in which the policy intentions of council are, at best, misguided, or are without legal authority, and staff have a responsibility to object in these situations.

How far staff should go in providing policy advice is also open to debate. On the one hand, they are expected, as professionals, to provide an objective and dispassionate analysis of the facts – although Lindblom and others have pointed out that there is no such thing as a decision based solely on the facts because facts are assembled, analyzed, and presented by people, individuals with their own backgrounds, experiences, values, and judgments that inevitably colour what is presented.[34] On the other hand, councils often express displeasure at advice that they regard as unrealistic, "pie in the sky," and not sufficiently sensitive to local political realities. Staff who provide advice that is technically sound but politically problematic are often criticized. Yet those who temper their advice to take into account political considerations may be criticized just as strongly by councillors who feel that all political considerations are their prerogative and preserve.

Siegel cautions that the more staff modify their advice in response to their perception of local political realities, the more their neutrality is compromised.[35] If their advice shows a sensitivity to the views of a majority of councillors, then they may antagonize the remaining councillors whose views were apparently not given as much weight. If

---

[32] David Siegel, "Politics, politicians, and public servants in non-partisan local governments," *Canadian Public Administration*, Spring 1994, p. 9.

[33] T. J. Plunkett and G. M. Betts, *The Management of Canadian Urban Government*, Kingston, Queen's University, 1978, p. 161.

[34] Charles Lindblom, *The Intelligence of Democracy*, New York, The Free Press, 1965, pp. 138-143 and Richard S. Rosenblom and John R. Russell, *New Tools for Urban Management*, Boston, Harvard University Press, 1971, p. 229.

[35] The discussion in this section is based on Siegel, "Politics, politicians," pp. 26-28.

they focus too much on providing advice that will be acceptable to council, they may recommend what they think council wants to hear rather than what it should hear – which is not a desirable state of affairs. When staff know that their best technical and professional advice will not be politically acceptable to council, Siegel suggests the following:[36]

> Public servants should recommend what they see as the best course of action for the municipality from their administrative perspective, regardless of its political consequences for any particular councillor or even for council as a whole. It is important for council to have the best possible objective and professional advice. If there are political factors to be injected into the decision-making process, it is council's job to introduce them.

The relationship between council and staff does not get any easier with respect to the implementation of policy. The staff have the primary role when it comes to enforcing by-laws, delivering programs, or administering services to the local community, but councillors also have a responsibility to provide a general oversight of these activities – to ensure that policies are being implemented as intended and with due regard for the tax dollar. As Crawford explains so well, different perspectives on the implementation of policy cause an inevitable tension between a council and staff in connection with policy implementation.[37] He points out that members of council are constantly approached by individuals who feel they are unfairly dealt with under the general application of municipal policies and regulations. They attempt to persuade the councillors that their case merits special consideration.

> Because he is elected to represent the people and under the system of popular election his political life depends on keeping his people satisfied, and because the individual's claim is usually plausible, the representative tends to be more concerned with the exceptions than the rule. The permanent officials, who in most cases have been long in office and expect to continue there, are more conscious of the difficulties which result from making exceptions to general rules and, in the interest of equity to all, tend to resist requests for special treatment.

The fact that elected and appointed personnel approach situations with a different background and perspective complicates their relationship but can also be positive and productive. It is widely

---

[36] *Ibid.*, p. 27.

[37] K. G. Crawford, *Canadian Municipal Government*, Toronto, University of Toronto Press, 1954, pp. 165-166.

perceived, for example, that politicians are keen to push ahead with new approaches, while staff are likely to encourage caution and respect for established ways of doing things. Too much of one approach or the other can be problematic, creating a tendency toward excessive change or stagnation, but together these tendencies can create a healthy tension that generates new ideas but also subjects them to thorough examination.

A recent analysis examines differing political and staff perspectives in Ontario municipalities. It seeks to determine if there are personality differences between elected and appointed personnel at the local level, reasoning that any such differences are important because of the close interaction of councillors and staff and the fact that much of it takes place in public meetings where these differences will be evident. While the differences were not as great as might have been anticipated, the analysis found that politicians are more outgoing and sociable and more curious and imaginative, while staff are inclined to be more focused on internal aspects of the municipality and its efficient operation.[38]

Clarifying Roles and Relationships

For much of the 20th century, efforts to clarify and improve the council-staff relationship tended to focus on the strict separation of the roles of council and staff, the former setting policy and the latter implementing it, as depicted in Figure 8.2 below. As will be discussed, this politics-administration dichotomy was reflected in the city manager or council manager governing model that became very popular in the United States and enjoyed more limited success in Canada. But a complete separation of policy and administration is artificial and prone to problems. It is not always evident whether something is a policy matter, and items that first appear to be of a routine administrative nature can quickly develop policy and political implications. This was reinforced by a Supreme Court of Canada ruling – on the powers of British Columbia's Ombudsman – on "what is a matter of administration": the court ruled that virtually "anything that governments do" is a matter of administration. Similarly, much of what it does is also policy.[39]

---

[38] A number of potentially different personality traits are examined in Michael Ashton, Joseph Kushner, and David Siegel, "Personality traits of municipal politicians and staff," *Canadian Public Administration*, Summer 2007, pp. 273-289.

[39] On this case see British Columbia Development Corporation v. Friedman (Ombudsman), [1984], 2 SCR. 447 and Patrick Smith, "Fairness Inc.: Administrative Justice in British Columbia: The OmbudsOffice @ 30," in Stuart Hyson (ed.), *Provincial and Territorial Ombudsman Offices in Canada,* Toronto, University of Toronto Press/ Institute of Public Administration of Canada, 2009, Ch. 3.

Moreover, since most policy arises from ongoing administration, too rigid a separation leaves councillors trying to make policy in a vacuum. As a result, there developed a growing appreciation that policy and administration should be viewed as a continuum (also illustrated in the figure below), with councillors more involved at one end and staff more involved at the other.

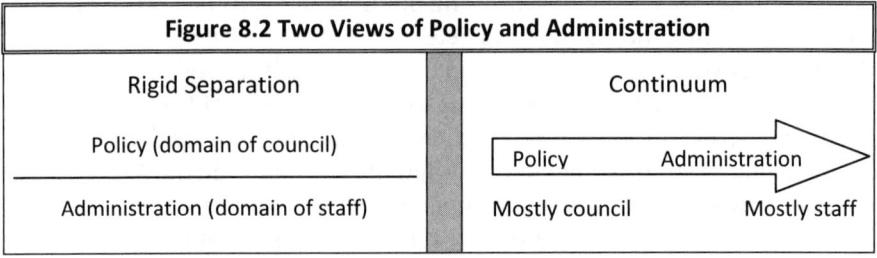

Figure 8.2 Two Views of Policy and Administration

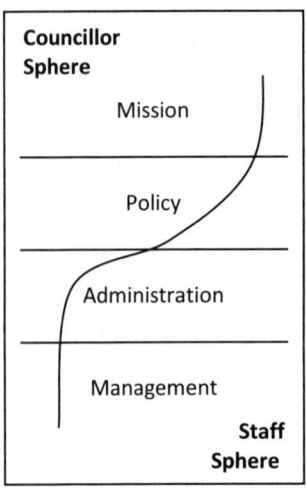

Svara provides a more refined version of the continuum view of staff and council roles by identifying four dimensions of the governmental process and showing how councillors and staff are involved in these dimensions to varying degrees.[40] As he sees it, councillors are particularly involved in setting out the purpose and mission of the municipality and in enacting policy, while staff play the predominant role in administration and management, leading to their combined involvement in the government process as illustrated in the accompanying chart.

The changing nature and context of municipal operations is reflected in the changing roles of the manager. As governments shifted their focus outward, to possible partners in the broader community, staff assumed new roles as broker and negotiator. By the 1990s, the International City Management Association's expanded list of manager roles included the following roles:[41]

---

[40] James Svara, "Dichotomy and Duality: Reconceptualizing the Relationship between Policy and Administration in Council-Manager Cities," *Public Administration Review*, 45, 1985.

[41] Jane G. Kazman, *Working Together, A Guide for Elected and Appointed Officials*, Washington, DC, International City Management Association, 2000, p. 17.

- consensus builder, translator, and interpreter of community values,
- convenor of interested parties and diverse community groups,
- change agent,
- facilitator of conflict resolution,
- champion of leadership development within the community,
- educator on community issues,
- problem solver,
- process leader,
- team builder/mentor,
- source of empowerment,
- champion of new technologies, and
- bearer of ethical standards

This range of roles is quite broad, and one could question whether such matters as interpreting community values, convening diverse community groups, and building consensus are more properly roles of councillors. But the list serves to illustrate the simplistic nature of earlier characterizations that essentially limited the roles of staff to advising on and implementing policy. The reality is that few matters are purely administrative and few matters are only policy – a view reinforced by renowned UK/Australian local government expert, Peter Self.[42]

Modifications to the Municipal Machinery

The internal governing structure of a municipality can influence the way in which councillors and staff carry out their roles and interact. A number of governing structures found in Canadian municipalities at both council and staff levels are briefly summarized below, beginning with the most basic – and historically most common – model, the standing committee system. The changes to governing machinery introduced over the years have mainly involved the introduction of executive committees to improve coordination and executive direction at the council level and coordinating officers to improve coordination and leadership at the staff level. The former have not been very effective, for the most part. The greater success with coordinating officer models has contributed to the service delivery and efficiency objectives of municipal government but somewhat at the expense of its political and representative role.

---

[42] See Peter Self, *Administrative Theories and Politics,* London, Allen & Unwin, 1977, Chapter 8.

The Standing Committee System

This governing model features the establishment of a number of ongoing committees, each focused on a major functional area of operations. The committees are normally responsible for overseeing the operations of one or more departments within their area and for making recommendations and presenting reports as requested by council – although sometimes the committees exercise only this latter, policy advisory role. They are composed of councillors, and may also include (infrequently) some citizen members. These committees are usually created entirely at council's discretion, and are not to be confused with the statutory committees and boards set up under the authority of provincial statutes. Examples of the latter would be committees of adjustment and land division committees which exercise planning responsibilities at the local level in Ontario. A typical committee system is depicted below.

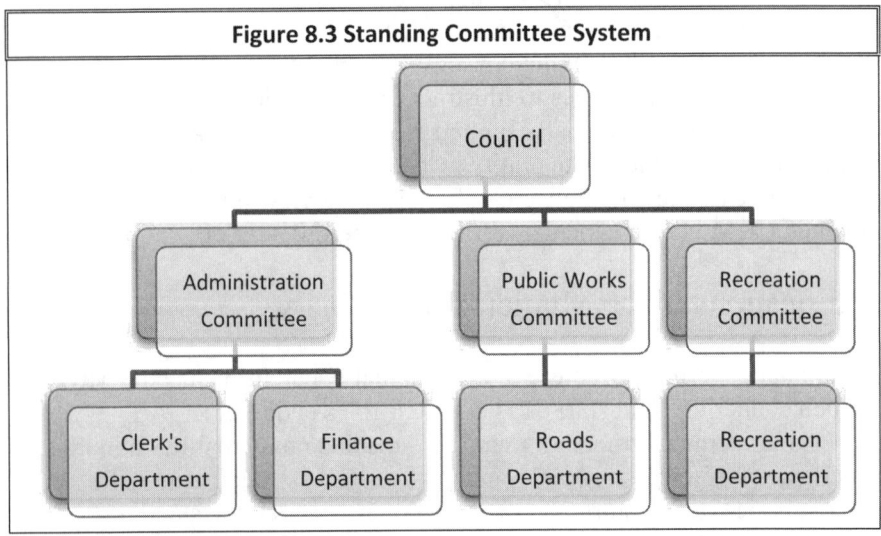

Figure 8.3 Standing Committee System

The use of a standing committee system is held to be advantageous because it speeds up work in council since the committee sifts through the details of an issue and presents a positive recommendation to council. It allows councillors to specialize in the areas of administration under the jurisdiction of their committees rather than trying to be knowledgeable in all fields. It is also alleged that the informal atmosphere of a committee meeting encourages more "give and take" in debate, facilitates participation by municipal officials, and also provides a good opportunity for interested groups or individuals to be heard. In this latter connection, it is argued that the delay built in when matters are referred to committee gives public opinion a chance to develop and to be heard and guards against overly precipitous action.

However, there are also a number of alleged disadvantages of the standing committee system. While some delay in decision making may be beneficial, referrals from council to one or more committees and back to council can create a very slow process and the opportunity for buck passing. If committee discussions are duplicated in council, much time is wasted and the value of the committee's specialized scrutiny is lost. There are often too many committees, with the result that a councillor's already limited time is seriously overburdened. An associated problem in many smaller municipalities is the tendency to establish standing committees when they are not necessary given the volume of work. Often such committees have no terms of reference, no regular schedule of meetings, and no systematic procedure of reporting to council. As a result, they are not an effective addition for managing the municipality.

Another criticism, of particular relevance for the ensuing discussion, is that standing committees tend to reinforce the departmentalization inherent in the municipal organization and thus contribute to a fragmented outlook. This is because members of a committee may put the interests of their particular department or departments first, an attitude which is hardly conducive to a coordinated approach or to a broad view of the municipality's needs. Often difficulties arise in this respect because the committee system has simply expanded with the increase in municipal departments. Yet the departments themselves may have grown without sufficient forethought and, if this structure is poorly organized for coordination, then what can one expect from a committee system similarly designed? Finally, it is argued that committee members tend to become overly preoccupied with matters of administrative detail and internal management of the departments under their jurisdiction. This is a common problem with councils generally but it is felt to be accentuated by the greater contact and familiarity with administration that the specialized scrutiny of committees permits.

Executive Committees

Over the years the most persistent method of attempting to provide political leadership and coordinated direction has been the establishment of executive committees of council. An early and prominent version of this structure was the board of control, introduced as part of the turn of the century reforms of 100 years ago. This model was quite widespread in Ontario during the first half of the 20th century. Other forms of executive committee were established, at least initially, in a number of large cities or metropolitan municipalities in an effort to duplicate a cabinet organization and a semblance of the parliamentary system. What was often missing here throughout Canada was any local party system paralleling that found in senior level parliamentary settings – an issue assessed in our concluding chapters.

Board of Control

As described in Chapter 2, the board of control first appeared in Canada in the City of Toronto in 1896. It was not really a board, but a statutory executive committee of council, assigned important responsibilities relating to such matters as budgets, contracts, and staffing. Its recommendations could only be overturned or altered by a two-thirds vote of council (of which the controllers were voting members). While it didn't make much of an impact in other provinces, the board of control became mandatory for cities over 100 000 in Ontario, although it could be dispensed with by a two-thirds vote of council if affirmed by the Ontario Municipal Board.

It was anticipated that the board of control would provide effective leadership and contribute to a more efficient management of the affairs of the municipality. But the board's similarity to a cabinet was superficial at best; instead of a body unified by the glue of party loyalty and discipline, the board was made up of individuals without necessarily any common purpose. With only four board members plus the mayor, the board became increasingly overburdened in attempting to oversee the administrative activities of the municipality and usually clashed with standing committees where they were retained. Most serious of all, however, was the friction between the board and the rest of council. The latter were particularly resentful of the two-thirds vote requirement for overturning board decisions. Gradually, municipalities took steps to abolish their boards of control, with the last one (in the City of London) disappearing at the end of the 2010 term of council.

Other Forms of Executive Committee

A variety of other executive committees are found in Canadian municipalities. Some are similar to a board of control in having a statutory foundation, including those established in a number of the reformed local municipal structures. There are also nonstatutory executive committees. By their nature they are much harder to categorize, especially since they do not always use the name "executive" committee. Their purpose is reflected in their composition, however, which usually comprises the chairs of the major standing committees in the municipality plus the head of council, and in their mandate, which usually includes responsibility for the budget and for providing leadership and coordination. The figure below illustrates this government structure.

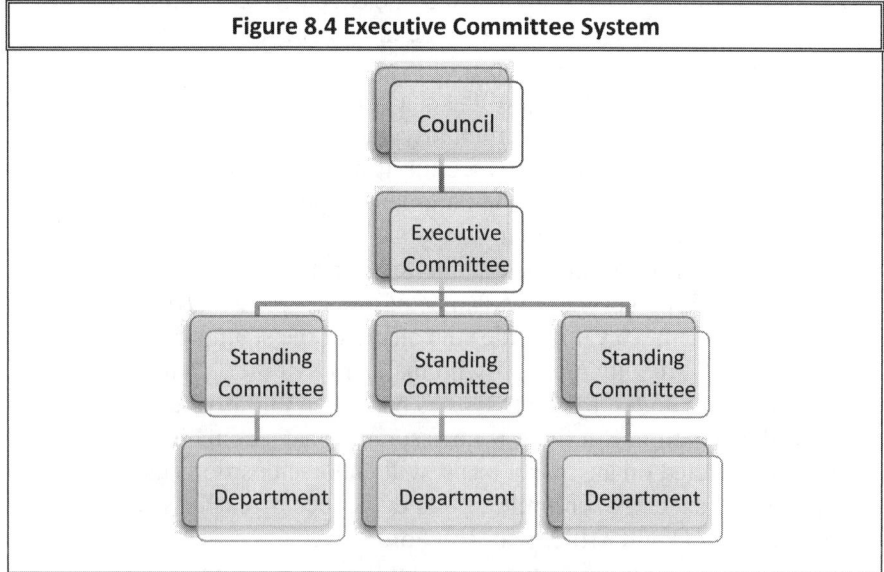

Figure 8.4 Executive Committee System

Montreal is likely the Canadian city with the longest experience with an executive committee, since there are references to such a body as early as the 1850s. By the 1960s, this committee had evolved into a powerful position because of the emergence of dominant political parties within Montreal's council. For example, during Jean Drapeau's long tenure as mayor (1960-1986), his choices for members of the executive committee were ratified by a council controlled by his Civic Party, and the committee could initiate actions with every expectation that it would be supported by the council. The cities of Quebec, Hull, and Laval established executive committees in the 1960s, after studies that found that their government machinery exhibited weaknesses of excessive council involvement in administrative detail, lack of executive direction, and uncoordinated administration. As with the situation in Montreal, the existence of local political parties within the municipal councils of these three cities provided a basis for strong political leadership.

In contrast, the executive committee established by the Municipality of Metropolitan Toronto in 1954 was unable to provide strong leadership. It was composed of the chair of the metro council, the mayors of the six lower tier municipalities in the system, and seven other specified representatives from the lower tier councils. With that many members, serving by virtue of a prior position elsewhere in the municipal structure, and without the unifying force of local political parties, the executive committee lacked cohesion or common focus, and also lacked a support base within the rest of council.

Similar constraints continued to affect the executive committee set up in the new City of Toronto, which came into existence in 1998. Known as the Strategic Policies and Priorities Committee, this body (no longer in existence) was made up of the chairs of Toronto's five standing committees, the chairs of its six community councils, the deputy mayor, the budget chief, and the mayor of Toronto. It was almost as large as a cabinet, but lacked cohesiveness and common purpose and depended upon the willingness of members to cooperate and work together.

As discussed earlier in this chapter, a new form of executive committee was created for Toronto in advance of the new *City of Toronto Act*. Headed by the mayor, it includes the chairs of the standing committees and the deputy mayor – who make up 8 of the 12 members and who are all appointed by the mayor as part of an initiative to strengthen this position. But there is no assurance that a council of 45 members, not elected on any party basis, will endorse positions taken by the mayor or the executive committee – as evidenced by earlier examples involving Mayors David Miller and Rob Ford.

Executive committees face a dilemma with respect to the extent of their power. The board of control model was rejected because it was seen as too powerful, owing to the two-thirds vote provision. Executive committees backed by political parties can be quite powerful (just as they have always been at the provincial and federal levels where they operate as the cabinet) but except in the province of Quebec (and in a few municipalities in British Columbia), voters have shown a great reluctance to support the introduction of political parties at the local level. In the absence of either of these options, we are left with executive committees that must rely on goodwill and persuasion to develop a position and then to obtain council support for it. While these may prevail on any one issue, they are hardly the basis for cohesion and concerted direction.

Coordinating Officers

Experiences with coordinating officers have been more varied, and more successful, than efforts to establish executive committees of council. The most common form of this position is the chief administrative officer, but it also embraces other forms of coordinating officer.

Chief Administrative Officer System

Chief administrative officers (CAOs) are found under a variety of names and with a variety of powers and responsibilities. Titles used include city administrator, city manager, commissioner, chief commissioner, and director general. Plunkett uses the term CAO to encompass all types of structure (including manager systems) that have a single appointed officer as head of the administration. On this basis, he found that by 1989 some 170 urban municipalities in Canada had adopted this structure.[43] Among the larger cities in this category were Vancouver, Edmonton, Calgary, Saskatoon, Regina, Winnipeg, Windsor, Hamilton, Toronto, Ottawa, Sudbury, Quebec City, Saint John, Halifax, and St. John's.[44]

The earliest and most powerful form of CAO is that of the city manager or council manager system, which spread into this country from the United States in the early 1900s. The first Canadian city manager was appointed in Westmount in 1913 and the system is still found mainly in Quebec, where legislation has authorized councils to appoint a manager since 1922. In contrast, not until a 1970 amendment did Ontario's *Municipal Act* give municipalities the authority to appoint any type of CAO. While the number of CAO positions has increased markedly since, most are not full fledged managers but rather weaker forms of coordinating officer or expanded clerk-treasurer, as described below.[45]

The Council Manager System

As it developed in the United States, this system is predicated on a complete separation of the policy and administrative activities of the municipality. It involves the appointment of a professional administrator (the manager) to whom is delegated complete responsibility for administering the programs of the municipality, including the coordination and supervision of all staff. The council, usually small in number, is elected at large and directs its attention to its representative role and the formulation of overall policies for the municipality. In the "pure" council manager systems found in the United States, there are not usually any

---

[43] T. J. Plunkett, *City Management in Canada: The Role of the Chief Administrative Officer*, Toronto, Institute of Public Administration of Canada, 1992, p. 21.

[44] *Ibid.*, p. 25.

[45] David Siegel, "The Leadership Qualities of Municipal Chief Administrative Officers," *Canadian Public Administration*, Summer 2010, pp. 139-61. This topic will be explored in more detail in a forthcoming publication by Siegel, *Leadership in Municipal Government: Lessons from the Front Line*, Social Sciences and Humanities Research Council project.

standing committees and therefore not any regular council contact with the administration except through the manager. The relatively simple, compact structure is depicted in the figure below.

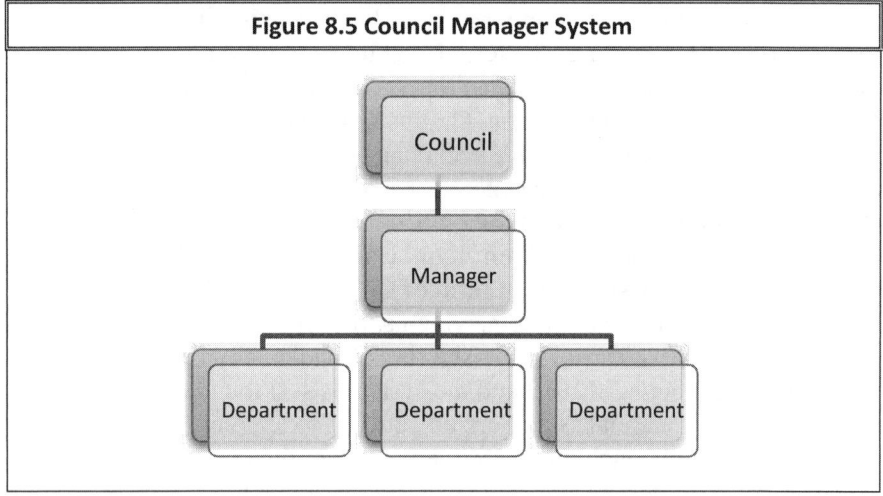

Figure 8.5 Council Manager System

Proponents of the council manager system contend that it provides for greatly improved coordination of administrative activities, frees the councillors from unnecessary detail, and allows them to concentrate on their primary role of policy making. While there is considerable potential for improved coordination in the organization of the manager system, its greatest weakness is the premise on which it is based – that it is possible to separate policy and administration in municipal government. To the contrary, as discussed earlier in this chapter, it is very difficult to identify in advance whether a particular issue is a routine administrative matter or has political implications. Even if this distinction could be made, it is not desirable to rigidly separate the two activities. In practice, much policy arises out of ongoing administration and the council's complete separation from the administrative activities of the municipality can leave it ill informed and "making policy in a vacuum."

While the system provides for a more efficient administrative structure, it does not provide for strong political leadership. Here, the distinction between efficiency and effectiveness, pointed out by Peter Drucker, comes into play: for Drucker, "efficiency is doing things right; effectiveness means doing the right things."[46] Indeed, because of the

---

[46] Peter Drucker, *The Essential Drucker:The Best of Sixty Years of Peter Drucker's Essential Writings on Management*, New York, Collins Business Essentials, 2008 and *Management, Tasks, Responsibilities, Practices*, Piscataway, N.J., Transaction Publishers, 1973.

focus on the manager, he or she is often a more conspicuous public figure than the members of council including the mayor. In addition to producing friction and jealousies that frequently result in the dismissal of managers, this situation also leads to managers becoming publicly identified with particular viewpoints and policies. If, as a result, they become embroiled in political controversies, their role as administrative leaders is impaired and they will likely be replaced. One book dryly observes that a manager's departure from work is often the result of illness or fatigue: "The council was sick and tired of him."[47]

The Manager System in Canada

As adapted to Canada, the council manager system has undergone certain modifications that minimize some of the problems noted above and, at the same time, minimize somewhat its strength and coordinating potential. Not surprisingly, these modifications reflect both the different governing principles of Canada and the United States, and the differing conditions that prevailed at the time of the system's introduction.

In most Canadian cities in the early 20th century the need for such an administrative reform seemed less pressing or necessary than in American cities. Corruption and the worst excesses of local party politics were much less evident in Canadian cities, and appointments based on merit were much more prevalent. Moreover, administrative coordination was being achieved informally by utilizing the potential of certain key municipal positions, notably that of clerk and treasurer. Especially where the positions were combined in people with leadership skills, their overall knowledge of the municipality's operations and the influence inherent in their responsibilities for preparing agendas, background reports, minutes, by-laws, budgets, and financial reports often made them unofficial chief administrative officers. Some municipalities confirmed the coordinating potential of these positions by formally designating the clerk or treasurer as something more – resulting in such positions as clerk-comptroller, clerk-treasurer-administrator, and clerk-coordinator.

Even where the council manager system was adopted, the Canadian version usually incorporated certain features designed to maintain the significance and prestige of the elected council.[48] First, the Canadian

---

[47] Wayne Anderson, Chester Newland, and Richard Stillman, *The Effective Local Government Manager*, Washington, International City Management Association, 1983, p. 68.

[48] See Dennis A. Young, "Canadian Local Government Development: Some Aspects of the Commissioner and City Manager Forms of Administration," in Lionel D. Feldman and Michael D. Goldrick (eds.), *Politics and Government of Urban Canada*, Toronto, Methuen, 1976, pp. 276-278.

council manager system does not attempt to enforce a complete separation between administration and policy. The council usually has a direct relationship with at least its main department heads as well as the manager. This is normally accomplished "by the attendance of the department heads at a meeting of a limited number of standing committees of council when matters affecting their particular areas of jurisdiction are under review."[49] Second, the responsibility of appointing staff is exercised by council, not the manager, although often council only acts after receiving recommendations from the manager.

With such modifications, Young feels that the Canadian version managed to avoid the fundamental problem of council's complete separation from administration. He explains that council in a Canadian manager system continues to concern itself with administration but "does so from a much broader viewpoint." The advice and recommendations of staff are coordinated by the manager, and "it is this opportunity and ability to place such recommendations within the broader perspective of the city's needs as a whole which represents his greatest value to the council in his capacity as policy advisor."[50]

The Commissioner System

This system involves the appointment of a few commissioners, who are charged with supervising and coordinating the various departments under their jurisdiction. They may also meet as a board of commissioners under the direction of a chief commissioner, to provide overall coordination of municipal operations.

The commissioner system is similar to a council manager system except in two important respects. Policy and administration are not as completely separated under the commissioner system, particularly when the mayor sometimes sits as a member of the board of commissioners – although the wisdom and effectiveness of this combination has been a matter of some debate. The second difference is that having more than one commissioner permits a degree of specialization not possible under the manager system where one person must supervise the entire administrative structure no matter how large and complex. Typically, one commissioner is responsible for hard services, another for soft services, and a third (if provided) for finance and planning, as illustrated in the following figure.

---

[49] *Ibid.*, p. 277.

[50] *Ibid.*, p. 278.

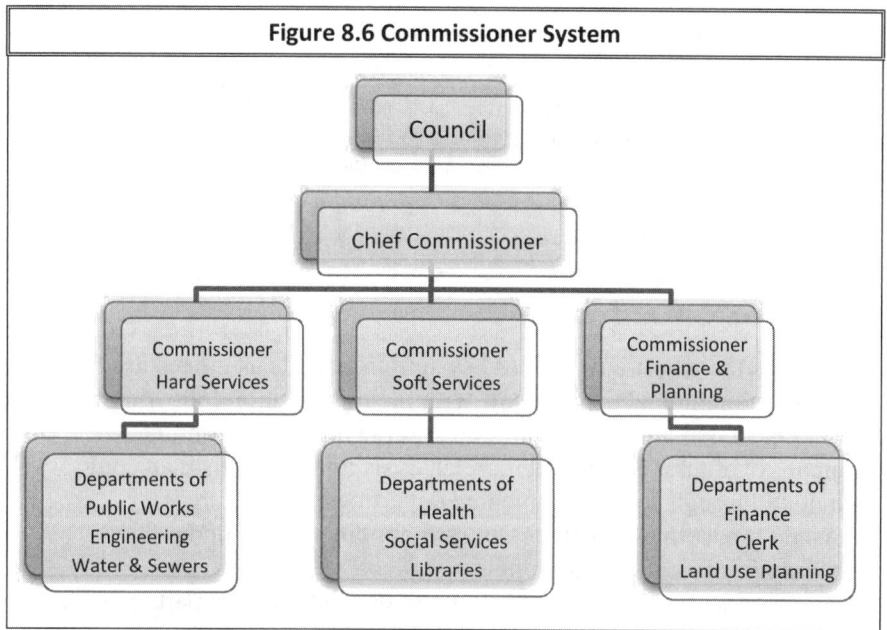

Figure 8.6 Commissioner System

The commissioner system was found mostly in Western Canada, but has gradually been replaced by manager or CAO positions over the past few decades. Some cities, such as Red Deer, Prince Albert, and Estevan, have appointed a single commissioner, in what amounts to a misnamed manager system.[51] Others, such as Edmonton and Winnipeg have abolished their commissioner systems (in 1984 and 1998 respectively) and replaced them with CAO systems. Ironically, as the commissioner system disappears in Western Canada, it is turning up in Ontario – albeit in modified form. The Ontario initiative involves the appointment of commissioners (also sometimes called directors) as senior staff in charge of groups of related departments. These senior staff may meet regularly with the CAO (and head of council) as a management committee, rather like the board of commissioners previously found in Western Canada.

This new model has appeared particularly in municipalities created as a result of Ontario's widespread amalgamations. It incorporates a distinction between internal, support services and services delivered to the public (or what used to be termed staff and line departments) and usually features four groups of related departments, along the lines of the table below. Note the similarity with the commissioner groupings.

---

[51] Plunkett, *Role of Chief Administrative Officer*, p. 53.

Table 8.1 New Coordinating Model in Ontario

Hard Services	Soft Services	Planning & Dev't	Corporate Services
Public works	Parks & recreation	Long range and strategic planning	Clerk
Transportation	Culture & heritage		Treasurer
Engineering	Libraries	Planning approvals	Legal services
Water/waste water	Seniors homes	Economic development	Human resources
Fleet & facilities	Emergency services		Computer services

Canadian CAOs Today

Plunkett sees the growth of the CAO system in Canada as the result of the growth in municipal departments with the urbanization following the Second World War and the recognition that the issues confronting municipal governments required more analysis and synthesis than could be provided through such a fragmented departmental structure. He explains that most municipalities can now appoint a CAO under the general municipal legislation of their province.

The success of any particular CAO will depend, in large part, on how well the individual is able to work with the diverse mix of department heads in the municipality. Some of these managers may have strongly opposed the introduction of a "senior coordinating officer," while others may have unsuccessfully sought the position themselves. In either case, they are unlikely to welcome a new CAO or to support the position. If standing committees have been retained, department heads may attempt to use these as a buffer or a means of blocking CAO initiatives.

Plunkett suggests that relationships between CAOs and department heads tend to fall into three categories:

i) *Passive*: CAOs who simply forward, without comment, reports received from department heads.
ii) *Active*: CAOs who include with departmental reports an accompanying memo setting out their comments.
iii) *Dominant*: CAOs who hold back reports from departments until these conform to their general policy viewpoint.[52]

The second category is probably the most common and certainly the most desirable. It ensures that both the technical knowledge of the specialist department head and the broader perspective of the CAO are sent forward, and it gives council the benefit of the most complete range of information on which to make a decision.

---

[52] *Ibid.*, pp. 28-29.

Another problematic relationship that can arise is between the CAO and the head of council, given the way the latter position is defined in provincial legislation. The potential for a clash exists if a mayor has a strong personality and a determination to provide "hands on" leadership consistent with his or her statutory authority to oversee subordinate officers and act as chief executive officer – as illustrated by the two examples that follow. While a CAO faced with such a conflict could appeal to council, which is ultimately responsible for the management of the municipality, such a course of action is by no means certain of success – especially since councillors are often inclined to view CAOs with suspicion and fear that they will become too dominant. Prudent CAOs make every effort to avoid an overt power struggle.

Box 8.4 Power Play in Ottawa[53]

A classic example of mayoral interference through excessive hands on involvement can be found in the actions of Larry O'Brien, the former businessman who was mayor of Ottawa in 2006-2010. O'Brien's multiple difficulties in settling into his new position demonstrate the fallacy of the popular notion that our problems can be solved by running municipal government more like a business. Claiming the need to get city spending under control, the mayor announced his intention to take over the approval of all hiring and contracts of over $10 000 until the end of 2007. Many members of council were less than enthused about this initiative (a sentiment shared by Ottawa's CAO), and the mayor accepted instead a modified process in which he and the city's CAO would jointly approve consulting contracts and any new hirings until the end of 2007.

Municipal expenditures are largely determined through an annual budget exercise carried out early in each year. There are well established procedures for the approval of individual expenditure items and for hirings within an approved staff complement. There is no doubt that a city of Ottawa's size and sophistication has such procedures in place. It also has a CAO who delegates authority to senior managers and holds them accountable for results – in the sort of managerial style that should appeal to a mayor with a business background. For the mayor to insert himself into city operations in this manner, essentially looking over the shoulder of the CAO, can only be viewed as a vote of non-confidence in the CAO and his senior staff that is likely to be harmful for morale.

O'Brien was defeated in the 2010 mayoral election.

---

[53] This issue was widely covered in the media at the time. The description that follows is partly based on Jake Rupert, "Mayor eases off City Hall power play," *Ottawa Citizen*, September 5, 2007.

> **Box 8.5 Gravy Train Derailed in Toronto?**[54]
>
> Toronto Mayor Rob Ford's core services review of 2011, undertaken to end the municipal "gravy train" in the city, is a further example of a mayor's heavy-handed intrusion into municipal operations. A series of reports by KPMG costing almost $1 million found few candidates for expenditure cuts that were not core municipal services – perhaps as little as $10-$15 million out of $1 billion for public works according to the City Manager. Under licensing, the report suggested that the city get out of the cat and dog licencing business and animal control. This lack of major gravy boats[55] to cut left the cutback oriented Toronto mayor musing about wage cuts as an alternative approach.

No matter how effectively a CAO system may work, it provides administrative, not political, leadership. Indeed, this system may even act as a constraint on political leadership and on the local political process in general. It is widely held, for example, that council-manager systems, "which emphasize the expert professionally trained manager as the effective executive," pay less attention to citizen demands and concerns than do mayor-council systems under which such demands are expressed more directly through the political process.[56]

New Business Models of Government

The new public management movement and values (discussed in the next chapter) influenced the introduction of business models of government that gained some popularity among larger municipalities over the past couple of decades.[57] Partly as a reaction against the silo perspective and turf protection mentality inherent in the traditional departmental structure organized on the basis of functional specialization, some municipalities restructured into core business areas, and then subdivided further into a number of business units for each area. These units were focused on the

---

[54] On the series of KPMG Reports see David Bider and Paul Moloney, "Little to trim in public works," *Toronto Star*, GT1, July 12, 2011. Subsequent reports are also available on Economic Development, Community Development and Recreation, Parks and Environment, Licensing and Standards, Government Management, Planning and Growth Management and Executive Committee, including arm's length agencies and such. On cutting labour costs see Elizabeth Church and Jill Maloney, "Ford vows to bring down city's labour costs," *The Globe and Mail*, July 16, 2011, p. A8.

[55] See Marcus Gee, "Municipal Spending: Mayor's financial numbers don't add up. With cuts looming, Rob Ford seems to prefer an axe to a scalpel," *The Globe and Mail*, July 16, 2011, p. A8.

[56] Harold Wolman and Michael Goldsmith, *Urban Politics and Policy: A Comparative Approach*, Oxford, Blackwell, 1992, p. 76.

[57] This discussion is partly based on C. Richard Tindal and Susan Nobes Tindal, *Guide to Good Municipal Governance*, St. Thomas, Municipal World Inc., 2007, pp. 28-29.

delivery of a particular municipal service, such as fleet maintenance, and were set up as separate cost/profit centres.

The rationale was that by bringing all activities associated with the delivery of a particular service into a single business unit, it would be easier for a municipality to determine the total cost of providing the service in question and to identify the total revenues (if any) arising from provision of the service. Isolating this financial information was seen as a necessary first step in promoting efforts to improve the cost revenue ratio and to move municipal operations closer to break even. The delineation of separate business units was also seen as an effective method of pinpointing responsibilities and heightening accountability. Performance contracts that established service standards to be met were also designed to enforce accountability. Alternative service delivery arrangements might be pursued with respect to municipal operations that failed to "measure up." Clearly, the new model was as much about different operating philosophies as it was about structure.

One of the pioneers of the business model for municipal government was the City of Waterloo (Ontario) and, as discussed in the next chapter, its experiences demonstrate the distinctive operating values underlying this model and the difficulty of reconciling these with other municipal values and objectives. Another example from Ontario is the amalgamated municipality of Chatham-Kent, which initially embraced a business model with the following features:[58]

> The Strategic Core reports to Council and is responsible for corporate and strategic planning, policy development, the business planning and budget process, and arranging the "contracts" or business plans with internal and external service providers that will directly provide services. The Service Centres are the "one-stop" contact points for residents and other clients requiring service from the municipality. The Service Delivery function will be carried out by Business Units within the administration or external contractors that will be responsible to deliver services at the level of service and level of cost agreed to by Council. The Strategic Core will monitor their performance. The Support Business Units will provide centralized services to all the other business units and provide input to policy and strategy development within the Strategic Core.

---

[58] Brian V. Bourns, KPMG Management Consultants, *Organizational Design, Municipality of Chatham-Kent*, November 4, 1997, p. 6, as quoted in Thomas R. Hollick and David Siegel, *Evolution, Revolution, Amalgamation: Restructuring in Three Ontario Municipalities*, Local Government Case Studies No. 10, London, University of Western Ontario, 2001, p. 219.

The outburst of business jargon that accompanied these reforms appears to have lost its momentum. Chatham-Kent reorganized in 2003, into four consolidated departments, although there are still 50 some operating divisions or operating units within this departmental framework, each responsible for a business plan. So the business philosophy continues but within a more traditional (understandable) structure. Windsor is another example of a municipality that reverted to departmental nomenclature after some years with business units.

This seems a sensible response and we would recommend that municipalities wishing to embrace this particular approach should concentrate more on these underlying changes in process and operating philosophy and be less preoccupied with couching everything in business terminology, no matter how fashionable that may have become with some provincial governments. It is permissible to go on calling departments "departments," even after they are regrouped into more effective combinations. The new public information centre can be called just that; it doesn't have to be known as one stop shopping or one window shopping. Employees can be challenged to strive for continuous improvement in performance (and rewarded accordingly), without there being a business plan, just as standards can be set, resources allocated, and results measured and monitored. What is actually being done is far more important than what it is called, especially when so much transplanted business terminology brings more confusion than enlightenment.

Effectiveness of the Modified Machinery

While generalizations are difficult, it is probably fair to say that reforms at the administrative level have been more successful than those at the political level. In particular, the establishment of a chief administrative officer system has the potential to effect improved coordination and integration of municipal programs and activities. This system may help to develop an expanded research and analytical capability and the provision of more comprehensive policy advice and recommendations to council, but much depends on whether complementary changes are introduced in the management and decision making process of the municipality.[59] Designating a CAO also provides a specific focus of accountability and responsibility for the administrative performance of the municipality.

---

[59] These changes relate to such matters as strategic and long term financial planning, and a top down, priority driven budget exercise. These process changes are at least as important as structural changes in bringing about improvements in municipal operations.

Perhaps surprisingly, reforms at the political level have largely ignored the strengthening of the position of head of council. Instead, the focus has been on the establishment of various forms of executive committee system, with quite limited success. Most of these committees have lacked political cohesion and have not had any means, except persuasion, to ensure that their initiatives receive the necessary support of council. The effectiveness of these committees has been dependent upon their method of selection and whether or not they are reinforced in their position and activities by the existence of organized political parties on council. In most cases, they are not, and the committees have lacked any power base as a result. On the other hand, bodies such as Ontario's board of control and the executive committees in Quebec backed by a block of party votes have been regarded as too strong and dominant. Striking a balance in these matters has been a challenge.

Are Political Parties the Answer?

Those seeking a strong executive within municipal government often call for the introduction of organized political parties, a topic of great controversy. What is it about parties that would create a strong executive and why are parties opposed so strongly?

The Case for Parties

Basically, parties perform the same task locally as they do at the senior levels; they organize the council into a governing group and an opposition group or groups. The creation of a governing party is significant because it provides the basis for concerted action. If heads of council are chosen by council, they would presumably be leading members of the majority party or majority group on council, and thus would have a power base to support their leadership. If they in turn choose their executive committee from the ruling group, then the committee has cohesiveness because of the common party affiliation and is somewhat analogous to a federal or provincial cabinet.

Political parties provide the potential for not only strong leadership but also more effective scrutiny of activities through an organized opposition or alternative governing group. As a result there is a group within council pledged to scrutinize and criticize municipal activities, an important role which is normally left to everybody – and nobody. With so many local politicians in Canada serving as part-timers, the balance in political-bureaucratic relations may tend toward the administrative side. The mayor and executive committee members under a local party system need to retain the confidence of council since they owe their positions to council, not the electorate.

In addition, with political parties the operations of council become more understandable and accountable to the public. Since councillors run as a group on the basis of specific programs, there is a greater likelihood that citizens will vote on the basis of substantive issues and policies instead of on the usual basis of selection among personalities. It is also argued that an election campaign organized around opposing parties and alternative approaches generates greater public interest and a higher voting turnout. In part this is because parties can be expected to play their usual roles of aggregating interests, mobilizing public support, and trying to draw more citizens into the political arena. More importantly, at the end of a term the public can attach responsibility for performance to the governing party since this group had the means to effect change. It is not possible for a ruling party to evade responsibility for action or inaction as individual councillors can and do.

How well things work will depend, of course, on the nature of the political parties involved. Proponents of party politics in local government assume a balanced situation with two or more parties that would alternate in power. If one party dominates council for a lengthy period, there is likely to be insensitivity to public opinion and other abuses, traits exhibited by the provincial and federal governments in the same situation. Another issue is whether there would be local parties, focused on local issues, or just branches of provincial or national parties. In the latter case, the concern is that local issues would be neglected and that local election results might reflect the popularity or unpopularity of "parent" parties. On the other hand, purely local parties are often temporary coalitions of local interests that display little cohesion or concerted action once elected. They may be more properly described as factions that reappear under a variety of names at election time and attempt to ensure the election of certain types of candidates, but do not exercise disciplined party voting within council.[60] Such factions clearly don't provide the basis for a strong governing group or opposition. Long established local parties do exist in settings such as Vancouver or Burnaby in British Columbia or Montreal in Quebec. These too may morph but have demonstrated as much stability as senior counterparts.

---

[60] Harold Kaplan, "Electoral Politics in the Metro Area," in Jack K. Masson and James Anderson (eds.), *Emerging Party Politics in Urban Canada*, Toronto, McClelland & Stewart, 1972, p. 147.

The Case Against Parties

Critics of political parties at the local level question the validity of a number of their alleged advantages.[61] For example, evidence from the senior levels of government hardly supports the claim that parties provide clear platforms and alternatives for the voter, or stick to their platforms after elected! Nor is it apparent that parties at the senior levels provide strong leadership – at least according to the complaints often heard from both those within the system and from the public. Accountability at the municipal level arises from the small scale of operations and ready accessibility of the decision makers (in most municipalities) and does not need parties to ensure it. In fact, it can be argued that parties make councillors less accountable to the voters because they are expected to vote with their party on issues. As for the likelihood of increased voter turnout with parties, how beneficial this would be depends on the reason for the turnout. If municipal electors had gone to the polls in record numbers in elections in the early 1990s to defeat Conservative candidates because they disliked Brian Mulroney and the GST he introduced, this would hardly be striking a blow for local democracy.[62]

There are, of course, a number of other arguments against the introduction of organized political parties at the local level. Chief among these is the assertion that parties introduce division where none exists or should exist. "There is no political way to build a road," claim proponents of this viewpoint which reflects the lingering notion that local government activities are administrative, not political, in nature. Yet if the actual construction of a road is a matter of engineering, not politics, the decision on where to locate a particular road is certainly political. The decision on whether the traffic problem in question should be solved through building a road or providing an alternative form of public transit is also clearly political. The decision on whether the scarce financial resources of the municipality should be used on transportation or some other pressing need is again political. Indeed, if the municipal council is concerned with establishing priorities in relation to conflicting public needs and demands, its role must be political.

Political decisions are an essential element of municipal operations, but they are not carried into the local arena by parties. Parties, however, may help to make the unavoidable political decisions more systematic and accountable to the public. At the same time, it must be

---

[61] See, for example, David Siegel, "City Hall Doesn't Need Parties," *Policy Options*, June 1987, pp. 26-27, on which the following points are based.

[62] *Ibid.*, p. 27.

acknowledged that parties tend to exaggerate differences and also to criticize excessively for purely partisan purposes. These traits have often been evident in the actions of the parties operating at the senior levels of government.

Another major objection to parties is the feeling that they bring corruption and unsavoury practices into local government. This feeling was undoubtedly strongly influenced by the excesses of party politics and the spoils system in the United States in the period leading up to the turn of the century reform era of the late 1800s/early 1900s. Nor were such practices entirely absent from Canadian local government, as illustrated by discussions in Chapter 2. However, it should be remembered that it is people who are potentially corruptible, not that specialized subgroup known as politicians. If there are opportunities for dishonesty and abuse, some people may succumb to the temptation, but they will presumably do so whether they are individual councillors or members of an organized political party.

Ultimately, it doesn't really matter how soundly based are the arguments for or against political parties in municipal government. In practice, there is a strong public antipathy towards any such move. As Chapter 10 illustrates, efforts by the national parties to contest local elections have usually been rebuffed. Yet voters have often elected coalitions of like minded candidates masquerading as non-parties and committed to the defeat of organized parties.

Concluding Comments

The various governing models used by municipalities over the years, and the governing philosophies underlying them have, for the most part, reflected a concern for efficiency and coordination in the delivery of services to the relative neglect of the representative and political aspects that are (or should be) equally a concern of municipal government. Because of the limited success of efforts to create effective executive committees, the most prevalent reform of coordinating machinery has been the chief administrative officer system. No matter how well this system works, however, it does nothing to strengthen political leadership and, to the contrary, may even detract from this objective by creating a bureaucratic system and by undermining the power and public status of the council.

Even more worrying are the developments in recent years that attempt to recast municipalities as businesses (or at least combinations of business units) and local citizens as consumers or clients. As one analysis describes the situation, "[u]nder various neo-liberal regimes of central government, local government structures and institutions in the global city have been radically transformed from democratic and representative into increasingly professionalized, marketized, entrepreneurial and managerial forms."[63] In the process, the importance of municipal government appears to have declined, with it now being increasingly portrayed as but one of many local service providers, public and private. The local citizen has been recast as a consumer of these services, diminishing both the importance of the citizenry and of local democracy. In light of these developments, the subject of Chapter 10 – the methods by which citizens participate in municipal government – takes on added importance.

---

[63] Evelyn S. Ruppert, "Who governs the global city,?" in Engin Isin (ed.), *Democracy, Citizenship and the Global City*, London, Routledge, 2000, p. 275.

Chapter 9
Municipal Governing Processes and Values

...governance is not about corporate structures or organizational models – or, at least, it is also about many other important aspects....Ultimately, good governance is an attitude or approach to governing based on a shared vision, common values, open processes, networking and collaboration, and respect for those within the municipal government and those they serve.[1]

Introduction

The governing of the municipality involves more than the internal governing structures described in the preceding chapter and the councillors and staff who comprise them. It also involves more than the structural changes inherent in the various restructuring and amalgamation initiatives that were pursued by several provincial governments in recent decades, as discussed in Chapters 4 and 5. A number of developments have shifted the focus to the broader notion of governance, which extends beyond the formal governing machinery to the other public, private, and voluntary bodies that are increasingly involved in the provision of services. While the term government refers to formal structures, governance is concerned with processes, with the way governing bodies assemble and deploy resources in pursuit of public goals. Governance as a framework moves beyond the structure of government "to a focus on how things are actually done, groups represented, priorities set and made, resources allocated, and services delivered and paid for."[2] The processes that are followed are a reflection of the prevailing values, both within the municipal organization and its surrounding community.

---

[1] C. Richard Tindal and Susan Nobes Tindal, *Guide to Good Municipal Governance*, St. Thomas, Municipal World Inc., 2007, p. 123.

[2] Laura A. Reese, "Recalibrating, Rescaling, Restructuring, Reinventing: Realistic Regoverning?," paper presented at the symposium on *A Global Look at Urban and Regional Governance*, Emory University, Atlanta, January 2007, p. 10.

The Importance of Values

It is increasingly recognized that the way things are actually done is less a reflection of the formal municipal structures in place than it is of the prevailing organizational culture and the values embraced by the local community. Values are "enduring beliefs that influence the choices made by individuals, groups or organizations from among available means and ends."[3] Organizational values are not always spelled out in any formal way. Community values, often referred to as the local political culture, are even less likely to be articulated. Measuring the existence and nature of a local culture is a far from precise exercise, but a social or ideological approach would focus on individual values and beliefs including political party preferences, liberal or conservative leanings, lifestyle choices, tolerance, and religious values.[4] Values are arguably the most important factor in determining how (and how well) a municipality operates – as will be evident from the discussion that follows.

Community Values

Even if they are not defined and articulated, organizational and community values are deeply rooted and continue to exert influence whatever structural changes may occur. Municipalities in the Ottawa area underwent a very dramatic restructuring just over a decade ago, with the creation of a unified city, a streamlined organization of municipal departments designed to be more businesslike in operation, and some decentralization of service delivery through former municipal offices in the area. According to a fairly recent study, the operations of the new city are strongly influenced by the prevailing local culture, and especially by the fact that this culture varied significantly among the municipalities that were merged to form the new city.[5] In addition to the usual urban

---

[3] Kenneth Kernaghan and David Siegel, *Public Administration in Canada*, 4th Edition, Toronto, Nelson/Thomson Publishing, 1999, p. 325.

[4] Reese, *Recalibrating, Rescaling*, pp. 24-25.

[5] Laura A. Reese and Davia S. Cox, "Local Culture and governmental change: The endurance of culture in the face of structural change," *Canadian Public Administration*, Summer 2007, pp. 245-271. See also Caroline Andrew, "Evaluating Municipal Reform in Ottawa-Gatineau: Building for a More Metropolitan Future" in Eran Razin and Patrick Smith (eds.), *Metropolitan Governing: Canadian Cases, Comparative Lessons*, Jerusalem, Magnes Press, Hebrew University of Jerusalem, 2006, pp. 75-94.

and rural differences, there were different and distinct cultures in several of the suburban municipalities, notably Kanata, Nepean, and Gloucester. "It appears that several distinct cultures remain present in the new city, apparently enduring more than five years after amalgamation."[6] These continuing differences are reflected in public perceptions of how and how well the amalgamation has worked.

Not only does the local political culture endure through structural changes and affect their impact and significance, but also it is important in its own right in defining a local community. Instead of focusing so much on changes in structure and governing machinery – which tend to have a minor and fleeting impact – those seeking to improve local communities might be better served by devoting more attention to the local culture, and strengthening it where appropriate. For example, those who subscribe to the Richard Florida thesis (discussed in Chapter 3 and Chapter 7) that communities need to be tolerant of diversity if they are to attract the talented "creative" workers needed in today's knowledge based economy will want to look at the evidence of tolerance in their own communities and how it can be encouraged and increased as necessary.[7]

To take another example, those of the view that municipalities need to join with various organizations in civil society to gain the capacity to address today's challenges should look at the extent to which civic, participatory values are evident in the community (and reinforced by the municipality). It is now widely appreciated that the broader processes of interaction and cooperation inherent in governance are much more likely to work effectively in communities blessed with extensive social capital. This term refers to "those stocks of social trust, norms and networks that people can draw upon to solve common problems. Networks of civic engagement, such as neighbourhood associations, sports clubs, and cooperatives, are an essential form of social capital, and the denser these networks, the more likely that members of a community will cooperate for mutual benefit."[8]

Social capital is enriched when people share common values and norms of behaviour and feel that they can trust their neighbours and the organizations in their community. This trust supports the notion of

---

[6] Reese and Cox, *Local Culture and Governmental Change*, pp. 264-265.

[7] Reese, *Recalibrating, Rescaling,* p. 25.

[8] Carmen Sirianni and Lewis Friedland, "Social Capital," in *Civic Dictionary*, Civic Practices Network, at www.cpn.org/tools/dictionary/capital.html, as quoted in Christa Freiler, *Why Strong Neighbourhoods Matter*, prepared for the Strong Neighbourhoods Task Force, Toronto, November 4, 2004, p. 11.

reciprocity, that efforts extended now on behalf of others will be returned (reciprocated) at some point in the future – and this belief facilitates cooperation for mutual benefit. The most vivid and intriguing definition of reciprocity was provided by that famous political scientist Yogi Berra, who warned: "If you don't go to somebody's funeral, they won't come to yours."[9]

According to Putnam, the decline in voting turnout in the United States is symptomatic of an underlying decline in public participation in everyday forms of community life. With more and more Americans "bowling alone," the title of his best selling examination of this topic, the social capital necessary for healthy communities has been severely eroded. As he describes the situation:[10]

> Television, two-career families, suburban sprawl, generational changes in values – these and other changes in American society have meant that fewer and fewer of us find that the League of Women Voters, or the United Way, or the Shriners, or the monthly bridge club, or even a Sunday picnic with friends fits the way we have come to live.

While his analysis focused on the United States, Canadian society is subject to the same pressures and demands and there is no less need for us to be mindful of social capital and dedicated to its enrichment. If the findings of a Statistics Canada survey in 2003 (discussed in Chapter 3) are any indication,[11] we appear to measure up reasonably well with respect to social capital, but have little cause for complacency. That survey found that the responses of immigrants who came to Canada since 1990 were not as positive as those who had come earlier and recent research by Putnam has raised some troubling questions about the presumed benefits of ethnic diversity in relation to social capital. According to his findings, residents of ethnically diverse communities tended to withdraw from collective life, to distrust their neighbours (no matter what colour their skin), to expect the worst from their community and its leaders, to volunteer less and give less to charity, to vote less, and to have less faith that they can actually make a difference. In Putnam's memorable phrasing, people living in ethnically diverse settings "appear

---

[9] Quoted in Robert D. Putnam, *Bowling Alone*, New York, Simon & Schuster, 2000, p. 20.

[10] *Ibid.*, p. 367.

[11] Statistics Canada, *2003 General Social Survey on Social Engagement, cycle 17: an overview of findings*, Ottawa, July 2004, accessed August 12, 2007 from www.statcan.gc.ca.

to 'hunker down' – that is, to pull in like a turtle."[12] These findings only serve to reinforce the need for governments, at all levels, to devote more attention and resources to what happens to immigrants *after* they arrive in this country and settle in particular local communities. As noted elsewhere in this volume, immigration is largely a federal responsibility; even though immigrant settlement is most strongly felt in Canada's major urban centres.[13]

Part of the answer is for municipalities to engage their citizens as fully as possible, a subject examined in the next chapter. Meaningful citizen engagement can help to build trust and strengthen relationships. If it is broadly based and inclusive, this engagement can also help to improve social cohesion. The benefits are quite significant. By helping to improve civic trust, in which "urban communities become places where people are able to influence how they are governed, to demonstrate their care for others through voluntary and community action, to respect and value differences ... and to discover their commonalities,"[14] community engagement has been found to produce positive effects in the areas of crime reduction, health, education, employment, and housing. Clearly, values and norms are real, important, and significant.

Organizational Values

Organizations benefit greatly from the existence of shared values, with "shared" being the key word. This was certainly the finding of Peters and

---

[12] Robert D. Putnam, "*E Pluribus Unum:* Diversity and Community in the Twenty-first Century, The 2006 Johan Skytte Prize Lecture," *Scandanavian Political Studies* 30 (2), 2007, p. 149.

[13] On this see Strategic Knowledge Cluster Workshop on "Immigration and Integration Policies in a System of Multi-Level Governance: A Canadian-European Comparison from an Urban Perspective," University of Victoria, B.C., March, 2009: including papers by Warren Magnusson, Serena Kataoka, and Mark Willson (University of Victoria), "Colonial Legacies: Immigrant Settlement in B.C.;" Caroline Andrew (University of Ottawa), "The Municipal Government Role in Immigrant Settlement in Canada: Governance and/or Government;" and Kristin Good (Dalhousie University), "Municipalities and Multiculturalism: Explaining Variation in Responsiveness to Immigrants and Ethno-Cultural Minorities in Vancouver and Toronto." These papers are all part of the MCRI research project on Multilevel Governance and Public Policy in Canadian Municipalities. See www.ppm-ppm.ca.

[14] Peter Clutterbuck, *Cross-Canada community soundings on building inclusive communities*, Toronto, Laidlaw Foundation, 2003, p. 44, as quoted in Glynis Maxwell, *Respect All Voices: Neighbourhood Councils as a Tool for Building Social Inclusion*, February 2007, p. 10.

Waterman when they went in search of excellence in the private sector.[15] It was also recognized by the public sector and by the mid-1980s "many public organizations at all levels of government had developed value statements as a partial basis for effective management."[16]

By that time, views were changing markedly about how government should operate and what its values should be. Traditionally, the most important values in government were neutrality, accountability, efficiency, effectiveness, responsiveness, representativeness, integrity, and – more recently – equity or fairness.[17] But there were growing criticisms of government at all levels because of mounting deficit and debt problems by the 1980s and growing global pressures to reduce regulations and tax levels. According to these "New Public Management" critics:[18]

- Governments had become too large and intrusive, largely because of the machinations of self serving bureaucrats and politicians (a view rooted in public choice theory and popularized by the *Yes, Minister* television series);
- Governments, as monopolies, were inefficient in delivering services and not sufficiently sensitive to the wishes of those receiving the services; and
- Internal controls to prevent abuses had become so widespread that they blurred accountability while stifling initiative. In making sure that public servants couldn't do anything bad, these controls also kept them from being able to do anything good.

New Public Management Values

A new ideology, increasingly referred to as neoliberalism, has come to the fore over the past thirty-plus years with its call for a much reduced role for government and a corresponding increase in activity by the private sector. French sociologist Michel Crozier has referred to the result as "The Modest State."[19] Further impetus for new approaches

---

[15] Thomas J. Peters and Robert H. Waterman Jr., *In Search of Excellence*, New York, Warner Books, 1982, p. 281.

[16] Mohamed Chirah and Arthur Daniels (eds.), *New Public Management and Public Administration in Canada*, Toronto, Institute of Public Administration of Canada, 1997, p. 52.

[17] Kernaghan and Siegel, *Public Administration in Canada*, p. 326.

[18] Chirah and Daniels, *New Public Management in Canada*, pp. 15-18.

[19] Michel Crozier, *L'Etat modern, L'Etat modeste*, Paris, Fayard, 1987.

came from a number of bestselling and much hyped books[20] that preached the need to reinvent government and to banish bureaucracy. The various new approaches being advocated from these and other sources became grouped together into what has become known as the new public management (NPM), the key features of which are summarized below.

Box 9.1 Features of the New Public Management

- Distinguishing more clearly between the policy and service delivery roles of government, along the lines of the steering versus rowing distinction made popular in the previously cited *Reinventing Government*.
- Increasing the autonomy of public managers so that they can operate with more of the freedom and flexibility associated with private sector operations. This was to be accomplished mainly by shifting service delivery responsibilities from the traditional departmental structure to separate operating agencies.
- Establishing performance standards and an increased customer focus as the primary method of ensuring accountability.
- Measuring and rewarding organizations and individuals on the basis of how well they meet standards and targets.
- Using performance contracts to reinforce accountability and to introduce a competitive atmosphere in which public servants must continually measure up to retain and renew contracts.
- Considering alternative service delivery options – including the not-for-profit and private sectors – to offer services traditionally provided directly by government.

NPM at the Local Level

A number of the features of the NPM have been quite prominent at the local level in Canada for some time, in some cases even before they were combined under this terminology.

Partnerships and Joint Ventures

One manifestation has been an increase in cooperation and coproduction between municipalities and various local bodies. Many community associations, for example, have become increasingly involved in "running sports, education and fitness programs; undertaking community environmental and aesthetic activities (parks maintenance, recycling);

---

[20] Leading examples of this genre are David Osborne and Ted Gaebler, *Reinventing Government*, New York, Penguin Books, 1993 and David Osborne and Peter Plastrik, *Banishing Bureaucracy*, New York, Penguin Books, 1998.

organizing social events (block parties and picnics); assisting in safety and security programs (block parents); and providing, independently or by contract with the municipality, charity, goodwill, and social services."[21] The voluntary sector, which used to play a very substantial role in the delivery of public services before the rise of the welfare state, is again being called upon to step up and take on more responsibility as governments retrench. The business sector has become more directly involved in the provision of some types of municipal services because of the attention now being directed to joint ventures and partnerships.

This collaborative approach was popularized by Osborne and Gaebler as part of the distinction between steering and rowing.[22] In their view, members of council should leave the rowing or service delivery to others, while concentrating on steering (setting direction) for the municipality. Moreover, a steering decision that certain services should be provided to address community needs did not necessarily mean the production of these services by the municipality. Part of steering involves assembling resources wherever they can be found in support of the municipality's objectives. Municipalities were encouraged to consider alternative service delivery (ASD) options, including:[23]

- purchasing a service from another municipality (or selling a service to them);
- joining with other municipalities for joint provision of a service;
- contracting with a private or nonprofit company for a service;
- offloading at least a portion of service delivery to voluntary or community organizations (as in the examples above); and
- privatizing the service by dropping it as a municipal responsibility and leaving its provision to the private sector.

Joint ventures with other local governing bodies have become increasingly common, including partnerships with local boards for bulk purchasing. Partners in such ventures sometimes include area hospitals and educational institutions. Some joint purchasing consortia gradually extend their activities to include such matters as education and training and combined contract negotiation for auditing and banking services.[24]

---

[21] Katherine A. Graham, Susan D. Phillips, and Allan M. Maslove, *Urban Governance in Canada*, Toronto, Harcourt Brace & Company, 1998, p. 128.

[22] Osborne and Gaebler, *Reinventing Government*, p. 217.

[23] The summary of options is based on Tindal and Tindal, *Municipal Good Governance Guide*, pp. 61-62.

[24] *Ibid.*, p. 64.

Unlike these public partnerships, public private partnerships (also referred to as PPP or P3) remain quite controversial. This is less the case where such partnerships are pursued in the delivery of day to day services – as in the use of private taxis to supplement municipal bus service in off peak hours or along low service routes. But P3s have often been promoted for capital projects, where they have been defined as "any situation where the costs, risks, and rewards of creating, refurbishing or expanding infrastructure are shared by government and the private sector."[25] Proponents of P3s argue that they are the best way to address the large backlog in infrastructure investment. Private companies may have expertise and experience lacking in municipal staff and because of specialization they usually have much more experience managing large capital projects. Private financing of such a project is also appealing to those municipalities reluctant to increase their long term debt.

But opinions are divided on whether P3s for capital purposes are really any cheaper. The experience of several provinces that pursued public private partnering for the construction of schools and hospitals has been one of higher costs and, in some cases, inferior construction standards.[26] A recent report prepared at the request of the Federation of Canadian Municipalities concludes that examples of municipal P3s such as the water system in Hamilton (Ontario) or the subway system in London (England) "do not show any clear benefits associated with P3s, either in terms of price or quality of service."[27]

Municipalities large enough to be engaged in financing major capital projects can usually borrow money at least as cheaply as private companies and the total cost of municipal operations does not have to include the profit margin required by private operations. Since private companies can't tax to generate the revenues that they need, it is obvious that a shift to privately owned capital facilities will be accompanied by a marked increase in user fees to finance such ventures. This raises the question of whether this arrangement is at least partly designed to allow governments to avoid the appearance of raising taxes on a tax weary

---

[25] Ministry of Municipal Affairs and Housing, *Study of Innovative Financing Approaches for Ontario Municipalities* (Price Waterhouse, Final Report), March 31, 1993.

[26] The Canadian Centre for Policy Alternatives has published a number of reports on this subject, including *Public-Private Partnerships, the True Cost of P3s*, Issue No. 2/P3s, April 2003 and *Value for Money? Cautionary Lessons About P3s from British Columbia*, June 2006. These reports are available at www.policyalternatives.ca.

[27] Pierre J. Hamel, *Public-Private Partnerships (P3s) and Municipalities: Beyond Principles*, *a Brief Overview of Practices*, Montreal, Urbanisation, Culture et Société, 2007, p. 8.

public, and whether user fees are ultimately the fairest way to pay for the operation of facilities from which a broader segment of the public than those paying the fees will benefit.[28]

In addition, it must be recognized that private companies operate with a degree of confidentiality and secrecy not easily reconciled with the openness and public accountability values (and, often, legal requirements) associated with municipal operations. Municipalities often have little or no experience in managing relationships with a private company and need to pay more attention to the handling of contracts with private service providers.[29] Anyone concerned about the ability of municipalities to monitor private operations sufficiently to protect the public interest can hardly be reassured by the experience of cities such as Toronto and Waterloo when they entered into finance contracts with a company known as MFP Financial Services (discussed later in this chapter). Judicial inquiries into the experiences of these cities underline the reality that there are major differences between public and private sector assumptions, values, and ethics, and that municipalities need to be more sensitive to these differences when dealing with the private sector.[30] To assist local governments with limited experience here, some municipal affairs ministries, as in British Columbia, developed best practice models/publications for assisting local learning on such.[31]

Measurement and Competition

Much of the NPM emphasis at the local level has been reflected in new practices and procedures that emphasize measurement, comparison, competition, and entrepreneurship. Municipalities make increasing use of such private sector concepts as performance measurement, benchmarking, and the search for best practices, as summarized below.

---

[28] Heather R. Douglas, "The Capital Investment Plan Act, 1993 and the Community Economic Development Act, 1993: New Opportunities for Public and Private Sector Partners in Capital Project Financing," in *Structuring and Financing Public-Private Partnerships*, Toronto, Insight Press, 1993, p. 103.

[29] Katherine Barrett and Richard Greene, "Short on Oversight," *Governing*, May 2006, www.governing.com.

[30] George Rust-D'Eye, "P3 Deals: Dangers of Compromise of Interest," *Municipal World*, January 2004, p. 23.

[31] See B.C. Ministry of Municipal Affairs, *Public Private Partnership: A Guide For Local Government*, Victoria, B.C., May 1999, available at www.cscd.gov.bc.ca/lgd/policy_research/library/public_private_partnerships.pdf.

Box 9.2 Measuring Municipalities

Performance Measurement	The primary measures that are receiving attention in government operations are the three Es – economy, efficiency, and effectiveness, with the last two being the main focus at the local level. *Economy* involves obtaining goods and services at the best cost. *Efficiency* is obtaining the best relationship between the input of resources and the output of goods or services. *Effectiveness* measures the quality of the goods being provided and the impact on the population being served.
Benchmarking	Pinpointing the superior performances, wherever found in public or private organizations, that establish the standard by which delivery of a particular good or service should be judged.
Best Practices	Determining the particular approaches and techniques used by the benchmarked organization, so that these can be applied to improve one's own operations.

There is no question that the use of such measures and practices can be beneficial in some respects. Having solid data on the cost of providing defined levels of output allows a municipality to build budgets on a realistic foundation. Budgets built in this manner provide an improved insight into the real causes of any overspending or underspending that may occur. They also indicate the results that are expected from the expenditures that are made. Performance measures can be used internally to set improved targets, year by year. These measures can provide a better basis for the annual budget discussions between councillors and staff, allowing council to exercise true policy control by establishing what services will be provided at what level, while leaving staff more freedom to use their experience and expertise – provided that they meet the standards specified within the budget allocation. Performance measures can also be used as the basis for new incentive and reward systems that can unleash creativity and improved productivity in municipal employees. If the costs of providing defined levels of output have been established, then employees who can meet (or exceed) the defined level for less money than budgeted can receive some portion of the resulting savings – in what is essentially a pay for performance scheme of the sort long found in the private sector.

The increasingly competitive atmosphere that develops from the use and comparison of performance measures is supposed to stimulate increased productivity in municipal operations. There is no doubt that competition can be very positive, if properly managed. Whether we are talking about the public or private sector, "when there's competition, you get better results, more cost-consciousness, and superior service delivery."[32] This reality is demonstrated by an interesting study of the solid waste experiences of two municipalities in the Greater Vancouver area.[33] One had periodic competition because of a contract with a private firm and the other had a permanent public monopoly under which city crews collected all solid waste. During the study period of the 1980s, crew productivity increased sharply for *both* municipalities. The key factor in explaining this pattern was the regional competitive pressure on solid waste producers in the Greater Vancouver area. The study authors explained that public producers were often exposed to unsolicited bids and to cost comparisons among municipalities in the region, though this is not the only explanation of high level performance in the delivery of public services by the public sector.

A well documented example of the positive impact of competition is that of Phoenix in the 1980s,[34] where the public works department lost out on several bids for garbage collection activities in various areas of the city, only to win a contract in its sixth year of competition. Morale soared as a result of this breakthrough. Management held a dinner for all staff and handed out hats with the city logo and the words "Sanitation #1." Employees knew that they had won the contract because they were the best and had demonstrated that fact in open competition. After 10 years, the department had won back contracts for garbage collection in all areas of the city. But employees can never rest on their laurels, because there are always contracts coming up for renewal. They must continue to demonstrate that they are the best.

While this experience was positive and motivating, competitive pressures can also be threatening to employees and harmful for morale – particularly if there is any indication that a reduction in staff or drops in pay will follow any increase in productivity. Price argues that the new public management is a direct threat to the municipal work force and to the power and resources of municipal departments. He points to the instability and insecurity in municipal employment with the constant competition and the threat of contracting out and downsizing.[35] If

---

[32] Auditor James Flanagan, as quoted in Osborne and Gaebler, *Reinventing Government*, p. 79.

[33] James McDavid and Gregory Schick, "Privatization versus union-management cooperation: the effects of competition on service efficiency in municipalities," *Canadian Public Administration*, Fall 1987, pp. 472-488.

[34] The description of Phoenix is based on Osborne and Gaebler, *Reinventing Government*, pp. 76-78.

[35] T. Price, "Council-Administration Relations in City Government," in James Lightbody (ed.), *Canadian Metropolitics*, Toronto, Copp Clark Ltd., 1995, p. 208.

measurement and competition are to provide a stimulus to increased productivity, there needs to be a climate of trust and confidence between council and staff, one that is often missing.

Rather than getting bogged down in what is often an increasingly ideological debate about the relative merits of public versus private provision, some municipalities have opted for an intermediate approach that is known as managed competition, which first came to prominence in Indianapolis in the 1990s. When a pro privatization mayor was elected in that city – over the strong opposition of a very concerned union movement – the first few months of the new administration were understandably strained.[36] However, the two sides gradually reached agreement on a new approach of managed competition instead of privatization, under which public sector employees and their managers compete with private firms for the right to provide a given service. To be competitive in this new operating environment, the union developed broader job descriptions that made staff more flexible and cross trained and upgraded employees, which led to savings from a reduction in supervisory personnel no longer needed. Bids submitted with union involvement were successful 80% of the time, and the new atmosphere in the city contributed to a decline in grievances from about 300 a year to about 20 a year. As the union leader sums up the situation, "we win 4 out of 5 contracts that the union bids. When we do the work we do it for 25% less than it was done in the past because of competition and because you start asking people to bring their brains to work instead of parking them at the door."[37]

Closer to home, the Region of Peel (Ontario) introduced managed competition in 2000 for services covered by the public works department. The municipality won five of the first eight contracts awarded through this process, including one that came back to the region after it had lost the contract in the first round of managed competition – an encouraging example of staff learning from the experience and coming up with an improved bid the second time around. With a gainsharing plan in place, 50% of savings realized under a contract stays with the region and the other 50% is distributed as a bonus to those working under that contract.[38]

---

[36] The description that follows is based on Peter Holle, "Enlightened Unionism," *Cordillera Institute Journal*, 1997, Issue 3, pp. 19-20.

[37] Quoted in *ibid.*, p. 20.

[38] Information provided by Region of Peel, August 2007.

There are problems and difficulties in applying measurement to government. As Keating points out, it is commonly found that increasing the number of police officers leads to a higher rate of reported crime, "not because police officers cause crime, but because they discover more of it."[39] Using performance measures to make external comparisons can also be quite misleading. Such comparisons can be "apples to oranges" because of differences in the way costs are allocated by competing organizations or other distinctions that render such comparisons invalid. In addition, external comparisons tend to focus on efficiency measures in the search for cheaper alternative delivery options, even though considerations of quality (effectiveness measures) are equally important. More fundamentally, efforts to find the cheapest service provider overlook the fact that municipalities exist for another, and more important, purpose – to act as a vehicle for communities to identify and address their collective concerns. The ultimate gauge of a municipality's performance is how well it serves the public interest not how well it measures up in a marketplace of competing service providers.[40]

Not all government programs lend themselves to quantitative measurement and, further, government decisions need to be based on more than these measures. Questions of value must frequently be addressed.[41] In the case of libraries, for example, is it "better" to build up the inventory of books through new acquisitions, to invest in conserving the inventory already in place, or to allocate resources to make the books more accessible to the public? This is a far from academic example, as is evident from the fierce battles waged in a number of communities when library boards have attempted to close small branch libraries and concentrate resources on fewer branches with longer operating hours.[42] These battles reflect the political reality that it is very difficult to cancel

---

[39] Michael Keating, "Size, Efficiency and Democracy: Consolidation, Fragmentation and Public Choice," in David Judge, Gerry Stoker, and Harold Wolman, *Theories of Urban Politics*, London, Sage Publications, 1995, p. 121.

[40] For a more general discussion of these themes, including some critical assessment of NPM, see also Peter Self, *Government by the Market: The Politics of Public Choice*, Boulder, CO, Westview, 1993, and Peter Aucoin, *The New Public Management: Canada in Comparative Perspective*, Montreal, IRPP, 1995.

[41] The example that follows is from Tindal and Tindal, *Municipal Good Governance Guide*, p. 41.

[42] In one such instance in our experience, the library board's plans to move holdings elsewhere and close a small branch were thwarted when the local municipality from which the library facility was rented changed the locks on the door thus denying entry to board personnel.

or curtail established programs, no matter what measurement and evaluation may suggest. In the inspired phrasing of an observer of the federal government's experience with variations of performance measurement:[43]

> Evaluation is like chastity; people support it in principle, but in practice they would prefer if it is mandatory for others and optional for them.

Rather than decrying the intrusion of political considerations, it can be argued that political priorities *should* prevail over measurement. For Cochrane, the preoccupation with measurement reflects an attempt to establish some sort of objective or rational means of determining how (and which) services should be provided locally, thus removing local service delivery from political controversy and, even more importantly, reducing local pressures to increase levels of spending. As a result, "stress has been placed on finding ways of standardising types of service to ensure that comparisons can be made in terms that focus on relative efficiency levels, rather than on differences in political approach."[44] In the process, financial or technical accountability replaces – quite inappropriately – democratic (political or electoral) accountability. Peter Self has suggested, more than 35 years ago, that this tension – between efficiency and accountability – is *the* central question in all of public administration.[45] He saw governing as more than the vision posed by NPM.

Citizen as Consumer

Another manifestation of new public management values is the notion of the local citizen as customer or client, interacting with the municipality as supplier of goods and services. Civic involvement is now equated with consumer processes, and strengthening the rights of citizens with opening up public services to market forces.[46] According to this view, given some choice among alternative service providers and provided

---

[43] Timothy Plumptre, *Beyond the Bottom Line: Management in Government*, Halifax, Institute for Research on Public Policy, 1988, p. 267.

[44] Allan Cochrane, "From Theories to Practices: Looking for Local Democracy in Britain," in Desmond King and Gerry Stoker (eds.), *Rethinking Local Democracy*, Houndmills, Macmillan Press, 1996, p. 198.

[45] See Peter Self, *Administrative Theories and Politics*, London, Harper Collins, 1977, Ch. 8.

[46] Vivien Lowndes, "Citizenship and Urban Politics," in Judge et al., *Theories of Urban Politics*, pp. 174-176.

with more information about standards of service and opportunities for complaint and redress, citizens can become active consumers instead of passive recipients of services.

There is nothing wrong with municipalities attempting to improve service delivery; indeed, there is much to recommend such an endeavour. Part of the way in which municipalities represent and act on behalf of their citizens is by providing them with quality services at a reasonable cost. It is not customer service, or its improvement, that is the problem. It is the tendency to depict local citizens as *nothing more than* customers and municipalities as *nothing more than* vehicles for service delivery that is the cause for concern.

Municipalities are not businesses. They don't have just occasional and specific contacts with customers; they have ongoing and complex relationships with citizens. "Citizens, unlike customers, have common purposes, obligations and rights, and among these are the right to be treated equitably."[47] Businesses, by contrast, practise target marketing, differentiate, discriminate, and take whatever actions are appropriate to increase market share or cut costs. If municipalities pursue business strategies, this approach opens up the possibility of inequities between individuals, "which runs counter to the equal and universalistic entitlements and obligations associated with citizenship."[48] As Seidle points out, such terms as customer or client do not capture the nature and complexity of the interaction that occurs when a government official services someone who is, among other things, "a taxpayer, a recipient of certain monetary benefits from the state, a voter and possibly a member of a political party and/or one or more voluntary organizations with an interest in public policy, and who carries expectations that extend beyond a particular contact with a particular public servant at a particular time."[49]

In the world of citizen as consumer, it is not the democratic aspects of government that are evaluated, but how municipalities apply such previously discussed private sector concepts as performance measurement, benchmarking, and best practices. Cochrane finds notions of accountability through accounting or the conversion of the citizen into

---

[47] Ole Ingstrup, *Public Service Renewal: From Means to Ends*, Ottawa, Canadian Centre for Management Development, 1995, p. 4.

[48] Jon Pierre, "The Marketization of the State," in Guy Peters and Donald Savoie (eds.), *Governance in a Changing Environment*, Montreal and Kingston, McGill-Queen's University Press, 1995, p. 57.

[49] F. Leslie Seidle, *Rethinking the Delivery of Public Services to Citizens*, Montreal, Institute for Research on Public Policy, 1995, p. 9.

consumer ultimately unsatisfactory "precisely because they attempt to depoliticise what are inevitably processes of political choice."[50]

It is also important to remember that not all relationships between citizens and municipal government are about service delivery. Citizens are, or can be, active participants in the process of government, not just consumers of services. "The consumer analogy takes the politics out of citizenship and local government," but "[I]f citizenship is reduced to consumerism and governance to shopkeeping, how are issues of collective choice to be resolved?"[51] A narrow focus on how well services are delivered to customers overlooks the fact that "the rationale of public services is not the satisfaction of individual demands, but meeting needs collectively within a framework of public policy."[52] Urbanists such as Jane Jacobs and Richard Florida have suggested that more complex calculations about "urban livability" need to be considered in the local/municipal/urban equation.

In a democracy, according to Carrel, "citizens must be recognized (and treated) as the *owners* of their government, not as its customers."[53] [emphasis in the original] As owners, citizens have responsibilities that are too often neglected. "A municipality's most serious liabilities are people who convince themselves that they are too busy to take an active interest in their municipality's affairs, who would rather complain that they are being victimized by government, and who look for scapegoats to be dumped in the next election."[54] Citizens, in the view of Carrel, "are the heart and soul of a democracy. If citizens do not actively participate in the shaping of public policy, democracy cannot function."[55] More importantly, to seek to truncate the discussion to that of customers does a great disservice to building healthy local democracies.

Value Clashes

As should be evident from preceding discussions, one of the challenges of values based operations is that organizations can be pursuing, simultaneously, values that are incompatible or in conflict. This has

---

[50] *Ibid.*, p. 200.

[51] Lowndes, "Citizenship and Urban Politics," p. 175.

[52] Dilys Hill, *Citizens and Cities*, Hemel Hempstead, Harvester Wheatsheaf, 1994, p. 228.

[53] André Carrel, *Citizens Hall,* Toronto, Between the Lines, 2001, p. 32.

[54] *Ibid.*, p. 65.

[55] *Ibid.*, p. 100.

become especially apparent with the widespread movement to embrace the values of the new public management movement. These essentially business values do not fit easily with traditional public sector values.

Traditional public management featured extensive controls to ensure propriety and accountability in the use of public funds. The new public management calls for freeing up managers to be more innovative and creative. But inherent in this approach is the possibility (indeed, the probability) that some mistakes will be made. An entrepreneurial organization accepts such mistakes, even welcomes them, provided that lessons are learned from the mistakes.[56] But it is difficult for governments to act in this manner, since any such mistakes become the focus of critical media coverage. It is particularly difficult for municipalities because of their scale of operations and the intensive public scrutiny they receive. The resulting atmosphere – often described as managing in a goldfish bowl – is not one conducive to the tolerance of mistakes.

Meeting Your Waterloo

While hardly a crushing defeat of the sort Napoleon suffered at the hands of the Duke of Wellington in his final battle, the City of Waterloo's dealings with MFP Financial Services were distinctly unsatisfactory and illustrate all too well the difficulties that can arise when embracing one set of values leads to the neglect of other, equally important values.[57]

Waterloo (Ontario) was in the forefront of those municipalities that embraced the new public management. It pioneered the establishment of a new organizational model in which traditional municipal departments were replaced by the establishment of five core businesses within which more than 20 business units were identified, each bringing together functions and processes that delivered specific products or services to local citizens. The new model, known as "Waterloo Inc.," conveyed the notion of businesslike operations in a competitive atmosphere focused on innovative ways of generating revenues and increasing efficiency.

The basic facts of the case involve arrangements entered into by the City of Waterloo with respect to the financing of RIM Park, a major recreation project containing a variety of facilities, fields, and parklands. The city signed a financing agreement with MFP that would supposedly

---

[56] Complaints are viewed as "a luscious, golden opportunity," rather than "as a disease to be got over," in the words of Tom Peters and Nancy Austin, *A Passion for Excellence*, New York, Random House, 1985, p. 83.

[57] The description that follows is partly based on Tindal and Tindal, *Municipal Good Governance Guide*, pp. 80-82.

cost less than 5% interest, only to find later that the actual rate of interest was twice that high (9.2%) and would cost the city $228 million, not the $112 million originally anticipated – although an out of court settlement eventually reduced the amount owed to $146 million.[58] The evidence provided to a judicial inquiry into this case by a representative of MFP was dismissed as lacking credibility and the inquiry found that he had perpetuated a scam usually referred to as a "bait and switch." But the inquiry was also critical of the lack of scrutiny of the MFP agreement on the part of municipal staff and council.[59]

The mayor of Waterloo who took office after the MFP deal referred to an underlying systemic problem arising from the culture associated with Waterloo Inc. – one that directed the city to operate as if it were a private corporation, and that conveyed the impression that the city was open for business, but not necessarily open to the public process.[60] The implication was that the business approach to government adopted by Waterloo contributed to a closed process that led to poor financial decision making.

It is clear from the judicial inquiry that operations were streamlined under Waterloo Inc. and the CAO was directed by council to delegate more responsibilities to his senior staff and to spend more time interacting with private sector enterprises and potential partners. But the inquiry was critical of inadequate oversight of senior officials (by council as well as by the CAO) and of the cosy relationship between staff and private companies. In its words:[61]

> The system of governance in Waterloo not only permitted but also encouraged 'schmoozing' with suppliers by senior staff. This led to economically unhealthy relationships between senior staff and suppliers. The system did not contain checks and balances that would head off situations that could have been more transparent.

It should be emphasized that none of the foregoing is meant to suggest that the Waterloo Inc. initiative was wrong or inappropriate. To the contrary, much of the emphasis of the Waterloo model was welcome and is still being pursued by progressive municipalities. The problems

---

[58] This summary of the facts is from Mary Louise McAllister, *Governing Ourselves?*, Vancouver, UBC Press, 2004, pp. 240-241.

[59] The Honourable Mr. Justice Ronald C. Sills, Commissioner, *RIM Park Financing Inquiry*, Final Report, City of Waterloo, October 2003. The report is available at www.waterlooinquiry.ca, accessed July 22, 2007.

[60] This assessment is found in McAllister, *Governing Ourselves?*, p. 242.

[61] Sills, *RIM Park Inquiry, Executive Summary*, p. 13.

that arose resulted from the values associated with the city's new model overwhelming other values of equal importance – such as public accountability. Further value clashes are evident in the public sector assumptions with respect to the boundaries of ethical behaviour and the more lenient assumptions of the private sector. "What some might call cronyism, undue influence and unacceptable lobbying may be considered by others to amount to no more than good salesmanship, the creation of goodwill and normal and traditional gestures of appreciation between those who do business with each other on a regular basis."[62]

This observation was made with respect to the findings of another judicial inquiry, also involving MFP Financial Services, this time with the City of Toronto. In this latter case, the misleading behaviour of MFP was overshadowed by serious ethical lapses on the part of a few city personnel. In response, an elaborate oversight regime has been introduced for Ontario municipalities, one intended to improve accountability but also one inimical to the new public management notion that management should be freed up to act in an innovative and entrepreneurial fashion. A closer look at ethics and accountability follows and will provide further insight into these values and the potential for clash and conflict.

Ethics and Accountability

Ethical issues and concerns have a long history in local government and were part of the impetus for the turn of the century reform movement of 100 years ago, described in Chapter 2. Patronage, political corruption, and blatant conflicts of interest prompted efforts to remove politics from local government, largely through elevating the role of the professional administrator and operating the municipality on the basis of sound management principles.

The rapid growth and urbanization in the years after World War Two provided many opportunities for overly close links and inappropriate behaviour between developers and members of council. Few questioned the desirability of growth, and the increased assessment and tax base that resulted, and supporting development projects was often seen as synonymous with acting in the public interest. While one could certainly dispute the accuracy of this perspective – and citizens groups increasingly did so in the postwar period – tunnel vision or poor judgment is not a crime. But supporting development for personal gain is quite another matter.

---

[62] Rust-D'Eye, *P3 Deals*, p. 26

Show Me the Money

Much of the concern has centred on the extent to which developers (and others in the business community) contribute to the campaign costs of municipal candidates and what considerations they expect (and receive) in return. Campaign costs have inevitably increased markedly in large and rapidly growing municipalities. It is estimated that the successful mayoralty candidates in large cities spent an average of $200 000 on their campaigns by the end of the 1990s. The mayor elected in Calgary in 2001 spent more than $1 million[63] (and media reports indicate that he raised at least $1 million toward his 2007 reelection.)[64] Similarly, in Vancouver, which has no expense or contribution limits, and at large elections, significant sums of money were raised/spent in recent civic elections.[65]

Without political parties at the local level (with limited exceptions), those running for local office must personally raise the funds they need. Lightbody finds that there are three main sources for campaign funds – people who do business with city hall, people who require city hall in order to do their business, and people who are relatives, friends, and associates. Incumbents raise and spend twice as much as challengers (a major factor in their continuity) because they can draw upon all three of these sources while challengers only have access to the last category.[66]

While the research on municipal election financing in Canada is limited, it indicates that the development industry is the overwhelming source of campaign contributions (apart from the funds provided by candidates themselves). A study of campaign financing[67] in the 2003 municipal elections for the city of Toronto and nine other urban municipalities containing the bulk of the population in the surrounding regions of Durham, York, and Peel, yielded the following findings:

---

[63] James Lightbody, *City Politics, Canada*, Peterborough, Broadview Press, 2006, pp. 205-206.

[64] C. Derworiz, "Mayor's $1 million scares off rivals," *Calgary Herald*, July 2, 2007.

[65] See, for example, Kennedy Stewart and Patrick Smith, "Improving Local Democracy in British Columbia," invited brief for the B.C. Local Government Election Task Force, Richmond, B.C., February, 2010.

[66] Lightbody, *City Politics, Canada*, pp. 258-259.

[67] This summary is based on Robert MacDermid, *Funding Municipal Elections in the Toronto Region*, paper presented to the annual general meeting of the Canadian Political Science Association, Toronto, 2006 and MacDermid, *Campaign Finance and Campaign Success in Municipal Elections in the Toronto Region*, paper presented to the annual general meeting of the Canadian Political Science Association, Saskatoon, 2007.

- Corporate contributions accounted for two-thirds of campaign donations to candidates in the suburban municipalities, over 70% in three of the nine, and a high of 81% in Vaughan. More than two-thirds of these corporate contributions were from the development industry.
- In the case of Toronto, corporate contributions represented just over one-third of the total, 45% of them from the development industry.
- One-quarter of the candidates surveyed received more than 80% of their funding from corporations and 22 candidates reported only corporate supporters. Vaughan once again topped the list, with the mayor receiving 93.5% of his funding from corporate contributions.
- Contributions from the development industry are carefully targeted and seldom wasted, with over 75% of their contributions going to winning candidates. In many instances, the support was provided to incumbents who had exhibited a pro development posture. An encouraging exception to this pattern was provided by the reelection of Mayor Steve Parish in Ajax. An outspoken opponent of poorly planned development, and someone who refused to take contributions from developers, Parish defeated a candidate generously backed by the development industry. Ajax, however, remains an exception to the norm.
- Contributions from trade unions were negligible in the suburban municipalities and not much more evident in Toronto, even with the financial support given to David Miller in his successful campaign for the mayor's chair.
- Individual contributions were quite low in most of the municipalities studied, with only 25 out of the 70 000 voters in Whitby, for example, donating more than $100 to a candidate.
- Toronto was a striking exception, with almost 55% of contributions coming from individuals. At least a partial explanation is found in the fact that Toronto provides a campaign contribution rebate program. While Ajax and Markham also have rebate programs, there were not widespread individual contributions in these municipalities in 2003. However data from the 2006 elections indicates that individual contributions in Ajax and Markham are growing faster than in municipalities without rebate systems, suggesting that rebate programs have a positive impact as the public becomes more aware of them.[68]

---

[68] Communication from Robert MacDermid, October 4, 2007.

The complete absence of limits on campaign donations or expenditures in British Columbia municipal elections has long been a cause for concern. Here again, contributions come particularly from interests associated with the property and development industries, according to a preliminary assessment of local election finance submissions from 2002, 2005, and 2008.[69]

Assuming that any applicable rules are followed, why should one fuss over the extent of corporate contributions to municipal election campaigns? If individual citizens are not going to provide financial support and if we are not going to limit the candidate pool to those wealthy enough simply to finance their own campaigns, where else could we expect candidates to find the increasingly large sums they now need? With future profits, and even economic survival, for companies in the property development industry dependent upon timely and supportive decisions by municipal councils, they quite understandably back the election of like minded individuals. For them, it is just one of the costs of doing business.

Crossing the Line

And yet, it is not quite that simple, or innocent. If a pro development stance brings financial support from the development community that bolsters the already strong reelection prospects of an incumbent, how do we break the cycle of councils dominated by individuals who favour the interests of developers over the broader community interest – or who have come to equate the two? The close relationships forged between members of council and the development community can result in collusion and entirely inappropriate behaviour. Lightbody described how during the 1980s in the York region, north of Toronto, municipal engineers, councillors, and developers got together regularly for rounds of golf and games of poker. Land acquired by those developers got serviced and approved for development at an impressive rate.[70] He also notes that in the early 1990s several councillors from Metro Toronto and suburban municipalities received lengthy prison terms for accepting bribes to support by-laws that assisted the developers' projects.[71]

The corrupt practices of Montreal Mayor Camillien Houde prompted a judicial inquiry led by Jean Drapeau who then succeeded Houde as

---

[69] Patrick J. Smith, "British Columbia Needs a Municipal Registrar of Lobbyists," *Influencing BC*, Vol. 2, No. 1, January 2012, pp. 1-5.

[70] Lightbody, *City Politics, Canada*, p. 213.

[71] *Ibid.*, p. 212.

mayor on a clean government platform. Ironically, the chair of the executive committee under Drapeau's administration had a country house built for him at no cost by a major contractor involved in the Montreal Olympics.[72]

It is hard to imagine a more compelling example of misguided behaviour than William "Wild Bill" Hawrelak, who was mayor of Edmonton for three periods from the beginning of the 1950s until the mid-1970s.[73]

Box 9.3 The Saga of William Hawrelak
Hawrelak's first tenure as mayor ran from 1951 through 1959. He exhibited "brash opportunism" and an inability to distinguish between public and private business activities, using the knowledge he acquired as mayor for personal and family gain. For example, he purchased land for motel development that had become possible because of zoning changes that he initiated, he bought land from the city at deflated prices for future construction, he swapped land with Chrysler for personal gain, and he voted in contravention of planning legislation. He was forced to resign for "gross misconduct" as a result of a judicial inquiry in 1959, but was reelected in 1964. Another violation of provincial rules (this time concerning conflict of interest) led to another judicial dismissal from office in 1965. Reelected in 1974 (for one last term), he appointed a disbarred lawyer to advise him on ethics.

Part of the explanation for Hawrelak's reelection (twice) following judicial inquiries and public disgrace is that he was able to exploit the notion that as a Ukranian Canadian he was being unfairly judged according to traditional and unwritten rules of British "fair play" that were being used in an attempt to keep non-Anglos from exercising power. Cultural minorities in Edmonton, led by the Slavs, remembered past discriminations and tended to feel, "so what if he made a buck, we all got rich and, in any case, he was one of us."[74] The possibility of culturally based differences with respect to what constitutes ethical behaviour is something that merits more attention now that so many of Canada's large cities have a sizeable and diverse immigrant population.

An extension of the inappropriate links between business interests and council is found in the lobbying activities that converge on city halls. Consider these few examples:

---

[72] Andrew Sancton, "Montreal," in Warren Magnusson and Andrew Sancton (eds.), *City Politics in Canada*, Toronto, University of Toronto Press, 1983, p. 74.

[73] The description that follows is based on Lightbody, *City Politics, Canada*, pp. 211-212 and p. 333.

[74] *Ibid.*, p. 216.

- The City of Edmonton made a number of concessions to the Ghermezian brothers with respect to the development of the West Edmonton Mall. Ralph Ghermezian sat in the council's public gallery during the final vote on the project and "so frantically gestured as to how to vote to his supporters on council that Nayor Purves inadvertently tried to summon 'alderman Ghermezian' to order."[75]
- A Toronto lobbyist who sat in the public gallery there and nodded to councillors when it was time for them to vote so annoyed Councillor Jack Layton that he suggested that the mayor "ask Mr. Blott to come and have a seat here (at the council table) so he can at least direct things from down here rather than from a seat in the council chamber."[76]
- Toronto's most famous/notorious municipal lobbyist was Jeff Lyons whose activities and questionable behaviour were well documented by the judicial inquiry triggered by Toronto's computer leasing arrangements with MFP Financial Services. He cultivated relationships by such means as his annual "Brother Jeff" charity golf tournament, countless tickets to all sorts of events, and delivery of election campaign money to candidates – which he made clear really came from him, regardless of the original source. He counted on favours for his clients in return.[77] So blatant were Lyons' interventions into city business that when a councillor raised a question in a council meeting about the leasing arrangements with MFP, he received a voice mail message from the lobbyist both critical and threatening, along with a call from an MFP employee expressing upset at the question and asserting MFP's right to the business. "The ship of state is well off course when a lobbyist and a salesperson chastise a councillor for asking a question in a Council meeting."[78]

---

[75] *Ibid.*, p. 214.

[76] Jock Ferguson and Paul Taylor, "Lawyer grows wealthy on development lobbying," *Globe and Mail*, December 17, 1987.

[77] The Honourable Madam Justice Denise E. Bellamy, Commissioner, Toronto Computer Leasing Inquiry, Toronto External Contracts Inquiry, *Report, Volume 4: Executive Summary*, pp. 22-23. All four volumes of the report of this inquiry are available at www.toronto.ca/inquiry.

[78] Bellamy, *Volume 1: Facts and Findings*, p. 40.

Moral Compass Missing

The Jeff Lyons saga, however, was merely a sideshow compared to the main drama that unfolded as the Toronto Computer Leasing Inquiry revealed a shocking story of completely unethical behaviour on the part of a very few Toronto personnel – primarily two senior staff and one member of council. Key findings of the inquiry include:

- A Treasurer who was instrumental in awarding a contract to a company owned by someone with whom she was having an affair at the time, who continued to promote successfully the interests of this individual in subsequent contracts after their affair (but not their close friendship) had apparently ended, and who maintained an inappropriately close – although not apparently sexual – relationship with the representative securing the contract for MFP Financial Services.
- A department head who had a "prodigious appetite for corporate freebies" (not just from MFP) and who between 1998 and 2001 "averaged at least one outing a month courtesy of other suppliers: golf, hockey games, a ski day, parties, lunches, dinners, cocktails." He also found time to fly to the Masters golf tournament in Georgia courtesy of a supplier and for a trip to England as well. The message he sent was of a public servant for sale.[79]
- A councillor who was shown to be "a calculating, strategic, and almost habitual liar" and who, on the witness stand during the inquiry, "drifted from lie to lie in a performance worthy of Pinocchio."[80]

Toronto's version of *Sex and the City* did not end with this sorry episode. Before the dust had settled from the Bellamy Report, a new scandal emerged with striking similarities to the indiscretions exhibited by the Treasurer. A senior manager admitted to a very close personal relationship with her immediate subordinate, indicating that he was her "soul mate," and she hoped to have a future with him (notwithstanding his married status). Because of this relationship, she allegedly used her influence to secure him promotions within the city and cooperated with him in improperly hiring personal friends of his. Both officials were suspended from their jobs when this story broke and were subsequently

---

[79] Bellamy, *Volume 4: Executive Summary*, p. 29.

[80] *Ibid.*, pp. 68 and 70.

fired – not for the personal relationship but because of conflicts of interest and inappropriate hiring and decision making.[81]

Governing as an Old Boys Club

It would be wrong, however, to leave the impression that unethical behaviour or corruption is confined to large cities and is a byproduct of growth pressures. While small municipalities may appear to be very open and accessible, they have often operated as an "old boys club" in a variety of inappropriate ways.[82]

A small and stable population and a relatively homogenous community result in the election of like minded individuals (traditionally, white, middle aged males) who find it fairly easy to reach consensus on most issues. In a small community, members of council will interact in a variety of settings – for example, through business contacts, social gatherings, and membership in local service clubs. Conversations often extend to municipal matters and councillors may even get together on a regular basis, for a morning coffee or an evening drink, to discuss issues facing the municipality. It becomes easier, and certainly more comfortable, to discuss and resolve issues during these informal discussions and then to process the issues expeditiously and with minimal debate at council meetings.

Over time, councillors begin to view municipal operations as their personal fiefdom. They know what is best and they try to minimize disputes and division. Within a small council (usually five members), an expression of a contrary view is angrily received as a personal attack. Councillors are also apt to become defensive when facing representations from the public with respect to agenda items. The following description of the municipal council in a small Manitoba village in the 1970s could probably apply to many Canadian municipalities of that era.

> There's always lots of correspondence and delegations but no spectators. It's considered in bad taste in small towns to attend

---

[81] The summary of this incident, which was widely covered in the Toronto media, is based on Shanti Fernando, *Ethics and Good Urban Governance in Toronto: The Tale of Two Love Affairs*, paper presented to the annual general meeting of the Canadian Political Science Association, Toronto, 2006, p. 9. The second "love affair" examined in this paper is, of course, the one involving Toronto's Treasurer, already noted above.

[82] The discussion that follows is partly based on David Siegel, "Small-town Canada," in John W. Langford and Allan Tupper (eds.), *Corruption, Character and Conduct: Essays on Canadian Government Ethics*, Toronto, Oxford University Press, 1993, but also reflects our experience and observations over several decades of municipal consulting.

meetings. The councillors are embarrassed at having to speak in public and they resent the implication that they are not doing their job.[83]

Vacancies on council are often filled by co-opting replacements who share the prevailing views, making it difficult for alternative points of view to find their way on to council – at least until the community grows and changes to the point where the greater diversity to be found can no longer be ignored. The style of operation in small municipalities is very personalized. Since members of council know almost everyone in the community, decisions may be made on the basis of the merits of the applicant, not the application – which has most notoriously happened in those instances where local administration of welfare led to lengthy discussions about which of those in need were worthy and deserving. Personal considerations may also influence decisions about hiring of staff and purchasing of supplies/awarding of contracts.

As a result of these features of small town operation, Siegel describes the following ethical problems:[84]

- ➢ Conflict of interest, often because councillors are also prominent business people who have dealings with the municipality.
- ➢ Benefiting personally from municipal resources, as in the example where the road running past the mayor's home receives extra maintenance work, which extends up the driveway.
- ➢ Allowing personal considerations to influence decisions that are made, as in the above example of welfare applicants.
- ➢ Being secretive and not sharing information with the public.
- ➢ Lack of objectivity, independence, and professionalism on the part of municipal staff who have obtained their positions through patronage or nepotism and are, therefore, reluctant to tell councillors things they don't want to hear but need to know.

Legislative Reponses

Most of the issues and concerns outlined above have been at least partly, although not always effectively, addressed by provincial legislation and requirements. For example:

- ➢ Provinces such as Ontario and Quebec have passed laws governing campaign financing. Ontario's legislation limits the contributions allowed from individuals, unions, and corporations

---

[83] Heather Robertson, *Grass Roots*, Toronto, James Lewis and Samuel, 1973, p. 126.

[84] Siegel, *Small-town Canada*, pp. 223-228.

(except for candidates and their spouses, who can donate any amount to their own campaigns), limits the amount candidates can spend, and requires identification of donors who contribute more than $100. A recent study of election experiences in Toronto and Calgary found that the greater regulation of election finances in Toronto had a "modest salutary effect on political competition" and, coupled with Toronto's campaign rebate program, left candidates in Toronto less reliant on corporate (including developer) sources than those in Calgary.[85] In other jurisdictions, such as British Columbia, there are no restrictions on either campaign contributions – local or foreign – or spending.

➢ Conflict of interest legislation has been in existence for several decades. As it applies to members of council, the legislation usually provides for them to declare situations in which they might have a potential financial interest in matters before council and to abstain from any discussion or voting related to such matters. This sensible arrangement allows those who would otherwise be ineligible for office to serve on the councils of their communities while absenting themselves from participation where appropriate. However, determining when one is in a situation of potential conflict is not always readily apparent, with the result that some overly cautious individuals declare excessively while others inadvertently breach the legislation.

➢ Freedom of information legislation (and associated provisions governing the right to privacy) has become increasingly common. In addition to requirements for public disclosure, such legislation usually provides an avenue for citizens to appeal when access to information has been denied.

➢ Open local government legislation or provisions have also received increased attention, in response to public demands and also court decisions that underline the need to conduct public business in public.

➢ Rules and requirements concerning the hiring of personnel and purchasing/contracting represent another avenue of legislating appropriate behaviour.

---

[85] Sam Austin and Lisa Young, *Party Finance in City Elections: Toronto and Calgary Compared*, paper presented to the annual general meeting of the Canadian Political Science Association, Toronto, 2006.

Legislative Overkill in Ontario?

While Ontario had legislation with respect to all of the above subjects, the provincial government has introduced an elaborate new oversight regime in amendments to its *Municipal Act* that took effect January 2007. The impetus for this new regime was the previously quoted Bellamy Report into the wrongdoings in Toronto. It recommended a number of new investigative and oversight agencies and these were warmly received by an apparently penitent Toronto. Included as mandatory provisions in the June 2006 *City of Toronto Act*, they require:

- The establishment of a code of conduct for members of council and local boards.
- The appointment of an Integrity Commissioner who reports to council and is responsible for performing in an independent manner the functions assigned by the municipality with respect to the application of the code of conduct and any rules, procedures, and policies governing ethical behaviour.
- The provision of a system of registration of persons who lobby public office holders, a requirement that they file returns and give information to the municipality, and the establishment of a code of conduct for such persons.
- The appointment of a registrar responsible for carrying out in an independent manner the functions assigned by the municipality with respect to the registry of lobbyists.
- The appointment of an ombudsman who reports to council and investigates any decision or recommendation made or act done or omitted in the course of the administration of the municipality and its local boards (in addition to the right of appeal or objection or review under any other Act or rule of law).
- The appointment of an auditor general who reports to council and is responsible for assisting council in holding itself and its administrators accountable for the quality of stewardship over public funds and for achievement of value for money in municipal operations.

All of these same provisions now apply to every other Ontario municipality through their inclusion in the revised *Municipal Act*. Granted, the provisions in the *Municipal Act* are optional, not mandatory, but municipalities that do not make use of the various powers provided can face criticism for failing to make every possible effort to protect the public. We are certainly not opposed to the use of these new powers; our concern is simply that those who do make use of the new provisions may mistakenly assume that they have done everything that needs to be done to ensure ethical behaviour.[86] But unless there is a foundation of ethical values in an organization, embraced by all employees, the new oversight regime won't make much difference.

Those who lack a moral compass are usually oblivious to rules that are meant for behaviour like theirs. When Toronto's Treasurer first crossed the line by supporting the awarding of a contract to her lover, the former City of North York, where she was then employed, had a code of ethics that forbade using one's position to secure favours for family or friends, and she had an employment contract that prohibited actual and apparent conflicts of interest.[87] When lawyer Jeff Lyons was lobbying on behalf of his corporate clients, he "didn't understand the City's conflict of interest policy, and nobody ever brought it up with him."[88]

More rules and more oversight agencies don't really address these fundamental human failings – a point iterated by Ken Kernaghan and John Langford in 2006.[89] In fairness, the importance of corporate culture and of self-regulation and self-responsibility was a point not lost on Justice Bellamy, who commented:[90]

> Key decision makers at the city were almost pathetically vulnerable to sales tactics in the guise of entertainment and favours. A *strong ethical culture* [emphasis added] in the public service should have been the first line of defence against those tactics. The existing culture offered no resistance.

As has been illustrated, if there are individuals lacking in basic standards of moral and ethical behaviour, they will ignore codes of conduct or will devote their energies and creativity to finding ways around whatever rules are put into place. In a similar behaviour pattern, we have written elsewhere how council members who are determined to meet in secret will find a way to do so, whatever the law may say. Instead of hoping that none of the optional grounds for which they are allowed to close a meeting will require them to do so, they instead treat

---

[86] The discussion in this section is based on Tindal and Tindal, *Municipal Good Governance Guide*, pp. 91-92.

[87] Bellamy, *Volume 4: Executive Summary*, p. 10.

[88] *Ibid.*, p. 23.

[89] See Ken Kernaghan and John Langford, *The Responsible Public Servant*, Montreal/Toronto, IRPP/IPAC, 2006.

[90] Bellamy, *Volume 1: Facts and Findings*, p. 164.

all these optional grounds as if they were mandatory and exploit them as a way of justifying more closed meetings.[91]

In Boyer's memorable phrase, "to define is to confine."[92] Any attempt to delineate a code of permissible behaviour is limited by the insightfulness and clarity of that definition. Anything not ruled out by the code becomes acceptable, even if it should not be. The Toronto manager dismissed for a personal relationship that led her to make decisions favourable to the object of her affection claimed that "the rules of conduct regarding office romance were unclear and there was no guidance given."[93] Even if that were the case, wouldn't elementary considerations of common sense and proper conduct tell you that it was not acceptable to make decisions that were influenced by the existence of that romance?

Going Beyond the Rules

Whatever rules there are governing ethical behaviour, they need to be reinforced and made operational in a variety of ways, including:[94]

> ➤ Modelling of appropriate behaviour by the senior staff and council. If the CAO or head of council seem to make every effort to maximize the perks attached to their positions, they should not be surprised to find that the clerk in the printshop is running off some personal photos on the municipality's colour printer.
> ➤ Recognizing that every major decision has ethical dimensions and ensuring that when the options in response to a particular situation are analyzed they include the question of right/wrong.
> ➤ Reviewing recruitment, performance appraisal, and reward systems to identify contributing factors that might lead to unethical behaviour and changing them as needed so that they reinforce an ethical climate.

Whatever the written rules, people need to be guided by their conscience. If they are worried about crossing the line, they are too close

---

[91] C. Richard Tindal and Susan Nobes Tindal, "Meeting Expectations," *Municipal World*, December 2005, pp. 9-12.

[92] J. Patrick Boyer, "Why It Is Easy to Get Tangled Up in Prescriptions for Ethical Conduct," in Nancy Averill (ed.), *Ethical Conduct and Public Office, Practices and Prescriptions*, Ottawa, Public Policy Forum, 2002, p. 47.

[93] Fernando, *Ethics and Good Urban Governance in Toronto*, p. 9.

[94] This summary, which is partly drawn from the Bellamy Report, is based on Tindal and Tindal, *Municipal Good Governance Guide*, pp. 93-94.

to it. If they would feel uncomfortable about seeing their planned action as a headline in tomorrow's paper, then they know they should not proceed. If they are rationalizing an action, in case it is challenged, then it should not be taken. If they wouldn't want their mother to find out what they had done, then they know it shouldn't be done – whatever the rules may allow.[95]

It should be reiterated that written rules are important, as long as they are not regarded as a complete response to the issue of ethical behaviour. Spelling out permissible behaviour in writing is the best way to try and ensure that everyone knows what the rules are and has the same understanding of their scope. This need is heightened in ethnically diverse communities where some cultures may have different views or standards concerning ethical behaviour – as was noted earlier in this chapter with respect to the continued electoral success of William Hawrelak even with two adverse judicial rulings. To take another example, Aboriginals come from a cultural tradition grounded by scarcity, where relatives often must come first (in sharing the proceeds from any successful hunt) and where nepotism is obligatory.[96] It would obviously not be sufficient to ask an Aboriginal office holder "what would your mother think?" Only through specific written rules could the different requirements and expected behaviour of those in municipal government be made clear.

When NPM Met MFP

An additional concern with a very elaborate oversight regime of the sort introduced in Ontario is the adverse impact that it may have on municipal operations. Municipal staff and members of council could become overly preoccupied with anticipating potential problems and trying to protect themselves from future scrutiny by one of the various oversight agents. Such a response seems almost certain to slow down operations and to work against the improved efficiency, streamlined operations, and expeditious decision making that municipalities have been urged to demonstrate over the past couple of decades.[97]

---

[95] C. Richard Tindal and Susan Nobes Tindal, "Keys To Good Governance IV: What Would Your Mother Think? Ethical Behaviour in Municipal Government," *Municipal World*, July 2007, pp. 9-12.

[96] Tom Pocklington and Sara Pocklington, "Aboriginal Political Ethics," in Langford and Tupper, *Essays on Canadian Government Ethics*, p. 51.

[97] Much the same concern has been expressed about the wide ranging accountability provisions introduced and promised by the federal government in the aftermath of the Gomery Report into the sponsorship scandal.

Similar concerns are evident in provinces such as British Columbia. As discussed in Chapter 7, plans to establish a Municipal Auditor General for B.C. have generated resistance to what is seen as provincial intrusion into municipal operations and an imposed "solution" for which there is no evident problem. British Columbia has also introduced, as of April 2010, a registrar for lobbyists – at the provincial level.[98] The establishment of the provincial registry has inevitably sparked discussion of extending a similar regime to the municipal level.[99] Such new procedures bring a learning curve – internally and externally – which could add to municipal concerns about provincial intervention into local matters. But Smith makes a persuasive case that B.C. needs a municipal registrar of lobbyists, as a means of providing some safeguard from abuses that could arise from the unregulated campaign financing arrangements in that province.[100]

In many ways, what has been happening is very reminiscent of the situation 100 years ago when reformers targeted corruption and machine politics (especially in American cities), and introduced rules and controls designed to prevent misuse of public money.[101] As a result of the law of unintended consequences, however, "in making it difficult to steal the public's money, we made it virtually impossible to manage the public's money."[102] By the second half of the 20th century, there were growing calls to "let the managers manage." As discussed earlier, the new public management (NPM) movement continued this new emphasis with its calls for a more flexible, businesslike, entrepreneurial, and innovative approach to government operations. But then NPM met MFP (Financial Services), not to mention a whole host of other dubious characters with names like Enron and Tyco, of American corporate notoriety, and the notion of streamlined, businesslike government operations as the new Holy Grail abruptly lost much of its lustre. Once again the pendulum is swinging and, as usual, it seems to be overcorrecting, especially in the Ontario context. Municipalities may find it quite a challenge to balance the requirements of oversight and accountability with their pursuit of more businesslike, efficient operations.

---

[98] See www.lobbyistsregistrar.bc.ca. Alberta, Newfoundland and Labrador, Nova Scotia, Ontario, and Quebec all have enacted parallel provincial legislation.

[99] Author discussion with Mary Carlson, Deputy Registrar of Lobbyists, B.C., Vancouver, August 22, 2011.

[100] Smith, *British Columbia Needs a Municipal Registrar of Lobbyists*.

[101] This section is based on Tindal and Tindal, *Municipal Good Governance Guide*, p. 93.

[102] Osborne and Gaebler, *Reinventing Government*, p. 14.

Accountability for What to Whom?

We also have another concern with the introduction of new investigative and oversight regimes and with increased requirements for municipalities to report annually on the basis of various efficiency and effectiveness measures. While these initiatives are usually couched in terms of improving accountability and public trust, it is arguable that this is not really their intent or their likely outcome. To understand the concern, we need to take a closer look at the concept of accountability itself. It can be viewed in at least three different ways:[103]

i) As a results oriented system, in which accountability involves measuring progress on performance and big ticket items;

ii) As an ethical framework, under which accountability is seen as the quest for good, through appropriate behaviour by elected and appointed officials; and

iii) As a "gotcha" mechanism, where accountable arrangements exist to catch wrongdoing.

According to Plumptre,[104] accountability often becomes a synonym for control, in what he terms a "financentric" view of management. The accountant and the auditor become key players and the paper trail of appropriate documentation is the focus. If accountability is equated with control, then the way to solve an accountability problem is to increase controls. But "the rise of inspectorates can paradoxically *reduce* the sense of responsibility and accountability in management"[105] [emphasis in the original]. Municipal staff could see less need to dwell on proprieties when there are so many other bodies to second guess administrative operations. If municipal operations meet the tests established by the oversight agencies but fail to meet the needs of the public, what have we gained? Gregory Inwood has posed this issue of accountability differently; he saw accountability as having five different meanings:[106]

---

[103] Institute on Governance, *Forum on Municipal Governance and Accountability: A Summary Report*, June 15, 2006, p. 1, accessed June 12, 2007 from www.iog.ca.

[104] Plumptre, *Beyond the Bottom Line*, p. 187.

[105] Francis Terry, *Public Management – Time for a Re-Launch*, Public Management and Policy Association, March 27, 2006, accessed June 2, 2007 from www.publicnet.co.uk.

[106] See Gregory Inwood, "Public Administration and Accountability," in Gregory J. Inwood, *Understanding Canadian Public Administration: An Introduction to Theory and Practice*, Toronto, Prentice-Hall, Allyn and Bacon Canada, 1999, p. 355.

i) Internal/hierarchical accountability to superiors,
ii) Internal political accountability to elected officials,
iii) Legal accountability to the law,
iv) Professional accountability, and
v) External political accountability to the public.

Plumptre argues that the challenge facing government is not an insufficiency of controls but "the apparent inability of governments to delegate in such a way that officials feel they have the tools they require to perform their jobs effectively and to make adequate use of their own judgment and initiative."[107] While legislative changes in several provinces now provide for somewhat greater municipal discretion and freedom to operate, the extensive new oversight regime in Ontario sends a contrary message and threatens to limit the newfound flexibility and freedom.

Accountability in a Democracy

Instead of, or at least in addition to, changes that increase the role of various appointed oversight agents such as auditors, ombudsmen, ethics commissioners, and lobbyist registrars, efforts to improve accountability in a local democracy should be directed more toward the relationship between the government and the governed. As discussed in the next chapter, aspects of that relationship include the following:

➢ What is the extent of the participation in the government of the municipality?
➢ How well do the councillors and staff reflect the nature and diversity of the community?
➢ What means are used (and could be used) to inform, involve, and engage the public more?

Concluding Comments

It is the theme of this chapter that the way things are done – the governing processes as opposed to the government structures of the preceding chapter – is largely a reflection of the organizational culture and the values of the local community. Traditional public sector values have

---

[107] Plumptre, *Beyond the Bottom Line*, p. 186.

gone through a major change over the past few decades with the new public management movement, and many municipalities have been in the forefront of initiatives to create more streamlined, businesslike operations. Accountability and improved performance were to be achieved through measurement and competition in the marketplace of alternative service providers.

Experience revealed, however, that the NPM values often conflicted with traditional public sector values. There are also limits on the measurement of government performance. It is difficult to develop measures for some government responsibilities (especially where questions of value must be addressed) and it can be argued that efforts to establish measures as the basis for evaluations are at the expense of political judgment and the associated responsibility to the electorate for the exercise of this judgment. Somewhat similar concerns have arisen about the NPM emphasis on the citizen as customer and civic involvement as a matter of improved consumer processes and more service choices.

As these concerns were calling into question some of the NPM values, a number of very high profile scandals occurred in the public and private sectors, in Canada, the United States, and elsewhere. As a result, proper procedures, crosschecks and safeguards, improved reporting and oversight mechanisms have all come to the fore, as especially illustrated with the Ontario experiences. This new emphasis is not supportive of the flexible and streamlined businesslike approach that had been espoused for municipal government. But neither is it helpful in strengthening the fundamental role of municipalities as democratic and accountable governments. That role receives overdue attention in the next chapter.

Chapter 10
Public Participation in Local Government

There are two competing views of local government explored in this book: top down and bottom up. Top down portrays local government as one of many possible service delivery agents of senior governments. Bottom up depicts local government as a vehicle through which residents directly shape their communities. This chapter focuses on the second view and outlines how local residents participate in their own governance, by considering aspects like the local election process, voting, candidacy, and local political parties. It also considers non-electoral or extra-electoral citizen participation and civic engagement between elections. Local politics is healthier than often portrayed when both electoral and non-electoral participation improves.

The Importance of Citizen Participation

A great many scholars not only believe public participation is the cornerstone of democracy, but also feel citizen input into policy making should in itself be viewed as a good practice to be pursued.[1] These scholars argue the more people participate in policy making, the more likely these policies will reflect the will of the people. They also suggest high participation rates increase the chance these people will continue to participate in future policy making processes and, more importantly, will more vigorously support any local government policy they help create. These ideas suggest the political role of local government should be revived and strengthened. In fact, since municipalities are "closest to the people" – in that local councils oversee the affairs of much smaller groups of people than provincial or national governments – there is every chance participation in local government might be even more important to a community than participation in provincial or national governance.

---

[1] For example, see C. B. Macpherson, *The Life and Times of Liberal Democracy*, Oxford, New York, Oxford University Press, 1977 and Carole Pateman, *Participation and Democratic Theory*, Cambridge, Cambridge University Press, 1970.

To a great extent, a municipal government's ability to push back against provincial and federal governments is also related to the extent that the local community members support local officials. By the same token, a disengaged citizenry can weaken the bargaining position of local officials. As Andrew notes, the push by local governments for greater autonomy from their provincial masters is more likely to succeed if backed by a popular base of support, which, in turn, depends partly on the extent to which local officials encourage local citizenship.[2] Immigration and amalgamation have combined to create some very large cities in Canada that could have considerable political weight and influence if citizens were more active. However, local officials will have to pay far more attention to how to interact with, and involve, citizens if they wish to draw more people into local decision making processes and strengthen their power to fend off unwanted provincial and national policies.

Local Government Elections

Modern local governments in Canada are expected to uphold the principle of representative government, in that members of the local population have the ability to elect officials to make decisions on behalf of the community. This was not always the case in Canada. As noted in earlier chapters, municipal governments began with a very restricted franchise favouring white male property owners. Early local election laws disenfranchised women, visible minorities, Aboriginals, those who had not yet reached middle-age, or those without property. However, the Canadian local government franchise is now much broader, allowing citizens 18 years and older who meet limited residency requirements to vote in local elections – although property owners often still have a right to vote in local elections even if they do not live in the municipality. The next few subsections explore voting and running in local elections as well as the activities of local political parties in several of our largest cities.

---

[2] Caroline Andrew, "City-States and City-Scapes in Canada: The Politics and Culture of Canadian Urban Diversity," August 2006, chapter for presentation at the conference *Managing Diversity: Prospects for a Post-Nationalist Politics*, Dublin, April 2004, pp. 18-19.

Voting in Local Elections

While the franchise has greatly expanded over the past decades, a great number of those eligible to cast ballots do not exercise their right to vote. For example, New Brunswick's chief electoral officer reports 336 398 residents were registered to vote in areas where there were contested municipal elections in 2008, with 162 660 ballots cast. These figures combine to produce an average voter turnout rate of 48% in municipalities across the province. To put these numbers into perspective, approximately 70% of those registered cast ballots in the 2010 New Brunswick provincial election, a rate 22 percentage points higher than that found at the local level.[3]

However, it is very important to remember the average turnout figure conceals wide variations in voter participation from municipality to municipality. For example, turnout rates in New Brunswick municipalities in 2008 ranged from as low as 20% in Woodstock and 22% in Beaubassin East Rural Community, to as high as 75% in Doaktown and 77% in Sainte-Anne-de-Madawaska.[4] This comparison shows that while the average voter turnout in all municipalities is 48%, the turnout rate is much lower than this average in some municipalities and in others it exceeds this average – and even that of provincial election turnout! Thus it is important not to assume every municipality suffers from a low turnout, but to look at each one on a case by case basis.

A plethora of academic studies[5] suggest that a number of factors combine to explain this variation in voter turnout rates. These include: the number of people living within the municipality, the type of electoral system, demographic variables, and the specifics of the local election races. Some studies suggest smaller municipalities demonstrate higher turnout rates than larger communities. Others show that municipalities with ward systems tend to have higher turnout rates than cities with at large elections. Still others indicate that turnout tends to be higher in municipalities with a large proportion of highly educated residents or

---

[3] Thirty-Seventh General Election, September 27, 2010, Report of the Chief Electoral Officer, at http://www.gnb.ca/elections/publications-e.asp.

[4] Quadrennial Municipal Elections, May 12, 2008, Report of the Municipal Electoral Officer, at http://www.gnb.ca/elections/publications-e.asp.

[5] See Joseph Kushner, David Siegel, and Hannah Stanwick, "Ontario Municipal Elections: Voting Trends and Determinants of Electoral Success in a Canadian Province," *Canadian Journal of Political Science*, September 1997 and Jacques Desmarais and Josée Perras, "Les élections municipales au Québec depuis 14 ans," *Municipalité,* août-septembre, 1996, pp. 17-20.

homeowners. The number of candidates, acclamations, concurrent referendums, and degree to which races are competitive are also often cited as affecting voting turnout rates.

Aside from these directly related causes of low turnout, some believe urban development patterns can also affect voter participation. For example, increasingly long commutes to work leave people less time to take an interest in municipal matters or participate in community activities and organizations. Little interest or interaction undermines local "social capital" – or the social connections, networks, and trust relationships facilitating cooperative action for mutual benefit within the community. Robert Putnam sees low voter turnout as a symptom of the general decline of local community spirit with voting as "an instructive proxy measure of broader social change" and weak electoral participation as "the most visible symptom of a broader disengagement from community life." For Putnam, the more people go "bowling alone," the less they tend to participate in their communities and/or vote.[6]

The structure of local government may also affect voter turnout. For example, municipal decision making may not seem relevant to local citizens because many of the issues of concern are handled by separate boards or by other service providers and not by elected municipal councils. Thus, voter turnout may drop because the electorate "perceives whether intuitively or through overt knowledge that the social, economic and even environmental problems which beset the city lie beyond the city council's power to solve."[7] A study by Stewart, Young, and MacIver of the 2005 Vancouver civic election shows that those who take the time to vote in local elections have very high levels of political knowledge. Local voters in Vancouver demonstrate a deep awareness of who they are voting for and what local officials can do to improve the city. Whether non-voters have the same level of political knowledge is open to debate.[8]

One Ontario study reports that 63% of respondents claimed they cast ballots in the 2003 St. Catharine's local election although official results show that only 30% of eligible voters turned out. These findings suggest many residents feel they should have voted and did not want to admit their failure to do so. The study also shows voting turnout was higher

---

[6] Robert D. Putnam, *Bowling Alone*, New York, Simon & Schuster, 2000, p. 35.

[7] Earl A. Levin, "Municipal Democracy and Citizen Participation," in Nancy Klos (ed.), *The State of Unicity – 25 Years Later*, Winnipeg, Institute of Urban Studies, 1998, p. 50.

[8] Kennedy Stewart, Patricia MacIver, and Stewart Young, "Testing and Improving Voters' Political Knowledge," *Canadian Public Policy*, Vol. 34, No. 4, December 2008, pp. 403-417.

among older people, homeowners, those with higher incomes, and those involved in community and political activity. Most interestingly, the study finds that non-voters claim their absence from the polls is due to being busy with work or family, polling station problems, or untrustworthy candidates. However, respondents cited factors such as apathy and laziness when asked to explain the absence of other non-voters, hinting people are willing to let themselves off the hook when it comes to non-voting, but are less forgiving to their neighbours for failing to go to the polls.[9]

Local Council Composition

Until recently, municipal council positions have been considered a part time responsibility, the preserve of the "gifted amateur" rather than the professional politician.[10] Given the strong influence business wields over municipal operations, it is not surprising most elected urban councillors are in business, the public service, education, or community organizations and are from the middle class, middle-aged, white, and male.[11] As a result, one of the challenges facing municipal governments is to encourage more representative councils, composed of members more accurately reflecting the composition of the local populations they are elected to represent. As a general rule, councils should mirror society. For example, if women comprise 50% of the population they should hold 50% of elected positions. The same logic holds for minority groups in society.[12]

In terms of gender representation, the percentage of women holding municipal council seats in major Canadian cities is higher than the percentage of seats held by women in provincial and national legislatures. This is hardly a cause for celebration, however, as Lightbody[13] reports that women held just 21% of the seats on municipal

---

[9] Joseph Kushner and David Siegel, "Why Do Municipal Electors Not Vote?," Winnipeg, *Canadian Journal of Urban Research*, Winter 2006, pp. 264-277.

[10] Andrew Sancton and Paul Woolner, "Full-time municipal councillors: a strategic challenge for Canadian urban government," *Canadian Public Administration*, Winter 1990, p. 385.

[11] Katherine Graham, Susan D. Phillips, and Allan M. Maslove, *Urban Governance in Canada*, Toronto, Harcourt Brace & Company, Canada, 1998, p. 99.

[12] Jeanette Ashe and Kennedy Stewart, "Legislative recruitment: Using diagnostic testing to explain underrepresentation," *Party Politics*, February 24, 2011, pp. 1-21.

[13] James Lightbody, *City Politics, Canada*, Peterborough, Broadview Press, 2006, p. 190.

councils in major Canadian cities in 2006. A similar study of British Columbia municipalities by Gavan-Koop and Smith finds:

> ...males dominate as both mayors and councillors across the province.... 125 mayors were male, while only 30 female mayors (19%) were in office.... there were still three times as many males on council as females, with 547 males and 270 females (33%).... In seven municipalities, there was no female representation on either council or as mayor. There were no councils with solely female representation.[14]

Some suggest women hold more seats on local councils than provincial and national legislatures because family responsibilities preclude women from travelling to and from federal and provincial legislatures and municipal issues are of more interest to women than men because the former are more connected to the local community than the latter.[15] Trimble dismisses these explanations as based on incorrect and unflattering assumptions about the nature of city politics and about women in general. She claims "women become involved in city government because of its profound influence on their lives; that is, women choose city politics because it is powerful in ways that matter to them."[16] Andrew makes a similar point by noting that the increasing involvement of women in organizations like shelters for battered women, food banks, and sexual assault crisis centres brings them into contact with local government and municipal policy and makes them more appreciative of the importance of municipal operations.[17]

Exploring another aspect of women in local politics, Smith and Gavan-Koop find women candidates to be more successful in smaller municipalities and in those without local political parties. In addition, the authors assert that the lack of regulations governing local campaign financing make it difficult for female candidates to match the fundraising abilities of male candidates. Finally, the authors conclude gender gaps

---

[14] Denisa Gavan-Koop and Patrick Smith, *Gender Governing in British Columbia*, paper for the British Columbia Political Studies Association, North Vancouver, 2004; see also Gavan-Koop and Smith, "Gendering Local Governing," in *Canadian Political Science Review*, Vol. 2, No. 3, 2008, pp. 152-171.

[15] Chantal Maillé, "Gender Concerns in City Life," in Timothy L. Thomas (ed.), *The Politics of the City*, Toronto, ITP Nelson, 1997, p. 109.

[16] Linda Trimble, "Politics Where We Live: Women and Cities," in James Lightbody (ed.), *Canadian Metropolitics*, Toronto, Copp Clark Ltd., 1995, pp. 93 and 110.

[17] Caroline Andrew, "Getting Women's Issues on the Municipal Agenda: Violence Against Women," in Judith A. Garber and Robyne S. Turner (eds.), *Gender in Urban Research, Urban Affairs Annual Review 42*, Thousand Oaks, Sage, 1995, p. 99.

will not be fixed by tinkering with rules, but may only be narrowed by using gender quotas to ensure a minimum number of women are elected to local councils. To this end, the Federation of Canadian Municipalities (FCM) launched a campaign to increase female representation on council to 30% by 2026, although the organization does not go as far as to endorse using gender quotas to achieve this aim.[18]

In contrast to the inroads being made by women in municipal politics, visible minorities remain very poorly represented on local councils. Even cities with ethnically diverse populations have very few minority candidates coming forward to stand for elections – let alone winning council seats. Visible minority underrepresentation undermines the democratic principles of equality and fairness as well as the legitimacy of local governments because the political process must be seen by all community members as open and inclusive if decisions are to be viewed as fair and acceptable. According to Canadian political philosopher Will Kymlicka, "this means, among other things, that the interests and perspectives of all groups be listened to and taken into account."[19] If local political processes lack this quality, there may be very little support for a decision, making its implementation more difficult.

In terms of visible minorities in major Canadian cities, many city councils remain white, middle class, and male despite growing heterogeneity among our urban populations.[20] Studies of various cities across the country indicate that "newcomers and minorities do not yet have even close to what could be described as an equitable numerical presence in elected office."[21] Montreal's minority representation, according to an analysis of the 2001 election results, did not reflect the city's ethnocultural landscape accurately as Italians and Jewish communities were overrepresented and Haitian and Chinese

---

[18] This summary is from speaking notes for Councillor Louise Poirier, *Community Mobilization Plan for Increasing Women's Participation in Municipal Government*, annual conference of the Federation of Canadian Municipalities, June 2, 2006. See https://fcm.ca/home/programs/women-in-local-government.htm for details on this initiative and various resources in support of it.

[19] Will Kymlicka, *Finding Our Way: Rethinking Ethnocultural Relations in Canada*, Toronto, Oxford University Press, 1998, p. 104.

[20] Karen Bird, "Obstacles to Ethnic Minority Representation in Local Government in Canada," in Caroline Andrew (ed.), *Our Diverse Cities*, Number 1, Spring 2004, p. 182, accessed at http://canada.metropolis.net/index_e.html, February 20, 2007.

[21] John Biles and Erin Tolley, "Getting Seats at the Table(s): The Political Participation of Newcomers and Minorities in Ottawa," in Andrew, *Our Diverse Cities*, p. 178.

communities were underrepresented.[22] A Vancouver study suggests that visible minorities are consistently underrepresented due to stereotyping and discrimination.[23]

Much attention has been directed to the election of Naheed Nenshi as mayor of Calgary in October 2010, a 38 year old Muslim whose parents came to this country from Tanzania. But this result is very much the exception that proves the rule in light of recent findings on minority representation. A new study[24] finds that while 40% of the population of the Greater Toronto Area comprises visible minorities, they make up only 7% of municipal councillors. Only 1 of 11 councillors in Brampton is from visible minorities even though they are 57% of the population. Mississauga's population is 49% visible minority, but there is not one representative among the 12 councillors. Even the City of Toronto which makes much of its diversity has but 5 members of council out of 45 from visible minorities.

Media coverage prompted by the GTA study provides further evidence of the underrepresentation of minorities.[25] Montreal currently has only 3 of its 64 councillors from visible minorities. Richmond (B.C.) with 65% of its population made up of visible minorities (according to the 2006 census) has only 1 councillor from that category. While the election of Mayor Naheed Nenshi has been explained, in part, by the fact that Calgary has become a very ethnically diverse community, he is the only representative of a visible minority on that city's council.

With the growing diversity of Canada's cities, it is increasingly important that electoral politics be made more attractive and accessible to minority communities. Compounding this challenge, as noted earlier, is the fact that recent immigrants are not integrating as quickly or easily as earlier generations did, or as successfully in terms of employment and income. While Canadian cities remain peaceful, recent riots in London and Paris suggest differences between communities can quickly turn

---

[22] Carolle Simard, "Municipal Elites in Quebec's Amalgamated Cities," in Andrew, *Our Diverse Cities*, p. 187.

[23] Yasmeen Abu-Laban, "Ethnic Politics in a Globalizing Metropolis: The Case of Vancouver," in Thomas, *The Politics of the City*, pp. 77-95.

[24] Myer Siemiatycki, *The Diversity Gap: The Electoral Under-Representation of Visible Minorities*, DiverseCity, The Greater Toronto Leadership Project, November 2011. See http://diversecitytoronto.ca/wp-content/uploads/Final-Report.pdf.

[25] The examples that follow are from Marcus Gee, "Visible minorities vastly under-represented in municipal politics," *Globe and Mail*, November 8, 2011 and Anna Mehler Paperny, "Visible minorities thin on the ground at Canadian city councils," *Globe and Mail*, November 9, 2011.

unpleasant – especially if the community actively alienates or discriminates against visible minorities. While Andrew argues "only a greater role for cities can ensure the successful management of diversity," much remains to be done to achieve this goal.[26]

Political Parties and Local Elections

In the United Kingdom, the Conservative and Labour parties run candidates in national and local elections. In the United States, Republican and Democratic candidates stand in national, state, and local elections. In Canada, however, the Conservative Party, Liberal Party, and New Democratic Party almost never formally venture into local election contests. As a result, while political parties dominate national and provincial level politics in Canada, they are present in very few local elections. The New Democratic Party (and its predecessor, the CCF) is the only national political party to make a concerted effort to elect candidates locally in Canada – an effort that has met with very limited success.

As described below on a city by city basis, those few local political parties that do exist in cities such as Vancouver and Montreal are not formal branches of provincial or national parties, although local parties on occasion informally cooperate with parties operating at senior levels. Often local parties – such as the Non-Partisan Association (NPA) in Vancouver and Winnipeg's Independent Citizen Election Committee (ICEC) – are really nothing more than loose coalitions of like-minded candidates with links to the business or development community concerned with preventing more left of centre candidates from gaining council seats. Members of these local parties usually present themselves as candidates interested in keeping parties out of local government – even though, ironically, they attempt to achieve this objective by coming together as a slate of candidates and behaving very much like a party.

Party Activity in Montreal

The province of Quebec has the best developed local political party system in Canada, mainly due to provincial legislation passed in the late 1970s allowing local parties to organize and raise funds. Originally applicable only to municipalities with at least 20 000 residents, this

---

[26] Andrew, *City-States and City-Scapes*, p. 1. See also Aude Claire Fourot, "Managing Religious Pluralism in Canadian Cities: Mosques in Montreal and Laval," in Tiziana Caponia and Maren Borkert (eds.), *The Local Dimension of Policy-Making*, Amsterdam, Amsterdam University Press, 2010, pp. 135-159.

legislation has been broadened to include all municipalities with a population of at least 5000. Currently there are more than 150 registered municipal political parties in Quebec with approximately one-third of municipalities within the province having at least one political party.[27]

Montreal is Quebec's largest city and also the city with the longest history of local party activity. Montreal has experienced well documented local political party activity for almost 60 years, beginning with the Civic Action League which ran candidates in the 1954 election – including a young lawyer named Jean Drapeau who was elected mayor.[28] In 1957, Drapeau was defeated as mayor and promptly formed a new political party – the Civic Party – and attracted to it most of the city councillors who had run for the Civic Action League. He returned to power as mayor in 1960 as head of this disciplined new party, a position that he was to hold until his retirement prior to the 1986 election.

The continued success of the Civic Party led to an increase in citizen participation in local affairs in Montreal as a reaction against the autocratic style of Drapeau who concentrated power in his office and in the executive committee that he appointed and controlled. By 1974, the growing opposition forces had come together to form the Montreal Citizens' Movement (MCM). The MCM made a surprisingly strong showing in the 1974 elections, but internal divisions weakened the party over the next few years. In addition, the MCM's socialist policy orientation alienated the newly elected provincial government of the Parti Québécois, which, in any event, was not anxious to tangle with Drapeau and was quite prepared to stay out of city politics if the mayor would keep his influential voice out of the Quebec sovereignty debate.

Following Drapeau's retirement, the MCM won a massive victory in 1986, with only one Civic Party councillor and two independents elected to council. In Milner's view, the MCM and its new leader, Jean Doré, "appeared reasonable and approachable, especially when contrasted with Drapeau's Gaullist style; its hammering at everyday bread and butter issues corresponded more closely to the emerging public mood than Drapeau's seeming preoccupation with grand projects."[29]

---

[27] See http://www.electionsquebec.qc.ca/english/municipal/rapeq/consultation-political-parties.php for current figures. See also William Brown, "Party time," *Forum*, May/June 2001, Ottawa, Federation of Canadian Municipalities, p. 27.

[28] Andrew Sancton, "Montreal," in Warren Magnusson and Sancton (eds.), *City Politics in Canada*, Toronto, University of Toronto Press, 1983, pp. 69-78, is the basis for much of the discussion of developments in Montreal.

[29] Henry Milner, "The Montreal Citizens' Movement: Then and Now," *Quebec Studies*, No. 6, 1988, p. 5.

In contrast to the autocratic, secretive style long followed by Drapeau, the Doré administration was cautious and consensual. Consultation was the watchword and was reflected in the establishment of five standing committees and the creation of district advisory committees for the nine planning areas into which the city was divided.[30] In spite of these positive initiatives, it wasn't long before the grassroots nature of the MCM began to weaken. Developers and business people began courting the new administration and party activists soon found little scope for their activities. Their best leaders had become city councillors or political advisors. Actions taken by the MCM in office increasingly alienated its traditional supporters.[31] When some of the MCM members began to voice concern over the actions being taken, rules were tightened up to enforce caucus confidentiality – the sort of muzzling action expected of old line parties.

Four MCM councillors defected during the first term, complaining of overwhelming pressure to follow the party line and the silencing of debate within the party. The MCM held on to power in 1990, but was reduced to six seats in the 1994 election and Doré lost the mayoralty to Pierre Bourque whose Vision Montreal party captured 38 other council seats. Bourque's first term was marked by controversy, including the defection from his party of no less than 15 members. There was also much criticism of Bourque's efforts to dismantle the public consultation machinery established by Doré and his return to the autocratic governing style associated with Drapeau. In spite of these developments, Bourque and the Vision Party captured the same number of seats in the 1998 election, but Doré finished a humiliating fourth in the mayoral contest.

There was no "third time lucky" for Bourque, who was defeated in 2001 in the first election of the amalgamated city of Montreal – rejected, in large part, by suburban voters opposed to the amalgamation and angry with Bourque for so strongly championing the merger. Victorious Mayor Gérald Tremblay had merged his original United Island of Montreal party with the MCM to form the Montreal Island Citizens Union. The result was a party described as "one very big tent: under it are people from the centre-right to the centre-left, suburbanites and city people, merger fans and de-merger advocates, and anglophones, francophones

---

[30] Pierre Hamel, "Urban Issues and New Public Policy Challenges: The Example of Public Consultation Policy in Montreal," in Caroline Andrew, Katherine A. Graham, and Susan D. Phillips (eds.), *Urban Affairs, Back on the Policy Agenda*, Montreal & Kingston, McGill-Queen's University Press, 2002, pp. 228-229.

[31] Timothy L. Thomas, "Political Representation and Community Politics," in Thomas, *The Politics of the City*, p. 214.

and allophones. It is the most heterogeneous Montreal party in memory, and by far."[32] While criticized during his first term for supporting the "no" side in the demerger votes that were held and for running a secretive administration, Tremblay defeated Bourque again in 2005.

Despite being assailed with accusations of corruption, in 2009 incumbent Mayor Gérald Tremblay led his (renamed) Union Montréal party to a third straight victory. He defeated Vision Montréal, led by former Parti Québécois member of the Assembly Louise Harel and Projet Montréal's mayoral candidate Richard Bergeron. Harel's promise to clean up city hall was undermined by a scandal involving former Vision leader Benoît Labonté who was forced to withdraw from politics. Polls shortly prior to the election had put Projet Montréal's leader Richard Bergeron neck and neck with the two other main candidates. Besides the party's main focus on public transit and urban planning, it emphasized ethics and running its campaign on a small budget. Tremblay still managed to win, but with less than 40% of the votes for mayor.

Party Activity in Toronto

There is no better example of public resistance to national and provincial parties moving into the municipal sphere than the 1969 Toronto municipal election. The Liberal Party of Canada, fresh from its 1968 national election victory under Pierre Trudeau, was anxious to establish a stronger base in Toronto, partly as a necessary prerequisite to the overthrow of the long entrenched Progressive Conservative provincial government. The decision to enter a slate of candidates for municipal office was hotly debated, however, and the internal split in the party on this issue resulted in a less than wholehearted effort in the ensuing election.[33] Whatever the reasons, the election results were not encouraging for the national parties extending their reach into local politics. The Liberal Party's candidate for mayor, Stephen Clarkson, finished third with fewer than half as many votes as the victorious William Dennison. Significantly, Dennison had refused to run as an NDP candidate even though he was closely associated with that party. Only three candidates formally associated with the NDP and two with the Liberal Party were elected to council.[34]

---

[32] Henry Aubin, "Suburbs win big," *Montreal Gazette*, November 5, 2001.

[33] See Stephen Clarkson, *City Lib*, Toronto, Hakkert, 1972 and the exchange between Clarkson and J. L. Granatstein in Jack K. Masson and James Anderson (eds.), *Emerging Party Politics in Urban Canada*, Toronto, McClelland & Stewart, 1972, pp. 60-67.

[34] Donald J. H. Higgins, *Urban Canada: Its Government and Politics*, Toronto, Macmillan, 1977, p. 239.

The 1969 election was also significant in demonstrating the influence of the citizens' movement of that era. It helped to elect a minority of reform candidates to council. The next election, in 1972, saw a dramatic breakthrough, with the election of a majority of reformers to council and a self-proclaimed member of the reform group – in the person of David Crombie – to the mayor's position. Once elected, however, Crombie operated as a moderate and, in fact, voted against the reform councillors on many of the major issues facing council.[35] While he was genuinely concerned about the threat to neighbourhoods posed by the excessively pro growth mentality of previous councils, Crombie was no less committed to private property and private enterprise. Rather, he wanted to find a way of providing continued development without the disruption and dislocation that had accompanied it in the recent past.[36]

The Crombie-led council was not radical enough for some and the reform group that had appeared to capture control of council in 1972 soon split into moderates and more militant reformers, with the latter becoming increasingly critical of Crombie's moderate policies. Ironically, while reform councillors continued to be elected throughout the 1970s, one of them, Michael Goldrick, persuasively argues that the election of 1972 was not the beginning but "the zenith of the reform movement." As he explains, the moderates were satisfied that the reform movement would ensure that neighbourhoods were protected, the automobile would be treated with common sense, and the style of development would be modified – all objectives of the middle class. But for the hard line reformers elected from working class wards, the real objective was to redistribute wealth and power:

> They wanted real, not token, decision-making power shifted to neighbourhoods, not only the style of development controlled but its pace, location and ownership subject to public decision; they challenged private property rights exercised by financial institutions and development corporations and attacked the fortresses of civil service power.[37]

John Sewell was undoubtedly the most conspicuous and widely identified member of the reform group, and a community activist who had been earlier associated with a number of the citizen confrontations

---

[35] Jon Caufield, *The Tiny Perfect Mayor*, Toronto, James Lorimer and Company, 1974.

[36] Magnusson, in Magnusson and Sancton, *City Politics in Canada*, p. 119.

[37] Michael Goldrick, "The Anatomy of Urban Reform in Toronto," *City Magazine*, May-June 1978, p. 36.

with city hall.[38] Sewell was a very independent minded politician and, while he had made some unsuccessful attempts to build a reform party around himself, he ran for mayor in 1978 as an independent candidate.[39] After one very controversial term, especially in relation to Sewell's defence of various inner city minorities and his demands for police reform, he was defeated by Arthur Eggleton, a Liberal-affiliated candidate with strong ties to the business community. Eggleton was elected throughout the 1980s.

In the meantime, however, reform councillors continued to be voted on council, although increasingly linked with the NDP. By 1980 they had 9 of the 23 seats on council, with all but one of the victorious candidates having run with official party endorsement.[40] But the economic decline in the early 1980s prompted councils to adopt an increasingly pro growth stance. An inevitable backlash against this stance occurred in the 1988 election, which saw the voters defeat two pro development aldermen, elect a majority of designated reform candidates, and choose reform candidates to fill six of the eight city positions on the Metropolitan Toronto council.[41] Another economic decline at the beginning of the 1990s influenced the 1991 election which saw a former police commissioner and councillor June Rowlands elected as mayor over Jack Layton (who subsequently became leader of the federal NDP and leader of Canada's official opposition). Six NDP-affiliated council members were elected, and were returned to office in 1994, along with an NDP-affiliated mayor, Barbara Hall.

By the next election in 1997, Metropolitan Toronto and all of its constituent municipalities were amalgamated to create a new City of Toronto. With the much larger city council needed to represent the 2.5 million people in this greatly enlarged municipality, the limited focus provided by political parties became more diffuse – even as, arguably, the need for the kind of cohesion that parties can provide became that much more pressing. In 1997, Barbara Hall was defeated by North York's long-time mayor, Mel Lastman, who was described as

---

[38] For his personal reflections on these experiences, see John Sewell, *Up Against City Hall*, Toronto, James Lewis and Samuel, 1972.

[39] Magnusson, in Magnusson and Sancton, *City Politics in Canada*, p. 123.

[40] *Ibid.*, p. 122.

[41] Michael Valpy, "Voters Demonstrate Power of Ballot Box," *Globe and Mail*, November 16, 1988.

"nominally conservative" and pro business in orientation.[42] The 56 members of the new council had as many differences as there are flavours of canned soup. A dozen or so members were affiliated with the NDP, with another 6 to 10 councillors voting with these members depending on the issue. There was also another group of perhaps 20 to 25 councillors who coalesced around Lastman.[43]

Instead of traditional left wing and right wing clashes, the new council tended to split more along geographic (old city versus old suburb) lines, notably with respect to such matters as property tax reform, transportation, and programs for the homeless. While some welcomed the apparent reduction of ideological clashes, the new council lacked a clear identity or any clear sense of purpose. It was characterized as "a debating society with 56 contesting opinions."[44]

The 2000 election was for a slightly smaller council (44 members, plus the mayor), but the result was similar in terms of a diverse makeup of members. According to James, Toronto's council had at least five distinct groups: "the hard right wingers, neo-conservatives really; the mushy middle, center right councillors who usually carry the vote; the NDPers, unabashed lefties; left wingers who don't want to be tarred as NDPers; and the lost souls whose votes are likely for sale in return for political favours or power."[45]

Lastman was defeated in 2003 by NDP-affiliated David Miller, who appeared with a broom on election night to demonstrate how he was going to sweep the city clean after the scandals and cronyism that had characterized the previous regime. Miller had the support of only about 15 left wing votes on council, only one-third of the total, which undermined his ability to push through his policies. Soon after Miller's reelection in 2006, city council gave the mayor additional powers, notably with respect to the appointment of an executive committee. With 13 supposedly guaranteed votes from this base, the expectation was that the mayor would be well placed to pick up the additional 10 votes needed to advance his agenda.[46] Yet his first major initiative, to make

---

[42] This apt description was used by Colin Vaughan, "Bright spots on council hard to find," *Toronto Star*, November 9, 1998.

[43] See Bruce Demara, "New united council a 'soup' of 57 varieties," *Toronto Star*, May 16, 1998, on which this discussion is based.

[44] Colin Vaughan, "Time for council to shape up," *Toronto Star*, June 8, 1998.

[45] Royson James, "Factionalism in full bloom at budget time," *Toronto Star*, April 30, 2001.

[46] Royson James, "Lack of support leaves mayor exposed," *Toronto Star*, July 17, 2007.

use of the taxing powers given to the city under its new legislation, resulted initially in an embarrassing defeat, demonstrating once again the difficulty of providing strong leadership within a large council without disciplined voting blocks through the use of parties.

In 2009, Mayor Miller announced he would not stand for reelection. This opened the field for candidates, with the right of centre and outspoken Rob Ford eventually winning with 47% of the vote. Centrist George Smitherman finished second with 36% and left of centre Joe Pantalone finished a distant third with 12% of the vote. The race was at times vicious, with all candidates suffering personal attacks. Ford's mayoralty has been marked by controversy, including the city's compliance audit committee ordering an audit of Ford's election campaign finances.[47] While the new mayor seemed to bulldoze his way through things in the early months of his term, he suffered a number of setbacks as 2011 drew to a close and it is not clear whether he will regain the momentum or find himself, as with Miller before him, thwarted by lack of sufficient support within Toronto's large council.[48]

Party Activity in Winnipeg

Local political activity in Winnipeg received a great stimulus in 1919, when the General Strike polarized the city. A Civic Election Committee was formed by downtown businesses to endorse, and raise funds for, anti-labour candidates. Until the end of the 1980s, this organization – later known as the Metropolitan Election Committee, the Greater Winnipeg Election Committee, and, finally, the Independent Citizen Election Committee (ICEC) – continued to elect a majority of the members of council against the efforts of candidates affiliated with the Independent Labour Party, the CCF, and, most recently, the NDP. While essentially a pro business local political party, the ICEC insisted that it was not a party at all and that support for its candidates would prevent parties – especially socialist parties – from bringing their politics and policies into the municipal council chamber. As a result, the ICEC was able to avoid accepting the responsibility for leadership in spite of its dominant numerical position within Winnipeg council over the decades.

As discussed in Chapter 4, a radically new form of municipal government was introduced in Winnipeg in 1972. In the view of Paul Thomas, the Unicity experiment was designed to weaken the alliance

---

[47] http://www.torontosun.com/2011/05/13/fords-election-campaign-to-undergo-audit.

[48] For one perspective on this question, see Marcus Gee, "Is it all downhill from here, Mayor Ford?, *Globe and Mail*, October 22, 2011.

between public officials and land-based business by promoting citizen involvement and placing "other political actors representing neighbourhoods, broader communities, ethno-cultural groups, non-profits and advocacy groups on a more equal footing with the business interests."[49] The anticipated increase in citizen participation did not fully materialize, however, in part because the centre right candidates of the ICEC dominated the Unicity council and entrenched a pro development regime in Winnipeg, one with little sympathy for citizen participation in politics.[50]

By the 1980 election the ICEC's veneer of nonpartisanship had worn thin, and the NDP-affiliated candidates scored a breakthrough by capturing seven seats on the Unicity council, with another nine going to independent candidates and the remaining twelve to ICEC candidates. Shortly before the 1983 election, the ICEC announced that it was disbanding, but the results were disappointing for those candidates affiliated with the NDP which lost one of its seven seats, and nearly lost two others, partly because of internal divisions between "old guard" members and newer, more progressive members. The NDP presence on council was reduced even further, with just two affiliated members, in the 1986 municipal election. The other 27 members elected were all independents, although the majority of them represented the disbanded ICEC. Indeed, one assessment identified 20 of these 27 "independents" as actively involved with the Progressive Conservative or Liberal parties, continuing the domination of the ICEC type candidate.[51]

In 1989, a reform coalition composed of New Democrat and Liberal-affiliated candidates formed under the hopeful name of WIN (Winnipeg into the Nineties).[52] It succeeded in electing members to one-third of the seats, establishing for the first time a cohesive reform block on Winnipeg city council. The response to this "threat" by the Conservative provincial government elected in 1990 was to abolish the right of political parties to make contributions to candidates running for city council, while authorizing donations from corporations and unions, actions which have been described as leading to the corporatization of civic government.[53]

---

[49] Paul Thomas, "Diagnosing the Health of Civic Democracy: 25 Years of Citizen Involvement with City Hall," in Klos, *The State of Unicity*, p. 47.

[50] Greg Selinger, "Urban Governance for the Twenty-First Century: What the Unicity Experience Tells Us," in Klos, *The State of Unicity*, p. 89.

[51] This is the assessment of Jeff Lowe, "Winnipeg: User-Unfriendly," *City Magazine*, Spring 1988, p. 9.

[52] Barton Reid, "City Beat," *City Magazine*, Winter '92/'93, p. 5.

[53] Selinger, "What the Unicity Experience Tells Us," p. 95.

In the 1992 election, WIN candidates retained their minority position, holding 5 seats on a council reduced from 21 to 15. But one commentator contends Winnipeg's longstanding schism disappeared in 1992 when the city council was slashed to 15 and civic politics became a full-time job. "The demands on councillors in the new environment pretty well drove off the last of the bright lights on the right and left, who no longer could pursue civic politics as a hobby."[54] WIN had disappeared by the time of the 1998 election. Former WIN member Glen Murray was elected mayor as an independent candidate and all members of council also sat as independents.[55] Murray was reelected in 2002, but resigned in 2004 to run, unsuccessfully, in the federal election that year. He was replaced by Sam Katz, who was reelected in 2006.

Sam Katz stood for reelection in 2010, winning a decisive victory over Judy Wasylycia-Leis. With ties to the Manitoba Conservative Party, Katz ran a low key election campaign, making only seven campaign announcements while running on his record, presenting himself as a competent financial manager and portraying Wasylycia-Leis as tied to unions and NDP involvement in the mayoral race. Wasylycia-Leis was a Manitoba cabinet minister in the NDP provincial government from 1986 to 1988 and a member of the Canadian House of Commons between 1997 and 2010.[56]

Party Activity in Vancouver

As with Winnipeg, a pro business party formed in Vancouver to counter the threat of political gains by the left in the city's formative years. Formal local party activity began in 1936, when three CCF candidates were elected in the city's first at large municipal election.[57] In response, business interests founded the Non-Partisan Association (NPA), the organization's very name designed to conceal its real status as a local political party. The NPA dominated city council over the next few decades. However, by the 1960s, concerns about the pace and location of development, especially about urban renewal and expressway projects, brought increased opposition to the NPA and led in 1968 to the formation of two new parties to challenge its vision of the city.

---

[54] G. Flood, "Civic Fight Sputters," *Winnipeg Free Press*, September 21, 1997.

[55] Brown, "Party time," p. 27.

[56] http://www.winnipegfreepress.com/breakingnews/Polls-have-closed-votes-being-counted-105919743.html.

[57] The CCF, forerunner of the NDP, was the Cooperative Commonwealth Federation.

The first new party was TEAM (The Electors Action Movement), a diverse coalition of reformers, especially anti expressway forces, more conservative business interests, community workers, and academics. The second party, the Committee of Progressive Electors (COPE), was formed by the Vancouver and District Labour Council, with the objective of bringing together labour, ratepayer groups, the NDP, and other interested groups to establish a base to enter municipal politics.

An important breakthrough appeared to occur in 1972 with the defeat of the NPA and the election of a municipal council controlled by TEAM. Leo concedes that TEAM was a liberal, establishment party, focused on middle class issues, with only a limited concern for matters like "affordable housing, inner-city education, homelessness, racism, and women's issues."[58] But he contends that TEAM made a valuable contribution by shifting attention from a conservative, development oriented approach to city planning to one that addressed issues of "livability." Whatever its accomplishments, within four years TEAM was badly divided and in the 1978 election the NPA reemerged as the major party on council.

Control of Vancouver council by the NPA faced new challenges in 1980 when Mike Harcourt, a provincial New Democrat, won the mayoralty as an independent candidate and COPE elected three councillors. Harcourt returned as mayor in 1982, along with four COPE councillors and two independent NDP councillors. Gutstein refers to this election result as the "first successful challenge to business dominance at the local level in the city's 96 year history."[59] However, there were some difficulties in maintaining a progressive voting bloc on council, and continuing problems with interference from the Social Credit provincial government. Indeed, one book during this period expressed concern that local autonomy was being threatened by the neoconservative forces in power at the provincial level and their view that local authorities should not be allowed to follow policies contrary to the market oriented revival being promoted provincially.[60]

On the surface, the 1984 election results were quite similar to those of 1982. Harcourt was reelected mayor, along with five progressive

---

[58] Christopher Leo, "The Urban Economy and the Power of the Local State," in Frisken, *The Changing Canadian Metropolis*, Vol. 2, p. 690.

[59] Donald Gutstein, "Vancouver: Progressive Majority Impotent," *City Magazine*, Winnipeg, Spring 1983, p. 12.

[60] Warren Magnusson, William K. Carroll, Charles Doyle, Monika Langer, and R. B. J. Walker (eds.), *The New Reality: The Politics of Restraint in British Columbia*, Vancouver, NewStar Books, 1984.

members – four of them from COPE. Opposing them were three members from the NPA and two from TEAM. According to Gutstein, the polarization of the city was complete with this election. As he saw it, Vancouver was really two cities: a working class east side city and a middle class west side city – which elect two entirely different councils.[61]

The 1986 election results were quite dramatic, bringing Vancouver's developers back into power at city hall. The NPA captured 9 of the 11 seats on council – including its mayoral candidate, developer Gordon Campbell (who continued on to become the Liberal Premier of British Columbia) – and 8 of 9 seats on the school board. Campbell easily won reelection in 1988 and 1990, although COPE managed to increase its representation on council from three to five. The 1993 election was a near sweep for the NPA, with COPE winning only one seat. In an ironic twist of fate, the right wing city council found itself having to contend with an NDP provincial government led by Mike Harcourt – much as Harcourt, when head of a left leaning council a decade earlier, had to contend with interference from a Social Credit provincial government.

Domination by the NPA continued throughout the 1990s, with the party winning all seats on the council and school board in 1996 and all but two council seats in 1999. Just when it seemed that COPE was finished, it came roaring back in the 2002 election, electing 8 out of 10 city councillors, 7 of 9 school trustees, and 5 of 7 members of the parks board. Also successful was its candidate for mayor, Larry Campbell, former RCMP officer and city coroner (who inspired the CBC television series *Da Vinci's Inquest*). To at least some extent, COPE's victory was seen as a rejection of the cost cutting actions taken by a right wing Liberal provincial government, headed by former Vancouver mayor Gordon Campbell, elected provincially in May 2001. Once again, contrasting ideologies set the stage for potential strife between the city and the province.

Before the end of its first term, COPE was torn apart by internal wrangling, with several moderate members eventually forming a new party, Vision Vancouver, to run in the 2005 election. COPE and Vision Vancouver agreed not to run candidates against each other to avoid splitting the left vote and handing victory to the NPA, but considerable public bickering made a mockery of their pledge.[62] Fed up with the

---

[61] Donald Gutstein, "Civic Election Wars," *City Magazine*, Summer 1985, p. 12.

[62] Patrick Smith and Kennedy Stewart, *The COPE Interlude: The (Predictable) Rise & Fall of Vancouver's Radical Civic Left 2002-2005*, presentation to annual meeting, Canadian Political Science Association, Toronto, June 2006.

drama of local politics, Mayor Campbell departed municipal politics to become a Liberal Senator before the 2005 election. COPE did not run a mayoral candidate, but the new Vision Vancouver mayoral candidate Jim Green was defeated by Sam Sullivan of the NPA, which also won six council seats to control council. Only one COPE councillor was elected, along with four Vision Vancouver councillors.

In the run up to the 2008 civic election, NPA councillor Peter Ladner announced he would challenge Sullivan for the position of NPA mayoralty candidate, with Ladner defeating Sullivan in a close vote among party members. Vision Vancouver nominated former NDP MLA and environmentalist Gregor Robertson as the party's mayoralty candidate. COPE backed Robertson and once again declined to run a candidate. Robertson defeated Lander by a wide margin. Vision won seven council positions, COPE two, with the NPA reduced to a single seat.

During Robertson's tenure as mayor, Vancouver successfully hosted the 2010 Olympics, brought more bicycle lanes to the city, and reduced street homelessness. However, his mayoralty was dogged by Robertson's decision to bail out the troubled Olympic Village, charges of inaction during the 2011 Stanley Cup Riots, and complaints that he did not take more decisive action to end the "Occupy Vancouver" squatters who camped out on the grounds of the Vancouver Art Gallery throughout the fall of 2011. The latter surfaced as an issue in the municipal elections in November 2011 but had little impact on the results. Vision Vancouver, Robertson's local party, won seven of ten council seats (with another being the city's first Green member) and also controlled the school board and parks board. Incumbents also prevailed in other elections in the Greater Vancouver area, with only one-quarter of the voters turning out in some cases. The mayor and her party took all the seats in Surrey and the leftist Burnaby Citizens Association won all council and school board seats for a second time, continuing their quarter century hold on power.

Non-Electoral Participation in Local Government

In addition to participating in electoral politics, citizens can become involved in municipal policy making between elections.[63] As shown in the table below, Stewart provides a list of 26 extra-electoral citizen

---

[63] See also C. Richard Tindal and Susan Nobes Tindal, *Guide to Good Municipal Governance*, St. Thomas, Municipal World Inc., 2007, Chapter 5.

participation mechanisms used by national, provincial, and municipal governments. Some of these mechanisms, such as surveys and newsletters, are commonplace at the local level, while others, such as study circles and participatory budgets, are less so.[64]

Table 10.1 Twenty-Six Extra-Electoral Participation Mechanism	
1. Advertising	14. Public Hearing/Inquiry
2. Citizen Advisory Board	15. Public Meeting (Q&A)
3. Citizens' Assembly	16. Public Service Announcement (PSA)
4. Citizens' Jury	17. Referendum
5. Focus Group	18. Research Panel
6. Green/Discussion Paper	19. Sponsored Lobby Group
7. Initiative	20. Stakeholder Forum
8. Interactive Website	21. Study Circle
9. Internet Chat Group	22. Survey (closed-ended questions)
10. Localized Government	23. Survey (deliberative)
11. Newsletter	24. Survey (open-ended questions)
12. Participatory Budget	25. Telepolling/Televoting
13. Plebiscite	26. White Paper

It is important to remember not all mechanisms are equal in the extent to which they facilitate citizen input into decision making. The key to evaluating the value of these mechanisms is to determine the extent to which they allow citizens to *control the outcome* of the participation exercise. Some mechanisms offer citizens substantial say over the final decisions, while others leave control with elected officials. The following sections discuss various citizen participation mechanisms according to the extent to which they are informative, consultative, or delegative in nature. *Informative* mechanisms offer the least decision making control to citizens and provide local officials vehicles by which to advertise their policy decisions. *Consultative* mechanisms formally allow citizens significant input during decision making processes, but final decisions are still made by local officials. *Delegative* mechanisms allow the most citizen control as citizens have the final say on how an issue will be addressed.

Informative Participation Mechanisms

Local governments provide information to the public using a variety of mechanisms, including advertising, newsletters, public meetings, and

---

[64] K. Stewart, "Write the Rules and Win: Understanding Citizen Participation Game Dynamics," *Public Administration Review* 67, 2007, pp. 1067–1076.

public service announcements. These one way means of communication allow citizens no direct control over what decisions are made, but are still very important as information helps citizens organize around particular issues and pressure civic officials. Unless the public are kept informed they are unlikely to participate in other governance activities and if the public participation is not informed often it will be less effective or constructive.

One way to inform the public is simply to ensure that information regarding municipal operations is accessible. Many councils broadcast meetings via the Internet or local cable channels and make meeting minutes readily available. However, some councils do not have the will or capacity to ensure this basic level of information is available and some even try to hide information from the public. A recent Supreme Court of Canada decision shows the balance is tipping toward increased transparency at the local level. The case involved the City of London (Ontario) meeting behind closed doors to discuss a by-law, then subsequently passing the by-law in an open council meeting without debate. The city argued in court that the *Planning Act* allows council to pass interim control by-laws without advance notice to the public provided the subject matter was something from which litigation might arise. The court rejected this argument, stating in the decision:

> Municipal law has changed to require that municipal governments hold meetings that are open to the public, in order to imbue municipal governments with a robust democratic legitimacy. The democratic legitimacy of municipal decisions does not spring solely from periodic elections, but also from a decision-making process that is transparent, accessible to the public, and mandated by law. When a municipal government improperly acts with secrecy, this undermines the democratic legitimacy of its decisions, and such decisions, even when *intra vires*, are less worthy of deference.[65]

While openness is a necessary starting point, informing the public also requires proactively distributing intelligible material to citizens. Incomprehensive, jargon-filled reports do little to inform and involve the public. Imposing excessive charges for copying materials being sought also effectively works against their wider circulation. Fortunately, many municipalities are using the Internet to make available at their websites a wealth of useful data – including agendas, minutes of meetings, strategic and other long term plans, official and other land use plans, annual

---

[65] *London (City) v. RSJ Holdings Inc*, 2007 SCC 29, p. 3, accessed August 8, 2007 from http://scc.lexum.org/en/2007/2007scc29/2007scc29.html.

financial statements, and, where available, municipal service delivery measurements. Some municipalities publish a brief newsletter or highlights report on their website within 24 hours of a meeting – avoiding the delay of one or two weeks before minutes are approved at the next council meeting and officially available to the public and also ensuring that meeting results are presented in a summary form that invites public perusal.

While council meetings have long been broadcast on local cable television stations, a growing number of municipalities are now streaming video of their meetings on the Internet. Videos of the meetings then remain available on-line, allowing those interested in particular items to scroll down and view that agenda item.[66] Catering even more to the way people access data today, some municipalities provide information that can be downloaded by iPod users who can keep up with municipal happenings while listening to their favourite tunes.

Some municipalities get off to a good start by welcoming new residents with a detailed information package containing such items as the most recent municipal newsletter, street maps, a brief outline of the history of the community, information on municipal personnel, the council meeting schedule, phone numbers and contact persons for municipal services, and a list of service clubs and organizations. Much of this information may be on the municipal website, but not everyone has Internet access and even those who do still find this "hard copy" convenient. To drive home the point that it is local citizens for whom the municipality exists, St. Paul, Minnesota entitles its information booklet "Owner's Manual."[67]

The most common way in which local governments inform citizens face to face is still the public meeting. These meetings involve either elected or appointed officials presenting information and often taking questions from the audience. Sometimes under-attended and sedate, sometimes overflowing and raucous, public meetings have for many years been the lifeblood of municipal political life between elections. While public meetings often have the appearance of being consultative, these meetings are really just another way for local officials to deliver information to citizens. While citizens can often ask questions at these meetings and perhaps even influence officials, citizens have no ability to control directly how council addresses the issues under discussion.

---

[66] Susan Kuczka, "Suburbs stream meetings on Web," *Chicago Tribune,* May 9, 2007, accessed May 14, 2007 from www.chicagotribune.com.

[67] David Osborne and Ted Gaebler, *Reinventing Government,* New York, Penguin Books, 1993, p. 74.

Figure 10.1 Municipal Public Meeting

Source: Ian MacAlpine, *Kingston-Whig Standard*. Reprinted with permission.

Informative participation mechanisms are important as they provide organized groups with information by which to interact with their municipal officials. As described in Chapter 2, organized groups have been forming since the turn of the century reform movement of 100 years ago and various residents' and ratepayers' associations have protected the interests of the property owners, the business community, and the middle class for decades.

The 1960s and 1970s saw a great increase in local groups formed around social and environmental causes such as resisting expressways and bulldozing neighbourhoods. One analysis describes the changes during this period as "the politicizing of urban life" and refers to professional and skilled workers of the information economy forming a broad new social category referred to as the "new middle class." [68] In Magnusson's view a new reform politics developed, one that questioned long held views about "sacrificing the neighbourhood to the larger community, observing the proprieties of bureaucratic procedure, respecting the judgments of professional planners, and accepting the leadership of

---

[68] Paul Villeneuve and Anne-Marie Séguin, "Power and Decision-Making in the City: Political Perspectives," in Trudi Bunting and Pierre Filion, *Canadian Cities in Transition*, 2nd Edition, Toronto, Oxford University Press, 2000, p. 554.

elected officials...."[69] These groups included the Strathcona Property Owners' and Tenants' Association established in 1968 to oppose Vancouver's urban renewal initiatives; ratepayers' and residents' groups from the Treffan Court area of Toronto responding to the threat of new high rises in their middle and upper class neighbourhoods;[70] and the Stop Spadina, Save Our City, Coordinating Committee (SSSOCCC) formed to stop the Spadina Expressway in Toronto.[71]

By the 1980s, the citizen activism that had emerged two decades earlier had largely dissipated. Sewell goes so far as to suggest that neighbourhood groups, which were the building blocks for reform efforts in the 1960s and 1970s, will be the stumbling block for any new reform movement because "[e]xclusivity has become the dominant characteristic of the urban area and the Not in My Backyard (NIMBY) lullaby is frequently sung to consistent applause."[72] Frisken explains modern citizen activism may now be aimed at preventing housing provision for low income families, keeping public transit out of residential areas, or otherwise discouraging initiatives disturbing the status quo.[73] Following this line of thought, Filion concludes "neighbourhood influence is associated with a tight focus on the immediate interests of residents and a narrow consideration of a decision's consequences, most negative externalities being likely to materialize elsewhere."[74]

There are, of course, still local groups agitating on behalf of various environmental and social issues. These include STORM, a coalition of 25 citizens' groups and individuals formed in 1989 out of concern for the economic integrity of the Oak Ridges Moraine in the Greater Toronto Area. It remains active and in September 2011, on the 10th anniversary of the *Oak Ridges Moraine Conservation Act*, STORM together with two other environmental groups (Earthroots and Ontario Nature) launched a

---

[69] Magnusson and Sancton (eds.), *City Politics in Canada*, pp. 33-34.

[70] Magnusson, "Toronto," in Magnusson and Sancton, *City Politics in Canada*, p. 115.

[71] The work of this committee and the expressway battle are outlined in Donald J. H. Higgins, *Local and Urban Politics in Canada*, Toronto, Gage, 1986, pp. 282-287.

[72] *Ibid.* Sewell has since elaborated his views about urban design in *The Shape of the City*, Toronto, University of Toronto Press, 1993.

[73] Frances Frisken, "Introduction," in Frisken (ed.), *The Changing Canadian Metropolis*, Vol. 1, p. 30.

[74] Pierre Filion, "Government Levels, Neighbourhood Influences and Urban Policy," in Henri Lustiger-Thaler (ed.), *Political Arrangements: Power and the City*, Montreal, Black Rose Books, 1992, pp. 176 and 180.

new campaign to draw attention to threats to the moraine.[75] Since 2002, Vancouver's *Think City* has helped citizens understand the issues facing their communities while developing collective solutions to protect the environment, strengthen local economies, advance democratic rights, and ensure access to quality public services.[76] However, the scattered handful of contemporary organized citizens groups still pale in comparison to the multitude of vibrant local organizations of the 1960s and 1970s.

Consulting with the Public

No matter how widely and creatively information is disseminated, informing is still a one way process. Consulting with the public is a two way process, in which opportunities are provided for local citizens to express their views and concerns, their vision and values. If the municipality exists as a vehicle for local citizens to articulate and express their collective concerns there must be avenues for such expression to take place.[77] Local governments use a variety of consultative mechanisms including: citizen advisory boards, citizen juries, focus groups, green papers, interactive websites, public inquiries, research panels, stakeholder forums, Internet chat groups, sponsored lobby groups, plebiscites, and surveys. A number of these mechanisms are discussed below.

- *Citizen Advisory Boards* are any type of permanent, government-appointed body struck to advise council on a particular issue. Composition can include any combination of elected members, professionals, or ordinary citizens. Small in size, advisory boards are struck and lightly resourced to investigate a specific range of issues. Recommendations are not usually binding on council.
- *Citizen Juries* are small, broadly representative groups of ordinary people recruited through random or representative sampling.[78] A citizen jury is formed to discuss specific policy issues and participants are allowed to call upon experts to help

---

[75] Details on STORM and its activities are available at www.stormcoalition.org, accessed October 25, 2011.

[76] See http://thinkcity.ca.

[77] These examples are partly drawn from Tindal and Tindal, *Municipal Good Governance Guide*, pp. 51-53, and also from municipal consulting experiences.

[78] The citizen jury process was invented by the Jefferson Centre (see www.jefferson-center.org). For information as to how this process has worked in the United Kingdom, see A. Coote and J. Lenaghan, "Citizens' Juries: Theory into Practice," Institute for Public Policy Research, London, 1997 (www.ippr.org.uk/home).

with their deliberations. While monitored by civic leaders, the citizen jury has no power to implement its verdicts and its role remains consultative.

- Widely used in the private sector, *focus groups* are small collections of people, often assembled through random sampling, brought together to refine product design and marketing strategies. Focus groups are also sometimes used by local councils to determine how community members will respond or are responding to certain policy changes.
- *Green papers* are official discussion papers containing a range of policy proposals. Published before a final decision is taken by elected officials, green papers outline a number of policy options for a specific community problem.
- *Plebiscites*, or non-binding referendums, are usually held in conjunction with elections. Voters are asked to record their opinions about specific policy options. Usually in a "yes/no" format, plebiscite questions sometimes can be multiple choice.
- The term "*public inquiry*" covers a broad range of activities such as task forces or commissions set up to investigate a specific policy problem. While rules vary, the reporting body has no power to implement final recommendations. However, depending on the length of the inquiry, public participation can be wide ranging and discussions of strategic issues can often emerge.
- *Sponsored lobby groups* only differ from organized citizens' groups discussed in the previous section in that they are either partially or fully funded by the city, although officials are under no obligation to heed the advice or pressures of lobbyists. Vancouver's Tenants' Rights Action Coalition (TRAC) provides an example of this mechanism. Partially sponsored by the City of Vancouver, TRAC is a coalition of groups and individuals advocating tenants' rights and various housing issues.[79]
- Officials wishing to gauge public opinion on specific issues often hire polling firms to ask a randomly selected sample of people to answer *survey* questions. These surveys can include "yes and no" questions or those in which respondents can provide more elaborate answers. Surveys can come in many forms. For example, as part of its SimpliCity system, Windsor (Ontario) introduced a 311 call centre that can provide responses

---

[79] www.tenants.bc.ca.

to over 150 languages at any city facility.[80] While the 311 line is chiefly just another mechanism by which the city informs the public, data drawn from 311 calls is used to generate statistics of a consultative nature regarding municipal services, including levels of satisfaction and effectiveness of response to complaints.

Consultative mechanisms allow city officials to provide information to citizens and then receive feedback from citizens about what they think about various proposals. They move beyond informative mechanisms and help organize the public input into decision making, reducing costs for citizens and the need for citizens to organize themselves into protest groups. However, as final decisions rest with civic officials, little or no control is relinquished by officials and citizens may weaken their position by abandoning their own groups and relying instead on these types of mechanisms.

Delegating to the Public

Informing and consulting with the public are important as far as they go, but these efforts still leave citizens playing a rather limited and reactive role. Consultations that never lead to policy change breed cynicism. At the same time, for the public to expect that a municipality will automatically embrace and implement every suggestion provided during a consultation process is unrealistic and unreasonable. A third avenue available, however, involves municipalities going beyond informing and consulting to *delegating* decision making authority to the public. A number of delegative participation mechanisms are discussed below, including referendums, study circles, citizens' assemblies, participatory budgets, initiatives, and localized government.

- *Referendums* are exercises in which qualified voters are asked to answer "yes" or "no" to questions specified by city leaders. While final decision making control is delegated to citizens, city officials still have control over the question. It is important not to confuse referendums with plebiscites as the former is binding (i.e., officials must abide by the results) while the latter is not (i.e., officials are under no obligation to abide by the results).
- A *study circle* is a small, self-formed group that meets regularly to talk over issues of concern to group members. The group sets its own rules for deliberation while city officials provide funds to

---

[80] Lisa Gordon, "Breaking down Barriers, Windsor's SimpliCity program keeps it simple," *Municipal Monitor*, November/December 2006, pp. 17-18.

hire facilitators, book meeting space, and provide administrative supplies. In Sweden, study circles are the primary mechanism for delivering continuing education, and at one stage were the chief vehicle for ensuring adult literacy.[81]

- While not currently used in cities and towns, the Government of British Columbia recently established a *Citizens' Assembly* to oversee electoral reform within the province. The provincial voters' list was used to randomly select a sample of 159 citizens (two for each constituency and an appointed chair), who were paid a small stipend to discuss changes to British Columbia's electoral system. After deliberating, the Assembly set a ballot question put to all provincial voters by means of a referendum.[82]

- *Participatory budgeting* is a device through which local councils extensively consult with the public to decide how a designated portion of their annual budget should be allocated. Facilitated by the local government, organized groups deliberate within their own neighbourhoods as to how money should be spent, and then compete with other groups for a share of the resources. As not all projects can be funded, groups build alliances to form stronger lobbies. While a wide range of processes can be used, council has final approval of the budget – although local groups often monitor implementation of the plan.[83]

- Perhaps best described as a citizen initiated referendum, *initiatives* begin by setting a referendum question then gathering signatures from those eligible to vote. If enough signatures are collected, the question is then put to the entire community. Initiatives are an option at the provincial level in British Columbia, including the recent successful effort to eliminate the Harmonized Sales Tax.[84] Another example comes from California where citizens passed Proposition 13 in 1968, capping property taxes and requiring a two-thirds local referendum to raise taxes. These measures led to severe fiscal and servicing difficulties for local municipalities as they gave control over tax

---

[81] For more information, see the Study Circles Resource Centre at www.studycircles.org.

[82] See www.citizensassembly.bc.ca/public.

[83] For a good overview, see *A Guide to Participatory Budgeting by the International Budget Project* at http://internationalbudget.org/wp-content/uploads/A-Guide-to-Participatory-Budgeting.pdf.

[84] See www.elections.bc.ca for more information.

increases to one-third of the population no matter how great the public need.

- *Localized government* represents a decision by government officials to decentralize decision making authority over a specified geographic area to local residents. For example, community centres in Vancouver are operated by locally elected community centre associations with support and guidance from the Vancouver Board of Parks and Recreation. The basis of this relationship is a joint operating agreement automatically renewed every two years. The operating budget for community centres is negotiated by each centre association and the Park Board. But the Park Board has ultimate control over the amount of funds given to the local associations. Community associations often supplement this revenue stream by, for example, imposing user fees.[85]

It is worthwhile discussing referendums, initiatives, and localized government in more detail as these mechanisms are commonly used at the local level in Canada. In terms of referendums, opinions are strongly divided on how these mechanisms affect public involvement and democracy. Those in favour argue decisions made through referendums are more legitimate because they reflect the will of the people and are more democratic as they provide a direct link between citizens and their government. Proponents also argue that during the period leading up to the referendum vote the municipality and the public engage in a thorough, informed debate on the issue which gets citizens more involved in their community and enhances their citizenship.[86]

However, turnout in referendum votes is often low, averaging only 35% in Switzerland for example.[87] American studies indicate that referendums have little drawing power in getting voters out when held in conjunction with elections and even lower voting turnout when they are held separately. There are also concerns that efforts required to get enough signatures to place a question on the ballot leads to domination

---

[85] The West Point Grey Community Centre Association has an excellent website outlining the details of the structure and agreements pertaining to all such groups within the City of Vancouver – including the joint operating agreement, association constitution, by-laws, and meeting minutes. See http://www.westpointgrey.org/ for more information.

[86] Louise Quesnel, *Public Consultation: A Tool for Democracy*, Toronto, ICURR Publications, August 2000, p. 26.

[87] Mark Charlton, "The Limits of Direct Democracy," in Charlton and Paul Barker (eds.), *Crosscurrents: Contemporary Political Issues*, 3rd Edition, Toronto, Nelson, 1998, p. 416.

by large special interest groups with the resources for the task. Indeed, some businesses specialize in gathering signatures, often in exchange for payment.[88] These practices seem rather far removed from the notion that referendums somehow transfer power to ordinary citizens.

Ontario legislation allows municipalities to submit referendum questions to their local electorate, the results of which are binding if there is a voting turnout of 50% of eligible voters and if 50% plus one of those voting answer "yes" to the question. Councils are required to act in a timely manner with respect to any such yes vote. If the voters reject the referendum question, then council cannot put that question to a vote again until after the next municipal election. However, the legislation has limitations. For example, referendum questions require provincial approval, and the province has used this power to reject questions on casino expansion, obviously a matter of the greatest local interest. In addition, councils are prohibited from spending money to support their position.

Carrel believes that "the referendum can play an important and legitimate role in a democracy *if* it is a tool in the hands of citizens, not a toy of the governing elite."[89] But holding an occasional referendum will accomplish little in the absence of other changes. The real value of the referendum occurs when it is provided as part of a series of changes that demonstrate a commitment to openness, consultation, and public participation on the part of the council and staff of a municipality. In Carrel's colourful words, "a referendum thrown to an angry and frustrated citizenry, like a bone to a hungry dog, is not a democratic act."[90] Carrel doesn't view referendum outcomes as a victory by citizens over council or of council over its citizens. Instead, "the decisions are realignments of the fence within which council roams freely."[91] Quesnel has a different view, warning that referendums can be instruments "by which the disadvantaged are excluded and the privileges of the affluent are protected."[92]

---

[88] Quesnel, *Public Consultation*, pp. 56-57.

[89] André Carrel, "Government: Its Legitimacy, Efficacy and Relationship to Citizens," presentation to Capilano College, January 1998, p. 7.

[90] André Carrel, "Municipal Government Leadership," presentation to Capilano College, March 14, 1997, p. 6.

[91] André Carrel, *Citizens' Hall*, Toronto, Between the Lines, p. 46.

[92] Quesnel, *Public Consultation*, p. 56.

Many Canadian provinces provide citizens with the ability to use initiatives, particularly when it comes to zoning, municipal borrowing, and bond issues.[93] Alberta laws order local council to publish proposed by-laws authorizing long term debt in local newspapers and for these by-laws to be submitted to the public for approval if at least 10% of the population signs a petition requesting such a vote within 60 days.[94] Similar laws exist in British Columbia.[95] However, André Carrel points out that as there is often no requirement for council to act on the results of a successful vote, these processes are more like citizen initiated plebiscites than citizen initiated referendums as results are not binding on council.[96]

Carrel is more positive about the initiative rules for municipalities in the Yukon, which authorize citizens to petition council for a referendum to initiate a new by-law or to amend or repeal an existing one. If sufficient signatures are collected, the results of the subsequent referendum are binding. However Carrel reports that the first time citizens attempted to use this power in Whitehorse – by demanding a by-law to protect the community's green spaces – the municipal council deliberately drafted a convoluted and confusing by-law and then mounted an aggressive and misleading campaign against it. Despite these efforts to undermine the initiative, local citizens narrowly approved the referendum, effectively telling the council to live with the consequences of its messily crafted by-law.[97]

Carrel speaks from experience, having been the administrator of the small British Columbia city of Rossland when it began an exciting exercise of direct democracy in 1990. Under local laws, citizens could subject a council decision to public confirmation by initiating a referendum within 30 days after the third reading of a by-law provided 20% of residents signed a petition. In addition, community members could initiate a referendum to force council to act on an issue again with 20% support. The most important outcome of the Rossland experience is not the number of initiatives presented or their outcome, but the changed atmosphere in the community. Instead of just complaining about council action or inaction, more people began discussing policy issues. Because

---

[93] *Ibid.*, pp. 33-49.

[94] Jack Masson and Edward C. LeSage Jr., *Alberta's Local Governments, Politics and Democracy*, Edmonton, University of Alberta Press, 1994, p. 302.

[95] Robert L. Bish, "The Draft Community Charter: Comments," a paper prepared for the Workshop on the Community Charter, University of Victoria, June 14, 2002, p. 3.

[96] André Carrel, *Democracy's Chador, Thought and Afterthought*, July 21, 2006.

[97] This analysis of the situation is based on *ibid.*

they had been given some say in municipal decisions, they felt a greater responsibility to be informed and to exercise their new power thoughtfully. They were also gaining a sense of ownership of city policy. Rossland's constitution by-law came to an end in 2005 when citizens initiated a petition that council feared would lead to the defeat of a planned development.[98]

The final type of delegative mechanism is localized government – when local groups are empowered to make binding decisions over particular geographic areas within a municipality. Localized governments are often created following municipal mergers in an effort to ensure an adequate voice for local citizens and communities within the enlarged municipal jurisdictions. The 13 community committees established during the Winnipeg Unicity amalgamation in 1972 are probably the best known (and documented) example of this type of body. They were originally seen as providing a forum for public involvement and a vehicle for political decentralization. Each committee was responsible for preparing its own budget for services with a local orientation that were assigned to it. Resident advisory groups (RAGs) were elected to advise and assist each committee. While these committees were initially seen as somehow taking the place of the former lower tier municipalities, they had very little authority to make binding decisions and were provided no taxing powers.[99] Enthusiasm for the resident advisory groups waned when the limited role of the community committees became apparent and the increasingly centralized civic administration began to undermine committee decisions.[100] The number of community committees and RAGs was gradually reduced over the years, with the RAGs abolished in 1992.

Montreal's experience with a localized government is also disappointing. While in opposition, the Montreal Citizen's Movement party had made much of the importance of neighbourhood councils with decision making power that would be part of a decentralized city government. Following its election in 1986, the MCM set up nine district (not neighbourhood) advisory (not decision making) councils. All power remained centralized in the city council and its executive committee and

---

[98] The discussion in this section is based on André Carrel, *"We" Styles vs. "Me" Styles, Thought and Afterthought*, October 7, 2005.

[99] Higgins, *Urban Canada: Its Government and Politics*, p. 150.

[100] Lloyd Axworthy, "The Best Laid Plans Oft Go Astray: The Case of Winnipeg," in M. O. Dickerson, S. Drabek, and J. T. Woods (eds.), *Problems of Change in Urban Government*, Waterloo, Wilfrid Laurier Press, 1980, pp. 116-117.

there was growing disillusionment with the weakness of the district advisory committees (DACs).[101]

A variation of this model was introduced following mergers in 2000 in Montreal. Borough councils (conseils d'arrondissement) were set up in the 27 boroughs in Montreal mostly based on the boundaries of the municipalities that were amalgamated. Since the demergers described in Chapter 4, there are now 19 boroughs. Borough councils do not have any separate taxing power, but essentially run a number of local services. Their status is enhanced by the fact that the borough council chairs are directly elected mayors who also sit on Montreal city council.

When the Halifax Regional Municipality was created, five community councils were established, each made up of the city councillors elected from districts located within their boundaries. These boundaries were drawn not to follow old municipal boundaries.[102] A sixth council was established in 1996. If authorized by city council, these community councils can exercise certain land use planning powers, monitor and make recommendations concerning the provision of services, and submit proposed operating and capital budgets annually with suggested services and projects for their areas. Vojnovic views these councils positively, stating they promote "a healthy local democracy by enabling residents to determine the characteristics of the service packages provided in their districts," but suggests that proposing budgets does not equate to actual decision making power.[103]

When the amalgamated City of Toronto came into existence in January 1998, six community councils were established, initially on the basis of the boundaries of the municipalities that had been amalgamated. Because these municipalities varied greatly in size, the result was councils with from 4 to 16 members (not counting the mayor, who was an ex officio member of all these councils). Six new communities were delineated in 2000, with boundaries more in harmony with those used for ward elections to city council and with reduced population disparities.[104] A further change occurred in 2003, with the six community councils

---

[101] Timothy L. Thomas, *A City With a Difference*, Montreal, Véhicule Press, 1997, pp. 108-109.

[102] This discussion is based on Louise Quesnel, *Large Cities: An Opportunity for Innovation in Sublocal Entities?*, paper presented at the Urban Affairs Association Annual Meeting, Boston, 2002, p. 3.

[103] Igor Vojnovic, "Municipal Consolidation, Regional Planning and Fiscal Accountability: The Recent Experience in Two Maritime Provinces," *Canadian Journal of Regional Science*, Special Issue, Spring 2000, p. 67.

[104] Quesnel, *Sublocal Entities*, p. 6.

reduced to four. The councils make recommendations to city council on local planning and development matters and also hold public meetings with respect to these matters – but their role is strictly advisory. Since every matter has to be ratified by city council, there is no real accountability at the community council level. Moreover, a great deal of time at city council can be spent on these local issues, to the neglect of the larger city-wide issues that should be the focus. The need for council to direct more attention to an overall vision and focus was evident in discussions leading up to the 2006 legislation strengthening the city.

Concluding Comments

This chapter explores electoral and non-electoral citizen participation. Citizens can participate in elections as voters or candidates of local political parties where they exist. There are a number of lessons to take away from the information provided in this chapter. Regarding voting, where many media and academic reports often suggest voter turnout is always low during local elections, this is clearly not the case. As the chapter shows, some municipalities have very high turnout – even surpassing that of provincial elections in some cases. However, the wide range of turnout rates across municipalities does not eliminate the need to understand why variation in turnout occurs between municipalities. Geys suggests that social scientists have uncovered core reasons to explain why voter turnout is higher in some jurisdictions, linking higher turnout to municipalities with small and stable populations, high levels of voting in past elections, close races, easier registration procedures, and proportional representation.[105] However more work is required to develop our understanding in this area – especially in Canada.

Moving to local election candidates, the research shows women and visible minorities are underrepresented on councils. Often this absence is attributed to a lack of supply of these types of candidates, meaning too few women and minorities come forward to fill the number of positions required to give them a proportion of council seats equal to these groups' proportion of the population. However, new research shows that the imbalance on council is more likely caused by lack of demand. In other

---

[105] Benny Geys, "Explaining voter turnout: A review of aggregate-level research," *Electoral Studies*, Vol. 25, Issue 4, December 2006, pp. 637-663.

words, women and minority candidates come forward in sufficient numbers, but biases within the process impede women and minorities from securing a proportional number of seats. Some suggest that the only way to remedy this situation is to follow the lead of other countries and impose quotas for these groups, guaranteeing women and minorities hold an appropriate number of seats.[106]

Finally, while many oppose political parties at the local level, their absence robs citizens of the many benefits of partisan activity. Parties can play a vital role in the local policy making process and those cities without local parties will likely fall behind those with vibrant party systems as the population increases. As Stewart and Smith state, local political parties:

> ...play a vital role of aggregating preferences into policy choice and providing labels that can be easily identified by voters. Non-partisan elections are generally personality contests devoid of substantive policy discussion as candidates do not fight under one common banner and have little capacity to develop policy platforms on which they collectively campaign or for which they can be held politically accountable. As such, once elected, candidates often have no common policy goals and are either free to forward their own private agendas, or, more commonly, to react to pressures from organized interests or civil servants. Simply stated, non-partisan politics in large cities undermines the capacity of decision-makers to generate a public agenda for elected officials to transform into a governmental agenda.[107]

Turning to non-electoral citizen participation, the review in this chapter suggests there are many ways local government officials can draw citizens into the policy making process between elections. However, what really matters is the extent to which the various mechanisms decentralize control to citizens. In many cases, councils will inform citizens, in some they will consult, but in very few instances will councils delegate control to local residents. However, it does appear that direct democracy is becoming more commonplace – with, for example, municipalities making more use of referendums. Whatever the case, some suggest participation is most likely to arise from processes

---

[106] Jeanette Ashe and Kennedy Stewart, "Legislative recruitment: Using diagnostic testing to explain underrepresentation," *Party Politics*, February 24, 2011, pp. 1-21.

[107] Kennedy Stewart and Patrick J. Smith, "Immature policy analysis: Building capacity in eight major Canadian cities," in L. Dobuzinskis, M. Howlett, and D. Laycock (eds.), *Policy Analysis in Canada: The State of the Art*, Toronto, University of Toronto Press, 2007, pp. 146-158.

promoting informed and continuing discussion between citizens and their government prior to a decision being made:

> The development of institutionalized processes whereby government can learn from citizens and citizens can learn from government opens up the process of public decision making to a wider range of ideas, interests, and influences than is available through the conventional system of political representation.[108]

Municipal councillors and staff today are often overwhelmed with changes and challenges within their jurisdictions. Faced with such pressures, there is often a reluctance to encourage public participation because of the fear that it will bring delays, probably opposition to changes, and much time and effort consumed in dealing with this opposition. It may also be that municipal personnel will neglect public consultation more through oversight than deliberate decision, being so preoccupied with everyday challenges that they forget to look outward to their communities. But efforts to engage the public have the potential to bring benefits on several fronts. For one, participation brings diverse views to bear on the issue in question, including those of segments of the local populace that are often underrepresented. For another, decisions will tend to have greater legitimacy and have a higher likelihood of successful implementation. Finally, connecting groups and organizations in the local community through participatory exercises builds working relationships and trust and, hence, encourages the development of valuable social capital and community cohesion.

---

[108] David Prior, John Stewart, and Kieron Walsh, *Citizenship: Rights, Community and Participation*, London, Pitman Publishing, 1995, p. 137.

Chapter 11
Municipal Policy Making

"Public Policy is whatever governments choose to do or not to do."[1] Municipal governments appear to be at a crossroads with respect to their public policy making role. While a number of constraints and complications affect this role, municipalities today also find themselves with an opportunity to take more initiative in policy making. If they rise to this challenge, they can better serve their local citizens while also enhancing their own stature and importance.

Introduction

The preceding chapters have raised a wide variety of policy issues relating to the operations of municipal governments in Canada. How municipalities respond to these issues, the policy decisions that they make, collectively and cumulatively, can have a major impact on the nature of a local community and the quality of life for those living within it. As a recent text on this subject explains, policies are important "because they define how local governments interact with their citizens" and provide "the 'face' of local government."[2]

Municipal policy decisions have traditionally focused on which services are to be provided and to what level or standard. A growing policy consideration over the past couple of decades is whether a needed service should be delivered directly by the municipality or by an alternative service provider. Besides issues of servicing, there are also important local policy decisions of a regulatory nature. These have to do with such matters as the establishment of permitted land uses within a municipality, the licensing of local businesses, and the enactment of rules

---

[1] Thomas Dye, *Understanding Public Policy,* Englewood Cliffs, N.J., Prentice-Hall Inc., 1972, p. 14.

[2] Edmund P. Fowler and David Siegel, "Introduction: Urban Public Policy at the Turn of the Century," in Edmund P. Fowler and David Siegel (eds.), *Urban Policy Issues*, 2nd Edition, 2002, Toronto, Oxford University Press, p. 1.

governing local behaviour – such as by-laws controlling noise and smoking.

It is precisely because local government decisions are local – that is, spatially specific – that gives them the potential to be so important. Depending on how these decisions are made, they can do a great deal to improve social justice and advance social change. Consider these examples:[3]

> ➢ Planning and zoning decisions largely shape settlement patterns, the extent of sprawl or compactness, the mix of land uses, and – as a result – the degree to which reliance on the automobile is necessary.
> ➢ Good public transportation services, effectively advertised, make it possible for the poor to travel to and from places of work.
> ➢ High quality day care services facilitate the pursuit of employment, especially in single parent (usually female) households.
> ➢ Cultural and recreational facilities that are dispersed, backed with adequate finances, and inclusive enhance the local quality of life.

Global economic developments in recent decades have increased social polarization and this trend is especially evident in large cities with their extensive, and growing, immigrant populations. The resulting challenges are also a wonderful opportunity for city governments to demonstrate their relevance and the substantial political role that they can play. To do so, they will have to move beyond their traditional role of servicing land – land that is then often developed in ways that exacerbate rather than reduce social inequities.

While attention tends to be directed to policy issues facing large municipalities (including transportation, housing and homelessness, and population diversity), small and rural municipalities also have important policy decisions to make. These relate to such issues as protecting the quality of groundwater supplies, dealing with the influx of "factory farms," and delivering protective services (including how to operate a combined force of volunteer and full time fire fighters).

---

[3] These examples are drawn from Caroline Andrew, "Municipal Restructuring, Urban Services, and the Potential for the Creation of Transformative Political Spaces," in Wallace Clement and Leah F. Vosko (eds.), *Changing Canada, Political Economy as Transformation*, Montreal & Kingston, McGill-Queen's University Press, 2003, p. 329.

Conflicting Perspectives on Policy Making

Faced with ever growing demands and needs and yet very limited financial and personnel resources, municipalities – and their senior, particularly provincial, authorities – have become increasingly concerned with methods and techniques for improving their efficiency and effectiveness. There has been growing recognition of the need for improved planning and priority setting, for more rigorous policy research and analysis, and for the measurement of performance or results to ensure value for the dollar spent. At the same time, citizens and citizens' groups have been demanding that the policy making process be open and responsive to their particular views and concerns. They believe that the views of the populace affected by a potential decision are just as valid in the decision making process as the testimony of technical experts. While people appreciate that governments need more research and analysis in relation to policy problems, they also believe that the elected representatives should remain in charge. As a result, a deep conflict runs through common attitudes toward policy making.[4]

> On the one hand, people want policy to be informed and well analyzed. On the other hand, they want policy making to be democratic, hence necessarily political.... On the one hand they want policy making to be scientific; on the other they want it to remain in the world of politics.

For municipal governments, this conflict represents the tension between their two basic administrative and representative roles, to which frequent reference has been made in this text. But the conflict is made more complex by the fact that even those who want local governments to be more democratic, to pay more attention to their representative role, often think that they don't want local governments to be political – thanks to the distorted legacy of the turn of the century reform movement of over 100 years ago that was discussed in Chapter 2. However, municipal councils do make (and should make) political decisions. They don't necessarily follow the recommendations made by their staff; nor do they necessarily follow the apparent wishes of local interests (although some interests are not easily ignored). Instead, councillors consider these factors as well as their own beliefs, values, and judgment, and make what they feel are appropriate decisions in the circumstances.

---

[4] Charles E. Lindblom, *The Policy Making Process*, Englewood Cliffs, Prentice-Hall Inc., 1980, p. 12.

Our exploration of municipal policy making will begin by illustrating the complexity of policy issues and then examining the changing context within which policy decisions are made. The consideration of external influences will extend to jurisdictional constraints and to the nature and sources of local political power and influence. We will then move "inside" to consider municipal structures and capacity before concluding with an examination of a typical municipal policy decision and how it can be explained.

The Complexity of Policy Making

Municipal policy making is complicated by a number of factors, starting with the policy making process itself. In addition, policies may get misidentified or misdiagnosed, policies often have unintended consequences, and many policy issues are interconnected and interdependent.

A Far From Tidy Process

The first complication is that the policy making process in practice is quite different from the logical series of interrelated steps suggested by the rational/comprehensive or classical model of policy making. That model begins with correct identification of the issue or problem, proceeds through a comprehensive analysis of alternatives, and culminates in the selection and implementation of the "correct" policy decision. This process may depict how many people feel that policy should be made, but it does not describe very accurately what happens in practice.

Probably the best known contrast to the rational model is found in the views of Charles Lindblom, who describes instead a policy making process of incrementalism or what he colourfully terms the "science of muddling through."[5] He argues that our problem solving capacity is too limited to encompass all of the options and potential outcomes that might arise, that there is usually insufficient information to assess accurately all options, and that comprehensive analysis is both too time consuming and too expensive. As will be discussed later in the chapter, all of these

---

[5] Charles E. Lindblom, "The Science of 'Muddling Through'," *Public Administration Review*, 19, Spring 1959, pp. 79-88.

points seem to apply to most municipalities in Canada, with their very limited research and analytical capacity.

Recognizing these realities, Lindblom claims, decision makers look for simpler approaches to problem solving. Instead of attempting to identify every possible course of action, they consider only those few alternatives that represent small or incremental changes from existing policies. Once again, this approach sounds consistent with municipal experience, given that the first question that is often asked about an issue is: "Did this ever come up before, and how did we handle it then?" Adjustments at the margin are more common in municipal decision making than are radical new policy directions – and this is true of more than just the annual municipal budget process.

Yates also rebuts the rational model of policy making, with the aid of metaphors based on three games that were prominent in the penny arcades of yesteryear. He compares the process of identifying the problems that require attention to being in a shooting gallery where targets keep popping up and passing by – forcing the player to decide which target (problem) to address, with the knowledge that choosing that target means letting others pass by without response. He goes on to suggest that the policy making characteristics of the problems that arise can vary just as randomly as the apples, oranges, and cherries that appear in various combinations in a slot machine. Those policy making variables include "the nature of the problem, the issue context, the stage of decision, the configuration of participants, the institutional setting, and the government function involved."[6] As a result, Yates contends that policy makers who follow a standard approach, or who rely upon one or two standard responses to policy issues, are likely to be off the mark much of the time. Finally, he compares the process of policy implementation to the operations of a pinball machine. "Given the central policy maker's weak control over his own administration, street-level bureaucrats, and higher-level governments, decisions once taken are likely to bounce around from decision point to decision point."[7]

In the real world of policy making, those responsible cannot select their problems and analyze them with detachment and thoroughness. This is especially true when they face a constant barrage of new or changing problems and service demands, which has certainly been the case for municipalities in recent years. It is not possible to stop the world, freeze a particular problem, and dissect it in clinical fashion.

---

[6] Douglas Yates, *The Ungovernable City*, Cambridge, M.I.T. Press, 1977, pp. 91-92.

[7] *Ibid.*, p. 93.

Moreover, policy makers regularly deal with problems that are not clearly understood or generate conflicting political pressures. Rather than undertaking thorough research and analysis, the more likely response is to grope for a plausible remedy and hope it works better than previous responses – emulating the incremental approach already discussed.

In light of the above, the rational model described above – with its tidy, sequential process and specific start and end – becomes instead a continuous process "in which a particular problem receives brief, often frantic attention; some kind of decision is made, which bounces around in the implementation phase; and then the problem pops up again in a new or slightly altered form."[8] Examples of this pattern include:

- When property standards are strictly enforced, an unintended result is often housing abandonment or higher rents, leading to housing shortages for low income residents.
- In an attempt to prevent strip development along rural roads, planning policies have traditionally encouraged infilling within existing hamlets – but in many cases the increased population in these hamlets led to well water pollution and triggered the need for very expensive piped water and sewage treatment systems.
- Garbage "bag tag" policies can be effective in encouraging recycling and in covering some of the costs of garbage collection, but they can also lead to an increase in garbage dumped along back roads or burned in backyard barrels.

Dror suggests a possible compromise position – between rationally comprehensive and "muddling through" – that he calls "economic rationality."[9] Dror notes that Lindblom may be right in describing how policy making occurs, but is wrong normatively in arguing that this is how policy making *should be* made. His compromise contention is that policy makers should seek to be as comprehensive as they can afford to be – in temporal, political, and economic terms. Given the increasingly complex nature of policy issues confronting local governments, and the multilevel jurisdictional settings in which solutions lie, this advice has some merit.

Policy Definition: More Movement or Less?

Complications can also arise at a very early stage because of the way the policy issue is defined, or sometimes misidentified. The standard policy

---

[8] *Ibid.*

[9] Y. Dror, "Muddling Through: Science or Inertia," *Public Administration Review,* 1964.

response to problems of urban transportation provides a classic example of this situation, as discussed next.[10]

Our policy responses with respect to urban transportation have proceeded from the assumption that the objective is to move more people to more places more quickly. So we spend ever increasing amounts of money and devote about half of our urban land to cars, in what seems to be a losing battle to reduce urban gridlock. This policy thrust is reinforced by the many participants in the "movement business" – such as those involved in selling gas and oil, manufacturing and selling cars, repairing cars, insuring cars, selling tires and other auto parts, and building roads.[11] Those in the property development industry also promote the expansion of transportation routes, since these routes provide access to vacant fields that can be developed for financial gain. But there are also losses, financial and social, as a result of our approach to urban transportation – in the form of air pollution, health costs, the loss of prime agricultural land, and the negative social impact on communities that feature major highways, heavy traffic flows, and constant commuting. Transportation policies devoted to increasing movement have focused on the construction of more roads to carry more cars, thereby worsening these adverse conditions.

Policy responses that can reduce the reliance on car travel include the following:[12]

> Limiting car use and movement through such means as traffic calming features (speed bumps, planter boxes in the middle of intersections, four way stops, and very low speed limits), closing roads in sections of the city centre, setting parking fees that reflect the actual cost of parking, and charging a toll on clogged, inner city roads.
> Expanding the use of public transit, which, of course, is difficult while we continue to allow sprawling, low density development. Instead of curtailing transit service in a usually futile attempt to reduce the transit deficit, we need to point out the far greater extent to which taxpayers subsidize roads. We need to look at greatly expanded transit service, such as is found in Brazil where articulated buses in Curitiba carry up to 270 passengers and

---

[10] Discussion of this issue is based on Edmund P. Fowler and Jack Layton, "Transportation Policy in Canadian Cities," in Fowler and Siegel, *Urban Policy Issues*, pp. 108-138.

[11] *Ibid.*, p. 116.

[12] *Ibid.*, pp. 129-133.

come by once a minute during rush hour, prompting even many who own cars (28% of bus users) to travel by bus.[13]
- ➤ Encouraging greater bicycle use, by such measures as the provision of bicycle lanes and even free bike programs.

Ultimately, the most effective way to address transportation problems, however, would be to shift the focus away from methods of *increasing* movement – whether by car or otherwise – and to concentrate instead on ways of *reducing* movement. If movement can be reduced (mainly through more compact development that incorporates mixed uses), many of the problems cited above can also be alleviated. But any such dramatic reversal of the approach to transportation policy would have to begin with a recognition of the link between transportation and land use and the policy decisions that influence the pattern of land use – to which we turn our attention in the next section.

Policy Linkages: Sprawl and All

Complicating municipal policy making is the fact that so many policy issues are interconnected and interdependent, as will be illustrated first through a review of the issue of urban sprawl. As Chapter 3 made clear, urban sprawl and all of its attendant problems present a major challenge for our urban areas and for the local governments that operate within and across them. No government would set out deliberately to create urban sprawl – although Rusk presents a chilling fable about how a shadowy group set out over 50 years ago to conquer America from within, by destroying its great cities through promotion of a new American Dream built around life in the suburbs. He then points out that no such imaginary group could have done a better job at this task than the federal government's own policies have done.[14]

To at least some extent, this same charge could be levied in Canada. The housing policies of the federal government, and especially the financial support for single family homes provided by the Canada Mortgage and Housing Corporation, encouraged low density residential development. Housing construction was a central component of the substantial government spending that Keynesian economics (the prevailing ideology in the postwar period) advocated as a key to economic growth. These policies responded to the housing preferences of

---

[13] *Ibid.*, p. 132.

[14] David Rusk, *Inside Game, Outside Game*, Washington, DC, Brookings Institution Press, 1999, pp. 82-86.

young married couples and pleased those in the development industry and their allies within government. Provincial governments also supported this pattern of growth, in part through providing substantial transfer payments, particularly for road construction. In many Canadian settings now the transfer of responsibility for major roads to the local level, where infrastructure dollars are more limited, may act as a constraint on such thinking and planning.

The municipal level must also accept its share of responsibility for the sprawl that occurred. Suburban municipalities were happy to accept the population overspill from central cities, gaining an increased tax base without having to provide city services, and using their resulting lower tax rates as a lure to attract further growth into their areas. Any municipal governments that might have been prepared to slow growth and limit sprawl faced the reality that if they didn't accommodate the growth pressures they would just find an outlet in a neighbouring municipality. Unless all were prepared to work together with a coordinated policy to manage growth, this objective could not be achieved. As long as a few of them made it clear that they were "open for business," all of them had to be receptive or face a loss of assessment and tax revenues. In fairness, it is not reasonable to expect municipalities to act any differently in this situation. It is for this reason that Leo argues for a stronger provincial role in planning and development in urban areas.[15]

If a variety of governmental actions and inactions give rise to the urban sprawl, it in turn unleashes a variety of other major problems – ranging from economic decline in the inner city to traffic gridlock and air pollution, to increased costs for servicing less dense development, to loss of agricultural land, pollution of groundwater, and social isolation. The figure below attempts to illustrate the variables inherent in this policy issue, although the arrows in a straight line depict a much tidier and more sequential process than really exists.

Figure 11.1 The Policy Dimensions of Sprawl

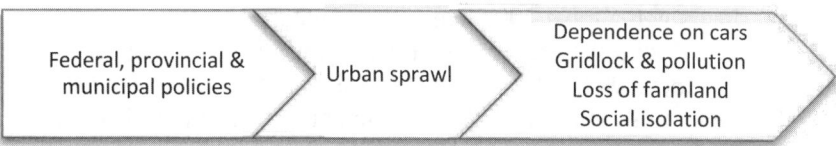

---

[15] Christopher Leo, "Urban Development: Planning Aspirations and Political Realities," in Fowler and Siegel, *Urban Policy Issues*, pp. 232-233.

As a result of these complexities, it is almost impossible for any one municipality to mount an effective policy response to urban sprawl. Particularly in the very large urban areas such as the Greater Toronto Area (GTA), it is arguable (as Leo contends above) that only the provincial government has the jurisdiction and resources to attempt to address this issue. The extensive municipal restructuring throughout the GTA did nothing to improve the situation, nor did the short lived experiment with the Greater Toronto Services Board, which wrestled with the problems of urban transportation without having any control over the underlying land use patterns that were unfolding. More promising, as described in Chapter 5, is the recent provincial initiative to designate green belts and growth centres as a way of concentrating growth and limiting sprawl in the Greater Golden Horseshoe.

Other metropolitan settings have taken somewhat different tacks. In Metro Vancouver, for example, the provincial government transferred transportation planning and implementation responsibilities to a regional authority, Translink, at the end of the 1990s. The province has since reorganized the governance of Translink's structure, limiting the capacity of local mayors to influence day to day decisions of the body, and has renamed it the South Coast British Columbia Transportation Authority (in place of the Greater Vancouver Transportation Authority, as noted in Chapter 5) anticipating a broader regional scope for its work.[16]

Policy Linkages: Pursuing Healthy Communities

Our second example to illustrate the complexity of municipal policy making is interesting in a variety of ways. Once again, all three levels of government are involved in this policy field, but the nature and extent of their involvement has changed significantly over the years. The interdependence of government initiatives is also illustrated, perhaps even more so in this example.

Local governments were in the forefront of the original public health movement that began almost 200 years ago.[17] That movement was largely concerned with the prevention of contagious diseases and epidemics. The focus was not on treating sickness but keeping people healthy by preventing sickness. Achieving this objective required action

---

[16] On this, see Patrick Smith, "Even Greater Vancouver: Metropolitan Morphing in Canada's Third Largest City Region," in Donald Phares (ed.), *Governing Metropolitan Regions in the 21st Century*, London, M. E. Sharpe, 2009, Chapter 13, pp. 237-263.

[17] The discussion in this section is substantially based on Trevor Hancock, "From Public Health to the Healthy City," in Fowler and Siegel, *Urban Policy Issues*, pp. 253-275.

by local governments with respect to sanitation, sewage, and treatment of drinking water. As discussed in Chapter 2, the newly incorporated City of Toronto established a board of health in 1834 and in Toronto and elsewhere the public works department grew out of the public health movement, as did urban planning, parks, housing, and social service functions.

Health was one of the responsibilities assigned to the provincial level in the *British North America Act* of 1867, but an even more important factor that directed attention away from the local role in this field was the development of the so called medical model of health care. As the 20th century unfolded, powerful diagnostic and therapeutic tools such as x-rays, antibiotics, and effective anaesthesia appeared in medicine. Clinical supremacy took over from the public health movement and better health became equated – in the minds of the public and their political leaders – with doctors and hospitals. Expenditures and emphasis on prevention programs declined as the provincial governments (and, increasingly, the federal government through transfer payments) became involved in supporting the newer tools of health care.

There has been a growing appreciation, however, that Canada's health care system has essentially developed into a sickness care system, one in which only about 5% of the health budget is actually devoted to prevention.[18] According to the 1986 Ottawa Charter on Health Promotion, the prerequisites for health include peace, shelter, education, food, income, a stable ecosystem, social justice, and equity. The Premier's Council on Health, Well-Being, and Social Justice in Ontario came to a similar conclusion, finding that human health and longevity are linked to national wealth, household income, employment status, social support networks, level of education, early childhood development, and the quality of our natural and built environment. Yet it is program areas such as social assistance, affordable housing, and environmental protection – prerequisites for healthy living – that have been adversely affected by the cutbacks and downsizing pursued by the federal and provincial governments over the past couple of decades in response to global pressures. Here again, we find a striking example of the unintended consequences of policy decisions.

The recognition that we must approach health care from a broader perspective that embraces social, economic, and environmental considerations is reflected in a healthy cities or healthy communities initiative spearheaded by the World Health Organization. Within a

---

[18] This section is based on C. Richard Tindal, *A Citizen's Guide To Government*, 3rd Edition, Whitby, McGraw-Hill Ryerson Limited, 2005, p. 297.

decade of its inception in 1986, the healthy communities movement had spread to several thousand cities, towns, and villages in Europe, North America, Latin America, Asia, Africa, and Australasia.[19] Within Canada, Mississauga's mayor, Hazel McCallion, worked with the World Health Organization's Centre for Health Development (in Kobe, Japan), to develop the Mississauga model as a tripartite initiative of the municipality, the Centre, and the University of Toronto at Mississauga. In May 2006 a *Healthy Mississauga 2010 Plan* was released,[20] including measures for tracking improvements in local health as the plan progresses. Progress is monitored through annual report cards from Mississauga's Healthy City Stewardship Centre.

As the focus returns to the central role played by the local level in maintaining health (as opposed to treating sickness), we are reminded that almost all policy areas addressed by municipalities have a direct impact on the creation of healthier communities. This interdependence of policies has been cited earlier as a major factor in the complexity of the municipal policy making. The notion that in government everything connects is nowhere more evident than in the health field. To illustrate:[21]

- Whether a municipality pursues economic growth without regard to the adverse impacts that may result or focuses on achieving growth that is environmentally and socially sustainable is obviously pertinent.
- Another key consideration is the pattern of development that is encouraged, permitted, or restricted by the land use policies of the municipality. To what extent do these policies allow low density sprawl which not only increases servicing costs but also our reliance on the automobile with all its attendant health costs?
- The provision of clean drinking water and the maintenance of effective sewage treatment and waste disposal systems were primary objectives of the original public health movement of more than 150 years ago. These services remain essential to the health of our communities, as has been demonstrated so dramatically in recent years in places such as Walkerton, Ontario, and North Battleford, Saskatchewan.
- The provision of adequate shelter is a basic determinant of good health, and the local role in this regard has increased as a result

---

[19] Hancock, "From Public Health to the Healthy City," p. 267.

[20] Go to http://www.mississauga.ca/file/COM/Executive_summary.pdf for an executive summary of the plan, accessed September 4, 2007.

[21] From Hancock, "From Public Health to the Healthy City," pp. 268-269.

of reduced federal and provincial support for affordable housing. A variety of studies, such as the Mayor's Task Force on Homelessness, in Toronto (1998-1999), have noted the increasing social pressures of affordability and homelessness. They also have concluded that any solutions will need to include local governments but be multilevel in nature.

➤ Transportation is a significant factor in health. "The automobile is associated with accidental injury and death, air pollution, the stress of commuting, a sedentary lifestyle, and a segregated-use urban sprawl that destroys a sense of community."[22] Through such actions as land use policies that limit sprawl, expanded public transit, and the promotion of a more pedestrian friendly and bike friendly urban design, municipalities can take steps that create a more healthy community.[23]

➤ The health of a community depends upon the human relations services available (such as education, health care, social services, recreation, and culture) and the adequacy of the social safety net. While it is mainly in Ontario that the local level has a major role in providing social services, municipalities or local boards and commissions are responsible for the other services cited.

➤ Police, fire, and emergency services have an obvious impact on the health and safety of the community.

It is clear from these examples that the policy decisions made by municipalities are potentially of great significance to the lives – and health – of their local citizens. It is also evident, however, that coordinated municipal policy initiatives are complicated by the extent to which policy issues are interconnected and also intertwined with policy decisions taken by separate local boards and by the provincial and federal governments. In the specific instance of health, Hancock notes that reforms of the health care system in almost every province have shifted responsibilities to separate regional health authorities, and expresses concerns that these arrangements sever the direct link that should exist between municipal government services and the health of the public.[24]

---

[22] *Ibid.*, p. 269.

[23] On such alternatives see Richard Gilbert and Anthony Perl, *Transport Revolutions: Moving People and Freight Without Oil,* Gabriola Island, B.C., New Society Publishers, 2010.

[24] Hancock, "From Public Health to the Healthy City," p. 261.

Influences on Municipal Policy Making

The most obvious factors affecting municipal policy making are found within the municipality itself and relate to such matters as governing structure, extent of authority, and adequacy of resources. But these matters, in turn, are related to external factors, notably the municipal subordination to the provincial level within the Canadian federal system. Even beyond the structure of governments and their interrelationships are numerous socio-economic constraints found in the surrounding environment. Each of these sets of influences, depicted in a general way in the figure below, will be examined in turn. Policy making, however, is almost never as straightforward and sequential as the tidy line of arrows below would suggest.

Figure 11.2 Influences on Policy Making

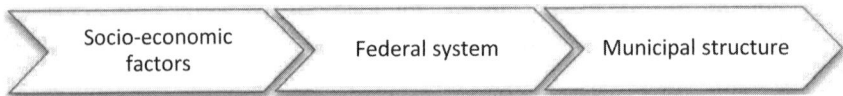

Socio-Economic Factors

This category embraces a number of factors including changes in the population, economic forces, interest groups, and the prevailing values or ideology.

Demographics

To the extent that government policies are developed in response to the wants and needs of society, the policy focus obviously changes – or should change – when society does. This point is best illustrated by the impact of demographics and the pattern of boom, bust, and echo made famous by David Foot.[25] With an increasing proportion of Canadian society now becoming senior citizens, there are profound implications for everything from pensions and health care to elementary and secondary schooling. The effect of changing demographics on municipal governments is illustrated by the following three examples:[26]

---

[25] David K. Foot, with Daniel Stoffman, *Boom, Bust & Echo*, Toronto, Macfarlane Walter & Ross, 1996.

[26] David K. Foot, "Urban Demographics in Canada," in Fowler and Siegel, *Urban Policy Issues*, pp. 30-33.

> A decline in the demand for public transit was experienced by the 1980s, as baby boomers got married, moved to the suburbs, started a family, and increasingly depended on the automobile.
> With the boomers now in their sixties, however, they are likely to prefer smaller homes, closer to shopping and transportation – and this raises questions about the future demand for monster homes in the suburbs.
> An older population is also less involved in the recreational programs and activities that have traditionally received municipal attention and more interested in the arts and culture.

Another noteworthy demographic is the extent of urban population now comprising immigrants and the policy challenges arising from this ethnic diversity. As noted earlier in this chapter, these challenges include the need for measures to reduce social inequities and promote social justice. Good finds that the "racial configuration of local societies structures urban regime formation and dynamics."[27] Biracial municipalities – that is, those with a high concentration of one racial minority, such as Vancouver, Richmond, and Surrey in British Columbia, and Markham in Ontario – have been responsive or somewhat responsive to the diversity of their populations. This may be at least partly explained by the fact that when a single immigrant group predominates, there is likely to be more community cohesion within the immigrant population, making it easier for them to act collectively and to encourage the development of responsive urban regimes.[28] In contrast, Mississauga and Brampton, Ontario, have a multiracial makeup and have been largely unresponsive to the needs of their residents. But Toronto does not follow this pattern, having both a multiracial population and the most highly developed and supportive immigrant policies and programs. However, as discussed in Chapter 6, the business community in Toronto has taken the lead in supporting a city role in immigration settlement and multiculturalism policy, through the work of bodies such as the Toronto City Summit Alliance and Toronto Region Immigrant Employment Council.

Economic Influences

Economic factors have a major influence on municipal policy making. The health of the local economy and of the municipal tax base imposes a basic constraint in terms of the capacity of the municipality to generate

---

[27] Kristin Good, "Patterns of Politics in Canada's Immigrant-Receiving Cities and Suburbs," *Policy Studies*, Vol. 26, Nos. 3/4, 2005, p. 276.

[28] *Ibid.*, p. 277.

financial resources. Growth or decline in the broader regional, provincial, and even national economy obviously provides a positive or restrictive climate for local initiatives. When the economy is booming, attention is often focused on the need to manage and control such growth, to avoid undesirable impacts on the community, and to protect the environment. Such concerns tend to take a back seat, however, during times of economic decline. For example, the City of Toronto's resolve to restrict the height and density of its downtown buildings weakened in the face of the economic slowdown that began in the mid-1970s and had become a severe recession by the early 1980s.[29] Another recession a decade later once again prompted the municipality to soften its approach, this time with respect to Cityplan 1991. A proposal, for example, that new development *must conform* to environmental standards became a proposal *to encourage* development to meet environmental objectives.[30]

Globalization has unleashed an increasingly competitive economic climate in which there is even more pressure on municipalities to pursue policies that support the interests of the business community. It is evident that the very mobile corporations of the new economic order have reduced the bargaining leverage of municipalities.[31] These international developments have also curtailed the activities of federal and provincial governments, and prompted their cuts in social spending and transfer payments, the result of which has been to shift more responsibility and expenditure burden to municipal governments. The resulting challenges are formidable, but they also create an opportunity for an enhanced local role for municipalities with the capacity and the political will to respond.

In some instances, particularly around local social issues and challenges, it is at the municipal level that the need for such action first manifests. In Vancouver, for example, the death of approximately 200 local residents from drug overdoses was what drove the city to initiate efforts to develop a harm reduction model of drug treatment with cooperation from the senior administrations provincially and federally. Establishing North America's only Supervised Injection Site (SIS) was the result of this local "eager beaver" initiative.

---

[29] Frances Frisken, *City Policy-Making in Theory and Practice: The Case of Toronto's Downtown Plan*, London, University of Western Ontario, Local Government Case Studies, No. 3, 1988, p. 99.

[30] Edmund P. Fowler, "Decision Time for Cityplan '91," *City Magazine*, Winter '93, pp. 10-11.

[31] Christopher Leo, "Planning Aspirations and Political Realities," in Fowler and Siegel, *Urban Policy Issues*, p. 222.

Prevailing Ideology

Yet another environmental factor is represented by the extent to which policy making is supported or constrained by the prevailing values and ideology. The neoliberal ideology accompanying and promoting globalization calls for a reduced role for government, reflected in tax cuts, cuts in social spending, and removal of rules and regulations – all in the name of freeing up businesses to be more competitive. One result has been to "hollow out" the nation state and to reduce its role "as an institutional buffer between localities and the machinations of the global economy."[32] While left more to their own devices, municipalities have also gained some additional responsibilities as a result of the decentralization promoted by neoliberalism. As already noted, this presents them with an opportunity to play an enhanced role – even as they face new fiscal challenges.

Neoliberalism is also reflected in the new public management (NPM) principles that have taken hold over the past couple of decades. According to the NPM perspective, whatever limited services remain with government should be provided on a more businesslike basis. This philosophy has been fairly widely embraced by municipalities with the result that 100 years after the turn of the century reform movement of the early 1900s, history is repeating itself. Once again, politics in municipal government is deplored and operating more like a business is encouraged. In response, there is some movement toward the privatization of previously public services or their provision through some form of public private partnership. With businesslike efficiency now to the forefront, there is also pressure to ensure that those services still provided directly by the municipality generate as many revenues and operate as close to break even as possible.

Interestingly, not all support such choices. In Mission, B.C., for example, local groups such as Water Watch have taken on the municipality of Mission and the City of Abbotsford over a P3 model for local water supply. Abbotsford has approved the public private venture. Mission which is smaller but shares in the same water supply has found the matter embroiled in local politics. Rather than accepting the efficiency arguments of P3 proponents, there have been calls for accountability to receive more consideration. Here politics and representativeness are central to local policy making.

---

[32] Jason Hackworth, *The Neoliberal City*, Ithaca, Cornell University Press, 2007, p. 12.

Limits of the Neoliberal Market Model

This market model of government ignores the concept of the municipality as an instrument through which a community can identify and address its collective concerns. It also ignores the notion that governments, including municipal governments, exist to provide public goods for the betterment of society. The municipality is judged by how well it manages the bottom line, not by how well it serves the needs of its community.

The impact of the market model can be illustrated with reference to the field of recreation.[33] With this model, recreation becomes an end in itself, and is evaluated on the basis of such measures as the number of participants and/or the revenues that each program generates. But evaluating recreation essentially on the return on investment defines it simply "as a commodity to be purchased and consumed rather than something that leads to a higher human or social goal."[34] Clearly the philosophy reflected in the market model dictates quite different municipal recreational policies than would arise from a broader perspective that sees recreation as a method of personal and social development, a vehicle for helping people to improve their quality of life.[35]

The market model is also affecting recreation more indirectly, in a classic example of the unintended consequences of policy decisions. A few years ago, it was reported that community sports and recreation groups were disappearing across Ontario as a result of escalating user charges for municipal and school facilities, increased competition for space, a growing shortage of rinks, gyms, pools, and playing fields, and the loss of volunteers driven away by the growing stress and workload.[36] A primary cause of this crisis was the supposedly solid business decisions made by municipalities and school boards to increase user fees to operate on more of a break-even basis and to generate much needed revenue without a property tax increase.

But what are the costs of replacing volunteers with paid staff? Given the links between recreational activities, fitness, and reduced vandalism and youth crime, what are the health, social, and criminal justice costs of the loss of community recreational activities? A business plan embracing

---

[33] This example is based on Bryan J. A. Smale and Donald G. Reid, "Public Policy on Recreation and Leisure in Urban Canada," in Fowler and Siegel, *Urban Policy Issues*, pp. 189-190.

[34] *Ibid.*, p. 189.

[35] *Ibid.*, p. 190.

[36] James Wallace, "Across Ontario, community groups struggle to survive as costs soar," *Kingston Whig Standard*, August 9, 2003.

these broader considerations would quickly demonstrate that increased user charges might be anything but a financial gain for local government or society. In fact, a more enlightened Ontario government introduced a $20 million community use of schools program in 2005 in an effort to reduce user fees, increase participation in community activities, and restore the traditional role of schools as "community hubs."[37]

Sources of Local Political Power

Interest groups and other sources of local political power interact with municipal councils and staff and help to shape policy outcomes. Over the years, a variety of theories and explanations have been advanced with respect to these sources of local power and influence.

Community Power Studies

Among the best known and widely debated early theories about local decision making were the community power studies of the 1950s and 1960s centred on the research of Hunter and Dahl.[38] Hunter's study of reputed influentials in Atlanta led him to conclude that power was concentrated in the hands of a socio-economic elite that dominated local decision making. In contrast, Dahl's study of issues in New Haven found that numerous individuals and groups had influence, which they might exercise depending on the issue involved, but not with respect to all issues. Dahl's pluralist model saw decisions arising from the interplay of various organized groups, while conceding that business interests were particularly well organized and influential.

Critics have argued that the approaches of both studies were flawed – Hunter's from asking those reputedly influential if they were, and Dahl's by selecting certain issues and not others and by ignoring those matters that were kept from the policy agenda and didn't even get to a decision. Their different findings could be explained, it has been argued, on the grounds that "what you see depends on how you look at it."[39] Whatever the merits of the two approaches, however, they both suggested that

---

[37] James Wallace, "Combat youth crime through sports and recreation, group urges," *Kingston Whig Standard*, February 2, 2006.

[38] Floyd Hunter, *Community Power Structure*, New York, Anchor Books, 1953 and Robert Dahl, *Who Governs?*, New Haven, Yale University Press, 1961.

[39] This explanation is discussed in E. Barbara Phillips and Richard T. LeGates (eds.), *City Lights: An Introduction to Urban Studies*, New York, Oxford University Press, 1981, Chapter 12.

"local power is concentrated in the hands of a relative few, be it some socio-economic elite (as the elitists argued) or a series of elites with different resource bases (as the pluralists argued)."[40]

Flawed approach or not, Dahl's work has been quite influential, and pluralist theory has been widely cited as an explanation of the policy outcomes of governments. Essentially, pluralists see government action as the outcome of a competition between organized groups that seek to protect or promote the interests of their members.[41] In this model, government is a rather passive arbiter and policy decisions emerge from the clash and interaction of these various groups.

Critics of the pluralist model point out that many citizens don't belong to groups, that groups vary greatly in their resources and effectiveness, and that not all groups have equal access to government. Too often, the apparently diversified influences implicit in the pluralist model serve to conceal or distract attention from the fact that one type of group – the business group – is by far the most dominant. This issue has been memorably summarized by Schattsneider in the comment that "the flaw in the pluralist heaven is that the heavenly chorus sings with a strong upper class accent."[42]

Business groups are certainly prominent at the municipal level in Canada and such organizations as the Urban Development Institute and the Canadian Home Builders Association, as well as more localized bodies such as chambers of commerce, promote the virtues of growth and development. The fact that councillors often receive from developers and others associated with the property development industry a substantial portion of the funds that they require to conduct their election campaigns certainly does nothing to reduce the influence of developers. But they are by no means the only groups active at the local level, as evident from the following few examples:

> ➤ Local residents and ratepayers groups have enjoyed some success in pressuring councils to hold the line on taxes, often at the expense of actions that should have been taken to upgrade infrastructure over the years.

---

[40] Harold Wolman and Michael Goldsmith, *Urban Politics and Policy: A Comparative Approach*, Cambridge, Mass, Blackwell Publishers, 1992, p. 13.

[41] Stephen Brooks and Lydia Miljan, *Public Policy in Canada: An Introduction*, Toronto, Oxford University Press, 4th Edition, 2003, p. 34.

[42] E. E. Schattsneider, *The Semi-Sovereign People*, New York, Holt, Rinehart and Winston, 1960, p. 35.

> Environmental groups continue to draw attention to the adverse impact of much growth and economic activity and have made some progress in injecting notions of smart growth and sustainable development into policy discussions.
> The increasing diversity of society, especially in larger cities, is reflected in the rise of groups representing ethnic, racial, and cultural communities and gay and lesbian rights, among other concerns.
> Advocacy groups for the poor and the homeless have also become more prominent.

Somewhat surprisingly, the first major study of community power in Canada, by Kaplan, concluded that if there was a dominant elite of any sort it was composed of the elected and appointed municipal officials.[43] However, this study from the mid-1960s focused on Metropolitan Toronto, an upper tier government, while many of the issues that would directly affect community groups were handled by lower tier municipalities within Metro Toronto. As Chapter 10 pointed out, citizens' groups and reform councillors became much more prominent in Toronto in the 1970s – largely in response to the perceived threat to existing communities from pro growth councillors too closely allied to the property industry.

One of the reform councillors of that period, subsequently mayor of Toronto, was John Sewell, who assessed the decision making process quite differently. Admittedly, he was writing about the City of Toronto, not Metro Toronto, and his political autobiography was hardly a scholarly analysis of the Kaplan variety.[44] Sewell emphasized the intimate links between councillors and the development industry. From his experience, councillors did represent and speak for outside interests – those of the developer – and power was concentrated outside the formal institutions. A similar viewpoint was echoed by a number of other writers during this period.[45] The discussion of ethics and values in Chapter 9 included examples that indicate the continuing close ties between municipal councils and business interests in places such as

---

[43] Harold Kaplan, *Urban Political Systems: A Functional Analysis of Metro Toronto*, New York, Columbia University Press, 1967.

[44] John Sewell, *Up Against City Hall*, Toronto, James Lewis and Samuel, 1972.

[45] See James Lorimer, *The Real World of City Politics*, and *A Citizen's Guide to City Politics*, Toronto, James Lewis and Samuel, 1970 and 1972; Lorimer, *The Developers*, Toronto, James Lorimer and Co., 1980; and Donald Gutstein, *Vancouver Ltd.*, Toronto, James Lorimer and Co., 1975.

Toronto and Edmonton. The influence of business interests is unlikely to wane in the current climate of global economics and neoliberalism.

For Cobb and Elder, when power is the focus, it is safe to assume certain "inherent biases."[46]

1. Any political system will work to the advantage of some and the disadvantage of others.
2. The range of issues that will be considered in any political system is restricted – by time, by resources, by jurisdictional questions, etc.
3. All political systems, municipal or otherwise, have a certain inertia; this means that getting your question or issue on to the local agenda has to overcome this bias. It also means that "there is a strong bias in favour of existing arrangements and agenda questions."

Public Choice Model

The alleged economic limits on local government are even more evident in public choice theory (known as the political economy model in the United States). It explains the behaviour of individuals and groups, and the policy decisions of governments, on the basis of concepts of classical economics about "economic man," motivated by self-interest, seeking to maximize gains or minimize losses in any economic situation. By extension, "political man" is presumed to operate on the same basis of rational self-interest, "seeking to maximize satisfaction at the least cost within the limits of the information at hand."[47] But basic economic forces don't work nearly as well when applied to public goods since government is a monopoly supplier (for most such goods) and it operates in ways that are biased toward excess growth and spending.[48] This happens because, as already noted, the natural instinct of politicians and bureaucrats is to pursue their own self-interest. For politicians, this means retaining voter support by promising more and better services to the

---

[46] See, for example, Roger Cobb and Charles Elder, "The Politics of Agenda Building," *Journal of Politics,* Vol. 73, No. 4, November 1971. See also their *Participation in American Politics: The Dynamics of Agenda Building*, Boston, Allyn and Bacon, 1972.

[47] Brooks and Miljan, *Public Policy in Canada*, p. 37.

[48] See Charles M. Tiebout, "A Pure Theory of Local Expenditure," *Journal of Political Economy* 64, No. 5, October 1956 and Vincent Ostrom, Robert Bish, and Elinor Ostrom, *Local Government in the United States*, San Francisco, Institute for Contemporary Analysis, 1988.

electorate. Expanded services are also supported by civil servants since their status in the hierarchy is enhanced by larger budgets and empires.

To offset the natural tendency to overproduction inherent in governments, public choice advocates support a fragmented local government structure, one in which multiple suppliers of goods and services at a variety of tax levels provide choice for local consumers. In response, the public can show its preferences for public goods and services through a variety of means including voting, lobbying, public opinion polls, petitions, public hearings, demonstrations, court proceedings, and even taxpayer revolts.[49] Ultimately, they can "vote with their feet" and move to a municipal jurisdiction providing a service and cost (tax) package that they find more acceptable.[50]

Critics of public choice question the extent to which local consumers have knowledge of the choices available to them and have the mobility to act upon this information. Such mobility is certainly not available to the poor and disadvantaged. As a result, one of the strongest criticisms of public choice theory is that it can serve to justify the establishment or preservation of separate jurisdictions that house the rich and privileged and keep out the poor and undesirable and their expensive servicing needs – although this practice is more evident in the multiple servicing districts and separate jurisdictions found in American urban areas.

But mobility is available to many businesses, increasingly so in today's world. As a result, local governments feel pressure to accommodate the interests of businesses or risk losing them to other locales (and even other countries). This idea has been taken to its limits, one might say, by Peterson,[51] who argues that the policies adopted by a city will be constrained and shaped by how those policies affect the city's overriding objective of promoting economic growth. In particular, he contends that redistributive policies (those that involve income transfers from higher to lower income segments of the population) will be avoided by cities as much as possible, lest they prompt businesses to respond to the extra tax burden by relocating. Peterson exemplifies the structural alternative to the pluralist approach, one that directs attention beyond the elites and interest groups that operate within a community to

---

[49] *Ibid.*, pp. 22-23.

[50] On this aspect, see Robert Bish, "Local Government Service Production in the Capital Region," at University of Victoria, Local Government Institute, School of Public Administration website: http://publicadmin.uvic.ca/aboutUs/FacultyPersonal/bish.php (accessed July 21, 2011) and "Municipalities are cheaper by the dozen," University of Victoria Press Release, July 7, 1999.

[51] Paul Peterson, *City Limits*, Chicago, University of Chicago Press, 1981.

more external constraints on municipal operations. Peterson's views have been criticized for excessively subordinating politics to the economic imperatives and for ignoring widespread examples of vigorous local political activity prevailing over business interests or preferences.

Regime Theory

Political scientists such as Clarence Stone[52] and John Mollenkopf,[53] among others, developed a kind of hybrid of the pluralist and structuralist perspectives. They recognize that municipal leaders have two kinds of interaction – with their local population/community interests and with their economic environment. Effective action requires collaboration between those able to generate electoral support and those who command economic resources. Alliances between municipal leaders and private partners often develop into mutually beneficial long term relationships or regimes that endure over several municipal administrations. Proponents of this regime theory suggest that it improves on pluralism by contemplating the possibility of diverse interests coming together in stable coalitions and improves on structuralism by giving due recognition to the influence of the political/electoral arena along with economic forces.[54]

The first election for the new City of Toronto in 1997 brought with it what can be seen as a regime change.[55] The shift from the old urban regime to a new, suburban regime was typified by the mayoralty results. The mayor of the old City of Toronto, Barbara Hall, active in the New Democratic Party, was defeated by Mel Lastman, former businessman and mayor of the City of North York, the largest of the former suburban municipalities. It seems likely that the regime change was the result of efforts by the Toronto business community, which was anxious to get rid of the progressive thrust of city council and to replace it with an administration more favourably disposed towards business. But a case can be made that this change was engineered by the amalgamation

---

[52] Clarence Stone, *Regime Politics: Governing Atlanta*, Lawrence, University Press of Kansas, 1989.

[53] John M. Mollenkopf, *The Contested City*, Princeton, Princeton University Press, 1983. See also Elizabeth A. Strom and John Mollenkopf (eds.), *The Urban Politics Reader*, New York, Routledge, 2007, for extensive readings on local politics and power. It is a Mollenkopf chapter in the latter source, pp. 99-109, that is the basis for this discussion.

[54] *Ibid.*, p. 107.

[55] The discussion that follows is based on Jean-Pierre Collin and Mélanie Robertson, *Metropolitan Change and Related Political Behaviour in Canadian Metropolises*, Montreal, INRS-Urbanisation, Culture et Société, working paper presented to the International Metropolitan Observatory Meeting, Bourdeaux, January 2004, pp. 78-80.

imposed on Toronto by the Conservative government of Mike Harris, which counted on the more conservative citizens and elected representatives from the suburban areas to rein in the left leaning, free spending politicians that had held sway on the old Toronto council. The fact that such political and ideological considerations occur in senior governments contemplating local governmental restructuring should not be that surprising. A similar motivation can be found in the reworking of the London (England) region – from the creation of the London County Council to its replacement by the Greater London Council, to the GLC's abolition during the Thatcher years and a restructured Greater London Authority under New Labour. Terrence Cook has termed this "Putting Power Where Pals Prevail."[56]

After serving a second term, Lastman was defeated in 2003 by David Miller. Miller, a member of the New Democratic Party, was reelected in 2006, but there is some evidence to suggest that the suburban and pro business regime that began with Lastman remains to some degree. This would help to explain, for example, the embarrassing defeat suffered by Miller with respect to his proposed tax increases in the summer of 2007. The influence of the business community and significance of business and municipal collaboration was also evident in the successful revival of that tax proposal, in modified form, in October 2007, following its endorsement by the Toronto Board of Trade. The election of former suburban Etobicoke councillor and right wing Mayor Rob Ford in 2010 was also tied to suburban and business interests in the amalgamated city.

Legal and Jurisdictional Constraints

Notwithstanding the improved municipal legislation enacted by most provinces over the past decade, municipal governments are still, in Clarkson's blunt phrasing, "the lowest form of political life in Canada."[57] Many of the policy issues that concern them – such as sprawl, pollution, homelessness, urban infrastructure, and preservation of farmland – can only be addressed, at least in a comprehensive way, by concerted action on the part of the provincial and/or federal levels of government as well. But a comprehensive policy response to these issues has certainly not been forthcoming from these governments.

---

[56] Terrence Cook, Eastern Washington University, "Putting Power Where Pals Prevail," paper for the Pacific Northwest Political Science Association, 1985.

[57] Stephen Clarkson, *Uncle Sam and Us, Globalization, Neoconservatism, and the Canadian State*, Toronto, University of Toronto Press, 2002, p. 103.

Federal Neglect

As discussed earlier in this text, the federal government has pursued many policies that affect the local level, but often with little apparent awareness of this impact. In more recent years, it has adopted policies that attempt to address problems *in* cities, but these separate initiatives do not constitute an urban policy – and the Harper Conservative government is most committed to working with the provinces to avoid intrusions into local matters. Nor have most federal initiatives shown sufficient appreciation of the growing importance of cities in the new international economic order. For example, an analysis of the infrastructure program introduced by the federal government in 1993 reveals that it was seen by them primarily as a method of job creation, was designed to minimize friction with the provinces, was preoccupied with *who* pays rather than *what* should be built, and gave priority to traditional basic elements of infrastructure – roads and bridges, and water and sewage systems.[58] With the 2008-2010 world recession as well, Canada's infrastructure investments program followed a similar path. As a result, the infrastructure expenditures did little to improve the capacity of cities to compete in the new knowledge based economy by developing a rich and diverse environment that attracts talented people, as discussed in Chapter 3.

It appeared that a new era in federal relations with the cities and their policy challenges had arrived with Paul Martin's "New Deal." But even before his short lived tenure had ended, the federal initiatives lost their focus in an egalitarian shift to "cities and communities." Under the current Harper administration there seems little prospect of new federal initiatives for cities – or any municipalities – since he has made it clear that his government will confine itself to matters of federal jurisdiction.

Provincial Paternalism

Provincial governments have also adversely affected municipal policy making in a number of ways. For much of the past century, they have supervised and controlled municipal decisions to such an extent that municipalities often lacked the autonomy to act. Even when they had some local scope for action, municipalities often lacked the confidence to proceed. After being treated like children by paternalistic provincial administrations, they have found it difficult to stand on their own feet when the opportunity arises. Even the exceptions, such as Vancouver's SIS initiative, tend to prove this point.

---

[58] Caroline Andrew and Jeff Morrison, "Infrastructure," in Fowler and Siegel, *Urban Policy Issues*, pp. 237-250.

The scope for local decision making has been broadened by recent legislative changes in a number of provinces that give municipalities natural person powers and broad spheres of authority in which to operate. But it remains to be seen if they will have access to sufficient resources to make full use of any expanded jurisdiction. Since "the devil is in the details," it is also too soon to tell how much operating freedom the new legislation actually brings; although limited, recent court decisions generally support expanded municipal discretion. In Toronto, the city has mostly rejected the use of new taxing powers; in Metro Vancouver, some of them have been embraced. In the summer of 2011 Translink's Mayors' Council approved a two cent gas tax hike to pay two-thirds of the regional costs of rapid transit expansion.

Provincial (and federal) influences on municipal actions may be motivated by a variety of considerations. Frisken suggests that what she aptly terms "parent government" intervention in local affairs "may represent a simple assertion of formal authority, an effort to protect or strengthen the local economy, a concern with keeping down the costs of local services, an interest in affecting a redistribution of the costs and benefits of public and private economic activity more equally among municipalities or among individual citizens, or an attempt to appease politically-influential local interests."[59] It follows that the nature and extent of senior government influence over local policy making activities is not uniform but may vary depending on the particular municipality, the local circumstances, and the objectives that are being pursued by the senior level(s).

Multilevel Governance

One encouraging development has been the growing tendency for governments to "think outside the constitutional box" when responding to issues that extend beyond one jurisdiction. In addition to intergovernmental collaboration focused on local delivery of programs established by the provincial or federal level, there is now greater appreciation of the insights and local knowledge that municipalities can provide if involved in the development of provincial and federal programs and policies. These new arrangements were referred to by various terms in Chapter 6, including multilevel governance and deep federalism, but whatever they are called they represent approaches to policy making and implementation less restricted by jurisdiction.

---

[59] Frisken, *Toronto's Downtown Plan*, p. 17.

The need for greater cooperation among levels of government was emphasized in a project on social sustainability carried out by the Canadian Policy Research Networks (CPRN). Because of the scale and complexity of urban issues and the linkages among them, participants called for such things as more cooperation among governments, an end to turf wars among the levels of government, having all players at the same table, and otherwise finding ways to bring together all levels of government (and other key players as well) to address urban policy issues such as housing, urban poverty, immigration, and the Aboriginal influx to urban areas.[60] Logical and desirable as a combined approach may be, Leo and Mulligan caution that the necessary sharing and cooperation will not easily be achieved. "Bureaucratic and political interests at all levels of government run to possessiveness and personal aggrandizement."[61] An example of what can be achieved, however, is found in Toronto's initiatives (described in Chapter 6) in developing "new political, fiscal and legislative relationships with upper levels of government in immigration policy."[62]

The Municipal Structure

There are also a number of constraints on policy making within the municipal structure itself. To begin with, a number of significant local matters are not directly under municipal council but are instead assigned to separate boards and commissions[63] that operate across the municipality or a combination of municipalities. These arrangements are found in most provinces with respect to such functions as education, public health, some social programs, utilities, water management, and

---

[60] F. Leslie Seidle, *The Federal Role in Canada's Cities: Overview of Issues and Proposed Actions*, Ottawa, Canadian Policy Research Networks Inc., January 2003, pp. 15-16. Available from http://www.cprn.org/doc.cfm?doc=158&1=en (accessed September 10, 2007).

[61] Christopher Leo, with Susan Mulligan, "City Politics: Globalization and Community Democracy," in Joan Grace and Bryon Sheldrick (eds.), *Canadian Politics, Democracy and Dissent,* Toronto, Pearson Education Canada Inc., 2006, p. 159. On MLG, see also, Andrew Sancton and Robert Young (eds.), *Multilevel Governing In Canada: Provincial Overviews,* Toronto, University of Toronto Press, 2009.

[62] Good, *Patterns of Politics*, p. 270.

[63] Separate boards and agencies are extensively used in Western Canada for the provision of health, social services, and education on a regional basis, as summarized in Evan Jones and Susan McFarlane, *Regional Approaches to Services in the West: Health, Social Services and Education*, Canada West Foundation, February 2002.

conservation. The governing boards of these bodies consist of appointed (most commonly) or elected officials and they are often quite dependent upon provincial governments for policy direction, resources, and even approval of local decision making. As a result, such important policy fields as policing and transit are largely beyond the jurisdiction of municipal councils.[64] The consolidation of school boards in most provinces, and centralization of decision making at the provincial level, has left very little scope for educational policy making at the local level.[65]

A different kind of fragmentation is found where there are a number of separate municipalities within one urban area. While common intermunicipal problems may call for coordinated action, individual municipalities are understandably motivated to do what best serves the needs of their residents and ratepayers. In the short run at least, this preoccupation may prompt them to focus quite narrowly on their own particular situation – leading them to compete vigorously with their neighbours for economic development, or to try to avoid paying toward regional facilities from which they may benefit, or to avoid contributing to the cost of social programs borne by the central city.

We know, for example, that different pricing policies with respect to taxes and development charges could help to limit sprawl, but there is little that a municipality in the urban core can accomplish in this regard if some surrounding municipalities are actively wooing new growth. Similarly, efforts by one municipality to pursue policies that address social and environmental problems may prompt residents and businesses that are mobile to relocate to another jurisdiction that eschews such policies in favour of lower taxes and fewer limits on business operations.

Within any one municipality, effective policy making is hampered by the lack of strong leadership and executive direction and the lack of cohesion and accountability within the council itself. As has often been stated, in municipal government everyone is responsible for everything, which also means that no one is really responsible for anything. This statement must be qualified to the extent that a municipality has a chief administrative officer and/or executive committee of council or where a strong mayor emerges in spite of the lack of formal powers attached to

---

[64] For a good discussion of the many local boards and commissions that operate in Canada, see Dale Richmond and David Siegel (eds.), *Agencies, Boards and Commissions in Canadian Local Government*, Monograph No. 15, Toronto, Institute of Public Administration of Canada, 1994.

[65] Peter Woolstencroft, "Education Policies: Challenges and Controversies," in Fowler and Siegel, *Urban Policy Issues*, pp. 276-297. For details on the arrangements for the administration of education in the various provinces, see Karin Treff and Deborah Ort, *Finances of the Nation 2010*, Toronto, Canadian Tax Foundation, 2011, Chapter 9.

that office. In those circumstances, there may be a focus for improved policy advice and policy direction. The widespread lack of such a focus, however, represents one of the Achilles' heels of local accountability.

Municipal Policy Analysis Capacity

Stewart and Smith's recent examination of eight of Canada's largest cities (Vancouver, Calgary, Edmonton, Winnipeg, Toronto, Ottawa, Montreal, and Halifax) found that the capacity of local decision makers is limited and that "civil servants drive and dominate the policy analysis process." Among the points that they make are:[66]

- There is little substantive policy discussion in the nonpartisan elections that are fought in most municipalities, elections that send individuals to council who have no common policy goals and little basis for developing and agreeing on a policy agenda.
- Widely used elections at large, coupled with the "first-past-the-post" system of vote counting, disenfranchise racial and ethnic minorities and lower voting turnout. Whatever agenda appears often reflects the preferences of a minority of local residents. The unequal access to local influence – noted above – often favours business interests.
- Minority interests, especially wealthy ones, have an increased opportunity to influence the local agenda when there are no limits on election spending.
- The limited salaries paid to most councillors usually require them to hold other jobs, leave them less time to devote to their duties, and make them more vulnerable to internal bureaucratic and other outside influences.
- The lack of personal staff available for most councillors limits their ability to oversee and evaluate the work of municipal staff.

After examining the eight cities in relation to these factors, Stewart and Smith found that "only Montreal avoids the pitfalls of nonpartisanship, at-large systems, and unlimited election spending and, from an electoral perspective at least, can be considered the study city most likely to play an effective role in the policy analysis process."[67] Vancouver, by

---

[66] The points that follow are based on Kennedy Stewart and Patrick J. Smith, "Immature Policy Analysis: Building Capacity in Eight Major Canadian Cities," in Laurent Dobuzinskis, Michael Howlett, and David Laycock (eds.), *Policy Analysis in Canada, The State of the Art*, Toronto, University of Toronto Press, 2007, pp. 265-287.

[67] *Ibid.*, p. 278.

contrast, receives the lowest ranking (in terms of its capacity to generate and impose a democratic mandate) because of "its at-large electoral system, unlimited election spending, low council salaries, no pensions, and low number of councillors and support staff...."[68] Even with a long established local party system, this is not enough to compensate.

Illustrating Municipal Policy Making

After discussing so many variables, constraints, and influences, the following example of a not untypical municipal issue provides an opportunity to review and apply these factors, as well as other considerations introduced in earlier chapters.

Box 11.1 Explaining a Municipal Policy Decision

A rapidly urbanizing township adjacent to a medium-sized city continues to experience strong growth pressures. There is little undeveloped land left within the city. The other nearby municipalities are small and rural, and lack the infrastructure necessary to support any large scale development. The urbanizing township has an abundance of serviced land and its council has been actively pursuing new growth for several years, believing that the increased assessment is the key to financial survival. A large corporation applies for a zoning amendment to allow a high tech industrial project. This application is referred to the township's Planning Advisory Committee, consisting mainly of citizen appointees – most with ties to the business community. The application is supported by the committee. There is some lobbying from a couple of local citizens' groups opposed to the rezoning – one being a hastily formed coalition of neighbours living adjacent to the proposed project. Another group expressing opposition is a rural based coalition of long time residents who feel that the township is neglecting its rural and farm interests in its obsession with growth and development. However, the rezoning is subsequently approved by council and upheld on appeal to the provincial tribunal responsible for such matters.

On the surface, this is a straightforward exercise of decision making power by the appropriately authorized bodies. Under provincial legislation, municipal councils have the authority to amend their zoning by-laws. Some provinces authorize councils to establish planning advisory committees to provide assistance in the planning process. Objections to a rezoning usually result in a hearing by a provincial tribunal, which then makes the final decision.

---

[68] *Ibid.*, p. 283.

But what explanations might be provided for the policy decision that was made by the municipality in this instance? Traditionally, the first explanation would look for answers in the formal machinery of municipal government. What we have here is a typically fragmented structure, with several different municipalities operating within one urban area (the city and its surrounding hinterland), each pursuing its own agenda. Thus, the pro growth township is able to attract most of the new development in the area, whether or not that might be the best location for it if viewed from a broader perspective.

Further fragmentation can be found within the structure of the township itself. While it is only advisory in nature, the planning committee does divide consideration of planning issues between council and this separate body. Moreover, the fact that the advisory committee consists mainly of citizen appointees increases the likelihood that it will have a different point of view than that of the council. The internal governing structure of the township may also be fragmented, depending on the specifics of its organization. Since it has been growing rapidly, it has almost certainly been adding new staff and departments in a rather ad hoc fashion. There may be a series of standing committees, each focused on the activities of their department(s) and perpetuating or even reinforcing, these specialized viewpoints. If there isn't any chief administrative officer, then the various department heads are officially equals. They will respond to development proposals such as the one outlined above largely on the basis of how such proposals might affect their departments. But what about the overall impact on the municipality? Where is that perspective found?

A second explanation for the planning decision outlined above is that it reflects the self-interest of the politicians, bureaucrats, and development interests involved. From this point of view, politicians seek to be elected and then to maintain themselves in power, while staff seek to expand their empires and therefore their own importance. Development interests are by definition "pro development." This public choice perspective (outlined earlier and familiar to those who have seen the *Yes, Minister* – and *Yes, Prime Minister* – television series) suggests that politicians would support the rezoning application because they see the resulting development and increased assessment as enhancing or at least maintaining their political support base. To the township staff, continued growth means an almost certain increase in their operations, responsibilities, staff complements, and budgets – in short, expanded empires which would, in turn, enhance their stature, and often remuneration.

The specific reaction of politicians, bureaucrats, and development interests to an issue of this sort would also be influenced by such factors as the perceived capacity of the media to influence public opinion and the ability of interest groups to mobilize supporters. This is not always a given regarding particular types of development. Proposals for big box store outlet developments are increasingly opposed by local citizens – and some old downtown business interests – as town destroying rather than locally contributing. This is the case across a broad range of Canadian municipal settings. Given the outcome of the scenario outlined above, it can be concluded that the media did not "run" with this issue for any length of time, and that the citizens' groups lined up against the rezoning were not considered to carry much weight.

The significance and influence of local groups within this municipality is at the heart of the third explanation of the planning decision. It sees decisions as the result of the interaction of groups, all seeking to influence policy outcomes. This pluralist perspective views the government as an essentially passive force and government decisions as the outcome of a competition between organized groups that seek to protect or promote the interests of their members. Given the planning decision that resulted, we must assume that, in addition to the citizens' groups opposed to the rezoning, there were other influential groups at work. These might include community economic development advocates, ratepayer groups, and fair tax coalitions pressuring the township council to hold the line on taxes. To most councillors, this goal can only be achieved by increasing assessment and, therefore, by supporting the rezoning. They would certainly include business groups such as a local chamber of commerce, construction association, and homebuilders' association. Pluralists would presumably explain the planning decision by conceding the stronger influence (and superior lobbying resources and tactics) usually exhibited by business groups. Cobb and Elder's view on agenda setting is consistent with this latter explanation, except where more widespread local democratic pressures emerge – as sometimes happens with big box proposals.

One might also explain the planning decision above as an indication of the pervasiveness of capitalist values within Canadian society. The virtues of private enterprise and pursuit of profit are seldom questioned. The role of local government is seen as providing the physical services needed to support growth and development. Government decisions are seen as the outcome of the lines of cleavage in Canadian society that, in turn, result from the way wealth is distributed. Thus, the economic power of the property development industry prevails.

In the case of the planning decision above, the prevalence on the planning advisory committee of citizens with ties to the business community is of note. There might also be a similar pattern of close linkages between many of the councillors and the business community, perhaps reinforced by financial support from the development industry for the election campaigns of these councillors. Here, adequate local election financing rules – including reporting – contribute to more democratic oversight of such links.

Neoliberalism and global economic pressures provide a further rationale for the decision taken. Future growth lies not in traditional manufacturing jobs, we are told, but in the employment of knowledge workers in high tech jobs of the sort being offered to the municipality in this example. If the municipality doesn't respond positively, those jobs will go elsewhere – not necessarily within the region, or even the country. Yet many of the jobs resulting from the successful advocacy of pro development forces are service sector based. While contributing to local employment, few are higher wage or unionized positions with a range of benefits attached. Indeed, in some big box developments – as in Quebec with Wal-Mart – when efforts to unionize are successful, the store development is shut down rather than allow a first contract to be negotiated.

Outwardly, the municipal planning decision depicted above is reflected in one or two council meetings, some staff reports, a citizen delegation or two, and a couple of articles in the local media. Underlying the official decision making process, however, are a wide variety of factors, forces, and influences that help to shape the policy outcome.

Concluding Comments

It is generally held that a primary role of municipal council is to enact policies on the basis of expert advice provided by staff and (one hopes) after taking into consideration local views, concerns, and input. In practice, as this chapter has attempted to demonstrate, the policy making process is considerably more complex and is subject to a number of influences and constraints. The latter include:

- Factors in the socio-economic environment such as demographics, economic influences, and interest groups;
- The prevailing political ideology;
- Legal and jurisdictional constraints; and
- The municipal structure and policy capacity.

Taking into account all of these constraints, together with the complexity of municipal policy making and the extent to which so many policy issues are interconnected and intertwined with provincial and federal jurisdictions, there might appear to be very little scope for municipal policy initiatives. On the other hand, it can be argued that circumstances today present municipalities with an opportunity to take more initiative in policy making. Certainly those municipalities that wish to act as "eager beavers" have more potential to be proactive. Those holding to this view cite such developments as the following:

- Without overstating the point, something of a vacuum has been created at the centre by the scaling back of federal and provincial government activities. This retrenchment has occurred because of the fiscal restraint pursued by the provincial and federal levels, arising from a sharp swing to the right in the prevailing political philosophy (neoliberalism) – in favour of downsizing and privatizing operations – and from restrictions imposed by transnational corporations and international trade agreements in this era of globalization.
- Many provincial transfer payments are gone, which means that the conditions that used to be attached to most of the payments, and which used to distort local decision making, are also gone. Less senior leverage is one result "eager beavers" can exploit where they are so inclined.
- Amalgamations in Central and Eastern Canada (well founded or not) have created a number of significantly larger municipalities that may be more prepared to challenge the restrictions imposed upon them by their provincial governments. Indeed, Canada now has metropolitan governments larger than some provinces.

It would appear that municipal governments are at something of a crossroads when it comes to policy making. One path, along which they are being pushed by at least some provincial governments, leads to a diminished role centred on the selection of the cheapest alternatives for the delivery of local services. The other path leads to an enhanced policy role, one in which municipalities and their local citizens decide together how they want to define their community and provide for it. This path proceeds from an acceptance of the inherently political nature of municipal government – and the resulting importance of a policy process centred in, and responsive to, the local community. Here representativeness and local accountability may trump anti-political efficiency arguments. As the 1979 *Royal Commission on Financial Management and Accountability* concluded, you cannot have efficiency in a democracy without accountability.[69]

---

[69] Royal Commission on Financial Management and Accountability (Allen Thomas Lambert, Commissioner), *Final Report*, Ottawa, March 1979.

Chapter 12
Future Prospects for Municipal Government

How well municipalities fare in the 21st century will depend, as always, on how successfully they maintain a balance between their two primary roles: representative/political and administrative/service delivery. The tension between these two roles is reflected in two contrasting images of municipal government – as a democratic institution that responds to community concerns and as but one of many players in a competitive marketplace in which individual interests prevail.

Introduction

This book began with fanciful suggestions about the 21st century belonging to Canada's municipalities. What have we learned in the more than 400 intervening pages that support or detract from this optimistic outlook? What needs to happen if this new century is to bring greater municipal significance?

Taking a New Look

The best way to start, especially for those in municipal government, is to turn upside down the usual way of looking at municipalities, a perspective which has them on the bottom of several levels of higher jurisdiction, as in the accompanying chart. According to this traditional view, municipalities are subordinate and subservient creatures of the provinces to which they owe their existence. They are

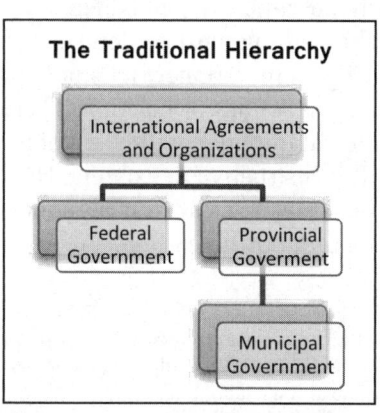

also dependent on the federal (and provincial) levels for financial assistance that, in practice, is limited and elusive and they are significantly affected by senior/federal government actions (and inaction). They are also increasingly constrained by international agreements and organizations and by global competitive pressures and a prevailing neoliberal ideological paradigm.

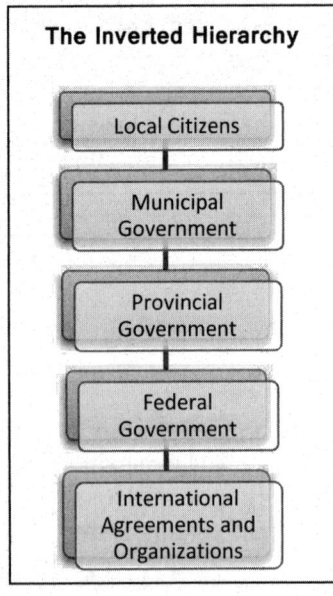

There is, however, an alternative way of looking at municipalities and their place in the world, unaccustomed as we are to considering it. What if we invert the traditional hierarchical view, as in the chart on this page? What if we see local governments as the first order of government? Let us consider the significance of such a reversal.

Globalization and the accompanying free trade regime are certainly forces to be reckoned with, but we shouldn't overstate their importance for day to day municipal operations. Not all firms are completely footloose and most would think long and hard before pulling up stakes and setting up shop in another country where culture, language, and other barriers may present quite a challenge. Since the terrorist attacks of September 11, 2001, many actions have been rationalized or justified "because of 9/11" – no matter how tenuous the link. The attacks have become an all too convenient cover or excuse for actions (especially adversely affecting individual rights and freedoms) that would not otherwise be tolerated. In much the same way, globalization is constantly invoked as the reason why something must be done or cannot be done. Without in any way denying its importance, let's not allow it to become an excuse for municipal actions or inaction. There is still considerable scope for municipal initiative within a global world.

It is instructive to examine Horak's analysis of the background to Toronto's New Deal campaign that ultimately led to the new *City of Toronto Act* of June 2006.[1] At first blush, one might interpret this

---

[1] Martin Horak, *Governance Reform From Below: Multilevel Politics and the 'New Deal' Campaign in Toronto,* Global Dialogue Series, No. 4, Nairobi, UN-Habitat, 2008, available at www.unhabitat.org/pmss/listItemDetails.aspx?publicationID=2494 (accessed October 30, 2011).

development as the inevitable response of a global city seeking out additional powers to strengthen its competitive position. But Horak found that the forces of global economic competition were not the key factors driving Toronto's New Deal campaign. Instead, he identified a number of developments that came together to create the impetus and opportunity for change, including:

- The provincially imposed amalgamation that created the City of Toronto;
- Provincial downloading of social programs that burdened the new municipality with substantial costs;
- Elections at all three levels of government that resulted in leaders (Martin, McGuinty, and Miller) predisposed to working together.

The size of the amalgamated municipality gave it increased clout, and the disparities in downloaded cost burdens between the new City of Toronto and the suburban municipalities in the surrounding Greater Toronto Area provided further stimulus for those seeking greater powers for Toronto. The arrival of the three Ms as heads of the three levels of government provided the other major factor favourable to a New Deal for Toronto. Horak's research into the Toronto case demonstrates that even in cities that are highly integrated into the global economy, the exigencies of global competition are not the only or necessarily even the primary influence. He concludes that "both the size of the new City and the sense of fiscal crisis that accompanied its birth were critical to the emergence of the New Deal campaign, in that they enabled and encouraged the new City to move beyond the passive intergovernmental stance that Canadian municipalities have typically assumed given their weak standing in the constitutional order."[2] Once again we have a welcome example of what "eager beavers" can accomplish.

Because the constraints imposed by globalization apply more to federal and provincial governments, it can even be argued that the net result is to liberate rather than to restrict municipalities. National borders are more porous and the nation state is challenged by international trade rules and agencies and scaled back by neoliberal preachings about the inherent superiority of private sector operations. These global and ideological pressures affect the local level as well, but municipalities also have an opportunity to move into the vacuum created at the centre by the reduced role of the federal and provincial levels. In fact, the municipal capacity to capitalize on this opportunity has been strengthened, unwittingly, by the actions taken by the federal and provincial levels in

---

[2] *Ibid.*, pp. 41-42.

response to globalization and neoliberalism. We refer, in particular, to the decentralization of responsibilities to the local level and the reduction in provincial and federal transfer payments and the conditions/requirements that accompanied most of them. Municipalities have more powers and greater financial self-sufficiency. The annual budget of the City of Vancouver, for example, now approaches $1 billion, but the financial contribution from the province has dropped to 1% of total revenues.[3]

The importance of municipal governments has been enhanced by a number of developments. With over 80% of the population now living in urban centres, how well municipalities operate is a matter of national concern. That the constitutional order established in Canada in the 1860s reflected a country which was almost 80% rural seems less of an issue today. As noted earlier in this text, many problems *in* the cities are not problems *of* the cities, but they end up being addressed – if at all – by the cities, by default. The economic health of Canada's large cities is widely viewed as critical to the international competitiveness of our nation, and studies have also shown that economic growth in these "hub" cities is the best way to bring about growth and prosperity in outlying areas as well. Jane Jacobs has convincingly made this point.[4]

Municipalities, especially large cities again, are also in the forefront as key players in the development of new forms of governance at the regional level in response to global pressures. They are also gaining status within growing multilevel governance arrangements that go beyond the formal constitutional division of powers and bring all levels of government together, along with community groups and other players as needed.

What's Missing?

Taken together, all of these factors suggest a very prominent, and increasing, role for Canadian municipalities. They sit at the top of the hierarchy (not the bottom), legitimized by local elections, providing

---

[3] Kennedy Stewart and Patrick J. Smith, "Immature Policy Analysis: Building Capacity in Eight Major Canadian Cities," in Laurent Dobuzinskis, Michael Howlett, and David Laycock (eds.), *Policy Analysis in Canada, The State of the Art*, Toronto, University of Toronto Press, 2007, p. 267.

[4] See Jane Jacobs, *Cities and the Wealth of Nations: Principles of Economic Life,* New York, Random House, 1984.

services essential to civilized living, contributing local insights that are now recognized as increasingly valuable in shaping provincial and federal policies with a spatial impact, and initiating and coordinating new, broader based governance models to respond more effectively to global competition. So what's keeping municipalities from playing the enhanced role that seems to be available to them? Why does the 21st century not yet belong to municipalities?

Historically, the answer has been that municipalities need constitutional recognition, or more empowering provincial legislation, or additional revenue sources – all matters beyond municipal control and unlikely to be provided. We suggest instead that the key missing element that keeps municipalities from being more powerful is their failure to harness the support of their local citizens – and to show leadership on issues which matter clearly to them.

A case in point is the new City of Toronto, one municipality containing over 2.5 million people. The mayor of Toronto is elected from that entire population, whereas a provincial or federal elected representative – including the Premier and the Prime Minister – is elected from a population of 100 000 or less. With such a mandate, the Toronto mayor must be a powerful political figure. Accounting for such a large portion of the population of Ontario and of its economic activity, Toronto must be a dominant force. And yet, consider the following events that unfolded in the summer of 2007.[5] Faced with its annual budget crisis, the City of Toronto wrestled with whether or not to use new taxing powers (that would not come close to balancing the budget). In the meantime, it pursued various expenditure cuts that would reduce services in the city. For example, the municipality projected savings of $160 000 by reducing by one month the season during which it maintains outdoor ice pads.

In the meantime, the Ontario government posted a $2.3 billion dollar surplus for the fiscal year ending in March 2007, even after an orgy of year end spending that led to a very critical report from the Provincial Auditor and the resignation of one member of the cabinet. That minister was responsible for a department (Citizenship) that dispatched large sums of money to various groups and associations without proper procedures and documentation. When the Ontario Cricket Association asked the ministry for $150 000, it received a cheque for $1 million the next day. If the Ontario government has money to spare of this magnitude, why are Torontonians facing the loss of ice rinks for a savings of $160 000? If big cities are the key to the country's economic

---

[5] The discussion of this example is largely based on John Barber, "Wage cuts? Rink closures? Seen from Queen's Park, it's all penny-ante," *Toronto Star*, September 1, 2007.

survival, why is the federal government looking at a $14 billion surplus while claiming that it is up to the provinces to redress any municipal fiscal imbalance? The situation into the second decade of the 21st century seems little different (except that the federal and most provincial governments are no longer flush with cash).

We are not suggesting that the province (or the federal government) should simply hand money to Toronto whenever it has a shortfall – as will be evident from our criticisms in Chapter 7 of Toronto's handling of its fiscal problems. The point of this example is to raise the question of why a city of 2.5 million people has so little apparent clout and political influence. In our view, a primary reason is that the municipal government does not have those 2.5 million people – or even a significant portion of them – solidly behind it. The council has failed to provide a vision for the city or to demonstrate its need for financial assistance in a way that would rally the populace behind it. With such support, the City of Toronto could not be ignored by other levels of government when they are rolling up budget surpluses. Without that support, the municipality's entreaties have been largely ignored. We have placed local citizens at the top of our second chart (on page 440), but they don't occupy that lofty position in the operations and attention of most municipalities. Local engagement in matters municipal in Canada remains historically low. Enhancing that democratic connectedness would considerably empower municipalities to clearer ongoing political influence.

Reviving the Political Role

If municipalities are to earn the public involvement and support that will legitimize their decisions and strengthen their position, they need to rediscover their political role. The term rediscover is used because municipalities were originally established with a political role that was at least as important as the service delivery role. If the settlers in Central Canada in the early 1800s had only been interested in receiving services, there would have been no need for them to push for elected municipal governments. They were already receiving local services from the Courts of Quarter Sessions. What they wanted, clearly, was something more – a say in those servicing decisions, a vehicle through which they could express collective concerns about their communities. No matter how many or what services are provided by municipalities, their primary importance is as an expression of local choice. As Clarke and Stewart explain, there would be no point, other than administrative convenience, in local governments providing services in which there was no significant local choice.[6]

A series of developments, described in earlier chapters, undermined the political role of municipal government, to the point where it receives far too little attention today. The first significant influence to be noted is the turn of the century reform movement of 100 years ago, from which came the notion – still widely held – that politics has no place in municipal government and only serves to interfere with the technical decisions that must be made by staff experts facing complex servicing issues. The irony, of course, is that the reform movement did not really succeed in eradicating politics from municipal decision making, nor was that really the objective of many reformers. What the reforms of that era did was ensure that the political power of business interests and the middle class continued to prevail. This truncated model of local democracy ill serves the broader citizenry of any municipality.

By the mid-20th century, municipalities had become closely intertwined with the operations of the provincial and federal governments and were increasingly seen as vehicles for servicing land in support of the economic growth objectives of these governments. Bradford, as noted in Chapter 3, refers to this period as "cities in the shadow of Keynesian space,"[7] in deference to the economic policies then being followed by the federal government. With the growing complexity of service demands arising from the rapid urbanization following World War Two, the importance of technical expertise as the basis for municipal decisions continued to hold sway. There appeared to be widespread support for municipal efforts to promote and accommodate rapid economic growth and municipal activities seemed more administrative than political in nature. Here again, as at the end of the 19th century, the reality was rather different. "Power was in the hands of politicians, bureaucrats, and developers, all of whom were involved in the transformation and expansion of cities – hence the focus was on efficiency and only limited debate occurred over policy orientations."[8]

---

[6] Michael Clarke and John Stewart, *The Choices for Local Government*, Harlow, Longman, 1991, p. 2.

[7] Neil Bradford, *Why Cities Matter: Policy Research Perspectives for Canada*, CPRN Discussion Paper No. F\23, Canadian Policy Research Networks, June 2002, p. 16.

[8] Paul Villeneuve and Anne-Marie Séguin, "Power and Decision-Making in the City: Political Perspectives," in Trudi Bunting and Pierre Filion, *Canadian Cities in Transition*, 2nd Edition, Toronto, Oxford University Press, 2000, p. 554.

Debate did intensify by the 1960s, as citizens and local groups increasingly mobilized to protest against the consequences of the pattern of economic growth and development underway. Urban renewal and expressway battles provided evidence of an increasingly politicized urban life – in settings such as Toronto and Vancouver. But many of the groups that sprang up during this period were very narrowly focused and cries of NIMBY (Not In My Back Yard) were frequently heard. By the 1980s, the citizens' movement had lost much of its momentum.

By this time as well, the political role of municipal government was increasingly constrained by changing economic and ideological forces. Deficit and debt reduction became the preoccupation of the provincial and federal governments, in part to ensure Canadian competitiveness in the global economy. Municipalities found themselves facing a growing revenue squeeze. They also faced an even greater threat in the form of provincially imposed or encouraged amalgamation initiatives in several provinces in the 1990s. A number of very big municipalities have resulted from these initiatives, and they face their own challenges in representing the interests of large and often diverse populations.

Whatever their size, municipalities are being urged to operate more like a business as the best way of meeting the challenges that they face. In some respects we have come full circle and are back in another turn of the century reform era in which the political role of municipalities is ignored in favour of the service delivery role. Here the great comic philosopher Pogo offers advice. He suggested "we have met the enemy and he is us." One of the major constraints on "more politics" in local governing comes from local citizens themselves. Confronted with local councils which seem inattentive to citizen concerns or too much tied to developer interests, many citizens in the 21st century ask "what can we do?" but balk at the suggestion that they might organize, take a run for council, perhaps form a local party grouping for municipal elections. Many citizens (often the same ones) also object if council engages in lengthy debates and struggles with decisions – rejecting this indication of a healthy local democracy as too much "politicking." The nonpartisan tradition seems so embedded in contemporary Canada's local governing that only Pogo's recognition will unseat it.[9]

If municipalities are to play an important role in the 21st century, they must reassert themselves as municipal *governments*, centred on elected bodies that make *political* decisions. The municipal council must be recognized as a political mechanism for expressing and responding to the collective concerns of members of the community. Among the

---

[9] On this Pogo cartoon see Walter Kelly, "Pogo," *New York Star,* Earth Day, 1971.

important implications of this conception of municipal government are the following points:[10]

> If the municipality is an extension of the community, its identity and its purpose derive from that community, not from the particular services it provides.
> The municipality has a legitimate right to take actions that are needed by that community. The right derives from the nature of the municipality as an extension of the community, and does not depend on what specific powers have been assigned to it.
> The municipality's primary role is concern for the problems and issues faced by its community. The interests and values of the community are expressed and resolved through the municipality. It is "a political institution for the authoritative determination of community values."[11]

Are municipalities that kind of institution? How often are community values discussed at budget time or during an election campaign? Holding the line on taxes is not the only community value, but one would never know that from the narrow minded focus of too many candidates for council. The 2006 municipal election results in Ottawa are a good case in point. Bob Chiarelli, the incumbent mayor, was expected to face a strong challenge from former councillor Alex Munter. However, the election was won by a late entrant to the campaign, Larry O'Brien, a successful businessman who promised a zero tax increase.

After his election, much of O'Brien's time and energy was spent attempting to convert the city to more businesslike operations and to find some way of keeping his increasingly unlikely promise of holding the line on taxes. Whatever his good intentions and his eventual successes, what there was not much of in his mandate (2006-2010) was any sense of vision for Ottawa of the sort that might inspire local citizens. The city's commitment to increased public transit was left in disarray following council's cancellation of a previously approved light rail project. The one term mayor's energies were too often focused on duplicating the role of the CAO (as discussed in Chapter 8). It is not readily apparent what positive accomplishments the O'Brien administration hoped to achieve, beyond holding the line on taxes; on that he failed as well. His successor (2010-2014) has championed new city light rapid transit development

---

[10] These points are largely based on John Stewart, "A Future for Local Authorities as Community Government," in John Stewart and Gerry Stoker (eds.), *The Future of Local Government*, London, Macmillan, 1989, Chapter 12.

[11] *Ibid.*, p. 241.

and brought clearer vision and direction while still being conscious of the taxpayer's bottom line.[12]

Improving the Service Delivery Role

Calling for a revived political role for municipalities does not mean ignoring suggestions for improving the service delivery role that have been promoted in recent decades under the rubric of reinventing government or pursuing new public management. As always, it is a case of striking a balance, of giving proper attention to the administrative *and* political roles of municipalities. Consider the following examples.

Escaping the Service Delivery Box

Municipalities have traditionally operated on a model of self sufficiency that equated responsibility for a service with direct provision of that service. As the demand for services grew, so did the municipal workload and the upward pressure on scarce resources – personnel as well as financial. Municipalities that continued to try to do all of the things they had always done found themselves facing an increasing crunch at budget time. Years of reducing expenditures across the board to keep tax increases to a minimum added up to "death by a thousand cuts," resulting in a skeleton operation in which services were provided more poorly and facilities maintained inadequately.

Instead, municipalities need to review their mandates (as many are doing) and to define the priorities that will dictate the allocation of their scarce resources. It may be that the community would prefer to see fewer services provided better. Or it may be that the community would accept paying more to avoid losing certain services. Municipalities need to find the answers to such questions. They need to reverse the backwards budget process that is still far too common, the one which starts with the objective of zero tax increases, achieved through a long process of cutting and pruning, often with insufficient appreciation of the impact and long term consequences of such actions. A sensible budget process

---

[12] See David Reevely, Joanne Chianello, and Neco Cockburn, "New LRT plans 'win-win' for riders, taxpayers: Changes to tunnel cuts $207 million from cost," *Ottawa Citizen,* July 8, 2011, pp. C1-2.

should start by identifying those services that the community needs and wants and is willing to fund. Such an approach could transform the budget process into a real exercise in setting community priorities. Toronto's Core Services Review process of 2011 might have contributed to that; instead Mayor Rob Ford's insistence that the municipality was bloated with gravy as a starting point left little room for such dialogue. Ford's reaction to the KPMG reports that identified little to trim which was not a core service represented a missed opportunity. It is difficult to accept his suggestion that simple wage cuts meant that there was a real engagement of the city's 2.5 million residents on whether they wished a leaner city administration or indeed cared more about the quality and breadth of city services.

Depending on how they are carried out, strategic planning exercises can be used to canvass local citizens (and other stakeholders) with respect to the challenges facing the community and the issues that most need to be addressed. These exercises can be a very effective way of involving the public, setting priorities, and reallocating scarce municipal resources accordingly. The debate and dialogue during the strategic planning process can lead to greater council awareness of what is important to the public and greater public understanding of the issues facing council and the difficult decisions that must be taken. The result is a much more solid foundation for fulfillment of the political role of municipal government. In Toronto's case, the 2011 review exercise was more limited by ideological input before any real public discussion got underway, and an opportunity at civic engagement was missed.

The municipality needs to be selective as well as strategic with respect to its service delivery decisions. It needs to step back from day to day service delivery and consider what it is doing and whether there are better alternatives. There may be instances (quite limited, we would suggest) where the municipality should divest itself of a service responsibility entirely, leaving the matter to be taken over by a private supplier if at all. There may be other instances (more common) where the municipality should consider partnering with other local governments, community groups, or the private sector to provide a service. Municipalities don't have to go on providing every service they once assumed. Nor do they need to produce themselves every service that they provide.

Municipalities need, in the words of Gaebler and Osborne, to do less rowing and more steering.[13] The strength of steering organizations is that they are not limited to the resources that they can directly allocate to the

---

[13] David Osborne and Ted Gaebler, *Reinventing Government*, New York, Penguin Books, 1993, Chapter 1.

matter at hand. Having defined the issue broadly, steering organizations can then "shop around" for the resources needed to deal with it. They may regulate, license, or otherwise monitor some activity, they may enter into a variety of partnership arrangements – the options are almost endless.[14] A rather similar perspective is found in the concept of the "enabling authority," described in writings about British local government.[15] Since the municipality is defined by the needs and problems facing its community, it obviously cannot and should not always act on its own; it has to work with others. An enabling municipality is one "which takes a broad responsibility for the social and economic issues confronting its area and uses all the means at its disposal to meet the needs of those living in the area."[16] Note as well how the steering organization is very compatible with the notions of governance, even multilevel governance, discussed earlier in the text.

The European Union has adapted such notions as opposed to stronger euro-constitutional provisions. In the second decade of the 21st century, the EU is utilizing what is termed the Open Method of Coordination (OMC) to develop social policy, etc. This "soft law" approach proceeds via best practice sharing and benchmarking/monitoring rather than directives from the centre.[17] As with subsidiarity principles, those responsible for local government in Canada might learn from this less institutional/constitutional approach for multilevel cooperation on policy making.

Promoting Community Responsibility

Greater involvement of the public through exercises such as strategic planning can help promote a greater sense of community responsibility for local issues and their resolution. All too often citizens respond to a problem by complaining "why doesn't the government do something

---

[14] Osborne and Gaebler identify 36 alternatives to standard service delivery. See *ibid.*, p. 31 and pp. 332-348.

[15] This term is used by a number of British authors, including John Stewart in Stewart and Stoker, *The Future of Local Government*, and Clarke and Stewart, *The Choices for Local Government*, Chapter 2, on which this discussion is partly based.

[16] Gerry Stoker, "Creating a Local Government for a Post-Fordist Society," in Stewart and Stoker, *The Future of Local Government*, p. 167.

[17] See, for example, Philippe Pochet, "The Open Method of Co-ordination and the Construction of Social Europe" in J. Zeitlin and P. Pochet (eds.), *The Open Method of Coordination in Action: The European Employment and Social Inclusion Strategies*, Brussels, Peter Lang, 2006.

about this," even as they decry the size of government and the heavy tax burden they bear. Adding to this paradoxical behaviour is the fact that more responsible actions on the part of citizens might avoid some of the problems that then lead to expensive responses from government. People used to undertake self help and community initiated ventures almost as a matter of course. But as the scope of government activity expanded over the past century, these tendencies disappeared. The notion somehow developed that once the government gets involved with some subject, then it is the government's problem, not ours. Governments have contributed to this unfortunate development by appearing to exclude the public, by acting as if only professionals and experts could have the answers.

Gradually this trend is being reversed. Progressive governments are working with communities to reduce the likelihood of problems arising in the first place. After a century of the medical model of health care, which consumes vast resources to treat people after they become sick, the "healthy cities" movement has revived efforts by municipalities and public health agencies to promote healthy communities and healthy lifestyles as primary methods of avoiding sickness and associated treatment costs. The same emphasis on prevention is evident in the shift to community policing, the opening of "storefront operations," and the provision of youth related recreational facilities in an effort to reduce crime. Progressive fire departments recognize that their primary task is not to fight fires but to prevent them from happening, and they have devoted increasing resources to public education activities. Members of the community have often led the way with respect to environmental matters, pushing their municipalities to adopt recycling and blue box programs and to promote the three Rs (reduce, reuse, and recycle).

To take one more example, many municipalities have recognized their financial limits and the importance of community involvement by setting up mechanisms which encourage local groups, organizations, or businesses to accept responsibility for providing or maintaining particular facilities or services. A common example is an arrangement under which the municipality provides the site and the boards, but a neighbourhood group accepts responsibility for maintaining an outdoor rink in its area. Schemes to "adopt a park" or "adopt a flower bed" are also widespread. A plaque at the site identifies the organization taking on this role.

There is a danger, of course, that these latter arrangements can become little more than a scheme to shift public responsibilities and costs on to private shoulders. If that is the only objective of the exercise, it is unlikely to succeed for long. Equally foolish is the situation in which governments call for greater efforts from volunteers and community associations at the very time that they have been cutting grant support to such associations in the name of fiscal restraint! Adequate government resources and true partnership arrangements are needed "to enable communities in their efforts to rehabilitate housing, create employment, get rid of drug dealers, pimps, and slum landlords, foster strong community schools, recover rivers for community use, and improve public health."[18] In Burnaby, British Columbia, city owned facilities created as part of the density bonus of a 46 storey project are then offered for bids to community non profit organizations. This is a good example of a municipality supporting and encouraging such community endeavours.[19]

Almost lost in all the recent talk about governments pursuing public private partnerships is the importance of a new partnership between governments and their citizens, one that can generate the volunteer and community efforts that are so needed today. It is scarcely an exaggeration to say that governments spent the first three decades following World War Two building a welfare state that largely pushed aside volunteer organizations, and the last three decades dismantling these social programs while underfunded charities struggled to pick up the pieces.[20] Municipalities today increasingly recognize the value of volunteers and the fact that they can be involved in many areas other than the traditional field of recreation. With municipal resources so strained and limited, it only makes sense to draw upon community resources and expertise wherever possible. In the words of a former community worker and municipal councillor from Western Canada (now Premier of Manitoba), "civic bureaucratic expertise combined with community initiative can lead to a more dynamic, engaged civic culture and to stronger local democracy."[21]

As this quote suggests, what makes a partnership between government and the community so valuable is not the reduction in government workload but the increased feeling of community responsibility and ownership. The "adopt a park" program cited earlier does help to defray

---

[18] Greg Selinger, "Urban Governance for the Twenty-First Century," in Nancy Klos (ed.), *The State of Unicity – 25 Years Later*, Winnipeg, Institute of Urban Studies, 1998, p. 99.

[19] See Wanda Chow, "South Burnaby Neighbourhood House to get new digs: Winning proposal for new city-owned non-profit space…," *Burnaby News Leader,* July 20, 2011, p. A15.

[20] This is the perspective of Carol Goar, "Don't mistake price tags for values," *Toronto Star*, February 13, 1999.

[21] Selinger, "Urban Governance for the Twenty-First Century," p. 99.

municipal program costs, but its main benefit is enhanced community involvement and a greater sense of ownership. This is reflected in reduced vandalism and general abuse of park facilities that are adopted in this manner. If members of the community have volunteered their time and energy to maintain a park, they view it quite differently; it is "their" park, not just a municipal park. They are not going to damage or neglect "their" park; nor are they likely to tolerate others being similarly inconsiderate. It was always their park, of course, since it was provided through tax dollars, but they didn't see it that way before.

Using Resources Wisely

Whatever planning and priority setting exercises may be carried out and however much community responsibility and collective ownership can be engendered, municipalities still face the challenge of providing a wide variety of services and programs to their citizens with severely constrained financial resources. As a result, they need to take steps to ensure that they are using their limited resources as wisely as possible. These steps often involve the use of tools and techniques from the business world – even though we have repeatedly rejected the notion that municipal governments should run more like a business. There is no inconsistency here. In seeking to use their resources wisely, municipalities should employ any tools that can *assist* them in their decisions. It is not the business tools *per se* to which we have objected, but situations in which business tools and market forces dictate decisions instead of simply providing background information on which political decisions are made by councils. Two examples will illustrate the point.

We have already noted that municipalities can be service providers without necessarily being service producers. They can consider a variety of alternative service delivery (ASD) options, as discussed in Chapter 9, and may decide to contract with another body for delivery of a service. But any such step should be taken only after a comprehensive analysis of the situation and ASD options should not be promoted as a euphemism for downsizing and privatizing. We find nothing inherently superior in private administration, and offer in support of our position the positive municipal experiences with managed competition in places such as Indianapolis and Phoenix, as described earlier in the text. There is much to be said for measuring, comparing, and introducing competitive pressures (in any organization). But a municipality considering the use of an alternative service supplier needs to consider such things as:

- How central is the service in question to the core mission and mandate of the municipality? Is it a service that should be kept under direct municipal control?
- Is there sufficient information on how costs are classified and apportioned by the alternative supplier and the municipality to be confident that the comparison is really "apples to apples"?
- In addition to cost and efficiency, has equal attention been given to the question of quality and effectiveness? What is the alternative supplier's track record in this regard?
- Will the alternative supplier be taking over full responsibility for the service in question (as opposed to, for example, being responsible for provision within a portion of the municipality's geographic area) and, if so, what happens to existing municipal staff who have been handling this service?
- If the municipality is no longer involved in providing this service, will it still have sufficient internal expertise to monitor the way it is being provided and to ensure that the service contract is being fulfilled?
- Has a "Yellow Pages test" been done to determine if there are several alternative suppliers of this particular service, in case the first one is no longer the preferred choice when the original contract comes up for renewal?

Our second example, also discussed in Chapter 9, concerns the increased municipal use of performance measurement, benchmarking, and best practices to improve their operations. These developments are welcome and the resulting information can enhance municipal decision making. But those pursuing an ideological agenda to downsize the public service and to enhance private sector operations can distort performance measures to advance their cause. For virtually every municipal service, it is probably possible to find a quote from somewhere that promises cheaper service delivery. But performance measures should not be used as a means of searching out the cheapest alternative. They are not intended for that purpose – or for the accountability "report card" mandated in municipal financial reports in Ontario since 2000 or the "Annual Reports" under B.C.'s *Community Charter* since 2004 – but as a way of helping managers to improve program implementation. Rather than asking "is anyone doing this cheaper?" the question should be "is staff performance showing desired improvement, year by year?" Steady progress of this sort is more effective than the "quick fix" of contracting out service provision to an apparently cheaper supplier.

Striking a Balance

The challenge for municipalities is to maintain a balance between two contrasting visions of what they are and how they should operate and a balance between the two primary roles that underlie these visions. For the purposes of this discussion, these two visions will be characterized as the vending machine and the barn raising.[22]

A Vending Machine or a Barn Raising?

The vending machine image reflects the municipality's role as service provider. This view has always been prominent and it has received even greater attention in recent years with the emphasis on municipalities being more businesslike and taking care of the customer. People drop money (tax payments) in the municipal vending machine, and the machine dispenses services. Sometimes the machine doesn't work, or is out of the particular product that people want, and they grumble and kick the machine. In response, people may be offered different products and different prices. They may be given a 1-800 number (or, more recently, a 311 number) to call; they may even be offered guarantees about product availability or quality. Ultimately, however, there is nothing to encourage a close allegiance between citizens and the municipal vending machine. It is just a service provider. All it wants is for people to deposit their money in exchange for the products. All the people want is the products that satisfy their particular needs. Instead of being citizens of a wider community who have an interest in the needs of others, they are individual consumers. The vending machine view is essentially an extension of public choice theory, focusing on individual choice through markets. It provides a marked contrast to traditional theories of local democracy that focus on the capacity for collective choice through voting.[23]

The barn raising image incorporates the notion of citizen and community responsibility. People have collective needs and concerns. Instead of saying "why doesn't the government do something?" when a

---

[22] These contrasting images of municipal government are described in Frank Benest, "Serving customers or engaging citizens: What is the future of local government?," an article originally published as an insert in the *International City Management Association Journal*, November 1996. Some of the ideas in this article provided the inspiration for the discussion in this section.

[23] Michael Keating, *Comparative Urban Politics*, Aldershot, Edward Elgar, 1991, p. 108.

problem arises, they are as likely to say "what are we going to do?" The "adopt a park" initiative, properly conducted, is consistent with the barn raising model of municipal government. So is a strategic planning exercise that draws upon the views and values, hopes and fears, of countless members of the community as a foundation for its planning and priority setting. Technical staff can write a strategic plan, but only the citizens of a community can provide the vision that illuminates such a plan – a point obviously not understood in Toronto's 2011 core services review. Storefront operations, efforts to involve and empower local groups and associations, initiatives to promote partnerships amongst groups to tackle community issues – all of these actions reflect the barn raising model. This model is consistent with the notion of the municipality as an extension of the community, the community governing itself.

The Representative or Administrative Role?

Underlying the two contrasting images of a barn raising versus a vending machine are the two roles of municipal government: representative/political and administrative/service delivery – and they may also be in conflict. If the first role is emphasized, the municipality is seen as a vehicle used by the community to address its collective concerns. This role conveys the notion of collective action to deal with shared problems and challenges (consistent with the image of the barn raising). Municipalities are viewed as local democratic institutions that respond to collective public concerns by providing public services financed from taxes. The ultimate measure of their performance is how effectively they respond to the elusive public interest.

If the administrative role is emphasized, as has certainly been the case in recent years, the municipality is seen as but one of many players in a competitive marketplace in which individuals are free to pursue their personal interests by seeking out the services that they find most attractive. The image is manifestly not one of the collective identification of issues and collective responses. A variety of alternative service providers is seen as offering the range of choice needed for individual consumers of services to pursue their best interests. Charging user fees for these services is favoured over payment through taxes because the former allows individuals to select only those services they want to use, and to pay accordingly (as in the vending machine analogy). The ultimate measurement of performance is how efficiently municipalities deliver services as reflected in their bottom line. The figure that follows depicts the key characteristics of these two contrasting views.

Figure 12.1 The Contrasting Characteristics

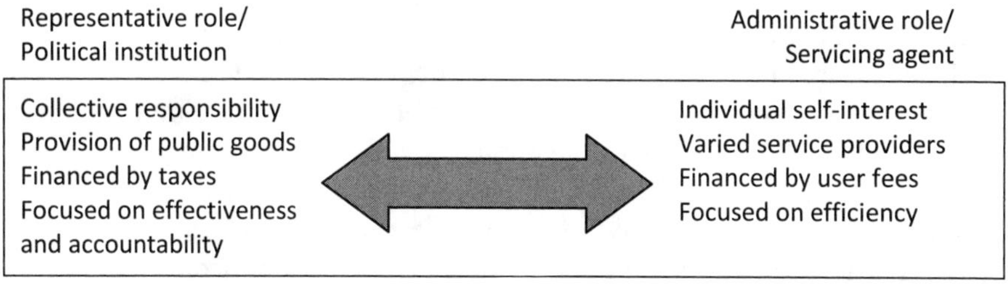

Representative role/ Political institution	Administrative role/ Servicing agent
Collective responsibility Provision of public goods Financed by taxes Focused on effectiveness and accountability	Individual self-interest Varied service providers Financed by user fees Focused on efficiency

U.K. and Australian local government expert Peter Self has described this relationship between representation/accountability versus service provision/efficiency as *the* classic dilemma in public administration. For Self, efficiency and accountability are competing values. In this zero-sum relationship, the more you add to one the more you take from the other.[24] Others have suggested something other than zero sum, arguing that in a democracy, governing cannot be efficient if it is not accountable.[25] However viewed, it is clear that undervaluing the political/representation/accountability side of the local governing equation – as many public choice advocates have done – is partly to blame for the truncating of local democracy.

The second role, of municipality as servicing agent, contains within it both positive elements and potential dangers, depending on the extent to which its key features are pushed. The benefits of a competitive atmosphere have long been evident in the public sector, and public choice proponents are persuasive when they contend that the choice for citizens is enhanced when there are multiple local service providers and when there is freedom to access a service or not by paying a user fee or not. As noted elsewhere in this text, there is considerable evidence to suggest that a fragmented municipal structure provides services less expensively than one large, consolidated unit. It is also well documented that "what gets measured, gets done,"[26] and that concerted efforts to promote and reward productivity improvements bear fruit.

On the other hand, we have also noted in this text that whatever efficiency benefits there may be from a fragmented municipal structure

---

[24] Peter Self, *Administrative Theories and Politics,* London, Allen and Unwin, 1977, Chapter 8, pp. 277-278.

[25] This view was strongly made in the Lambert Royal Commission on Financial Management and Accountability, *Final Report*, Ottawa, March 1979, particularly in the section on "Closing the Accountability Gap."

[26] Osborne and Gaebler, *Reinventing Government*, p. 146.

are potentially offset by problems caused by the lack of a unified approach to intermunicipal issues and by the perpetuation of servicing and financing inequities. With a number of separate municipalities, individuals are free to choose the one which provides whatever combination of services and charges best meet their needs – assuming that they have both knowledge of the choices available and the mobility to act upon this knowledge. But this structural arrangement may also allow the creation or preservation of communities of relatively wealthy individuals who need minimal government services and are taxed accordingly, and who aren't obliged to contribute, thanks to their separate governing jurisdiction, to the costs of the many government services needed by the less fortunate in society, who are located in other jurisdictions. Carried to an extreme, this can result in a kind of social apartheid, in which the elite "feel increasingly justified in paying only what is necessary to insure that everyone in their community is sufficiently well educated and has access to the public services they need to succeed."[27] It is clear that the pursuit of individual self-interest can work better for some individuals than it does for others. Along with what is best for the individual, as measured in strictly financial terms, there has to be some consideration of what is best for the broader community and region in which one moves and interacts.

Similarly, a preoccupation with the efficiency of service delivery and a tendency to measure municipal operations in the same way as a business, can lead to some harmful distortions. It must be remembered that many of the services provided by government are not provided by the private sector because they do not, and cannot, generate a profit or even come close to operating at break even. This bad bottom line doesn't make such services a candidate for termination; it is why they belong in the public domain. User charges have their benefits, applied selectively, but any widespread expansion of their use can be self-defeating. Once again, the self-interested individual will attempt to minimize costs. The wealthier citizens have no need of services such as public transit. They can forego public parks in favour of cottages and private resorts, and may even feel less need for police services thanks to their secure access high rise or gated community. Indeed, there are now far more private security forces than there are public police. But public programs and services certainly cannot be financed solely from user charges paid by the less wealthy in society.

---

[27] Robert Reich, "Secession of the Successful," *New York Times Magazine*, January 6, 1991, as quoted in Murray Dobbin, *The Myth of the Good Corporate Citizen*, Toronto, Stoddart, 1998, pp. 128-129.

Consider the example of municipal transit services. These services never operate at break even, a fact which causes great controversy – even though the public roads provided for the convenience of cars and which are much more heavily subsidized by government also never come close to operating at break even. Yet a typical response to a transit deficit is to increase the fees and reduce the service, actions hardly conducive to an improvement in the situation. A totally different way of looking at public transit would be to view it as an essential public good which is also cost effective when one factors in the costs that would arise without it, in the form of increased air pollution and traffic congestion, greater traffic control costs, time and money lost in commuting, more "fender-benders" and other accidents, and more associated police and court costs. When everything is taken into consideration, it might even be that the much maligned municipal transit system is a bargain. But when the focus is only on the bottom line, rather than on the broader benefits to society, we are likely to be guilty of shortsighted bookkeeping.

Concluding Comments

The contrasting images and roles that we have been examining are not either/or options for municipalities. They represent gradations of behaviour and orientation, and it is certainly possible (and highly desirable) to combine the best of both. Our favoured combination would keep the vending machine in the back of the barn. In other words, we believe that the representative/political role should be paramount, but that features of the service delivery role are also valuable in moderation and within the framework of the first role. Efficient and economical use of municipal resources is a desirable objective, provided that such measures are balanced by considerations of effectiveness. The pursuit of the bottom line cannot be allowed to take precedence over pursuit of the public interest.

Under different circumstances, it should not be that difficult to add businesslike, competitive features to local democratic institutions. Presently, however, we face the added challenge that the institutions of government (at all levels) seem to be under attack, as a result of the global economy, the dictates of international capitalism, and the anti-governmental neoliberal ideology that has held sway for the past couple of decades. Not content to have government act in a more businesslike manner, there are many who wish to go further and downgrade the role and significance of government in our society, while elevating the importance of the private sector.

One manifestation of this viewpoint is the widespread attitude that virtually all spending by government is inherently less desirable than spending by and on the private sector, and that no further tax increases can be tolerated. But the bill for local government services is something of a bargain, as vividly illustrated by Jim Sharpe's comment that:

> ...although the local government bill is not small, it provides education, public health, social services, highways, libraries, fire, police, refuse collection, and a whole range of other public services which most people need and demand, at a total cost that is no larger than the amount we collectively spend on such things as wine and beer, cigarettes, eye shadow, tennis rackets and a flutter on the horses.[28]

It is highly unlikely that paying taxes will ever become a popular pastime in Canada. But it is through such taxes that a society provides the goods and services that serve and enhance the public good. This community need and collective responsibility provide a marked contrast to the emphasis on individual preferences and choices that has been receiving growing attention. Unless and until citizens themselves show more commitment to governments and to their responsibilities within the governmental system, municipalities will remain vulnerable to the pressures to convert them into quasi businesses. To resist these pressures, therefore, municipalities need to do as much as possible to demonstrate their value and relevance to their communities. Starting with a reengagement of local citizens is an essential first step.

There is an additional, and compelling, reason for municipalities to reassert their political role and to reforge links with their citizens. As noted earlier in this chapter, this relationship represents the best hope for municipalities in the future. Experience has shown that there is little to be gained by relying on the provincial and federal levels and waiting to see what may trickle down from above. Galbraith has referred to trickle down as the relationship of the sparrow to the horse. Far better to build strength upward from the community, from the citizens whom municipalities exist to serve. That means taking into account the views and concerns of all citizens, not just propertied or business interests. It means being efficient where possible, but also being prepared to provide services or programs which aren't necessarily cost effective, if they are

---

[28] L. J. Sharpe (ed.), *The Local Fiscal Crisis in Western Europe, Myths and Realities*, London, Sage Publications, 1981, p. 224.

required to address a public need. It means being mindful of the bottom line but also dedicated to the public interest. And it means showing local citizens and taxpayers vision, leadership, and how municipal initiatives benefit all in the community.

As Jane Jacobs and Caroline Andrew argue in Chapter 6, municipal governments must get beyond their mindset of dependency and become more assertive. Patrick Smith and Kennedy Stewart demonstrate in that chapter that constitutional and statutory inferiority need not be a complete barrier for creative and aggressive municipalities that take advantage of any bargaining leverage that they may temporarily enjoy. Chris Leo and Susan Mulligan, in the same chapter and in Chapter 10, envisage an enhanced role for municipalities in fine tuning the local application of federal and provincial policies and programs.

Moving from a war on drugs to harm reduction in Vancouver took vision and leadership – now through four different mayors/ councils representing three different local political parties. This initiative succeeded by demonstrating to local communities in the city, some with serious reservations, that it was not only the right thing to do, but that it was cost effective. When North America's senior governments across the continent abandoned efforts to achieve the environmental standards of the Kyoto Accord, local governments stepped up and committed to meeting Kyoto targets on greenhouse gases. In doing so, they spoke for their local citizenry. These examples are part of that difficult work of building trust and engagement. Local democracy is essential to our well being. The work of local democracy falls to us all.

Instead of being preoccupied with their place in the hierarchy of governments in Canada, municipalities need to look outward to the other local actors that they can bring together into more inclusive governing regimes. They need to stop lamenting their status as constitutional orphans and seek adoption by their local communities. Building trust and developing close links with local citizens will be a slow and difficult process. But it is something within the power of municipalities to do. Successfully carried out, it is the key to their enhanced role in the 21st century.

Select Bibliography

Advisory Commission on Intergovernmental Relations, *A Look to the North: Canadian Regional Experience*, Washington, DC, 1974.

Anderson, Wayne, Chester Nowland, and Richard J. Stillman, *The Effective Local Government Manager*, Washington, DC, International City Management Association, 1983.

Andrew, Caroline, "Evaluating Municipal Reform in Ottawa-Gatineau: Building a More Metropolitan Future," in Eran Razin and Patrick Smith (eds.), *Metropolitan Governing: Canadian Cases: Comparative Lessons*, Jerusalem, Hebrew University Magnes Press, 2006, pp. 75-94.

_____, "City-States and City-Scapes in Canada: The Politics and Culture of Canadian Urban Diversity," August 2006, chapter for presentation for the conference *Managing Diversity: Prospects for a Post-Nationalist Politics*, Dublin, April 2004.

_____ (ed.), *Our Diverse Cities*, Number 1, Metropolis Project, Citizenship and Immigration Canada, Spring 2004.

_____, "The shame of (ignoring) the cities," *Journal of Canadian Studies*, Winter 2001.

_____, John Biles, Myer Siemiatycki, and Erin Tolley (eds.), *Electing a Diverse Canada: The Representation of Immigrants, Minorities and Women*, Vancouver, University of British Columbia Press, 2008.

_____, Katherine A. Graham, and Susan D. Phillips (eds.), *Urban Affairs: Back on the Policy Agenda*, Montreal and Kingston, McGill-Queen's University Press, 2002.

_____ and Patrick Smith, "World Class Cities: Can – or Should – Canada Play?" in Caroline Andrew, Pat Armstrong and André Lapierre (eds.), *World Class Cities: Can Canada Play?*, Ottawa, University of Ottawa Press, 1999, pp. 5-25.

Antoft, Kell and Jack Novack, *Grassroots Democracy: Local Government in the Maritimes*, Halifax, Centre for Public Management, Dalhousie University, 1998.

Ashe, Jeanette and Kennedy Stewart, "Legislative recruitment: Using diagnostic testing to explain underrepresentation," *Party Politics*, February 24, 2011.

Association of Municipalities of Ontario, *Local Governance in the Future: Issues and Trends*, Toronto, 1994.

_____, *Ontario Charter: A Proposed Bill of Rights for Local Government*, Toronto, 1994.

Aucoin, Peter, *The New Public Management in Canada in Comparative Perspective*, Montreal, Institute for Research on Public Policy, 1995.

Austin, Sam and Lisa Young, *Party Finance in City Elections: Toronto and Calgary Compared*, paper presented to the annual general meeting of the Canadian Political Science Association, Toronto, 2006.

Bell, David and Mark Jayne (eds.), *Small Cities: Urban Experience Beyond the Metropolis*, New York, Routledge, 2006.
Bellamy, Honourable Madam Justice Denise E., *Toronto Computer Leasing Inquiry, Toronto External Contracts Inquiry* (4 vol.), 2005.
Bird, Richard (ed.), *Who Decides? Government in the New Millennium*, Montreal, C. D. Howe Institute, August 2004.
_____ and Enid Slack, *Fiscal Aspects of Metropolitan Governance*, Toronto, University of Toronto, January 2004.
_____ and Slack, *Urban Public Finance in Canada*, Toronto, Butterworths, 1983 and Toronto, John Wiley & Sons, 1993.
Bish, Robert L., "The Draft Community Charter: Comments," a paper prepared for the Workshop on the Community Charter, University of Victoria, June 14, 2002.
_____, *Local Government Amalgamations: Discredited Nineteenth-Century Ideals Alive in the Twenty-First*, Commentary No. 150, C. D. Howe Institute, March 2001.
_____, "Evolutionary Alternatives for Metropolitan Areas: The Capital Region of British Columbia," *Canadian Journal of Regional Science*, Special Issue, Spring 2000.
_____ and Eric Clemens, *Local Government in British Columbia*, 4th Edition, Richmond, B.C., Union of B.C. Municipalities, 2008.
_____ and Eric Clemens, *Local Government in British Columbia*, 3rd Edition, Richmond, Union of British Columbia Municipalities, 1999.
Blais, Pamela, *Inching Toward Sustainability: The Evolving Urban Structure of the GTA*, Report to the Neptis Foundation, March 2000.
Booth, Philip and Bernard Jouve (eds.), *Metropolitan Democracies*, Burlington, Ashgate Publishing Limited, 2005.
Borins, Sandford, "The new public management is here to stay," *Canadian Public Administration*, Spring 1995.
Boudreau, Julie-Anne, "The Politics of Territorialization: Regionalism, Localism and Other Isms ... The Case of Montreal," *Journal of Urban Affairs*, Vol. 25, No. 2, 2003.
_____, *MegaCity Saga*, Montreal, Black Rose Books, 2000.
_____, Pierre Hamel, Bernard Jouve, and Roger Keil, "New State Spaces in Canada: Metropolitanization in Montreal and Toronto Compared," *Urban Geography*, 28, 2007.
Bourne, Larry, *People and Times: A Portrait of the Evolving Social Character of the Greater Toronto Region*, Toronto, Neptis Foundation, 2000.
_____ and Jim Simmons, "New Fault Lines, Recent Trends in the Canadian Urban System and Their Implications for Planning and Public Policy," *Canadian Journal of Urban Research*, Vol. 12, Issue 1, Summer 2003.
Boyer, J. Patrick, *Lawmaking by the People: Referendums and Plebiscites in Canada*, Toronto, Butterworths, 1982.
Bradford, Neil, *Whither the Federal Urban Agenda? A New Deal in Transition*, Research Report F/65, Ottawa, Canadian Policy Research Networks, February 2007.

_____, *Creative Cities Structured Policy Dialogue Backgrounder*, Ottawa, Canadian Policy Research Networks, August 2004.

_____, *Why Cities Matter: Policy Research Perspective for Canada*, CPRN Discussion Paper F\23, Canadian Policy Research Networks, June 2002.

Broadbent, Alan, *Urban Nation: Why We Need To Give Power Back to the Cities To Make Canada Strong*, Toronto, Harper Collins, 2008.

_____, *The Place of Cities in Canada: Inside the Constitutional Box and Out*, Ottawa, Caledon Institute of Social Policy, June 2002.

Brooks, Stephen and Lydia Miljan, *Public Policy in Canada: An Introduction*, 4th Edition, Toronto, Oxford University Press, 2003.

Brunet-Jailly, Emmanuel and John Martin (eds.), *Local Governance in a Global World: Australia and Canada in Comparative Perspective,* Toronto, University of Toronto Press, 2010.

Bunting, Trudi, Pierre Filion and Ryan Walker (eds.), *Canadian Cities in Transition: New Directions in the 21st Century,* Toronto, Oxford University Press, 2010.

Bunting, Trudi and Pierre Filion (eds.), *Canadian Cities in Transition*, 2nd Edition, Toronto, Oxford University Press, 2000.

Burke, Mike, Colin Mooers, and John Shields, *Restructuring and Resistance: Canadian Public Policy in an Age of Global Capitalism*, Halifax, Fernwood Publishing, 2000.

Cameron, David M., "Provincial responsibilities for municipal government," *Canadian Public Administration*, Summer 1980.

Cameron, John R., *Provincial-Municipal Relations in the Maritime Provinces*, Fredericton, Maritime Union Study, 1970.

Canada West Foundation, *Urban Policy Priorities and Assessing Governments* (Loleen Berdahl), April 2007.

_____, *Apples or Oranges? Urban Size and the Municipal-Provincial Relationship* (Kari Roberts and Roger Gibbins), October 2005.

_____, *Rationale for Renewal* (Casey Vander Ploeg), September 2005.

_____, *Tightening Our Beltways: Urban Sprawl in Western Canada* (Liam Stone, with Roger Gibbins), October 2002.

_____, *Big City Revenues: A Canada-U.S. Comparison of Municipal Tax Tools and Revenue Levers* (Casey Vander Ploeg), September 2002.

_____, *Cities at the Crossroads: Addressing Intergovernmental Structures for Western Canada's Cities* (Denis Wong), August 2002.

_____, *Regional Approaches to Services in the West: Health, Social Services and Education* (Evan Jones and Susan McFarlane), February 2002.

_____, *Framing a Fiscal Fix-Up: Options for Strengthening the Finances of Western Canada's Big Cities* (Casey Vander Ploeg), January 2002.

_____, *Building Better Cities: Regional Cooperation in Western Canada* (Susan McFarlane), October 2001.

Canadian Centre for Policy Alternatives, *Value for Money? Cautionary Lessons About P3 from British Columbia*, June 2006.

_____, *Public-Private Partnerships, the True Cost of P3s*, Issue No. 2/P3s, April 2003.
Canadian Federation of Mayors and Municipalities, *Puppets on a Shoestring*, Ottawa, April 28, 1976.
Canadian Urban Institute, *Smart Growth in Canada*, Toronto, March 2001.
_____, *The Future of Greater Montreal: Lessons for the Greater Toronto Area?*, Conference Proceedings, Toronto, 1994.
_____, *Disentangling Local Government Responsibilities: International Comparisons*, Toronto, 1993.
Carrel, André, *Citizen's Hall*, Toronto, Between the Lines, 2001.
Caufield, Jon, *The Tiny Perfect Mayor*, Toronto, James Lorimer and Co., 1974.
Chenier, John, "The Evolving Role of the Federation of Canadian Municipalities," in *Canadian Public Administration,* Vol. 52, No. 3, Autumn 2009, pp. 395-416.
Chirah, Mohamed and Arthur Daniels (eds.), *New Public Management and Public Administration in Canada*, Toronto, Institute of Public Administration of Canada, 1997.
Clarke, Michael and John Stewart, *The Choices for Local Government*, Harlow, Longman, 1991.
Clarke, Terry Nichols and Michael Rempel (eds.), *Citizen Politics in Post Industrial Societies*, Boulder, Westview Press, 1997.
Clarkson, Stephen, *Uncle Sam and Us, Globalization, Neoconservatism, and the Canadian State*, Toronto, University of Toronto Press, 2002.
_____, *City Lib*, Toronto, Hakkert, 1972.
Clement, Wallace and Leah F. Vosko (eds.), *Changing Canada, Political Economy as Transformation*, Montreal and Kingston, McGill-Queen's University Press, 2003.
Cochrane, Allan, *Whatever Happened to Local Government?*, Buckingham, Open University Press, 1993.
Coleman, Stephen and Donald F. Norris, *A New Agenda for E-Democracy*, Oxford Internet Institute, Forum Discussion Paper No. 4, January 2005.
Colton, Timothy J., *Big Daddy*, Toronto, University of Toronto Press, 1980.
Conference Board of Canada, *Mission Possible: Successful Canadian Cities*, The Canadian Project Final Report, Vol. III, 2007.
_____, *Canada by Picasso: The Faces of Federalism*, Ottawa, 2006.
Courchene, Thomas J., *Global Futures for Canada's Global Cities*, IRPP Policy Matters, Vol. 8, No. 2, June 2007.
_____, *CitiStates and the State of Cities*, Montreal, Institute for Research on Public Policy, June 2005.
_____, *A State of Minds*, Montreal, Institute of Research on Public Policy, 2001.
_____, *Celebrating Flexibility: An Interpretive Essay on the Evolution of Canadian Federalism*, Montreal, C. D. Howe Institute, 1995.
Craig, Gerald M. (ed.), *Lord Durham's Report*, Toronto, McClelland & Stewart Limited, 1963.

Crawford, K. G., *Canadian Municipal Government*, Toronto, University of Toronto Press, 1954.
Cuff, George B., *Making a Difference: Cuff's Guide for Municipal Leaders*, Vols. 1 and 2, St. Thomas, Municipal World Inc., 2002 and 2007.
_____, David Siegel, and C. Richard Tindal, "Representation Riddle: Conflicting demands on the local councillor," *Municipal World*, December 2004.
Davis, Jonathan and David Imbroscio (eds.), *Theories of Urban Politics*, 2nd Edition, Los Angeles, Sage, 2009.
Davis, Mike, *City of Quartz: Excavating the Future of Los Angeles*, New York, Verso Publishing, 2006; New York, Vintage Books, 1990.
Dickerson, M. O., S. Drabek, and J. T. Woods (eds.), *Problems of Change in Urban Government*, Waterloo, Wilfrid Laurier University Press, 1980.
Dobuzinskis, Laurent, Michael Howlett, and David Laycock (eds.), *Policy Analysis in Canada, The State of the Art*, Toronto, University of Toronto Press, 2007.
Doucet, Clive, *Urban Meltdown, Cities, Climate Change and Politics as Usual*, Gabriola Island (B.C.), New Society Publishers, 2007.
Downey, T. J. and R. J. Williams, "Provincial agendas, local responses: the 'common sense' restructuring of Ontario's municipal governments," *Canadian Public Administration*, Summer 1998.
Dreier, Peter, John Mollenkopf, and Todd Swanstrom, *Place Matters: Metropolitics for the Twenty-First Century*, Lawrence, University Press of Kansas, 2001.
Dupre, J. Stefan, *Intergovernmental Finance in Ontario: A Provincial-Local Perspective*, Toronto, Queen's Printer, 1968.
d'Entremont, Harley and Patrick Robardet, "More Reform in New Brunswick: Rural Municipalities," *Canadian Public Administration*, Fall 1997.
External Advisory Committee on Cities and Communities, *From Restless Communities to Resilient Places: Building a Stronger Future for All Canadians*, Ottawa, 2006.
Fainstein, Susan and Scott Campbell (eds.), *Readings in Urban Theory*, Cambridge, Blackwell Publishers Inc., 1996.
Federation of Canadian Municipalities, *Building Prosperity From the Ground Up: Restoring Municipal Fiscal Balance*, June 2006.
_____, *Our Cities, Our Future*, Big City Mayors' Caucus, June 2006.
_____, *The Municipal Fiscal Imbalance By the Numbers*, 2006.
_____, *Quality of Life in Canadian Communities*, Theme Report #3, 2005.
_____, *Early Warning: Will Canadian Cities Compete?*, May 2001.
Feldman, Lionel D., "Tribunals, Politics and the Public Interest: The Edmonton Annexation Case – A Response," *Canadian Public Policy*, Spring 1982.
_____ (ed.), *Politics and Government of Urban Canada*, Toronto, Methuen, 1981.
_____ and Katherine Graham, *Bargaining for Cities*, Toronto, Butterworths, 1979.

Fernando, Shanti, *Ethics and Good Urban Governance in Toronto: The Tale of Two Love Affairs*, paper presented to the annual general meeting of the Canadian Political Science Association, Toronto, 2006.

Filion, Pierre, *The Urban Growth Centres Strategy in the Greater Golden Horseshoe*, Toronto, Neptis Foundation, May 2007.

Final Report of the Capital Region Review Panel, Manitoba, 1999.

Final Report, Prime Minister's Caucus Task Force on Urban Issues (Judy Sgro, Chair), *Canada's Urban Strategy: A Blueprint for Action*, November 2002.

Final Report, *Task Force on Municipal Regionalization*, St. John's, September 1997.

Florida, Richard, *The Great Reset: How New Ways of Working and Living Drive Post Crash Posterity*, New York, HarperCollins, 2010.

_____, *Whose Your City?*, Toronto, Random House, 2009.

_____, *The Flight of the Creative Class*, London, HarperCollins, 2005.

_____, *The Rise of the Creative Class*, New York, Basic Books, 2002.

_____, *The Economic Geography of Talent*, Pittsburgh, Carnegie Mellon University, 2001.

Foot, David K., with Daniel Stoffman, *Boom, Bust & Echo*, Toronto, Macfarlane Walter & Ross, 1996.

Fourot, Aude Claire, "Managing Religious Pluralism in Canadian Cities: Mosques in Montreal and Laval," in Tiziana Caponio and Maren Borkert (eds.), *The Local Dimension of Policy-Making,* Amsterdam, Amsterdam University Press, 2010, pp. 135-159.

Fowler, Edmund P., *Building Cities That Work*, Montreal and Kingston, McGill-Queen's University Press, 1992.

_____, and David Siegel, *Urban Policy Issues*, 2nd Edition, Toronto, Oxford University Press, 2002.

Fraser, Graham, *Fighting Back*, Toronto, Hakkert, 1972.

Frisken, Frances, The Public Metropolis: The Political Dimension of Urban Expansion in the Toronto Region, 1924-2003, Toronto, Canadian Scholars Press, 2007.

_____, (ed.), *The Changing Canadian Metropolis: A Public Policy Perspective*, 2 vol., Toronto, Canadian Urban Institute, 1994.

_____, *City Policy-Making in Theory and Practice: The Case of Toronto's Downtown Plan*, Local Government Case Study No. 3, London, University of Western Ontario, 1988.

Garcea, Joseph and Edward C. LeSage Jr. (eds.), *Municipal Reform in Canada*, Toronto, Oxford University Press, 2005.

Garreau, Joel, *Edge City: Life on the New Frontier,* New York, Doubleday, 1991.

Gaunthier, Pierre, Jochen Jaeger and Jason Prince, *Montreal at the Crossroads: Superhighways, The Turcot and the Environment*, Montreal, Black Rose Books, 2009.

Gertler, L. O. and R. W. Crowley, *Changing Canadian Cities: The Next 25 Years*, Toronto, McClelland & Stewart Limited, 1977.

Gertler, Meric S., "City-Regions in the Global Economy: Choices Facing Toronto," *Policy Options*, September 1996.
Ghitter, Geoff and Alan Smart, "Mad Cows, Regional Governance and Urban Sprawl: Path Dependence and Unintended Consequences in the Calgary Region," *Urban Affairs Review*, Vol. 44, No. 5, 2009, pp. 617-645.
Gilbert, Richard and Anthony Perl, *Transport Revolutions: Moving people and freight without oil*, Gabriola Island (B.C.), New Society Publishers, 2010.
Gillham, Oliver, *The Limitless City: A Primer on the Urban Sprawl Debate*, Washington, DC, Island Press, 2002.
Goetz, Edward G. and Susan E. Clarke (eds.), *The New Localism*, Newbury Park, Sage Publications, 1993.
Good, Kristin R., *Municipalities and Multiculturalism: The Politics of Immigration in Toronto and Vancouver,* Toronto, University of Toronto Press, 2009.
_____, *Urban Regime-Building as a Strategy of Intergovernmental Reform: The Case of Toronto's Role in Immigrant Settlement*, paper presented to the Canadian Political Science Association Annual Conference, Saskatoon, May 30-June 1, 2007.
_____, "Patterns of Politics in Canada's Immigrant-Receiving Cities and Suburbs," *Policy Studies*, Vol. 26, Nos. 3/4, 2005.
Gould, Ellen, *International Trade and Investment Agreements: A Primer for Local Governments*, Richmond, Union of British Columbia Municipalities, June 2001.
Grace, Joan and Bryon Sheldrick (eds.), *Canadian Politics, Democracy and Dissent*, Toronto, Pearson Education Canada Inc., 2006.
Graham, Katherine A., Susan D. Phillips, and Allan M. Maslove, *Urban Governance in Canada*, Toronto, Harcourt Brace & Company, 1998.
Graham, Katherine A. and Susan D. Phillips, *Citizen Engagement: Lessons in Participation from Local Government*, Toronto, Institute of Public Administration of Canada, 1998.
_____, "Who Does What in Ontario: The Process of Provincial-Municipal Disentanglement," *Canadian Public Administration*, Summer 1998.
_____, "Customer engagement: beyond the customer revolution," *Canadian Public Administration*, Summer 1997.
Granatstein, J. L., *Marlborough Marathon*, Toronto, Hakkert and James Lewis and Samuel, 1971.
Gutstein, Donald, *Vancouver Ltd.*, Toronto, James Lorimer and Co., 1975.
Gyford, John, *Local Politics in Britain*, London, Croom Helm Ltd., 1976.
_____, Steve Leach, and Chris Game, *The Changing Politics of Local Government*, London, Unwin Hyman, 1989.
Hackworth, Jason, *The Neoliberal City*, Ithaca, Cornell University Press, 2007.
Hambleton, Robin, Hank V. Savitch, and Murray Stewart (eds.), *Globalism and Local Democracy*, London, Palgrave Macmillan, 2002.
Hamel, Pierre J., *Public-Private Partnerships (P3s) and Municipalities: Beyond Principles, a Brief Overview of Practices*, Montreal, Urbanisation, Culture et Société, 2007.

Harcourt, Michael and Ken Cameron (with Sean Rossiter), *City Making in Paradise: Nine Decisions that Saved Vancouver,* Vancouver, Douglas and McIntyre, 2007.

Haus, Michael, Hubert Heinelt, and Murray Stewart (eds.), *Urban Governance and Democracy*, New York, Routledge, 2005.

Headrick, T. E., *The Town Clerk in English Local Government*, London, George Allen & Unwin, 1962.

Herland, Karen, *People, Potholes and City Politics*, Montreal, Black Rose Books, 1992.

Herrschel, Tassilo, *Urban Governance, the 'Virtual Region' and Policy Making: Moving Towards 'Integrated' City-Regionalism?*, paper presented at the Urban Affairs Association annual conference, Seattle, April 25-28, 2007.

_____ and Peter Newman, *Scale, 'Virtual Regions' and Structures in City Regional Government – a North American – and European Perspective*, paper prepared for the City Futures Conference, Chicago, 2004.

Higgins, Donald J. H., *Local and Urban Politics in Canada*, Toronto, Gage, 1986.

_____, *Urban Canada: Its Government and Politics*, Toronto, Macmillan, 1977.

Hill, Dilys, *Citizens and Cities*, Hemel Hempstead, Harvester Wheatsheaf, 1994.

Hiller, Harry (ed.), *Urban Canada,* 2nd Edition, Toronto, Oxford University Press, 2010.

Hobson, Paul A. R. and France St-Hilaire (eds.), *Urban Governance and Finance*, Montreal, Institute of Research on Public Policy, 1997.

Hodge, Gerald and David L. A. Gordon, *Planning Canadian Communities: An Introduction to the Principles, Practice and Participants*, 5th Edition, Toronto, Nelson, 2008.

_____ and Ira M. Robinson, *Planning Canadian Regions*, Vancouver, UBC Press, 2001.

_____ and Mohammed Qadeer, *Towns and Villages in Canada: The Importance of Being Unimportant*, Toronto, Butterworths, 1983.

Hollick, Thomas R. and David Siegel, *Evolution, Revolution, Amalgamation: Restructuring in Three Ontario Municipalities*, Local Government Case Studies No. 10, London, University of Western Ontario, 2001.

Institute on Governance, *Forum on Municipal Governance and Accountability: A Summary Report*, Ottawa, June 15, 2006.

Isin, Engin F. (ed.), *Democracy, Citizenship and the Global City*, London, Routledge, 2000.

_____, *Cities Without Citizens*, Montreal, Black Rose Books, 1992.

Jacobs, Jane, *Cities and the Wealth of Nations: Principles of Economic Life*, New York, Random House, 1984.

_____, *The Death and Life of Great American Cities*, New York, Random House, 1961.

Jones, George and John Stewart, *The Case for Local Government*, London, Allen & Unwin Inc., 1985.

Jones, Victor, "Beavers and Cats: Federal-Local Relations in the United States and Canada," in H. Peter Oberlander and Hilda Symonds (eds.), *Meech Lake from Centre to Periphery*," Vancouver, Centre for Human Settlements, University of British Columbia, 1986, pp. 88-115.

_____, *Metropolitan Government*, Chicago, University of Chicago, 1942.

Judge, David, Gerry Stoker, and Harold Wolman (eds.), *Theories of Urban Politics*, London, Sage Publications, 1995.

Kaplan, Harold, *Reform, Planning and City Politics: Montreal, Winnipeg, Toronto*, Toronto, University of Toronto Press, 1982.

_____, *Urban Political Systems: A Functional Analysis of Metro Toronto*, New York, Columbia University Press, 1967.

Keating, Michael, *Comparative Urban Politics*, Aldershot, Edward Elgar, 1991.

Kernaghan, Kenneth, Brian Marson, and Sandford Borins, *The New Public Organization*, Toronto, Institute of Public Administration of Canada, 2000.

_____ and John Langford, *The Responsible Public Servant*, Montreal, IRRP, 1990.

_____ and David Siegel, *Public Administration in Canada: A Text*, Toronto, Methuen, 1987.

King, Desmond and Jon Pierre (eds.), *Challenges to Local Government*, London, Sage Publications, 1990.

_____ and Gerry Stoker (eds.), *Rethinking Local Democracy*, Houndmills, Macmillan Press Ltd, 1996.

Kitchen, Harry, *A State of Disrepair: How to Fix the Financing of Municipal Infrastructure in Canada*, Toronto, C. D. Howe Institute, December 2006.

_____, *Financing City Services: A Prescription for the Future*, Atlantic Institute for Market Studies, September 2004.

_____, *Municipal Revenue and Expenditure Issues in Canada*, CanadianTax Paper No. 107, Toronto, Canadian Tax Foundation, 2002.

_____, *Municipal Finance in a New Fiscal Environment*, Commentary No. 147, C. D. Howe Institute, November 2000.

Klos, Nancy (ed.), *The State of Unicity – 25 Years Later*, Winnipeg, Institute of Urban Studies, 1998.

Kneebone, Ronald D., *Following the Money, Federal and Provincial Budget Balances with Canada's Major Cities*, Commentary No. 249, C. D. Howe Institute, June 2007.

Kushner, Joseph and David Siegel, "Why Do Municipal Electors Not Vote?" *Canadian Journal of Urban Research*, Vol. 15, No. 2, 2006, pp. 264-277.

_____, "Do Municipal Amalgamations Result in More Efficient Service Delivery?," *Municipal World*, January 2006.

_____, "Do municipal amalgamations reduce political representation and accessibility?," *Municipal World*, May 2004.

Kushner, Joseph, I. Masse, T. Peters, and L. Soroka, "The determinants of municipal expenditures in Ontario," *Canadian Tax Journal* (1996), Vol. 44, No. 2.

Laffin, Martin, and Ken Young, *Professionalism in Local Government*, Harlow, Longman, 1990.

Landon, Fred, *Western Ontario and the American Frontier*, Toronto, McClelland & Stewart Limited, 1967.
Lang, Vernon, *The Service State Emerges in Ontario*, Toronto, Ontario Economic Council, 1974.
Langford, John W. and Allan Tupper (eds.), *Corruption, Character and Conduct: Essays on Canadian Government Ethics*, Toronto, Oxford University Press, 1993.
Lazar, Harvey and Christian Leuprecht (eds.), *Spheres of Governance*, Montreal and Kingston, McGill-Queen's University Press, 2007.
Lennon, Richard and Christopher Leo, *Stopping the Sprawl: How Winnipeg Could Benefit From Metropolitan Growth Strategies for a Slow-Growth Region*, Canadian Centre for Policy Alternatives, January 2001.
Leo, Christopher, "Deep Federalism: Respecting Community Differences in National Policy," *Canadian Journal of Political Science*, September 2006.
_____, *The Politics of Urban Development: Canadian Urban Expressway Disputes*, Monographs on Canadian Urban Government, No. 3, Toronto, Institute of Public Administration, 1977.
_____ and Kathryn Anderson, "Being Realistic About Urban Growth," *Journal of Urban Affairs*, Vol. 28, No. 2, 2006.
_____ and Mark Piel, "Winnipeg UNICITY: Superannuated at 35," in Eran Razin and Patrick Smith (eds.), *Metropolitan Governing: Canadian Cases: Comparative Lessons*, Jerusalem, Hebrew University Magnes Press, 2006, pp. 121-146.
Levine, Allan (ed.), *Your Worship: The Lives of Eight of Canada's Most Unforgettable Mayors*, Toronto, James Lorimer, 1989.
Lidstone, Donald, "Recent British Columbia Legislation: The Community Charter," *UBC Law Review*, Vol. 40, No. 1, 2007.
_____, "Municipal Acts of the Provinces and Territories: A Report Card," Ottawa, Federation of Canadian Municipalities, Summer 2003.
Lightbody, James, "Defining a Canadian Approach to Municipal Consolidations," *Commonwealth Journal of Local Governance*, Vol. 3, May 2009, pp. 8-30.
_____, *City Politics, Canada*, Peterborough, Broadview Press, 2006.
_____, "Finding the Trolls under Your Bridge: The New Case for Overt Partisanship in Canadian City Politics," *Journal of Canadian Studies*, Vol. 39, Spring 1999, pp. 172-183.
_____, "Canada's Seraglio Cities: Political Barriers to Regional Governance," *Canadian Journal of Sociology*, July 1999, pp. 175-191.
_____, "Council Multiplicity and the Cost of Governance in Canadian Metropolitan Areas," *Canadian Journal of Urban Research*, June 1998, pp. 27-46.
_____, "A new perspective on clothing the emperor: Canadian metropolitan form, function and frontiers," in *Canadian Public Administration*, Fall 1997.
_____ (ed.), *Canadian Metropolitics: Governing Our Cities*, Toronto, Copp Clark Ltd., 1995.

Lindblom, Charles E., *The Policy Making Process*, Englewood Cliffs, Prentice-Hall Inc., 1980.
Lithwick, N. H., *Urban Canada: Problems and Prospects*, Ottawa, Central Mortgage and Housing Corporation, 1970.
Lorimer, James, *The Developers*, Toronto, James Lorimer, 1978.
_____, *A Citizen's Guide to City Politics*, Toronto, James Lewis and Samuel, 1972.
_____, *The Real World of City Politics*, Toronto, James Lewis and Samuel, 1970.
_____ and Carolyn MacGregor (eds.), *After the Developers*, Toronto, James Lorimer, 1981.
Lorinc, John, *The New City*, Toronto, Penguin Group, 2006.
Lowi, Theodore, *The End of Liberalism*, 2nd Edition, New York, W. W. Norton, 1979.
Lustiger-Thaler, Henri (ed.), *Political Arrangements: Power and the City*, Montreal, Black Rose Books, 1992.
MacDermid, Robert, *Campaign Finance and Campaign Success in Municipal Elections in the Toronto Region*, paper presented to the annual general meeting of the Canadian Political Science Association, Saskatoon, 2007.
_____, *Funding Municipal Elections in the Toronto Region*, paper presented to the annual general meeting of the Canadian Political Science Association, Toronto, 2006.
Mackenzie, Hugh, *The Art of the Impossible: Fiscal Federalism and Fiscal Balance in Canada*, Canadian Centre for Policy Alternatives, July 2006.
Magnusson, Warren, "Protecting the Right of Local Self Government," *Canadian Journal of Political Science,* Vol. 38, No. 4, 2005, pp. 897-922.
_____, "Urbanism, Cities and Local Self Government," *Canadian Public Administration,* Vol. 48, No. 1, 2005, pp. 95-123.
_____, *The Search for Political Space*, Toronto, University of Toronto Press, 1996.
_____, "The Local State in Canada: Theoretical Perspectives," *Canadian Public Administration*, Vol. 28, No. 4, Winter 1985, pp. 575-599.
_____ and Andrew Sancton (eds.), *City Politics in Canada*, Toronto, University of Toronto Press, 1983.
Mancuso, Maureen, Richard Price, and Ronald Wagenberg (eds.), *Leaders and Leadership in Canada*, Toronto, Oxford University Press, 1994.
Manitoba, Government of, *Proposals for Urban Reorganization in the Greater Winnipeg Area (White Paper)*, Winnipeg, Queen's Printer, 1970.
Marquand, David, *Decline of the Public: The Hollowing-out of Citzenship*, Cambridge, Polity Press, 2004.
Martin, Geoffrey R., "Municipal Reform in New Brunswick: Minor Tinkering in Light of Major Problems," *Journal of Canadian Studies*, Winter 2007.
Masson, Jack, with Edward C. Lesage Jr., *Alberta's Local Governments: Politics and Democracy*, Edmonton, University of Alberta Press, 1994.
_____ and James D. Anderson (eds.), *Emerging Party Politics in Urban Canada*, Toronto, McClelland & Stewart Limited, 1972.

McAllister, Mary Louise, *Governing Ourselves? The Politics of Canadian Communities*, Vancouver, UBC Press, 2004.

McBride, Stephen, *Paradigm Shift*, Halifax, Fernwood, 2005.

_____ and John Shields, *Dismantling a Nation: The Transition to Corporate Rule in Canada*, 2nd Edition, Halifax, Fernwood, 1997.

McDavid, James and Annette Mueller, "A Cross-Canada Analysis of the Efficiency of Residential Recycling Services," *Canadian Public Administration*, Vol. 51, No. 4, 2008, pp. 569-588.

McDavid, James, "The impacts of amalgamation on police services in the Halifax Regional Municipality," *Canadian Public Administration*, Winter 2002.

_____, "Solid Waste Contracting Out: Competition and Bidding Practices amongst Canadian Local Governments," *Canadian Public Administration*, Vol. 44, No. 1, 2001, pp. 1-25.

_____ and Brian Marson (eds.), *The Well-Performing Government Organization*, Toronto, Institute of Public Administration, 1991.

McDonald, Robert, *Making Vancouver: Class, Status and Social Boundaries*, Vancouver, UBC Press, 1996.

McEvoy, John M., *The Ontario Township*, University of Toronto, Political Studies, 1st Series No. 1, 1889.

McIver, J. M., "Survey of the City Manager Plan in Canada," *Canadian Public Administration*, Fall 1960.

Meligrana, John (ed.), *ReDrawing Local Government Boundaries*, Vancouver, UBC Press, 2004.

Mellon, Hugh, "Reforming the Electoral System of Metropolitan Toronto," *Canadian Public Administration*, Toronto, Spring 1993.

Milner, Henry, "The Montreal Citizens' Movement: Then and Now," Hanover, *Quebec Studies*, No. 6, 1988.

Minister of Urban Affairs, *Strengthening Local Government in Winnipeg: Proposals for Changes to the City of Winnipeg Act, Discussion Paper*, Winnipeg, February 27, 1987.

Ministry of Municipal Affairs (ON), *Study of Innovative Financing Approaches for Ontario Municipalities* (Price Waterhouse), March 31, 1993.

Mintz, Jack M. and Tom Roberts, *Running on Empty: A Proposal to Improve City Finances*, Toronto, C. D. Howe Institute, February 2006.

Mizra, Saeed, *Danger Ahead: The Coming Collapse of Canada's Municipal Infrastructure*, Ottawa, Federation of Canadian Municipalities, November 2007.

Mollenkopf, John H., *The Contested City*, Princeton, Princeton University Press, 1983.

Murray, Heather L., *Re-Thinking Intergovernmental Relations in Canada? An Analysis of City-Provincial Relations in Winnipeg and Vancouver*, paper presented to the Canadian Political Science Association Annual Conference, Toronto, June 1, 2006.

New Brunswick, Government of, *Local Government Review Panel, Miramichi City: Our Future – Strength Through Unicity,* and *Greater Moncton Urban Community: Strength Through Cooperation,* April 1994.

———, *The Commission on Land Use and the Rural Environment: Summary Report,* Fredericton, April 1993.

———, *Strengthening Municipal Government in New Brunswick's Urban Centres,* Ministry of Municipalities, Culture and Housing, December 1992.

Norris, Donald F., *Current Issues and Trends in E-Government Research,* Hershey, CyberTech Publishing, 2007.

Northwest Territories, Ministry of Municipal and Community Affairs, *The New Deal for NWT Community Governments,* Fall 2006.

Nova Scotia, Government of, *Interim Report of the Municipal Reform Commissioner, Cape Breton County,* Department of Municipal Affairs, July 1993.

———, *Task Force on Local Government,* April 1992.

Oberlander, H. Peter and Patrick J. Smith, "Governing Metropolitan Vancouver: Regional Intergovernmental Relations in British Columbia," in Donald N. Rothblatt and Andrew Sancton (eds.), *Metropolitan Governance: American/Canadian Intergovernmental Perspectives,* Berkeley, CA, Institute of Governmental Studies Press, University of California, 1993, pp. 329-373.

——— and Hilda Symonds (eds.), *Meech Lake from Centre to Periphery,* Vancouver, Centre for Human Settlements, University of British Columbia, 1986.

O'Brien, Allan, *Municipal Consolidation in Canada and Its Alternatives,* Toronto, ICURR Publications, May 1993.

———, "The Ministry of State for Urban Affairs: A Municipal Perspective," *Canadian Journal of Regional Science,* Halifax, Spring 1982.

———, "Local Government Priorities for the Eighties," *Canadian Public Administration,* Spring 1976.

Oheming, Frank and John Grant, "When Markets Fail To Deliver: An Examination of the Privatization and Deprivatization of Water and Wastewater Delivery in Hamilton, Canada," *Canadian Public Administration,* Vol. 51, No. 3, 2008, pp. 475-499.

Orfield, Myron, *Metropolitics: A Regional Agenda for Community and Stability,* Washington, DC, Brookings Institution Press, 1997.

Osborne, David and Ted Gaebler, *Reinventing Government,* New York, Penguin Books, 1993.

Ostrom, Vincent, Robert Bish, and Elinor Ostrom, *Local Government in the United States,* San Francisco, Institute for Contemporary Analysis, 1988.

Peirce, Neal R., *CitiStates: How Urban America Can Prosper in a Competitive World,* Washington, DC, Seven Locks Press, 1993.

Peters, Thomas J., *Thriving on Chaos,* New York, HarperCollins Publishers, 1988.

——— and Nancy Austin, *A Passion for Excellence,* New York, Random House, 1985.

——— and Robert H. Waterman Jr., *In Search of Excellence,* New York, Warner Books, 1982.

Phares, Don (ed.), *Governing Metropolitan Regions in the 21st Century*, Armonk, NY, M.E. Sharpe, 2009.
Peterson, Paul E., *City Limits*, Chicago, University of Chicago Press, 1981.
Phillips, E. Barbara and Richard T. LeGates (eds.), *City Lights: An Introduction to Urban Studies*, New York, Oxford University Press, 1981.
Plunkett, T. J., "A Nation of Cities Awaits Paul Martin's 'New Deal' – Federal Funds for 'Creatures of the Provinces'," *Policy Options*, February 2004.
_____, *City Management in Canada: The Role of the Chief Administrative Officer*, Toronto, Institute of Public Administration, 1992.
_____, *Urban Canada and Its Government*, Toronto, Macmillan, 1968.
_____ and Meyer Brownstone, *Metropolitan Winnipeg: Politics and Reform of Local Government*, Berkeley, CA, University of California Press, 1983.
_____ and Katherine Graham, "Whither Municipal Government," *Canadian Public Administration*, Winter 1982.
_____ and James Lightbody, "Tribunals, Politics and the Public Interest: The Edmonton Annexation Case," in *Canadian Public Policy*, Spring 1982.
_____ and G. M. Betts, *The Management of Canadian Urban Government*, Kingston, Queen's University, 1978.
Poel, Dale H., "Amalgamation Perspectives: Citizen Responses to Municipal Consolidation," *Canadian Journal of Regional Science*, Special Issue, Spring 2000.
Polese, Mario, *The Wealth and Poverty of Regions: Why Cities Matter,* Chicago, University of Chicago Press, 2009.
_____ and Richard Stren (eds.), *Social Sustainability of Cities: Diversity and the Management of Change*, Toronto, University of Toronto Press, 2000.
Prior, David, John Stewart, and Kieron Walsh, *Citizenship: Rights, Community & Participation*, London, Pitman Publishing, 1995.
Putnam, Robert, "E Pluribus Unum: Diversity and Community in the Twenty-first Century, The 2006 Johan Skytte Prize Lecture," *Scandinavian Political Studies* 30 (2), 2007.
_____, *Bowling Alone*, New York, Simon & Schuster, 2000.
Quesnel, Louise, with Éric Kerrouche, *Is Local Democracy Sacrificed to Metropolitan Governance? The Recent Québec Experience*, paper presented at Urban Affairs Association annual meeting, Montreal, May 2006.
_____, *Large Cities: An Opportunity for Innovation in Sublocal Entities?*, paper presented at the Urban Affairs Association annual meeting, Boston, 2002.
_____, *Public Consultations: A Tool for Democracy*, Toronto, ICURR Publications, August 2000.
_____, "Municipal Reorganization in Quebec," *Canadian Journal of Regional Science*, Special Issue, Spring 2000.
Razin, Eran and Patrick Smith (eds.), *Metropolitan Governing: Canadian Cases, Comparative Lessons*, Jerusalem, Hebrew University Magnes Press, 2006.

Reese, Laura A., "Recalibrating, Rescaling, Restructuring, Reinventing: Realistic Regoverning?," paper presented at the symposium on *A Global Look at Urban and Regional Governance*, Atlanta, January 2007.
_____ and Davia S. Cox, "Local culture and governmental change: The endurance of culture in the face of structural change, *Canadian Public Administration*, Summer 2007.
Regional District Survey Committee, *Summary Report of the Regional District Survey Committee*, Victoria, Queen's Printer, 1986.
Report and Recommendations, Committee of Review, City of Winnipeg Act, Winnipeg, Queen's Printer, October 1976.
Report of the Advisory Committee to the Minister of Municipal Affairs, on the Provincial-Municipal Relationship (Hopcroft Report) Toronto, January 1991.
Report of the GTA Task Force, *Greater Toronto* (Golden Report) Queen's Printer, January 1996.
Report of the Municipal Study Commission (Parizeau Report), Montreal, Union of Quebec Municipalities, December 1986.
Report of the Special Representative, *Constitutional Development in the Northwest Territories* (Drury Report), Ottawa, 1980.
Report of the Task Force on Nonincorporated Areas in New Brunswick, Fredericton, Queen's Printer, 1976.
Report to the Government of Nova Scotia, *Task Force on Local Government*, April 1992.
Richardson, Boyce, *The Future of Canadian Cities*, Toronto, New Press, 1972.
Richmond, Dale and David Siegel (eds.), *Agencies, Boards and Commissions in Canadian Local Government*, Toronto, Institute of Public Administration of Canada, 1994.
Rothblatt, Donald and Andrew Sancton (eds.), *Metropolitan Governance Revisited: American/Canadian Intergovernmental Perspectives*, Berkeley, CA, IGS Press, 1998.
_____ and Andrew Sancton (eds.), *Metropolitan Governance: American/ Canadian Intergovernmental Perspectives*, Berkeley, CA, Institute of Governmental Studies Press, 1993.
Roussopoulos, Dimitri (ed.), *The City and Radical Social Change*, Montreal, Black Rose Books Ltd., 1982.
Rowe, Mary, *Toronto: Considering Self-Government*, Owen Sound, The Ginger Press, Inc., 2000.
Roy, Jeffrey, *E-Government in Canada*, Ottawa, University of Ottawa Press, 2006.
Royal Commission on Education, Public Services, and Provincial-Municipal Relations in Nova Scotia. Report (John Graham, Commissioner), Halifax, Queen's Printer, 1974.
Royal Commission on Metropolitan Toronto, Report (H. Carl Goldenburg, Commissioner), Toronto, Queen's Printer, 1965.
Royal Commission on Metropolitan Toronto, Report (John Robarts, Commissioner), Toronto, Queen's Printer, June 1977.

Royal Commission on Municipal Government in Newfoundland and Labrador. Report (H. Whalen, Commissioner), St. John's, Queen's Printer, 1974.

Rusk, David, *Inside Game Outside Game*, Washington, DC, Brookings Institution Press, 1999.

_____, *Cities Without Suburbs*, Washington, DC, Woodrow Wilson Centre Press, 1993.

Rust-D'Eye, George, "P3 Deals: Dangers of Compromise of Interest," *Municipal World*, January 2004.

Rutherford, Paul (ed.), *Saving the Canadian City: The First Phase 1880-1920*, Toronto, University of Toronto Press, 1974.

Sancton, Andrew, *Canadian Local Government*, Don Mills, ON, Oxford University Press, 2011.

_____, "A Review of Canadian Metropolitan Regions: Governance and Government," in Don Phares (ed.), *Governing Metropolitan Regions in the 21st Century*, Armonk, NY, M. E. Sharpe, 2009, pp. 221-236.

_____, *The Limits of Boundaries: Why City Regions Cannot Become Self Governing,* Montreal and Kingston, McGill-Queen's University Press, 2008.

_____, *The Limits of Boundaries: Can City-Regions Be Self-Governing?*, paper presented to the Urban Affairs Association annual conference, Montreal, April 22, 2006.

_____, *Municipal Mergers and Demergers in Quebec and Ontario*, paper prepared for the Colloque sur les réalisations du gouvernement Charest, Université Laval, December 9-10, 2005.

_____, "The Governance of Metropolitan Areas in Canada," *Public Administration and Development* 25, 2005.

_____, "Canadian Cities and the New Regionalism," *Journal of Urban Affairs*, Vol. 23, No. 5, 2001.

_____, *Merger Mania*, Montreal and Kingston, McGill-Queen's University Press, 2000.

_____, "Globalization Does Not Require Amalgamation," *Policy Options*, November 1999.

_____, "Reducing costs by consolidating municipalities: New Brunswick, Nova Scotia and Ontario," *Canadian Public Administration*, Fall 1996.

_____, *Governing Canada's City Regions: Adapting Form to Function*, Montreal, Institute for Research on Public Policy, 1994.

_____, *Local Government Reorganization in Canada Since 1975*, Toronto, ICURR Press, April 1991.

_____, "Montreal's Metropolitan Government," Hanover, *Quebec Studies*, No. 6, 1988.

_____ and Robert Young (eds.), *Foundations of Governance: Municipal Governance In Canada's Provinces,* Toronto, University of Toronto Press, 2009.

_____, Rebecca James, and Rick Ramsay, *Amalgamation vs. Inter-Municipal Cooperation: Financing Local and Infrastructure Services*, Toronto, ICURR Press, July 2000.

_____ and Paul Woolner, "Full-time municipal councillors: a strategic challenge for Canadian urban government," *Canadian Public Administration*, Winter 1990.
Savara, James, "Dichotomy and Duality: Reconceptualizing the Relationship between Policy and Administration in Council-Manager Cities," *Public Administration Review* 45, 1985.
Savitch, H. V. and Paul Kantor, *Cities in the International Marketplace*, Princeton, Princeton University Press, 2002.
Savoie, Donald J., "What is wrong with the new public management?," *Canadian Public Administration*, Spring 1995.
Schneider, Mark, *The Competitive City*, Pittsburgh, University of Pittsburgh Press, 1989.
Scott, Allen J. (ed.), *Global City Regions, Trends, Theory, Policy*, Oxford, Oxford University Press, 2001.
Seidle, Leslie, *The Federal Role in Canada's Cities: Overview of Issues and Proposed Actions*, Ottawa, Canadian Policy Research Network Inc., December 2002.
_____ (ed.), *Rethinking the Delivery of Public Services to Citizens*, Montreal, Institute for Research on Public Policy, 1995.
_____, *Rethinking Government: Reform or Revolution?*, Montreal, Institute for Research on Public Policy, 1993.
Self, Peter, *Administrative Theories and Politics*, London, Allen & Unwin, 1977.
Sewell, John, *The Shape of the City*, Toronto, University of Toronto Press, 1993.
_____, *Up Against City Hall*, Toronto, James Lewis and Samuel, 1972.
Sharpe, L. J., *The Government of World Cities: The Future of the Metropolitan Model*, Chicester, John Wiley & Sons, 1995.
_____, "Failure of Local Government Modernization in Britain," *Canadian Public Administration*, Spring 1981.
_____ (ed.), *The Local Fiscal Crisis in Western Europe, Myths and Realities*, London, Sage Publications, 1981.
_____ and K. Newton, *Does Politics Matter?*, Oxford, Clarendon Press, 1984.
Shields, John and B. Mitchell Evans, *Shrinking the State: Globalization and Public Administration "Reform,"* Halifax, Fernwood Publishing, 1998.
Shortt, Adam, *Municipal Government in Ontario, An Historical Sketch*, Toronto, University of Toronto Studies, History and Economics, Vol. II, No. 2, undated.
_____ and Arthur G. Doughty (eds.), *Canada and Its Provinces: A History of the Canadian People and Their Institutions*, Toronto, Glasgow, Brook and Company, 1914, Vol. XVIII.
Siegel, David, "The Leadership Role of the Municipal Chief Administrative Officer," *Canadian Public Administration,* Vol. 53, No. 2, 2010.
_____, "Politics, politicians, and public servants in non-partisan local governments," *Canadian Public Administration*, Spring 1994.

_____, "City Hall Doesn't Need Parties," *Policy Options*, June 1987.

_____, "Provincial-Municipal Relations in Canada: An Overview," *Canadian Public Administration*, Summer 1980.

_____ and C. Richard Tindal, "Changing the Municipal Culture: From Comfortable Subordination to Assertive Maturity," *Municipal World*, March and April 2006.

Sills, Honourable Mr. Justice Ronald C., *RIM Park Financing Inquiry*, Final Report, City of Waterloo, October 2003.

Slack, Enid, *The Impact of Municipal Finance and Governance on Urban Sprawl*, paper presented to the International Symposium on Urban Impacts: Global Lessons for the Great Lakes Basin, Chicago, September 2006.

_____, *Intergovernmental Fiscal Relations and Canadian Municipalities: Current Situation and Prospects*, Report to the Federation of Canadian Municipalities, May 8, 2002.

_____, *Municipal Finance and the Pattern of Urban Growth*, Commentary No. 160, C. D. Howe Institute, February 2002.

_____ and Richard M. Bird, *Cities in Canadian Federalism*, ITP Paper 0603, University of Toronto, May 2006.

Smith, Patrick J., "British Columbia Needs a Municipal Registrar of Lobbyists," in *Influencing B.C.*, Vol. 1, No. 4, December 2011, pp. 2-6.

_____, "Even Greater Vancouver: Metropolitan Morphing in Canada's Third Largest City Region," in Don Phares (ed.), *Governing Metropolitan Regions in the 21st Century*, Armonk, NY, M. E. Sharpe, 2009, pp. 237-263.

_____, "Global City-Region Policy Options: The Case of Cascadia," in *Korean Local Government Review*, Vol. 7, No. 3, 2006, pp. 143-174.

_____, "Transborder Cascadia: Opportunities and Obstacles," *Journal of Borderland Studies*, Vol. 19, No. 1, Spring 2004, pp. 99-121.

_____, "Globalist vs. Globalized Cities: Redefining Urban Responses to Globalization," in T. H. Cohn, S. McBride and J. Wiseman (eds.), *Power in the Global Era: Globalization and Its Discontents*, London, Macmillan, 2000, pp. 141-154.

_____, "More than One Way Towards Economic Development: Public Participation and Policy Making in the Vancouver Region," in Katherine Graham and Susan Phillips (eds.), *Citizen Engagement: Lessons in Participation from Local Government*, Toronto, IPAC/ICURR, 1998, pp. 49-77.

_____, "Restructuring Metropolitan Governance: Vancouver and BC Reforms," *Policy Options*, September 1996.

_____, "British Columbia: Public Policy and Perceptions of Governance," in James P. Bickerton and Alain G. Gagnon (eds.), *Canadian Politics*, 2nd Edition, Peterborough, Broadview, 1994, Ch. 26, pp. 506-526.

_____, "Local Government" in Michael Howlett and David Laycock (eds.), *The Puzzles of Power: An Introduction to Political Science*, Toronto, Copp Clark Longman, 1994, Part 12, pp. 485-492.

_____, "The Making of a Global City: Fifty Years of Constituent Diplomacy – The Case of Vancouver," *Canadian Journal of Urban Research*, Vol. 1, No. 1, June 1992, pp. 90-112.

_____, "Local-Federal Government Relations: Canadian Perspectives, American Comparisons," in H. Peter Oberlander and Hilda Symonds (eds.), *Meech Lake: From Centre to Periphery*," Vancouver, Centre for Human Settlements, University of British Columbia, 1986, pp. 117-136.

_____, "Regional Governance in British Columbia," *Planning and Administration* 13, 1986.

_____ and T. H. Cohn, "Developing Global Cities in the Pacific Northwest: The Cases of Vancouver and Seattle," in Peter K. Kresl and Gary Gappert (eds.), *North American Cities and the Global Economy: Challenges and Opportunities*, Thousand Oaks, CA., Sage, 1995, in *Urban Affairs Annual Review*, No. 44, Ch. 11, pp. 251-285.

_____, Kevin Ginnell and Peter Oberlander, "Making Biggest Bigger: Port Metro Vancouver's 21st Century Re-Structuring – Global Meets Local," *Canadian Political Science Review*, Vol. 2, No. 4, December 2008, pp. 76-92.

_____ and Denisa Gavan Koop, "Gendering Local Governing: Canadian and Comparative Lessons – The Case of Metropolitan Vancouver," *Canadian Political Science Review*, Vol. 2, No. 3, Autumn 2008, pp. 152-171.

_____ and Kennedy Stewart, "British Columbia," in Andrew Sancton and Robert Young (eds.), *Foundations of Governance: Municipal Government in Canada's Provinces*, Toronto, University of Toronto Press, 2009, pp. 282-313.

_____ and Kennedy Stewart, *Global Calgary: A Globalist Strategy for the City of Calgary*, Ottawa, Canadian Policy Research Network, April 2006.

_____ and Kennedy Stewart, "Local Whole-of-Government Policymaking in Vancouver: Beavers, Cats and the Mushy Middle Thesis," in Robert Young and Christian Leuprecht (eds.), *Canada: The State of the Federation 2004: Municipal-Federal-Provincial Relations in Canada*, Montreal and Kingston, McGill-Queen's University Press, 2006.

_____ and Kennedy Stewart, *The "COPE Interlude:" The (Predictable) Rise & Fall of Vancouver's Radical Civic Left 2002-2005*, presentation to annual meeting, Canadian Political Science Association, Toronto, June 2006.

_____ and Kennedy Stewart, "Beavers and Cats Revisited:...Canadian-American Comparisons/ Vancouver and British Columbia Lessons," *Korean Local Government Review*, Vol. 6, No. 1, 2004, pp. 123-156.

_____ and Kennedy Stewart, *Making Accountability Work in British Columbia*, report for the Ministry of Municipal Affairs and Housing, June 1998.

Stein, David Lewis, *Toronto for Sale: The Destruction of a City*, Toronto, New Press, 1972.

Stelter, Gilbert A. and Alan F. Artibise (eds.), *Power and Place: Canadian Urban Development in the North American City*, Vancouver, University of British Columbia Press, 1986.

_____, *Shaping the Urban Landscape: Aspects of the Canadian City-Building Process*, Ottawa, Carleton University Press, 1982.

_____, *The Canadian City: Essays in Urban History*, Toronto, McClelland & Stewart Limited, 1977.

Stephens, G. Ross, and Nelson Wikstrom, *Metropolitan Government and Governance*, Oxford, Oxford University Press, 2000.

Stewart, John, *The Responsive Local Authority*, London, Charles Knight and Co. Ltd., 1974.

_____ and Gerry Stoker (eds.), *Local Government in the 1990s*, Houndmills, The Macmillan Press Ltd., 1995.

Stewart, Kennedy, "Inaction Costs: Understanding Metropolitan Governmental System Reform Dynamics in Toronto," *Canadian Political Science Review*, 2008, Vol. 2, No. 1, pp. 16-34.

_____, "Write the Rules and Win: Understanding Citizen Participation Game Dynamics," *Public Administration Review* 67, 2007, pp. 1067-1076.

_____, "Why Insulate New Institutions: Evaluating Pre and Post-Change Support for Metropolitan Reform in Greater London and Toronto," in Eran Razin and Patrick Smith (eds.), *Metropolitan Governing: Canadian Cases: Comparative Lessons*, Jerusalem, Hebrew University Magnes Press, 2006.

_____, *Think Democracy: Options for Local Democratic Reform in Vancouver*, Vancouver, Institute of Governance Studies, Simon Fraser University, 2003.

_____ and Patrick Smith, "Immature Policy Analysis: Building Capacity in Eight Major Canadian Cities," in Laurent Dobuzinskis, Michael Howlett and David Laycock (eds.), *Policy Analysis in Canada: The State of the Art*, Toronto, University of Toronto Press, 2007, pp. 265-287.

Stoker, Gerry, *The Politics of Local Government*, London, Macmillan Education Ltd., 1988.

_____ and Stephen Young, *Cities in the 1990s*, Harlow, Longman, 1993.

Stone, Clarence N. and Heywood T. Sanders (eds.), *The Politics of Urban Development*, Lawrence, University Press of Kansas, 1987.

Stoney, Christopher and Katherine Graham, "Federal-Municipal Relations in Canada: The Changing Organizational Landscape," *Canadian Public Administration*, Vol. 52, No. 3, 2009, pp. 371-394.

Strom, Elizabeth A. and John Mollenkopf (eds.), *The Urban Political Reader*, New York, Routledge, 2007.

Sutcliffe, John, *Municipal Influences in a Multi-national Setting? The Windsor-Detroit Border Crossing*, paper presented to the Canadian Political Science Association annual conference, Toronto, June 2006.

Swenarchuk, Michelle, *From Global to Local: GATS Impacts on Canadian Municipalities*, Ottawa, Canadian Centre for Policy Alternatives, May 2002.

Task Force on Housing and Urban Development. Report, Ottawa, Queen's Printer, 1969.

Task Force on Municipal Legislative Renewal, *Municipal Governance for Saskatchewan in the 21st Century, Options 2000: A Framework for Municipal Renewal – Summary of Final Report*, August 2000.

Task Force on Nonincorporated Areas in New Brunswick. Report, Fredericton, Queen's Printer, 1976.

Tennant, Paul and David Zirnhelt, "Metropolitan Government in Vancouver: the strategy of gentle imposition," *Canadian Public Administration*, Spring 1973.

Thomas, Timothy L. (ed.), *The Politics of the City*, Toronto, ITP Nelson, 1997.

_____, *A City With a Difference*, Montreal, Véhicule Press, 1997.

Tiebout, Charles, "A Pure Theory of Local Expenditures," *Journal of Political Economy*, Vol. 64, No. 5, October 1956.

Tindal, C. Richard, *A Citizen's Guide to Government*, 3rd Edition, Whitby, McGraw-Hill Ryerson Limited, 2005.

_____, *Structural Changes in Local Government: Government for Urban Regions*, Monographs on Canadian Urban Government, No. 2, Toronto, Institute of Public Administration of Canada, 1977.

_____ and David Siegel, "Municipal Time Bombs Need a Municipal Bomb Squad," *Municipal World*, October 2011, pp. 23-25.

_____ and Susan Nobes Tindal, *Guide to Good Municipal Governance*, St. Thomas, Municipal World Inc., 2007.

_____, "Keys To Good Governance IV: What Would Your Mother Think? Ethical Behaviour in Municipal Government," *Municipal World*, July 2007.

_____, "Meeting Expectations," *Municipal World*, December 2005.

Tomalty, Ray, *The Compact Metropolis: Growth Management and Intensification in Vancouver, Toronto and Montreal*, Toronto, ICURR Press, 1997.

_____ and Andrejs Skaburskis, "Development Charges and City Planning Objectives: The Ontario Disconnect," *Canadian Journal of Urban Research*, Vol. 12, Issue 1, Summer 2003.

Toronto Dominion Bank, *An Update to TD Economics' 2002 Report on the Greater Toronto Area (GTA) Economy*, July 2007.

_____, *The Greater Toronto Area (GTA): Canada's Primary Economic Locomotive In Need of Repairs*, May 2002.

_____, *A Choice Between Investing in Canada's Cities or Disinvesting in Canada's Future*, April 2002.

Treff, Karin and Deborah Ort, *Finances of the Nation 2010*, Toronto, Canadian Tax Foundation, 2011.

Urbaniak, Tom, *Her Worship: Hazel McCallion and the Development of Mississauga*, Toronto, University of Toronto Press, 2009.

Vaillancourt, F., "Financing Local Governments in Quebec: New Arrangements for the 1990s," *Canadian Tax Journal*, Vol. 40, No. 5, 1992.

Vojnovic, Igor, "Municipal Consolidation, Regional Planning and Fiscal Accountability: The Recent Experiences in Two Maritime Provinces," *Canadian Journal of Regional Science*, Special Edition, Spring 2000.

_____, "The fiscal distribution of the provincial-municipal service exchange in Nova Scotia," *Canadian Public Administration*, Winter 1999.

_____, *Municipal Consolidation in the 1990s: An Analysis of Five Canadian Municipalities*, Toronto, ICURR Press, 1997.

Weaver, John C., *Shaping the Canadian City: Essays on Urban Politics and Policy, 1890-1920*, Monographs on Canadian Urban Government, No. 1, Toronto, Institute of Public Administration of Canada, 1977.

Whalen, H. J., *The Development of Local Government in New Brunswick*, Fredericton, 1963.

Wichern, Phil H., Jr., *Evaluating Winnipeg's Unicity: The City of Winnipeg Act Review Committee, 1984-1986*, Research and Working Paper No. 26, Winnipeg, Institute of Urban Studies, University of Winnipeg, 1986.

_____, "Evaluating Winnipeg's Unicity: Citizen Participation and Resident Advisory Groups, 1971-1984," Winnipeg, Institute of Urban Studies Report, 1984.

Winfield, Mark S., *Analysis of the Government of Ontario's Greater Golden Horseshoe Growth Plan*, Pembina Institute, July 2006.

Wolfe, Jeanne M., "A National Urban Policy for Canada? Prospects and Challenges," *Canadian Journal of Urban Research*, Vol. 12, Issue 1, Summer 2003.

Wolman, Harold and Michael Goldsmith, *Urban Politics and Policy: A Comparative Approach*, Cambridge, Mass, Blackwell Publishers, 1992.

Woodbridge, Roy, "Provisioning Cities – A New Urban Agenda," *Policy Options*, July-August 2005.

Wynn, Graeme and Tim Oke (eds.), *Vancouver and Its Region*, Vancouver, UBC Press, 1992.

Yates, Douglas, *The Ungovernable City*, Cambridge, M.I.T. Press, 1977.

Young, Robert and Christian Leuprecht (eds.), *Canada: The State of the Federation 2004: Municipal-Federal-Provincial Relations in Canada*, Montreal and Kingston, McGill-Queen's University Press, 2006.

Zimmerman, J. F., *State-Local Relations: A Partnership Approach*, Westport, CT, Praeger, 1995.

Using the Internet

Listing all of the websites pertinent to local government would require as many entries as the preceding "hard copy" items. The brief annotated list that follows brings together, for convenient reference, the main web addresses cited in footnotes in this book. It also contains information on a few general sites that deal with broad categories or contain numerous links to other sites. The main municipal associations are listed separately below. All of these sites were active at the time this book was written.

www.canada.gc.ca	Website for government of Canada with links to provincial and territorial governments. Using this site, you can access any provincial department of municipal affairs, or comparable organization.
www.statcan.gc.ca	Statistics Canada, the source of population figures and several reports cited in this text.
www.canlii.org.	Canadian Legal Information Institute site, containing statutes from all 10 provinces and the 3 territories as well as from the federal government.
www.acjnet.org	Access to Justice Network also contains federal and provincial statutes, and case law as well.
www.municipalworld.com	*Municipal World* magazine. This site also has extensive links to other local government websites.
www.fcm.ca	Federation of Canadian Municipalities, source of extensive material and several reports cited in this text.
www.cwf.ca	Canada West Foundation, which publishes reports on a variety of local government topics, some cited herein.
www.cpsa-ascp.ca	Canadian Political Science Association. Website contains papers from annual conferences, several cited herein.
www.cprn.org	Canadian Policy Research Networks, another source of reports on various topics, including local government. This organization is no longer operating, but the web site and its many publications are still available at this site.
www.policyalternatives.ca	Canadian Centre for Policy Alternatives. As the name implies, this organization often questions the conventional view on issues.
www.cdhowe.org	C. D. Howe Institute, which publishes on a wide variety of topics, including a local government series.
www.civicnet.bc.ca	British Columbia local government information

Municipal Associations in Canada

Most of the municipal associations in the various provinces have their own websites. These are usually cited in the links in the entries noted above, but are also listed in the table that follows.

Association	Web Address
Alberta Association of Municipal Districts & Counties (AAMD & C)	www.aamdc.com
Alberta Urban Municipalities Association (AUMA)	www.auma.ca
Association of Manitoba Municipalities	www.amm.mb.ca
Association of Municipal Administrators of New Brunswick AMANB/ AAMNB	www.amanb-aamnb.ca
Association of Municipal Administrators, Nova Scotia (AMANS)	www.amans.ca
Association of Municipal Managers, Clerks and Treasurers of Ontario (AMCTO)	www.acmto.com
Association of Municipalities of Ontario	www.amo.on.ca
Association of Yukon Communities (AYC)	www.ayc.yk.ca
Canadian Association of Municipal Administrators	www.camacam.ca
Federation of Canadian Municipalities	www.fcm.ca
Federation of Prince Edward Island Municipalities	www.fpeim.ca
Local Government Administration Association of Alberta (LGAA)	www.lgaa.ab.ca
Local Government Management Association of British Columbia	www.lgma.ca
Manitoba Municipal Administrators Association (MMAA)	www.mmaa.mb.ca
Municipal Finance Officers Association of Ontario	www.mfoa.on.ca
Newfoundland and Labrador Federation of Municipalities (NLFM)	www.municipalitiesnl.com
North West Territories Association of Municipalities	www.nwtac.com
Nunavut Association of Municipalities	www.nmto.ca
Ontario Municipal Administrators' Association	www.omaa.on.ca
Ontario Municipal Management Institute	www.ommi.on.ca
Rural Municipal Administrators' Association of Saskatchewan	www.rmaa.ca
Rural Ontario Municipal Association	www.roma.on.ca
Saskatchewan Association of Rural Municipalities	www.sarm.ca
Society of Local Government Managers of Alberta	www.clgm.net
Union des municipalités du Québec	www.umq.qc.ca
Union of British Columbia Municipalities	www.ubcm.ca
Urban Municipalities Administrators Association of Saskatchewan (UMAAS)	www.umaas.ca

Index

A
Abbotsford, BC, 92, 419
Aboriginals. *See* Native Canadians
Acadia, 37
Accountability, 361–362
Accounting Standards Oversight Board (ASOB), 282n
Act Respecting Rural Communities (NB, 2005), 127
Adams, Thomas, 54, 55
Administration (staff), 295–297
Agencies, boards, and commissions (ABCs), 7, 58, 60, 100, 101, 128, 182, 187, 263, 299, 334, 415, 431
Agglomeration council (Montreal), 121, 122, 272
Alberta
    grants, 249–250
    historical overview, 43
    intermunicipal agencies/agreements, 94–97
    provincial-local relations, 207
    restructuring, 93–97
    revenue sharing, 253, 254
Alberta Capital Region Forum, 96, 142
Alberta Capital Regional Alliance (ACRA), 96
Alberta Capital Regional Governance Review, 96
Aldermen, 36, 39, 50, 53, 55, 56, 57
Allegheny Conference on Community Development, 176
Alternative service delivery (ASD), 334, 453–454
Alward, David, 128, 193
Amalgamated single tier municipalities, 143, 149–150
Amalgamations (and annexations). 92, 93-94, 98, 100, 112, 115-116, 117, 119-120,121, 129, 130, 132, 133-134, 135, 154, 157, 169, 180
Anti-sprawl movements, 80–81
Assessment. *See* Property tax
Association of Municipalities of Ontario (AMO), 197, 198, 205, 212
Atchison, Don, 294–295
Auditor general, 356
Axworthy, Lloyd, 220

B
Baby boomers, 17
Baldwin, Robert, 34

Baldwin Act, 35, 59. *See also* Municipal Act (ON)
B.C. Housing, 164
"Beavers" *vs.* "cats," 201–202, 232–235, 437, 441
Bellamy Report. *See* Toronto Computer Leasing Inquiry
Benchmarking, 337. *See also* Performance measurement
Bergeron, Richard, 376
Berra, Yogi, 330
Best practices, 337. *See also* Performance measurement
Big City Mayors Caucus, 215
Board of control, 56-57, 60, 307, 308, 310, 321
Boards and commissions. *See* agencies, boards, and commissions
Boosterism, 51
Border crossing (Detroit-Windsor), 227–228. *See also* Multilevel relations
Bourque, Pierre, 171, 375
Brampton, 372, 417
British Columbia
    historical overview, 43–44
    provincial-local relations, 210–212
    regional districts, 89–92
    restructuring, 88–92
    revenue sharing, 253
British North America (BNA) Act, 4, 33, 201, 243, 413
Bruntland Commission, 81–82
Building Canada Fund, 251
Building Manitoba Fund, 253
Burke, Edmund, 291
Burnaby Citizens Association, 385
Business model of government, 318–320
Byrne Commission, 122, 190, 192

C

C5 (Five Cities), 221, 235
Calgary, 43, 46, 49, 56, 64, 93, 94, 97, 154, 216-217, 253, 347, 355, 372
Calgary Metropolitan Plan, 97
Calgary Regional Partnership (CRP), 97
Campaign financing. *See* election financing
Campbell, Gordon, 210, 384, 385
Campbell, Larry, 233, 384
Canada Assistance Plan, 244
Canada Health and Social Transfer (CHST), 244
Canada Infrastructure Works program, 220, 251

Index   489

Canada Mortgage and Housing Corporation (CMHC), 68
Canadian Federation of Mayors and Municipalities (CFMM), 219
Canadian Home Builders Association, 422
CAO. *See* Chief Administrative Officer
Cape Breton, 143
Cape Breton Regional Municipality, 130
Capital Region Committee, 105
Carrel, André, 296, 396, 397
"Cats." *See* "Beavers" *vs.* "cats"
Census metropolitan areas (CMAs), 64, 98, 119
Charest, Jean, 121
Charlottetown (PE), 38, 133-134
Charter cities, 215-216
Charter communities, 45
Chatham-Kent (ON), 143, 319
Chiarelli, Bob, 294, 447
Chief administrative officer (CAO), 311, 316–318, 324
Cities Act (SK, 2002), 99, 209
Cities, Towns and Villages Act (NT), 138
Citizen participation. *See* Public participation
Citizens for Local Democracy (C4LD), 234
City beautiful movement, 51
City charter. *See* Charter cities
City efficient movement, 53–54
City healthy movement, 52–53
City manager. *See* council manager
City of Toronto Act (2006), 206, 213, 272, 293, 356, 440
City of Winnipeg Act (1998), 292
City of Winnipeg Charter Act (2002), 208
Civic Action League (Montreal), 374
Civic Election Committee (Winnipeg), 380
Clark, Christy, 261
Cold Lake (AB), 94
Commission for the Conservation of Natural Resources (CCNR), 54
Commission of the Three Communities (NB), 126, 142
Commission on the Future of Local Governance (NB, 2008), 193
Commissioner system, 314–315
Committee of Progressive Electors (COPE), 383
Community Charter (BC, 2003), 92, 210, 211
Community councils, 399–400
Community policing, 451
Community power studies, 421–424

Community values, 328–331. *See also* Values
Comox Valley Regional District (BC), 92
Competition, in municipal government. *See also* Performance measurement
Conditional grants, 246, 247. *See also* Transfer payments
Conflict of interest legislation, 355
Conseils d'arrondisement, 120, 399
Consolidated Municipal Act (BC, 1871), 43
Constitution Act (1982). *See also* British North America Act
Constitutional Act, 1791, 31
Consulting the public, 391–393
Continuing Protection of Property Taxpayers Act (ON, 2000), 260
Coordinating officer, 310–318
Corruption, municipal, 49–50, 60-61, 298, 324, 346-353, 360
Council. *See* Municipal council
Council manager system, 311–314, 318
Council-staff relations, 297–305
Counties Act (NB, 1877), 39
County Incorporation Act (NS, 1879), 37, 38
County Restructuring Program (ON), 112. *See also* Regional governments
Courts, role in interpreting municipal powers, 201-204, 216-217
Courts of Quarter Sessions, 29, 30, 37, 39
Creative class, 73-74, 269
Crombie, David, 109, 197, 377

D

Dawson City (NT), 3, 45, 296
Dartmouth (NS), 129, 131
Deep federalism, 230, 231, 429. *See also* Multilevel relations
Delegating to the public, 393–400
Demergers (QC), 121, 399
Demographics, 16-18, 416–417
Dennison, William, 376
Depression of 1930s, impact of, 71, 75, 186, 188
Denver Regional Council of Governments (DRCOG), 176–177
Design for Development, 111n, 114
Development charges, 265–266, 279
Dexter, Darrell, 133, 196
Dieppe (NB), 126
Dillon's Rule, 203, 204
Direct democracy. *See* Referendum

Direct and indirect election, 91, 107, 111, 150
Disentanglement, 189–201
District advisory committee (QC), 398–399
District Councils Act (ON, 1841), 34
Dominion Housing Act (1935), 68
Doré, Jean, 374, 375
Downloading, 155, 189, 199-200, 441
Drapeau, Jean, 117, 294, 309, 349–350, 374
Drumheller (AB), 94
Dunderdale, Kathy, 137
Durham Lord, 12, 33

E
Eager beavers, 437, 441. *See also* "Beavers" *vs.* "cats"
Economic forces affecting municipal government, 18-22, 70-71, 378, 404, 417-418, 424-426, 436
Economies of scale, 70, 151
Edmonton, 43, 46, 49, 57, 64, 72, 93-94, 95, 96, 97, 154, 253, 254, 277, 288, 315, 350, 351, 432
Edmonton Commitment, 252
Edmunston (NB), 143
Education financing, 259, 260, 268, 276
Efficiency-accountability dilemma, 285, 341, 457
Efficiency *vs.* effectiveness, 312, 337, 340
Eggleton, Arthur, 378
Election by general vote, 289, 290
Election financing, 347-349, 354-355
Elections, municipal. *See* Municipal franchise
Enabling authority (municipality), 450
Environmental issues, 61, 74, 76, 77, 79, 82, 158, 248, 389, 423
Equal Opportunity Program, 125–126, 166
Equity issues, 161–169
Established Program Financing (EPF), 244
Estevan (SK), 315
Ethics, 346–360. *See also* Corruption, municipal and Values
Ethnic enclaves, 76–77
European Union (EU), 232, 450
Evergreen Line, 166
Executive committee, 57, 307–310. *See also* Board of Control
Executive Policy Committee (Winnipeg), 292
External Advisory Committee on Cities and Communities, 222, 229
Extra-electoral participation mechanisms, 385-386

F

Farnworth, Mike, 210
Federal grants. *See* Transfer payments
Federal-local relations, 185, 217–223, 228, 230, 231, 236
Federation of Canadian Municipalities (FCM), 76, 205, 221, 241, 371
Fewer Politicians Act (ON, 1996), 114
Finances. *See* Local government finances
First Nations governments, 9, 27-28, 45, 99
Fiscal neutrality, 197, 198, 199
Ford, Rob, 110, 274, 283, 310, 318, 380, 427, 449
Fredericton (NB), 39, 56
Free trade. *See* Globalization
Freedom of information legislation, 355
Frustration thesis, 188

G

Gardiner, Fred, 101, 107
Gas tax sharing, 251, 271, 272
Gatineau-Hull (QC), 143
General Agreement on Trade in Services (GATS), 225
Ghermezian, Ralph, 351
Giles Report (QC, 1990), 118
Globalization, 24, 174–177, 223–227, 418
GO Transit (ON), 165
Godfrey, John, 221, 222
Golden Report (Report of the GTA Task Force, 1996), 109
Governance, 8, 175, 232, 236, 286, 327
Governing structures. *See* Municipal governing structures
Graham, Shawn, 128, 193
Graham Commission (Royal Commission on Education, Public Services, and Provincial-Municipal Relations in Nova Scotia), 129, 190
Grants. *See* Transfer payments
Grants in Lieu of Taxes Act, 251
Greater Golden Horseshoe (GGH), 65. 83, 110, 115, 160, 165, 412
Greater Toronto Services Board (GTSB), 110, 142, 412
Greater Toronto Transportation Authority, 110. *See also* Metrolinx
Greater Vancouver Regional District (GVRD), 91, 225
Greater Winnipeg Election Committee, 380
Greater Winnipeg Investigating Commission (1959), 101
Green Energy Act (ON, 2009), 160
Greenbelt Act (ON, 2004), 160
Growing pains, 46–50

Growth Strategies Act (BC, 1995), 90, 158
Guelph (ON), 57

H
Haldimand-Norfolk, 143
Halifax and Halifax Regional Municipality (NS), 6, 131, 169, 174, 399
Hall, Barbara, 378, 426
Hamilton and Hamilton-Wentworth (ON), 53, 113, 147, 153, 170, 311, 335
Hamm, John, 196
Harcourt, Mike, 383, 384
Harel, Louise, 376
Harper, Stephen, 222, 223, 236, 249, 276, 428
Harris, Mike, 112, 139, 197, 246, 276, 289, 427
Hawrelak, William, 350
Head of council, 292–295, 317-318
Healthy cities and communities, 412-415, 451
Highway Improvement Act (ON, 1901), 249
Home rule, 182, 202-203, 204, 232
Hopcroft Report (ON, 1991), 197
Houde, Camillien, 349
Housing, 17, 47, 51, 52, 54, 61, 68, 69-70, 75, 80, 82, 107, 164, 167, 199-200, 231, 278, 283, 390, 408, 411, 415
Hudson's Bay Company, 41, 42, 44
Hull-Gatineau (QC), 120

I
Immigration, 17-18, 32, 37, 48, 67, 83-84, 234-235, 248, 276, 417. *See also* United Empire Loyalists
Independent Citizen Election Committee (ICEC), 380, 381
Indianapolis, 339
Informative participation mechanisms, 386–391
Infrastructure, 241, 242, 275, 282, 428
Initiative, 394, 397–398. *See also* Referendum
Integrity commissioner, 214, 356
Intergovernmental relations. *See* Federal-local relations and Provincial-local relations
Intermunicipal boards, 142, 145–146
Intermunicipal clashes/turf wars, 169–171
International relations, 223–227
Investigative and oversight agencies, 356, 359

J

Jackson, Lois, 181
Jacobs, Jane, 81
Joined up governance. *See* Multilevel relations
Joint boards. *See* Intermunicipal boards and Agencies, boards, and commissions
Juba, Stephen, 294
Justices of the peace. See Courts of Quarter Sessions
Justifications for Municipal Government, 9-16

K

Katz, Sam, 382
Kawartha Lakes (ON), 143
Keynes, John Maynard (and Keynesian economics), 19, 69
Kingston (ON), 30, 154
Kyoto accord (and Kyoto protocol), 248, 461

L

Labonté, Benoit, 376
Ladner, Peter, 385
Land Use Planning and Development Act (QC, 1979), 116
Lastman, Mel, 378–379, 426
Layton, Jack, 351, 378
Lesage, Jean, 115
Lethbridge (AB), 43
Lévis (QC), 143
Livable Region Strategic Plan (Greater Vancouver Regional District), 158
Lobbying, municipal, 260, 346, 350-351, 352, 357, 433, 435
Local council. *See* Municipal council
Local governance. *See* Governance
Local Government Act (BC), 210
Local government elections. *See* Municipal franchise
Local government finances. *See* Municipal revenues
Local groups, 8, 389-391, 422-423, 435
Local political culture, 328, 329
Local political parties. *See* Political parties
Local services districts (NB), 127
Local services realignment (LSR), 167, 197
Local state. *See* Civil society
Localized government, 395, 398–400
London (UK), 427

Longueuil (QC), 143
Lord, Bernard, 126, 128, 193
Lower Canada Municipal and Road Act (QC, 1855), 36
Loyalists. *See* United Empire Loyalists
Lyons, Jeff, 351, 357

M
Macdonald, John A., 67
Managed competition, 339
Manitoba
    historical overview, 41–42
    provincial-local relations, 207–208
    restructuring, 99–105
    revenue sharing, 253
    Winnipeg. *See* Winnipeg
Manitoba Capital Region Committee, 142
Market forces (and market model), 82, 208, 214, 341-342, 420-421, 453.
    See also economic factors affecting municipal government
Markham (ON), 277, 348, 417
Martin, Paul, 20, 222, 249, 276, 428
Mayor. *See* Head of Council
Mayoralty elections
    Montreal, 373–376
    Ottawa, 447
    Toronto, 376–380, 426, 427
    Vancouver, 382–385
    Winnipeg, 380–382
Mayor's Task Force on Homelessness (Toronto), 415
McCallion, Hazel, 274, 295, 414
McGuinty, Dalton, 114
McKenna, Frank, 193
Merger. *See* Annexations and amalgamations
Metrolinx, 110, 165
Metropolitan Authority of Halifax, 142
Metropolitan communities (QC), 119, 123
Metropolitan Toronto. *See* Toronto
Metropolitan Transportation Agency (Montreal), 168
MFP Financial Services, 344–346, 351
Miller, David, 273, 310, 348, 379–380, 427
Milton (ON), 65
Ministry of State for Urban Affairs (MSUA), 218–220, 249
Minneapolis-St. Paul, 163

Minority representation on council, 371–372, 400–401
Miramichi (NB), 143
Mission, BC, 419
Mississauga, 236, 273–274, 288–289, 372, 414, 417
Mitchener Commission (MB), 190
Montreal
    amalgamation, 143
    mayoralty elections, 373–376
    minority representation on council, 371–372
    political parties, 322, 373–376
    taxing powers, 272–273
Montreal agglomeration council, 122
Montreal Citizen's Movement (MCM), 374, 398
Montreal Metropolitan Community (MMC), 119, 142, 181
Montreal Metropolitan Corporation, 117
Montreal Urban Community (MUC), 117–118
Multilevel relations, 8, 228–232, 236
Municipal Act (ON, 2001), 206, 212, 213, 292, 296
Municipal auditor general (BC), 261, 360
Municipal Clauses Act (BC, 1892), 44
Municipal corruption. *See* Corruption, municipal
Municipal council, 287–305
    composition, 287, 369–373
    female representation, 369–371, 400–401
    method of election, 289–291
    minority representation, 371–372, 400–401
    roles of council members, 287, 288-289
    staff, relations with, 297–305
Municipal expenditures and revenues, 240–243
Municipal Finance Authority (BC), 89
Municipal franchise, 366-385
Municipal governing structures, 285–325
    board of control, 308
    business model of government, 318–320
    chief administrative officer (CAO), 311, 316–318, 324
    commissioner system, 314–315
    coordinating officer, 310–318
    council manager system, 311–314
    executive committee, 307–310
    standing committee system, 306–307
Municipal Government Act (AB, 1994) 206, 207
Municipal Government Act (MB, 1996) 207

Municipal Government Act (NS, 1999) 133, 208
Municipal infrastructure. *See* Infrastructure
Municipal lobbyists. *See* Lobbying, municipal
Municipal policy analysis capacity, 432–433
Municipal policy making, 403–438
    complexities and conflicting perspectives, 405-408
    legal and jurisdictional constraints, 427–430
    municipal policy analysis capacity, 432–433
    pluralist theory, 421, 422
    public choice theory, 424–426
    regime theory, 426–427
Municipal restructuring. *See* restructuring *by province*
Municipal-Rural Infrastructure Fund Agreement (ON), 115
Municipal staff, 295–305
    Roles of, 295-297. *See also* Council-staff relations
Municipal revenues
    new revenue sources, 270-275
    sources in other countries, 266-269
    See also Development charges, Property tax, Transfer payments, and User fees
Municipal transit services. *See* Transportation
Municipalities Act (NB, 1877), 39
Municipalities Act (NL, 1999), 209
Municipalities Act (SK, 2006), 99
Municipality, characteristics of, 4
Municipality, classifications of, 5, 35
Murray, Glen, 279
Mushy middle, 202, 204, 232–235

N
Native Canadians, 8-9, 27-28, 63, 64, 359
Natural person powers, 206
Neighbourhood groups. *See* Local groups
Neighbourhood Improvement Program (NIP), 230
Nenshi, Naheed, 372
Neoliberal (and neoconservative), 22-23, 115, 332, 383, 419-421, 442, 459-460
Networked federalism. *See* Multilevel relations
New Brunswick
    Equal Opportunity Program, 125–126, 166, 192–193
    historical overview, 38–39
    restructuring, 125–128

498   Index

New Deal, for municipalities, 222, 223
New Deal, for Winnipeg, 279–280
New Democratic Party, in municipal elections, 373
New public management (NPM), 332–343
    benchmarking, 337
    best practices, 337
    features, 333
    measurement and competition, 336–341, 363
New regionalism (and old regionalism), 178–180
New Urbanism movement. *See* Smart growth
New Westminster (BC), 43, 165
Newfoundland
    historical overview, 40
    provincial-local relations, 209
    restructuring, 134–137
NIMBY (Not in My Back Yard), 446
Non-electoral participation, 385–400, 401
Non-Partisan Association (NPA), 233, 373, 382-385
North American Free Trade Agreement (NAFTA), 21, 224, 225, 226
Northern Ontario Heritage Fund, 66
Northern Territories
    historical overview, 44–45
    restructuring, 138
    transfer payments, 250
Northwest Territories. *See* Northern Territories
Nova Scotia
    Graham Commission, 129
    historical overview, 37–38
    provincial-local relations, 195–196, 208–209
    restructuring, 129–133
Nunavut. *See* Northern Territories

O
Oak Ridges Moraine (ON), 160, 390–391
O'Brien, Larry, 317, 447
"Occupy Vancouver" squatters, 385
Ombudsman, 303, 356
Ontario
    historical overview, 31–35
    provincial-local relations, 197–199, 212–214
    restructuring, 106–115
    Toronto. *See* Toronto

Open federalism. *See* Multilevel relations
Open local government legislation, 355
Oppal, Wally, 191
Organizational values. *See* Values
Ottawa, 143, 167, 170, 447
Outaouais Urban Community, 118. *See also* Hull-Gatineau
Owen, Phillip, 233

P
Pantalone, Joe, 380
Parish, Steve, 348
Parish and Town Officers Act (ON, 1793), 31
Parti Quebecois, 118, 119, 374, 376
Partnerships and joint ventures, 333–336. *See also* Public private partnerships
Pawley, Howard, 20
Payments in lieu of taxes. *See* Transfer payments
Peel, Region of (ON), 339, 348
Performance measurement, 337, 340, 363, 454
Phoenix, 338
Pichette Task Force (QC, 1993), 119
Pittsburgh, 175–176
Places to Grow Act (ON, 2005), 160
Planning, municipal, 53, 54-55, 81-83, 158-159, 411-412
Plebiscite. *See* Referendum
Pluralist theory, 421, 422
Policy making. *See* Municipal policy making
Political parties, in local government
    Montreal, 373–376
    pros/cons, 321–324
    Toronto, 376–380
    Vancouver, 382–385
    Winnipeg, 380–382
Political role of municipal government, 11, 14-15, 365, 404, 444-448, 459-460. *See also* Representative role
Poverty, 74, 75-76, 83-84, 85, 162
Prime Minister's Caucus Task Force on Urban Issues (2002), 221
Prince Albert (AB), 57, 315
Prince Edward Island
    historical overview, 38
    restructuring, 133–134
Professionalism, in local government, 298–300

Property tax
    burden of, 277, 278
    fairness/efficiency, 255, 277, 278
    provincial incursion, 258-261
    tax and expenditure limits, 268
    visibility, 256

Proposition 13, 268, 394

Provincial-local relations
    disentanglement, 189–201
    historical overview, 186–188
    legal relationship, 201–214
    See also Provincial-local relations *by province*

Provincial-Municipal Fiscal and Service Delivery Review (ON, 2008), 168

Public choice theory, 155, 424–426

Public health movement, 412–413

Public meetings. *See* Public participation

Public participation, 365–402
    consultative mechanisms, 391–393
    delegative participation mechanisms, 393–400
    informative participation mechanisms, 386–391
    initiative, 394, 397–398
    public meetings, 388, 389
    referendum, 393, 395–396

Public policy. *See* Municipal policy making

Public private partnership (P3), 225, 335

Public Sector Accounting Board (PSAB), 282

Public transit. *See* Transportation

Q

Quebec
    historical overview, 36
    Montreal. *See* Montreal
    political parties, 374
    provincial-local relations, 193–195
    restructuring, 115–124

Quebec Act, 29

Quebec City, 143

Queens, Region of (NS), 131-132

Quiet Revolution, 115

R

Rae, Bob, 197
Rational model of policy making, 406. *See also* Municipal policy making
Real property tax. *See* Property tax
Reciprocity, 330
Red Deer (AB), 97, 315
Red tape, 281
Referendum, 393, 395–396, 401
Regime theory, 426–427
Regional community municipality (QC), 116–117
Regional districts (BC), 89–92
Regional governments (ON), 106, 108, 109, 111-114, 119
Regional health authorities (AB), 95
Regional planning commissions (AB), 95
Regional services commissions (AB), 95
Representative role of municipal government, 102, 288-292, 311, 366, 405, 457. *See also* Political role
Resident advisory groups (MB), 102, 398
Restructuring. *See* restructuring *by province*
Revenue sharing agreements, 163, 247, 252–254
Richmond (BC), 372, 417
RIM Park Financing Inquiry (Waterloo, ON), 344
Riverview (NB), 126
Robertson, Gregor, 233, 385
Rossland (BC), 296, 397-398
Rowlands, June, 378
Royal Commission on Finance and Municipal Taxation (NB, 1963), 122, 190, 192. *See also* Byrne Commission
Royal Commission on Education, Public Services, and Provincial-Municipal Relations in the Province of Nova Scotia (1974), 129, 190
Royal Commission on Local Government Organization and Finance (MB, 1964), 125
Royal Commission on the Land (PE, 1990), 133
Royal seigniories, 31
Rusk, David, 161, 410

S

St. Albert (AB), 93, 156
St. John's (NL), 143
St. John's Metropolitan Area Board (NL), 142
Saint John (NB), 215

Saskatchewan
    historical overview, 42
    provincial-local relations, 209
    restructuring, 98–99
    revenue sharing, 254
Saulnier, Lucien, 117
Savings and Restructuring Act (ON, 1996), 112
School boards, 7, 259, 431. *See also* Education financing
Scientific management, 53
Service delivery role, of municipal government, 448–450
Settlement patterns, 69–70, 77
Sewell, John, 377–378, 390, 423
Sgro Report. *See* Prime Minister's Caucus Task Force on Urban Issues
Significant Projects Streamlining Act (BC, 2003), 189, 212
Silicon Valley Civic Network, 176
Simcoe, J. G., 31
Smart Growth, 81
Smitherman, George, 380
Social capital, 329, 368
Social polarization, 404
Social Union Framework Agreement, 244
Société de Transport de Montreal (STM), 168
South Coast British Columbia Transportation Authority, 168, 412
Spadina expressway, 81, 107, 390
Special purpose bodies. *See* Agencies, boards, and commissions
Spheres of authority (or jurisdiction), 206–207
Sprawl. *See* Urban sprawl
Standing committee system, 306–307
Steele, Barbara, 261
Steering (versus rowing) organizations, 449–450
Stikine Region (BC), 89
Stop Spadina, Save Our City, Coordinating Committee (SSSOCCC), 390
Strategic planning, 449, 456
Strategic Policies and Priorities Committee (Toronto), 310
Strathcona Property Owners' and Tenants' Association, 390
Strathcona Regional District (BC), 92
Sudbury (ON), 143
Sullivan, Sam, 233, 385
Summerside, PEI, 143
Sustainable development, 81
Sustainable Region Initiative (Greater Vancouver Regional District), 158
Sydenham, Lord, 33, 34, 36

T

Task Force on Local Government (NS, 1992), 195
Task Force on Municipal Legislative Renewal (SK, 1998), 98
Tax and expenditure limits (TELs), 268
Tax sharing. *See* Revenue sharing agreements
Taxing powers, new municipal, 272–274
TEAM (The Electors Action Movement), 383
Tenants' Rights Action Coalition (Vancouver), 392
Thatcher, Margaret, 22, 427
Think City, 391
Three Es (economy, efficiency, effectiveness), 337
Three Rs (reduce, reuse, and recycle), 451
Three Ts (technology, talent, and tolerance), 73
Tiers, one or two tier, 143, 146-150
Tolls. *See* Transportation. *See also* Municipal revenues
Toronto
    community councils, 399–400
    executive committee, 309–310
    mayoralty elections, 376–380, 426, 427
    political parties, 376–380
    restructuring, 106–111
    revenue raising power, 215–216, 272-274
Toronto Centred Region Plan, 159
Toronto City Summit Alliance, 179, 234, 417
Toronto Computer Leasing Inquiry, 352, 356, 357
Toronto Region Immigrant Employment Council, 234–235, 417
Town Incorporation Act (NB, 1896), 39
Towns Incorporation Act (NS, 1888), 38
Transfer payments, 246–254, 274–276
Transit. *See* Transportation
Translink, 91, 166, 168–169, 283, 412
Transportation, 165, 264, 271, 409–410, 459
Tremblay, Gerald, 171, 375, 376
Turn of century reform era
    boards and commissions, 58
    boards of control, 56
    city beautiful movement, 51
    city efficient movement, 53–54
    city healthy movement, 52–53
    city managers/executive committees, 57
    electoral process, 55–56
    professional planners and planning, 54–55

Two Hills (AB), 94
Two tier systems. *See* Tiers, one or two

U
Unconditional grants, 246, 247, 249. *See also* Transfer payments
Unethical behaviour, 352–354. *See also* Corruption, municipal
Unfunded mandates, 242
Unicity. *See* Winnipeg
Union Act (1840), 33, 36
Union of British Columbia Municipalities (UBCM), 205, 261
Union of Nova Scotia Municipalities (UNSM), 205
United Empire Loyalists, 24, 30, 31, 38
United Island of Montreal Party, 375
Upper Canada. *See* Ontario
Urban Development Institute, 422
Urban growth. *See* Urbanization
Urban renewal, 52, 68, 231, 382, 390, 446
Urban sprawl, 78–83, 155, 157–161, 181, 278, 410–412
Urbanization, 18, 63-64, 66-70, 78, 80, 240, 346, 445. *See also* Census metropolitan areas
User fees, 262–265, 279, 420

V
Values, municipal, 328, 343–346
Vancouver
    campaign contributions, 347
    "eager beaver" tendencies, 202, 233, 234
    mayoralty elections, 382–385
    minority representation on council, 372
    political parties, 382–385
    real property tax, 257–258
Vancouver Agreement, 231, 233
Vaughan (ON), 277, 348
Victoria (BC), 43, 47, 89, 155, 164
Village Municipalities (BC, 1920), 44
Virtual region, 179
Visible minority underrepresentation, 371–372
Vision Montreal party, 375
Vision Vancouver party, 384
Voluntary Amalgamation Act (QC, 1965), 115
Voter turnout, 367–369, 400. *See also* Municipal franchise

W

Ward elections, 55, 170, 289-291
Warden, 34
Water supply (and sewage disposal), 52, 100, 101, 106, 107, 134, 225, 263, 419
Waterloo (ON), 319, 344-345. *See also* Rim Park Financing Inquiry
Wayne, Elsie, 294
Wells, Andy, 295
Wells, Clyde, 135
Westmount (QC), 156, 311
White Paper on Municipal Reform (PE, 1993), 134
Whitehorse (NT), 138, 296, 397
Who Does What panel, 109, 190, 197, 198
Whole of Government policy making. *See* Multilevel relations
Williams, Danny, 137
WIN (Winnipeg into the Nineties party), 381, 382
Windsor (ON), 320, 392–393
Windsor-Detroit border crossing, 227–228. *See also* Multilevel relations
Winnipeg
    charter, 208, 215
    mayor, 292–293
    New Deal, 279–280
    political parties, 380–382
    restructuring, 100–105
Winnipeg general strike, 49, 380
Winnipeg Housing and Homeless Initiative, 231
Wolfville, NS, 6
World Bank, 19
World Trade Organization (WTO), 224, 226

X-Y-Z

Yellow Pages test, 454
Yellowknife (NT), 45, 138
Yukon. *See* Northern Territories